The History of Non-League Football Grounds

Kerry Miller

Published by
POLAR PRINT GROUP

The main stand at Braintree Town FC during the winter of 1963.

DEDICATION

To the memory of Dorothy May Bentley
K.M.

First published in Great Britain 1996 by
Polar Print Group Ltd
2, Uxbridge Road, Leicester LE4 7ST
England

Text copyright © Kerry Miller 1996
Design Copyright Polar Print Group Ltd ©1996

ISBN 1 899538 11 9

Edited by
Julian Baskcomb and Julia Byrne

Designed and Printed by
Polar Print Group Ltd
2, Uxbridge Road, Leicester LE4 7ST
Telephone: (0116) 261 0800

Maps painstakingly drawn by 'Charlie Cartographer'

Front Cover photographs:
Top: The Shed End at Fakenham Town (left) and (right) the City Ground, Darlaston.
Bottom: Nene Park, Rushden & Diamonds (top left), Marlborough Park, Ilfracombe
Town (bottom left), Clarence Park, St. Albans City (right).

Back Cover photographs:
Top Section - Clockwise: York Street, Boston United FC; A flooded Park View Stadium,
Erith & Belvedere; Osberton Radiators; An aerial view of Millbay Park, Plymouth;
Wolverton Park, Wolverton Town; The old Catterick Racecourse stand at Spennymoor
United; Horton Road, Darenth Heathside FC;
Bottom - Spectators at Malvern Town's Langlands Stadium in the 1950's.

Foreword

by Simon Inglis

Author of 'The Football Grounds of Great Britain'
and 'The Football Grounds of Europe'

Whether they are prepared to admit it or not, anyone with the remotest understanding of the history of English football, its culture and its role in the life of the nation knows, deep down, that the true essence of the game, even now, lies not in the glitzy superbowls of the Premiership but in the wooden shelters, farm-yard covers and neighbourhood clubhouses of non-League football.

Away from the circus of overpaid, mollycoddled players, arrogant and greedy managers, and overpriced gentrified stadiums, the non-League game shines out as a constant reminder of where football's real roots lie.

But that is only one of the many reasons I welcome and delight in Kerry Miller's astonishing efforts as laid before you now.

On a personal note, within these pages I find the first football ground I ever encountered (two or three years even before my first inside experience of Villa Park as a goggle-eyed seven year old). I was walking in a park with my aunt on an Easter holiday when we passed what seemed to me then a giant, green-corrugated barn, from which ripples of cheering, 'oohs and aahs' seeped out like the overheard rituals of a secret society.

Within those battered fences lay the home of Chelmsford City, but it might have been anywhere. A life-long addiction, affliction even, had begun.

Now, thanks to Kerry Miller, at long last I know something of that weird little ground I (and no doubt many others) always make a point of looking out for as the train rushes through Wolverton. All those wonderful back street grounds in the West Midlands I once visited as a teenager on my spluttering BSA motorbike - Bilston, Darlaston, Stourbridge and Moor Green - now I know for sure that my eccentric joy in them was not misplaced.

Indeed this book allows me to revisit so many of the grounds I have been drawn to over the years, usually en route to somewhere else, often late for an appointment but lured nevertheless by a set of floodlights or the glimpse of a stand revealed between a gap in the houses. Always the same compulsion, always the same guilt as I ask my travelling companion to wait, always the same insistence, 'Just five minutes'.

And although my own adult efforts and researches have since been confined largely to the senior grounds and stadiums of world sport, I have never lost that fascination for the quirky sheds, decaying shelters, spindly pylons and lumpy turf of England's small towns, obscure suburbs and rural villages.

Since embarking as an author upon my own football odyssey in the early 1980's I have often been asked if I would ever write a book on non-League grounds. Each time my answer has been in the negative. Trying to keep up with a hundred or so senior grounds is tough enough, but the challenge of visiting and researching hundreds of non-League grounds, each with their own special charms and quirky stories, was, I would always frankly admit, beyond my capabilities and energies.

For that reason alone, Kerry Miller has my unbounded admiration, and my gratitude - and that of thousands more ground buffs, no doubt - for producing a book which will now, surely, accompany every travelling football fan in the country.

This is a book which has long been overdue, but which on the evidence of these pages, has been well worth the wait.

Simon Inglis
November 1995

Contents

Woodside Road, Worthing.

West Cornwall & Penwith	9
East Cornwall & The Clays Hills	14
Dartmoor, Plymouth & Torbay	19
Exmoor & North Devon	23
West Somerset	32
Dorset	38

Grove Corner, Portland.

West Sussex	86
East Sussex	93
East Kent	97
Central Kent & The Docks	106
North Sussex & Surrey	112
North Downs & South Berkshire	120
M25 Inner West	124
M25 Inner East	131
Middlesex and its Borders	137
M25 North East	145
South & West Essex	151

The Mendips & The Levels	47
Bristol & Bath	54
Salisbury & The Plains	61
Mid-Wiltshire	65
Gloucestershire	69
South West Hampshire & The Isle of Wight	76
South & East Hampshire	81

Buryfield, Ware.

Chiltern Hills & The Thames Valley	155
Oxford & The Berkshire Downs	163
North Oxon & Buckinghamshire	169
Hertfordshire	173
Rural Essex	180
Ipswich & West Suffolk	188

Victoria Park, Salisbury.

Cambridge	193
Bedford & District	198
Northants & East Warwicks	201
Worcestershire & Surrounds	208
Birmingham & Black Country	216
Herefordshire & Shropshire	225
Stafford & North Birmingham	230
Nuneaton to Leicester	236
Burton, Derby & Matlock	240
Nottingham	248
Fenland	251
Lincolnshire	254
Norfolk & North Suffolk	260
Humberside & North Yorkshire Moors	266
Sheffield Area	271
The Potteries & The Peaks	278
North Cheshire	284
Merseyside & The Coast	288
Manchester	295
South Lancs	301

Coles Lane, Sutton Coldfield.

Central Lancashire & The Coast	306
West Yorkshire & Harrogate	314
Durham Coalfields across to Teesside	321
Durham North & Wearside	328
Cumbria	333
Newcastle & The North	338
Welsh clubs in England	343
Subscribers	350

Tow Law Town.

OPENING
OF THE
Wolverton Park and Recreation Ground

(*Kindly presented by the Directors of the London and North Western Railway Company*).

The celebration of above will take place on August 3rd, 1885, when the Chairman of the Company, accompanied by the Directors, Nobility and Gentry of the neighbourhood, will declare the Park and Recreation Ground open.

The Workmen, their Children, and Friendly Societies will march in procession, accompanied by five Bands, from the Works to the Park and Recreation Ground.

The proceedings in the Park will be as follows:—

ADDRESS BY THE CHAIRMAN.
CHILDREN SINGING.
BANDS PLAYING.
BICYCLE, FLAT, AND OTHER RACES.
TUG OF WAR, &c.
FIRE BALLOONS.   FIREWORKS.

The day's festivities to conclude with

A BALL IN THE WORKS,
WHEN THE
Wolverton Rifle Volunteer Band

Will play under the leadership of Mr. PINFOLD.

ADMISSION 6D.

Stewards—Chairman, R. BORE, Esq., Messrs. C. A. PARK, W. PANTER, J. B. WILLIAMS, W. WILLIAMS, H. M. WILLIAMS, W. PURSLOW, and R. KING. Hon. Secretary, Mr. G. M. FITZSIMONS.

POOLE TOWN FOOTBALL CLUB.

The Committee request the pleasure of your company
at the
Opening Football Match
on the NEW SPORTS ARENA, Wimborne Road, Poole.
POOLE TOWN v. WELLS CITY
ON SATURDAY NEXT, AUGUST 26TH, 1933
At 3-15 p.m.

The MAYOR OF POOLE (Coun. W. C. J. Shortt)
has kindly consented to kick-off.

COMPLIMENTARY TICKET
of Admission to Ground and Stand.
This portion to be retained.

H. S. STOKES, Hon. Sec.,
Marwin, Longfleet, Poole.
This portion to be given up at Entrance.

YORKSHIRE AMATEUR A F.C.
BRACKEN EDGE, HAREHILLS LANE, LEEDS.
Colours : Light and Dark Blue Quarters.

OFFICIAL PROGRAMME

SATURDAY, Feb. 27th, 1932
YORKSHIRE AMATEURS
v.
WIMBLEDON
AT BRACKEN EDGE.
F.A. Amateur Cup—4th Round Replay.
Extra Time if necessary.

AT BRACKEN EDGE.
Saturday, March 5th.
Leeds & District F.A. Senior Cup.
LEEDS U.Y.M.I.
v.
WYKEBECK ATHLETIC
Kick-off 3-15 p.m.

Youngmans, Printers, 68, New Briggate, Leeds.

MOOR GREEN FOOTBALL CLUB

"The Moorlands," Sherwood Road, Hall Green.
(Off HIGHFIELD ROAD)
(2 minutes from the Robin Hood Picture House)

WATCH AMATEUR FOOTBALL.
MATCHES EVERY SATURDAY.

Admission Ground and Stand - 6d.

Membership Tickets 10s. 6d.   Ladies' Ticket 5s.

Introduction

SIMON INGLIS wrote as an introduction to his superb Football Grounds of England and Wales, "Anyone who has been to a football match will know that rush of excitement when first catching sight of the floodlights and stands".

That one sentence neatly sums up my reaction, when a ground comes into view or just peeks out from behind some houses, or simply beckons me to it from afar. But that rush of excitement can lead to the frustration of spotting a set of lights or a little wooden stand in the distance whilst hurtling along on British Rail's finest, without having a clue where you are.

In my formative footballing years, I travelled the length and breadth of the country searching for the elusive Watford away win. Each away game seemed to find me at some far flung northern industrial town, craning out of the window for an early glimpse of the ground, or a chance to read the track-side graffiti. Whatever happened to Shaun of Darlo? And did their bootboys really rule?

Non-League football in its senior guise entered my life on May 4th 1974, when, for reasons long now forgotten, I found myself at Lower Mead, to witness Wealdstone's championship winning side take on Trowbridge Town. Some 1000 or so new grounds later, the anticipation of the coming Saturday's trip is still with me, albeit in a different mode. As I hope will become apparent, no visit is complete without the background of the place being ferreted out. Was it once a vastly bigger stadium with stands, thousands of fans streaming in, or has it quietly ambled along, occasionally witnessing some minor cup triumph, the photo of which adorns the wall of the club skittle alley?

My local side as a kid, before successive adults began escorting me to Vicarage Road, provided my Saturday afternoon football in the Watford and District League. Mill End, who played then, as now, in Watford's Gold and Black were all-conquering in the early and mid sixties, and it seemed to me were always playing cup matches at places like Wheathampstead and one year for some obscure reason, Surbiton Byron. In those days the fact that most of the matches were

played on park pitches, and our home ground consisted of a dilapidated wooden cricket pavilion did not seem to matter. They were my team. The fearsome tackling of Dickie Hams, the awesome shooting power of `Trout', and the bandy-legged wizardry of Dave Hutton are all as clear now as they were then, some thirty years ago. And now when I drive past `The Field', I still experience a tingle, I can still see the banners propped up on the fence, and the shout from Bill Critcher of "Come on the Bay", a reference to the village's old nickname of Tiger Bay. But the fence is gone, the pavilion is long gone and Mr. Girdler who chased us out of the nets is long gone too.

Those memories are mine, but in this book I have attempted to jog other peoples' memories, and to provide a background to many of the fascinating grounds around the country. As the book unfolds, it will become noticeable that it is not always the spick and span new stadia, nor the most successful clubs who feature more heavily. Some grounds have an instant appeal which is often difficult to evaluate, such as Tow Law Town or Netherfield. Others have a kind of Gothic quality about them, particularly when empty, such as Crook Town, and still others, one in particular at Cockfield, are simply so steeped in history that it is of no concern that there is virtually nothing left to look at. The past is all-enveloping.

In addition, the sites of numerous former grounds were visited, most sadly now covered by houses or supermarkets, or motorways, but now and again a little gem will crop up, almost qualifying as Industrial Archaeology. The terracing at Rugby Town's old ground, or the large pile of metal and concrete that once fenced in the pitch at Sharpness.

It is the never ending search for information, and the knowledge that as I pass my 1000th ground, I am showing no signs of slowing down, that keep me going.

The last decade or so has seen the loss of many of our well-established and much-loved football grounds, both in the professional and semi-professional game.

Somerton Park, Fellows Park, The Old

Show Ground, Eastville, Leeds Road and others in the Football League, and Green Pond Road, Lower Mead, Western Road, Granleigh Road, Champion Hill, Central Ground, Moat Field, West Street, Cross Keys and Turnfurlong Lane amongst others in non-League.

Many more clubs are in the process of moving, folding, amalgamating or sharing as ground grading, lack of income and apathy take a hold on our game as it approaches 140 years old.

The blanket coverage of all Premiership, Football League and European matches with live games on one channel or other, most nights of the week, has had a serious effect on crowds that had shown signs of improving until the last couple of seasons.

It was with these facts firmly at the front of my mind that I began to investigate the possibility of exploring the history of our non-League grounds whilst the majority of them still existed. Two other factors were instrumental in setting me off on what has become a three year quest for information.

Firstly, the inspiration gleaned from Inglis's book, which was first published in 1983 and describes the Football League grounds on which the vast majority of us were weaned, and its subsequent re-print after the Bradford fire. It is now an invaluable reference to the memory of the grounds that have been transformed from idiosyncrasy to blandness by the Taylor and Hillsborough Reports.

Secondly, my involvement with James Wright's awesome FA Cup Club-by-Club Records which I proof-read and cross-referenced. Initially, my ambition was to somehow collate information on every ground that had hosted FA Cup football since the war, but that soon turned out to be nigh on impossible for many of the records within the bowels of the FA were incomplete and the results unknown, let alone the venue at which the match was played.

Eventually, it became apparent that a geographically arranged work, covering all major venues within the pyramid, exploring their development from the earliest days would be appropriate, with reference made to former grounds where known. This threw up a major problem. With some 800 senior clubs within the so-called pyramid, and many more that had long since dropped into lesser leagues but had retained interesting grounds, the problem of where to draw the metaphorical line arose.

Many clubs such as Stonehouse, Wells City, Portland United, Nanpean Rovers, Cromer, Whitchurch Alport and Prestwich Heys still played on fascinating grounds, and so in the interests of brevity and sanity only a passing reference is given to some of them.

As the research continued and the replies to the initial 600 or so requests for information dried up, I soon realised that tens of thousands of miles would be racked up in visiting librarians and historians, and the slightly less onerous task of visiting or re-visiting grounds on matchdays would be important. The desperately disappointing aspect of the first phase of work was the lack of co-operation given by seven out of eight of the secretaries who did not give me the courtesy of a reply. Even more irritating, having travelled across the country to visit a club I was often confronted with "Well, I can't give you the information you want, but I'll forward it to you if you give me your name and address", which would be the last communication either way, which then put me back to square one.

Of course many clubs are blessed with dedicated historians whose information and knowledge was readily made available to me and it was most fortunate that two of my most favoured grounds, those at Gresley Rovers and Gravesend and Northfleet are superbly documented.

This book does not set out to be a strictly accurate and thorough representation of every change seen at the grounds since they were first set out, but moreover it aims to give an insight into the antiquity, or otherwise, of a club's home and attempts to convey to the reader something of its character.

As in most walks of life, there are things and places that please, as there are many that do not. During my travels, on more than one occasion my initial reaction to a ground when approaching it or viewing it for the first time was one of disappointment at its blandness, or possibly the way an old grandstand had been pulled down to make way for a car-park. Or, as in the case of a number of Home Counties-based clubs, how their chosen leagues insistence on a hideous eight foot tall perimeter fence or wall had wrecked the ground's previously charming vista.

On those occasions it was not unknown for me to go back a second or third time at a later date when the ground was empty and possibly my thoughts were not clouded by the actions of unco-operative or disinterested club officials. Human nature will dictate that the reader's first reaction to the book will be to turn to his or her chosen club to hopefully read reams of text never before having seen

the light of day. In many cases, happily, that will be the case, for ultimately the vast majority of grounds are given coverage, although, as will become apparent, one or two are not. With those, despite several requests to secretaries, programme editors, Chairmen and Chief Librarians, nothing was forthcoming. It was then that the barest of information was gleaned from senior club supporters at matches. To those whose grounds are not given glowing references, then I ask you not to take it personally, but to accept it as one man's point of view. In very few cases have I actively expressed a dislike for a ground, maybe no more than a handful, for the intention of this book was not to give opinions, but to explore how, and from what, a ground had developed over the years. If, however, that very development has created an ugly and uncomfortable arena for football in my opinion, then it will not be difficult to read between the lines.

The `History of Non-League Football Grounds' has completely taken over my private and working life for the last three years and it will take some while to get used to not waking up in the back of my car in some service station on a Saturday morning, having driven 300 miles the night before to visit a ground on matchday.

To this end I must thank my wife Lynn for her love, patience and tolerance when things were going haywire, and my daughter Katie who three years ago at the age of six took on the role of Junior Correspondence Co-ordinator. Also thanks to Effie, my Canine Mobile Security Operative who guarded the car with enthusiasm on dozens of occasions and asked for nothing more than an inexhaustible supply of strokes, and chips in gravy.

As to individual contributions, I have detailed them elsewhere, where a separate message of thanks is added. If you are not listed, then please accept my apologies for the oversight, and my assurances that your contribution was most welcome and appreciated. Special thanks go to Andy Molden, Chris Bedford, Jon Weaver, Andrew Chitty, Andrew Luscombe, David Kirby and James Wright who helped in various ways and with various clubs.

Thanks also go to Apex Reprographics of Bedminster for unlimited use of stationary and postage, and to Gavin Ellis-Neville, Paul Dennis, Andy Dakin, Mike Floate, Dean Walton and Chris Gibbs amongst many others, for their camera work.

Finally, thanks to Harland, Jungle Head and Chris `Viscosity' Baker for a total of 60 years of unbroken friendship. Here's to the good times.

Kerry Miller
November 1995

Bibliography

- Wembley F.C. A History of Wembley *Geoffrey Hewlett*
- Chorley F.C. 1883-1983 Centenary
- Chorley F.C. Historical & Pictorial Review 1875-1946
- Clutton F.C. Clutton Football Club 100 years
- Trowbridge Town F.C. Centenary 1880-1980
- Nantwich Town FC. Centenary Dabbers, a history of Nantwich Town Football Club 1884-1984 *by Michael Chatwin*
- Bromsgrove Rovers F.C. Centenary 1885-1985 *Bill Kings*
- Ryde Sports F.C. Ryde for Pride *Mike Bull*
- Emley AFC. 90 Years of History 1903-1993 *Alec F. Hardy*
- Workington AFC So Sad, So Very Sad Part 1 *Martin Wingfield*
- Workington AFC 1884-1984 *Steve Durham*
- Liskeard Athletic FC 100 years of football in Liskeard. *E.K.Brown*
- Ware FC An Intention To Play *by Steve King*
- FA Cup Club-by-Club Records. *James Wright*
- Official Centenary of the Southern League. *Leigh Edwards*
- The Grounds of Rugby League. *Trevor Delaney*
- The Football Grounds of England and Wales. *Simon Inglis*
- A View From The Terraces. One Hundred Years Of The Western League. *Sandie and Doug Webb*
- Gone But Not Forgotten 1-6. *Dave Twydell*
- Arlesey Town, The First Hundred Years.
- Northants FA Centenary Souvenir. *David Thorpe*
- Kings of Amateur Soccer, Bishop Auckland. *Chris Foote-Wood*
- Northern Goalfields. History of the Northern League. *Brian Hunt*
- Grays Athletic First Hundred Years.
- Centenary Story of Kidderminster Harriers. *Colin Youngblood*
- From Reds To Raiders. History of Football in Shepshed. *David Kirkby*
- Defunct FC and More Defunct. *Dave Twydell*
- Sutton United 75th Anniversary.
- Early History of Buxton FC. *Ian Cruddas*
- Newmarket Town and the Suffolk Cups. *EJ Wybrew*
- Newmarket Town and the FA Cup. *EJ Wybrew*
- History of Guiseley FC
- Droylsden FC, The First 60 Years. *David Siddall*
- Wellington Street to Wembley. Burton Albion. *Rex Page*
- St Margaretsbury FC Centenary
- Cray Wanderers FC. A History.
- Hednesford Town FC 100 Years of Soccer. *Dave Shaw*
- Official History of Colne Dynamoes FC. *Philip Terry*

West Cornwall and Penwith

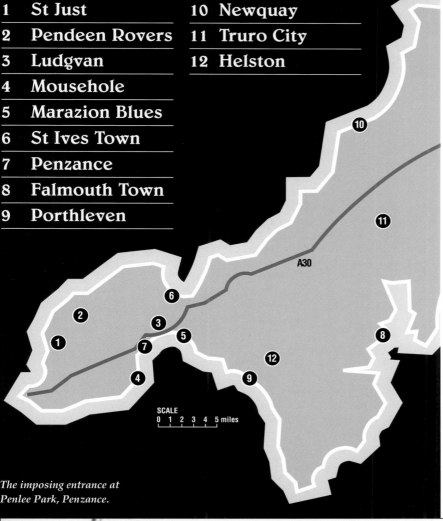

1   St Just
2   Pendeen Rovers
3   Ludgvan
4   Mousehole
5   Marazion Blues
6   St Ives Town
7   Penzance
8   Falmouth Town
9   Porthleven
10 Newquay
11 Truro City
12 Helston

The imposing entrance at Penlee Park, Penzance.

THE REGION of Penwith, the westerly tip of Cornwall, boasts six senior grounds apart from Penzance's Penlee Park. All belong to clubs playing in the Cornwall Combination.

West Cornwall has always been a strong sporting area for football and rugby, but due to its geographical position, there has been no desperate need for clubs to substantially develop their grounds, as Southern League football has always been a distant idea and nothing more, even for all conquering Western League side Falmouth Town.

The western-most senior ground in England (the most westerly overall, incidentally, is that of Sennen who play in the West Penwith League), is Lafrowda Park, home of **ST JUST A.F.C.** It is reached through a honeycomb of squat terraced streets to the south of the former tin mining town. Just beyond a pay-gate is a smart gabled clubhouse, built in the late 1980s and sporting an impressive club logo painted in green, black and white. Beyond the club and changing rooms a small stand turns its back against the winds that howl into this exposed ground off the Atlantic.

St Just's near neighbours are **PENDEEN ROVERS**, whose ground is named after the family from whom it was acquired in the 1950s. Borlaise Park is tucked in behind of row of houses that skirt the B3306 St Just-St Ives road, but the entrance is off the lane that winds down to Pendeen lighthouse. Rovers previously played on a pitch on the other side of this lane, and before that at a site near the Geevor tin mine from where the club's players were traditionally recruited. The closure of the mine's social club in the late 1980s led to the construction of a clubhouse on the ground itself. The ground, once very run-down, has been been tidied considerably since the building of the clubhouse. The pitch, with a freshly painted permanent surround, slopes up towards the changing

PENLEE PARK
Penzance A.F.C.

The Main Stand at Penlee Park.

According to Greg Nicholas's centenary history of Penzance A.F.C., a national newspaper recorded the opening of Penlee Park thus: "Roll up your sleeves. If you love sport and want British boys and girls to lead the world follow the example of the `Penzance Pioneers' who built a football stadium for their town".

The newspaper was alluding to the hundreds of thousands of hours hard labour invested by committee members and volunteers between early 1951 and the summer of 1952. 20,000 tons of earth and other material were shifted and levelled, two miles of drains were laid, and several marriages are believed to have veered dangerously towards collapse as husbands absented themselves from home to toil in a sea of mud caused by weeks of heavy rain. The fruit of their labour was described as `the finest football stadium in the West', and officially opened on 25th August 1952 by Football League secretary Sir Stanley Rous, and a Luton Town team who defeated their hosts 10-0.

Those among the tireless unpaid labourers who still visit Penlee Park today will no doubt feel a sense of frustration that their efforts have not been matched in recent years - the ground has slipped into a sorry state of disrepair as the Magpies have wallowed from one financial crisis to another throughout the eighties and nineties. Only recently has it begun to be respected again, with the stand being repaired and the impressive banking reclaimed. The entrance/turnstile block has been repainted and gives an excellent

first impression to the ground that is situated close to the seafront and a few yards from the equally impressive Penzance and Newlyn Rugby Club. The formerly impenetrable fence separating Penlee Park from a public park of the same name has been breached leaving this town centre stadium prey to vandals. A far cry from the heady days of the fifties and sixties when four-figure crowds regularly watched the Magpies excel in the Cornwall Senior Cup and the new semi-professional South Western League. A supporters club then boasted a 3,000-strong membership and handed over tidy sums of money for the development of the ground.

Penlee Park had undoubtedly gone to seed in recent years but this famous old club looks to be coming out of its shell once more. The ground remains a typically impressive seaside venue. The capacious grandstand, holding seven rows of bench seats, is sufficiently robust to withstand the buffeting of rain, wind and vandals,

whilst the grass bank that rolls up to a second entrance, off a lane at the back of Morrab Road, provides a spectacular viewing point in pleasant weather.

An unusual feature is the perimeter fence which is solidly made of concrete posts with a protruding lip with bolt holes in each one. This is a legacy of the early days of the ground, before the main stand was built, where wooden bench seating ran all around the pitch attached to the fence. When the stand was built, the club decided not to replace the benches when they became damaged as spectators were using them instead of paying for a stand seat and so they were allowed to eventually disappear!

Previous grounds were at Trereife Farm, near to the current ground of local junior side Trelawny, Sona Merg Park in Heamoor, and St Clare - again near Heamoor and now the home of Penzance Cricket Club.

rooms. These back on to the terraced houses and have an overhang that offers limited spectator cover. Floodlights are in place, but are bright enough only for training.

LUDGVAN's Fairfield ground is the most basic on the Penwith peninsular, its main feature being the massive double-storey village hall/community centre that towers behind one goal and is clearly visible from the main A30 near Crowlas. The playing area, used for cricket in summer months, boasts two pitches, the nearest of which is roped off. Spectators tend to congregate under the overhang of the village hall. This raised area houses a tea hatch and affords an excellent view down the pitch and across to St Michaels Mount beyond.

To find the home of **MARAZION BLUES** one takes the steep hill out of Marazion centre and turns left up an even steeper slope (Shop Hill) opposite the Fire Engine pub. As the gradient levels out, Marazion Community Centre lies to one's right. The players change in this and walk across the

road, through an entrance where a gate is collected (off spectators, that is!), and into the ground. The club pulled off a coup in 1991 when they installed floodlights, but these have since been dismantled and the venue is quite spartan, the only cover being an overhang at the front of an equipment shed.

MOUSEHOLE's is perhaps the peninsular's most interesting ground. As the fishing village of Mousehole clings precariously round a steep hillside, the nearest terrain level enough to accommodate a pitch lies nearly two miles inland at the village of Paul. Trungle Park is concealed at the end of a long unmetalled lane, and cars are parked on a gentle slope behind the near goal. A squat brick-built structure, painted in the club colours of green and white, above the far halfway line houses changing rooms and limited cover. This, the focal point of the ground from its 1960 construction, is now buttressed by a brand new clubhouse - previously the Seagulls' H.Q. had been a small social club opened in Mousehole village in the late

1970s. In the summer of 1987 the ground was transformed when the visit of Manchester United for a friendly necessitated the erection of temporary spectator accommodation. The match was the official celebration of the Mousehole's purchase of Trungle Park.

ST IVES TOWN joined the ranks of senior football when they moved into the Cornwall Combination from the Mining Division League in 1992. Their smart ground, at Lelant Saltings, is unusual in a number of ways. Firstly, it is several miles east of the bustling tourist town of St Ives, which like Mousehole suffers an acute shortage of flat land. Secondly, the ground is divided from the mud-flats of Hayle Estuary only by the embankments of the St Ives branch line - Lelant Saltings station abuts the ground, though St Erth main-line station is only fifteen minutes walk distant. Finally, the only vehicular access to the ground is through a garish tourist theme park just off the A3074 St Ives road.

BICKLAND PARK
Falmouth Town FC

Considering that Bickland Park is less than 40 years old, it has already acquired a neat and tidy but well used look which normally indicates a much higher level of antiquity. Its enormous grass bank either side of the main stand and steep concrete terraces at the car-park end, together with rudimentary cover on the three other sides make it without question the finest football ground in Cornwall. Falmouth Town settled at Bickland Park in 1957 having had several homes in the seven years since their formation.

The very first game was played at Union Corner Rec which stood just yards from where Bickland Park is now but later that season a few games were played at the Rugby Ground which is still used for that purpose today.

In 1952 the club began playing at the Ashfield ground which was terraced with changing rooms on the site. It was home until Shell BP offered to purchase the riverside site for the then staggering sum of £20,000 with an option of building Bickland Park. This they did and the new ground opened on August 28th 1957 with a game against the Cornish County side. The impressive main stand has been there since the start, housing board rooms and changing facilities and a small area of cover was provided along with the concrete terracing which stretches all along the car-park wall. Over the years all three sides have gained and lost their cover as the winds have torn them off and destroyed or damaged them a number of times. The far side cover is now much shorter than in the past having been re-built in 1984.

Floodlighting was put in in 1973 but not used until April 10th 1974 when Porthleven played there in a league game. Bristol City eventually came down to switch them on. The entrance is dominated by a lovingly cherished pay-box which was a gift from a supporter in 1953 and by the clubhouse which dates from the seventies. The pay-box formerly stood at Ashfield, and was transported following the move. Despite its undoubted claim to be the biggest ground in the county, it has a capacity of 6,000 which was reached back in 1962 when Oxford City were the visitors for an FA Cup 1st Round tie.

Bickland Park remains the only Cornish ground to stage a match in the FA Cup proper.

Two views showing the elevated areas at Bickland Park. Note the pink pay-box (below) which was originally at the old Ashville ground.

MOUNT WISE
Newquay FC

The first game of football of any note in Newquay took place in January 1890 involving a Grammar School side, and from this the club was born, playing on a field behind what is now Trenance Infants School. By 1894 the club were playing on the Jib Field by consent of the owner and landlord of the Red Lion Inn. Around 1900 Jib Field had acquired a grandstand, but the cost of playing there where spectators viewed for free had caused a problem for the club and so Newquay moved to Ennors Meadow situated behind the New Hotel.

Much the same thing happened there, with more outside than in, and the club eventually were suspended for not paying fees. Within weeks the club were reformed and returned to the Jib Field until 1912 when the ground was turned into a golf links and the club went back to Ennors Road for the remainder of the season. In September there appeared no sign of football in the town, and

The large crowd for a league match between Newquay and Tavistock at Mount Wise in November 1955 and (right) the same view 40 years later.

with disciplinary problems and a debt over their head, the club went under.

In November 1913 Newquay Juniors were formed, playing at Pentire before the Great War and at Glendorgal after, and in 1920, a Newquay United team was formed who were forced to play at Tregunnel as the War had taken care of all pitches in Newquay itself. Moving to a pitch near Trethellan Terrace (opposite the Mount Wise Cemetery) the club immediately had a problem as the road was on a higher level to the hedge and acted as a free grandstand. A hessian fence was hastily erected to prevent any gratis viewing. By the following season football had taken off in the town, and gates of 1,000 were common, the club having moved back to Tregunnel.

After years of moving from one field to another, and from one crisis to another, the club finally were granted a lease to play on a piece of land formerly used as an allotment, and as a result Newquay United played at Mount Wise for the first time in August 1922.

Within three months a Committee was formed to finance the building of a grandstand, and on 25th April 1923 the biggest stand in the county was opened. For a while crowds flocked to football with gates of 2,000 regular for Plymouth and District League matches, but once again serious financial problems saw the club fail to start the next season and they never played again. However Rovers were still going strong and they moved into Mount Wise for some ten years before finally disbanding in January 1937. In the two years prior to the War only junior sides played in the town, Newquay Electric using Mount Wise for a year.

A new Newquay FC was formed just two months short of the War, merging Newquay Electric Co with a new club. They were almost immediately shut down for the hostilities and Mount Wise was used as a truck depot and a baseball pitch with the grandstand being badly damaged and broken up for firewood. The club was eventually reformed in 1946 and due to the state of

Mount Wise a pitch at Whitegate was used, later the site of a youth club. The return to Mount Wise came in 1947 to a ground which at the time had no boundary walls, no pitch fencing, no banking, no cover of any kind and no baths or electric. By 1950 improvements were made at the ground, the stand had been repaired and changing-rooms added under it, and shortly after banking and terracing using railway sleepers was provided. Two covered ends soon followed with a boundary wall and entrance, and the whole transformation was celebrated on December 1st 1951 with a grand re-opening of the ground. Some thirty years later, the mayor of Restormel opened a new changing room block at the car-park end of the ground and three years from then major work costing some £8,000 was carried out on the old grandstand. Mount Wise has aged gently in the last few years and apart from the floodlights which went up in 1988 little has changed in this windswept area of Cornwall.

Mount Wise, showing its exposed position.

Truro City

TREYEW ROAD
Truro City FC

Truro's long and illustrious history is almost matched in length by the Treyew Road ground itself, which has been more or less on the same site since 1898.

Very early on in the 1900's, a grandstand was built and situated close to where the current one is now. The banked ground has had many minor changes to it, but none so radical as in the mid seventies when the Council required some land for road widening purposes, and the pitch was moved forwards, the covered terracing behind the town goal disappearing and the levelling of the pitch forming some excellent grass banking.

The ability to stage a game with a crowd of 12,000 went then too, although crowds for Cornish Senior Cup ties had long since tailed off from the heady days of the forties. Treyew Road was once the home of Truro Cricket Club with the square being on a plateau and the outfield and pavilion being roughly where the lorry park is now. An old wooden grandstand with dressing rooms stood on the half way line in the gap between the banking which can be clearly seen next to the new stand. Cricket finished around 30 years ago at Treyew Road and the club now play at the stunning Boscawen Park, next to the river.

With the new clubhouse, and revamped ground came a celebration game against Tottenham Hotspur, on 3rd May 1978.

Since then Treyew Road has had floodlights installed in 1986, Oxford United providing the opposition for the switch on.

Photos in this section by: Pat Brunning, Andy Dakin, Dean Watson, James Wright and from the Newquay Centenary History book.

GALA PARC
Porthleven FC

Porthleven's long awaited move to the newly created Playing Fields called Gala Parc, came in 1956, although it was short-lived as the ground was found to be unready, and they were forced to play on a pitch at the top of Preachers Lane until moving in for good in May 1957, where they lost the first game 7-3 to the Devon and Cornwall Police.

Prior to these comings and goings, the club began after the War at Treza Downs for several years until moving to Sunset Farm. The idea of the Playing Fields was first mooted back in 1946 when the Gala Committee suggested that the need was there. Some eight years later the land was bought, and it was eventually opened by The Duke of Edinburgh a year after Porthleven FC moved in, in 1958.

In 1964, a pavilion complete with changing rooms was built, and six years later a covered stand was added to the ground, which in turn gained tip-up seats in 1993, when Gala Parc hosted the South Western League Cup Final between Truro and Falmouth.

KELLAWAY PARC
Helston FC

Club records indicate that Helston Football Club played their football along Clodgey Lane at at least five different venues, before moving to the current ground which they now own. In 1949 they moved to Beacon Parc which had banking, a pavilion and an entrance with a double set of pay boxes, and the ground was the envy of many, and indeed the stand with its changing rooms below, was copied by Bugle at their Molinnis ground.

The final game was in 1972 when Newquay provided the opposition for the club's last game in the South-Western League. Beacon Parc had been built just after the War with the help of German PoW's and this splendid ground is now underneath a mobile home site. Kellaway Parc was created from a pitch rented to the club by a Franklyn Moyle, and subsequently bought with help from a Dr Kellaway after whom the ground was named. A large wooden shed was used as a clubhouse, and was only superceded by an £80,000 purpose built structure opened in 1988 which has a lean-to which acts as a cover for the spectators. In the early days at the ground the players used the cricket club to change in until another wooden shed was acquired for that purpose. Helston have taken a long while to recover from the double loss of league and ground but seem to be on the way back.

East Cornwall and the Clay Hills

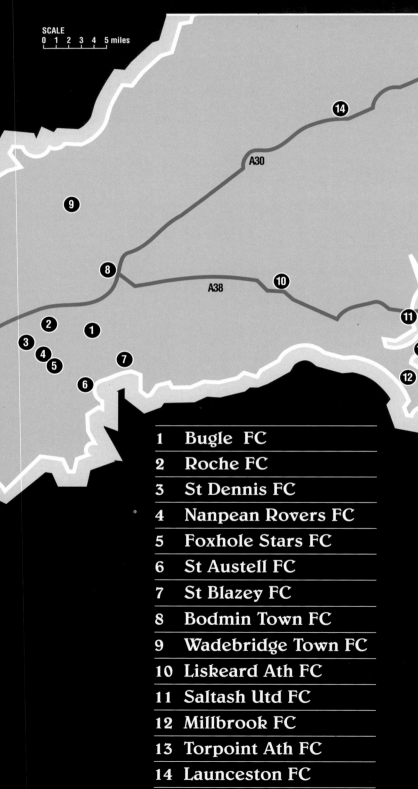

SCALE
0 1 2 3 4 5 miles

A30

A38

1 **Bugle FC**

2 **Roche FC**

3 **St Dennis FC**

4 **Nanpean Rovers FC**

5 **Foxhole Stars FC**

6 **St Austell FC**

7 **St Blazey FC**

8 **Bodmin Town FC**

9 **Wadebridge Town FC**

10 **Liskeard Ath FC**

11 **Saltash Utd FC**

12 **Millbrook FC**

13 **Torpoint Ath FC**

14 **Launceston FC**

CORNWALL'S soccer heartland is the China Clay Hills to the north of St Austell, an eerie almost lunar landscape of conical waste heaps, some now overgrown with bracken and gorse. Former mining villages are embedded into the steep hills and valleys, five boasting thriving, or once thriving, East Cornwall Premier League clubs.

BUGLE were for many years a major force in the South Western League, but their Molinnis Park ground now bears testimony to a dramatic decline in the early 1990s. The recently organised social club went bankrupt in 1991, necessitating the club's drop to the East Cornwall League the following summer, and now the building stands forlornly boarded up on the eastern side of the pitch. Directly across the halfway line looms a narrow lofty stand with four rows of bench seats and a disused press cabin perched high above the changing rooms. This stand, painted like all the other facilities (tea-bar, toilets, pay-box, post and rail pitch surround) in the club colours of black and white, backs tightly on to a row of houses (Molinnis Road) and was built after the club borrowed the plans for the stand at Beacon Parc in Helston.

Contrasting starkly with the sad aura of neglect at Bugle is the primness of Trezaise Park three miles west. **ROCHE** moved to this ground from a field just behind the parish church (only a few hundred yards away) in quite recent times, and have developed a functional set-up. Driving into a spacious car park off the B3274 just south of the village, one is greeted by a wooden pay-kiosk, a sparkling new clubhouse, a floodlit training area and a level playing surface enclosed by a concrete post and wire surround. The most striking feature of this ground, however, has nothing to do with the club; Roche Cliff, an outlandish outcrop of granite topped by a minute fifteenth century chapel, towers imposingly beyond the eastern touchline.

Bugle's stand, based on the stand at Helston's former ground.

The Cliff at Roche FC.

ST DENNIS nestles under the North Western fringe of the clay hills, and the club's pretty ground lies in a low valley a quarter mile west of the village centre. Boscawen Park was fashioned out of an area of wasteland in 1952, the club having occupied a number of different pitches in the immediate vicinity since their 1903 formation. A clubhouse, opened in 1972 by Lord Falmouth (who still owns the entire site), stands behind the goal nearest the entrance. Green and white predominate everywhere - on the changing room block, tea-hut and the obliga-

tory pay-box. The playing area, which has a cross-pitch slope, is enclosed by a post and wire surround, and a second pitch, to run parallel, is being levelled on the side furthest from the entrance.

A little over a mile south of St Dennis on the B3279 lies the home of former South Western League members **NANPEAN ROVERS**. Victoria Bottoms was a clay quarry until its 1936 conversion into a football ground, and its ampitheatrical qualities make it a quite unique sporting arena. The faces of the former quarry, now verdantly

covered in foliage, rise sharply behind both goals and the eastern touchline, and a myriad of small pathways offers the adventurous spectator countless different vantage points. Two recognised viewing spots, one at each end, have been covered by 'bus shelter type' accommodation, accessed again by narrow paths. The topography of the ground dictates that all amenities are clustered on its western flank. A children's swing and roundabout greet you as you penetrate the narrow entrance, and beyond a small car park lie two modern club rooms. A final oddity about this remarkable venue, which is beautifully maintained by the Playing Fields Committee, is that the pavilion housing the changing rooms doubles as a memorial to local men who fell in the 1939-45 war - their initials decorate granite slabs between the dressing room doors.

Half a mile further down the B3279, **FOXHOLE A.F.C.** complete the quintet of senior clay hills clubs. This very old venue could until recently be accessed only via a poky, easily-missed, lane between two houses on Goverseth Terrace, but a new, if somewhat circuitous, track has been constructed leading one straight to the equally new clubhouse. (The club H.Q. was previously the local Working Men's Club). The pitch runs parallel to Goverseth Terrace so balls frequently plop into back yards. Brick-built dug-outs are situated on either side of the field, and a small floodlit training area completes what is now a tidy, if unspectacular, ground.

POLTAIR
St Austell FC

St Austell's stark concrete main stand looks out over a banked ground that was the venue for the highest ever attendance for a football match in Cornwall when an estimated 15,000 people paid over £1,000 to watch the Cornish Senior Cup final of 1949 between St Austell and Penzance.

Today Poltair Park is much the same with the grassy banks all around and the 1930's vintage concrete stand showing signs of age. It could have been a whole lot different for during the War years the club were offered the chance to have the pitch levelled and a stand built behind the Town goal by the US forces who were using the ground at the time, but the club turned them down and as a result Poltair is virtually unchanged. There are three turnstiles in place that date from around 1950 at the Brewery Gate, Park Gate and the Poltair Gate entrances with the fourth now used for car-parking. The more modern clubhouse behind the stand was opened in 1982.

The Cornwall Senior Cup Final at Poltair in 1953 (right) and a somewhat quieter Poltair today (below)

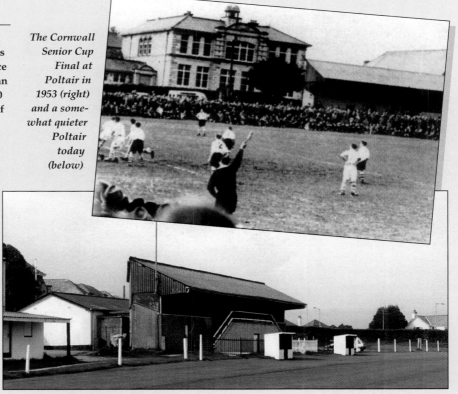

Blaise Park with the Royal Box in the centre.

ST BLAISE PARK
St Blazey FC

St Blazey Football Club are preparing for their centenary celebrations next year, having been formed to play on a pitch which adjoined the site now covered by St Blaise Park, in 1896. From there the club moved to a field in Back Lane, behind the Packhorse Hotel, which was the club's headquarters in those days.

St Blaise Park was first used in 1906, thence up until the outbreak of the Great War when the pitch was dug up and sand taken from it to fill sandbags, the site having been on reclaimed land from a former estuary. The field was re-filled with rubbish and re-seeded and the club moved back having played in the meantime at Kitts Moor, known now as Middleway. At the end of the 1930-31 season the present grandstand was constructed, and in 1957 a Royal Box was built into it for the visit of HRH The Duke of Edinburgh for a match between Cornwall and the Combined Services with proceeds given to the National Playing Fields Association. The match was played under floodlighting which at the time was the only system in Cornwall. It had been erected by voluntary labour and paid for by way of £1 shares.

After the War there were restrictions on spending within the building trade, and in 1949 the club were allowed £350 to construct a committee room and dressing rooms which did service until 1988. The ground is currently owned by Restormel Council, and is on a long term lease to the club. Back in September 1956, however, St Blazey bought a pocket of land next door which belonged to the St Blazey and District Co-op with the objective of building a clubhouse, but this did not materialise until December 15th 1972. Within two years a large room with dance floor was built and then extended, and in 1988 Gerry Francis, manager of Bristol Rovers, opened a further extension which incorporated dressing rooms and a snooker complex.

The original floodlights were not wholly successful and in the main were used for training, but on 7th November 1989, Ken Brown, manager of Plymouth Argyle, switched on the new set and The Pilgrims played a match to commemorate it.

St Blaise Park is complete with banking which was used to good measure back in 1949 when a derby game in the prestigious Cornwall Senior Cup against St Austell attracted a crowd of over 6,500. Today, the ground has a capacity of half that number, but is none the worse for that.

PRIORY PARK
Bodmin Town FC

Possibly one of the happier aspects of being geographically out of the mainstream is that with no real ambition of going any further than the Western League at a push, clubs in this area do not have to worry too much about ground gradings at a higher level. This is one of the reasons why grounds have remained more or less unspoilt by change for donkey's years.

Bodmin's delightful home is situated close to the town centre in what looks like a natural bowl with a perfectly adequate grandstand with around 400 seats which was built in September 1958 at a cost of £2,500. It replaced an older galvanised structure which the club brought with them from West Heath some time after the War when they lost the ground they had shared with St Lawrence's Hospital FC and the cricket club. That ground is now covered with housing. Other earlier homes included Coldharbour, which was the Duke of Cornwall Light Infantry drill field which is still used for football, and a field in Barn Lane.

Priory Park is leased from the council and the club originally played on the second pitch before moving across. The floodlights were erected in 1971 and fourteen years later the clubhouse, which was extended a few years ago, was built.

BODIEVE PARK
Wadebridge Town FC

The Bridger's wonderfully old fashioned switchback ground with its 70 year-old grandstand and Nissen hut dressing rooms is under two pronged attack from the planners and bureaucrats who have all but consigned it to the ever increasing list of lost grounds. Having stood without incident since shortly after the ground was opened, the largely timber stand was declared unsafe, and as a result the innards were ripped out and burned on Guy Fawkes Night, 1994, leaving just the shell.

It is strongly rumoured that the club will be vacating the ground to make way for a supermarket and move across the road to a purpose-built arena with all mod cons. This will mean leaving the Nissen hut which was bought and converted in 1951 by the Supporters' Club and, apart from an extension for the referees, has remained there ever since.

Wadebridge's stand before the bureaucrats got at it!

The covered end at Bodieve Park is of indeterminate vintage, but has been re-erected more than once following high winds. The banking which surrounded the ground is still more or less intact with just the bottom end near the clubhouse missing. The years after the Second War were a boom time on and off the pitch with the ground bought in 1949 for £900 and the Nissen hut dressing rooms which came from RAF St. Eval going up. During the War years the ground reverted to a corn field and the stand served as a barn which meant matches were played at Egloshayle Playing Fields. The club entered the South Western League and the FA Cup in 1951 and crowds of 3-4,000 were not uncommon, especially for local derbies with Camelford. The original entrance to the ground was in the corner by the main road until the sixties when a road widening scheme nibbled away a small area of the land and necessitated creating a new entrance at the other end. In 1979, after much volunteer work, the clubhouse opened and remains the last significant positive development at the ground. Bodieve Park may well shortly become either a supermarket or a newly developed ground on the other side of the road. Its switchback pitch - so similar to Horwich RMI's late ground - and its gutted stand may well, sadly, be doomed.

PENNYGILLAM
Launceston FC

There have been three grounds called Pennygillam all within a few yards of each other. The building of the town by-pass put paid to number two which stood alongside the A30 but number three soon followed and remains home.

The first known pitch was at Hurdon which was home until taken over by rugby around the time of the Second War. It was then that the first Pennygillam ground was used, which was roughly on the site of the current one, but the ground was shared with cricket and had a pitch at 45 degrees to its present position. Soon after their own ground was prepared over the road on Pennygillam 2, a covered enclosure was put up which ran along the touchline parallel with what is now the access road to the current home. An old hut - which had served at a Prisoner of War camp in a previous life - stood in one corner as changing rooms. When the building of the town by-pass took away part of the ground and hastened the development of the Pennygillam Industrial Estate which now surrounds it, the club moved back over the road to the original Pennygillam which by now had changed in shape and was complete with a pre-fabricated clubhouse built from an old cow-shed at a cost of £1,300. The second Pennygillam is now under a combination of the new road and the premises of Abru Ltd directly opposite the club entrance.

The enclosure was transferred over and is now replete with 150 seats and room for the same amount standing. A new L-shaped club room with dressing rooms combined has recently opened, tucked away in one corner of the latest Pennygillam which has a number of mature firs behind the far goal to break up the monotony of the Industrial Estate which engulfs this most un-Cornish of football grounds.

Bodmin Town

LUX PARK
Liskeard Athletic FC

There has been football played in and around Liskeard since 1890. Various clubs came and went including a YMCA side which played on the cricket field. The very first Cornwall Senior Cup final was also held there in 1893 and the following year a Liskeard team reached the final although it is not certain if this was the YMCA club. Other grounds in the area included Lux Cross and Evely's field; the former stood where the Post Office is now.

Lux Park had been used for cricket since 1851 and when the ground went up for auction in 1912 both sporting teams were shocked as they had enjoyed tenancy for a nominal rent of 1/- a year until then. The owner, Viscount Clifden agreed to sell for £300 providing the ground was used for sports. The funds were raised and the ground was later given to the Borough. The War years prevented any progress being made to develop the ground, but in 1921 a new grandstand was built on the cricket ground which had 200 seats and was painted chocolate and amber. Changing rooms were situated under the structure which was decorated with a copper shield inscribed in honour of those fallen in the War. The stand was in use as a cricket changing room until the new complex was built, when it began to fall prey to vandals. The seats were stolen and eventually another bit of history disappeared when it was taken down in the 70's.

In the Spring of 1922 the adjoining field became available and was purchased for £500. Deals were struck with a local man who had a slaughter house in one corner and soon the pitch was laid out along with a bowling green, tennis courts and a cycle track which would run around both fields. The dividing hedge was taken away and the first game was played on September 9th 1922 against Woodland Villa. The initial enthusiasm waned and the club were forced to fold in 1935 with heavy debts. Rugby was played at Lux Park during this period and indeed it was not until after the Second War that the modern Liskeard Athletic were formed during 1946. Moorswater FC used the ground for one year but Liskeard eventually took over.

Lux Park continued much the same until 1961 when dressing rooms were built where the St.Cleer Road entrance is now. These only lasted around seven years, as a road improvement scheme wiped them out. In 1965 a fixed post and rail system went up around the pitch which had an old stand, of indeterminate age, along one side which had been added to around 1960. A new standing enclosure was built in the late eighties which, along with three pylons and the cricket field fence was destroyed in the gales of January 1990. These were all soon replaced along with a new dressing room complex with hospitality rooms.

Lux Park has seen good times and bad and has developed into a pleasant Western League ground. Due to the club's geographical position it is extremely unlikely that Southern League football will ever be sought and therefore the shape of the ground will only ever be determined by committee men and acts of God rather than by stringent League rules for which the Western League are happily not renowned. Indeed for the 1995-96 season Liskeard have returned to the South Western League, increasing the likelihood of Lux Park remaining as it is.

THE MILL
Torpoint Athletic FC

Torpoint Athletic had to endure losing their ground to another club for some years in a similar way to that which befell Hampton FC, when Twickenham removed them from the Beveree for a while. Both clubs eventually returned, in this case eleven years later, after playing on the HMS Defiance pitch whilst St Columba's Rugby Club used the Mill.

It had been home since before the War,

THE MILL
Millbrook FC

Millbrook's Mill ground has only been in existence since 1977 when a rubbish tip was fashioned into a football ground, following the club's move from their spartan home at Insworke Park. A wooden shed which came from HMS Raleigh and was formerly a mess hut, was converted into a small clubhouse, with dressing rooms adjoined and along with a perimeter post and rail, the ground was good enough for the South Western League. More recently, in 1990 floodlights were installed and new dressing rooms were erected along with a covered stand, which was named in memory of the Chairman's son, Neil Townsend.

Millbrook's previous ground had the main problem of low hanging telephone wires which often altered the flight of the ball, and along with the lack of changing facilities - the players used the Liberal Hall - Insworke Park eventually reverted back to an unused field. Much earlier Millbrook sides before the War played on a pitch at Mill View now covered by a housing estate.

although little developed, until 1960 when forced to move away. It is only in the last twenty odd years that the ground has gained its clubhouse, changing rooms and new stand, which replaced the original buildings, the latter in 1991. More recently a gatehouse has improved the entrance to what is a pleasant little South Western League ground in Plymouth, just a short ferry trip away from foreign lands.

KIMBERLEY STADIUM
Saltash United FC

Saltash United have also taken voluntary redundancy from the Western League and have gone into the South-Western for the 1995-96 season which will automatically make Kimberley

Stadium one of the more developed grounds in the league. The high grass banking behind the town end goal and along one side, combined with the stand, creates a capacity of around 3,000, a thousand less than watched an Amateur Cup tie in 1951 in what was then a new stadium.

The early Saltash side played on a pitch in Town Park, in Fore Street before moving to Longstone and later to a Corporation ground in Maunders Field. After the War, the club re-formed as Saltash United, and from 1948, played at Wearde Road in St Stephens. Finally, in 1951 Kimberley Stadium was opened. The stand, which incorporates dressing rooms and a canteen as well as a press box was opened in 1969, followed by the original clubhouse in 1978. This was extended to include the Sapphire Lounge in 1989.

Photos in this section by: Pat Brunning, Andy Dakin, James Wright and from the Newquay Centenary History.

Kimberley Stadium, Saltash.

Dartmoor, Plymouth and Torbay

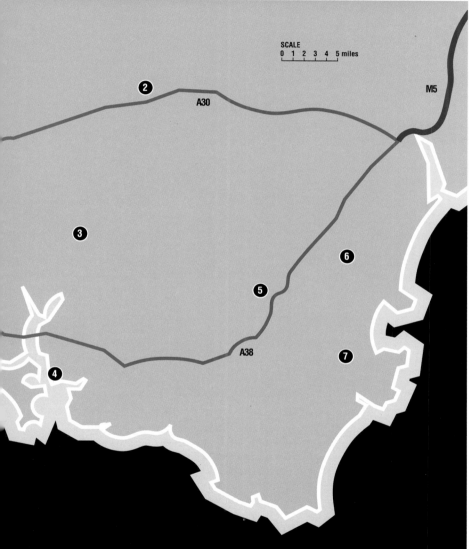

THIS AREA is rich in old football grounds which have either seen higher levels of football in the past, or were once part of leagues which were more significant than of late.

Wall Park in Brixham saw Western League football before the club fell on hard times, Teignmouth's Coombe Valley ground is again hosting senior football and Moretonhampstead's Wadley Brook ground has a stand which would not look out of place in a higher grade.

Elsewhere the new Devon County League contains a number of clubs whose grounds are yet to develop despite being at a higher level, such as Ivybridge's Erne Fields, Weston Mill's Sports Ground, and Chagford's Padley Common.

UPCOTT FIELD
Holsworthy FC

From founding until the time of the Second World War, Holsworthy played their football on the Recreation Ground. It was blessed with a fine wooden grandstand, which seated 300 and had glass sides and dressing rooms underneath. The sadness is that the stand was built in the mid-thirties and only survived a handful of years before the ground was requisitioned for the War effort and turned into a Prisoner of War camp. The temporary buildings were converted into homes and the area is now a housing estate.

For a couple of seasons in peace time, the club played on a pitch next to the cricket ground in Stanhope Park, until the owner of the land where Upcott Fields now stands, Mr Eric Axtell, sold it to the Council on the proviso that it was always used for football. Thus the club moved in and have been there ever since. In the early years before the brick built dressing rooms were erected, away players changed in the Huntsman pub with local based players changing at home. There was little in the way of facilities, save a small chicken run which stood on the site of the new covered area until its demise in 1994. The first part of the clubhouse was opened in 1981 and a further function room extension went up in 1994.

1	Holsworthy FC
2	Okehampton Argyle FC
3	Tavistock FC
4	Millbay Park
5	Buckfastleigh FC
6	Newton Abbot FC
7	Stoke Gabriel FC

Wall Park, Brixham

*Millbay Park, former home of Devon &
Cornwall Police, this year home to
Plymouth Command.*

Upcott Field is another in a long list of
pleasant, typically rural grounds which have
potential but are unlikely to be changed,
other than through necessity. The remoteness
of the town and the unlikelihood of the club
wishing to go into the Western League and
latterly Southern League, has meant that
grounds such as these do not need to expand
for the few dozen regulars that watch football in the 90's.

It must be hoped that the proposed entry
into the pyramid by the South-Western
League does not mean that the ridiculously
unwarranted intrusion of seven foot high
corrugated fences, caged walkways, and
seated capacities for God knows how many
hundreds of imaginary spectators, does not
ruin the atmosphere and character of places
like Holsworthy, Tavistock and St Blazey.

MILLBAY PARK

**The casual visitor to Plymouth Hoe cannot fail to be impressed by the former home
of the Devon and Cornwall Police Football Club, situated as it is between Millbay
Docks, the city centre and the Hoe itself. Sadly, due to pressure from above, the
Police side have been forced to withdraw from regular league football, leaving
Millbay Park up for grabs, possibly by Plymouth Command FC.**

Although the ground has been in existence since the early 30's, it has had no
significant changes made to it, but it is no worse for all that. The site of Millbay Park is
steeped in history, and is believed to have been covered by mills before the first of
Plymouth's naval prisons were established there. Some 230 years later, the area was
made into a football ground and has staged many Services matches, as well as in the
past being the home of a selection of local sides.

Until 1995, the Police had sole use of it for their South-Western League matches
and occasional Rep. games. For the 1995-96 season Plymouth Command FC have
moved in, playing in the Devon County League. The playing area is surrounded on
three sides by a broad hedge which completely hems in the park to such an extent that
many people are not aware of its presence. Two of the sides have grass terrace kept in
place by retaining boards, with the remaining areas being flat standing. The players
change in the small white-roofed building tucked into the corner of what is a delightful
ground which can be appreciated by those who do not necessarily need hugely
developed arenas to enjoy their football.

SIMMONS PARK
Okehampton Argyle FC

Simmons Park is a fine example of how a football ground need not be ultra developed to be attractive and worth visiting. Argyle have played in Simmons Park since 1929 when they began in the West Devon League, playing on a pitch which stood roughly where today's ground is. On the outbreak of the Second War football closed down and the pitch was taken up temporarily for the War effort, and on the resumption, a pitch was used which is still marked out for junior football between the bowling green and the river, just behind the present day swimming pool. Home players changed in the bowling pavilion with the visitors having to make do with a room in the Labour club in the town.

In the early fifties the club began playing where they are now, with no more than a wooden shed for the referee and a stone barn for the players to change in. This continued until 1982 when the changing room complex which stands behind the town end goal was built, along with a small area to stand undercover. The ground only developed within the last four years after the club were admitted into the South-Western League, when a permanent pitch barrier replaced the standard post and rope, and a small covered stand went up on the halfway line. An extension to the first building now houses the clubhouse and bar which was opened in November 1993. Although Simmons Park is one of the less developed of the Devon area grounds, the rushing stream alongside and stunning wooded valley which stretches out behind give it a setting which is difficult to match anywhere.

DUCKSPOND
Buckfastleigh Rangers FC

The Duckspond ground was little more than a recreation ground with a pitch on it until the 1980's when Rangers became the first club in the South Devon League to erect floodlights. This was the beginning of the superb development at Buckfastleigh which can be seen from the nearby A38 when zooming into, or away from, Torbay.

The club were formed around the turn of the century and played at the recreation ground which was shared with cricket and rugby until the mid sixties, when the cricket club bought the Rec and Rangers were forced to go elsewhere.

The Rec at one time boasted a grandstand which was shared for both winter sports but there is no longer any trace. A few yards down the lane from the Rec is Oaklands Park where Rangers play their South Devon and Youth team matches, and where the first team played for three years while their Duckspond ground was repaired after a culvert collapsed.

Oaklands Park is a field with ricketty dressing rooms and an undulating pitch reminiscent of The Creek at Bristol Manor Farm until it was improved. The Duckspond is somewhat different with a large clubhouse housing snooker, skittles, and games and function rooms with the dressing room complex next door. A steep bank has been terraced in front of the dressing rooms and a natural grass bank at the opposite end gives the ground a bowl like shape.

LANGSFORD PARK
Tavistock FC

Tavy Football Club are as old as the Devon FA themselves, and were founded following a meeting called by sporting businessman Herbert Spencer, on September 8th 1888.

The new club played on the old Tavistock Grammar School Playing Fields in Russell Street with immediate success before moving to a pitch in Green Lane, owned by the landlord of the Bedford Hotel, in 1892. The pre-War years saw the club move again, first back to the school and then to the sports field in Green Hill before using a pitch in Sandy Park. This ground had a small timber stand and was used by the club until the Second War. For many years it reverted back to farmland but is now used by a rugby club although the stand is gone.

For three years after the War, the club played on a pitch with a small changing hut in Green Lane, now covered by Dulvin Road school, until moving into Langsford Park in 1949. The club President, Herbert Langsford, a local quarry owner, had purchased the land in 1947 and gave it to the club under trust.

Much ex War Department surplus was used in the building of the ground, with the stand made solidly of concrete with redundant railway sleepers being used for the floor and seating in a similar manner to that further north at Barnstaple. The curving roof was also government surplus and was victim of high winds on several occasions before finally being replaced a couple of years ago after the stand went a season without one. Two ex-Army huts were placed in one corner for changing and these were eventually swept away when the new block was built in 1974 and opened by Exeter City. Three years later the Social Club was opened and in 1994 the floodlights were installed.

Tavistock Football Club are in the fortunate position of being situated in one of the most scenic areas in the country. Langsford Park overlooks a rippling river and rolling Devon hills which set off the charm of the place which is relatively undeveloped but a perfect place to watch raw, unpretentious football.

NEWTON ABBOT

The town of Newton Abbot currently has around half a dozen teams of which the most well known are Spurs and Newton Abbot F.C., formerly Dynamos.

Newton Abbot Spurs are the oldest by some way, playing after the war on a ground called Bradley Meadow and then Bakers Park, a ground now used by Newton United from the lower reaches of the South Devon League. In 1950 the club moved to the Recreation Ground in Marsh Road, causing something of a stir by uprooting the well established All Whites rugby union team who were resident.

In the early days of football on the Rec. the pitch was at a different angle to today's set-up with a large wooden stand and changing room on the side roughly where the tennis courts are now. The ground has seen large crowds in recent seasons when chosen to stage the prestigious Herald Cup Final.

Newton Abbot F.C. were formed in 1964 as a youth team and played part of the first season on Sandringham Park recreation ground before club officials persuaded the manager of the Centrax company to allow them to use the Sports Ground until they could find something more permanent. The Centrax was to be their home for 24 years, eight of which were in the South-Western League. To comply with league rulings the club erected post and rails around the pitch and provided some cover. On resigning from the league, Newton Abbot moved to a former school cricket pitch which had a battered pavilion and little else. In the short time since then, an extension has been put on to the refurbished pavilion and a permanent barrier installed around the pitch. The new County F.A. headquarters has been completed and has new changing rooms underneath it replacing those at the back of the pavilion. The ground is very pleasant to visit with a vista of wooded Devon hills overlooking it, and the waft of newly-cooked burgers emanating from the canteen in the clubhouse!

The beautiful Devon backdrop at Stoke Gabriel and the programme from the official opening of the G.J. Churchward Memorial Ground.

G.J. CHURCHWARD MEMORIAL GROUND

Stoke Gabriel FC

Founder members of the newly formed Devon County League, Stoke spent many years playing on a variety of farmers fields before their picturesque home in Broadley Lane was opened with a match against Torquay United on August 1st 1984.

The history books show that Stoke used Oxland Park, Vicarage Road, Wilkenden, Pound Field, Cater Field, Kings Rydon, Paignton Road, Broadpath, and Whitehill and quite possibly some others before settling at the Memorial Field. The sloping field cost the club some £12,250 with a further £5,000 spent on levelling and reseeding and building of the changing rooms which are tucked away on the bank which runs along the railed off pitch. Although undeveloped, the rolling Devonian countryside in which it is set creates an ideal backdrop for a ground dedicated to the memory of the railway engineer who was born in the village nearly 140 years ago.

Stoke Gabriel Football Club

STOKE GABRIEL F.C.
1984 Herald Cup Winners

v.

TORQUAY UNITED
Football League Division 4

OFFICIAL OPENING MATCH
at the
G. J. Churchward Memorial Ground
Broadley Lane, Stoke Gabriel

Wednesday, August 1st, 1984
Kick-off 6.45

Admission by Programme 60p

Child/OAP 30p

Photos in this section by: Sam Balsdon, Devon & Cornwall Police and Pat Brunning.

Exeter and East Devon

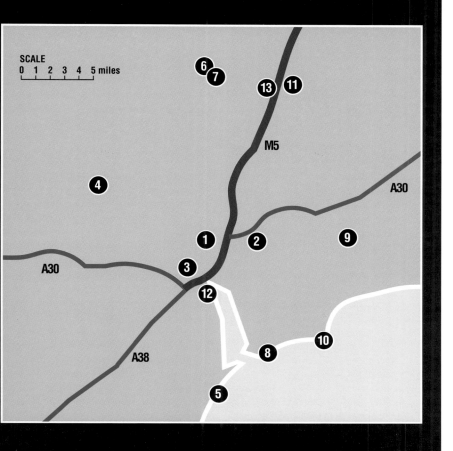

SCALE
0 1 2 3 4 5 miles

M5

A30

A30

A38

1	**Heavitree Utd FC**
2	**Clyst Rovers FC**
3	**Alphington FC**
4	**Crediton Utd FC**
5	**Dawlish Town FC**
6	**Tiverton Town FC**
7	**Elmore FC**
8	**Exmouth Town FC**
9	**Ottery St Mary FC**
10	**Budleigh Salterton FC**
11	**Willand Rovers FC**
12	**Topsham Town FC**
13	**Cullompton Rangers FC**

THE legacy of Devon and Exeter and Western League competition can be seen in many of the grounds in this area, which is home to a number of clubs who have tasted success in recent times and who have improved their grounds accordingly.

As in the Torbay area, there are also many clubs who have facilities which would enable them to play in a higher standard, should enthusiasm and playing success catapult them there.

LADYSMEAD
Tiverton Town FC

Of the small group of non-league grounds clustered in and around Tivy, Ladysmead is by far the most advanced, although possibly not the prettiest, being wedged between a petrol station and an industrial unit.

The club began playing when the Rugby club folded in 1912 and a football club was formed from the ashes a year later. Most sport in Tiverton in those days was played on the Agricultural Show Ground, later known as the Athletic Fields, which had a huge wooden pavilion with a seated verandah. For one season before the Great War, and up to 1920, Tiverton Football Club used it until the Society Committee decided to allow the re-formed rugby club exclusive use, and the football club moved to the Elm Field, a rugby ground in Blundell Road, a stone's throw from the Athletic Fields. This remained home until 1939, at which point the ground was used as a coal dump next to the gas works during the War, and never saw football again. The Elms had a wooden, 150 seater stand on one side, opened amidst much pomp in September 1925 with a grass bank at each end, and was named after the large house in whose gardens it was originally laid out.

Today, the site is covered by the Blundell Road car-park although the house still stands. After the War, Tivy moved to

Ladysmead Stand, Tiverton, soon to make way for a new complex stretching most of the pitch length.

Construction of the new covered end at Ladysmead.

Ladysmead, which was undeveloped but had seen football previously. Part of the old stand from the Elms was salvaged and re-sited at the ground which in the early days had the pitch running at right angles to its current position. It was replaced by the structure which stands on the same site. Today's Ladysmead stands on the extreme edge of town, close to the connecting road to North Devon, and is reached via an unmade road next to a garage. In 1993, the club fenced off the ground from the car-park, and created a new entrance away from the clubhouse. Inside, alongside the club, a high area of covered standing supported by 12 stanchions has been erected. Opposite this, a pitch-length complex with seating, changing rooms and offices is planned to sweep away the groundsman's sheds, changing rooms, old clubhouse and stand, thus transforming Ladysmead into a fine ground in time for the expected promotion to the Southern League.

A covered terraced area built at the main road end in time for the start of the 1995-96 season has transformed the ground by giving it a more enclosed feeling. Next to the stand is the old clubhouse which served the club from 1962 until the new one was built in 1984, and next to it stand the tea-bar and changing-rooms. Behind the far goal is flat standing, close up to a group of rather sad looking trees, and opposite is a new area of terracing which was laid down in 1995.

Tivy's pride and joy is the splendid clubhouse which dominates the ground and was first opened on March 5th 1984 by Mick Channon. Previous to that a Lounge Bar had been opened in time for Christmas 1983 by Gerry Francis, former captain of England.

A road now cuts the old Coronation Field in half, with the Rugby club next door, and the Athletic Fields are now smaller in size, but still used for football, and called Amory Park. The pavilion was replaced by a standard brick changing room complex in the mid-seventies and all that remains is a plaque which once hung above the entrance but is now on display in the town museum.

SILVER STREET
Willand Rovers FC

Just occasionally, a visit to a ground of which nothing was previously known can be a delight. Anyone diverting off the M5 through the village of Willand will be afforded such pleasure when espying the Silver Street ground.

The peculiarly shaped stand proudly displays the club name and the surrounding area is beautifully manicured. The iron gates give way to a newly Tarmacadam-surfaced approach to the clubhouse which was opened in 1987 and has been extended more recently. A long larch lap fence enclosing a new estate is fronted by a series of stiles. These now lead nowhere, but are used to speed the recovery of balls from the orchard that gave way to the housing.

The seated stand looks like an immaculately kept fifty year-old in its design, but in fact is only half that age, and bears the club's training lights on top and maintenance equipment at its rear. The Devonian feel is completed with an L-shaped thatched cottage quietly watching proceedings from the corner on the main road.

Willand Rovers were founded in 1946. For their first half dozen years they played on a ground in Station Road, which is now under an industrial estate, before moving to a barren field with no facilities. A large hedge was removed to create space for the club, and endless endeavour meant players could vacate the village hall across the road and change in comfort. Since these early days, Silver Street has matured into a ground which would grace the Western League. Its popularity with Devon County F.A. officials was confirmed on Saturday August 22nd 1992 when it was selected to host the official opening of the new Devon County League.

HORSDON PARK
Elmore FC

Horsdon Park, home of Elmore is the most unsung of the grounds in the Tiverton area. Ladysmead is changing and moving on as the team continue to be successful and Willand Rovers' delightful home amongst the thatched cottages modestly hosts Devon County football. Speeds Meadow, home of Cullompton Rangers is admired briefly by hundreds of thousands of rubber necking motorists who roar past it each year on the M5. But Horsdon Park, which has been in existence since 1958 has seen Western League football for 17 years and has quietly got on with it in the shadow of its neighbour which bears the town name.

Elmore Sports Club was formed in 1947 and the first few seasons were spent on farmers fields in and around the town which has expanded greatly in the last twenty years. Prior to moving to the current ground, the club played on a pitch just a couple of

KING GEORGE V GROUND, SOUTHERN ROAD
Exmouth Town FC

For a club that enjoyed so much success all through the eighties, Exmouth's riverside ground is surprisingly undeveloped. Its small square stand, built in the late 1960's, is the only structure for spectators, other than a small covered area tucked away in the corner, built from the proceeds of the FA Vase run. The rest of the ground is open hard standing all round, with the clubhouse and changing rooms incorporated near the entrance.

It has been home since 1964, when they left the Maer Cricket Ground for the second time, having re-formed there after the War.

Strangely, the cricket ground is far more interesting; it still has a substantial football artifact, namely a long covered stand, roofed with corrugated asbestos but now partially relieved of its railway sleeper terracing and most of the bench seating. The stand, still in very good nick, is perched on the grass bank which ran the length of the ground. Used by cricket spectators, although a long way from the boundary in some instances, it is a glorious reminder of Exmouth's relatively distant past.

The club were originally formed to play in the Exeter and District League in 1933 playing at the Cricket Ground for all but one year, which was spent at Raleigh Park in Withycombe just before the War.

Exmouth's success culminated in an FA Vase semi-final appearance in 1985 where a large crowd saw Fleetwood gain a first leg draw, however the record attendance is 2,395 for a friendly with Liverpool Reserves in July 1987.

The new stand and dressing rooms at Elmore FC.

LORD'S MEADOW
Crediton United FC

The small Devon town of Crediton has seen various football teams since the beginning of the century, but United have been in existence since 1945 when they entered the newly formed Exeter and District League.

The club played at the Newcombes Playing Fields eventually gaining senior status in 1963, but the scope for development was not there and when the Lord's Meadow Sports Centre was opened in 1976 they moved on to a fenced off pitch on the site.

Since then a clubhouse has been built, in 1979, and the ground now has two stands, one with around 150 seats and has a modern dressing room complex in one corner. Floodlights were installed in time for the club to be promoted to the Premier Division of the Western League which they joined in 1990.

The fir trees planted around the pitch now give a much more enclosed feel to what is a pleasant ground in a very sport-minded area.

hundred yards away, now covered by a poultry packing works, although the changing room building still exists. The area all around Horsdon Park has changed dramatically since the demise of the Tiverton to Dulverton railway which ran alongside the ground until the early sixties. As the town expanded and the need for link roads became apparent then the railway track bed was swallowed up allowing much easier access to the ground which was previously entered via a lane and a railway crossing. This also accelerated the building process at the ground which was a field used by a slaughterer until bought by the club for £1000. The outbuildings were used as changing rooms for a while until substantial work was done to infill the area which the River Lowman had eroded and re-route it. In 1966 the first clubhouse was built by joining together two pre-fabricated buildings, and this has been substantially altered and expanded since. A small corrugated roofed stand was erected in 1970, and this stood on the half-way line until 1993, when it was demolished and replaced with a modern red-brick structure which houses changing rooms. The ground today benefits immensely from the mature trees that have grown up alongside the main road and now give the place a much more secure look to that of just three or four years ago. The slaughterer's field is now a distant memory.

▼ *An early view of Crediton United. The trees are maturing fast around the ground, and another covered terrace is built to the left of the entrance. The ground is now floodlit.*

Washbrook Meadow, Ottery.

WASHBROOK MEADOW
Ottery St Mary FC

The Otters have been in existence since 1911, but did not enjoy the luxury of a well-appointed ground until after the Second War when the open spaces of Washbrook Meadow became available.

Various fields had been used, including Shoots Mead and Slade Road and for a while Kings School College grounds were home, but the current ground first became established around 1950 when a tiny tin and timber shed was erected in the corner of the ground and used for changing. A change from the previous arrangements when the Volunteer pub in the square was used.

In the early days there were two pitches end to end on each other with one tight against the road where the training pitch is now, although at right angles. The club's main stand, a square building made of what looks like the same materials as the changing rooms seems to date from around the same time as it is still in use complete with stencilled seating arrangements on the back wall. Indeed the original shed is still there, now ivy covered and in use for storage.

The large and impressive clubhouse has been extended and has had changing rooms built on to it but these were made redundant when a new block was built next to the stand in 1994. The second team pitch lies in the next field and is complete with a small area of cover used as a dug-out which may well be the one which originally stood across from the stand on the main pitch many years ago.

The capacity at this cosy little ground nestling in a stunning Devon valley was tested to the full ten years ago when Nottingham Forest played a friendly at Washbrook Meadow.

WATERSLADE PARK
Clyst Rovers FC

Reached by driving up a narrow lane off the A30, Clyst Rovers' compact little ground has been transformed within the last four years since their entry into the Western League from the South-Western League.

The ground is unusually situated on the extreme edge of Exeter Airport, and indeed was at one time part of it as can be seen by the modernised Nissen hut which has been utilised for the Social Club behind the near goal. Other huts were dotted around the place and were used in various ways until the serious work began. A seated covered area was provided on the site of one of them to replace a basic piece of cover, and on the opposite side more cover was provided with conifers bordering the ground. Behind the far goal the area is rough and stretches right across to the airport.

Information on the club's history is sketchy to say the least, but it is known that Rovers previously played at the Fairoak ground until just after the War, but on reforming the club in the Exeter and District League, and later the Sunday version of that, they moved to the present site, which needed extensive work on it to build up the playing area using rubble from the M5 construction.

THE CHRONICLES
Alphington FC

Alphington is an area of Exeter close to the City itself and has had a sports ground at the Chronicles since the 1890's.

The ground has only been developed in a similar way to that at Buckfastleigh since the late 80's when the splendid long low clubhouse was built with an overhang which acts as cover. The pitch railings went in in 1993 and have to be part removed as the ground is used for cricket. The post War years saw a Nissen hut used for dressing rooms at what is now a council owned ground which may well prove to be a hindrance to the club as they are unable to install floodlights to enable the club to go forward.

● *Another interesting venue close to Exeter is the former Western League home of St Lukes College at the Cat and Fiddle ground in Clyst St Mary. Now used as the training ground for Exeter City, it still bears the old Rothman's Western League score-board on the pavilion.*

PLAYING FIELDS
Dawlish Town FC

The open spaces of the Playing Fields in which Dawlish's ground is set, are not ideal when having to accommodate a large crowd, as it is not possible to fully enclose it, a problem shared with Minehead in the same league. A canvas sheet is erected around the chain fence in the old fashioned way to prevent a free view, But Dawlish have made great strides since opening their adjacent Social Club in 1982, and have built a new dressing room complex and erected floodlights in 1987 and 1988 respectively.

The site has been home to the club since the turn of the century, before which they used pitches at Elm Grove Road, near Elm Grove House, and later in Sandy Lane, next to Bowerman's Sawmills, which is approximately where the pitch is today. At odd times matches were played on a field belonging to a Mr Newberry which was where Coronation Avenue is now.

GREENWAY LANE
Budleigh Salterton FC

For many years the club played in a local park and on a pitch now covered by the bowls and tennis clubs in Cricketfield Lane which they shared with rugby.

In 1953 the council offered the club a piece of land which was protected by a covenant which provides for sport only on the site. They began playing there, changing in the old Drill Hall but a clubhouse and changing rooms which have been extended several times since went up in 1962. Around 1983 the post and rail barrier was put in place and was soon followed by the small bus stop type stand. The new dressing room building on the half way line is four years old.

In an area not exactly awash with top grade non-League football Budleigh have one of the best appointed grounds which is well qualified for the Devon County League which they joined in 1995, and frankly, is as good as some Western League grounds.

During the War, it was used as a base for military personnel and it was around this time that the old stand was put up which now holds 200 seats. The area all around the ground is used for sports and Dawlish Football Club are well established in one of the most pleasant towns in Devon.

CORONATION FIELD
Topsham Town FC

Topsham St Margarets were first established in 1908, playing on a pitch on the Bowling Green Marshes until after the Second War. They moved briefly to a ground called the Retreat before buying Pynes Fields in 1953 and re-naming it Coronation Field. A small wooden hut with a tin bath sufficed for changing and this did not improve until 1969 when the new dressing room block which is used today was built.

The club headquarters at the time were at the Lord Nelson pub and it was not until 1981 that years of graft and fundraising brought about the Social Club. In 1985 the changing block was extended and later planning permission for floodlights was obtained although lack of funds has prevented them to date.

Despite the closeness of the M5/A38 which thunders by next door, the ground is pleasant in a wealthy looking area close to Exeter and is beautifully maintained.

WINGFIELD PARK
Heavitree United FC

Situated minutes from St James's Park, Heavitree are always going to struggle to compete against their big brothers at Exeter City. That appears to be the least of their problems, however, for building work next door to the ground meant the narrowing of what was already a tight enclosure thus making any kind of expansion impossible.

United were formed in 1885 and are believed to have played in Heavitree Park on various pitches up to the Second War. At the time Wingfield Park was just part of an estate owned and run by a sporting benefactor who left the field and her house to the Social Club who still occupy the building today. The area was mainly rural and was not part of the City as such which meant that the ground was laid out in open space with just an old red brick wall running down one side. During the War United States forces occupied the field, using it as a camp site, and at various times the Royal Artillery who were stationed nearby played Polo on it when it wasn't required as an animal paddock.

Initially the football field was laid out at 45 degrees to its current position and was flanked by the stables of the house. Later a grass bank was formed when the pitch was turned and the entrance was from the corner to the right of where the gate is now. In the

The main stand at Heavitree. Same stand, different seasons.

sixties a small area of cover was erected over the bank and players changed in an old hut near to the entrance. Later, hard standing was put down in 1982 on the site of the bank, the cover of which by then had been blown down in a gale. The old wooden stand which straddles the half way line is in fact not as old as it looks for it was erected with the help of loyal club man Harry Wood and named after him back in 1970. Since then it has been regularly painted, re-boarded and mended, and as a result seems to look different every couple of seasons although it is the same stand.

Today the players change in a pre-fabricated building which was erected close to the site of the original stables in what is now the car-park.

Photos in this section by: Kerry Miller, Tony Colliver, Pat Brunning, Dean Walton and Chris Gillard.

SPEEDS MEADOW
Cullompton Rangers FC

There have been a number of sides come and go in the small town of Cullompton and the current one is Rangers, whose Speeds Meadow ground can be clearly seen from the M5. They have played there since the early 70's but it was only recently that the stand was erected and this enabled the club to go into the new Devon County League.

The first clubhouse was an old site hut from extension works on the A38 and cost £100. Ten years later a new clubhouse was built on the same site.

Amongst the former grounds used were Court Drive, Exeter Road and a pitch close to the old railway station which is now under the approach road from the M5.

Exmoor and North Devon

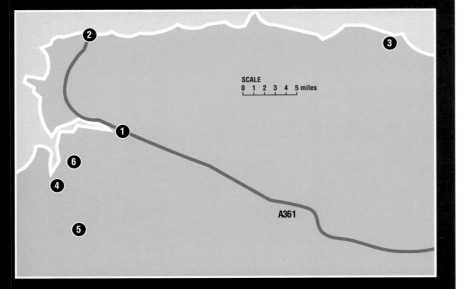

SCALE
0 1 2 3 4 5 miles

A361

1	**Barnstaple Town FC**
2	**Ilfracombe Town FC**
3	**Minehead FC**
4	**Bideford FC**
5	**Torrington FC**
6	**Appledore FC**

NORTH DEVON and West Somerset enjoy some of the wildest and most beautiful landscapes in the south of the country. In the days between the Wars the East Devon and North Devon Leagues were strong with almost every village proudly supporting a football team: Bampton, Silverton, North and South Molton and Dulverton were just a number who had much success.

Now, the North Devon League has one or two clubs who have either built up, or retained developed grounds of sorts, such as those at South Molton, but in the main the most senior grounds are those which currently stage Western League Football.

MILL ROAD
Barnstaple Town FC

Barnstaple's pre-War home has undergone a transformation in recent years which has re-established it as one of North Devon's premier football grounds. The old chicken run which had stretched down the side opposite the main stand since the late 1950's was swept away and replaced by a neat new version, which complements nicely the rest

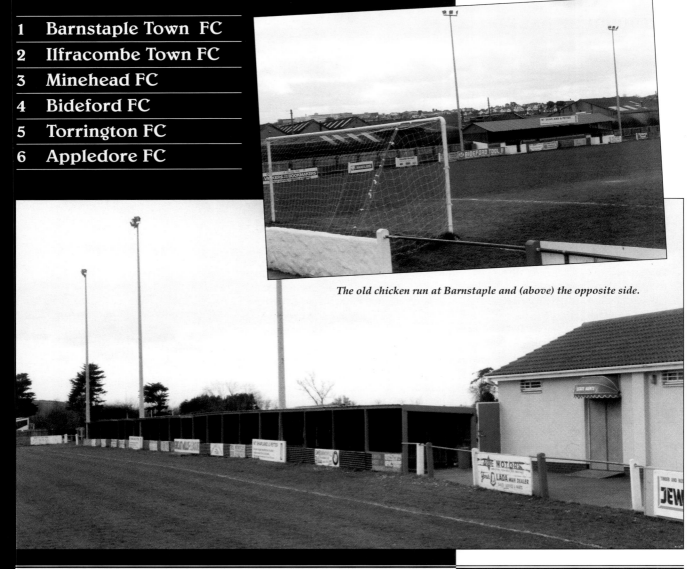

The old chicken run at Barnstaple and (above) the opposite side.

of the ground although it is somewhat over-shadowed by the rugby ground next door.

Barum began playing on Town Wharf before the Great War, when they had a number of grounds, none developed, including Highfield Road, Newport and pitches in Pilton and Rock Parks. The move to Mill Road is believed to have been around 1936, and shortly after, the old main stand was built into the grass banking which surrounded the pitch. Today, the old railway sleepers which rested on the bank and were used as seats within the stand are still in place, as is much of the banking.

The original changing rooms were superceded by replacements on the same spot built around 1980, as was the impressive entrance, named the George Bishop Gate. The clubhouse was built in 1984 after the original, which had an overhang as cover was taken down. To the right of the entrance is a bank which is partly enclosed and looks as if it may have been covered at one time, although research did not reveal any information.

Mill Lane has seen a crowd of over 6,000 for an FA Cup tie back in 1954 when Bournemouth came to town, and the current capacity is still a healthy 5,000 with the new stand covering 1,000.

MARLBOROUGH PARK
Ilfracombe Town FC

Marlborough Park was opened by Alderman Rowe on October 2nd 1924, before the club's prestigious friendly with Bristol City played before a crowd of 3,000 which stands as a ground record to this day.

The club had moved from Killacleave, close by, which was the playing fields for the Grammar School, having also used a pitch at Shaftesbury Field. The Grammar School is now comprehensive and the fields are still used.

Extensive engineering work was needed to level what was a sloping piece of farmland, and on completion of that, a perimeter fence and a post and wire around the pitch were in place. A small wooden cover stood on the half way line with the dressing rooms cut into the slope behind it .

Very little changed at the ground until the club began to go into decline around the late fifties and left the Western League. The old stand was burnt down in the mid sixties and the dressing rooms became derelict to an extent that players changed in the nearby comprehensive school. Things began to change for the better in 1978 when the old dressing rooms were refurbished and a clubhouse was planned and started with volunteer help. It took two years to complete and the club and ground were on the move.

1982 saw a car-park created and the following year a covered enclosure was built behind one goal and hard-standing laid down along with dug-outs.

The thriving supporters' club was extended in 1985 and a small amount of cover added as the club returned to the Western League after an absence of 25 years.

More recently floodlights were installed for the first time and a tannoy and new gate entrance added to further improve the ground that Alderman Rowe had dreamed of 70 years ago.

MARSHFORD
Appledore/BAAC

The small town of Appledore is curious in that it is neither a full-blown tourist area, taking advantage of the stunning scenery around the Torridge estuary, nor is it a heavily industrialised place, despite the small docks area which dominate parts of it.

In a similar way, the football ground is 70 years old but has never fully realised its potential, set as it is with glorious vistas of land and sea.

The early Appledore sides played on pitches on the flat lands beneath the town, known as the Burrows, and at Diddywell. The posts were removed after each game and stored at a farm, and this continued until 1925 when land became available at Marshford, with a barn in the next field for the home team to change in, the visitors having to make do with the bakehouse in the town. A couple of spartan huts were all that stood on the ground until around 1973 when changing rooms were finally erected, and a more recent addition to the ground is the clubhouse that has an overhang which doubles as covered accommodation.

The rather curious name came about after a merger with the successful Bideford Amateur Athletic Club in the late seventies whose football team shared the ground.

Ilfracombe Town

RECREATION GROUND, IRNHAM ROAD

Minehead FC

It is only a dozen years ago that Minehead played in the Southern League, in the club's golden era, that included five appearances in the competition proper of the FA Cup in six years, and a crowd of 3,600 for a match against Exeter City in Christmas week, 1977.

Minehead finished as runners-up to Wimbledon in the season that the Dons reached the Football League, and with a little luck could have taken the title. Times have changed. In May 1988, the Dons walked away from Wembley with the FA Cup, having beaten Liverpool 1-0, and fifteen months later Minehead walked away from Wordsworth Drive, Taunton, having been beaten 9-1 in a Preliminary Round tie in the same competition.

Despite the up and down fortunes of the club in the last years, the Recreation Ground, is still in beautiful condition, with the focal point, the 26 year old grandstand, dominating the area completely.

The whole ground is now owned by the local Council, and is unusual in that it is a senior football ground surrounded by a public park, which includes a children's play area.

Irnham Road was first opened in 1899, when seven acres of ground, complete with a wooden grandstand with seats for 200, was opened for polo, cricket and athletics, as well as football. The stand only lasted until the early 1900's when it burnt down, and it was not replaced until 1920.

From the outset the land was owned by a local landlord and squire, whose home was in Dunster Castle. The land was administered through a lease until 1950 when the squire died, and a great deal of his estate was sold off, the Rec. included. The Urban District Council took over the

land and have used it for recreational purposes ever since.

In 1969, the old wooden stand was condemned as a fire hazard, and the Committee and supporters, with the permission of the Council and a grant of £5,000, erected the grandstand with club room and dressing rooms underneath. It was opened before a match with Bristol City on August 27th, in the company of a wealth of guests from various committees and clubs.

Some five years later in December 1974, Minehead took advantage of the sad demise of Guildford City's St. Joseph's Road ground when they purchased the floodlight pylons and lights. It was around this time that cricket was last played on the ground, for until then the pitch actually encroached on to the football surface, with

the added problem of shortening the season for the footballers.

In recent years the stand has been extended towards the pitch to create a bar and skittle alley, which meant removing the terracing in the paddock area and now, other than a pathway along the stand side, the ground is flat grass standing all around.

A comparison to Irnham Road would be the Playing Field at Dawlish, which is also an open space, but with a far less imposing stand. Minehead's home has not changed dramatically in shape for it is protected by a covenant which ensures sport will be always be played there and, although the club will not again grace the upper echelons of non-League football, the Recreation Ground will remain precisely that.

SATURDAY, AUGUST 30, 1969

MINEHEAD A.F.C.'s NEW GRANDSTAND OPENED

Red-Letter Day For Local Soccer

Before Minehead A.F.C.'s match with Bristol City Colts on Wednesday evening, the new grandstand was officially opened by the Minehead president, Mr. Marshall Coneley, when, after with others he had been introduced to the players and match officials on the pitch, he cut the white ribbon across the entrances to the dressing rooms, &c., and the accommodation above associated with presen...

purposes, and a kitchen from which there is a servery for the half-time cups of tea and other light refreshments.

"A LOT TO BE DONE"

In a statement issued with the program... above the signature of M... ...ted out that the new ...ream of the club ...ars out until ...ark was ...because

Sports Ground, Bideford

SPORTS GROUND
Bideford AFC

The massive Sports Ground is close to the town centre of Bideford and was donated to the people of the town before the last War by a group of businessmen, and is now administered by the local council. Just after the War the ground was shared by the football and rugby clubs until the early fifties when the football club bought another site in the town and moved on their own to the Hansen Ground. It was not a success with the public not supporting them at the new site, and so a deal was struck whereby the two clubs swopped grounds, and this remains the case to this day.

Over the years both the Council and the football club have made improvements to the ground and the grandstand, which was condemned after the Bradford fire and replaced by a steel structure in 1990. The covered standing area opposite, the clubhouse and floodlights were all erected and paid for by the club who pay a substantial rent for the privilege of playing there. The cover can hold around 1,000 spectators and the new stand has around 120 seats. The splendid lighting system dates from 1982 and was opened by Manchester City, whose first team played a friendly to commemorate the occasion.

The pitch is circled by a track and athletics meetings are still held there and for a while greyhound racing was tried but without success. The size of the place can be gauged by the record crowd of nearly 6,000 which saw the FA Cup 4th Qualifying Round tie with Gloucester City in 1949.

VICARAGE FIELD
Torrington AFC

Tucked away a dozen miles south of Barnstaple, the pleasant North Devon town of Torrington has seen football on its Vicarage Field since the club was formed in 1908. Whilst never reaching the heights of its neighbours at Bideford and Barnstaple, Torrington have slowly developed their ground until it is one of the more attractive of the Western League's venues.

The first major building was the covered stand on the south side which went up in 1958, and was filled with around 100 seats in 1994. Opposite, the north side stand was built in 1984 when the club moved up from the South-Western League.

The clubhouse has seen two extensions since it was built in 1978, with a lounge and an office added in 1983 and 1993 respectively. In 1983 the pitch was extended to comply with FA rules, the dug-outs being removed from the north side and put down on the south.

Torrington boasted a goalscorer just after the War by the name of Sid Trickett who is believed to have scored 11 goals, all with his head, in one 18-0 win over Ilfracombe. His ashes are buried near the top goal and a small plaque commemorating the event is screwed to the goal-post in recognition of a feat which made the Guinness Book of Records.

Photos in this section by: Pat Brunning, Roger Turner and James Wright.

West Somerset

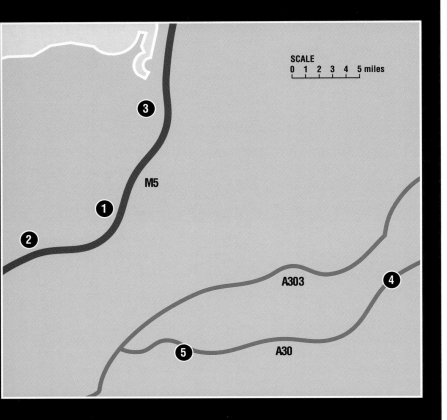

SCALE
0 1 2 3 4 5 miles

③

M5

①

②

A303

④

A30

⑤

1	Taunton Town FC
2	Wellington FC
3	Bridgwater Town FC
4	Yeovil Town FC
5	Chard Town FC

Below: Ilminster Town. The green stand has since been re-clad. With the cricket now transferred behind the ground, it could easily become a four-sided Western League ground.

OF THE clubs in this area, three have played Southern League football in recent times, Yeovil moving on to higher things and newer grounds.

Now languishing in the lower reaches of the Somerset Senior League are Ilminster Town who until 1982 were in the Western League. A run of only twelve wins in three years meant a drop to County Football. Their ground is unchanged with the old stands still in good shape, although not used quite so regularly.

WORDSWORTH DRIVE
Taunton Town FC

There are dozens of grounds around the country that seem to mirror the area in which they are set. Oswestry Town's former home at Victoria Park was a classic example of a slightly seedy, yet homely, place which echoed the town it served.

In a similar vein, Wordsworth Drive, Taunton gives off an air of rustic charm to match the county in which it belongs. Its tall elegant trees behind the far goal mask the view into a local park, and the seated stand situated on the same side as the well-patronised Peacock Club is solid and unpretentious.

Surprisingly the ground is only 40 years old, having been leased to the club by the local authority, who initially used the land as a rubbish tip, before converting it to a football ground, which at first suffered from having a 6in. deep cycle track running across it.

The club reformed in 1947, playing mainly friendlies before being accepted into the Somerset Senior League. The first season was spent at the Police ground at Mountfields, now home of the Wyvern Club, before moving to Ash Meadows (near Taunton Deane Cricket Club and now part of a golf course) and Rose Meadows, the Huish School playing fields now covered by Bloomfield Close.

Victoria Park was next stop for a year before Denmans Park, in Haines Hill where

*Wordsworth Drive, Taunton, in 1970 (above)
and the same stand 25 years later (right).*

the club had two caravans, one for changing and one used as a refreshment room. The transition from Somerset Senior to Western League football came in 1953 and two years later the club moved to the present ground which in those days was known as Hamilton Road. Since then, they have purchased the ground and continued to improve it, regularly renovating the popular side, when successive galvanised iron sections began giving up the ghost.

The small main stand was built around 1960 after a covered area with ash and railway sleeper standing had gone up opposite. This has since been rebuilt and extended with a tea bar, now unused. The Peacock Club dates from around 1971, the original building being a hut on the Army camp at Norton Fitzwarren. Most of the changes at the ground occurred before 1977 when the club entered the Southern League. Floodlights and terracing went in and car-parking followed. More recently the top end has gained concrete terracing as Wordsworth Drive continues to be one of the best grounds in the Western League.

The record attendance for a competitive match at the ground is 2,960 for a Western League match against Torquay United in 1958, although in March 1994, Taunton Town played Tiverton Town in a top of the table Western League game which almost matched it.

The original Taunton club played on the superb Priory Park until they folded, the ground being sold to the local rugby club in September 1935. Happily, the ground complete with massive wooden grandstand is still in use today, and little appears to have altered. Over the years the town has seen a number of grounds as the once-strong Somerset Senior League matches attracted large crowds just after the War. Somerset Police played on the Mountfields ground before Town, and the main rivals to Town in

their early days, Taunton British Rail, played on a ground at Obridge, on the other side of the railway from the rugby ground. The railway ground still exists and is used by a club called British Rail in the local junior league.

The concrete terracing at Wordsworth Drive is crumbling, but is more or less in place and the rusting corrugated tin sheeting which originally covered it, and was put up in 1952, now lays scattered against the wall in the dense undergrowth. There are strong rumours that the area is going to be developed and it could be that yet another piece of history will be lost before too long.

Above: Obridge, former home of Taunton B.R., a strong Somerset Senior League side of the 1950's and '60's.

Left: What's left of the covered terrace. The ground is still used for junior football but will soon be gone.

Below: Priory Park, former home of Taunton United, who folded in 1935. Since then it has been the home of Taunton Rugby Football Club.

WELLINGTON PLAYING FIELDS
Wellington AFC

The club was formed back in 1892 and for the first 70 years of its life played in the Taunton and Tiverton leagues on local pitches. Their previous homes included a field in Popes Lane, Rockwell Green and another at Pyles Thorn both since built on, and Courtlands Road School which is still there and was home until 1954.

A year previously the local council had taken over part of the grounds of a private house, since converted into old peoples homes, and created a dual purpose sports ground for the cricket and football clubs. The footballers changed in either the Ship or the Dolphin pubs, normally in the skittle alleys, until around 1960 when the cricket pavilion was built on the ground.

In 1966 the council built the small concrete stand with three terraces and this was put to good use when Ipswich Town played a friendly in front of the record crowd at the Playing Fields of 1,100. Seven years later the dressing rooms and clubhouse were built, and when the club joined the Western League in 1978 referees rooms were added. Further improvements were made in 1986, when a skittle alley and function room were built at the back of the stand and floodlights were erected before a game with Southampton. Since then there have been further alterations as Wellington strive to improve the social side at a ground where the presence of the cricket square means that all the facilities are situated down the side nearest the car-park with the rest of the ground completely open.

Further ground regulations could mean problems for the club, equidistant from the larger towns of Taunton and Tiverton, but until then their basic yet homely ground will continue to host Western League football.

Bridgwater Town in 1994

FAIRFAX PARK and CASTLEFIELDS
Bridgwater Town FC

The demise of Bridgwater Town was as sudden as it was sad and hastened the loss of an excellent football ground, more recently mirrored in the town by the loss of the Bridgwater and Albion Rugby Ground. Happily, both clubs are now re-established next door to one another by the side of the local college.

There have been several Bridgwater clubs during the last 100 years, the first played for just four seasons in the Somerset Senior League, and the second, a local factory side called Wills Athletic, adopted· the name

Bridgwater Town just after the Great War, and lasted until 1933.

In 1947 another junior side, Crown Dynamo, who played on an undeveloped ground in Cranleigh Gardens, joined the Somerset Senior League and also called themselves Bridgwater Town. Castlefields soon developed in an area which is now completely surrounded by an industrial estate and as early as 1956 had a floodlighting system installed. The slightly banked ground had a capacity of 5,000 at its peak and had covered terrace behind one goal and a stand which seated 300. In 1963 a large clubhouse was built which, when completely refurbished twenty years later, proved to be the final nail in the club's coffin. Having won

Western League honours in the previous two years, the Southern League beckoned but financial collapse was just around the corner.

Castlefields was left to rot, tucked away off the main road. It was partly destroyed, as the clubhouse was knocked down and the terrace roof left on the pitch. Within three years the pitch had become a jungle and eventually a service road was laid across it. Today, warehouses stand on the site which is named Robins Drive after the club's nickname.

Within a year, supporters had reformed the club and were in the lower reaches of the Somerset Senior League. Rapid progress was made, and in 1986 a long lease was signed on the field at Bridgwater College which was home. The lack of changing facilities meant using the college itself, a task not always performed without problems, as witnessed by a certain referee, named Miller, who got lost during the half-time interval of a game against Weston-super-Mare and, much to his embarrassment, was ten minutes late for the second half!

In 1988, the impressive cantilever stand, which seats 180 people, was built backing on to the railway line, and a post and rail was put in. The rise of the club continued with a welcome return to the Western League in 1994, by which time changing rooms, dugouts, refreshment facilities and offices had all been added to Fairfax Park.

DENING SPORTS GROUND
Chard Town FC

The home of Chard Town FC is known variously as the Town Ground, Dening Sports Field or simply Zembard Lane, the name of the rough track which led to the ground before the building of the nearby school meant it was upgraded.

The football ground is just a part of a much bigger complex which is owned by Bass Brewers who let it to the Council who in turn sub-let it to the cricket, tennis and football clubs. The field has been in existence since the cricket club began some 150 years ago but the football part was not created until the late twenties when Chard moved from their Bonfire Close ground, taking their wooden grandstand with them.

The formidable end to end slope seen today was considerably more pronounced at the beginning until a concerted effort saw earth transported from the top to the bottom of the ground. The evidence can be seen behind the bottom goal where the cricket area slopes away showing the pitch to be on a plateau. Early photos show an old Nissen hut which is still in use as a changing room for the minor sides but was used by all until the clubhouse and changing room complex was built in 1974. The old grandstand survived until then but was demolished to make way. Prior to the hut, players made do with the George Hotel in the town, walking to the ground with an overcoat on top of their kit.

A large flint wall ran behind the top goal with a galvanised fence stretching all down the Lane side, but these have been replaced by a concrete panel fence and a huge wall, part of the works which has been built next door. Three sides are enclosed by trees with the clubhouse and its overhang acting as cover on one side with a rather ugly area of cover opposite.

On first viewing the Town Ground looks almost freakish with its ten foot drop from end to end, very similar to that at Darlaston, but seen from certain angles the slope is much less pronounced giving the impression of an optical illusion. However, it is reasonable to assume that there is no more pronounced slope anywhere in senior non-League football.

THE HUISH and HUISH PARK
Yeovil Town FC

Yeovil Town are a club that by rights and with the correct amount of luck and forward planning should not appear in this book at all. They are ideally placed and well enough supported to have long since gained Football League status, but instead find themselves out of the top flight once again.

They have been fortunate enough to have played on the most famous non-League

ground in the country which once held over 16,000 people and was still in good condition when sold. They have also built a futuristic new stadium at Houndstone, well away from civilisation that gives ample room for expansion.

The building of the new stadium, easily the largest new non-League ground built in this country for decades, has brought problems, for its massive cost has put untold financial strain on the club and has meant that the two ends are unlikely now to be covered as was originally planned.

The two sides of the ground are symmetrical inside with seating for a total of over 5,000 with both uncovered ends large enough for a further 3,500. The capacity was reached all bar a couple of hundred when Arsenal visited in the FA Cup in 1993 and, despite the team's poor showing on the field, the crowds continue to come in.

The initial seeds were sown way back in March 1985 when discussions opened with Bartlett Construction with a view to selling Huish and moving to Houndstone. At that time a figure of £680,000 was quoted for the sale, which eventually rose to £2.8m over several years. A public enquiry was held in September 1987 but the results were not published until February 1989 and work began in time for the start of the 1990-91 season.

The Huish Athletic Ground was first coveted in 1897 by the fledgling club, then called Yeovil Casuals, when Brutton's Brewery were approached with a view to buying it outright.

The club were unsuccessful and continued playing on their ground at Pen Mill, between the station and the hotel of the same name. They took the name Town and changed to green and white in 1908, just prior to the founding of a new club, Petters United who had a pitch in Brickyard Lane. The two clubs merged in 1914 and after the Great War steps were taken to drastically

Aerial views of the old Huish ground (above), scene of several FA Cup giant-killing acts, and (below) Yeovil's new Huish Park Stadium, the largest non-league ground built in this country for decades.

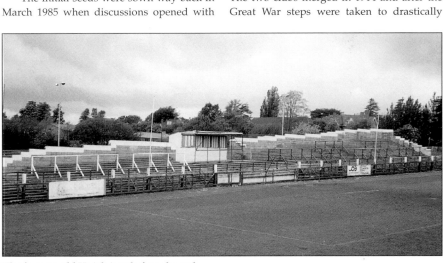

The famous old Huish just before the end.

improve the ground at Pen Mill which had a 300 seater stand but no changing facilities, the hotel being used.

A second attempt to buy the Huish was successful, Bruttons accepting £1,725 with a covenant placed that they had first refusal to buy back the land at the original figure. The early footballing days at the Huish saw flat terraces with the old stand brought with them from Pen Mill. In 1922 dressing rooms with sunken baths were built and the stand extended as they geared themselves up for Southern League football. The pitch was lengthened by four yards and the Queen Street end saw 750 loads of earth deposited to form terracing before more materials and 1000 railway sleepers were laid down to add steps. The following years saw the Supporters' Club formed and they installed three tea huts at the ground. Such was the size of the place that 5,500 saw an FA Cup tie against Bournemouth and Boscombe in 1924 and before the next round the Brutton Road end had been terraced. November 1926 saw the Queen Street end covered which was the last work at the Huish until 1931.

They had gained the freehold of the ground by then and had bought more land at the Brewery end to increase the capacity, and four years later enjoyed another FA Cup run,

Liverpool visiting the Huish on this occasion. In the two weeks leading up to the game, a small stand was built to hold 100 people and afterwards this was used as a Directors' box until the new stand was built.

In 1939 a new record gate of 14,329 saw Sheffield Wednesday visit for an FA Cup replay with thousands more locked out and the Queen Street end was severely damaged by people viewing from the roof. That proved to be the last major occasion before the War during which time the ground was used first as an ammunition store and then by the American Army who offered to level the pitch to play baseball, an invitation that was refused.

1949 saw the famous match against Sunderland when over 16,000 crammed in to the Huish to watch Yeovil win 2-1 in one of the most famous Cup upsets of all time. The funds from that Cup run were put to good use over the next five years when the sleepers and waste materials were removed from around the ground and replaced by concrete terracing. Sadly the cover on the Queen Street end never recovered from the Sheffield game and was removed to enable the terracing to go down. The North Terrace was then covered for the first time as the costs approached £5,000, with a wall and the first

set of floodlights being added in 1955. Work was completed when the back of the North Terrace was closed in and the Huish again was left alone until the Summer of 1963 when the old stand and a tea hut were demolished to make way for the 2,000 seater stand with dressing rooms which was finished along with the new Social Club in December of that year. It had cost £60,000 and was officially opened on 22nd March 1965.

Between then and the end in 1990 some £200,000 was spent on ground safety at the Huish installing crash barriers, staircases, fireproofing and segregated areas. However, it was all wasted effort as, after five years of negotiations, the ground was sold to Bartlett Construction and with almost indecent haste the famous sloping pitch was covered by another Tesco superstore.

Photos in this section by:
Kerry Miller, Pat Brunning and Dean Walton.

Dorset

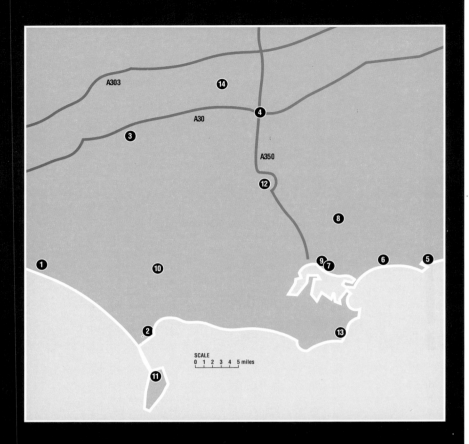

A303
A30
A350

SCALE
0 1 2 3 4 5 miles

1   Bridport FC
2   Weymouth FC
3   Sherborne Town FC
4   Shaftesbury FC
5   Christchurch FC
6   Bournemouth FC
7   Poole Town FC
8   Wimborne Town FC
9   Hamworthy United FC
10 Dorchester Town FC
11 Portland United FC
12 Blandford United FC
13 Swanage Town & Herston FC
14 Gillingham FC

THE County of Dorset is blessed with a number of long established clubs that have graced the Southern and Western Leagues over the years as well as some that are succeeding in the relatively new Wessex League. Along with the Dorset Combination which also thrives, this pedigree has meant many well developed grounds in the area, including a number of brand new stadia, one of which should be the blueprint for the future.

Of the less well known grounds in Dorset, **Gillingham**'s Hardings Lane ground with its now condemned main stand is of interest, having been originally the home of the Gillingham Show Society. The club moved there between the Wars, having played at Chantry Fields and, later on, a field just behind the Police Station. The modern clubhouse dates from 1977.

Blandford United FC are an amalgam of a number of clubs in the town and played, amongst other places, on a pitch in the local park opposite the hospital with an entrance through the Crown Meadows. Soon after the First War the club began playing at the Recreation Ground and in 1933 they built a large wooden grandstand which seated more than 200 and survived until around ten years ago when, having deteriorated, it was condemned and taken down.

Sherborne FC play at Raleigh Grove, a ground with a new clubhouse and covered area which has a bank down one side and gives the impression of antiquity although only a dozen or so years old. The club moved across from the Terrace Playing Fields where the facilities were far more basic than those at Raleigh Grove.

WEYMOUTH FC GROUNDS
Since 1890

Weymouth Football Club were founded in 1890 and for the first three seasons of their existence played on a field at Lodmoor. In 1893 the club moved to Westham where they changed at the Rock Hotel, in Abbotsbury Road.

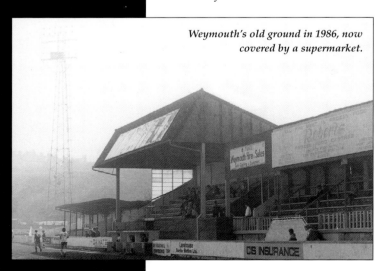

Weymouth's old ground in 1986, now covered by a supermarket.

The old Recreation Ground in Weymouth.

In 1897 they leased a recreation ground in Newstead Road from the Weymouth Corporation, and remained there for the next 90 years.

In the early days of the Rec, there were two wooden stands one containing changing rooms underneath. The stands accommodated only a few hundred and it was not until 1960 that a new modern stand was built which straddled the half-way line and could at a pinch seat 800. Soon after, a Directors' stand was built with Supporters' Club offices underneath, and terracing was laid at one end with a covered enclosure for 1,500 along the side opposite the main stand. Around 1967 the new Supporters' Club was built in one corner of the ground near the turnstiles.

The Rec was one of the earliest grounds to receive floodlighting, in 1953, and some years later came the modern version with its 130 foot high pylons. It had a capacity of around 10,000 at the end with some 6,500 covered. The record attendance at the ground was the 12,512 who packed into the Rec to see the FA Cup 2nd Round tie with Yeovil Town in December 1948.

When a supermarket chain began to covet the prime area site on which the ground stood, the Council snapped up the deal and Weymouth were on the move to a brand new stadium in Radipole Lane constructed more or less on the spot of the old Weymouth Speedway Stadium. The £1m site was built to Alliance League standards with terraced cover on all four sides and a capacity of 10,000. The first match at the new ground was on August 26th 1987 when Weymouth beat Lincoln City 3-0 in the Conference and the official opening came two months later on October 21st 1987 when Manchester United were the guests for a prestigious friendly.

A fine view of Weymouth's Wessex Stadium.

WEYMOUTH AVENUE and THE AVENUE GROUND
Dorchester Town FC

The start of the 1990-91 season saw the inauguration of three new stadia at the top of the pyramid. Those of Conference giants Wycombe Wanderers and Yeovil Town received most attention and acclaim, somewhat overshadowing Dorchester Town's magnificent achievement at the Avenue Stadium. That was unfortunate as Dorchester's is certainly the most innovative football ground built in England for many years.

Dorchester Town have been edging their way seawards down Weymouth Avenue (now the A354), for the best part of a century. Originally the club were sited at a basic recreation field which survives today as such, then in 1929 they moved 'over the hedge' to the ground that was to remain their home for sixty years, taking the name of the road on which it stood. A railway coach was moved to the ground to house the players' and officials' changing facilities and remained in situ until the construction of a permanent pavilion four years later. 1930 saw the erection of the 300 seat stand that backed on to the main road and became distinctive in its latter years for the fascia prominently advertising Huntsman Ales. The stand cost £300, a figure that was met by a contribution of £50 from each of six benefactors, including one Harry Crocker whose nephew, Peter Aitken, played the leading role in the development of the new stadium sixty years later.

The whole site, including a rugby club to the immediate south of the football ground, was owned by the Duchy of Cornwall who stipulated that it be used for sport all year round - the Lord's Taverners provided an

*Right: **The last match at Dorchester's old ground. Two days later the demolition men moved in and** (above) **as the old ground is dismantled the new stadium can be seen nearing completion in the background.***

artificial wicket at the football ground, but it was unpopular with local cricketers.

The seeds of change at Weymouth Avenue were sown as early as 1985 when a developer, learning of the planned construction of a major by-pass route skirting the southern fringe of the rugby ground, realised the potential of the site and approached the club. Brushing aside an opportunist attempt by Dorchester Town to buy the freehold, the Duchy of Cornwall were insistent that any development take place through them, and the culmination of five years' frenzied activity was a bout of musical chairs; Tesco supermarket took over the site of Dorchester Town F.C., Dorchester Town F.C. moved next-door to Dorchester R.F.C., and Dorchester R.F.C. relocated to Coburg Park.

The Avenue Stadium, built by McIntyre Construction, was designed by the Duchy's architects. The Duke of Cornwall himself, Prince Charles, was generous with his advice, as widely reported in the national press at the time, and paid two official visits, and several others unofficially. Club chairman, Peter Aitken, fought the football club's corner with great gusto, and the end result was as far removed from a 'hideous carbuncle' as one could possibly hope.

On Saturday 18th August 1990, Worcester City were defeated 3-2 in the first competitive fixture at the Avenue Stadium, and two months later Chelsea drew a crowd of 4,000 when they visited to officially open the ground. His Royal Highness's attendance record at football is not well documented, but if he had any say in the interior design of the stadium, then he must possess a football fan's eye for there are few venues around that offer such comfortable viewing.

The grandiose gabled stand sports 710 moulded plastic seats. Most are white, but some have been blackened to boldly depict 'D.T.F.C.'. The stand also boasts a capacious glass-fronted press box, and is accessed via stairways from turnstiles on either flank and from the V.I.P. lounge at its core.

The remainder of the stadium is symmetrically and conveniently steeply terraced. A turnstile block between two turrets on the eastern side offers access from the main car park to the terracing. A tea bar stands to the north of this entrance, a small club shop to its south. The Duchy covered the southern end with a tasteful slated roof, and the football club covered the eastern side, in the same style, at their own expense to maintain the aesthetic symmetry.

The whole ground was constructed at a cost of around £3million, of which £110,000 was spent on the playing surface. 32,000 tons of chalk were laid to ensure the good drainage of a pitch that was prepared fully eighteen months before the completion of the stadium. The chalk lies one metre deep at one end and three metres deep at the other to ensure flatness, something that was notably lacking at the previous ground which suffered an eight foot end to end, and twelve foot corner to corner, slope.

Other impressive features of the ground are the palatial foyer, V.I.P. lounge and boardroom, changing rooms, club laundry, and treatment room - all of which are situated under the main stand. The only notable absence is that of a supporters' social club. Permission for one, outside the ground, has been granted, but its planned construction fell through when the brewery pulled out.

The superb management of the relocation is highlighted by the fact that the club raised £11,000 from selling the fixtures and fittings of their old ground. The cover that shielded the terracing was off-loaded to Waterlooville F.C. and has been erected behind one goal at Jubilee Park, Dorchester R.F.C. purchased the floodlights to illuminate their new set-up, the turf from the pitch was sold by a resourceful director, Mr Stacey Gould, to a local contractor, and the dressing rooms were bought by a farmer and now house chickens!

Dorchester Town came out of the move so well primarily because of the constructive co-operation between all three parties; supermarket, football club and land-owner. They are financially better off, and the move from a spartan sloping old ground to an ultra-modern stadium has resulted in a dramatic increase in support despite the fact that on-the-field performances have remained uninspiring.

Dorchester's superb new Avenue Ground was designed by the Duke of Cornwall's architects.

THE CUTHBURY
Wimborne FC

It is believed that football has been played on the Cuthbury since the Wimborne club were formed back in 1878. It was used for rugby and soccer until eventually used exclusively by the football club.

The first structure of any significance was a timber stand with changing rooms beneath and 100 bench seats. This was constructed in 1920 and stood astride the halfway line opposite the current buildings. It just about survived to see its Golden Anniversary for it was pulled down in 1970 and replaced with a small covered area on the near side of the ground, leaving the far side open, as it has been ever since.

In 1950 a brick-built changing room complex was put up which was used until 1978 when it was transformed into a small clubhouse, and temporary dressing facilities were bought in. Two years later a new clubhouse and changing room took shape.

The first lights at the Cuthbury were training lights put in around 1970, but in 1982 the new set was unveiled for full scale use, Portsmouth being the visitors. Around the same time the covered enclosure for 300 was built and this sufficed for some 12 years until a further area was put up behind one goal. A small stand was built for directors to the right of the club in 1990 and two years later the lights were upgraded as the club enjoyed success. A run in the FA Vase which culminated in a Wembley appearance in 1992 saw the record attendance figure shattered when the club played Bamber Bridge in the second leg of the semi-final. Estimates of upwards of 5,000 crammed into Cuthbury, although the official record is 3,250.

DAYS PARK
Swanage Town & Herston FC

Days Park is a throw back to the old rustic grounds of the Western League which the club played in all too briefly for fifteen years before joining the Wessex League in 1990.

Swanage Albion was originally formed in 1898 playing on a field at what is now the Middle School on the edge of town. Around 1925 they moved to Days Park, named after the Mayor who left it to the town for its sole use as a football ground. The facilities were spartan and it was not until 1951 that the pitch was levelled, thus removing the fearsome end to end slope. The grass banking around the pitch gives a clue to the camber which the players were forced to cope with. Herston FC was formed in 1956 as a way of giving veteran players a game, but the club did so well that they eventually merged with the parent club and took the current name in 1956. The ricketty wooden stand has 150 or so wooden seats and dates from sometime around the late 40's

COCKRAMS
Shaftesbury FC

The Cockrams ground in the pleasant Dorset town of Shaftesbury is another that comes as a surprise when seen in context with the modest league in which it hosts its football.

Situated by the main town car-park it has twin covered standing areas either side of the matching dug-outs and is railed off all round. The frontage is dominated by the clubhouse and changing complex, built in 1974 when the club moved from their previous ground in Barton Hill which had been home since 1923. The Recreation Ground had a pavilion, and in the early days was rented at £1 per year by the club who, at various times, have used the cricket field and Stratton's Field as well as Park Walk in the town.

CHRISTCHURCH SPORTING CLUB
Christchurch FC

The Hurn Bridge ground of Wessex League side Christchurch has only been home since 1984 when they moved off their Barrack Road Recreation Ground, believed to have been home for the best part of 100 years.

The new ground is situated close to Hurn Airport and is surrounded by woods with the barest of covered areas to the left of one goal. Stricter grading levels in the Wessex League have cast serious doubts over this old club, whose ground is also headquarters to the Bournemouth FA and needs far more upgrading than the club can cope with at the moment and so a drop into the Hampshire League or even closure are both sad possibilities.

BEEHIVE, ST MARY'S FIELD
Bridport FC

The Beehive has changed very little since 1953 when the club moved from the Crown Field, West Bay Road. It is a typical Western League ground with a low wooden, slightly ramshackle stand which came up from the Crown Field with them, and straddles the half way line. Slightly upgraded by the breeze block wall at the front and sides, it seats 200. The covered area dates from the sixties and at a squeeze can hold 400.

Prior to the Beehive, Bridport used the Crown Field from 1930, a site now covered by a nursery, and from 1897 shared the cricket ground. Other early pitches were at Wanderwell, just off West Bay Road, Wrixon Mead in Bradpole Road and Pymore Road. The record attendance stands at 1,150 against Exeter City in 1981, with the Crown Field once holding 3,000 for a match against Chelsea in 1950.

The Beehive, Bridport

Victoria Park - tucked away in the suburbs of Bournemouth.

VICTORIA PARK
Bournemouth FC

Universally known as the Poppies, the club have played at Victoria Park since before the First War, having spent their earlier years on a field at East Common and later on part of Dean Park, close to Dean Court, home of AFC Bournemouth.

Victoria Park was formed out of a farmer's old field and boasted a stand and dressing rooms much earlier than several more advanced clubs. The Poppies leased the ground from July 1923 and the changing rooms and stand were repaired and rebuilt soon afterwards. In 1944 the council took the unusual step of buying back the ground and renting it to the club for £1 a year. Conditions attached to the agreement dictated that the club enjoyed the use of the ground every Saturday and Bank Holiday throughout the season plus six Wednesdays, with the added proviso that they keep the gate money.

The pitch was roped off until the early seventies when a barrier was put up. Subsequently a new clubhouse with all mod cons was erected next to the current version of the seated stand which replaced the original, burnt down twenty years ago.

Nowadays tucked away among Bournemouth's suburbia, Victoria Park is a not unpleasant ground but it would need transforming before the Southern League could ever consider it worthy. Whether the Council, or indeed the locals, might accept wholesale changes with acres of fencing or walling is debatable.

NURSERY GROUND
Hamworthy United FC and Poole Town FC

The first club to play in the area were Hamworthy St Michaels, a church lads' team who played on a pitch in Rectory Gardens, covered since the fifties by a school. The move to the Nursery Ground, now officially the County Ground, took place just after the War when it was enclosed by a wall built by club members.

In 1956 Sir Stanley Rous opened the club's main stand which remains in its original form today. At that time the club were using the classrooms of the nursery next door as dressing rooms, but when that closed in 1974 and became a remedial education unit, the club then leased it from the council.

The building is currently the headquarters of the Dorset County FA as they now lease the ground with the two clubs as ten-

ants. Since 1994 Poole Town's appearance has led to a number of changes at the ground to bring it up to Southern League standard.

POOLE STADIUM
Former home of Poole Town FC

Over 60 years of football at Wimborne Road came to a close on 23rd April 1994, when Erith and Belvedere were the last ever visitors to Poole Town's cavernous stadium. Unusually, it was not the end for either ground or club, for the club have moved into the Dorset HQ ground to share with Hamworthy United and the stadium remains intact, hosting speedway and greyhound racing.

The original Poole Football Club were formed through a merger of Poole Rovers and Poole Hornets on September 20th 1890. Their early home matches were held on a pitch at Sterte, so close to Poole Harbour that

The Nursery Ground, home of Hamworthy United and Poole Town.

the pitch was often covered in seaweed! When the club resumed after the Great War, they took up residence on a ground in Breakheart Lane - now Linthorpe Road - and used changing rooms at The Shah of Persia pub. The club entered the Western League in 1923 and the Southern League three years later but fell on hard times and folded in 1930, whereupon they re-formed as an amateur outfit.

Now called Poole Town, they re-entered the Western League but lost Breakheart Lane and all but folded again, until rescued by a benefactor who lent the club, rent free, a field which adjoined his premises.

Supporters, officials and players worked to level the pitch and erect a stand before the 1930-31 season and there they remained until promised use of the brand new stadium in Wimborne Road. A few games were played at the back of the new ground before it was ready on a pitch which is now utilised by the boys of Henry Harbin School.

The opening match at the stadium was against Wells City in the Western League on 26th August 1933 amidst much pomp and pageantry, the Mayor of Poole kicking-off. The original facilities at the ground consisted of banked standing areas behind a track, with a long covered stand stretching down one side. Various ancillary buildings were also dotted about, but little happened

POOLE TOWN FOOTBALL CLUB
AND
POOLE TOWN FOOTBALL SUPPORTERS' CLUB

Official Opening
of the
New Football Stand

by

SIR STANLEY ROUS, C.B.E., J.P.
(Secretary of the Football Association)

Saturday, 19th August, 1961

prior to the Southern League Division One match

POOLE TOWN 3
v.
HASTINGS UNITED 0

POOLE TOWN FOOTBALL CLUB.

The Committee request the pleasure of your company
at the
Opening Football Match
on the NEW SPORTS ARENA, Wimborne Road, Poole.
POOLE TOWN v. WELLS CITY
ON SATURDAY NEXT, AUGUST 26TH, 1933
At 3-15 p.m.

The MAYOR OF POOLE (Coun. W. C. J. Shortt)
has kindly consented to kick-off.

COMPLIMENTARY TICKET
of Admission to Ground and Stand.
This portion to be retained.

H. S. STOKES, Hon. Sec.,
Marwin, Longfleet, Poole.
This portion to be given up at Entrance.

Right: Poole Stadium in Wimborne Road, now used for speedway, boasts a record crowd of over 11,000 for an FA Cup tie between Poole Town and Watford in 1962.

Above: An invitation to the stadium opening in August 1933 and, some 28 years later, Sir Stanley Rous was guest of honour at Poole to open the new 1,400-seater main stand.

to change the ground until after the Second War.

During hostilities, the stadium was commissioned for the War effort but on resumption plans soon surfaced for the club to adopt professionalism and this came to fruition in 1952. Two years later the inaugural floodlights were switched on with a friendly against near-neighbours Bournemouth and Boscombe Athletic on 20th October 1954.

Good times came with a Western League title win and the Southern League once again took the club on board in 1957. The ground continued to develop and in 1961 the club officially opened their 1,400 seater main stand, the inevitable Stanley Rous performing the ceremony before a match with Hastings United on August 19th. The second set of lights went in a year later.

From then on the ground has developed with speedway in mind as much as football. Indeed, it is probably the continuation of that sport that has saved the stadium from a fate worse than Tesco or Asda. A further grandstand is now opposite the main stand and the old covered banks have been converted to high covered terracing.

The scale of the ground can be gauged by the record crowd which gathered to see the FA Cup tie with Watford in 1962, 11,155 cramming into Wimborne Road.

Although often lost in the acreage of the old ground, the club must feel claustrophobic playing in the tight confines of Hamworthy United's domain.

GROVE CORNER
Portland United FC

Grove Corner almost went out with a bang during the winter of 1994. Having been vacated and demolished in readiness for the area to be quarried, a huge unexploded wartime bomb was found lying underneath one of the penalty areas. It necessitated the sealing off of the entire island as the bomb was made safe.

It is perhaps a blessing that Liverpool's roly-poly Tommy Lawrence never played in goal at Grove Corner, or the ground may not have reached the ripe old age of 72 years! The summer of 1994 proved a sad one, for the glorious former Western League ground saw its last game on May 9th, when Weymouth came across Chesil Beach to play a friendly.

At the end the old girl looked as though she had had enough, although still clinging on to some self-respect. The entrance was through the remains of a gateway leading to a pay-box which poignantly thanked everyone for their support during the last 72 years.

There was a covered terraced area behind the near goal which had lost its roof with weed infested banking along the side and a further covered area straddling the half way line. A stone wall ran along the back goal and a storage shed stood next to the rusting old main stand. The roof fascia was in an advanced state of decay but the all-wooden interior was still sound. Another store-room and the burnt remains of the clubhouse were on the near side and in the corner were the corrugated iron changing rooms painted blue and white.

With a few days to go before demolition, Grove Corner was only short of some weed-killer and a few sheets of corrugated iron to return to its splendour as a Western League ground when 3,000 or more would pack in.

The whole site has now been quarried but Portland United have moved a few hundred yards further up the road, ironically to a piece of land which was reclaimed after having been quarried. They have developed a banked ground with a superb clubhouse behind one goal; the club lives on but dear old Grove Corner is no more.

Photos in this section by: Tony Colliver, Andy Dakin, G.M. Ellis-Neville, Kerry Miller and Dean Walton.

Three views of the now demolished Grove Corner at Portland.

The Mendips & The Levels

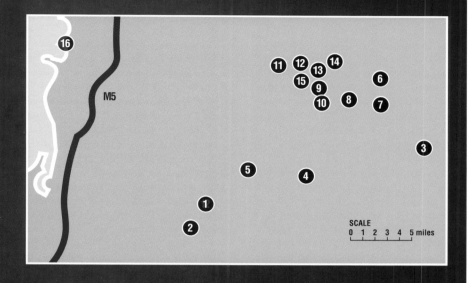

THE area which bounds the Mendip Hills and includes the North Somerset Coal Fields to the south of Bristol and the Somerset Levels around Glastonbury is another steeped in history, much of it emanating from the strength of the Western League. The mining areas around Radstock were rich with football clubs, many of whom have faded but it is still a stronghold despite Radstock Town themselves dropping from the Western League into Division One of the Somerset Senior.

The gritty mining village of Peasedown first saw Western League football in 1911 when Peasedown St John played through until 1924. For one season before the Second War and then through to 1960 when they finished bottom, Peasedown Miners Welfare were in the league. They now play in the village as **Peasedown Athletic** on the Welfare Ground which has a small concrete stand and ancient corrugated changing rooms behind the Bath end goal. As is sadly the case with most Welfare Grounds today, it is no longer the focal point of the village, up until the 70's having staged fetes, fairs and flower shows and providing tennis courts, a bowling green and a skittle alley. It is the fourth

1	Glastonbury FC
2	Street FC
3	Frome Town FC
4	Shepton Mallet FC
5	Wells City FC
6	Peasedown Athletic FC
7	Clandown FC
8	Radstock Town FC
9	Paulton Rovers FC
10	Welton Rovers FC
11	Bishop Sutton FC
12	Clutton FC
13	Tunley Athletic FC
14	Timsbury Athletic FC
15	Temple Cloud FC
16	Weston-Super-Mare FC

The homes of Radstock Town (above) and Peasedown Athletic (right), former Western League clubs now playing in the Somerset Senior League.

ground to be used, the others having been on a field near the Red Post Inn situated between two lodge houses, behind what is now Arleen's Coaches yard and at the cricket ground before the Welfare was created in the early twenties.

Peasedown Mycor FC were accepted into the Senior League for 1995 and will play at the cricket ground.

CLANDOWN F.C., situated a couple of miles south of Peasedown, enjoyed a prolonged spell in Western League football at their Thynne Field ground, until dwindling support hastened their resignation. As a result the reserves became the first team and they are currently in the lower reaches of the Somerset Senior League. The ground suffered during one of the terrible storms of the early 1990's when the clubhouse literally blew down, dealing the club a major blow. However, the old jet black stand somehow withstood the impact and continues to give a degree of comfort, if a touch on the ricketty side.

Tunley, Timsbury, Temple Cloud, and Clutton are all neighbouring villages with clubs in the Somerset Senior League .

TUNLEY ATHLETIC have played on the Recreation Field, formerly the Miners Welfare for over 80 years. Originally Tunley Rovers, and later Tunley M.W, the club went to great lengths to provide good facilities back in 1970, when the pitch was turned round to its present position then levelled, and a small stand erected the following year.

TIMSBURY ATHLETIC play now at the Conygre, home also of the cricket club, which hasn't always been a happy marriage. A number of seasons ago, they were forced to play at Radstock Town's ground, the club being in dispute with the owners of the ground, but are now back in the village. The club's one and only FA Cup tie in the Extra-Preliminary Round of 1949, against

Chippenham Town, was played on their old ground, which sadly is no more, on the other side of the crossroads in the village.

TEMPLE CLOUD play at the Cameley Playing Fields, and have been in existence on and off for 80 years or more

CLUTTON F.C. celebrated their centenary with a match at their Warwick Arms ground against Bristol City in 1990. The club have had a fascinating history for such a small club, first playing at Nine Acres and had two pitches with changing facilities, situated in the next field to the present Warwick Field ground. This ground was used until around 1930, apart from a couple of years at Tile Down, a spartan site in neighbouring Temple Cloud. Through the thirties the club played at Red Hayes, a ground with no changing facilities, where the players had to walk half a mile to the Miners Welfare Hall (now Village Hall).

It is not clear when the club moved to Warwick Field but it has been in use continuously since the War. Facilities have improved immensely over the years, and the most ambitious project was to level out the fearsome slope in 1978. Prior to that, in 1962, the first dressing rooms were built - a wooden structure with asbestos roof and tin baths - which meant the men no longer had to change in the pub stables!

A small green wooden stand was erected to celebrate the club's promotion to the First Division of the Bristol & District League, but only lasted 17 years and has been replaced by the Centenary Stand, a small building incorporating dug-outs. The clubhouse is made up of some old classrooms from Monkton Combe Junior School. These were split in two, the other half going to Backwell United for the same purpose.

RADSTOCK TOWN play at Southfields, another Miners Welfare Ground which has seen happier times. The club are

now in Division One of the Somerset Senior League with much work to do to regain their old status. The wood and tin main stand has been renovated in recent years, as have the changing rooms which are tucked away in the corner by the entrance. Walsall FC brought a side down to commemorate their opening a few years ago.

WEST CLEWES
Welton Rovers FC

West Clewes is the oldest of the established football grounds within the area bounded by the old Somerset Coal Fields. Situated close to the centre of Midsomer Norton, it has been in existence since the 1880's, when Welton Rovers were formed.

At the time of the formation the club bought the ground, but during the early twenties they experienced severe financial difficulties, and were forced to relinquish West Clewes to the Miners Welfare who, as was standard in many parts of the country, contributed a penny a week for its continued existence as a recreational outlet.

Just before the Second World War, the grandstand was built, initially holding 150 seats, and much later after continued success on the pitch, the club created banking which was terraced in 1965. Soon after, however, the declining coal industry brought about a change of circumstance, and the Welfare decided to donate the ground to the local authority for its continued use by the football club and Welton now lease it from the local council.

Today, West Clewes fights hard to remain a comfortable and pleasant ground to visit, although the main stand, which has been extended since its opening, is looking a little weary and pale around the gills. Within the last couple of years the entrance has had a wooden hut placed next to it, for the use of

West Clewes is the oldest of the established grounds within the area bounded by the old Somerset coalfields.

Tannery Field, Street, (above) and the Athletic Ground, Wells (below), the latter another Western League ground now hosting Somerset Senior League football.

TANNERY FIELD
Street FC

Street are a club who fell from grace during the last twenty odd years but have had a new lease of life and are looking to regain their Western League place.

As a Western League club, their Victoria Field ground was often crammed full to watch derbies with Glastonbury and Frome in the FA Cup, and their current home, since 1975, is the Tannery Field, a spacious, walled off ground amongst many residences that have been built up around it. The field was given to Street Urban District Council by the Co-Op Tannery, whose works playing fields it originally was. The club have leased it ever since.

The move to the Tannery was forced on them by the building of the Street by-pass which sliced through the Turnpike ground which they had used for just six years. The turnpike building which gave the ground its name and acted as changing rooms is still standing, by the roundabout leading to the by-pass. The pitch was situated roughly between it and the road. The club had erected a small pre-cast cover at the Turnpike, and that is now to be found at the Tannery. The club's spiritual home was the Victoria Field, played on since the 1900's. It was a three-sided ground with two small wooden stands, and a Nissen hut acting as a dressing room in between the two. The ground was shared with the cricket club, and today cricket is still played there, although there is no trace of the football artifacts. In fact one of the stands is now at West Shepton Playing Fields, home of another Somerset Senior League Club, Shepton Mallet FC, whilst sadly the other one never quite made it.

The Tannery is a ground which would not need much altering to bring it up to Western League standards, and with the continued support that this fallen giant still enjoys, it could easily become the third ground in the town to witness FA Cup football in the space of 30 years.

the Supporters' Club, the car-park being immediately in front. The club-house in its current state was built as a shell around the original wooden building which was then gutted, in a similar move to that at Atherton Collieries. The changing rooms are situated behind the stand in a dank and dark area reached by a narrow walk-way. An area of terracing is still intact to the left of the stand, and this curves round to a sloping area with a small playground, which was almost certainly terraced as well at one time. All down one side, on a lower level, a row of modern looking residences are seemingly cowering under an onslaught of footballs, which somehow, surprisingly never seems to come, despite there being only a six foot wall to stop them! The whole area was dominated by mining over the years, and the last coal was taken as recently as 1975; the remains of one of the pit heaps can still be seen from the ground.

WINTERSTOKE ROAD
Paulton Rovers FC

It is not known precisely how long Paulton Rovers have played at the Athletic Ground in Winterstoke Road. Certainly since their formation in 1881 several grounds have been used, including the Chapel Field and the Cricket Ground and, for a couple of seasons after the War, the Recreation Ground in the village.

ATHLETIC GROUND
Wells City FC

Wells City's Rowden Road ground is one of those fascinating places which, without the visitor having any prior knowledge about them, give off an aura suggesting much early history. Wells City were members of the Western League until 1960 and were regular entrants into the FA Cup, once reaching the Fourth Qualifying Round in 1954. Their home is shared with cricket and has a substantial timber and brick main stand on the far side which has been patched up and altered over the years.

The changing rooms and clubhouse now overlook the cricket pitch which has another football pitch alongside it for Sunday sides.

The ground as it is now began to take shape in 1967 when the Social Club bought an old RAF hut, re-erected it on the ground and were granted a licence. Soon plans were drawn up to obtain a mortgage to fund the building of bigger premises and a skittle alley. To do this the playing area was turned round 90 degrees to its present position, and the clubhouse was built roughly where one of the penalty areas was before.

A new changing room block was built behind an old covered enclosure near the half way line in 1972, around the same time as the clubhouse was extended. In recent years the ground has improved immensely with a new stand being built capable of seating 138 people and a tarmac car-park has been laid behind the near goal. The large wall in front replaced a post and rail barrier and is at an ideal height to view from, as the pitch is a few feet below level giving an excellent vantage point.

The high hedge down the opposite side to the stand with perimeter wall gives the ground a nicely rural feel, and there are reminders all around the area that Paulton is above the North Somerset coalfield, as behind the far goal in the distance stands an old colliery tip now scarred from walkers and bike riders but adding to the interest of what is a pleasant West Country ground.

LAKE VIEW
Bishop Sutton FC

A few miles to the West is the long village of Bishop Sutton which has had its current football club since 1977 when they were formed as a youth team. Earlier village teams played next door on the recreation ground where the cricket club are now, and the Lake View ground, less exotically known as the Butchers Arms until recently, dates from soon after.

Situated behind the pub and originally entered through its car-park, the ground has changed considerably with a new clubhouse, changing room area and a car park behind one goal. A small timber covered area which straddles the half way line is the only spectator facility as yet although as the club adapt to life in the Western League there are many plans. The stunning Chew Valley Lake forms a backdrop to this pleasant ground.

BADGERS HILL
Frome Town FC

Football has been played at Badgers Hill since the formation of Frome Town Football Club in 1904. The first competitive match played there was a Wiltshire League fixture against Wootton Bassett in front of a crowd of 400. At that time the area was simply a rectangular piece of grass, roughly enclosed, with no amenities at all.

Before the dressing rooms were built as was the custom up and down the land, the players changed in a town centre public house, but Frome quite often were then paraded up to the ground led by a marching band! The earliest reference to any kind of building on the ground is dated 1907, and mentions a grandstand being in place, which

may well have been on the site of the disjointed but quaintly attractive stand on the Berkley Road side, which is believed to date back to around 1930.

The ground did not change with any great significance until 1954, when Town embarked on their best ever FA Cup run, culminating in a 1st Round home draw with Leyton Orient. To enable the club to stage the game, much work was done to transform the ground. Lorry loads of rubble and clay were deposited to form banking around parts of the ground, and a terraced enclosure was built at a slight angle opposite the old stand which held 400 people. Further additional covered terracing was built next to the stand, and a remarkable 8,500 crammed in to witness Town bow out 3-0. This remains the highest ever attendance at the ground.

Above: The grandstand at Frome Town which has clearly seen better days! Below: The far side terrace, built at an angle to the touchline for the Leyton Orient FA Cup tie in 1954.

Several years later there were tentative plans drawn up for a dog track to be introduced at Badgers Hill, but mercifully this came to nothing and indeed the next major change wasn't until 1970 when fire destroyed the old dressing rooms and the club were forced to build new ones to the side of the grandstand. In the middle of the decade the clubhouse was built which, although not the most attractively designed building in football, has certainly done the job, and is one of the biggest clubhouses in the Western League, with a raised path outside giving a fine view down onto the pitch.

Floodlighting was installed in 1980 at a cost of £6,000, and new refreshment and programme shops were erected, both sadly now unused, which in a way neatly encapsulates the way the fortunes of this club and ground have wavered in the last decade or so. The ground despite its rather run-down appearance, still has a certain charm and character about it, so reminiscent of many old small market town grounds, and is still a pleasure to visit, particularly when the club is doing well.

WEST SHEPTON
Shepton Mallet FC

Without question the best football ground in the Somerset Senior League, ignoring reserve sides, is to be found at Shepton Mallet. Situated behind the old Eye Hospital near the town centre, it has the look of a much older ground, despite having been first used in 1956.

The club had played for many years on a pitch in Whitstone Park, on the Frome to Shepton Mallet road, until the Council decided to use the land to build a school. Fortunately, an area of agricultural land was found, and with the help of a public subscription and financial backing from the Council, the £5,000 was found to buy the ground. Changing rooms were built almost immediately, where they are today, but these were burnt down some five years later and while they were being replaced the players were forced to use a hut in the Eye Hospital grounds. In the sixties, when Street Football Club moved from their home in Victoria Park, Shepton took one of the wooden stands, the other, unfortunately being unusable. It was erected straddling the half-way line and is still in use today. Much later, a committee man at the club managed to obtain some old lorry trailers from Showerings, which were going free and, having had them cut in half, placed them down the touch line opposite the main stand to make perfectly adequate covered standing, and these too are doing sterling service.

Floodlights were installed in time for the club's entry into the Western League around 1977, and all seemed well until the mid-eighties when the original Town club crashed with vast debts. The current club was formed from the ashes and has consolidated. Recently it began a new dressing room complex next to the old lorries, which hopefully will grace Western League football again very soon!

WOODSPRING PARK
Weston-Super-Mare FC

Weston has had at least one football team in the town since the turn of the century with Ashcombe Rangers being prominent before the War and Weston-Super-Mare Borough Employees following on. There have been grounds in Ashcombe Park itself and close by in Milton Road but the modern day Weston club, who originally went under the catchy title of Borough of Weston-Super-Mare FC moved onto what was called the Great Ground, in Locking Road in 1948.

This site, now covered by housing, stood opposite where Macs Garage is, and had a turnstile next to the road from where spectators had to walk a further 50 or 60 yards to the pitch which had posts and wire around it. Players at first changed in a marquee before

Above: The site of Woodspring Park before development.
Below: The same view today shows a breezeblock stand at Weston's latest ground.

the club hired an old wooden stand with rudimentary baths underneath. It lasted less than six years for, unbeknown to them, permission had been granted for housing on the site and when marker pegs sprouted across the pitch one morning they took the hint and looked elsewhere.

Elsewhere was an old filled in clay pit in Langford Road which they covered with soil and seeded, only expecting to be there for a season or so. Weston ended up staying for 30 years having at first used an old Nissen hut as a refreshment room until social club status came with a bar. Concrete changing rooms were added just beside it and a wooden structure with telegraph poles holding up a corrugated roof did the job of a covered side. A post and wire stretched around the ground where spectators could park next to the pitch to view from their cars. Later a small area of concrete terracing was laid along the side which backed onto the housing. As the club was extended a skittle alley was built with a roof providing a kind of shelter behind the near goal.

The ground was eventually sold to Marble Mosaics Ltd who evicted the club in 1982 and they came within an inch of extinction. The local Council, however, made available a piece of land which they converted into a ground fit for Western League football, erecting a breeze block stand and an impressive headquarters which faces on to the pitch and provides the changing and hospitality facilities. The pitch was enclosed by banking which was transformed into flat covered standing at the car-park end in recent times and the whole ground is now concreted as per Southern League instructions. A railway wagon bought from BR now houses the club shop and, although the ground still looks half-finished, it is good enough for the Beazer Homes League.

Back in the town, the old Langford Road site can, at the time of writing, still be seen. The entrance gates are still there just in front of a jungle of shrubs which are rapidly camouflaging the foundations of the club and changing rooms. A few perimeter posts remain in place, as does the small area of terracing against the retaining wall. The pitch is knee deep in foliage but with well defined walkways across which have encouraged the usual sorry dumping of everything from prams to tyres. An eerie place, it almost defies belief that Western League football was played there only a dozen years ago.

Photos in this section by: Andy Dakin, Leigh Edwards, Les Heal of Glastonbury FC, Steve Jupp and Kerry Miller.

ABBEY MOOR STADIUM
Glastonbury FC

Glastonbury took the agonising decision in 1980 to move from their home for 60 years in the grounds of Glastonbury Abbey to an altogether less salubrious site, at a newly-built dog track which is now just to the south of the new by-pass.

The contrast between the two could not be more marked, with the Abbey ground having a long low stand - which was opened in February 1934 and remained until it was re-erected in part at Abbey Moor before being replaced a few years ago.

The current ground is designed more for the greyhound racing with various covered areas tagged on to the main clubhouse and dressing room building, the rest of the area being unmade.

The club were formed in 1890 and played on several sites including the Athletic Field which is now covered by the Tor Leisure Centre, and Dyehouse Lane. Abbey Field became available in 1919, the players using a building in the market for changing in until the dressing rooms were built just after the War.

The move was forced on the club by the continued refusal of permission to erect floodlights or a clubhouse on the site and although these are both available at Abbey Moor they cannot compensate for the lack of immediate scenery given by the Abbey and the Tor. The site of the old ground is barely visible, the only real sign being the large stone wall which ran along one side of the ground, and some foundations of the stand.

Two views of the old Glastonbury FC ground 20 years ago and (inset) pictures taken from the same viewpoint in the summer of 1995. Above: Looking towards the Tor, now even the big tree on the right is gone. Below: Footings from the old stand can still be found at the base of the wall.

Bristol and Bath

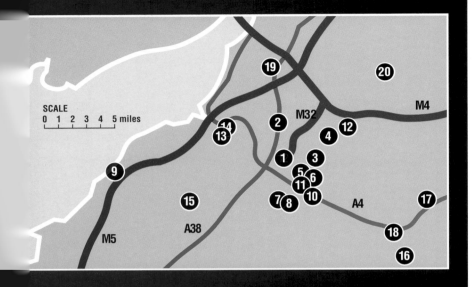

SCALE
0 1 2 3 4 5 miles

BRISTOL is the very soul of the Western League and has a rich pedigree, including within the area Bristol St George, Almondsbury Greenway, and Clevedon all of whom have had their glory days .

The more central location of the city has meant that progress has not been hindered by geography, and as a result a number of local clubs are now either playing, or aspiring to, Southern League football.

Bath, of course is dominated by Bath City, who host League football through their tie up with Bristol Rovers, their continued reign at or near the top of the pyramid has possibly had some bearing on the relative lack of forward movement with one or two neighbouring clubs.

The fact that Bath is home to arguably the most successful Rugby Union club in the country does not help.

Below: The homes of Somerset League side Winscombe FC and new Gloucester County League club Bitton AFC (bottom).

1 Bristol St George FC
2 Bristol Aerospace FC
3 Douglas FC
4 Soundwell FC
5 Hanham Mount FC
6 Hanham FC
7 St Philips Mas FC
8 Hengrove Athletic FC
9 Clevedon Town FC
10 Keynsham Town FC
11 Brislington FC
12 Mangotsfield United FC
13 Bristol Manor Farm FC
14 Portway-Bristol FC
15 Backwell United FC
16 Odd Down FC
17 Larkhall Athletic FC
18 Bath City FC
19 Almondsbury FC
20 Yate Town FC

4

BRISTOL CLUBS IN THE FA CUP

THERE have been a number of clubs in the Bristol area who came to prominence either in the Amateur Cup or the FA Cup, most of whom have quietly continued in local football, many of their members oblivious to past fame or triumphs.

Possibly the saddest tale is that of Bristol St George FC who were the top amateur side in the city for many years and played, and still play, at Bell Hill on a ground owned and shared by the cricket club. The wooden stand which saw such exploits in the fifties is still in situ although in a sad state as are the club themselves, having been denied re-entry into the Gloucestershire County League, and hence the pyramid, by an alleged problem with changing facilities a few years ago.

Bristol Aerospace Company FC played in the Western League and the FA Cup for three seasons immediately after the War before returning to local football where, as BARR United, they still play at the BAC Ground in Southmead Road. The pitch was next to the ornate pavilion which was only pulled down around four years ago and replaced by a modern facility. The grounds now stage cricket and American Football as well as having several soccer pitches.

Douglas FC were the works side for the company and played on a splendid ground just behind Kingswood High Street in Wood Road. Complete with terracing and stands it saw Western League football as Aero Engines FC until the name change and subsequent resignation in 1950. They eventually folded in the sixties but the ground continued to be used by both Bristol City and Rovers for their Colts sides. It was eventually pulled down and covered by a car-park.

Another of Bristol's prominent sides of the fifties and sixties were Soundwell whose home ground was on the impressive sounding Star Ground, named after the local pub. In truth the Star was a roped off pitch with a small dressing room building and remains so to this day. Soundwell drifted along before amalgamating with Victoria Park FC in the eighties to become Soundwell Victoria, playing in the Avon Premier Combination, a feeder to the Glos County League.

The suburb of Hanham, cut off from the south of Bristol by the River Avon, has had two teams in the post-War FA Cup with Hanham Athletic FC competing for nine seasons, once reaching the Second Qualifying Round after winning through three ties. The club were relegated from the Glos County League and are now in the Avon Premier Combination, still playing at Vicarage Road, a ground threatened more than once by development.

Their one time neighbours Hanham Mount FC played as Mount Hill Enterprise on a ground now covered by housing. They had relative success in the FA Amateur Cup but faded slowly and folded some years ago.

St Philips Marsh Adult School, known locally as "The Adult School" were a power in the sixties playing on their own enclosed ground just off the Feeder Road in the city. A wooden grandstand provided cover for many years until the land was sold. It is now covered by the offices of SWEB. The club were in the wilderness for some while but eventually took over playing on the old Harvey's Sports Ground in Norton Lane, Whitchurch, just a few hundred yards away from the home of Hengrove Athletic FC of the Somerset Senior League, and once of the FA Vase.

HAND STADIUM and TEIGNMOUTH ROAD
Clevedon Town FC

Clevedon Town have come a long way from their roots playing on Dial Hill, home of the Clevedon Cricket Club back in the 1890's. Dial Hill more recently has seen County 2nd XI cricket as it continues as one of the oldest sporting venues in the area.

In 1904, the club, then known as Clevedon FC, moved to a ground situated next to the old Portishead to Clevedon Light Railway, adjacent to a gas works and a saw mill. The main entrance at the ground (known in those days as Old Street, as Teignmouth Road did not exist) was through the saw mill on a set of planks to avoid the mud therein. There was a small wooden stand just big enough to accommodate 120 people at a squeeze with a further entrance from Parnall Road which ran alongside the railway. The ground was bought for £450 in 1949, a fine investment considering it was eventually sold for £1.3m in 1991.

A long cover was constructed which ran the length of the pitch opposite the stand and took a fearful pounding over the years, being patched up many times. Terracing stretched under it with a few seats in the centre area although they were never the most comfortable and anyone more than six foot tall stood a good chance of a dented head from the roof. The stand lasted until 1968 when it was burnt to the ground - apparently at the hands of children - and it was never replaced; instead a large social club was built close to the site.

The ground was slowly swallowed up by housing which went up all around it, so much so that a certain less than charitable neighbour would confiscate any balls which avoided the netting behind the far goal and ended up on his property. His problem was solved in 1992 when, instead of having a football match next door once a fortnight, he gained a housing estate overlooking his property 24 hours a day. Each to their own.

Teignmouth Road was certainly looking its age when sold for development and it was only a matter of weeks after the final game at the ground, against Weston-Super-Mare on Easter Monday, that almost everything disappeared along with the social club, and access roads were built across the pitch.

History preserves the ground which hosted football for nearly 90 years and once saw 2,300 attend an FA Amateur Cup tie with Billingham Synthonia in 1949.

The Hand Stadium is beautifully sited close to the M5 with plenty of room to manoeuvre and has all its administrative and social facilities built into the all-purpose structure which has a 300 seater stand at its rear.

Opposite, in a similar way to that at Gloucester, a full length covered terrace is provided, mercifully now without the ridiculous breeze block dug-outs which spoiled the view from 50 per cent of it until last season. Both ends are uncovered but, unlike a number of less inspired new grounds, they are terraced and provide a good view.

The old floodlights from Teignmouth Road now adorn the training pitch next door to what is an excellent new ground, built with improvement and the Conference in mind.

COSSHAM STREET
Mangotsfield United FC

Football has been played at the sports ground in the village of Mangotsfield since before the War. The ground is now split in two by the outside wall of the football ground, with the remaining half used only for training purposes.

In its heyday, the ground was a large space used for cricket and tennis as well as football. It boasted a generously-sized club room brought over from Salisbury Plain, as a relic of the Great War, and erected on the Cossham Street side of the ground.

The club room contained snooker tables and was the focal point for the sporting side of the village, until being demolished and replaced by the original version of the clubhouse which is used today.

Mangotsfield United. The fellow on the extreme left is not a groundhopper, but the one next to him definitely is!

During the War the field was used as a timber store and as a result was unavailable for sports, but shortly after, in 1950 the present club was formed and began playing on part of the field. Wooden dressing rooms were erected, roughly on the site of the new stand, and at one time a small area of cover which did service for a few years before proving unsafe was donated to the club by Kettering Town. Club officials then went about obtaining cycle sheds from one of the many Wills tobacco factories in Bristol, and these went up to provide some cover close to the old changing rooms.

At the turn of the seventies the whole outlook and geography of the Cossham Street ground changed after one season in the Western League. The eastern half was fenced off to provide an enclosed site, and a small scratching shed was erected down the middle of the ground bisecting the field. Other than a new changing room complex, things remained the same until a resurgence in the late eighties saw success on the field and bigger crowds. With the Western League title came the chance to apply for entry to the Southern League. Despite replacing the cycle sheds with a splendid new seated stand, updating the shed on the opposite side with a newer, less ricketty version, and fencing around the whole site, promotion was still denied them. Consequently Cossham Street remains one of the better grounds in the Western League, and certainly the best non-League ground in Bristol.

IRONMOULD LANE
Brislington FC

The village of Brislington still exists proudly, although it has been swallowed up by the march of big brother Bristol. The ground however, is some way out of the village and is tucked away in rural surroundings just off the A4 and within yelling distance of Crown Meadow, home of rivals Keynsham Town.

'Briz' have played there since escaping from their Council-run recreation ground pitch at Victory Park in 1978 to begin fashioning a pitch out of what was a cow field at the back of Brislington Cricket Club. Their earlier football as a re-formed club in 1956 was played at Arnos Court Park, before moving to Victory Park on entry into the Suburban League. In 1971 the club moved into the Somerset Senior League and twenty years later, the Western League.

Ironmould Lane has developed significantly within the last four years, with a small covered stand and a post and rail barrier going up along with a new brick refreshment area, dressing rooms and clubhouse, which meant an end to sharing the cricket club's facilities just behind.

The cricket ground has staged a Sunday League match for Somerset in the past, and the outfield was once home to the famous old Bristol club Clifton St Vincents who were in the Gloucestershire County League but now play on the Downs. Next door on the other side of the lane is another ground which at one time was home to BGH FC (Bristol General Hospital) in the Somerset Senior League.

They moved around eight years ago to Farleigh Hospital grounds, changing their name in the process and latterly have been known as Farleigh Sports. Avon St Philips FC used the ground after them, changing their name to Archway St Philips following amalgamation.

RECREATION GROUND
Backwell United FC

Despite its proximity to Bristol, and the fact that the village and its neighbours are being devoured by housing projects, Backwell retains its country feel, and the football ground does nothing to alter that, being heavily tree-lined and distinctly Somerset-flavoured.

When the village club re-formed after the Second World War, they immediately moved onto the recreation ground having spent the early years at various basic venues in the area whilst in the Clevedon and District and Church of England Leagues.

It wasn't until the start of the seventies that the ground began to develop when, to prepare for life in the Somerset Senior League, new changing rooms with showers and electric central heating were built on the south side of the Rec.

Following success on the pitch, a small clubhouse was built which in recent times has been extended, and further minor alterations took place after the club entered the Western League in 1983. Since that time the club have had protracted battles to gain planning permission to erect floodlights, and

LODGE ROAD
Yate Town FC

Yate Town are a club who, when given the chance to relocate to a new ground in a rural setting, with easy access, wisely chose not to opt for anything grandiose and instead built a functional, friendly-on-the-eye home which without too much fuss could be updated from the Hellenic League standing that they had at the time to the Southern League, which they duly reached.

To comply with the requirements of that league, a small seated stand was built tucked away in the top corner of the ground, and turnstiles installed along with enclosing fencing. An unusual feature is the pitch side barrier, which is made up entirely of halved tree trunks, built at a comfortable height and curving round behind the goals.

Also inside the ground and giving it a very enclosed feel are an army of rapidly maturing fir trees around three sides, with the stand, committee room, turnstiles, and treatment room all completing the fourth side.

The lane which leads from the Iron Acton road, eventually leads into a large unmade car-park, behind the social club, a lively place decorated with old team photos, many of which were taken at the club's previous ground in Sunnyside Lane which they left for Lodge Road in 1984.

only in 1993 did they finally achieve that aim, playing their first match against Tiverton Town in the League Cup, in front of a record crowd.

New changing rooms and a gymnasium were also built in 1993, prior to the start of the season. The recreation ground has all the facilities on one side with just a permanent rail down the north side, and a high chain link fence behind one goal, with the green painted shell of a lorry behind the other acting as a store. A row of trees and bushes form a natural barrier which separates the ground from the rest of the recreational area which has another unconnected pitch and a rugby club.

The whole area is reached by an entrance off the main road, emblazoned by a club name board welcoming visitors to what is a pleasant and unusual ground.

Promotion to the Premier Division of the league meant another battle ensued to gain planning permission to erect a stand opposite the clubhouse to comply with rules. As this book goes to print it is hoped the battle has been won.

THE CREEK
Bristol Manor Farm FC

The riverside home of "The Farm" has only reached its current state of development during the last ten years since the club has been a member of the Western League. Before that, in the Somerset Senior League, a rough extension to the club room which chiefly consisted of scaffolding poles and corrugated iron, did service as cover. Slowly, the ground has improved due in no small way to the efforts of the club's main sponsor, a local fencing firm.

The whole area is now fenced off with a wooden cover straddling the half-way line on the railway side and a small but beautifully formed seated stand directly opposite in front of the clubhouse. As a result of the terrible storms which swept the West Country in the late 1980's the original cover was destroyed and in its place a sturdier covered standing area was built around the same time as extensive levelling of the pitch took place.

The Creek, not surprisingly, gets its name from the tidal creek which is adjacent to the ground and has in the past caused problems to such an extent that one particular match finished with the waters of the River Avon lapping around the goal-line at the Bristol end.

Below: Two views of the Creek during the '80's... The covered area was destroyed and eventually replaced with a sturdier version... The creek itself is just a few yards behind the goal at the unfenced ground.

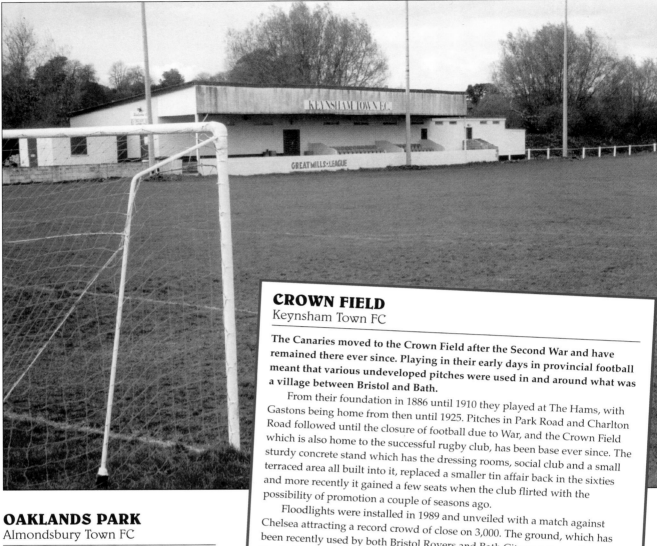

CROWN FIELD
Keynsham Town FC

The Canaries moved to the Crown Field after the Second War and have remained there ever since. Playing in their early days in provincial football meant that various undeveloped pitches were used in and around what was a village between Bristol and Bath.

From their foundation in 1886 until 1910 they played at The Hams, with Gastons being home from then until 1925. Pitches in Park Road and Charlton Road followed until the closure of football due to War, and the Crown Field which is also home to the successful rugby club, has been base ever since. The sturdy concrete stand which has the dressing rooms, social club and a small terraced area all built into it, replaced a smaller tin affair back in the sixties and more recently it gained a few seats when the club flirted with the possibility of promotion a couple of seasons ago.

Floodlights were installed in 1989 and unveiled with a match against Chelsea attracting a record crowd of close on 3,000. The ground, which has been recently used by both Bristol Rovers and Bath City as a venue for Football Combination games, has more than once accommodated crowds of 2,000 for derbies between Rovers and City. Crown Field also staged American Football when its initial popularity was at its peak and for some time a temporary stand was in place along the far touchline between the two grounds.

OAKLANDS PARK
Almondsbury Town FC

Almondsbury Football Club appear to have lurched from one crisis to another ever since their wonderful achievement in reaching the FA Vase final in 1979, having got as far as the semi-final a year earlier.

There have been two ground moves and at least five changes of name as the struggle to survive has intensified under the noses of successful clubs such as Yate, Mangotsfield and Bristol Manor Farm, and with the bare minimum of support. Oaklands Park is unusual in that it boasts a splendid social club with dressing rooms and a canteen with a function room, floodlights and an adequate car-park yet has no covered accommodation whatsoever, with rough standing around most of the ground which sits in the shadow of a Police motorway control building.

The original club played at the other side of the A38 on the Recreation Ground which had always been home to the cricket club until a purpose-built ground, barriered all round and with portakabins behind the far goal, was created next door. After more grief and name changes, Almondsbury moved over the A38 to their current home in the late eighties and installed floodlights in 1991.

The planned covered stand, to run down the high wall which separates the football from the rugby club, has not materialised, nor has the purchase of the ground by the Gloucestershire FA which was seen as a potential life saver for the ailing club.

PLAIN HAM
Larkhall Athletic FC

Plain Ham may be one of the least developed grounds in the Western League, but it is far from being the least attractive, perched as it is high on the side of a hill forming part of the Cotswold range.

The early Larkhall sides played wherever they could, often on pitches on the flat land close to the river on the edge of Bath, until settling after the War at Plain Ham. The only structure of note on the ground was a small hut which sufficed until 1964 when a pre-fabricated bungalow was brought from the Bannerdown area of the city, and was the beginning of what is now a much extended clubhouse. A post and rope arrangement ran around the ground until three years ago when a more permanent barrier went up, the small car-park being enlarged about the same time .

The tiny shack which acts as a cover on this windswept ground began life as a cabinet-maker's bike shed and it arrived about the same time as the awesome slope was partially removed from the pitch, around 20 years ago.

TWERTON PARK
Bath City FC

There have been several instances in recent years where non-league grounds have been utilised for League football through ground-share agreements. **Chester City shared Moss Rose with Macclesfield Town while the Deva Stadium was under construction, and Maidstone United moved into the Watling Street home of Dartford when they quit their London Road ground.**

Twerton Park has hosted League football since Bristol Rovers left Eastville in 1986, despite severe problems with crowd regulations and residential complaints in what is, in truth, a heavily populated area. Locals may have been unconcerned that 18,000 crammed the ground back in 1960, but are now anxious to avoid the heavy congestion that each Rovers game brings, despite crowds being down to five or six thousand.

Twerton Park itself has certainly not suffered from the ground-share. Indeed, it has been regularly tidied, has had a family stand built alongside the old main stand, a temporary stand erected and then dismantled, and has survived a major fire which all but destroyed the grandstand in 1991.

Whilst the overall shape and atmosphere of the ground has changed little since the concrete banking was created over thirty years ago, various alterations have been forced, firstly by the demands of the Alliance

Premier League (Conference) and secondly by those of the Football League. The Bristol end, steep open terracing, is now stringently segregated for visiting supporters, and the Bath end, a low open terrace, has been fenced off from the walkway behind. And, whilst it is still adequate for the needs of the 1990s, the massive covered 'popular side' was reduced when land behind was sold for housing. The main stand was, before the fire, looking a touch seedy on the outside although within, the offices, clubrooms, lounges and changing rooms were all wearing well and beautifully maintained. Today the whole structure is a footballing equivalent of Elizabeth Taylor - everyone knows her age, but she's still attractive.

Twerton Park is the third home of Bath City Football Club, the first having been the Belvoir Ground, situated in East Twerton adjoining the railway on a site now occupied by Stothert and Pitts. It was typically basic, sufficing the club's needs until the Great War ended and a tenancy was negotiated with the Bath Horse Show Committee for use of the Lambridge Ground at the other end of the city on the old London Road. The rental of £100 per annum was considered exorbitant at the time, particularly as the club could not play when there was a horse show. These shows often necessitated the digging of a huge hole in the pitch for a water jump, and a further problem was the frequent flooding of the nearby River Avon. However, Lambridge

was far more advanced than Belvoir, possessing supporters' huts and a wooden stand nearly as long as the pitch, and the club soon joined the powerful Southern League. To finance this, a limited company was founded under the chairmanship of Alderman Hunt who was also chairman of Bath Board of Guardians, the old Social Security.

The club was dogged by financial worries, nonetheless, and despite the formation of a supporters club, plus regular donations from the public and a local newspaper, they continued to struggle. At one stage in the early 1920s with the depression looming, the club asked fans to return their season tickets halfway through the campaign. On three separate occasions, Blackburn Rovers brought down their full side, including many internationals, to raise funds for City whose exploits in the FA Cup had yet to materialise.

A run through the qualifying rounds of the Cup in 1931 led to the beating of Crystal Palace in the Second Round in front of a crowd of 7,000 who each paid 1/6d. In the next round, City lost 0-2 at Brentford, but the proceeds of the run, and two astute transfers, meant the club could consider purchasing their own ground. Today Lambridge, minus the stand, is used as a training ground by Bath Rugby Club.

City bid £2,000 to secure a site just off Twerton High Street on the edge of the steep Innox Park, and were immediately granted a mortgage by the Football Association. The

Twerton Park in the Georgian city of Bath. The houses nearest the camera mask the covered terrace which once stretched much further back.

area suffered a 45 degree slope (today's visitor can visualise the gradient by beholding the terrain behind the popular side) and it took the best part of three years to shift 15,000 tons of soil and several trees to create a playing surface and perimeter banking.

The first Southern League match at the newly named Twerton Park was against Bristol Rovers Reserves and, as there was no grandstand, spectators were seated on forms around the pitch. The club soon shelled out a further £2,000 for the present main stand, built by Lysaghts of Bristol, and later a covered stand was added to the popular side of the ground, a forerunner to the current structure. It had been originally ordered by Weston-Super-Mare Rugby Club who did not take delivery for financial reasons.

Bath City flourished during the War years with many service camps in the area. Some of the great names of the time were stationed near Twerton and were eager for a game, the Football Association permitting payment of thirty shillings a match. As the conflict progressed, part of the banking was used for allotments for the war effort and the popular side was badly damaged by bombing but, incredibly, 17,000 once assembled for a war-time cup tie with Aston Villa.

As peace reigned and throughout the 1950s, Bath City began to develop the ground further, securing floodlights and a clubhouse, mainly due to the fund raising activities of the supporters' club and various FA Cup runs which brought five-figure crowds to Twerton. The banking was replaced by terracing, a cover was placed over the popular side, and up sprang new dressing rooms, club premises and offices. The club gained promotions through the Southern League in the '70s to the Alliance Premier. Although the playing side held its own, the financial side did not and, with falling gate receipts and regular end-of-term losses, City struggled until the welcome life-line of the Bristol Rovers ground-share was dangled in 1986.

Today, Twerton Park is a splendid non-League ground, although as a League ground it is a touch clumsy. Viewed from the slope behind the housing, it blends well with the beauty of Georgian Bath and the distant Cotswold foothills. The brilliant white roof of the refurbished main stand and the deep blue interior of the family stand contrast well. The large concrete terrace at the Bristol end is now no longer swallowed up by the hideous temporary stand erected after the 1991 fire, and the covered terrace remains the popular haunt of City and Rovers fans alike.

With the continued apathy of the Bristol powers-that-be denying Rovers the chance to go home, Bath City will continue to challenge for the Conference title safe in the knowledge that a championship would guarantee them promotion to the Football League.

Photos in this section by: Iain Anderson, Keith Brookman, Tony Colliver, Andy Dakin, Tony Lees and James Wright.

The splendidly refurbished stand at Bath City.

COOMBE HAY LANE
Odd Down FC

Situated on the opposite side of Bath, high on the road leading to Radstock, is the village of Odd Down. The football ground is tucked away just off the main road and has been home since the early thirties when there was just one pitch as opposed to the two which stand side by side today.

The five and a half acre site has undergone a number of changes in its 60 odd years, having once been home to Fairway Cricket Club who had a small pavilion where the new changing room building is now.

Having spent their early days on pitches at Stirtingate Farm, in Englishcombe Lane, and at the Quarr Ground (later covered by the Clarks Shoe Factory amongst others), Odd Down moved to Coombe Hay Lane, changing in a small shack and washing by means of milk churns full of cold water bought from the Burnthouse Inn on the main road. After the War a redundant building which stood at the back of a house called The Limes was transported across and used until it burnt down.

On removing Fairway Cricket Club the footballers used the little pavilion until it was replaced around ten years ago by the newer version. The second pitch was created around 1960 and much later was segregated by a wall which was extended when the club gained promotion to the Premier Division of the Western League three years ago.

About the same time as the wall went up, the club erected a small covered area on the half way line which was extended when the alterations went on in the 1990's. Odd Down's thriving clubhouse was built by members over a period of five years and finally opened in 1973. It remains much the same to this day.

Coombe Hay Lane is a ground made much more attractive by its location high above the Georgian City of Bath, although it can be blustery in the winter.

The cover at Penpole Lane didn't last long. When Portway Bristol folded it was knocked down and dumped in the woods at the back. Shirehampton FC continue to play there, as before.

Salisbury and The Plains

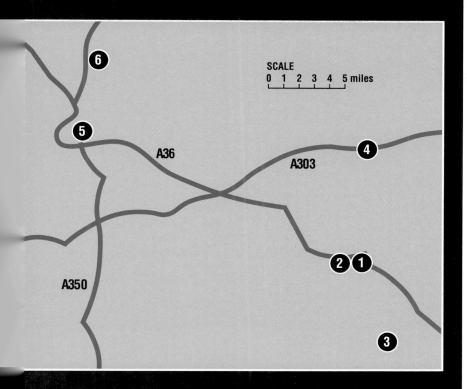

1 **Salisbury Town FC**

2 **Bemerton Heath Harlequins FC**

3 **Downton FC**

4 **Amesbury Town FC**

5 **Warminster Town FC**

6 **Westbury United FC**

THE area to the West of the city of Salisbury and around the Plains themselves is sparsely populated and has but a handful of senior clubs, two of whom have recently changed grounds.

VICTORIA PARK
Salisbury City FC

The delightfully situated, but nowadays impractical, Victoria Park ground has been under a cloud for some time, the projected move to Old Sarum due to take place during the summer of 1995, having been deferred yet again. Should the relocation go ahead, the football club will remove the two areas of covered terrace and the floodlights, but the main stand will remain as it is owned by the council.

Also the pagoda-style pavilion, which has housed the board room, changing rooms and bar in the past, won't be going far as it is a listed building, and rightly so. The area of the park within which the ground itself is built, has seen football since the turn of the century.

Before any developments were done the pavilion, which was originally built in 1899 for cricket purposes, was the only relevant building until a large wooden stand was erected by the council to cater for the two senior football clubs in the city, namely City and Corinthians. The latter, as the more senior, had first refusal on a Saturday afternoon, often relegating City to the lesser

Sylvan setting at Salisbury

The pavilion at Salisbury - one of the very few listed buildings in non-league football.

ground along Stratford Road at what is now the rugby ground.

Also, whenever Wiltshire's county rugby team were in town, they enjoyed preference over football. Shortly after the war, due to extreme financial problems both City and Corinthians were forced to fold, however the natural successor to them both, formed in 1947, was known as Salisbury F.C.

As the recreation ground remained just that, the club were unable to improve it and as a result it has stayed more or less in the state it was when the club started. On either side of the now re-vamped stand are two areas of covered terrace, although they are going to Old Sarum, and a grey railing now squares off the pitch from the circular track which surrounds the pitch and goes round the back of the stand.

The wonderful pavilion has been patched up slightly and modified inside to extend outwards. It is much the same as it always was and looks out over the now naked recreation ground which will no doubt revert to its original state. Some may still reflect back on how 8,902 people witnessed a Western League game there in 1948 .

The splendid new home of Bemerton Heath Harlequins

RECREATION GROUND
Amesbury Town FC

The small town of Amesbury, perfectly situated just off the A303 and on the banks of the River Avon, has had a football team playing on the Rec since just after the Great War, when the ground was created from an old rubbish dump. Until 1994 when the club made the big step into the Western League the playing area was simply roped off, with a pre-cast concrete pavilion on a bank behind the goal.

All that changed with the move from the Wiltshire League, and an impressive floodlighting system now graces the ground. A permanent barrier surrounds the pitch, and a small covered stand straddles the half way line. The pavilion, built in 1967 to replace a pair of wooden huts which acted as dressing rooms, has a kitchen and small club room as well as the changing facilities and has a covered pathway in front on the top of the bank which gives an elevated view.

On matchdays a green net is erected along the open side to enclose the ground and various advertising boards are stood along the stand side, transforming what is a Recreation ground with a small stand into a Western League ground with character.

WEYMOUTH STREET
Warminster Town FC

One of football's fast disappearing collection of ricketty old structures bit the dust during 1993 when the gloriously wobbly main stand was taken down, having gazed down from its position high above the Wiltshire town since it was built, complete with changing rooms at the rear, in 1923 .

Strange as it may seem at the time the club had the choice between buying the ground outright for £500 or building the grandstand and, unwisely, they chose the latter. Although she gave wonderful service for 70 years, the ground today is in the hands of the West Wilts District Council and Warminster Town are still fighting for planning permission to erect floodlights at Weymouth Street.

The club moved to the ground which is situated on sloping land overlooking the town, in 1882, and the first building of any description was the stand which provided changing rooms, previously situated in pubs. Much later a pre-fabricated building, which served as a clubhouse until it was

Weymouth Street, Warminster, before the old stand and clubhouse was replaced.

WESTWOOD RECREATION GROUND
Bemerton Heath Harlequins FC

The new club and new ground have come a long way in the six years since the amalgamation of Bemerton Athletic, Bemerton Boys and Moon FCs.

The first season was spent in the Wessex League at their traditional home at the Salisbury and South Wilts Sports Club, known less formally as the Cricket Field, where they had played since the War. For one season only a fence and floodlights were erected around the pitch which had a small amount of cover and dug-outs on the half-way line.

On the move to Westwood in August 1990 the lighting went with them but the dug-outs remain, as does the pitch which is still used. The new ground is in fact on the site of a council pitch which used to run at right angles to its present position and was levelled and made fit by Army personnel in the late sixties. The council even provided a pre-fabricated building for changing in and this is now tucked away behind the clubhouse and used as a tractor shed. The clubhouse complex is impressive, having been built through voluntary labour at a cost of around £100,000 and opened in December 1989.

For the first couple of seasons a temporary covered area was erected on the opposite side to the new stand and lasted until Christmas Eve when it blew down taking 50 feet of chain link fencing with it. The current stand is built to sturdy proportions and presumably needed to be of some length to fit in the legend 'Bemerton Heath Harlequins FC' along the roof. It has concrete terracing under it with a small group of seats for guests and the playing area is post and railed off with three sides being further enclosed by immature pine tress which are doing a fine job in breaking up the ugly lines of the 8ft fence around the ground. The myriad advertising boards, new red brick wall and turnstile entrance enhance what is becoming an excellent new venue.

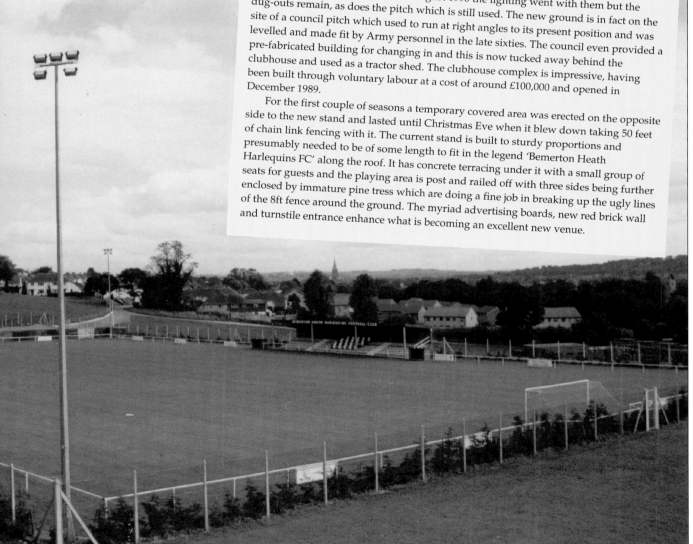

replaced in 1993, was purchased in sections and put up by the committee. The spanking new multi-purpose affair built on the site of the stand houses the bar, changing rooms, and boardroom and has an extension with around 100 seats. Next to it in marvellous contrast are the Headquarters of the South Road Pigeon Club in a small hut!

Whilst in the middle of the development the players were housed in a breeze-block building which acted as temporary accommodation and is now a store room.

The rest of the ground is, and always has been, undeveloped with a rustic fence down the bottom side and high netting behind the goals. Although having lost the classic old stand with its huge name board proclaiming Warminster Town Football Club which could be seen from far away, the 90's version was well overdue and finally wipes away the vestiges of the club's Wiltshire League days.

MEADOW LANE
Westbury United FC

The town centre home of the White Horsemen has been in existence since it was purchased by the club in 1934 for £475. The site then was a farmer's field and Meadow Lane was precisely that, with just one dwelling near the newly-named Jubilee Playing Field. A celebratory match against Bristol City took place with takings of £17. 19s. 0d. being banked.

The club in its established guise was formed in 1921 with the merger of Westbury Old Comrades and Westbury G.W.R. The original ground prior to the move stood in Redland Lane and to the this day the club's various youth sides continue to play on it. The old wooden stand which the club at one time contemplated purchasing and re-siting at Meadow Lane has long since disappeared. At the time of the ground opening the

BRIAN WHITEHEAD SPORTS GROUND
Downton FC

Downton's well-kept ground is another in the Salisbury area which is a baby in footballing terms, having been opened in 1982 following the club's move from the shared ground at Long Close Park, still the village cricket ground, and home to Downton FC from the late 60's.

Prior to that, a pitch in Barford Lane was home from 1952 until it reverted back to agricultural use for some years before being currently being used for rugby. The club's main home for nearly fifty years was called Barlings, situated opposite the White Horse pub and now used as farm land.

The area which became the new ground was set out for the use of bowls, football and tennis and was once part of a gravel pit with an animal pound and allotments all swallowed up in its making. The Parish Council bought the six acres of land and the sports ground was named after a local doctor and prominent sportsman in the village at the behest of his widow.

The club room began life as the offices of the CID at Amesbury Police Station and was transported and erected at the entrance to the ground using volunteer labour. It now sports a splendid name board welcoming all-comers to the home of the Robins. In January 1994 the new seated stand was erected in place of the small overhang which jutted out from the front of the tractor shed. It has transformed a pleasantly situated semi-rural ground into a comfortable one nestling as it does, a little off the beaten track.

amenities were fairly basic, as was the norm, with the emphasis on providing playing facilities first, and spectators' accommodation later.

It wasn't until the 1950's that the corrugated iron club rooms were added to the ground in place of the old huts which the players had changed in previously, and a covered standing area was erected, just in front of the club house to the left of the Town end goal, and paid for by the hard working Supporters' Club. The current brick built changing room complex also dates from the mid-fifties, and stands between the clubhouse and the concrete stand, built to replace the original wooden one which burnt down in 1971.

Since then the club have progressed off

the pitch to the Western League and in 1988 erected floodlighting which was again celebrated, this time with a match against Southampton. This decision paid dividends in 1992 when the club won Division One of the Western League, promotion to which would not have taken place without the lights. Currently the ground is pleasantly situated in an area surrounded by residential development. It is slightly lop-sided with the facilities in one corner and a large open area within the enclosed ground put aside for car-parking.

Meadow Lane's largest crowd came just before the war, when over 4,000 spectators crammed in to watch an F.A.Cup tie against Llanelli which the club are always proud to point out was on the pools coupons!

Meadow Lane, Westbury

Mid-Wiltshire

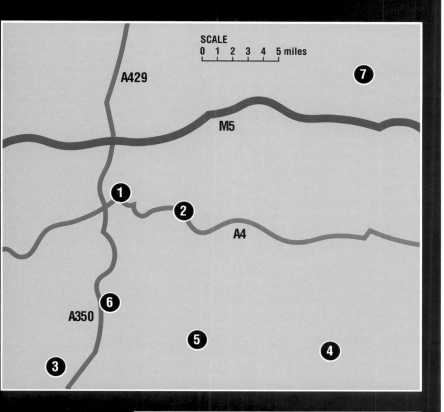

SCALE
0 1 2 3 4 5 miles

A429

M5

A4

A350

1 **Chippenham Town FC**

2 **Calne Town FC**

3 **Trowbridge Town FC**

4 **Pewsey Vale FC**

5 **Devizes Town FC**

6 **Melksham Town FC**

7 **Swindon Supermarine FC**

THE area around and to the south and west of Swindon is not short of interesting grounds although it is a mystery why none of the resident clubs, with the possible exception of Trowbridge Town have made any in-roads into the pyramid. There are a number of clubs who currently play in the Hellenic League and seem happy to stay there without the problems of ground grading which seems to be a little less financially exhausting than in other leagues. The Western League is well represented too, with Melksham's Conigre ground worth a visit.

Wootton Bassett, **Purton** and **Highworth** are all plying their trade in the lower reaches of the Hellenic League on relatively undeveloped grounds. **Corsham Town**'s Southbank ground appears virtually unchanged from the early fifties when they were regular entrants into the FA Cup, apart from a new clubhouse which would do many Western League clubs proud.

FROME ROAD
Trowbridge Town FC

Frome Road has lived a perilous existence ever since a series of events, starting with a devastating fire which threatened not only the ground but the club as a whole.

On the morning of September 20th 1986, a massive blaze destroyed the main stand which had served the club for 63 years, effectively putting paid to any chance of returning to the Alliance. The fierceness of the blaze melted some of the floodlighting and wiped out a significant part of the club's history. In the wake of this, the future of the ground was again jeopardised when provisional plans were made to route a relief road through part of the site, which meant that no development of facilities could take place to replace the stand.

To further undermine the club's standing the covered banking behind the far goal was declared unsafe and has since been fenced

Wiltshire League Corsham Town's Southbank home.

Photos in this section by:
Pat Brunning, Mike Floate,
Kerry Miller and James Wright.

off. Finally, in 1993 the club announced plans to relocate to a site on the edge of the town which would incorporate all the major sporting clubs in the area.

Through all this turmoil, to the credit of the club and their supporters, a high standard of football has been maintained, and the crowds are still very good compared with many others.

The origins of Trowbridge football date back to 1880, when matches of both codes were played on a field at the top of Timbrell Street, which is now covered by the County Ground. In 1887 a move was made to Wingfield Road where John O'Gaunt School is now, but it was not popular or successful and three years later the Flower Show Field was used. With the club growing fast the new ground was regularly filled, but not everyone was happy with the use of the site for football, as it was also required for fetes, funfairs etc. It is now the Stallards Rec.

However, the club re-started after the Great War on the same ground, and it wasn't until 1923 that they moved to the quaintly named Bythesea Road, which boasted high banking on three sides and a splendid wooden stand, provided by the parents of a local man who was killed in action in 1916, whilst serving as a major in the Royal Wilts Yeomanry.

Sadly, the council at the time coveted the central site for their new County Hall, and only 10 years on from its opening Bythesea Road ground was gone, and the club acquired a new site at Frome Road. Happily the stand was able to be transported and so graced the new headquarters. The football club suffered from an apathetic reaction to the council's bullying tactics, and the opening games were played without any ceremonies and on a site not then completed by the contractors.

Over the years with the club on a firm footing, development of the ground went on apace, and with the continued financial and physical help from the Supporters' Club, the lower stand, popular bank and North Stand were all erected and the ground bought up to a level which enabled the club to be accepted into the newly formed Alliance Premier League in 1981.

Today, the ground viewed from certain angles is a forlorn site with the condemned cover, high on banking now fenced off by chain-link, rusting and unwanted. The area where the main stand stood is now a wide open space, with portakabins at the back in use as dressing rooms. The covered end is still very popular and houses a tea-bar, and next to it the club's entrance and turnstiles now face the relief road which was intended to go through the ground.

This has been a mixed blessing for the club, for it has meant that the frontage is now clearly visible from the road whereas before it was approached down a lane from Frome Road. On the negative side, the passing traffic is a touch hazardous to spectators entering or leaving the ground. The administration block and clubhouse are situated behind the long covered terrace which now has sufficient seating under it to placate the Southern League.

Trowbridge Town are to be praised for conquering the myriad problems thrown at them, and are sure to view a move to a new site with more relish than their predecessors did when leaving Bythesea Road.

The old main stand at Melksham, since demolished and replaced.

THE CONIGRE
Melksham Town FC

The Conigre is the absolute epitome of small market town grounds, situated in the middle of what is a busy and active Wiltshire town. Records and newspapers are not clear as to the exact date of the first match on the ground, although there is mention of the club playing on a pitch 'in the centre of town' in September 1884. As the other club grounds were at Challeymead until 1883, when they moved to a field adjoining the Bear Inn, then it seems fair to assume the Conigre is 111 years old.

Again, the date the classic old wooden stand was built is not immediately available, but to judge by the style of it via old photos, the thirties would seem a good guess. Certainly the post and rail all around the ground was erected in November 1957, by players and supporters, and when a Supporters' Club was formed in May 1968, they soon began to raise funds to build the impressive covered enclosures that stand today behind one goal and all down the side opposite the clubhouse, which was also the work of the supporters.

Sadly, the stand was dismantled four years ago, leaving an ugly weal on what is a delightfully old-fashioned looking ground. A new stand now covers the spot but sadly is low and set back and not designed to give a good view. The green-painted covered terrace has a welcome - clearly visible on entering - emblazoned all down one side. The entrance is through a car-park used in the main by council officers housed in the mansion next door.

The loss of the stand, and the club's demotion from the Western League back to the Wiltshire League was a double blow, and it would have surprised few outside of the town, if Melksham had simply faded into obscurity. To the credit of all concerned, promotion back to the Western League was achieved at once, and the new stand has neatly helped to cover up the unhappy scar and restore the Conigre to something like its original splendour.

NURSTEED ROAD
Devizes Town FC

The ground as it appears today at Nursteed Road was laid out in 1961 when the club played on a pitch next door and purchased the ground in readiness for a stand to be built. The playing area was levelled and drained and a stand which could hold 350 people was completed with tiny changing rooms below. It was a box shaped structure which had extremely shallow stepped seats, similar to those at Minehead.

The original outlay for the purchase of ground and stand was £7,000, which included a running track that, although built, was never maintained and was eventually grassed over. The new ground was opened in 1965 by Mr. Dennis Fellows before a friendly match with Walthamstow Avenue. In 1968 the social club was built which had a gymnasium attached to it and this has been altered over the years to combine a skittle alley, a vital part of the social scene in this part of the world.

The stand did not endure too well, and by the eighties was looking a touch second hand, almost the footballing equivalent of Barbara Cartland, where the paint seemed to be all that stopped it from falling over. It was condemned and demolished in 1994 and almost immediately replaced with a similarly shaped structure with new dressing rooms extending out of the back. To the left of the old stand was a large hut which housed the tea bar until it was destroyed by arson around four years ago and this area is now cleared and has a floodlit training area next to it.

On entering the ground down a lane between houses the openness and size of the place is immediately evident. A second pitch runs at right angles to the main one and the clubhouse is at the end of the straggling car-park. Attached to the back of the clubhouse is one of the most interesting, and possibly ugliest, buildings on any non-League

Nursteed Road, Devizes, with old stand, now replaced, and the site of the old ground behind.

ground. The huge corrugated iron structure which dominates that area of the ground has had a mixed history, having come from a military base on Salisbury Plain before being transported to Nursteed Road and used first as a gymnasium and indoor pitch and latterly as a night club which bit the dust when the noise levels upset the neighbours.

It is now hired out to all and sundry including the local table tennis club whose County headquarters stand in the top corner of the ground, neatly tucked away.

GREEN STREET
Roundway Hospital FC

Nursteed Road was not the first purpose-built football ground in Devizes, as after the War and into the sixties Roundway Hospital played their Wiltshire League games on their own ground in Green Street.

Situated by the side of the old Maternity Hospital with a wooden stand on the half

way line and a hedge bordering the pitch all down one side, Wiltshire County Mental Hospital FC, as they were unceremoniously called until 1950, played five FA Cup ties on the ground reaching the second qualifying round in 1947.

The site of the pitch is still there, as council pitches now straddle it, although there is no trace of the stand which was close to the group of changing huts currently in use. A large oak tree still gives a good clue to the siting of it.

RECREATION GROUND
Pewsey Vale FC

Pewsey Vale are the most easterly of all the Western League clubs and their relatively undeveloped ground has been home, in the main in the Wiltshire League, since 1950. They were originally known as Pewsey YM and for three seasons just after the War entered the FA Cup, playing just one home game at Swan Meadow against Trowbridge Town.

Pewsey remained there until 1950, when they moved to the Recreation Ground. It started with a basic dressing room complex which then had a small clubhouse attached, but only in recent times with their promotion to the Western League, have the club provided a modest stand.

Kennet District Council have refused the club permission to erect floodlights and so the future was in some doubt as the 1995-96 season approached.

BREMHILL VIEW
Calne Town FC

Bremhill View is one of a number of grounds which has seen progress from Wiltshire to Western League in recent memory. The club is over 100 years old having been formed around 1886 as Calne Town before amalgamating with the works team from the local bacon factory to become Calne and Harris United.

Home had always been the recreation ground in Anchor Road which was shared with Calne Cricket Club who still use it today. The changing facilities were shared and the pitch was roped off but had no other facilities, and in 1967 the club moved to its own ground in Bremhill View which had been formed from what was no more than a barely-used field.

Today it boasts a small concrete stand with an older looking wooden changing room building with an extension on the front as cover. A well-used clubhouse stands close to the entrance and in fact is on part of the original pitch which had to be moved to accommodate it. Floodlights were put up soon after the club were accepted into the Western League in 1986, and a year later, in July 1987, Swindon Town were the visitors to Bremhill View when the record crowd of 1,100 watched a friendly.

Above: Hardenhuish Park, Chippenham.   Below: The popular side at Frome Road, Trowbridge is now seated following the destruction of the grandstand.

THE FIRS
Chippenham United FC

The lesser known of the two major Chippenham sides lasted only 15 years, yet arguably, in that time, created a ground superior to their great rivals at Hardenhuish Park. United were formed by a breakaway group from Town in 1947 and soon obtained, and began to develop, a piece of land surrounded by fir trees .

After fencing off the pitch, the club erected a small shelter and dressing rooms and when the playing surface was levelled the top soil was shaped into banking at either end. The shelter was later extended and in the late 50's a grandstand was built capable of seating 600 people. The size of the ground can be gauged by the record crowd at the Firs which is 5,624 against Bath City in the FA Cup in 1951. Initial enthusiasm soon waned and in 1962 the possibility was discussed that the two clubs merge back into one, but nothing came of it and the club folded in September of that year.

The ground soon disappeared under a housing estate although the three rows of fir trees still exist to give a clear indication of the old site in Hungerdown Road.

HARDENHUISH PARK
Chippenham Town FC

Hardenhuish Park, pronounced locally as 'Harnish' Park, has been home to the Town club since the first game on September 24th 1919. The old main stand is clearly visible from the main Bristol Road and from the back looks rather bigger and more imposing than it actually is.

Its age is unknown but it has been renovated more than once and has had changing rooms underneath it from the start which were themselves modernised back in 1985. There was a popular stand on the far side of the pitch which has been replaced twice and was eventually destroyed in storms and subsequently replaced again by a more modern structure in 1993, with hard standing to add to the small amount of terracing next to the stand.

In 1979 a new clubhouse was built onto the back of the old stand which has a vantage point through on to the pitch from behind glass windows. In 1986 floodlights came to Harnish Park which although 75 years old, seems to stay at the same level despite continued membership of the Premier Division of the Western League.

HIGHWORTH ROAD
Swindon Supermarine FC

The club have been in this form for only three years, following the amalgamation of Swindon Athletic and Supermarine Football Clubs. In turn, Swindon Athletic were known as Penhill Youth Club and Penhill FC, playing on the Southbrook ground on Pinehurst Road.

The main pitch still has a covered stand which is now used by junior sides, whereas the lesser pitch was used towards the end by Swindon Town for their South-East Counties games. In 1992 the clubs merged, playing on the Highworth Road complex which is shared by a number of sports although the football ground is now separate.

Supermarine were formed as Vickers FC and played on a pitch adjacent to the social club. On moving to the current pitch, the small stand that seats 50 or so was taken with them and re-erected, and a post and rope was put around the ground. In recent times, with success in the Hellenic League, floodlights have gone up and a clubhouse has been built next to the stand as the new club consolidate their good start to the marriage.

Swindon Supermarine before the merger.

Gloucestershire

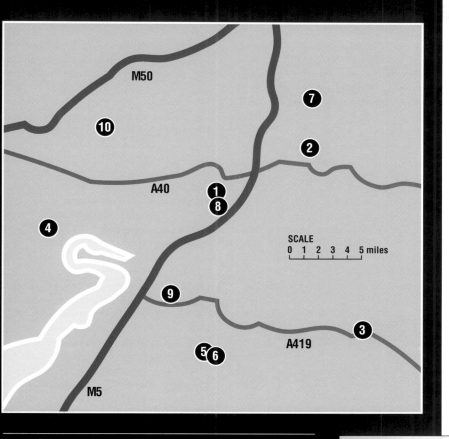

LOUCESTERSHIRE is rich in senior non-League football, with Cheltenham Town, Gloucester City, Cinderford Town and Forest Green Rovers all in the Southern League, and Tuffley Rovers, Shortwood United and Bishops Cleeve in the Hellenic.

At the other end of the scale there are a number of clubs who have fallen away in recent years, namely **Lydney**, who dropped from the Hellenic to Division Two of the Gloucester Northern Senior League, and **Berkeley, Frampton Utd, Lydbrook, Worrall Hill, Viney St Swithens, Brimscombe** and **Thrupp, GALA Wilton** and **Newent** who are all ex-members of the County League. **Sharpness** now play on a school pitch after losing their lovely dockside ground a few years ago and **Stonehouse** are still at Oldends Lane, 35 years after dropping out of the Western League.

THE HOMES OF
Gloucester City FC

The early grounds on which the club played are not well-documented and from formation in 1889 all that is known is that the Budding Field was home until 1895, with the Avenue Ground, off Tuffley Road being used for the first time during the next two years. Both grounds were used in the next 20 years, as was the Co-op ground in India Road, just the other side of the railway from

1	Gloucester City FC
2	Cheltenham Town FC
3	Cirencester Town FC
4	Cinderford Town FC
5	Forest Green Rovers FC
6	Shortwood United FC
7	Bishops Cleeve FC
8	Tuffley Rovers FC
9	Stonehouse FC
10	Newent FC

Above: Meadow Park, Gloucester, under construction around 1986.

Right: Four year later.

the site of Horton Road ground which was built in 1964.

Things become clearer from 1925 when City were on the Avenue ground once more which was described as being an asset to the club as it was on the tram route and was naturally banked to be visible by all. It tended to become a quagmire in wet weather and in 1927 they were on the move again, this time to a field at Sutgrove. It had two entrances, one in Carlton Road and one in Stroud Road and had ample space for the large crowds. It was also enclosed, which allowed the club to do away with the canvas sheeting which went around the other grounds preventing free view-points. Dressing rooms were erected at Sutgrove in 1927 and a small stand joined them two years later, and by 1930 work had started on a second stand but, due to unforeseen problems, it was never completed. City obtained a five year lease at Sutgrove but within months due to clashes with reserve team cup games were forced to play matches at the Bon Marche ground in Estcourt Road, and with Sutgrove also suffering from excessive boggy conditions City were on the move again permanently in 1933.

The old stand at Sutgrove was taken down and re-assembled, only this time with added materials it was much larger and a pavilion went up which incorporated changing rooms. Gloucester City turned semi-professional in 1935 and once more were looking for pastures new. A new field was bought in Longlevens, and immediately work on a members' stand commenced. It had two entrances, the main one in Elmbridge Court Lane next to the greyhound track and another where a concrete bridge spanned the brook.

A third entrance direct from Cheltenham Road was later put in. 1,200 spectators saw the opening game against Weston-Super-Mare and a further 2,000 saw the stand opened officially on October 5th 1935 before a league game with Market Harborough. The stand had changing rooms beneath and by January 1936 was joined by another on the opposite side of the pitch which became known as the 'Tin Run'. Behind each goal was raised banking which doubled the capacity.

In 1952 floodlighting was installed for the first time with a number of friendlies played, including one against Tottenham Hotspur. The ground continued to develop but its out-of-town location was a problem as was the lack of parking and in 1960 they sold Longlevens for housing and bought a 14.5 acre site in Horton Road with the aim of building a fully-equipped sports stadium.

It was ready four years later and was set in a bowl shape with a large stand incorporating both covered seating and terraced standing with a clubhouse built alongside. The lack of support for the club at the time meant the original plans for Horton Road were never fulfilled and the ground remained virtually unchanged in the 22 years of its existence. A track ran round the pitch which initially was laid down for athletics but was used briefly in the seventies for dog racing.

Again City suffered badly from poor drainage and when the chance came to sell Horton Road to developers and move to a purpose-built stadium in Sudmeadow Road it was accepted. The deal was signed in 1979, around the same time as the floodlights were installed at Horton Road, but it was not until August 1986 that the new ground was ready for the club to move into. The first plan was for a combined greyhound and football stadium, but mercifully this came to nothing and the new home opened on August 9th 1986 when Leicester City were the visitors. Billy Wright returned to the area some 27 years after opening Stonehouse's ground, to unveil a plaque. The 300 seater stand along one side also incorporated an impressive changing room complex, with a social club and directors' accommodation while opposite, running the full length of the pitch, covered terracing was installed. Both ends were flat and open until 1990 when terracing was added and these are expected to be covered during the 1995-96 season.

A new regime at City has bought about much change to the perimeter of the ground which at first was referred to as Sudmeadow Road, then Meadow Park and is now known as the City Stadium. A new pitch, up to Hellenic League standards is being put down outside the ground on the old Fieldings sports ground site and with improvements to the parking and social side it seems that, at long last, Gloucester City have settled down.

A very rare photograph of Gloucester City's Longlevens ground in the mid-50's. It was sold for housing development in 1960.

VICTORY GROUND, WHADDON ROAD
Cheltenham Town FC

The Victory Ground has seen many changes since its opening, but happily the basic lay-out remains the same. With a strong looking main stand and long low covered enclosure on the Wymans Road side, it is not difficult to imagine the ground, in slightly smaller form as it was when Cheltenham Original Brewers opened it in 1927.

Cheltenham had been playing in the Birmingham Combination at Whaddon Lane, and prior to that on ground 200 yards away called Carters Field. Six years later the club was secure enough to turn professional.

In its infancy, the Victory Ground had a low wooden stand where the main stand is now, which the club filled with seats collected from Gloucestershire C.C.C. at the end of the summer and returned again in the spring. A wooden fence surrounded the pitch and remained in one form or another until the hurricanes of 1987 destroyed both a chunk of it and the old chicken run, which was completely split apart, the right half being swept over the roofs of the houses in Wymers Road, ripping off chimneys before coming to rest half a mile away.

The brewery decided to give the ground over to the Corporation at the end of the war, with the proviso that football must be played on it, and it is that agreement which protects the ground and secures its future.

Remarkably, floodlighting was installed as early as 1950, upgraded with the present pylons ten years later, and soon after that the club embarked on the project to replace the wooden stand with the present structure at a cost of £25,000.

Cheltenham's impressive stand is capable of seating 1,200 people, and was soon

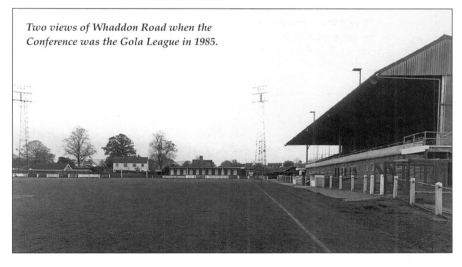

Two views of Whaddon Road when the Conference was the Gola League in 1985.

copied as several other clubs, including Morecambe and Chorley erected identical stands around the same time. Since those heady days, the ground has seen few major changes other than those forced on it by Acts of God or acts of stupidity by the League ground grading rules.

The pitch surrounds were already being replaced when the big wind hit, but the ground had to suffer the indignity of having part of itself put out of bounds until the impressive new full length covered terrace was opened in 1990 to replace the wrecked chicken run. Sadly, to comply with the stringent ground regulations laid down for clubs at the top of the non-league pyramid, an ugly red slatted fence was erected behind the far goal, in front of what was a grassy bank with a small terrace in front, to enclose the ground further - a somewhat futile gesture as there is a deep slope with a stream immediately behind it.

This fence, although permanent looks temporary and could be improved with a

less-sudden colour scheme, or removal while the club is out of the top flight, as from some angles it ruins what could be a splendid ground. At the town end an old area of cover remains set back from the pitch, but acts as a gentle reminder of what the old chicken run was like.

On the other side of the goal is another steeper terrace backed by a high fence protecting a bungalow behind, which building, incidentally, prevents the club from developing that area. A jumbled group of temporary huts stand in front of an L-shaped two-storey structure which houses a bowling club, to the side of the stand containing the entire administration, changing, and recreational facilities.

The area behind the stand was reclaimed from overgrown allotments around 20 years ago and is now a part of a large car-park, the envy of many. Whaddon Road ground is comfortable, neat and tidy but, as are so many grounds in the Southern League, is tantalisingly short of being splendid.

THE LAWN
Forest Green Rovers FC

The small town of Nailsworth, situated in one of the five valleys which radiate in or out of Stroud, has two senior football teams, on either side of the valley, and within sight of each other. The more senior ground, The Lawn, has grown from a field surrounded by hedges and, with no buildings of any kind, into a Southern League ground which staged an FA Vase semi-final.

The precise date of the move to the Lawn is not available, but what is known is that the area at the time was isolated a mile up the hill from the town in a location called Forest Green. The players then had to trek from the Jovial Foresters pub where they changed, to the pitch. The first building of any kind was an old wooden and tin stand which was given to the club, having previously stood at the King George V Field in the town, some time after the First World War.

Very little changed at the ground until servicemen returning from World War Two formed a supporters' club and with the funds generated from this, and the help given by a local dignitary, the solid brick built changing rooms which are still in use today were erected and opened on August 30th 1950.

The pitch was barriered off, and towards the end of the decade the committee of the time decided, having studied the grounds of clubs in different areas, that they wished to substantially build up the Lawn into a complete football stadium. The plans were drawn up and, to enable the work to go ahead, the Lawn was closed for a season and home matches were played on a field further up the lane, with the players using the club changing rooms.

When the ground was officially re-opened on August 19th 1961, it had terracing around the ground, with cover behind the far goal, and a new entrance in the corner nearest to the town. The stand, a pleasant black and white structure, sits on the site of the original one and looks over a pitch which was levelled, giving the appearance of being on a small plateau. Today, on entering the ground, the pitch is considerably higher than the walkway on the dressing room side which gives an indication as to the previous severity of the slope.

Since those major changes, a social club has been built in 1968, and altered and extended in 1980, and in the early seventies a covered training area was provided in the space between the covered end and the dressing rooms. This area is now used for storage and as a covered area for spectators, and has since had a canteen built under it.

Surprisingly, for a club which had built up its ground from virtually nothing in 1959, having purchased it some twenty years earlier, they did not install floodlights until 1981. Since then, the club offices have moved into ugly portakabins - the old wooden ones were removed in 1994 - which do little for what is otherwise a comfortable and attractive country ground.

The Lawn, although happily retaining its rustic feel, is no longer isolated for developments have crept up the hill, and it is now surrounded by housing. A nostalgic reminder of other teams' glories comes at the ground entrance, where spectators pay at turnstiles which previously stood at the Eyrie, the sadly demolished former home of Bedford Town FC.

MEADOW BANK
Shortwood United FC

The topography surrounding the Cotswold town of Nailsworth from where Shortwood United originate is so hilly it comes as quite a surprise to discover that at least three different fields have been used by them since their beginnings in the early part of the century.

Tableland was a field at Wallow Green that had little or no facilities and the players changed at the Rising Sun. It had a small lean-to made of corrugated tin and little else. A nearby pitch was home from the fifties where cow muck was shovelled off before kick off and the players had the luxury of changing rooms on site, indeed the foundations are still there today.

In 1975 the present pitch was dug out of the side of a hill and levelled and the changing rooms opened. The small stand dates from around four years afterwards and can seat 50 with a further 150 standing. The popular clubhouse was opened by Bristol Rovers in 1984.

The capacity of Meadow Bank is given as 5,000 which would not be allowed in any event as the ground is only reached up a narrow residential lane which is barely wide enough for team buses. However the record crowd stands at around 1,000 which saw the local derby with Forest Green Rovers in 1982.

The Lawn floodlights are clearly visible across the valley from United's ground and provoke the question of how many other small towns of Nailsworth's size are home to two senior football clubs of the stature of Shortwood and Forest Green?

*Below: **Meadow Bank, home of Shortwood United. The pitch was dug out of the side of a hill.***

CAUSEWAY GROUND
Cinderford Town FC

The recent alterations to Cinderford's fascinating ground have managed to achieve the club's objectives without spoiling what is a lovely old-fashioned ground set high in the town with views over much of the Forest of Dean.

The levelling of the pitch has meant the excavation and lowering of the surface so that there are now steep banks at one end and along one side which are perfect for the terracing that at some point will doubtless be a pre-requisite for any promotion. The three stands are still as they were, with their stepped appearance giving an indication of the slope which has now been done away with.

Cinderford have played at the Causeway since 1947, having lost their Mousel Barn ground during the War. The first days were spent on a field behind the Royal Oak pub before moving to Mousel Lane, behind the Red Lion and then the Royal Oak prior to Mousel Barn in 1932. The club naively left their playing equipment in a shed at the ground and returned after the War to find that not only had the store been rifled but the ground was sold!

Fundraising began in an effort to find enough cash to purchase land of their own, and eventually three fields on the Causeway - an area described in those days as bleak and inhospitable - were bought, incurring a debt of £1,000.

Other than the immediate area around the football ground it is now covered by the biggest housing estate in the town. The first stand, converted from an old shed, was put up in 1947 and two years later the Chairman launched an appeal for funds which were used to erect the other two stands, all three of which survive today. The referee's changing quarters were built in 1951 and in September of the following year the Town formally opened the new changing room block, believed to be the best in the Western League at the time.

Between then and 1994 the ground remained more or less the same with just the clubhouse being built behind the stands. The recent changes included a new fence which segregates the car-park and wholesale tidying up of what is now a fine bowl-shaped ground with much potential.

Before, during and after the major works to get rid of the slope at Cinderford's Causeway ground. As a result of the levelling of the pitch there are now steep banks at one end and along one side of the ground which will be perfect for any future terracing.

FOOTBALL IN STONEHOUSE

Football in the Stroud Valley does not follow any logical boundaries, and seems to have grown up away from the town rather than in it. Whilst Stroud is strong at cricket and rugby, there is no senior non-League football team of any description, nor has there been in living memory.

However, in the adjoining smaller town of Stonehouse, football was hugely popular with Stonehouse FC having graced the Somerset Senior League, and the Western League until leaving on the same day as Street FC in 1960. Opened by Billy Wright on 25th August 1949 before a match with Cheltenham Town, their now sadly decaying ground is still spectacular when put in context with their current standing.

Two years later 5,500 crammed in, a record attendance, to see an FA Cup tie with Gloucester City which was lost 2-1 but emphasises the size of the ground. It is much the same now as it was when first built, with a large covered end and equally impressive seated stand on the half-way line, but the sale of the clubhouse some years back accelerated a decline which now sees the club in the Gloucester Senior League (North), a feeder to the County League.

Further along Oldends Lane is the Hoffmanns factory which spawned Hoffmann Athletic, a club which had its own ground, now sadly gone, by the side of the factory. They played alongside Stonehouse in the FA Cup until 1950 but have long since gone under as have their sister team of the same name, based in Chelmsford.

Just east of Stroud is Thrupp, a small village which boasts a club, Brimscombe and Thrupp. They are now out of the Gloucester County League but, in their time, created a splendid ground on the main road complete with small wooden stand on a bank.

They too are sadly in decline, but that cannot be said of the neighbouring clubs in the small town of Nailsworth, just south of Stroud. The two clubs there vie for top spot in the area, Forest Green edging it at the moment by dint of their precarious membership of the Southern League.

THE STADIUM
Cirencester Town FC

Cirencester's attractive Hellenic League ground, ideally situated by the main Fosseway road, is a curious mixture of the old and the new, with a grey-brick clubhouse dominating the ground. An overhang from the front of the club provides cover, as do the two astonishing matching dug-outs, topped with advertising hoardings.

A ricketty covered area behind the town goal, erected around 12 years ago, was sadly severely damaged in the gales of December 8th 1993, and partly collapsed. It has since been renovated and has a small number of seats behind its black and red timbered front

Just behind the clubhouse stand the old changing rooms, now used for storage and made redundant from their original use around 15 years ago when the clubhouse was built. The ground has been in use since the late fifties when a lease was taken out with the permission of the land-owner Lord Bathurst. Ten years later the club bought the land, parts of which have been sold over the years for different reasons.

When the council decided to create a roundabout next to the ground, taking a small pocket of the club's land in the process, the pitch was moved from north/south to its current west to east position. A small timber and tin shack which stood on the half way line was removed and a barrier put up.

Later the stand went up behind the goal, in the main to prevent people from gaining a free view of the game from beyond the fence. In recent times an all-weather area and floodlights have been installed at what is a very pleasant ground in an area not known for its intense following of football.

Above: **The two old stands at Stonehouse FC, opened by the late Billy Wright in 1949.**

GLEVUM PARK
Tuffley Rovers FC

Tuffley Rovers are a good example of a club that has taken more than 60 years to become an overnight success! Living in the shadow of Gloucester City is not easy, but the off-shoot of that club's financial windfall has meant the lower clubs in the area have been able to compete for those better standard players who are not in the frame for Southern League football.

Tuffley have developed their club and ground since taking over some waste land in 1984 owned by Gloucester Gas and have now created something plenty good enough for the Hellenic League.

The changing room complex went up soon after they moved from the more basic Beaufort School pitch, which is still home to the third team, and a pitch barrier and dug-outs soon followed. A small stand seating around 40 was erected in 1993 and a year later floodlights were installed as Rovers sought to consolidate their position as the number two club in the area.

The clubhouse at Wildsmith Meadow, home of Newent Town FC.

WILDSMITH MEADOW
Newent Town FC

When Newent Town moved from their Recreation Ground home 14 years ago, the major engineering work to be done before any play could commence was the removal of part of the disused railway bank which curved around the site, thereby enabling the pitch to be laid out.

The remains of the track-bed of the former Ledbury to Gloucester line are still visible, overlooking the clubhouse and changing rooms heavily fortified against unwanted visitors. Although that mode of transport is gone, the ground is now threatened by another, with the suggested A40 route being proposed to go right across it.

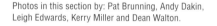

Photos in this section by: Pat Brunning, Andy Dakin, Leigh Edwards, Kerry Miller and Dean Walton.

The Meadow, picturesque ground of Gloucestershire Northern Senior League club Brimscombe & Thrupp.

South-west Hampshire & the Isle Wight

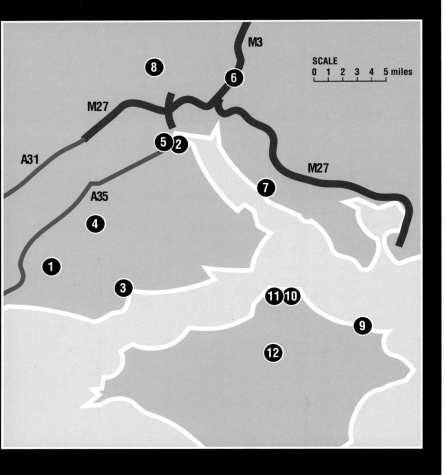

SCALE
0 1 2 3 4 5 miles

1   **Bashley FC**
2   **AFC Totton**
3   **AFC Lymington**
4   **Brockenhurst FC**
5   **B.A.T.FC**
6   **Eastleigh FC**
7   **Aerostructures FC**
8   **Romsey Town FC**
9   **Ryde Sports FC**
10 **East Cowes Vics FC**
11 **Cowes Sports FC**
12 **Newport IOW FC**

THE Hampshire League is responsible for the wealth of grounds in this area although it has to be said that only Bashley have made any real progress up the pyramid, and in no time at all.

Nearly 100 years of football in that league has seen many teams come and go, and only **Winchester City** look back on playing at a higher level, having spent two seasons in the Southern League from 1971. **Road Sea Southampton**'s Marchwood ground is still used after that former Sunday club were elevated to Southern League status in 1982 and disappeared again four years later. Southampton FC use the ground for their reserve team Combination games as well as occasional youth team games.

Most of the grounds in this area now host Wessex League football, which in one or two cases is proving to be a hardship, as it forms a feeder to the Southern League with ever burgeoning ground grading rules.

SPORTS GROUND
AFC Lymington

The recent changes to the ground regulations imposed by the Wessex League have cast serious doubts on the Linnets' continued membership of that body. The three-sided nature of the ground which is shared with cricket plus the cramped changing rooms fall outside the criteria laid down and are causing the club much of grief.

AFC Lymington as such only date from 1988 when the old Lymington Town amalgamated with Wellworthy Athletic to form the new club. Town were the natural progression of a selection of teams in the early days such as Albion, Turks, Borough, White Star, Harriers, Athletic, Comrades, Territorials and Rovers among others, many of whom at one stage used the Sports Field.

The cricket and football pavilion, built and opened in May 1913, lasted until burnt to the ground in 1968 but was subsequently replaced. The football grandstand, a square,

The old grandstand at Lymington, pictured in the early 70's.

wooden structure opened in 1929 stood until demolished, being replaced with the new sleeker 200-seater stand which was opened on March 1st 1989.

The ground, which has been floodlit since 1981 has a record attendance of just over 1,000 for the stand-opening friendly with Southampton, although some unconfirmed records indicate a 2,000 crowd for an FA Cup tie around 1950.

Wellworthy Athletic played at the Ampress Ground, within the factory site in Southampton Road until the amalgamation and the pitch still exists at the time of writing although in a poor state of repair.

RECREATION GROUND
Bashley FC

The official history of Bashley Football Club states that in the early days after the War the only football played were friendly matches due to a stream and hedge running through the middle of the pitch. A more credible view from the club is that this is nonsense although the ground originally had two pitches running parallel at 90 degrees to the current one and so there may have been a stream or hedge dividing the two.

What is certain is that the club was formed in 1947 and joined the Bournemouth League three years later. The Recreation Ground in those days was open and bordered by trees on three sides and players changed in an old Nissen hut which stood roughly where the clubhouse is now. The village hall which stands in front of the ground had the club bar built onto the side of it in the early eighties when Bashley took off, leaving the Bournemouth League for the Hampshire League and, three years later, the Wessex League. The permanent perimeter fence was put down in time for the first game in the Wessex League, and the galvanised metal stand with wooden bench seating was opened by AFC Bournemouth manager Harry Redknapp on December 13th 1988, before a celebration game with Tottenham Hotspur. As the club rose to the Southern League so it was obliged to improve the ground again, and in 1991 a much larger covered enclosure was put together and transported to the ground where it was erected next to the stand. This was added to when a smaller structure, used for a secretaries office with a VIP seating area was placed on the opposite end of the main stand. Behind all this is a bank of changing rooms, committee rooms, a board room, a treatment room and a refreshment area, all of which are tucked away, leaving the ground itself, although delightfully rural and very comfortable, a bit lopsided all the facilities being on one side. Directly opposite the ground is an equally impressive cricket ground which emphasises how fortunate are the sporting fraternity in the tiny village of Bashley.

TEN ACRES
Eastleigh FC

*Above: **The Ten Acres ground under construction in 1957.***
*Below: **A similar view, nearly 40 years on.***

Along with countless others, Swaythling Athletic Football Club first saw the light of day in 1946. Their very first matches in the Southampton Junior League were played on `The Flats', on Southampton Common, behind the Cowherds Inn off The Avenue.

Before the end of the first season, they were playing at Westfield, in Walnut Avenue, Swaythling. Conditions were extremely primitive with cold washing water collected in buckets and storm lanterns supplying the light in the dressing rooms which were an ARP wardens' surface shelter from the War with two-foot thick walls and no windows.

Conditions improved as the club progressed into senior football, and by 1957, after much hard work and dedication by club members, the new ground at Ten Acres was ready. A wooden pavilion with changing rooms was up and running and the pitch, which ran east to west in those days had been prepared. The pavilion was improved in 1959 and a verandah built as cover for

spectators although in the changes since this has been removed.

A stand was erected in 1971 when the pitch was turned north to south with a concrete path laid down to it and four years later the floodlighting system was switched on with a match against Saints on 30th September 1975 watched by 2,500 people. In 1980, the club re-named itself Eastleigh F.C. and became founder members of the Wessex League in 1986, constructing a barrier around the pitch at the time.

The pavilion and clubhouse has been constantly improved upon since it opened and now has a splendid bar and skittle alley, with kitchen and offices.

Today, Ten Acres stands on a roundabout which acts as a slip road for the M27, and is directly opposite the Southampton University Ground, home to their senior side as well as Saints juniors. The ground is not short of space as the name might imply, with the unused area frequently taken up by caravans.

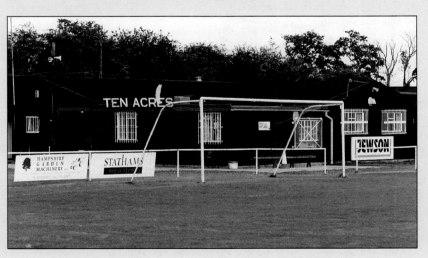

RINGWOOD ROAD SPORTS GROUND
B.A.T. Sports FC

BAT Sports were founded back in 1925 as Bramtoco FC, an abbreviation of the British and American Tobacco Company. Their sports ground has catered for all company activities since opening in 1929, but only within the last decade have alterations been made to enable the club to move into the likes of the Wessex League.

In the summer of 1989 a fixed barrier was placed around the pitch and a small covered spectator area built to partly segregate the football from the cricket. Floodlights were also installed at that time and in 1993 hard standing was laid in accordance with League rules.

formed around the Second War, the company making parts for civil and defence aircraft, and played on various pitches within their sports complex before alighting on the current pitch.

For the first season in the Wessex League the club installed floodlights and a pitch barrier, with two bus shelter type covered areas. In 1994 these were replaced by a small 50 seater stand which was extended during the summer of 1995 to accommodate a further 100.

GRIGG LANE
Brockenhurst FC

The small town of Brockenhurst, mid-way between Lyndhurst and Lymington in the depths of the New Forest, has had a football club for close on 100 years. In that time, they have played on at least nine different grounds, finally settling at Grigg Lane in 1950 where they began draining the ground, laying down supplies of water and electricity and building dressing rooms, later adding a small stand.

In 1972 a social club was built at a cost of £4,000 and the original floodlights were erected at the same time, both using voluntary labour. Six years later, the clubs quaint, square-shaped stand was built for £27,000, complete with dressing rooms underneath and seating above, and this enabled the club to add a snooker room to the social club. More recently, in 1991 the modern floodlights went up as Grigg Lane entered a new phase.

The early Brock grounds were scattered all around what was a village, with the first being behind the Baptist Chapel in Lyndhurst Road before the club moved on to a field in Wide Lane, off Sway Road. From there, after the Great War they moved to the Polo Field which is now part of the Brockenhurst College grounds and in the late twenties played on Father's Field until that was required for housing by the Council.

Next was a field in the Black Knoll grounds, having to play on the open forest at the end of one season to allow the ground to recover and in 1934 they again switched to Oberfield, in Rhinefield Road until the War. County Council land in Tile Barn was next stop after the War for three years until the final move to the more enclosed Grigg Lane ground where they remain today.

FOLLANDS PARK
Aerostructures SSC FC

Another club to pull out all the stops to play in Wessex League football were Aerostructures, the works side formerly known as Folland Sports. They were

BY-PASS GROUND
Romsey Town FC

Romsey Town have plunged down hill since their Wessex League triumph of 1990. With the team moving on and funds drying up, the club went through to Hampshire League Division Two before a revival last season.

By-pass Ground quite possibly would not be acceptable to the league today, having no seats in the small stand which straddles the half-way line. It has been home since 1956 when the club moved from their long-time residence at Priestlands and is now right next to the by-pass on the junction of the A31 and A27. The clubhouse, which is part of the dressing room complex was put up in 1978 and was full to the brim for the last big match to when Littlehampton Town visited for the FA Cup 4th Qualifying Round match in 1990. Although having their best-ever Cup run and finishing fourth in the league, the following four years have been a nightmare for this proud club.

TESTWOOD PARK
AFC Totton

Totton Football Club are 110 years old, which makes them a year older than the Hants FC themselves. The area which surrounds the ground today was part of a private estate called South Testwood Park and the early football was played on a field within the grounds.

A number of fields were used between the Wars and when the estate became available for purchase the club bought an area, part of which they then sold off for more housing, and this financed the laying out of the pitch. A proposal to amalgamate with a local cricket club was thrown out and for years the ground was undeveloped with the visitors changing in the Travellers Rest pub before a rudimentary changing hut was provided.

It wasn't until the late fifties that cover was provided, the small stand lasting until 1983 when gale force winds lashed the ground during an FA Cup tie with Waterlooville and spectators were moved out as the stand rocked. The game was abandoned and the stand pulled down soon after.

Totton amalgamated with Totton Athletic in 1975 which proved to be a milestone year as floodlights were installed and a club room and bar opened. Ten years later, to replace the stand, the modern 200 seater was built and more recently hard standing has gone down to allow the club to remain in the Wessex League.

Totton's main entrance in 1972.

SMALLBROOK STADIUM
Ryde Sports FC

In 1990, Ryde Sports vacated their Partlands Ground, just two years after their centenary, and two years short of the ground's century. At the time of writing, the overgrown site is just recognisable as a former ground, with remnants of the fencing still more or less in place, and a small green corrugated iron hut just visible through the jungle.

In total contrast, the Smallbrook Stadium is spick and span, catering not only for football but track and field athletics. Its splendid frontage is vaguely reminiscent of the Avenue Stadium, Dorchester, and leads to a playing area sited some way back from the seated stand which stretches the length of the ground. Its 300 seats are set somewhat clumsily behind four floodlight pylons, and the press box and tea bar are in the middle of the stand.

Ryde followed Newport in vacating their traditional home, but whereas Newport have a purpose-built football ground, up to Southern League standards, Ryde have a huge arena which, despite its modern outlook, may not fit the Southern League bill should the case arise.

Ryde Sports began as a rugby team, but switched codes and the football club as it is now known was formed in 1898. The early seasons were spent playing at the Isle of Wight College at Appley, now St. Cecilia's Convent, and four years later they moved to Partlands. Early newspaper reports indicate the club soon erected a wooden stand capable of seating 500 people, but when the club fell on bad times prior to the Great War, the stand was sold to pay off debts.

Following the end of the War, the club reformed and, with debts paid, the ground began to develop. The football and cricket clubs had amalgamated, both using the ground at the time, and there was a new stand. There was also a pavilion which was used for offices and changing facilities, and was previously used as a duty office for the anti-aircraft gun on what is now the golf course.

Church Litten, Newport, not long before closure.

In 1936 Ryde attracted over 5,000 for their FA Cup tie with Gillingham, which remains the biggest crowd ever assembled at Partlands, and in that same season, the club played three Hampshire Senior Cup ties against RASC Aldershot, which were watched by over 10,000 people, many of whom had to travel to The Dell twice for the privilege.

The Second World War saw Partlands badly damaged, chiefly by the ARP unit that had occupied it, but the club soon overcame that and with the post war boom the crowds flocked back to the ground.

Partlands was never to change dramatically, for the club did not aspire to glories other than the Hampshire League, and indeed in 1981 voted to drop down to the Island League, but an eleventh hour change of heart saved the day.

With the area around the ground having been developed post war, Partlands became a valuable asset and, an astute financial arrangement in the late fifties, which saw the ground purchased for £2,000, meant that thirty years later, with the value having risen to £400,000 or more, the decision to sell up and move on was taken, along with the club's elevation to the semi-professional Wessex League, alongside East Cowes Vics.

The new ground will see a higher standard of football than Partlands did, but whether it will be as entertaining is open to question. Smallbrook Stadium is vast, clean, neat and tidy, and the facilities on offer are far in advance of anything Ryde football has seen before. A new era has dawned.

ST. GEORGES' PARK and CHURCH LITTEN
Newport (IOW) FC

Newport Football Club was possibly better known for its atmospheric country ground at Church Litten than it ever will be at the new St Georges Park home. That is not to say that the new ground is in any way unsatisfactory considering it was built during the age of the antiseptic concrete edifice. It is simply that Church Litten was a hundred years old, give or take a few months, and its character will never be recaptured.

Originally known as Wellsfield, in its infancy it had a small enclosure and a rope around the pitch. It was not until 1930 that a much larger timber stand was built in its place which seated over 600 and had dressing rooms and committee rooms in its bowels and being similar appearance to the stand at Shepton Mallet. This completed a splendid era for the club, having purchased Church Litten for £3,000 back in 1924 from Winchester College.

The club enjoyed a number of FA Cup runs in the early fifties and the proceeds of the second of two meetings with Swindon Town brought about the covering of the Medina Road end in 1954 at a cost of £517. Another run in 1956 saw the ground record of 6,000 set when Watford were the visitors.

The market end remained open until the neighbouring builders merchants took a parcel of land from the club on lease which wiped out their debts overnight. To accommodate this, the pitch was turned round in the same style as at Moor Green and and the huge grass bank which ran down the whole of the side opposite the stand was flattened, leaving the main stand sitting behind one goal. The clubhouse under the stand was extended as Church Litten underwent major surgery, blissfully unaware of its impending doom.

Floodlights were installed in 1976 and in a masterly stroke of timing FA Cup holders Southampton brought the trophy to Church Litten for the illumination ceremony.

In the late 1980's the first rumblings were heard that a sale of the ground might become possible; the lure of £2.5m proved too much and the old girl swiftly became a supermarket.

Smallbrook, home of Ryde Sports since 1990.

St. Georges' Park, Newport.

The new purpose-built ground was close by and the massive complex which includes the clubhouse, administration offices, boardroom and dressing rooms was built and available before the pitch was ready.

Eventually, St Georges Park saw its first game in August 1988 and the ground-opener against Fulham attracted a crowd of 1,500 which remains the attendance record to date. Little has changed in the seven years since it was built, and the 300 seater stand and 1,000 capacity standing cover is perfectly adequate for life in the Southern League.

WESTWOOD PARK
Cowes Sports FC

The Yachtsmen of Cowes have played on two quite substantial grounds in their history, which can be traced to 1881, although the club has reformed on more than one occasion since then.

The first site, called the Brooklyn Ground, stood in Park Road, just next to the Recreation Ground. In 1899, much work was done to bring the ground up to scratch, with the pitch levelled, re-turfed and fenced in,

and more seats added to the grandstand, which had a dressing room built on to it. The Brooklyn was often full, with 3,000 watching the Island derby with Ryde, and a further stand was built on the eastern side to seat 700. The move up to the Southern League's top division however proved disastrous, for results went against them, gates fell, and the directors had no option but to disband the club in 1900.

In 1903, a new Cowes Football Club began playing. Having changed their name from White Star, and used the Brooklyn Ground once again, the newly-named club were immediately successful, and for nine further years played at Brooklyn, until the owner, a Mr. Butcher wanted the land for residential purposes and evicted the club. They did not have far to go, however, as a piece of land across the road on the Ward Estate was offered, and accepted.

The new pitch was first used on September 21st 1912, although it wasn't officially opened until November 2nd, when it was named the Westwood Ground. The imposing wooden stand, has received its fair amount of stick over the years and was in a very sorry state, as was the rest of the ground, until wholesale tidying up occurred a few years ago. Most of the outside of the stand has been re-clad and painted, but the interior is more or less the same.

Whilst the bank of turnstiles at the entrance are now surplus bar one, the move up to the Wessex League has rejuvenated the old place which is almost exactly the same age as its neighbour in Beatrice Avenue. There have been a number of minor changes; the small covered stand opposite the main stand is now gone, courtesy of two devastating storms, and part of the land behind the near goal has been sold off, but Westwood Park is more or less unscathed after 83 years and is a pleasant ground to visit.

Photos in this section by: Derek Brooks, Pat Brunning, Andrew Chitty, Joe Reed, Richard Wall, James Wright and courtesy of Newport I.O.W. First 100 Years.

BEATRICE AVENUE
East Cowes Victoria Athletic FC

Beatrice Avenue is about to suffer its first major change in nearly fifty years when the original grandstand disappears to make way for a sanitised alternative, thanks to the Wessex League's condemning of it in 1994. It is one of the oldest stands anywhere in non-League football and certainly the oldest on the island, having been built by volunteers from the ranks of the unemployed in 1912, soon after the land was first played on.

East Cowes Vics first played on a pitch close to the hospital in York Avenue before moving across to another, near to Norris Castle. Just prior to the Great War a piece of Crown land next to the current ground but nearer the main road was used, but when a 21 year lease was obtained the ground was laid out and the stand built complete with changing rooms underneath, a very modern and sought-after amenity in those days.

The ground changed little until after the Second World War when toilets and a tea hut were installed and a lean-to, stretching from the stand to one corner was put up. It still has a single row of seating for around 100 spectators and was erected in 1950 as crowds came back in numbers.

A further 20 years elapsed before the ground went up for sale, but there was, and still is, a covenant protecting it from all building, meaning that it must always be used as playing fields or an open space. Despite this, the club received permission to build their much needed clubhouse in 1976, and ten years later put up a post and rail and floodlights to gain entry to the fledgling Wessex League.

Beatrice Avenue is a throw back to earlier times, and is welcome for that. It remains to be seen just what the loss of the ancient stand will do to the oldest remaining football ground on the island.

An aerial view of Beatrice Avenue, home of East Cowes FC.

South & East Hampshire

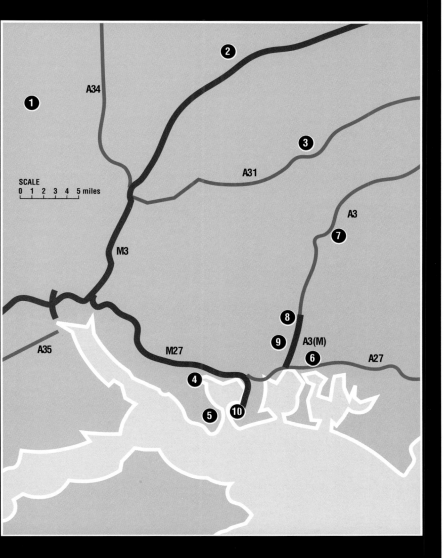

SCALE
0 1 2 3 4 5 miles

A34

M3

A35

M27

A31

A3

A3(M)

A27

1. **Andover FC**
2. **Basingstoke Town FC**
3. **Bass Alton FC**
4. **Fareham Town FC**
5. **Gosport Borough FC**
6. **Havant Town FC**
7. **Petersfield Town FC**
8. **Horndean FC**
9. **Waterlooville FC**
10. **Portsmouth RN**

IN relation to the rest of the county, this area has fared much better with Andover, Basingstoke, Fareham, Gosport, Havant and Waterlooville all playing, or having played in the Southern League. Again, the Wessex League has proved a salvation for several clubs - Andover are a prime example - who are able to lick their wounds and try again with renewed interest.

Whitchurch United have gone from the Hampshire League to the Wessex League twice at their Longmeadow ground and **Portsmouth RN** have done well to retain their status in the Wessex League. Their splendid stadium in Burnaby Road West has been home since 1987 when the famous Victory Stadium was vacated. The whole area around the stadium is dedicated to sport with cricket grounds and United Services rugby ground all close by.

The football ground has an official capacity of 1,500 but in truth many more could gather around its grass banking should they be able to get past Checkpoint Charlie on the security gate. The stand holds 500 seats and gives a fine view over the stadium which is never used to its full advantage. The remaining part of the Victory Ground has only recently been gobbled up, a road having dissected the pitch a few years back leaving some tantalising terracing crumbling away for the connoisseur to drool over!

PORTWAY STADIUM
Andover FC

As far as has been established, Andover were formed in 1883, although press reports from the time are vague and earlier references may be of the rugby code. The first seasons were spent on a pitch owned by a Mr Stride on Weyhill Road, before the club moved to the Walled Meadow, playing their first league game there against Guilder Rovers, a Salisbury side, on September 15th 1894.

The former home of Andover FC

The club entered the Southern League in 1898 for one season and were not to return for 73 years, by which time the Walled Meadow had gained two small stands, floodlights and a clubhouse.

The Walled Meadow was always one of the more basic, yet homely, of the Southern League grounds before the spiralling pyramid all but extinguished any sense of idiosyncrasy. Its small patched up grandstand was built by Knight and Pool in 1934 for £350 and remained to the end, with a covered standing area opposite. 1961 saw the installation of floodlights similar to those already in use at Folkestone, Ashford and Ramsgate and the ground changed little until its last game. A social club was opened in 1973 but the club struggled for many years and when finally the ground was sold to developers, Andover moved out in May 1989 after over a hundred years of football.

The new Portway Stadium was ready for action in November of the same year, and unlike many new grounds has proved both successful and popular. Andover finally gave up the ghost with the Southern League in 1993 and took voluntary relegation to the Wessex League where they have undergone a renaissance. The new ground was opened before a match with Leicester City in front of 1,100 spectators which remains a record. Looking back, the top crowd at the Walled Meadow was the 3,484 who saw the FA Cup First Round tie with Gillingham in 1962, the only time to date the club has reached the competition proper.

CAMROSE GROUND
Basingstoke Town FC

The Camrose has seen many changes since it was first opened as the Winchester Road ground on December 1st 1945 before a match with Southampton Borough Police. Today, the ground is ideally placed next to one of the umpteen major roads which seem to slice up the town, the main entrance being just off a roundabout. Indeed, wherever any ground is built in Basingstoke, the entrance would not be far from a roundabout!

For many years, a small wooden stand with grass banking around the pitch topped by railway sleeper terracing was home to the club until re-development took place as the Southern League beckoned. A new clubhouse went up in the car-park area in 1969, and in 1970 the impressive looking 800-seater main stand was built, complete with dressing rooms underneath. Concrete terracing was started opposite and floodlights were erected and opened before a game with the Metropolitan Police.

As the Camrose took shape as one of the Premier grounds in Hampshire, the terracing was covered during the seventies and has since been repaired following storm damage. In 1991 further cover was put up to the left of

ANSTEY PARK and BASS SPORTS GROUNDS
Bass Alton Town

The town of Alton, in Hampshire, is blessed with an abundance of sports fields, most of which are situated in the area around Anstey Park, original home of Alton Town F.C. Virtually next door, and across the road is the sports ground home of Bass (Alton) from the Hampshire League.

Three years ago, a merger took place between the two clubs which spawned Bass Alton Town. For the first season the new club played on at Anstey Park, with the reserves at the Sports Field, until the cost of continuing at the Park proved prohibitive, and the lease was given up.

The Bass Sports Ground has existed for cricketing purposes for as long as anyone can remember, although the football stand, built around 1960, is far younger than it looks, delightful though it is. Originally, players would change in an old Nissen hut which was situated in what is now the car-park at the rear of the clubhouse, before the new changing rooms were built.

These were subsequently transformed into the clubhouse and players now change in the cricket pavilion in the far corner of the ground. The wooden stand is very similar in design to that of its cousin up the road, and has a glass fronted lean-to tacked onto the back of it for the attendant bowling club.

Anstey Park, happily, is still in use, and the lease is now held by a new team, Alton United, who play in the Aldershot Senior League. The ground is believed to have been opened by the local council just after the war, with the stand being put up around 1955.

Directly opposite is a substantial area of covered terrace which followed on soon after. The whole area is surrounded by high fencing, and is still at the time of writing in good shape, with a portakabin acting as a club house for the new incumbents.

The covered terrace at Alton Town. The club merged with Bass Alton and the ground is now used by a club in local leagues.

the stand over the terrace which was finally completed this year.

The Camrose came about when the club moved from their long time home at Castlefields after the final game there in October 1945. They played a few matches at West Ham Park, home of Thorneycroft Athletic before moving two months later. Castlefield is still used for sport, as the home of Basingstoke Cricket Club's 3rd and 4th teams, being situated close to Mays Bounty Cricket Ground, and is used for football by Fairfield School.

CAMS ALDERS
Fareham Town FC

Cams Alders has been a football ground since September 1975, when the club, realising that Southern League football was never going to come at their spartan Bath Lane home, moved into the newly built stadium, which at the time consisted of the main concrete built stand and a pitch with no perimeter fence.

The area was previously a meadow, and is now covered by the recently extended stand, with a huge car-park and open recreational area, which gives the football ground an air of remoteness. In 1983 a cinder running track, which soon fell into disuse, was laid around the ground. It is now an eye-sore and a nuisance as it distances the pitch from the spectators in what is already an open and vast arena.

The lack of elevation around the pitch has been partially rectified recently in a similar way to that at Bedworth United, where the track around the ground is now ignored and the pitch perimeter fence has been squared off to bring the crowd closer to the action. To comply with League rules, a small area of cover has been stuck up to the left of the stand, seemingly as an afterthought and quite possibly against the club's wishes, again on similar lines to Wellesbourne, who were forced to erect a peculiar stand they didn't want.

The Bath Lane ground had a small cover and changing rooms with a roped-off pitch, and has staged football since before the 1920's. The sports ground now hosts hockey and cricket. Prior to that, the old Fareham FC used a ground along Beaconsfield Road which is now a housing estate.

Above: **Cams Alders**

Left: Fareham's former Bath Lane ground, still in use for hockey.

WEST LEIGH PARK
Havant Town FC

Havant Town's marvellous West Leigh Park ground is a rare commodity in that it is only 12 years old yet was built in a style which echoes some of our old market town grounds of the pre-war days. It was built on what was once a very boggy area that took two years to drain before the club could move in with a 99 year lease.

A post and rail was first erected and the hard standing put down around the playing area while the clubhouse opened in the first season. When the club entered the Wessex League the main stand was built. Apart from

the small area of cover by the entrance, the remainder was put up to protect 1,400 people in readiness for the Southern League, as was the retaining wall.

The ground now has the regulation three turnstiles, one of which came from Fratton Park, Portsmouth.

The pleasing part is that whether through necessity or design, the indiscriminate use of concrete has been avoided, and the same principal has been kept throughout its development into a Southern League ground capable of holding 6,000 people. The main bulk of the work has gone on since 1990 when the club reached the Southern League having won the Wessex League that season.

The original corrugated fence still runs down the length of the ground which has a sloping grass bank, which gives a good view when dry, at the back of a retaining wall. The current record crowd stands at 3,000 which saw Havant take on Wisbech in the FA Vase Quarter-final of 1986.

The club's previous ground called the Front Lawn was fenced off with a roped-off pitch and dressing rooms in one corner. Although the fence has been broken up and taken away, the club still use the ground for their 'A' team matches.

LOVE LANE
Petersfield Town FC

The recent history of Love Lane and the Petersfield club has been somewhat traumatic to say the least. The refusal of the Council to renew the club's lease and the demise of United and formation of Town have all been hammer blows which they have done well to survive.

Little is known of the club's original tenure at Love Lane until they moved to a field owned by a Mr Seward along Princes Road in 1926. The ground had a 300-seater wooden stand along one side with dressing huts opposite and was bordered on three sides by hedges with a high wood and netting fence on the side nearest the road. Just after the War the owner died and Princes Road became available to purchase but the club did not have the capital so the solicitors evicted them and the land was sold for housing.

The site of the current home was farm land which was flattened and converted to a pitch in 1948. An old Army hut for changing was eventually provided by the Council from a site at Woodbury Avenue in the town. Prior to that players were forced to change in the old workhouse 100 yards away from the ground.

The Supporters' Club raised the capital to erect the small wooden stand in 1962.

West Leigh Park, Havant

Love Lane, Petersfield.

It has given good service for over thirty years with only minor modifications in that time. Back then the ground was fenced off but had an old green hut just outside the ground which acted as a clubhouse and this was replaced in the early eighties, when the modern structure was built incorporating dressing rooms, boardroom and a kitchen.

Further cover went up in 1984 by which time Love Lane had been floodlit, the original lighting being improved two years later. Petersfield took a voluntary drop into the Wessex League in 1993 from the Isthmian League which removed the necessity to

upgrade the ground even further at a time when money was tight and problems were lurking just around the corner.

JUBILEE PARK
Waterlooville FC

Waterlooville Football Club first saw the light of day in October 1902 and initially played at Hart Plain Park, land which has since been built on, around half a mile north of their current home. In 1910 they moved to Stakes Road, former home of Purbrook of the Portsmouth North End

League, but some time later they moved again to share with Waterlooville Cricket Club.

This arrangement came to an end in 1923 when for the first time the club took the bold step of obtaining a ground for their exclusive use, again in Stakes Road. The move was largely welcomed as there had been problems sharing the cricket ground, although there were worries as the ground was some distance from the main road. 1927 saw them back at the cricket ground for one season until the new Recreation Ground in Jubilee Road became available. It was to be home to the Ville for the next 29 years as they rose to the Hampshire League. Being part of a public area the ground was never fully enclosed but was roped off for matches and a collection taken at half time in lieu of admission.

A club headquarters containing changing rooms, baths, a club room and a kitchen was built and opened on Easter Monday 1948, while in the early fifties a small covered stand was put up by the Supporters' Club. The changing rooms are still on the recreation ground to this day, although the small stand was taken down and transported to the new site during the move.

In Spring 1954 the club bought some land 200 yards south of the Rec. with the intention of developing their own ground. Work began but was soon halted as finances dried up. In October 1955 players and supporters began working on levelling and seeding the pitch, but appeals to the public and to the FA for financial help were not a success.

PRIVETT PARK
Gosport Borough FC

Surprisingly, the fourteen years spent in the Southern League did not have a major influence on Privett Park until the club were obliged to spend some £18,000 on an 8ft tall motorway style fence which now surrounds the whole ground.

Since 1937 when the sports ground was first opened and the old Gosport FC used it in the Hampshire League, it has not changed. Indeed, the original main stand, now capable

of seating around 500 was the only accommodation until a group of supporters who occupy the same site each match, built their own little cover a few years ago.

Privett Park was part of a larger area which was segregated off from the cricket ground and used exclusively for football. The early changing rooms were in the cricket pavilion until much later when new ones were incorporated into the stand. The clubhouse opened in 1972 and now has an overhang which acts as a small area of cover, complying with Wessex League rules.

Voluntary labour had to be used and so a further two years elapsed before Jubilee Park was opened in September 1957.

The small covered stand was transferred from the Recreation Ground to the east side and a further covered stand was built along half the length of the west side. Initially the teams would change in the club headquarters and had to cross the road but this soon altered when new changing rooms were built.

Upon entering the Southern League in 1971 the club were required to provide covered seating and during the 1971-72 season the 560-seater main stand was opened, and concrete terracing and walkways were put down all round the pitch. The following season saw floodlights at Jubilee Park and three years later the social and sports complex was built. During the summer of 1982 the last remaining area of grass banking disappeared being replaced by four steps of terracing at the south end of the ground. A roof was built over the popular north end in 1991, closely followed by a covered area at the other end which came from Dorchester's old Avenue ground when they relocated.

The ground today is approached through an industrial estate in a similar fashion to Stratford Town's Masons Road and is dominated by the massive night club and snooker complex which backs onto the main stand. Jubilee Park is best viewed from opposite the stand on the flat standing area backed by an intermittent line of trees. A selection of club rooms built on separate levels are to the left

Jubilee Park, Waterlooville.

of the huge main stand, whose seats are steeply banked to give a splendid view of the pitch. Covered terrace is provided at each end and to the right of the stand is another area of covered terrace which is not dissimilar to that at West Court, East Grinstead.

Jubilee Park is a comfortable ground which would possibly look far more attractive if it were set anywhere other than in the middle of the industrial units which have sprung up all around it.

Photos in this section by: Andrew Chitty and Richard Wall.

FIVE HEADS PARK
Horndean FC

Horndean's modest ground has been home since 1969 when they moved from the Recreation Ground. Situated in Five Heads Road, it was not developed to any degree until the start of the eighties when the clubhouse was built. This was followed by a perimeter fence around the ground and a small 50 seater stand, with another small section of cover on the half way line.

Floodlights were installed in 1980 and despite the activity in the early eighties, the ground has not gone on from there, although regulations will perhaps force Horndean into a corner very soon.

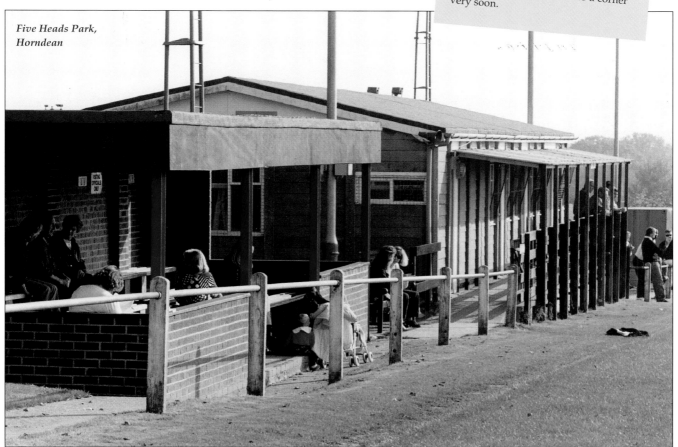

Five Heads Park, Horndean

West Sussex

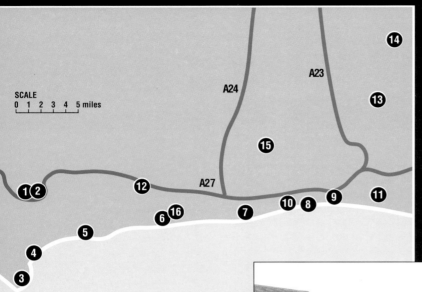

SUSSEX is a beautiful and fascinating county with its contrasts of rolling down lands and busy coastal towns; witness for instance the genteel slumberings of Eastbourne matched by the aggressive liveliness of Brighton. Its well-established football administration has nurtured possibly the best County League in the country, which has produced one or two Southern and Isthmian League participants as well as a number of clubs with delightful grounds which grace the league today.

In the far west, **Selsey** and **Midhurst & Easebourne** both have well cared-for grounds, the latter sharing with cricket, whereas in the far east of the county **Haywards Heath** are still in their Hanbury Park home which held over 5,000 people for a Metropolitan League game in the fifties. Its imposing stand is going to waste as the club sadly vegetates awaiting the loss of its ground to town planners.

1	Chichester City FC
2	Portfield FC
3	Selsey FC
4	Pagham FC
5	Bognor Regis FC
6	Littlehampton Town FC
7	Worthing FC
8	Shoreham FC
9	Southwick FC
10	Lancing FC
11	Whitehawk FC
12	Arundel FC
13	Burgess Hill FC
14	Haywards Heath FC
15	Steyning FC
16	Wick FC

Above: Selsey FC

Midhurst & Easebourne FC

Oaklands Park, home of Chichester City FC.

OAKLANDS PARK
Chichester City FC

Chichester Football Club were formed in 1873, when a local newspaper of the time related that "We are glad to be able to record the formation of a football club in the City, promoted by several gentlemen of athletic tastes". As was common in the very early days, both codes were played until 1883 when, with the club already established at Priory Park, they concentrated on Association Football.

The only major honour to come their way at Priory Park was the Sussex Senior Cup won in 1926, and it wasn't until the club moved to their present ground at Oaklands

Park that they had easily their most successful spell, winning the County League title two years running and reaching the First Round of the FA Cup. In the previous round the ground record crowd of 2,500 saw Dorchester beaten 4-1.

On moving to Oaklands Park, the club had to start from scratch as the site was bare. Their first task was to create some changing rooms, which were roughly west of where the current changing rooms are now. This was followed in 1960 by the erection of a large bus shelter from the centre of the town which was bodily moved, and placed to the east of the pitch on the half-way line. This stand lasted 20 years until it was removed due to its dilapidated state, but the base can still be seen. Soon after, two small stands were erected and they still exist.

At about the same time a clubhouse, which lasted until it was replaced along with the changing rooms in 1981, was built behind the southern goal.

Today the ground is perfectly functional for the crowds now visiting Oaklands Park, and is situated in an area put aside for recreational activities of all kinds.

CHURCH ROAD
Portfield FC

Church Road is home to possibly the slightly lesser known of the two Chichester clubs, although the current playing record indicates that Portfield have taken over as the top side at the moment. It has been home since a move from the local recreation ground in 1958 which ended a trek around a succession of pitches in the area, mainly farm fields, which were often spartan, with players changing in a railway coach, a groundsman's shed and a timber garage.

It took many years of fundraising before the clubhouse, complete with changing rooms, was finally built and it has since expanded creating the funds for the impressive separate changing block, built in 1983. The ground has a small stand with seating, which was recently rebuilt and has hard standing all round which sets off the ground nicely.

NYETIMBER LANE
Pagham FC

Although Pagham Football Club have been in existence since 1903 they were a junior or intermediate side playing on various farmers' fields until 1950 when they moved onto a field adjoining the cricket club and began playing in the West Sussex League.

A small wooden shed was thoughtfully provided by a local farmer for the players to change in and this sufficed until the club applied to enter the County League in 1970. A cricket pavilion type building went up alongside a breeze block stand which at the time had no seats. A wooden building belonging to a local grocer was wheeled down to the ground in one piece and used as a bar for some five years before the whole lot was removed and replaced with a more modern clubhouse and changing room building some time later. The ground was unfenced and open until their County League days and was not segregated fully from the cricket until 1988. Around that time the new floodlights went up which replaced a training set destroyed in the 1987 hurricane. Opposite the stand there is an area of open terracing which was laid down in 1980 and there are plans, which have been approved, to cover this and the far end of the ground.

The ground is happily protected by a National Playing Fields Trust which dates to when the field was left to the cricket club and the football club in the 50's. At one time Pagham were aiming for Southern League membership and were close to it but the goal posts have been moved some distance now and Nyetimber Lane has settled for being one of the more attractive County League grounds.

Church Road, Portfield.

NYEWOOD LANE
Bognor Regis Town FC

Nyewood Lane is one of the more unsung seaside grounds that maybe does not get the full praise it deserves. Having come out of the County League in 1972, Bognor, somewhat geographically out on a limb, have spent roughly equal lengths of time in the Southern and Isthmian Leagues.

They have not been without success in this period, reaching the 2nd Round of the FA Cup three times, and the 1st Round a further three times. The 1984 replay with Swansea City brought a gate record of 3,642, a total well within the reach of the club whose capacity is 6,000, although it would take a relaxing of police restrictions to fill the ground to that figure.

Bognor Football Club were formed in 1893 and at first used farmers' fields around the west end of the town before moving to Nyewood Road around 80 years ago. A small wooden stand was built with two dressing rooms and a first-aid room, while a storage shed was put up at the rear. Referees were required to change in another hut by the side of the stand, which had wooden terraced seats for around 150 people.

The pitch was enclosed with old wooden posts linked by thick rope, and for many years all remained virtually unchanged as the club played in the County League. Bognor were given permission to use the name Regis by King George V, after he stayed at the town whilst convalescing in 1935.

The Supporters' Club was formed around 1960 and it was their fund raising that enabled turnstiles to be built and a canteen added soon after. The club's first floodlights were bought from Wembley Stadium, and were fitted on telegraph poles. They were amongst the first to be seen in Sussex football. Two ex-RAF huts were acquired in 1970, and these were fashioned into a clubhouse with a bar, the funds raised through a club lottery. It has since been updated and metal cladding now surrounds the original building.

Since entering the Southern League,

St. Flora's Road, Littlehampton.

Nyewood Lane has changed considerably with three covered stands built around the ground to hold a total of more than 3,000 people The newer stand complete with dressing rooms and a boardroom holds 200 people.

ST FLORA'S ROAD
Littlehampton Town FC

Littlehampton Town's sports centre ground should be viewed from the corner nearest to the cricket pavilion to fully appreciate its qualities. Just as many of our seaside resorts are becoming somewhat seedy, but still retain hidden charms amongst the tat, then St. Flora's Road is unmistakably a seaside ground.

Forever held back by the presence of the cricket square since moving there in 1920 from their previous home at Lobbs Wood, it has nevertheless retained its position as one of the top grounds in the Sussex County League. The grand old lady of a main stand, built around 1930, is frayed at the edges and has a weather-beaten yellow and black name board, but happily is now flanked by two sturdy covered stands with concrete steps, built between 1948 and 1950, which for all the world appear to be guarding her in case

she falls over. She too was improved with seating for 200 at the same time.

Behind the goal nearest the entrance is the huge cricket scoreboard and less secure looking supporters' club hut. This stands in front of the hideous grey, mushroom-shaped 1970's style sports centre, which has been stuck straight in front of the entrance, and provides a grating contrast to the charming cricket pavilion by the side of it, which the club used up until 1975.

The pitch-side fence was first put in place in 1984 along with sponsorship boards and floodlights arriving four years later. The whole of the playing area is enclosed by a wooden barrier, part of which is removed during the cricket season along with many of the colourful advertising hoardings which brighten up the ground.

The club, and more importantly the Police, were sufficiently happy to allow the televised FA Cup 1st Round match against Northampton Town in 1990 when a record crowd of 4,000 - the capacity - packed the ground. In the same successful season, when the club reached the semi-final of the FA Vase, took the League title, and were runners-up in the County Cup, the ground was also well-attended.

WOODSIDE ROAD
Worthing FC

At one time during the club's 110 year history Worthing FC owned not only the football ground but also most of the other land down to the main road and railway. A generous benefactor and local sportsman Mr Brazier donated the land to the club but it was gradually whittled away as the area all around became developed.

It is believed the club have always played on the current ground, although at one time the pitch ran at right angles to its present position with one goal roughly where the bowling club is today. When it became more permanent the surrounds were banked up to allow better viewing and this

Nyewood Lane, Bognor Regis.

The Main Stand at Worthing.

was well demonstrated when some 4,500 people crammed in to watch the Amateur Cup quarter-final against the Depot Battalion Royal Engineers in 1908. That remains the highest-ever attendance at Woodside Road and with the current capacity set at the same figure it is unlikely to be exceeded.

For many years the players changed in a building on the corner of Pavilion Road and Woodside Road and then walked the 100 yards or so to the ground. The structure still remains but is now home to a charity organisation. The first building on the ground was the old low wooden stand which dated from around the mid twenties and had an asbestos roof and room for 740. On a bleak night just two weeks before the Bradford fire it was destroyed in a blaze. The only other building was a small shelter which stood close to where the clubhouse is now and was used by the players at half-time, as the clubhouse was further down the road. After the War the thriving Supporters' Club laid the terracing around the ground and soon after the clubhouse was built incorporating the first dressing rooms on the ground - and these survive to this day.

One unusual aspect of the site was the installation of a large static water tank during the War to combat the threat of fire from incendiary bombs. It survived until converted into a training area which in turn was sold for the development of flats. It was around this time that the small stand opposite was built, quite possibly as a gesture by the developers. It has since been altered and re-roofed but remains intact. Much later, in 1976 the club installed floodlights for the first time and soon after the banking in front of the

club was removed and the earth used to further raise the north side of the ground as a covered area was built.

After the fire a considerable amount of time and effort was spent in replacing the stand, its eventual arrival in 1986 again transforming the ground. Underneath is a VIP lounge and bar plus a boardroom and it is, from some angles, a replica of those larger stands at Cheltenham and Kings Lynn. Today Woodside Road ground is tailored to survive in the Isthmian League and has a solid in-fill around the pitch and intrusive

exterior fences but nevertheless still retains a certain charm quite often seen at seaside grounds.

MIDDLE ROAD
Shoreham FC

Shoreham's Middle Road, formerly part of a much larger public park, has been their home since 1970. Situated between housing and a long narrow industrial estate, it suffers from being somewhat inaccessible with the main entrance some distance from the

OLD BARN WAY
Southwick FC

The Wickers celebrated 100 years of football in 1882 and for all but 14 of those years have played their football on the recreation ground, although nowadays their home is segregated from the Rec by a wall and a huge indoor bowls club and is reached only via Old Barn Way.

The early football was played on pitches on or near what is now Southwick Cricket Club until 1896 when the council rented the club a site partly enclosed with changing facilities at the east end of the Rec. To enable them to become founder members of the County League the club moved to its present pitch site, building a small stand which still exists in abstract form today, patched up and world-weary but still usable despite the twin threats of the 1987 storms and the Lord Justice Taylor Report. The dressing rooms continued to be used right up until the opening of the clubhouse in its original form in 1972 which incorporated the long awaited replacements.

The first floodlights went up in 1968 and the Wickers were the first side to play a County League game under lighting, heralding the start of major changes at Old Barn Way. New regulations from the League demanded a fully enclosed ground which was achieved along with the twin area of cover either side of the stand in 1972. Further cover went up at the north end in 1989.

Today Old Barn Way is a fascinating collection of buildings which seem to gel into an atmospheric ground, particularly when Shoreham are the visitors - a meeting which even now in the days of double figure attendances still brings the in crowds .

main road and a gloomy dark carpar. Another, less used, entrance is tucked away behind some warehouses.

In the early days, canvas sheeting would be erected and dismantled on matchdays to screen the ground, and there was no cover or clubhouse. Successive championships in the Sussex County League Division Two meant that improved facilities were necessary, and the concrete boundary wall was built along with the covered accommodation on the south side of the ground.

It soon became apparent to the club that licensed headquarters were essential if their high standing was to be maintained, and this came to fruition in April 1985. A friendly against neighbours Brighton & Hove Albion marked the opening of the club, and eighteen months later Wimbledon were guests to celebrate the installation of floodlights. The attendance of 1,342 for the latter game remains a ground record. Prior to the move to Middle Road, the club played on a sloping pitch in Buckingham Park, a public area half a mile away which, as in the early Middle Road days, was 'canvassed off'. With no entrance charge, a collection box boosted the coffers, especially at Boxing Day derbies with Southwick.

MILL ROAD
Arundel FC

Arundel Football Club were formed at a meeting held in the vicarage by the Rev. P.A. Butler, a junior curate of Arundel. Permission was sought from the Duke of Norfolk to play under Association Rules

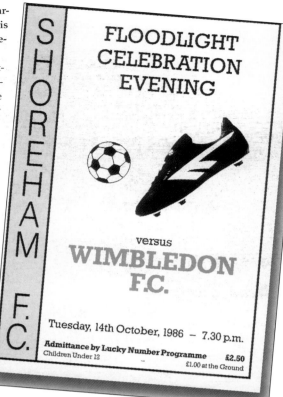

within Arundel Park, and the go-ahead was given. After training twice a week for a month the new club staged their first game at the park on October 17th 1889, when the captain's team took on the sub-captain's side.

Sadly very little is known about the club up to the thirties when a small wooden stand, which stood until 1971, was erected at the ground. After the war Arundel joined the strong County League, and around the beginning of the sixties much work was done to the pitch and its surrounds, but it became unplayable, and games were transferred to Walberton for a spell. A further scheme to improve the ground at a cost of £850 was introduced, and ten years later in 1971 new

changing rooms were opened at a cost of £2,000, which proved to be the beginning of the transformation of Mill Road.

A post and rail fence was put up around the pitch, and new training lights added, before the old stand was pulled down and a new white painted brick-built structure erected in its place. Since then a further small area of cover has been provided close to the changing rooms and clubhouse.

The club suffers from the fact that its home is overlooked by Arundel Castle, and as a result could never be changed sufficiently for it to progress to any greater level. Conversely, the ground is already delightful as a typical Sussex County League ground, with a picturesque leafy entrance, further enhanced by the presence of the Castle in very much the same way that Worcestershire's Cricket Ground is completed by the Cathedral in the background.

THE ENCLOSED GROUND
Whitehawk FC

East Brighton Park had been home, in one way or another, since the club's inception in 1945. The original pitch was on a lower part of the park and the players used the cricket pavilion to change in. In the late fifties the need became apparent for an enclosed ground, and the club moved to their present site, which at the time had two pitches, which were converted into one, and turned round 90 degrees.

In 1960, with a council grant of £300, the club planted trees and shrubs and created dressing rooms and a covered enclosure, which in later years had eight rows of steps built under it. During this period players changed in a building within the nearby camp site. In 1980, the Social Club was erected, using a building which formerly stood in a builder's yard, and this has since been

The Mill Road ground is overlooked by Arundel Castle.

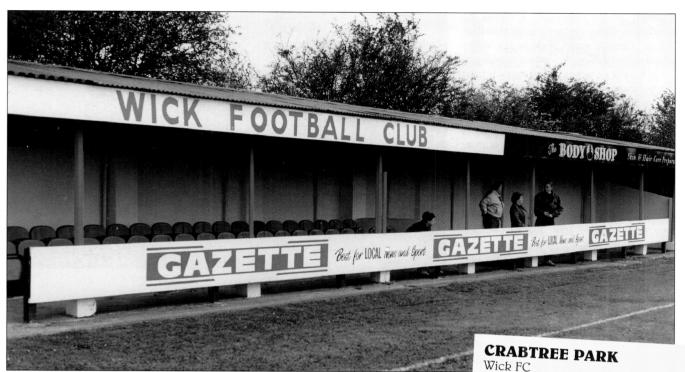

The half-pitch length stand at Crabtree Park, Wick.

improved and extended to include a committee room and a kitchen. A year later the fixed post and rail was put up around the pitch.

1988 saw the club reach the fourth qualifying round of the FA Cup, where they took Bognor Regis to a replay at the Goldstone Ground, in front of a crowd of 2,100. In the same year the floodlights at the enclosed ground were opened before a game with Luton Town.

LEYLANDS PARK
Burgess Hill Town FC

On the 2nd October, 1882, at the conclusion of the Annual General Meeting of the Burgess Hill Cricket Club it was decided to form a football club. Initial games were played on fields and meadows lent by sympathetic farmers, and parks, recreation grounds and pleasure gardens.

This nomadic existence continued after they became founder members of the Mid-Sussex League in 1900, using mainly St John's Park, Janes Lane and Fairfield Road Rec until the Second War. They resumed in 1947 at Janes Lane, then Mr Woolgar's Station Road Meadow, St Wilfred's Road and then back to Fairfield Road, changing at the Royal George Inn, courtesy of Jack De Caux, landlord and club Chairman.

Burgess Hill settled there, and had a pavilion built by members and supporters from funds raised in the town. The official opening was on September 5th 1958.

In 1969, now playing in the Sussex County League, the club merged with Worlds End FC to become Burgess Hill Town, and the Urban District Council played a major part in preparing an enclosed pitch

and providing the shell of a pavilion as well as laying an access road to a site north of the town, known as Leylands Park.

Four dressing rooms with showers, two offices and a club room and bar were soon erected and on April 24th 1971 the ground was opened at the end of the final league game of the season against Bognor Regis Town, in which both sides gained promotion. A year later, a covered stand for around 250 was built and paid for by the club's match with a Showbiz XI team. A lounge bar extension was provided in 1974 and again in 1982, and a year earlier the new floodlighting system was installed ready for the 1981-82 season.

The last main activity at Leylands Park was the opening of the all-weather training pitch before a friendly with Watford FC in October 1989.

CULVER ROAD
Lancing FC and Sussex County HQ

When the Sussex County Football Association bought the Culver Road ground in 1981 they secured its future but in doing so sentenced its marvellous 40 year-old stand to a lingering death, for the club room of the SFA was positioned in such a way that it blocks the view of a good proportion of the pitch regardless of where the punter sits.

The bungalow style building is set forward from the stand only feet from the touchline and is designed with a gap built into the facing wall to allow for a floodlight pylon. Why an equal amount of thought was not given to the dear old stand is anyone's guess.

CRABTREE PARK
Wick FC

The village of Wick, now all but swallowed up by the expansion of Littlehampton, has had a football team since 1892. The Crabtree ground, by the Six Bells pub was used until 1968, when their tenancy was ended by the owner, who wished to use the land for his livestock. The club were reduced to a small hut to change in at the finish, having spent many years using the True Blue pub and walking to the ground. For two seasons the Southfields Recreation Ground became home, until a field became available close to the railway and bordered by a housing estate.

Building began almost at once to fence off the site and to erect the covered enclosure in the bottom corner of the ground, and the square, two-storey clubhouse with dressing rooms, kitchen, and offices. The complex was opened on November 14th 1970.

Crabtree Park today is not much changed from 25 years ago, with the half pitch length stand now providing seating. Either through accident or design, the stand is very similar, though on a smaller scale, to the marvellous covered terrace at Queen Street, in Horsham, and it provides the only shelter on the ground. The opposite side is hemmed in by a railway line, which has to be warily and illegally traversed whenever the high netting fails to do its duty. In recent times a splendid brick turnstile block was built, at the back of the car-park, which fronts what is now a pleasant and comfortable Sussex County League ground.

The wonderful Dripping Pan at Lewes.

THE DRIPPING PAN
Lewes FC

Modern folklore has it that the Dripping Pan is so named due to its natural shape, having a sloping grass bank around most of its playing surface. However it almost certainly originates from the days when monks used to pan for salt in the nearby river, the adjacent ground being known as The Priory.

What is certain. however, is that a group of men met in the Royal Oak pub on September 23rd 1885 and formed Lewes Football Club which began playing at the Dripping Pan and has done ever since.

Very little appears to have been documented on the changes at the ground which has a ricketty stand seating 400 perched on those grassy banks which give the ground its distinctive shape. The slightly ambitious official capacity of 5,000 has never been tested,

with the highest crowd believed to be for a game against Newhaven in the County League on Boxing Day 1947.

CABURN PAVILION
Ringmer FC

The Caburn Pavilion, Ringmer is without question one of the most attractive of Sussex's grounds, and has the added bonus of being situated in an equally attractive setting, just east of Lewes.

The social club which fronts onto the car-park gives an indication that the rest of the ground is neat and well cared-for, and this is borne out once inside. The whole of the car-park side of the ground is taken up by a line of red brick buildings. The clubhouse has an extension which acts as a shelter, and next to it are the changing rooms which look big enough to house four teams, never mind two, while a further brick building, albeit window-less, is currently home to the village rifle club.

Behind both goals, the club has installed netting, and assorted trees and shrubs act as a natural barrier. A brand new stand, small but beautifully designed and seating 100 or so has been erected opposite the club on the halfway line and replaces the small brick shelter and dug-outs which did service there. The area behind the new stand, and the slightly incongruous set of cricket nets tucked away in the corner, suggest this was until recently a shared ground, and it comes

PIDDINGHOE AVENUE
Peacehaven and Telscombe FC

The football ground at Peacehaven and the immediate surroundings have altered considerably in the 65 years of its existence, although it has never at any time been substantially developed, being perfectly adequate for the club's needs.

Peacehaven Rangers and Telscombe Tye merged in 1923, and played on a piece of land called The Tye owned by the local squire. In 1930 came the move to Piddinghoe Avenue in Peacehaven, where the club shared the ground with cricket until 1958. The first buildings on the ground were wooden changing rooms, and in the mid-60's, the club acquired a Nissen hut from an old army base. This was soon replaced by a small stand capable of housing 100 people. Around this time the ground was enclosed with a concrete fence, effectively squaring it off for the first time since the cricket disappeared. The long clubhouse and dressing rooms which dominate the seaward side of the ground were initially built in 1978, and have been added to over the years, not least by the covered extension in 1993. A year before, the floodlights were erected.

Piddinghoe Avenue is just one of many identical roads that make up Peacehaven. The ground is part of a council-owned complex featuring bowls and tennis, as well as a Community Centre and play areas, all of which share the car-park with the football club. The ground itself is fairly ordinary, but is enhanced by the stunning scenery inland, with rich farmland and rolling hills providing the backdrop to Peacehaven and Telscombe Football Club.

as quite a surprise to find that has never been the case.

Part of the deal when erecting the flood-lights was they should be of the collapsible variety and so, other than on match days, the pylons lay as broken flowers with their bulbs just feet from the ground.

Football in Ringmer is believed to go back to 1910, and was played on a field only yards from the present ground, just south-east of the Anchor Inn. It was reached by a public footpath, after the players had changed in the beer storage room of the pub. Unfortunately, it was a working field, and the goal posts had to be taken down after each match ..... and the cowpats removed before!

The foundations for the club in its present form were laid down in the early sixties, when they reached Intermediate football and were offered use of a field at the back of the Post Office, with an option to buy. The first priority was to build changing rooms, which were completed with the help of local men, and were wooden, with a centre hall-way.

A season later a breeze-block bathroom was added at the rear, and a smaller hut erected alongside the building for refreshments. The area around the ground had begun to change dramatically, with new roads cutting in from the main road, and eventually it was agreed that the ground be moved 40 yards or so to its present spot, to enable the road and subsequent housing to be completed.

To once again solve the problem of changing, a large pre-fabricated building was bought from the old Croydon Airport. After hours of meticulous planning the clubhouse was re-erected on its present spot, the Council duly building a village car-park in front to afford access. It was opened on December 2nd 1967, and christened the Caburn Pavilion, which is now the universally accepted name of the ground.

THE OVAL
Eastbourne United FC

The history of the club goes back exactly 100 years when 1st Sussex Royal Engineers began playing. Home matches were held at Clifton House School ground, where Saffrons Road and Arlington Road now meet, and the South Lynn ground in Tutts Barn Road.

During the Great War the club were posted overseas and continued playing together until their return when the name was changed to Eastbourne Royal Engineers Old Comrades. Success came and the club moved to a new ground at King's Drive in Lynchmere which is now covered by the Thomas A'Beckett School. The pitch was enclosed and facilities improved enough to enter the County League in 1921 when they dropped the R.E. part of the name.

After the Second War the Lynchmere ground was sold for development and the club moved on to the Princes Park Oval in 1946. The Council improved the site by laying a pitch, an athletics track and a grass cycle track. A hugely successful fund-raising scheme enabled the club to erect a clubhouse, dressing rooms, medical room and supporters' facilities which replaced a Nissen hut. Later the grandstand was built and a covered terrace added on the Wartling Road side with open terrace in front of the stand. A Press Box was built into the stand and the bench seating was later replaced by a tip-up variety. Floodlighting was installed and then improved much later.

As is often the case with clubs who have dropped down the pyramid in recent years, the club are going through a tough patch and the council owned ground has now seen better days.

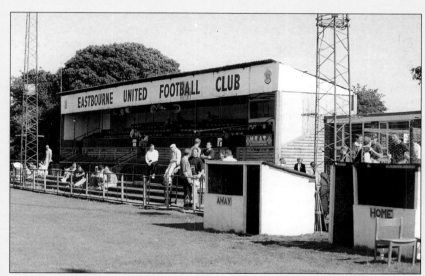

The Oval, home of Eastbourne United FC.

THE SAFFRONS
Eastbourne Town FC

Town are currently the middle standing of the three teams around the town, with United seemingly going backwards at the same rate that Langney are progressing.

The Saffrons is a superb sporting centre which is possibly better known for being a county cricket venue as well as being home to a strong hockey club. Eastbourne Town have played there for over 100 years with varying degrees of success and are in the process of improving the football side of the ground which suffered damage to one of its stands during storms which wrecked the roof. The portakabins which have been used for changing since the pavilion was taken over by the hockey club are shortly to be no more as a new block is to go in.

Apart from the main cricket pavilion, there was once a large wooden football stand which stood approximately where the terraced cover is now. Sadly, it succumbed to fire in the sixties and was replaced by the current cover.

The Saffrons has seen huge sporting crowds over the years, with county cricket and football both extremely popular, particularly in the early fifties, when over 7,000 crammed in to watch a local derby with Hastings United in the FA Cup in 1953.

PRIORY LANE
Langney Sports FC

The origins of Langney Sports go back to 1964 when Langney FC were formed and played in the Eastbourne and District League on the Village Recreation Ground and Princes Park in Eastbourne. As Sussex County League football beckoned, the club made great strides, with a clubhouse being started in 1983.

Early matches in the league saw the club obliged to erect a hessian barrier to comply with the relevant rules and the first stand on the ground consisted of a converted wooden container. It was replaced by a small cover which still stands over-looking the second pitch, and following promotion to Division One in 1988 a new ground was laid out adjacent to the original one, with a large covered stand along one touchline. In 1990, Crystal Palace attracted a 1,000 plus crowd which remains the highest to date, to officially open the new lights. Since then, the ground has improved and developed each season, with hard standing all around, an impressive new turnstile block and last year a new administration building, dressing rooms, President's club and a new covered stand behind one goal.

Langney Sports have now comfortably overtaken the two long established Eastbourne clubs and Priory Lane goes from strength to strength.

Rebuilding at Langney Sports

Hastings Athletic FC, Rock-a-Nore FC, Hastings St Leonards FC, Hastings Town FC, Hastings Utd FC, STAMCO FC

Rather than try to detail every intimate minor detail that has happened in the grounds around Hastings, it is far more worthwhile to record the chronology of the various clubs involved and their homes.

Organised football was first seen around 1887, played side by side with rugby on pitches marked out at the Central Ground, in Queens Road, home of Hastings and Sussex County Cricket in later years. There were a number of minor clubs set up at that time, playing friendlies, until the Hastings FA was formed in 1892 and various cup competitions were played for.

Hastings & St Leonards FC were formed in 1904 and entered the South-Eastern League, playing at the Central Ground before amalgamating with **St Leonards Utd FC**. Financial problems saw their demise after they played in the Southern League Second Division but lost a play-off with Stoke for a promotion place. After United, **St Leonards Amateurs FC** were the leading side, playing on the Briscoe Ground at White Rock, winning the Sussex Senior Cup and playing in the Athenian League just prior to the Great War.

In 1920, **Rock-a-Nore FC** were re-formed, having previously played as a junior side on Hickman's Field, later to be called The Oval in Bohemia Road. They had initially been refused permission to play at the Central Ground, which saw no further football after the first St Leonards side. Through various efforts the club obtained permission from the Corporation to play on a large meadow at the Pilot Field. The first match to be played there, on the upper pitch was late in 1920 when the club met Chichester in the newly-formed County League. The pitch was marked out with whitewash and a tuft of grass, the spectators occupying seats borrowed from the Corporation. At the end of the season Rock-a-Nore merged with **All Saints FC** and became known as **Hastings & St Leonards FC**.

In 1921 the Council brought forward a £6,000 scheme for excavating and laying out two pitches but, because of the substantial slope, hundreds of tons of earth had to be shifted and moved across to build up the area where the grandstand is now. By the time the work was complete it had cost £32,000 with a further £8,000 for the massive stand which followed two years later.

After problems with drainage had been sorted out, the club moved down from the upper pitch to play regularly on Pilot Field from 1923. Three years later, after a series of disagreements with the Corporation, the club had talks about the possibility of transferring to the Bulverhythe pitch (where, ironically, they moved some fifty years later), and an agreement was made but not signed for them to play at the Central Ground at £400 per annum. However, the status quo continued and they remained at Pilot Field.

In 1948, a newly formed professional side, **Hastings United FC**, took over at Pilot Field with the Amateurs moving up to the top pitch. It was not long before the ground was hosting greyhound racing and for a short spell, speedway came to the Field and indeed there are still vestiges of the banked track to be seen today. The enormity of the place with its grass banking which sadly is now out of bounds, covered terrace at one end and 1,000-seater stand has spawned much folklore concerning the size of crowds in the days between the Wars, but the confirmed highest attendance is 12,727 which saw the FA Cup 3rd Round tie with Norwich City on the 9th January, 1954. United continued playing there until June 1985 when, with massive debts, they resigned from the Southern League and folded.

St Leonards had continued throughout this time on the upper pitch at Pilot Field, apart from a brief three year spell at Bulverhythe whilst the upper pitch was brought up to scratch. In 1976, they changed their name to **Hastings Town**, and when they returned to the upper pitch, now called `The Firs', it had been substantially levelled and new dressing rooms had been built.

The Firs is also blessed with steep banking on two levels which enabled nearly 2,000 people to watch **STAMCO**'s FA Vase 5th Round tie with Tiverton Town in 1995 which broke the ground record three times over.

When United folded, Hastings Town applied for, and were accepted into, the Southern League, continuing to use the Firs for reserve and Sunday games after moving back down to the Pilot Field following an absence of 37 years. Even now, some ten years on, there are still signs around the ground which refer to United.

STAMCO FC orginated as a works team for the Sussex Turnery and Moulding Company in 1971. For five years the club used Borough pitches until purchasing land at Pannel Lane, Pett in 1976. Their picturesque ground is still used by them, but in 1993 The Firs was acquired, complete with clubhouse and stand which was built around 1981. In the two years they have been there, floodlighting has been erected, concrete standing has been laid all round and a wooden post and rail put up around the pitch. A six foot wooden fence now surrounds half the ground, and the clubhouse and dressing rooms have been completely renovated.

The whole place reflects the nature of the company and, as a result of the banking created by two sessions of earth-moving since the twenties, the ground boasts marvellous viewing areas.

The Pilot Field and The Firs have virtually identical gaily coloured brick entrances which with the segregation of the top field are now the only reminders that the grounds were formerly one and the same.

Photos in this section by: Gavin Ellis-Neville and Dean Walton.

East Kent

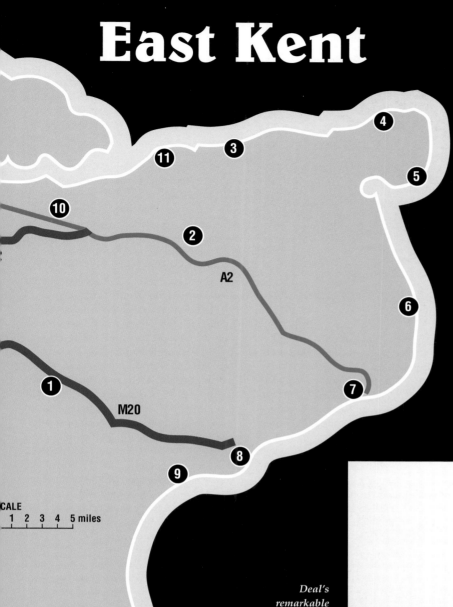

CHARLES SPORTS GROUND
Deal Town FC

Prior to the First World War the club played on a site occupied now by the local hospital. This was built as a memorial to those who fell in the War and as a result the club was moved to a site just opposite their present ground.

In 1920, they either merged with, or took over from Cinque Ports FC who had formed in 1908, and continued on that field until the mid-thirties when a local benefactor, Sir Justice Charles, donated the present ground, along with a wooden stand and dressing rooms for the "benefit of the young people of Deal".

SCALE
1 2 3 4 5 miles

1   Ashford Town FC
2   Canterbury City FC
3   Herne Bay FC
4   Margate FC
5   Ramsgate FC
6   Deal Town FC
7   Dover Athletic FC
8   Folkestone Invicta FC
9   Hythe United FC
10 Faversham Town FC
11 Whitstable Town FC

Deal's remarkable 65-year-old stand.

Inside Deal's old wooden stand.

Upon his death in 1950, his will stipulated that Deal Town should have sole use of the ground for two twenty-year periods, at a nominal rent payable to Dover District Council who became trustees of the ground. When these periods expired the ground was taken over by the Charity Commissioners. The Council have granted an interim lease but the Commission have vetoed any further leasing which has put the ground in jeopardy.

During the heyday of the Kent League in the mid fifties many clubs began developing their grounds and Deal Town were no exception, fully terracing the Mill Road end. A showbiz match featuring a Billy Wright X1 attracted over 4,000 in 1961 and this remains the record gate for any match on the ground. A few years later the smaller terrace on the Charles Road side was laid down and a set of floodlights acquired from Oxford United for £200.

The Charles Sports Ground is typical of so many former Southern League grounds in that it possesses real character within its slightly run-down appearance. The pitch has a post and rail all around it with the old wooden stand along one side and terraced enclosure opposite. The clubhouse and tea-bar have recently been improved, but the floodlights have sadly deteriorated over the years and been reduced to training duties only. The club hope to develop the ground into a multi-purpose sporting centre which would at least guarantee football in Deal although the traditional Kent League ground would be no more.

CRABBLE ATHLETIC GROUND
Dover Athletic FC

There has been football on the Crabble for nearly a century, as the first Dover club began playing on the bottom pitch whilst in the Kent League in 1897. Nowadays it is used for rugby and cricket with Kent County Cricket Club gracing it sporadically during the summer.

During the formation of the professional Dover Football Club in 1947, the Corporation examined plans for a grandstand on the open side of the top ground, opposite the existing stand which was built by Army personnel at the end of the War, and made an application for a loan from the Ministry of Health. This was turned down which posed a major problem for the club. In 1950 the club again approached the Corporation, and eventually, in October of that year, the loan was sanctioned and in January 1951 work began on extending the stand at either end to bring the seating up to around 950. In April of the same year Dover moved up to the top pitch for good and the first game was a friendly against a Fulham XI, and two weeks later a crowd of 5,000 packed in to see the semi-final of the Kent Senior Shield.

It was originally proposed that new dressing rooms would be constructed adjacent to the pitch and on the opposite side to the new grandstand. However due to the isolated position, the installing of the power supplies would not be cost-effective and so it was decided to split the main pavilion, with the footballers using the dressing rooms upstairs. At that time the football club were paying the Town Council £300 per year in rent whereas the rugby club on the bottom pitch were charged 25/- a match.

The new grandstand was officially opened by the Deputy Mayor before a match with Folkestone on August 25th 1951, and a year later it was announced that the Supporters' Association were to finance a project to provide covered terracing on the bank behind the town goal at a cost of around £3,000. This was good news for the regulars who had been used to sliding around on perilous muddy slopes.

The club had already installed floodlighting at the Crabble and Chelsea sent a team to celebrate the event which included Alan Harris and Terry Venables. The Crabble remained more or less unchanged as the original Dover folded and Dover Athletic took their place, and as the club reached the top of the Southern League promotion to the Conference beckoned. The extensive alterations which were required meant initial heartbreak for the club as they were turned down for promotion on the basis that the work was not completed by May of that year, 1990. New turnstiles had already been built at the top of the slope and by July 1990 areas of terracing had been repaired or replaced, both the covered ends were taken down and replaced and all the old seats in the main stand were substituted with new plastic ones. Having finally gained promotion in 1993 the club were once again obliged to add 250 extra seats in a brand new stand which was built on the open side, thus bringing to fruition a plan that first came to light back in 1947.

The Crabble, Dover.

CHERITON ROAD
Folkestone Invicta FC

Cheriton Road is an area rich in sporting facilities to this day. The County Cricket Ground is next door and lawn tennis and hockey are both catered for in the complex. The football ground emerged in 1914 when the club moved from the old Gas Works ground at Canterbury Road Rec. They had been there under the shadow of the viaduct since moving from the Moorhall Rec, behind the Electricity Works in 1894. The very early sides played on spartan pitches on the Plains and in the grounds of Sutherland House, near the old bandstand on the Leas.

Between the Wars the original Folkestone built a long low wooden grandstand all along one side, quite possibly when entering the Southern League in 1923, and followed that with an area of cover at the Cheriton End. The players changed in the pavilion which stood where the Black and Amber club was later built. Much later, when floodlights were introduced in 1959 a covered terrace was built along the Cheriton Road side. The lights were opened with a match against Burnley on September 30th 1959 as the club again prepared for Southern League football,

Folkestone Invicta now play at Cheriton Road, former home of defunct Folkestone Town.

SALTERS LANE
Faversham Town FC

The Town have been at Salters Lane since around 1958 when they vacated the Gordon Square pitch in favour of a ground purchased by the Supporters' Club for the football club. The layout has changed little since major work went on to build up the place in the early sixties.

Originally, as well as the seated stand there was another which was taken down when the clubhouse was built, and the covered standing followed around 1968. Four years later the club installed floodlights which were recently upgraded.

Prior to the move to Salters Lane the club had two homes, firstly on a field off Ashford Road called The Mall until the War, and then for a dozen years on farmland in Gordon Square which reverted back to agriculture when the club moved on.

The record gate for the club is at Gordon Square, when a local derby with neighbours Sheppey United was watched by 1,400. Since Sheppey lost their Botany Road ground they have shared with Faversham and indeed, very recently won the Kent League title, something which must surely rankle more than a little amongst the home fans.

left behind at the outbreak of the War.

The old stand lasted until January 1974 when it was burnt down and subsequently replaced eight months later by today's structure which can seat 900. Folkestone Town became Folkestone and Shepway as they struggled through the 80's and they went under in 1990. Happily a team called Invicta which had played its football in the Kent County League moved in and Cheriton Road continues to stage football into its 81st year. It would be nice to dream that one day the ground record of 7,801 which attended the Senior Cup tie against Margate in 1958 would be broken, but somehow it looks unlikely.

REACHFIELDS
Hythe United FC

Hythe United were formed from the ashes of the successful Hythe Town FC that for an all too brief moment sampled the delights

of a semi and a quarter-final in the FA Vase and a three year tenure in the Southern League before the the club crashed amid the apparent folly of too great a reliance on one man's promises.

It has, however, left the legacy of a fine ground which should grace the Kent League again in 1995/96 just as it did seven years ago, albeit this time on a humbler scale.

The original Hythe Town date from 1910 when they broke away from the established Hythe Wanderers. They played on a council-owned field in South Road until in 1973 acquiring Reachfields, an old Army sports ground and training area. Three years later having gained senior status they entered the Kent League. Reachfields at that time consisted of a single-storey clubhouse with dressing rooms and hard standing on the south side and in front of the club. A small shelter for a few dozen people which included the dugouts was halfway along the south side. The pitch was enclosed by a post and rail.

Reachfields ground at Hythe before the turmoil.

Further improvements were made ten years later when the ground was enclosed by railings and a covered area known as the Burlington Insurance Stand was erected, which had bench style seating for 120 but was destroyed in the hurricane the following year.

In January 1988 the club tied up with a local businessman who began planning immediately for the Southern League. The whole ground was concreted from pitch to outside wall and a new two-storey main stand was built on the site of the old one. The whole south side was covered and the roof extended to include the entire east end in front of the clubhouse. The south side was on one level whilst opposite were steps and four turnstiles. A toilet and refreshment kiosk with built-in shelter was then put up next to the main stand.

By February 1989 the work was virtually complete, and the main stand had a bar with six viewing balconies upstairs and seating for 250 with spacious dressing rooms and a medical room. The seating was later extended to 400 with the addition of another single-storey building alongside. Floodlighting was installed at the same time, as Reachfields was transformed within weeks. Soon after a single step was put in place all along the south stand and work began to develop the interior of the stand. This, sadly, was never completed, nor was the large stand planned for the open end on which work had started before another storm wrecked the scaffolding. It was never finished.

The Vase runs brought in some fair crowds to Reachfields which has a capacity of around 3,000, mostly covered. The record attendance currently stands at the 2,147 which watched the first leg of the FA Vase semi-final against Yeading in 1990.

The demise of the club is not a subject for this book, but positive moves were made to retain football in the town and the new club was formed in the Kent County League, re-gaining senior status with a welcome return to the Kent League.

BELMONT GROUND
Whitstable Town FC

The Belmont Ground is unquestionably one of the most pleasant in Kent, and is undoubtedly one of the oldest, having first staged football in 1888 by the original Whitstable side. The field was then owned by a Mr George Holden who lent it out periodically.

The club had already been in existence for three years, playing on Saddleston's Fields, and used this field along with another at Westmeads, in Cromwell Road before returning to Belmont in 1896. The following years saw a split with two clubs Town and United; Town stayed at Belmont whilst United played elsewhere, quite possibly on a pitch in Joy Lane.

1900 saw the clubs come together once more, and the Belmont was again home, although some matches were played at the Manor House. They stayed this time for eight years before moving to a new ground in Church Road, which was not a success for within a year they were once again back at the Belmont, where they have remained ever since.

The first building of any note was put up in 1909, and consisted of a timber stand with glass sides and dressing

rooms underneath. These remained unchanged until after the Great War when a covered enclosure was added to the front. Many of the Kent grounds were put out of bounds during the Second War due to their proximity to the Docks, and the Belmont's stand and dressing rooms were demolished and the ground requisitioned by the War Department.

When the War was over, the club obtained permission to play at the ground once more, and a cafe building was bought over from Tankerton Slopes and converted into dressing rooms. A committee room was built, fences erected around the ground and a post and rail put in. Three years later a concrete stand was built opposite the dressing rooms, costing £600, and in 1954 a covered terrace was constructed behind the goal at the Gasworks end.

Since the seventies there has been little change other than cosmetic, as the club continues in Kent League football. The clubhouse went up in 1972 and floodlights were installed in 1989, but Belmont is relatively unscathed. Its capacity of 2,000 is perfectly adequate, and is only 500 short of the highest-ever attendance at the ground, for an FA Cup tie with Gravesend and Northfleet in 1957.

ESSELLA PARK
and HOMELANDS
Ashford Town FC

Essella Park existed for 56 years as a football ground, from 1931, when the then recently formed club moved in, until 1987, when as runners-up in the Southern League Southern Division they were forced to move temporarily to play at Cheriton Road, Folkestone, as the new ground several miles out of town was not ready.

Essella Park, former home of Ashford Town and (above) the new ground, Homelands.

The old ground never did quite elevate itself to the stature of some of the more well appointed stadia, being crammed in amongst housing for the majority of its life. The main stand, a low structure in two uneven parts, managed to see out the ground's life-span, although looked decidedly second-hand at the end. The other three sides of the ground were covered either fully or partially, and a social club and tea-bar stood on the same side as the stand.

The club had the good sense to purchase the ground from the then President, Mr. Norman, for just over £2,000 in the fifties, and it was this that enabled the club to sell Essella Park for development, and build Homelands on a green-field site at Kingsnorth, four miles from the town centre.

In contrast to Essella Park, Homelands is approached by a long lane, which leads to a series of un-made car-parks in front of the ground. The remoteness of the site is accentuated on inclement days when rather open seating is vulnerable. Virtually all of the facilities at the ground are situated in, or next to, the huge building which extends out towards the pitch to provide seats for 500, in a capacity of 3,500. Inside, the offices and function rooms are superb, and a committee-room looks out over the pitch through a glass viewing area, thus enabling some spectators to keep warm when the wind blows in the wrong direction. One end is covered along its width, with plans for the other to be similarly adorned, and the whole site is enclosed by concrete panel fencing.

The football watching public of Ashford have gone from enduring the spartan, yet homely and accessible Essella Park, to the luxurious, but inaccessible and slightly soulless Homelands. Sadly, it seems the best of both worlds is often out of reach.

Whitstable Town FC.

WINCH'S FIELD
Herne Bay FC

The earliest section of Winch's Field, as it appears today, is the railway embankment that runs along the entire south side of the ground. This was created in 1863 when the line was laid through. It formed one boundary of the Winch's Brickyard which stood on the site around the turn of the century.

Stanley Gardens, the postal address of the ground, was developed in the 1920's while the area to the east remained clear and contained a pond at the Canterbury Road end of the ground. There was also the remains of one of the brickyard buildings that were converted into a private laundry. Air raid shelters were constructed on the waste ground and they remain below the pitch to this day.

Herne Bay Football Club had played their home matches on the town's Memorial Park after its transformation from a rubbish tip in the early twenties, until a pitch was laid out at Winch's Field. On August 26th 1953, over 1,000 spectators turned up to see the first fixture, a 2-2 draw with Tunbridge Wells in the Kent League. That match was the culmination of some £5,000 being spent on creating a venue to call their own.

Since that time the ground has slowly developed, and in 1970 a crowd record of 2,303 was set for an FA Cup 4th Qualifying Round tie with Margate. In 1971 a new clubhouse was built which still remains and is now used as a boardroom while covered accommodation also went up. Floodlights were installed in 1992 and two years later a new stand with terracing on the west side of the ground gave the club the distinction of cover on all four sides.

Winch's Field, Herne Bay.

HARTSDOWN PARK
Margate FC

Hartsdown Park Football Ground was laid out in the grounds of Hartsdown House in 1929. The players at that time changed in the big house before walking across the fields to the ground. Margate Corporation had provided it for the newly-formed team, the previous club which played at Dreamland having folded in 1928. It was decreed that the new club would play in the professional Kent League, and as such, a new company was formed with a share capital of £1,000.

By November of the same year work had commenced on the fencing, gates, and a 500-seater stand. The first match was a friendly on August 31st 1929 against Folkestone. Within five years the town council had agreed to commence work beneath the stand on new dressing rooms and toilets, and the club had altered the size of their pitch to equate with Arsenal's, as Margate had become that major club's nursery. Some time during this period a further stand was erected opposite the original one.

This boom time for the club, which included many lucrative FA Cup ties, came to an abrupt halt when the nursery agree-

Hartsdown Park, Margate.

ment collapsed. Having joined the Southern League, they were forced to return to the Kent League, and in 1938 the club closed down. A year later they re-formed, but almost immediately war broke out, and again the club folded, only to re-appear six years later.

Since the early fifties, Hartsdown Park has been steadily changed and improved, with an additional wooden stand being donated to the club by Mr. Arthur Weston

and re-erected in 1952, after it had blown down in a gale. It stood at the end now occupied by the clubhouse which was built fifteen years later. In 1956 the Cornhill stand and terracing was developed at the opposite end and, shortly after, more substantial walling and terracing was put down, while floodlighting costing £3,783 was introduced for the first time. The lights were erected on eight pylons, three on each side with one behind each goal. They were replaced in

THE FOOTBALL GROUNDS OF THE CITY OF CANTERBURY

Football in Canterbury has never been the number one pastime of the locals and during the early part of the century the lack of interest led to three City clubs folding prior to 1921. Journalists wrote that the game would never catch on in such a cricket-orientated place, as it had done in Faversham, Folkestone and the Medway towns. But it did through some lads forming a team called Waverley, and again after the Second War via Robert Brett and the then Mayor, Mrs Hews.

There have been at least six grounds where senior football took place in Canterbury, three of which were only used in county football for a short time. The facilities on each, if any, are not recorded.

THE RISING SUN

The Rising Sun ground existed from 1900 until the First War and was situated on Sturry Road, now the A28 to Ramsgate, behind the pub and just in front of some marsh land. Local clubs used the ground and in 1909-10 it was home to the 21st (Empress of India) Lancers who won the Kent Amateur Cup. The pub is now a refuge for battered wives and the marshland has long been drained and lost, along with the ground.

VICTORIA RECREATION GROUND

On the A2 Faversham Road with the Rheims Way dual carriageway alongside it, there is a fine view of the Cathedral from the ground where football and cricket are still played today. In 1919 to 1921 the third Canterbury side used it but soon ceased to operate there as they were refused permission for a stand or to take gate money.

MILITARY ROAD

There had been sports grounds between Military Road and Sturry Road, which run parallel, for a century until the last decade, when the MOD had an estate built called Brymore along with local Council offices. In 1945, the 12th Infantry Training Corps joined the Kent League, but withdrew in 1947 when their players returned to civvies. It was used in the 60's and 70's by local sides and had a changing pavilion at the Old Park end.

WINCHEAP GROVE

Senior league football started at Wincheap Grove in 1904, and in November of that year a stand was opened by the Mayor, Sir George Collard, which included new

dressing rooms, 140 seats and was built at a cost of £70. The Grove had seen football during the latter part of the last century. Canterbury Waverley moved from the Victoria Ground in the twenties and shared it with the Gas and Water Company who owned the land. By then the ground did not have a stand but there was terracing in front of the social club which was on the railway side and eventually a stand with dressing rooms and two large coke-heated baths were built. They were around half way along the touch line at the furthest end of the ground and opposite the official entrance in Wincheap Grove which was close to the Norman Castle and a small terraced street which came off the junction of Castle Street and Wincheap. The entrance had a terraced house on one side and a fifteen foot wall on the other, which belonged to the BRS lorry depot.

The pitch ran close to the back gardens of the houses and the BRS wall ran along to the railway bank which looked down onto the pitch. Today the houses are under the Rheims Way at the Wincheap end, with Habitat built on the BRS depot and BT buildings on the pitch.

The dressing rooms were brick-built with timber and the pitch was roped-off with railings behind the goals. The Waverley built a stand between the

1964, with a system that cost a similar amount to the original ones, and they in turn were replaced by those salvaged from Dartford's Watling Street ground. Sadly, in 1989 the second stand had deteriorated to such an extent it was condemned by the local fire brigade and declared out of bounds. The rear and sides were removed leaving just the roof on poles, but this too was declared unsafe and eventually the whole area was completely cleared and covered in gravel.

Southwood Stadium, Ramsgate.

SOUTHWOOD STADIUM
Ramsgate FC

There was a club in the Kent League who played as Ramsgate between 1909 and 1914, and a Ramsgate Town were formed when football resumed after the Great War. Mr. and Lady Weigall provided the ground at Southwood for the club from the start, but success was short-lived, and the club folded in 1924, and the ground was taken over by Ramsgate Grenville, who had played previously at the Warre Rec.

A new club, Ramsgate Press Wanderers, originally formed out of a group of news-boys, played on a ground called Dumpton, donated to them by the Harrison family. A crowd of 2,000 watched their first match in the Kent League, and for a while Dumpton was the scene of various grandiose schemes, but the support was never there, the club eventually folded, and Dumpton was sold.

Ramsgate Grenville never reformed after

Above: A glorious view of Wincheap Grove, home of Canterbury Waverley until after the War.

dressing rooms and the Gas and Water club backing onto the railway line, and a walk-way was laid down on the railway side for spectators. In the 30's a covered enclosure was built behind the Wincheap Grove goal. The gardens' side had duck-boards and during the summer cricket and 'bat and trap' was played. After the War Waverley were not allowed to play there, but the Gas and Water continued until the ground was sold to a wholesale fruit company, and later to BT.

BRETTS SPORTS GROUND

Bretts Corner had sport played on it for 100 years. Before the Brett Company bought the ground it was owned by Pays and known as the Pays Sports Ground and the land on which Brett's have their main building was part of the playing field. It was also called the Athletics Ground and an area of banking used for cycling can be seen today.

Bank holiday sports days and boxing were held there in its heyday. Football was played by local clubs or Army sides in the 1900's and after Brett's bought the ground, their works side played on it before the War.

Soon after, a meeting between Robert Brett and Mayor Mrs Hews brought about the birth of Canterbury City football at Brett's Corner from 1947 to 1958. The pitch was small and ran east to west with fencing on three sides. Opposite the stand and just beyond the fence was a cricket table and duck-boards were used on those three sides. Whenever large crowds gathered, bench seating was placed either side of the goal inside the fence. On the works side there were three stands. The main one on the halfway line was for season ticket holders, had a concrete floor and wooden seats with a brick wall facing the pitch and a steel staircase at the back. To the right was another cover made of scaffold poles and corrugated tin which was

Above: ***The home of former Kent League club Snowdon CW, FA Cup entrants until 1979.***

watch the derby with Margate in 1955. In August 1958, the Supporters' Club built a stand for the club, which is still in use, and was of concrete with bench seats not dissimilar to that at Maidstone Road, Chatham. In earlier times, there was a barrel roofed stand made of corrugated iron on the site. The new stand was built with dressing rooms underneath and ticket booths at each end, with a central tunnel.

In the sixties, Southwood was possibly at its peak, with the club playing in the Southern League. Both ends by then had been covered and terraced, with dressing rooms next to the bank of turnstiles by the clubhouse. For some reason those under the stand were never used for the purpose intended. The cover consisted of corrugated iron on a frame of scaffolding poles, with one end having a brick wall backing and the other made of corrugated iron.

Since leaving the Southern League in 1975, the ground has suffered. The council condemned both areas of cover, and they were dismantled, and a concrete panel fence erected in place of the iron. That too did not last long, and most of it has since gone.

The kitchens and committee room were damaged when rain got in through the leaking roof, and a tarmac training area which

terraced underneath. The third stand was seated on terraced flooring with wooden seats on four levels running half the length of the pitch. It had steel uprights and a tin roof with three large trees growing right through it! The whole of the south side was under cover. The changing rooms were behind it with referees room. The Supporters' Club had an office facing the only entrance and backed onto the stand at the Thanington Road end with a window facing the pitch. Brett's social club was part brick and part timber and was built next to the training area.

Because Brett's business section was at the corner of the main road the crowd had a 75-yard walk down a private road to the turnstiles which were inside the green painted 8ft fence. Like the Grove, Brett's had a railway line alongside it although it was disused by 1952. Also like the Grove, the River Stour ran within 100 yards of the pitch but was the least affected of the two. The stands at the ground were officially opened on January 24th 1948 with a fixture against Gillingham, the ground having already been in use since August 1947 when Aylesford Paper Mills played the first ever game there.

Brett's was home for just eleven years before City moved to the purpose built Kingsmead after playing their last match

Derelict stands at the old Bretts Sports Ground.

against Margate on a Friday night in May, 1958. The highest attendance on the ground was 4,998 in October 1948 for a Kent League match with Dover.

Bretts Corner has become one of the most photographed and famous of all disused football grounds in non-league football due to the continued presence of the now derelict stands. The ground has always been used for junior football since City departed and only recently has it been the target of a supermarket chain who want to buy but cannot get permission for a petrol station on the site.

the Second World War, but Southwood was again used, this time by a new club, Ramsgate Athletic, who were immediately successful, and won the League Cup, at Southwood in front of 4,000 spectators, which was a record until 5,083 packed in to

KINGSMEAD STADIUM

During 1954-55 Robert Brett gave City notice to leave and resigned as Chairman. They had three years to raise money to build a new stadium. A number of sites were viewed, but an old rubbish dump was chosen. The ground took two years to complete, built on the lines of a mini-Wembley. The main stand was all concrete and had seats for 600, but the whole thing was pyloned into the ground some 60 feet due to the ground's siting on an island created by the River Stour running around it.

Right: Aylesford Paper Mills' ground at Cobdown Ditton. The club played in the Kent League until 1954, competing in the FA Cup until 1950, and are now in the Kent County League.

was provided with the aid of a grant has been removed and the open side is now used for parking.

In more recent times there have been moves to create new sporting stadia incorporating a ground for Ramsgate, and so it remains to be seen whether Southwood can overcome this latest threat to its existence, or whether it will join Dumpton in the Ramsgate footballing archive.

Photos in this section by: Paul Bates, Pat Brunning, Mike Floate, Roger Turner and courtesy of the Kentish Gazette.

A supporters' building and a committee room with a viewing tower went up, and between that and the main stand was a tea bar. Opposite was a stand with terracing and a green-painted 50 yard long cover fashioned out of scaffolding and corrugated tin with the club name on the fascia board. On the Kingsmead Road end of the stand there was another tea hut.

In the early 60's a brick stand was built behind the Kingsmead Road end, again for standing, and a small amount of terracing was laid just inside the main entrance to the ground which had a running track around it for Canterbury Athletic Club. The main entrance is unchanged today with two turnstiles. Later, a large wooden social club was built to the right of the entrance; nowadays this building has been renovated and is a refreshment hut.

Over the years Kingsmead has changed somewhat for the worse, with two stands

gone and the third converted into a fully covered-in restaurant. The supporters' tower and rooms are now part of the greyhound racing facilities, although for a while they were out of bounds until the floodlights, pitch and outbuildings were renovated in 1989. Around and above the dog track is a walk-way while in the top south-east corner there is a concrete platform for viewing the match and alongside it a shed which once housed the pits for the speedway riders. The arrival of speedway saved the club, but to the detriment of the ground as the racers made alterations to cater for their own needs. The stands were taken down and the pitch moved to create the track as racing took hold in the late sixties and seventies. On the demise of the speedway, dog racing took over but despite renovation the ground still lacks any atmosphere due to the pitch being some distance from the fans.

The first game at Kingsmead was on August 30th 1958 when Ashford Town were the visitors for a Kent League match, and the official opening was a week later and performed by the omnipresent Mr Stanley Rous CBE.

The first home game in the Southern League was against Kettering Town two years later and the first floodlit game on September 22nd 1964 in the Southern League against Dover. The lights were bought from Margate and later sold to Whitstable Town in 1989.

The record gate at the ground is 4,100 for a Schoolboy International between England and Wales in March 1960.

Kingsmead as a football stadium is on borrowed time as Council plans are in hand for a new stadium at an unused recreation ground on the main A28. It cannot come soon enough for Canterbury City Football Club.

Central Kent and the Docks

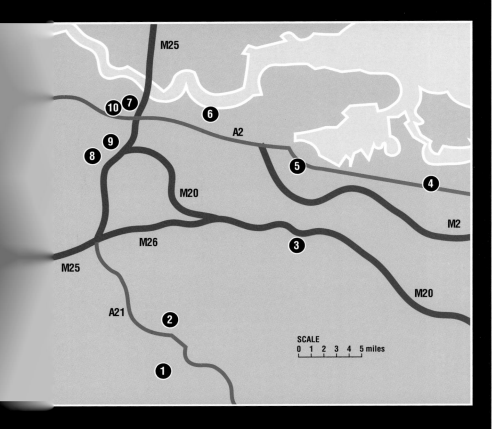

1 Tunbridge Wells FC
2 Tonbridge AFC
3 Maidstone United FC
4 Sittingbourne FC
5 Chatham Town FC
6 Gravesend & Northfleet FC
7 Dartford FC
8 Crockenhill FC
9 Alma Swanley (Furness FC)
10 Darenth Heathside FC

THE area around the Medway towns and the Docks has always produced strong football clubs and highly developed grounds but in recent times it has become a footballing graveyard with a number of clubs either collapsing or losing their grounds, while in Sittingbourne's case, selling up and attempting to build a new ground could prove their undoing.

The whole process stems downwards from Gillingham FC, a Football League club who have struggled desperately in recent times to stay afloat.

CULVERDEN STADIUM
Tunbridge Wells FC

The current Tunbridge Wells club is less than 30 years old, and Culverden Stadium dates from 1962; but the original club was formed in 1886, playing in the Southern League 10 years later

Eventually Tunbridge Wells Rangers became the dominant force, having played on the Nevil Ground, also home to Kent County Cricket Club. The Amateurs played on a field in Down Lane before moving to Ferndale, whereas Rangers used Combley Park and Swiss Cottage, a ground close to Culverden Stadium.

Between the Wars, the first major football ground in the area was developed at Down Farm. It had a wooden stand on one side with dressing rooms underneath and a small covered area opposite, with a form of terracing at one end. It was home until 1939 when the club closed down for the War and the ground was requisitioned. The stand was sold and the site was not used again, although it still remains as open land and the pitch area is still visible.

On reforming in 1947, the club moved back to Down Farm, but on a pitch a little further down the lane. It was not as substantial as the original and in 1951 the club moved again to the huge Agricultural Show Ground in Eridge Road at the other end of

Culverden Stadium, Tunbridge Wells.

town close to the Nevil. It had a barn type stand down one side with rudimentary shelters opposite, and was home until 1962, when following success in the Kent League, the club had joined the Southern League. Culverden Stadium was built over scrubland on part of Sir John Blunt's Estate, and from the start had a low seated stand, built to adjust to the slope of the pitch. Changing rooms were put up behind the stand and the pitch was surrounded by a post and wire while the top end banking was terraced with ash and railway sleepers.

It is a pleasantly rural ground to this day, having been more or less left alone by league regulations, and other than a clubhouse and floodlights, which were switched on in 1992, Culverden Stadium has changed little.

Longmead Stadium showing the main stand Tonbridge brought over from the Angel.

ANGEL GROUND and LONGMEAD
Tonbridge AFC

Tonbridge Football Club finally vacated the Angel, their home for 32 years, in 1980. After legal wrangling which had gone on since 1977, when plans were first drawn up by the Council to sell off the Angel for a supermarket, the club were unexpectedly handed a generous settlement, which enabled them to commence work on their new ground at Longmead. What was no more than a field soon became a football pitch, and the covered enclosure which ran the length of the pitch at the Angel was transported down and rebuilt as the centre-piece of the new ground.

The Angel only became a football ground in 1948, some ten years after it had ceased to be a cricket ground. From the 1890's up to the Second World War, it was utilised solely for cricket, and indeed, was a County ground used by Kent albeit sporadically towards the end. Because of this, when purely a football ground, it suffered from being rather lopsided due to the redundant open areas.

The 400 seater main stand at the Angel sat at an angle to the pitch, almost behind the near-side goal, presumably following the contours of the cricket outfield. The enclosure which was rescued, ran along the west side parallel with the High Street, and in the opposite corner to the stand, was the former cricket pavilion, housing the dressing rooms. The rest of the ground was undeveloped, save for an area of banking by the main stand.

Despite the paucity of facilities in some areas of the ground, a record crowd of 8,236 were present to see the FA Cup tie with Aldershot in 1951. The following year another big crowd saw Norwich City held to a draw at the Angel. Crowds gradually dwindled during the sixties and seventies, and the original club went into liquidation in 1976, but an immediate re-birth saw football saved.

The move to Longmead was not exactly a path paved with gold, for the club dropped into the Kent League for a spell before returning to the Southern League, their ground having been improved to league specifications.

LONDON ROAD
Maidstone United FC

The demise of the London Road sports ground and, more importantly, Maidstone United Football Club was one of the great lasting sorrows of the early nineties. Having moved to share Dartford's Watling Street ground after selling London Road, their brief sojourn into the Football League ended in 1992 with debts of over £650,000. Football lives on, however, ironically right next door to the site of the old ground where Maidstone Invicta play on what was United's training pitch.

London Road was originally built and known as the Athletic Ground back in 1893 when what was once a hop garden and orchard was transformed into a cricket ground. Agricultural shows had been held on the field for ten years before much work and money went into creating a football and cricket pitch with a running track on the west side. The whole area was surrounded by a cinder cycling track with a sturdy wooden fence behind it and an area of seating for around 500. On a higher level above the ground were tennis courts and a pavilion with three dressing rooms and various offices and kitchens.

In its early state the ground had just one entrance from London Road itself. A number of events and sports days had already been held when the ground was officially opened on May 22nd 1895. Maidstone United bought the ground which was often used during the twenties and thirties for Kent Senior Cup Finals and its amphitheatrical shape could hold crowds of 10-12,000 with ease. In 1950 the Scotsmans Stand was built for £1,200 and four years later floodlighting was introduced. In the mid-seventies the ground was given a huge facelift with terracing, improved floodlighting and stand rebuilding and to commemorate this, was re-named Maidstone Stadium. Greyhound racing made its debut in September 1976 which didn't seem to hamper the club's plans, as Bob Lord of the Football League passed the ground fit for League status should they poll enough votes.

Sadly, although League football finally came, it wasn't to be at London Road as the old girl had already unceremoniously been consigned to history.

BULL GROUND and CENTRAL PARK
Sittingbourne FC

Sittingbourne realised the dream of virtually every club in the country when their old Bull Ground became a prime development target and was eventually sold for a staggering £6.52m back in February 1990. Whether they have been able to take full advantage of this windfall, or the enormity of it all was just too much for the club to cope with remains to be seen.

Certainly in the early part of 1995, Sittingbourne FC were in financial turmoil having massively overspent and with the

*Above: **The Bull Ground in Sittingbourne, now demolished but as yet still undeveloped.***

proposed 40,000 capacity stadium less than half finished. The plans were for an all-seater stadium incorporating greyhound racing, hockey, netball, basketball and a nightclub. The first phase is all but finished, with the temporary stand and covered enclosure in front of it. What will be the new greyhound track is waiting to be moved to the second team pitch, laid out on a different section of the 23 acre site.

All this optimism was certainly borne out off the pitch with a record crowd of nearly 6,000 watching a friendly with Spurs and over 3,000 attending a local derby with Gravesend and Northfleet.

Still lying undeveloped in the town centre is the old Bull Ground. Although the interior artifacts have been removed, the outer wall and clubhouse remain intact, but creeping vegetation has, over five years, made the pitch and terraces unrecognisable.

The club was formed back in 1881 as Sittingbourne United and played at the recreation ground near the Bull in Albany Road until 1890 when they moved to the Gore Court Cricket Ground for two seasons, an area that still exists and is very close to the works ground of Bowaters, whose side were prominent in the FA Cup in the forties and fifties. The Bull ground opened in 1892 in preparation for the club's move into the Kent League and slowly developed until the main stand, with 450 seats was built complete with a paddock in front, for which a small extra charge was made for entry.

Later a covered enclosure went up opposite the stand over the concrete terracing which went around the ground from the early sixties. The largest crowd at the Bull came in 1960 when Gravesend visited for an FA Cup tie and attracted over 5,500 spectators. Sometime during the sixties both ends were covered as the capacity and the available seating were reduced substantially.

Today the site is forlorn, made even more so by the sad proceedings at the new ground which the club must pray fervently does not become an albatross around their necks.

MEDWAY SPORTS GROUND
Chatham Town FC

Sadly, the middle history of Chatham's delightfully kept ground is a bit of a mystery, although there is some information at either end of its 100 plus year lifespan.

Records indicate that Chatham played at the Great Lines in New Brompton, a vast open space situated off Marlborough Road containing a number of pitches. Gillingham FC also started life there, although on a pitch next to the main road, before moving to their new ground in 1893. Chatham's home was the bigger, indeed for many important matches stands were hired to allow huge attendances to be posted, none more so than the reported, but improbable 20,000 which saw the FA Cup ties with West Bromwich Albion and Nottingham Forest in 1889. Chatham were prompted to move to Maidstone Road in 1890 possibly by to the lack of facilities on the Great Lines or the fact that gate money could not be taken on the Army-owned land.

The site was owned by a benefactor George Winch who allowed the club to enclose the ground and build a pavilion with seats in front at a cost of £125. There was an entrance to the south-west with another at

the east and at first the club prospered, but the second Boer War took many local men away from the area, and the decision soon after to completely fence in the ground almost broke the club.

The chronology of the ground throughout its middle years has never been established, although it is believed large wooden stands were erected on either side of the pitch in between the Wars, and lasted until the mid-fifties. The grass banking around the rest of the ground stayed more or less intact until the fifties when terracing began to appear and a new stand with dressing rooms and a bar was built. Originally, it was part-standing and part-seated but now extra seats have gone in to plug the gaps. When the Southern League accepted the club back after a break of 54 years, they set about laying hard standing all round the ground and a complete overhaul and redecoration saw a return to its former splendour. The nineties see plans for the Sports Ground to have a covered stand at the Masons Road end as Chatham attempt to gain promotion to the Southern League for the fourth time. Meanwhile, the Great Lines is an eerie venue. Part of it is now covered by military housing but the old pitches, unused since the forties and fifties have reverted to common land. Gillingham FC's training ground and youth team home venue, with its covered terrace and grassy banks, is on the edge of the Great Lines, separated by the War Memorial which stands high overlooking the Medway town.

GREEN COURT ROAD GROUND
Furness FC

The elevated home of Furness was built originally in 1980 for the use of Alma Swanley FC, a club was formed in 1963 from players who used the Alma pub in the town. For some 17 years they played on a council pitch in St Mary's recreation ground

Chatham Town's neat and tidy home, now over 100 years old.

Alma Swanley FC folded and their ground is now home to Furness FC.

which was roped off and screened for big games, before the site of a former concrete batching plant that had been used to construct the nearby motorway became available.

It was raised to create a dry, flat surface and a red brick clubhouse was built in 1982 as they became successful in the Kent League. A small scaffolding stand was eventually replaced by the more modern structure which is used today, and later tip-up seats were installed courtesy of Charlton Athletic FC.

FURNESS FC is the current name for Furness Withy FC who were formed in 1968 following the merger of several shipping company sides and began playing at Brackley Road, Beckenham. Several grounds were used including the Dock Labour Board ground in Chislehurst, now called Flamingo Park and the Castaways Ground in Southwood Road. In 1982 the parent company withdrew support and they became Furness. In 1991 Furness took over the ailing Danson (Bexley Borough) club to form Danson Furness United playing at the Crook Log Ground, until a ground-share agreement with Alma Swanley came about in 1992. When Swanley folded the club took over the tenancy and reverted to the old name of Furness FC.

The Crook Log is currently used by a junior side.

WESTED MEADOW
Crockenhill FC

Wested Meadow has no real pretentions to become a top non-League ground, and perhaps because of that it retains a quaint charm amidst its country setting. The present Crockenhill side were formed during the boom period immediately after the Second War, and began playing at Wested, as had their predecessors.

Pre-War, the ground was undeveloped with no facilities and was commissioned as a site for a barrage balloon, with a Nissen hut built on concrete footings. The owner of the land, a Mr Miller, was a football enthusiast

and lent the field to the reformed club. By 1951 the club had erected a small grandstand plus dressing rooms, a tea bar, office and a loudspeaker system. Some 45 years later, the stand still exists, albeit with a new roof; the canteen, having been a physio room, is now the club shop and the grass banks which were formed around the pitch are also intact.

A simple entrance was built from corrugated iron and to the east a small covered area was put up with railway sleeper terracing, which lasted well into the eighties.

During the sixties, with the club's rise in

status, the clubhouse was created around the old Nissen hut and the entrance extended to include a superb old turnstile which came from the ground of Thamesside Amateurs. It is thought it once did service at Gravesend United's old ground before the War and may even date back to Southern League days in the 1890's.

Crockenhill and the ground went through a terrible spell in the seventies and eighties which came to a head when the 1987 hurricane deposited a tree through the roof of the clubhouse, closing it for two months. Later, the stand had its roof removed with the chairman of the time stating intentions to replace it, but this did not transpire and only the hard work of a couple of committee men put it right.

More recently a small terrace has been laid to the west of the stand and the clubhouse renovated as Wested Meadow continues to host football in its own special way.

STONEBRIDGE ROAD
Gravesend and Northfleet FC

It is, of course, a matter of personal choice, but there must be many devotees of football architecture who consider Stonebridge Road to be one of the classic football grounds in this country. It has miraculously

Crockenhill's glorious rickety stand pictured in the 50's (above) is still there in modified form some 40 years later (below).

A superb view of Stonebridge Road, Gravesend, one of the truly classic non-league football grounds in this country.

come through the various reports on stadium safety, ground grading regulations and two World Wars with the Docklands close by, to retain its charm (and its aged grandstand), against all odds.

Founded in 1890 Northfleet United were the first club to play on the ground. Following use of a number of fields, they moved to what was described as a "nice little plot of level ground at the bottom of Stonebridge Road". It was owned by APCM (now Blue Circle Industries), and had a 7ft fence, changing rooms, a small shelter and a tea bar all erected in time for the first game against East Ham Athletic on September 2nd 1905.

Gradually improvements were made with a small stand, which came from Rosterville Gardens in 1908, on the Stonebridge Road side of the ground and then the glorious main stand, built in 1914.

The two large covered stands were added in post War years, the first behind the Stonebridge Road goal around 1952, and the covered side was completed in 1959 after the

small stand had been taken down and the area terraced a few years earlier.

The final major work at the ground came in 1980 when the Swanscombe End was re-terraced with crash barriers and the roadways around the ground were tarred, most of the finance coming from the sale of goalkeeper Lee Smelt to Nottingham Forest.

Northfleet United did not survive the Second War, and the two leading clubs in the area, Northfleet and Gravesend United amalgamated with Gravesend vacating their Central Avenue ground. The club enjoyed much success, none more so than in the 1962-63 season when they embarked on an FA Cup run which started in September at the First Qualifying Round and went on to a Fourth Round replay at Sunderland.

With the big freeze of that year, the five months and ten days from first game to last is a record for the competition. The first Sunderland game, at Stonebridge Road, attracted a crowd of 12,036 which saw a 1-1 draw, an attendance which will never be surpassed, unless the old ground is radically altered, which hopefully, will not be the case.

HORTON ROAD
Darenth Heathside FC

Heathside's pleasantly rural home is the former Horton Kirby Paper Mill sportsground which at one time housed bowls, cricket and football. The club have played there since the early sixties, at various times alternating their sides with another ground at Bexley Hospital. When the club bought the ground cricket ceased and a form of barrier went around the pitch, which was later updated for the Kent League.

The old clubhouse is still in use, and a small stand with 200 seats was built close to it in the late 70's. The whole ground is topped off by the immense railway viaduct which runs across the front of the site and adds to what is a small but attractive Kent League home just a few miles from the built-up excesses of Dartford. Sadly the club were reported to have folded during the summer of 1995 and as a consequence, the future of the ground is uncertain.

Darenth Heathside folded in 1995 but the ground remains.

THE GROUNDS OF DARTFORD FC

The splendidly researched history of Dartford FC carried out by John Anthony, Michael Brett-Smith and Tony Brown has unearthed a detailed story of how that club finally settled at Watling Street in the 20's before their sad and controversial departure 70 years on. Now re-grouped, the club have been using the ground belonging to Erith and Belvedere in the Kent League.

The first serious club were Dartford Working Mens Club and Institute FC who began playing on Dartford Brent in 1888, which is now part of Hesketh Park, changing in all probability in the Wat Tyler Coffee Tavern. They were soon to move on to a pitch laid out behind Westgate House, but that was short lived as the site was needed for a new housing and road scheme, and they moved again to Lowfield Street.

This area was to be home for many years, but on a variety of sites. Various names were used for the meadows, and it is not clear precisely where they were or whether they changed ownership, and therefore name, or were simply the same place. What is known is that Mr Potter's Meadow became home in 1891 and at some point a small stand was built for officials.

1894 found the club playing on Summer's Meadow on the old Cranford Hall Estate, also in Lowfield Street. Again a grandstand was built, in September 1895, at a cost of £90, but this and a poor showing on the pitch led to financial problems and by 1899 the club, by now known simply as Dartford, had begun playing at Engley's Meadow, which might very well be the same spot as Potter's Meadow.

Dartford FC were wound up in 1900, but a new club, Dartford United were formed, only to last one season, and Dartford Rangers, an amateur club who had shared the ground, took over. This outfit were soon known simply as Dartford FC, and played on Summer's Meadow, where some dressing rooms were built. Engley's Meadow was eventually developed into a recreation ground with a bandstand and a shelter, while the old stand was also renovated.

Summer's Meadow was improved with fencing at the town end and more changing accommodation, and the club stayed put until War broke out in 1914.

They re-formed in 1921 and soon raised funds to buy five acres of land in Watling Street for £1,000. Six tennis courts were laid out, and a corrugated fence ringed the site which had an enclosure and substantial backing, all of which cost around £500, plus a further £88 for turnstiles. A large seated grandstand was built at a cost of some £2,900 and opened on Saturday, November 19th 1921 before a crowd of around 4,000. It was to be short-lived, for in February 1926, along with the dressing rooms, offices and boardroom, it was destroyed in a fierce fire.

A fund was set up to deal with replacing the uninsured items, and a new stand was opened officially in March 1927. Capable of seating 1,000 it was of steel construction with dressing rooms, offices, recreation rooms and baths underneath. Watling Street continued to expand and in 1930 a covered enclosure 150 feet long was built opposite the stand, and with the erection of more turnstiles at the main entrance, the ground was to remain unchanged until the Second War.

Despite its close proximity to the docks, the ground escaped relatively unscathed by bombing, but although Dartford Amateurs played from 1943, professional football did not start up until 1946. Within a year terracing had been laid at the Watling Street end and in 1949 the Supporters' Club donated an extension to the covered side. The enclosure in front of the stand was terraced in 1950 and by 1955, new turnstiles were in place and the popular side cover had all been terraced.

In October 1963, Dartford opened their new £6,000 floodlights, and possibly to help fund this and other improvements, surplus land including the tennis courts was sold off to enlarge Brent School playing fields. The car-park was tarred, the wooden fencing around the pitch was replaced by a wall, and the terracing on the popular side was raised and widened in the late sixties. Further sterling work was done by the Supporters' Association during the 70's and the ground reached its peak around this time.

Sadly, events beyond the control of mere mortals were to catch up with and ultimately overwhelm Watling Street during the 80's. Maidstone United lost their London Road home and moved in to share with Dartford FC. The club seemed to lose their identity as Maidstone played in the Football League and the ground was now painted in the yellow and black colours of the Stones. The oppressive fencing and segregation cages ruined what was an excellent arena, and when Maidstone's short and ill-fated run in the League came to an expensive end in May 1992, they effectively brought Dartford down with them.

Watling Street was razed to the ground with almost indecent haste and has been obliterated with new housing.

Although Dartford managed to start the 1992-93 season playing at Welling FC, it lasted just four matches before the club resigned. Since those sad days, the Darts have used Cray Wanderers ground as well as that of Erith and although as yet they have no new home on the horizon, they are still in there fighting.

Photos in this section by: Andrew Chitty, Alan Coombes, Gavin Ellis-Neville and Mike Floate.

Watling Street, Dartford, now demolished and built on.

North Sussex and Surrey

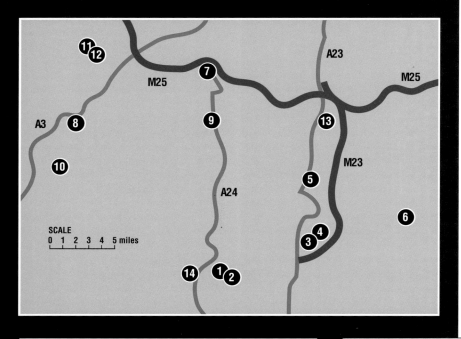

1	Horsham FC
2	Horsham YMCA FC
3	Crawley Town FC
4	Oakwood FC
5	Horley Town FC
6	East Grinstead FC
7	Leatherhead FC
8	Guildford City FC
9	Dorking FC
10	Godalming & Guildford FC
11	Woking FC
12	Westfield FC
13	Redhill FC
14	Broadbridge Heath FC

THE area of north Sussex and south Surrey is now dominated by Woking who have taken over the berth of top club vacated by Guildford City, and have also surpassed both Leatherhead and Crawley. Other than at Woking, the affluence of the area is not reflected in the fortunes of many of the clubs, with only Crawley Town maintaining a presence near the top.

QUEEN STREET
Horsham FC

There are precious few football grounds still in existence that retain their character, despite all that league regulations, safety reports and inclement weather can throw at them. Tickhill Square at Denaby is one, and so is Borough Park, Workington. Queen Street, home of Horsham Football Club is another.

It has been a football ground since around 1904, when having had a request to play at the local cricket ground opposed, arrangements were made with the local brewery to rent the site for the sum of £25 per annum. Prior to the move, Horsham began life in 1885 at Springfield Park, and later moved to Hurst Park which was home until 1896, when, with interest increasing along-

The main stand at Queen Street, Horsham, under construction in 1928. The original stand brought over from Springfield Park, can be seen in front of new building (left).

The same Horsham stand seen under construction on the facing page, pictured 57 years on.

side the crowds, the club were asked to find a new ground. They eventually returned to Springfield Park in 1897, and shortly after erected a small corrugated iron and wood stand.

In 1904, the owner of the Park decided to open a school on the site, and once more the club were homeless. The field was in a very rough state and scarred all over with plough furrows, but soon the pitch was levelled and work got under way to prepare for the next season. The stand at Springfield Park was re-erected, and remained in use up to 1928, until subsequently demolished when the current stand was built behind it.

In 1926 Horsham won the West Sussex Senior League, were accepted into the County League, and at the same time acquired at auction the ground plus other areas of land nearby. In 1928 following a public appeal for help, work started on the new stand and changing facilities, with over 100 people turning up at the ground to help. By the opening game of the 1928-29 season, the new stand was open and in public use, funds for the project having been raised by subscription, with anyone donating half a crown entitled to have a brick inscribed with their name.

Opposite the stand, a long corrugated asbestos covered terrace was constructed twenty years later with the proceeds of the club's FA Cup run which came to an end in front of 28,000 people at Notts County. A further eighteen years later, to cater for the club's entry into the Athenian League, more covered terrace was added at the Gorings Mead end. This proved a wise investment for in November 1966, Horsham entertained Swindon Town in the FA Cup, and posted their record crowd of over 8,000.

Today, Queen Street remains much the same as thirty years ago, although the capacity is only half what it was. The entry to this splendid tree-lined ground is down a narrow lane, which leads to the delightful slate roofed turnstiles and the car-park inside. Viewing the flat topped main stand from the side it looks for all the world like the chang-

ing room at a sea-front or lido. The paddock is enclosed by a solid wall with ornate gates, and is terraced in a curved style, with symmetrical wooden steps leading into the stand itself. The front wall is white with arches picked out in brown which give the impression of having been bricked up, but photographic evidence in the clubhouse shows the stand looking virtually identical in its early days, other than the deckledged roof front which is sadly now covered by advertising hoardings. It is to be hoped this marvellous structure remains in good repair for many years to come, and manages to avoid any calamity. Authority 'jobsworths' declaring it dangerous, or well-meaning benefactors wishing to replace it with some garish breeze-blocked nonsense would be nothing short of obscene.

The end nearest to the neighbouring YMCA ground at Gorings Mead is also covered terrace, although it is showing signs of wear and tear, and fighting a losing battle against the vegetation. To skilfully avoid

official interference, when the end was declared out of bounds, a handful of seats were installed to give a capacity of a couple of dozen, thus avoiding the loss of the cover.

Happily its elder brother, which stretches the full length of the ground, is in superb condition and one of the best preserved examples of steeply angled covered terrace at this level of football. Purposely built to arch into the centre of the terrace to improve the view, it is supported by twenty poles embedded into concrete blocks in a similar style to that at Chorley.

The whole of this atmospheric ground has been described as very reminiscent of Marlow's, but without their gardening expert's colourful touches. With a pair of shears and a pot of paint Queen Street, at nearly ninety years old, would be a match for any ground in the country.

GORINGS MEAD
Horsham YMCA FC

The area known now as Gorings Mead has been used for football since the mid-twenties, but the history of the site, pre-football is well-documented. The ground is built on part of the estate of Chesworth Manor which was given to one of William the Conqueror's men, William de Braose. The ownership eventually passed via the Howard and Mowbray families to Queen Elizabeth I, and became Crown land until acquired by the Eversfields of Denne. Throughout the 19th century the land was almost certainly a meadow, and at the turn of the century, a row of cottages were built, which still stand by the narrow entrance from the Brighton Road.

By 1905 the local branch of the YMCA had formed a football team which first played at Gorings Mead in the mid-twenties.

1960s action at Gorings Mead, Horsham YMCA. Horsham FC is behind the bushes at the back.

It is believed the ground was rented until 1929, when a large part of the estate was put up for auction, and bought by a Mr H. Blackiston who in turn re-sold the ground to the YMCA trustees, on May 7th. From that date the club has owned the ground provided that "no noisome noxious or offensive business" shall be carried on!

The club's first league game on their newly acquired ground was on September 28th 1929, by which time improvements were already made. The southern end of the ground had a pronounced downwards slope, and with the help of a vast amount of soil deposited from various parts of the town, they were able to extend the playing area. This is believed to be the site of a 'fulling mill pond', which is clearly marked on surveyors' reports, but is now covered by the clubhouse.

After the war when the club were dormant, cricket was played on the ground, and in 1956 dressing rooms were built at the north end, and water, electricity and drainage installed. The small extension was added in 1964. After much discussion and securing of loans, work began on the new clubhouse in June 1970 and, almost entirely through the work of volunteers, four years later it was officially opened.

For eight years from 1954, the pitch ran north to south with one goal situated close to the ditch which separates the YMCA from neighbours Horsham F.C. It was eventually turned round 90 degrees and in the early seventies the seated stand which straddles the half-way line was built, and the overhang to the old dressing rooms taken down. The footings can still be seen in front of the building which is now a store.

Some ten years later the impressive floodlighting system was provided at a ground by then deemed good enough to stage representative matches and happily, still does so. The record attendance stands officially at 600 for an Amateur Cup match against next door neighbours Horsham F.C., although it is possible that one of the many cup finals staged at Gorings Mead over the years may have attracted more. YMCA's promotion to the top division of the County League means there is but one division between them and their neighbours.

TOWN MEAD
Crawley Town FC

The early years of Crawley Town reflect the modesty of what was once a small Sussex village side playing on a series of central fields. How times change, as now it is in an area within one of the country's first and biggest New Towns.

Crawley were formed around 1895 and began on a field at Malthouse Farm, about a mile south east of the present ground on the other side of the railway. This arrangement lasted until after the Great War when they

TINSLEY LANE
Oakwood FC

Oakwood Football Club was founded in 1962 by a group of teenagers and were known as St Wilfred Youth Wing, but in 1966 changed their name to Oakwood, the estate where the school was situated in Crawley. They played on Crawley Council pitches until whilst playing in the Southern Counties Combination they took over a disused sports ground in Tinsley Lane, Three Bridges in 1983.

Since that time they have transformed it into a fine Sussex County League ground with a clubhouse, overhang and a handful of seats. In 1989 the pitch was drained and a Directors' and guests room constructed while the following year saw a concrete path laid behind the near goal. Floodlights and a further area of cover have also been added in recent times, but it may well all be academic for Oakwood are looking to re-locate and purchase another ground as the club was running fourteen teams in the 1994-95 season and has out-grown its present site.

moved to Victoria Hall which was no more than 200 yards from the current ground in the High Street. Tithe maps from the time show the area of the ground although little or nothing is known about it. Later Town shared a pitch with the local rugby club at Rectory Field before an altercation sent them back to Malthouse Farm until the Second World War. On the resumption the club took up residence at Yetmans Field in Northgate which was situated behind the old bus garage and they remained there until the new ground was made ready around 1952.

Town Meadow as it was known then was simply a slightly banked pitch which was eventually graced with a small seated stand on the south side of the ground in readiness for the club's entry into the Metropolitan League in 1956. The changing rooms, which were put in place not long after the opening, stood where they stand now at the car-park end behind the goal. As the ground began to take shape two areas of covered standing were put up either side of the main stand during the 1957-58 season and with the other three sides open there was little change at the

Crawley FC

Mead for some eight years. The visit of an Arsenal XI changed all that when 2,000 crammed in to see the ceremonial floodlit match in March 1966, although the lights had been operational all that season.

The car-park end was terraced in 1969 and soon after, the solid-looking enclosure went up over it bringing an end to development until 1980, when the new offices and changing rooms were built on the site of the old ones.

By now Town Mead was a town centre ground surrounded by development with a Fire Station at the far end but still had an open space and a grass bank down the side opposite the stand and behind the far goal. This all altered from 1990 when the club's improved standing saw them complete the terracing of the whole ground and even install crash barriers for the FA Cup tie with Northampton Town. The perimeter wall was infilled, the lights upgraded and in 1994 the original main stand with its one remaining covered area was taken down - the other had blown down years previously. A new 400-seater stand with a boardroom above went up in its place and the fire station end was also covered for the first time. With a metal fence replacing the wooden one, Town Mead has come a very long way much in a parallel fashion to the town itself. How ironic then, that just as the ground has reached an acceptable level for the top League, it is threatened with demolition as the club look to re-locate out of town.

EAST COURT
East Grinstead FC

A meeting held at the Public Hall on Wednesday, May 8th 1890, led to the formation of East Grinstead Football Club.

Friendlies were arranged for the first few years, until County Cup football was entered, and then in 1900 the club joined the Mid-Sussex League, playing at West Street, home of the town's cricket club, who owned

THE DEFENCE
Horley Town FC

The pleasant town of Horley, just sufficiently north of Crawley to remain in Surrey, has a ground to match its surroundings, which was given to the club by Major Jennings, a local landowner, in 1949. He asked for the ground to be named in remembrance of the men who fell in the Second World War, hence the name, `The Defence'.

For nearly fifty years from their inception, Horley Town had played on a ground in Balcombe Road which was owned by an official of the club who decreed it to them, but died before completing his Will, and it was later sold to the Gas Company who have an old gasometer on the site to this day.

The Gasworks Ground had a small stand made of corrugated tin with dressing rooms in the adjoining field. It was roped off for important cup games and during the War, was used as an ATC centre.

The new ground consisted of 10 acres of woodland and cornfield and was used by the BBC for recording the songs of the nightingale.

Work started on clearing the ground in 1947, but the first official match was not until August 1951 when neighbours Redhill were the visitors. The clubhouse was originally a temporary bank building at the Manor Royal Estate in Crawley, and it was moved to its present site where it was re-designed to include a board room, changing rooms, hall, kitchen and bar, and was opened on the 27th May 1967.

There have been various covered areas over the years which have succumbed to age or weather but the current structure was built in 1980. The Defence is a modest ground, perfectly adequate for the Combined Counties League with floodlights and a capacity for around 1,000, the precise figure which was posted for a pre-season friendly with Tottenham Hotspur in 1983.

the land. It was close to the centre of town, easily accessible, and as a result support was good. Often crowds would number 1,000, and in the boom years immediately after the First World War, they were at their peak, with the record being 2,006 who lined the ground to see an Amateur Cup tie with Lancing in 1947.

The players changed at the pavilion in the corner of the ground. The pitch was roped off and it wasn't until 1958, after 68 years, that a small stand was put up for the spectators, and the pavilion was improved to provide washing facilities.

Within months however, the football club faced a notice to quit, and were forced to apply to the War Memorial Committee in an

effort to buy a plot near the council offices in East Court. They were unsuccessful in purchasing the land, but given a lease at £30 a year, and a contractor was brought in to start work on the pitch, car-park and access road at a cost of nearly £5,000. At this point the club were hopeful of starting the 1962-63 season at East Court, but the whole site was beset with problems, including persistent failures in the drainage.

At this point the club played its last ever game at West Street, on Easter Monday 1962, and was officially homeless. The local council came to the club's rescue, and they turned out at King George's Field until a new contractor sorted out the mess. The club moved in on August 26th 1967, when they played Bexhill. The ground looked not entirely dissimilar to its current state. The changing rooms were originally a bungalow, and had a shower and referee's room added on, built by committee members, while the corrugated stand with concrete terracing was erected at a cost of £414.

Four years later the present clubhouse was built, again by members, and in 1981, despite much opposition from residents, a floodlit training court was built and opened by the late Ted Croker, Secretary of the FA.

In more recent times the ground has been floodlit to accommodate the wishes of the County League, and these were officially switched on by Ian Wright of England and Arsenal prior to a game against Crystal Palace on April 22nd 1992. There are plans to

East Grinstead FC

build new dressing rooms and a boardroom at East Court which has developed slowly but sensibly to keep in line with the requirements of the modern game.

East Court is reached via a long, unmarked lane, which leads to a car-park and the small, rather fortified, clubhouse. The changing rooms are situated at the top of a long path which eventually reaches the pitch by the raised covered terrace area. The whole ground is surrounded by trees and is some distance from the main road, leaving the whole place somewhat vulnerable to vandalism, and as such the clubhouse and changing rooms are both boarded up and in need of some care and attention.

FETCHAM GROVE
Leatherhead FC

The present Leatherhead Football Club was formed in 1946 following the amalgamation of the Rose and United clubs from the town, and began its life at Fetcham Grove which had been staging football matches since the twenties at least and possibly before that.

Leatherhead Rose played from formation in 1907 until 1933 at the Kingston Road recreation ground, and then until the War at a private ground just off Barnett Wood Lane. A pavilion with baths was built through the work of volunteers but, sadly, the ground was lost when the land was claimed for the war effort.

Meanwhile, a club called Leatherhead Juniors had been formed around 1920, playing at Fortyfoot Road Rec. Four years later they changed their name to United, and shortly after moved to Fetcham Grove.

During the first season back after the War, officials from United and Rose agreed on amalgamation with the new team going straight into a senior league, and the President of the old United gave his permission for Fetcham Grove to be used. However,

Above: Fetcham Grove main stand in 1995 and (left) the same stand nearly 50 years earlier.

the war effort had taken its toll on the ground, as it had been occupied by the military, and much work had to be done to bring it up to a playable standard. Dressing rooms were put in order and enlarged, plunge-baths installed in each, and the pitch cleared, all through volunteer labour. A cinder track was laid around what was still a very spartan ground at that stage, but in 1948 the club made great strides when a new stand, club room, dressing rooms, referees room, committee room, and canteen were all completed. Fetcham Grove was then possibly the best ground in the Surrey Senior League, and indeed, the stand still forms part of the present structure. As the fifties came, further improvements were made as the club progressed to a higher standard. The entrance end was banked in order to increase the capacity, and a social club provided for the use of members and players alike.

The playing area by then was enclosed by metal tubing rather than by a wire, and in 1954 Fetcham Grove had its first licensed bar. Soon after, the stands were extended to increase the covered terracing, which then boasted 500 seats and cover for 2,000.

Slowly but surely during the next twenty years the ground changed cosmetically, although never lost its rustic appeal. Having survived the big freeze of 1962-63, when the club was the first in the country to clear its pitch of snow, floodlights were installed during the following winter, and used for the first time in November 1963 for a game with Fulham. New pay-boxes and entrance gates were next, with a public address system in 1968.

At long last in 1970, the perimeter fence was built which segregated the club from the waste land adjoining the cricket club (this is now the leisure centre car-park), and with new dressing rooms, bar and boardroom at the far end of the ground, Fetcham Grove more or less reached the stage that it is now, apart from some additional banking which was built prior to the FA Cup tie with Colchester United in 1974. This remains the record attendance at Leatherhead, when 3,500 crammed in to watch the Tanners win 1-0 and prolong their epic run which reached a sad but glorious end at Leicester City, two rounds later.

In the twenty years since those heady days the ground has at best stood still. The pitch is surrounded by ugly corrugated material which does nothing for the general appearance, and the mere fact the club is not doing so well on the pitch has led to a dramatic decline in support, although of course, Leatherhead are not alone there.

The Crawley home of Unijet Sussex County League side Three Bridges.

Godalming & Guildford's stand, much of which, along with the post and rails, came from the defunct Addlestone & Weybridge ground in 1985.

WEYCOURT
Godalming and Guildford FC

Prior to 1971 Godalming United played most of its football on the council owned Recreation Ground in Holloway Hill, collecting jugs of tea from the groundsman's wife at the end of the match at a cost of 50p. Farncombe FC had failed to re-enter the Surrey Senior League in 1970 due to a lack of players which left the ground at Meadrow unused other than by a youth club on Sunday mornings. Officers from United met and took over the running of the club, together with the debts and formed Godalming and Farncombe United FC.

Around that time the pitch was moved on to the site of an old council rubbish dump (later named Weycourt) just behind the clubhouse, as the Rec became a sheltered home for the elderly. The new pitch had a post and wire fence down one side and due to subsidence the playing surface suffered badly from water-logging. New drainage was installed with the help of Waverley Council and more top soil added, but during alterations the club were forced to play on a pitch at Broadwater Park. A tarmac car-park was laid, the clubhouse improved and when the club were accepted into the Combined Counties League as Godalming Town FC the pitch had its first posts and rope around it and the fence to the north was moved back to make way for a training area and lighting.

In 1985 Addlestone and Weybridge's old ground was being dismantled and club officials bought the cast-iron railing around the pitch for £50 along with some 125 concrete posts as well as agreeing with the landowners to buy for £225 the old stand capable of seating 200. A working party removed the stand and re-erected it at Weycourt where it now resides complete with added changing rooms which were opened in 1988 courtesy

of a generous grant from the Football Trust. In 1991 the Guildford Football Appeal granted a sum of money for the provision of floodlights on the understanding that the name of Guildford should be incorporated into that of the club, and members again rallied round and the inaugural match took place on November 3rd 1992 against Woking.

The following summer the hard standing around the ground was completed and in 1994 a turnstile was obtained from The Den at Millwall and placed just inside the gate. Today Weycourt is undoubtedly one of the better grounds in the area and the League. It will never be another Guildford City, but then very few will.

KINGFIELD
Woking FC

The Kingfield home of Woking FC has managed to retain part of its old world charm during the major changes that have taken place within the last few years. The splendid pair of steel framed stands, built in 1922, and 1930 respectively, remain defiant, surrounded by the concrete redevelopment that has occurred to enable Woking to take their place in the top flight of non-league football.

It is all a million miles away from the clubs humble beginnings in 1889, where they played their first competitive match at a ground in Brewery Road, almost completely devoid of any facilities. In the early 1900's, the club moved to a ground in Pembroke Road, and at the resumption of football after the first war, Hobb's Meadow was used. This was part of Hobb's Farm at Kingfield,

where it is believed, access was achieved through the old Woking recreation ground and refuse tip with a wooden bridge over the River Bourne. There was a temporary wooden framed stand with corrugated iron cladding seating 80 people with small dressing rooms below.

In the season of 1921/22, Woking F.C. joined forces with Woking Football and Sports Grounds Co. Ltd., the latter acquiring ten acres of land at Kingfield where two football pitches, one cricket pitch, a hockey pitch and 12 tennis courts were laid out.

A former cricket pavilion was used for changing, and an ex-Army tea hut was provided by the cricket club. The steel-framed stand was erected by Palmers of Merton, with dressing rooms underneath and this remains today in its pomp.

Eight years later the Supporters' Club financed the construction of a second stand which also remains today next to its older brother. Immediately after the Second World War, and a massive fund raising campaign, the freehold of approximately 11.5 acres was acquired by Woking F.C., and this undoubtedly is the club's main asset. Since that time a number of improvements have been carried out in stages until a wholesale turnaround in the 1990's. Additional terracing was provided, some of which was covered, and five years later on the 19th of November 1964, four 100ft floodlighting towers were utilised for the first time. Around the same period, a new club room complex, which had a main hall, members' bar, kitchen and toilets was built replacing the original.

The late 1970's saw the demise of tennis and hockey at the site and it began to change significantly when the club came to prominence by reaching the top of the non-league pyramid, and also embarked on an FA Cup run which saw a demolition of West Bromwich Albion at the Hawthorns. Since then new terracing has gone up along the full length of the pitch opposite the stands, and most of the Kingfield End is now covered terrace as well. The Westfield end has also been improved with new seating, as has the main stand.

New toilets, entrance, and security fencing complete the picture of the almost total transformation of Kingfield, which seems to have been done with thought rather than

Kingfield, Woking FC.

simply with the relevant league rules in mind. The ultimate irony is that on-going negotiations may render all the improvements irrelevant if the club's aims of moving to a purpose built sports complex come to fruition. That would spell the end for the two ageing gentlemen who have stood side by side near the touchline since the 1930's, and seen hundreds of thousands come and go. They could never be replaced as they really don't build stands like that anymore.

BROADBRIDGE HEATH SPORTS CENTRE
Broadbridge Heath FC

Broadbridge Heath is a small village on the edge of Horsham, but is home to a massive Sports Centre which is used by the local club in the Sussex County League. Although not ideal for watching football it is an impressive facility financed by the sale of land to Tesco's in 1987.

It is built on the site of a former army camp vacated just after the last War and subsequently sold to the council for a nominal sum for the purposes of recreation. For many years it was a collection of ex-Army huts, an overgrown parade square and two rather tatty football pitches until the owners were obliged to plough some of the Tesco profits into the new Sports Centre and cater for the existing tenants, namely Broadbridge Heath FC, Horsham Table Tennis Club, Arum Badminton Club and the local Operatic Society. The football club were granted a lease for a club room and have use of the main arena which has an eight lane running track around it and a 300-seater stand, all enclosed inside an imposing amphitheatre shape. Sadly, the floodlights installed are not adequate for football and still remain so despite the club's pleas for an upgrade.

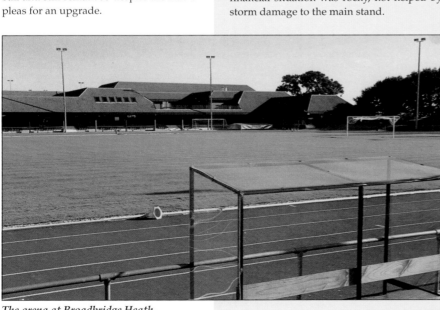

The arena at Broadbridge Heath.

FOOTBALL IN GUILDFORD AND GODALMING

Other than for one match in the mid-eighties at the University Ground, Guildford has seen no senior football since the sad and controversial demise of Guildford City in 1974. The original club in the area was Guildford FC, who were known as the `Pinks', and played from their inception in 1877 at the Guildford Working Men's Cricket Ground before moving to the Woodbridge Road Sports Ground which is today a splendid site still used by the town's cricket club and occasionally stages Surrey County matches.

It was capable of holding crowds of upwards of 4,000, and in 1920 when Brentford FC played a friendly match there, in front of a crowd of over 3,000, various sportsmen in the area saw the potential for football in the town and two months later Guildford United were formed. When a local land owner Mr Turner made available some land in St Joseph's Road they were up and running.

The ground soon began to take shape and a main stand was built with bench seating for nearly 400 and dressing rooms underneath was built while grass banking was created to provide an optimistic capacity of 8,000. Casuals FC shared the ground for a season before moving on to Crystal Palace and the following year the Pinks moved over to share St Joseph's Road with United. The summer of 1926 saw the name change from United to City as Guildford became a diocese and thus gained a cathedral. At the ground a second covered area was erected by the active Supporters' Club and a threat of greyhound racing came and went, but despite the generous gift of the ground by the owner and chairman Mr Turner, the club were in dire trouble by 1929. They survived, but despite regular well-attended FA Cup matches, the financial situation was rocky, not helped by storm damage to the main stand.

In 1931 the Supporters' Club built their own headquarters at a cost of £85 and two years later the Pinks moved out to be replaced by Old Guildfordians. The thirties saw mixed fortunes as attendances fluctuated and the club lurched along, finding time to apply for Football League status in the meantime. By 1938, the ground had extended its capacity to around 10,000 and had covered stands on three sides with banking which was some years later partly terraced by prisoners of war. In December 1938 Aldershot came to St Joseph's Road for an FA Cup 1st Round Replay which attracted the record attendance of 9,934 and the following April, 9,943 saw the league game with Colchester United who eventually pipped City for the title.

The War came and went with the club closing down for the duration, and on its resumption initial optimism soon waned,

which was mirrored at the Pinks, who had continued at the Cricket Ground but subsequently moved to Stoke Road Recreation Ground where the taking of gate money was not possible. They continued until the summer of 1954 when they sadly folded, no doubt rueing the day they invited Brentford FC to play a friendly.

St Joseph's Road changed little for many years, and a somewhat unsuccessful floodlight appeal meant it was October 1960 before Chelsea played a match to commemorate their long awaited switch on. The sixties saw a gradual decline in attendances and the ground slowly began to show signs of age. Although a new social club was built to hopefully create some capital, the prospects were bleak, and in April 1970 news broke that the site was to be sold for re-development and the club forced to move elsewhere. The club were informed that although sold,

the ground was available until 1973, but the supporters were unaware that even though the sale had raised some £200,000, the new owners wanted the club to pay the interest charges of £26,000 per year on the land. The proposed new site, a rubbish tip at Slyfield was not available until 1976. The end came in sight during 1974 when the directors voted to merge with Dorking FC and played the last few matches of the season at Imber Court and Meadowbank. The final game played at St Joseph's Road was on February 12th against Folkestone and prompted the last in a series of pitch demonstrations by supporters bitterly incensed at the way their club had been allowed to die in such dubious circumstances.

The new club, Guildford and Dorking United took over from Dorking FC who resigned from their league the previous season, but they lasted no more than two years

in the Southern League and folded in December 1976. A new team Dorking Town was formed immediately but were denied senior status.

Throughout all this the Supporters' Club of the City were still active and after several broken promises from the authorities to re-house the club, they agreed to help create Guildford and Worplesdon FC by merging with the latter, and the club joined the Combined Counties League playing at the Memorial Ground which was open and had no scope for development. The club were eventually thrown out of the league for playing a game on an unrecognised ground, namely the University and subsequently folded in 1984.

St Joseph's Road ground did not survive long after the club's demise and in 1977 it was demolished and built on.

The biggest ever crowd at Guildford City, nearly 10,000, for an FA Cup 1st round replay with Aldershot in December 1938. The visitors won 4-3.

North Downs and South Berkshire

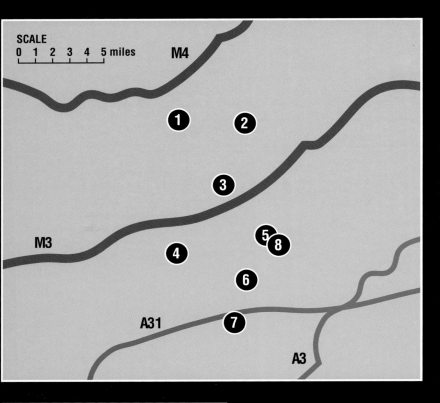

SCALE
0 1 2 3 4 5 miles

M4

M3

A31

A3

1   Wokingham FC
2   Bracknell Town FC
3   Camberley Town FC
4   Fleet Town FC
5   Farnborough Town FC
6   Aldershot Town FC
7   Farnham Town FC
8   Cove FC

NON-LEAGUE football in the area was given a major boost with the forming of Aldershot Town from the ashes of the famous League club. Already well represented by Farnborough who reached the Conference, there is a full spectrum of interesting grounds, ranging from Farnham's modest home through to the Rec at Aldershot which is virtually unchanged despite all the turmoil.

FINCHAMPSTEAD ROAD
Wokingham Town FC

At the time of writing plans are well advanced for Wokingham Town's new stadium, replacing the club's home which has stood tight against the railway in Finchampstead Road since 1906. The original club was formed as long ago as 1875, and played on a field in Oxford Road before moving to the cricket ground in Wellington Road, and then for ten seasons at Langborough Road, before settling at their present home in 1906. This was owned by a Mr. John Walker of Bearwood who rented it to the former Mayor of Wokingham, Mr. T. Wescott who in turn let it to the club.

Although successful in the various leagues and cups, the ground was not significantly developed until just before the Second World War, when the tiny stand was opened with a game against Chelsea in April 1939, which the club won 5-2 in front of 900 people. Nine years earlier the purchase of the ground was completed, and throughout the war and post war period the club, backed tremendously by their fund raising Supporters' Club rose to the senior ranks by joining the Metropolitan, and then later the Delphian League.

Finchampstead Road, Wokingham.

Floodlighting was first installed in 1966 when the club played in the Athenian League and was celebrated with a game against Fulham. As the years went by and the ground fell below the necessary standards demanded by the league, the club were forced to vacate and for three months in 1990 played home matches at Reading's Elm Park.

The ground today is seemingly doomed, but remains defiant, the cheerful tiny stand continuing to provide cover for the various V.I.P.'s. From a distance it looks as if a gust of wind might blow it away, but closer inspection reveals it to be solidly brick-built with a wooden interior housing six rows of seats. To the side a long clubhouse and changing room complex has an extended cover protruding from it suspended by permanent scaffolding poles. Behind the railway goal is flat standing leading to a fresh area of raised terracing to the side of the new stand, now replete with bucket seating. Behind the far goal is an unusual concentrically shaped terrace backed by a white wall, and topped by an ugly semi-derelict porta-cabin.

Finchampstead Road is a curious mixture of the ugly and attractive; a horrible black exterior wall uninviting and stark, next to the pleasantly designed entrance and clubhouse. Inside, the less than inspired breeze block infill of the perimeter wall is countered by the friendly little main stand.

Wokingham have been in the higher echelons of non-league football for many years, but whether they continue at Finchampstead Road or at pastures new remains to be seen.

The sad burnt out stand at Krooner Park (right) and the excellent new facilities which followed (above).

LARGES LANE
Bracknell Town FC

The original Bracknell club, known as the Wanderers, came into being in 1896 and played on a field near the Devonshire Arms before moving half a mile to a site near to the station, now covered by Ranelagh Grammar School .

The move to Larges Lane came in the thirties. There was a small shed tucked away in one corner for dressing but little else. The new town and the expansion of club and area were still long off, and it was not until the mid fifties that the sloping pitch was levelled using material from the burgeoning housing developments all around.

The club changed their name to Bracknell Town in 1962 and a local benefactor, Sir Raymond Brown, gave a substantial amount of money to build a clubhouse with changing rooms, a referees' room and a hall complete with an overhang for spectators, all of which was opened by Stanley Rous.

1971 saw the ground test the new facilities for the first time when Newquay attracted 2,500 to Larges Lane for an Amateur Cup tie.

More expansion came in the late 80's when a further brick stand and some cover were added as the club moved up, and in 1994 another area of cover for around 300 people went up behind one goal as Larges Lane attempted to keep pace with the Isthmian League regulations.

KROONER PARK
Camberley Town FC

Krooner Park has recovered well from the catastrophe which befell on August 5th 1990. A huge fire destroyed the club's old stand, taking with it playing kit and training equipment as well as scorching part of the pitch. The damage was estimated at some £100,000, but to their credit the club had replaced the stand by November and were back at the ground.

It has been home since 1922 when bought to coincide with Camberley's status as founder members of the Surrey Senior League. It brought to an end the search for a permanent home which had started at the London Recreation Ground in 1898 which they rented from the council just a year after it was opened. By 1905 they were playing on a pitch in Southwell Park Road, with headquarters and changing rooms at the Aspen Tree pub. When the area began to develop, the club were forced to seek another ground and for the 1909-10 season they played on Martin's Meadow in London Road, with their HQ transferring to the Hope pub. It was not long before some matches were taking place back at the London Road Rec to accommodate the large crowds and the following

season saw them return there. It was to remain home until the purchase of Krooner Park. St Mary's Hall nearby was pressed into service as changing rooms and in 1925 a Supporters' Club was formed to raise funds to build the stand. The £500 collected, the stand was completed inside two years and officially opened on February 12th 1927.

Despite success on the field, the club had financial problems and were forced to sell the ground to the council for £900 just prior to the War, but the new-found enthusiasm when football returned saw Krooner Park tidied up and re-opened for a game against Arsenal. The club remained much the same for many years in the Surrey Senior League until in 1974 floodlights were installed in readiness for an application to join the Athenian League. Crystal Palace played the first match in front of a record crowd of 3,146 on October 14th of that year. Three years later a new entrance in Hunts Lane was constructed and the long awaited development of the new clubhouse took place as the club stepped up into the Isthmian League.

The fire which set the club back so badly started around 5pm on August 5th 1990. It heralded a frantic three months during which a splendid 200 seater stand went up in place of the old wooden structure as Krooner Park returned to normal.

CALTHORPE PARK
Fleet Town FC

Such have been the improvements at Calthorpe Park in recent years, that the Southern League accepted Fleet's promotion following their successful year in 1995. It seems the catalyst was the fire which destroyed the old wooden stand in 1991

Fleet Town, new to the Southern League, built the Calvin Tyrer Stand after a blaze.

tripping off a chain of events which saw the completion of the new Calvin Tyrer Stand, toilet blocks, new turnstiles, refreshment facilities and an ambulance bay.

The ground has been home to Fleet Town since 1923 when Lord Calthorpe of Eltham Hall presented the club with the site and they moved in March of that year. Subsequently the ground was bequeathed to the local Council with the proviso that it would remain in continued use as a football ground by Fleet Town.

Formed in 1953, the Supporters' Club became the driving force behind the laying of a new pitch and the building of the pavilion with the subsequent installation of floodlights. However, the ground was never completely developed and decline set in when entry to the Athenian League was refused. The arrival of a fresh regime saw improvements made with perimeter barriers put in

and the Wessex League accepted the club. More improvements were carried out in 1991 when the old clubhouse was re-furbished, the pitch re-seeded and the whole ground fenced in. When the old pavilion-type stand burnt down, the current layout of Calthorpe Park developed and that brought Southern League football to the town.

MEMORIAL GROUND
Farnham Town FC

The pleasant Memorial Ground has been in existence as a playing field since 1910 when the land was given to a local side by Farnham United Brewers who stipulated its continued use as a recreational facility. The Memorial Hall next door provides the changing rooms while the ground was increased in length by 10 yards back in 1975 to help gain senior status.

The small covered area perched on the bank behind one goal was erected about the same time. The permanent barrier around the pitch went up in 1980 followed ten years later by the floodlighting system. More improvements are imminent with hard standing and perimeter fencing as Farnham battle back after recently being refused entry into the Isthmian League.

RECREATION GROUND
Aldershot Town FC

The Town club were formed just three years ago following the sad demise under sorry circumstances of the old Football League club which had played at the council owned Recreation Ground for 65 years. With commendable haste, all parties formed a new club and a fresh atmosphere of anticipation replaced the apathy, echoing in some ways the events of the pre-Great War era, when clubs often seemed able to re-form with almost the same personnel and found the public still came in droves.

The ground was unique in the Football League, with the end nearest the main road laid out with lawns and flower beds leading to a flat, undeveloped end which may quite possibly hinder the new club as they progress. They will also have to deal with the fact there are many mature trees close by, which St Albans City found to their cost, are lovely to look at but outlawed by certain leagues.

The ground was already a public park but by skilful interpretation of the Public Health Act, the Council were able to lease the ground to Aldershot FC thus enabling them to close off the site on match days.

Farnham Town FC

The untouched Recreation Ground, Aldershot, now thriving again in the Isthmian League.

OAK FARM
Cove FC

Cove Football Club suffer from one main problem, which is the close proximity of Farnborough Town, just a few hundred yards away. They did well to transform what was no more than a pitch laid on a reclaimed sewage farm into an Isthmian League standard ground ready to move up from the Combined Counties in 1990.

The site was infilled using building waste from the construction of the M3 at Bagshot and for some time was an open space with pitches until the playing area was enclosed and a clubhouse built in 1973. A high surrounding wall now entombs the ground which has seating for 75 people and a covered area for another 400. Aldershot brought their Football League side down to play the first game under floodlights on April 18th 1989 and it is ironic that Cove's highest-ever attendance is against the new Aldershot Town's Isthmian League side four years later when 1,800 saw the local derby in Division Three.

The first game was played on August 27th 1927 at what was an undeveloped ground but within two years it gained a small stand on the railway side. This was sufficient for the club to enter the Football League in 1930, but it wasn't until just prior to the Second War that the North Stand opposite was built, at that time with no seating. The original wooden changing rooms were built behind the South Stand and as the War ended the terrace at the east end was covered leaving the ground looking more or less as it does today. There have been changes, of course, but the shape and general appearance are remarkably similar to fifty years ago.

Floodlighting first went up in 1954 and was renewed eight years later and in 1970 a new office complex and changing rooms were built behind the North Stand which was seated soon after.

The Recreation Ground enjoyed a crowd of nearly 20,000, only 25 years ago for an FA Cup tie with Carlisle, and in League days the capacity was still around 12,000 at the death. For current purposes the limit is set at 5,000, all of which could stay dry at a ground that could still easily shelter 15,000 people.

JOHN ROBERTS GROUND
Farnborough Town FC

Twenty years ago the football ground at Cherrywood Road was scrub land and Town were playing on an unenclosed council pitch in Queens Road which had been their home since 1967.

The club's quite astonishing rise to prominence through the Surrey Senior, Spartan, Athenian and Isthmian Leagues to the Alliance Premier in that time has meant the ground has been constantly changing to accommodate the various ground gradings and, although not the prettiest, it is not uncomfortable, with cover for over 1,200 spectators. The first structure to go up was the main stand which is more of an extension to the clubhouse and administration areas which are all lumped together in an impressive brick building extending out into the car-park. The terracing around the playing area has been progressed with the first covered standing area on the far side from the stand going up to allow for entry into the Alliance in 1989. This area now has seating for around 250 on a raised terrace which gives a fine view of the proceedings.

The remaining terrace is rather shallow in places which is commonplace at many new grounds built within the last twenty years, although Avenue Stadium and the Huish are exceptions. More recently much urgent attention was given to Cherrywood Road to prepare it for a return to the top grade, with the addition of a small brick stand, seemingly glued onto the original plus further basic cover behind one goal and the completion of more terrace, all work done on a commendable voluntary basis by supporters, officials and players alike.

The John Roberts Ground is a prime example of thrifty cloth cutting where the club have dispensed with the frills off the pitch and reaped the benefits on it, having twice reached the top level of non-League football. Whilst not having the character of an older ground it does look homely and due to its gradual development has not been hastily thrown together as have so many of the ugly concrete monoliths which have been touted around as the modern way ahead.

Photos in this section by: Andrew Chitty, Kerry Miller and James Wright.

The extension to the main stand at Farnborough.

M25 Inner West

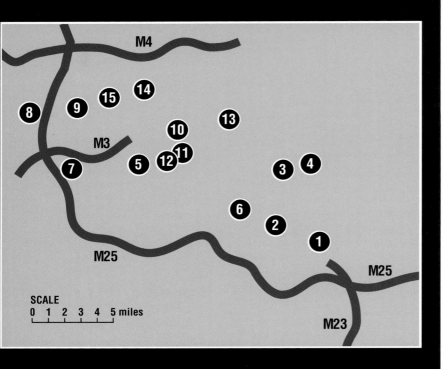

1	Chipstead FC
2	Banstead Athletic FC
3	Sutton United FC
4	Carshalton Athletic FC
5	Epsom & Ewell FC
6	Walton & Hersham FC
7	Chertsey Town FC
8	Egham Town FC
9	Staines Town FC
10	Hampton FC
11	Metropolitan Police FC
12	Molesey FC
13	Kingstonian FC
14	Feltham FC
15	Ashford Town FC

THE densely populated commuter belt area around Surrey and Middlesex is the heartland of the Isthmian League, with a sprinkling of Combined Counties clubs for good measure. Curiously the only two Southern League grounds of the modern era are sadly no more, namely Hounslow and Addlestone.

After 67 years Epsom and Ewell's West Street ground succumbed in 1993 to housing while Malden Vale survived a crisis at their relatively recently developed Grand Drive ground, by dropping into the Combined Counties League from the Isthmian. Bedfont and Ashford Town, both close to Heathrow Airport are now slowly developing their grounds, the former on what was an old orchard directly under one of the main flight-paths.

HIGH ROAD
Chipstead FC

Chipstead Football Club have been in existence for close on 90 years, with most of that time spent at Junior or Intermediate level.

Equipped with little other than the basic facilities, the field at High Road was not developed until 1979, when the thriving clubhouse and changing rooms were built that have enabled the club to slowly expand the ground up to its current state. A small wooden stand with cover for around 100 now perches on the half way line and the car-park is fenced off from the ground, which has been floodlit since 1991.

Action at the War Memorial ground Carshalton showing the staggered roofed terracing.

MERLAND RISE
Banstead Athletic FC

Banstead Athletic started as Banstead Juniors in 1944 playing on a pitch on the Tattenham Way Recreation Ground, owned by the Banstead UDC. After two seasons at junior level the County wanted the club to find a new name, and as the pre-war clubs Banstead FC and Banstead Hospital FC did not reform at the time the club re-named itself Athletic.

The pitch at the Rec was one of several on the site which was roped off and this remained home until April 1950 when the Council offered the use of a field at Merland Rise, a mile west of the village. There was a small wooden building which was used as a clubhouse and dressing room and shared with other organisations. For two years matches were played on a pitch to the south of it. Because the area was used by the general public, the Council then offered a field on the other side, eight and a half acres in total, for the sole use of the club and that is the area leased today.

For fifteen seasons the ground remained undeveloped, other than a small covered shelter built in 1954. Although there was much success on the pitch, the lack of a long lease made the club hesitant. When in 1966 Athletic finally got a 30 year deal, the cover was re-built and extended and is still in use today. A year later the field was fenced in and with the granting of a license, a clubhouse was built and opened in August 1969.

*Above: **A damp Merland Rise, Banstead.***
*Right: **The opening of the club's pavilion in 1950 which was used as dressing rooms until 1979.***

A further hall for functions was built behind the first clubhouse and opened in 1972.

Aiming for the Athenian League, new dressing rooms were built in 1979 nearer the pitch, which made the old Council building redundant, and shortly after Banstead's first floodlights were installed. In 1983 the club secured a loan from Whitbreads Brewery enabling them to rebuild the stand and extend the bar. A large car-park was built and a concrete walkway laid down around the whole ground. With extra dressing rooms added, the club were able to take their place in the Isthmian League when the Athenian folded.

The club survived a crisis in 1990 when a dispute between tenant and landlord developed, but having obtained a further 25 year lease more improvements have been made to Merland Rise since 1992. Floodlighting on the main pitch was doubled and equal lighting was added to the second pitch. A six foot high solid metal fence and two areas of covered terracing have been built along with a new toilet block and at the time of writing the club hold a 'B' grade with little more to do to move into the coveted 'A' bracket.

Crowds at Banstead have always been fairly modest in an area that is not short of football, and this is borne out by the record attendance of 1,400 to watch an FA Amateur Cup match against Leytonstone in 1953 when the ground was no more than a roped off pitch with dressing rooms. With a capacity of 3,000 there is at least potential at this vastly improved Isthmian League ground.

WAR MEMORIAL SPORTS GROUND
Carshalton Athletic FC

Mill Lane Mission were formed in 1903, and four years later changed their name to Carshalton Athletic. Another local side, St. Andrews merged with them at the end of that season. The newly-named club then played on the Wrythe Recreation Ground until 1914 when war broke out.

The land was used for agricultural purposes at that stage, and when football recommenced, the Rec. was not available, so a local market gardener lent the club a field half a mile away known as Culvers Park, and this was used for a year or so until the Urban District Council announced they wished to build an estate there. Carshalton wrote to the UDC requesting the lease on five acres of land which was no longer needed for agriculture, and mindful that plans existed for housing, a school and a link road close by, permission was quickly given to the club to fence in the ground and build a small club house and dressing rooms. The estimated cost of the work was £1,000, and the opening match was played on New Year's Day 1921 against Thornhill, some seven months before the work had actually been completed. The ground was named in memory of those players and officials lost in the Great War.

During the summer of 1926, the club acquired the Jockey Club grandstand from Epsom Racecourse, which was no longer required following rebuilding work, and it was transported and re-erected by supporters and officials, and stood for a further 42 years, until severe gales demolished it.

The stepped, covered terracing at Carshalton.

banked and terraced with railway sleepers, while a car park was created between the ground and the railway. A £3,000, 1,100 seater main stand was proposed and with financial help from the Council as part of the Coronation celebrations, and much voluntary labour, the long awaited grandstand was opened in 1953 and is still in use today .

It was a full eight years before the club accommodation under the stand was completed, including dressing rooms, club rooms and bars, and this was soon followed by floodlights as the club entered one of their greatest eras with a visit to the Amateur Cup Finals of 1963 and 1969 and the famous FA Cup run of 1969-70 which culminated in a 14,000 crowd crammed in to the ground for the Fourth Round visit of Leeds United.

Staging the match was never going to be easy, but the council stepped in and strengthened the terracing, renewed banking, fences and gates and enabled the game to go ahead. Bench seating was borrowed from the Oval Cricket Ground and arranged around the track and, although the 0-6 scoreline was conclusive, the club reaped the benefits.

Gander Green Lane returned to normal and it was ten years before the next significant change occurred when the original lights were replaced, and a further five before the club took over the running of the ground from the Council, which was the catalyst for the next round of change. The Athletics Club which had shared the ground moved out, and the club replaced the two original stands with the present structure in time for the entry into the Conference in 1986. The track was of course no longer required and it was squared off at the Gander Green Lane end and terracing built.

Since those heady days the big time returned just once for the famous FA Cup victory over Coventry City in 1989, and while Isthmian League regulations have brought more minor changes to the Borough Sports Ground, it has seen its fair share of action in 80 odd years.

A temporary stand sufficed for four years courtesy of the UDC, and the current structure went up in the spring of 1972. Extensive concrete terracing was laid down along the recreation ground side as early as 1949, and was extended around the top end in time for the visit of Tooting and Mitcham United in the 3rd Qualifying round of the FA Cup on October 28th 1950, when a ground record crowd of 8,200 crammed into Colston Avenue. The opposite side was concreted in 1953, and in the next ten years was covered in sections to give the stepped appearance seen today. In the autumn of 1959 a clubhouse was built, and eight years later floodlights were officially switched on with a match against Crystal Palace in front of 1,600 spectators. In more recent times a covered terrace with new turnstiles was completed with the removal of banking from one end. This has enhanced what was already a pleasant ground, well capable of keeping virtually all of its paying visitors dry.

GANDER GREEN LANE
Sutton United FC

The early history of football in Sutton, and the use of the grounds in particular is well documented, and shows two clubs Sutton Association and Sutton Guild Rovers merging in 1898 to form the current club.

Both clubs' grounds, those at Western Road and at Manor Lane, were retained, enabling the new body to field more than one side. The set-up lasted one season, as Western Road was not available the following year and all matches were played at Manor Lane which proved problematical, as spectators had a free view of the match from the road. The ground was roped off for that season but an enclosed site became essential, and funds became available to fence it off a couple of years later.

Manor Lane stayed home until grounds at Rose Hill, Fairfield at Collingham and London Road were used, prior to United

gaining the use of a pitch called 'The Find', in Grove Road. They had planned to play at the newly opened Adult School Sports Ground in Gander Green Lane but this was not available as they had decided to field a team of their own. In fact it was not until after the Great War, that the ground was secured and the first game played in August 1919. By then it had been open for seven years and had gained a small wooden stand which was added to during the summer of 1924 at a cost of £69. At this stage the Sports Ground, to be re-named the Borough Sports Ground following the Council's purchase of it from the school in 1934, had a cinder running-track with a post and rail and picket fencing around the playing area. The two stands were at the side of the ground and rough banking stretched around the oval-shaped site. There was a fence which divided the ground from the Rec next door and the site of the much later new stand was outside the ground altogether.

It was after the Second War that the shape began to change, with the Collingwood Road end being extended,

The main stand at Sutton United.

Stompond Lane, Walton and Hersham.

down the first cinder track in the area which was utilised by the athletics club which was formed in 1942 and has shared the ground ever since.

As Walton became Walton and Hersham after the war the Supporters' Club built a tea hut and covered the area opposite the stand, which remains to this day. In 1957 the club battled through to the first round of the FA Cup where they met Southampton, and much work was done to accommodate the anticipated crowd, with the grass banking either side of the stand made safe and chairs placed behind the goals. At that stage concrete terrace had already gone down behind the Hersham Road goal and the ground was roughly the shape it is today. During the sixties floodlights were introduced and the old wooden stand was eventually taken down and replaced with a 600-seater structure with dressing rooms underneath. This enabled the club to turn the old dressing rooms into a club room which still exists today. More recently cosmetic improvements have been done to keep pace with the Isthmian League's ever changing rule book, and the council owners have laid a synthetic running track to replace the old cinder one, but Stompond Lane is more or less unscathed.

STOMPOND LANE
Walton and Hersham FC

The first official information regarding the creation of Stompond Lane comes from the Council owners whose official hand-out on their open spaces mentions that an area of land belonging to Mr J.S. Sassoon, totalling 10 acres, was offered to them at £500 an acre way back in 1908. It was turned down but much later, in 1933, the ground was bought for £7,000.

Walton FC played on Stompond Lane in those pre-war years, the pitch then angled at 45 degrees to its present position. The building of the first grandstand, a green-painted wooden affair which stood on the site of the current one saw the pitch turned round and soon changing rooms were added next to it. Just before the war, the council owners laid

ALWYNS LANE
Chertsey Town FC

The very early days of Chertsey Town Football Club were spent on a number of fields including The Grange, up to the First War, and later The Hollows until the ground at Alwyns Lane was donated to the "premier club in the parish" by Sir Edward Stern, who provided a similar trust to the cricket club next door. The facilities from the start were spartan with the players changing in The Bell, a public house some 300 yards across the fields. However, a wooden dressing room was soon built and was in fact situated precisely where the the present one now stands.

After the war a substantial grass bank was created behind the Alwyns Lane end goal, and this proved very popular but over the years it was gradually cut back until its original 10ft by 30ft dimensions disappeared altogether in the early eighties. The brick built main stand was built in the mid-fifties using volunteer labour. It straddles the half way line on the church side of the ground, and today is looking better than possibly it has ever done. A corrugated shelter was built at the Gogmore Farm end in 1960, but it proved a

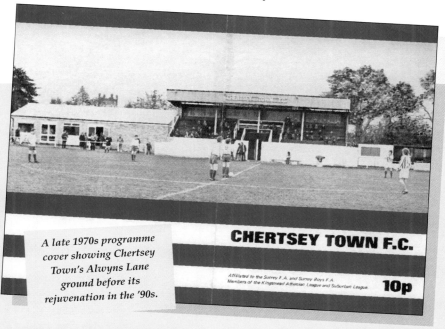

A late 1970s programme cover showing Chertsey Town's Alwyns Lane ground before its rejuvenation in the '90s.

poor investment for it was destroyed in gales three years later and never replaced. Around the same time, the original pre-fabricated clubhouse was built and lasted 16 years until replaced with the present brick built structure which has since been extended on the same site.

The new dressing rooms were built in 1988, and the rooms below the stand were then turned into a physio and kit room. Opposite the stand a bus shelter type covered area has stood since 1963, and stretches around a third of the pitch length. To gain the necessary ground grading to qualify for promotion, extensive concrete terracing has been laid down around the pitch, and a training area and additional turnstiles have also appeared within the last few years.

Today, Alwyns Lane is a pleasant if unspectacular ground in an equally pleasant Surrey town. With the two stands virtually unchanged since they were built and no other major developments taking place the ground has a contented look about it, glowing in the light of the success which has come on the pitch in recent years.

Egham Town in 1990.

TEMPEST ROAD
Egham Town FC

The current Egham side have only been in existence since 1963, and have developed their ground from very humble beginnings. The original club were founded in 1896, and played at the Anglers Rest Hotel, (now the Runnymede Hotel), until the outbreak of the Great War. On commencement of football in 1919 they moved grounds to Manorcroft, in the centre of the town, and the Headquarters moved to the Foresters Arms pub. In 1926 they were on the move again, this time to Vicarage Road and there they stayed until the Second World War when again the club disbanded, this time for good.

Football there was dormant until 1963, when a group of enthusiasts called a public meeting at the Egham Literary Institute to re-activate the club and a collection was taken. A ground was leased from the then Egham Urban District Council, whose offices were used for changing and soon after two small covered areas were erected. Around ten years later a small stand went up capable of seating just over 200 and sits adjacent to the half way line. Gradually shallow terracing was laid down around the ground which was not fully enclosed until 1989 when major changes occurred at Tempest Road. Since then the two ends of the ground have been covered and two further stands built either side of the original opposite the main stand. An impressive clubhouse and function room with a gym now stands just outside what has become an excellently appointed home in an area populated by at least a dozen senior non-League sides all vying against each other.

THE BEVEREE
Hampton FC

The Beveree ground, tucked away close to the centre of Hampton is one of the unsung homes in Isthmian League football that seems to escape the headlines year after year as the club goes quietly on. It was certainly not always that way, as controversy reigned in the early days of the Beveree when, after playing on the as yet undeveloped site from the War, Hampton and local rivals **Twickenham Town were invited to tender for the lease on the ground.**

Twickenham, whose Chairman just happened to be the Mayor at the time were given the right to play there and Hampton were forced to play on Hatherop Rec for seven years until Twickenham were thrown off having been out-manoevred by the club, who let them believe they were offering double the rent at tender!

They eventually dropped into local football and soon folded leaving Hampton to move in to reap the benefits of Twickenham's tenure.

A post and rail system was in place and a small covered area stood on the site of the current stand although it was frequently under water and as such rarely used.

The Beveree is named after the large house which still overlooks it today and in whose grounds the pitch was first laid out. Built on the site of a 17th century house and named Rose Villa, it dates from around 1825, and was at one time rented by Edward Jesse, Deputy Surveyor of Royal Parks and Palaces.

It much later became the home of a Captain Christie Crawford, was renamed the Beveree, and is now a preparatory school. When his family left the grounds to the Council around the time of the war it was soon converted into a football ground. Much earlier it is believed to have been the venue for athletics meetings, polo and fetes and right up to ten years ago was only segregated from the by now developed ground, by nothing more than a three foot high chain link fence. The first few years were spent using the old stables as changing rooms which stood just in front of the current building and this sufficed until 1962 when an army building was acquired from the airport which in a modernised form still is in use today.

The sixties saw the ground take on the shape it has now with the small 200-seater stand replacing the old shack while a large clubhouse and floodlighting both appeared

WHEATSHEAF PARK
Staines Town FC

There have been many teams in the Staines area and it is not easy to accurately piece together the history. What is known is that Staines FC were in the Surrey Cup in the 1880's and St Peter's Institute entered the FA Cup in 1879, before the two clubs merged in 1895. The accepted founding date for the Town is actually 1892.

The Great War killed off the first version of the club, with football continuing through the works sides of Lagonda and Projectile. When the war ended Staines Lagonda emerged and in 1925 changed their name to Staines Town but within ten years the club had ceased trading after unsuccessful attempts to merge with other local sides such as Staines Linoleum, Staines Athletic and Staines Lammas. The name Staines Vale was used towards the end of the Second World War, reverting again to Town soon after.

It is known that St Peters played at Edgell Road, not far from the church, with Staines playing at The Lammas, also known as Ashby Recreation Ground in Wraysbury Road. They moved to another ground on Shortwood Common and between the wars played on a ground at Mill Mead, also known as Hammond's Farm or Wicks' Farm, close to the Lino Sports Ground. Whilst at Mill Mead, players changed at the White Lion pub in the High Street, walking to the ground through the town. The Lino Sports Ground is now under a housing estate, and Mill Mead was lost to the Corporation around the time of the war, when the land was taken for construction of the reservoir. Indeed, the stand was used right to the end as a store for the engineers' equipment. The club moved out of Mill Mead in 1935 selling the stand to the land owner before playing their remaining games away. Eventually a temporary home was found in Shepperton Road, Laleham where they stayed until the new ground at the Wheatsheaf was built and opened in 1951. Originally the land was earmarked for housing, but it was found to be unsuitable and so the football ground was born instead.

The first structure was a multi-purpose building known as the Green Hut which housed changing rooms, a boardroom and a tea hut and stood behind what is now the main stand until it fell into disrepair and was knocked down around six years ago. The stand itself once straddled the half way line with a covered enclosure behind the right hand goal, both dating from the sixties, but when a pocket of land was sold for housing in 1981, the pitch was moved forward and the cover taken down, which leaves a narrow space at that end.

by 1967, the latter after a celebration match between the Spartan League and an England Amateur X1. In 1970 the large covered terrace which stretches down half the length of the pitch was erected transforming the ground and providing cover for 800. This was followed by the hard standing around part of the pitch which was not fully completed until many years later when Kingstonian used the Beveree while their new ground was being built, the Premier Division ruling having demanded that the whole ground be terraced.

More recently the stand has had the addition of some seats from Plough Lane, Wimbledon which replaced the benches and were alongside some earlier imports from the demolished Granleigh Road, home of Leytonstone.

One other nostalgic item at the Beveree is found at the impressive entrance to the ground where the club's turnstiles still do business, having been rescued from the lamented Hurst Park racecourse, which stood until the early sixties a few furlongs away across the river.

The main stand at Molesey FC.

IMBER COURT
Metropolitan Police FC

As should be expected of a club representing the Police Force in London, everything about Imber Court is immaculate, tidy, efficient and structured. From the huge multi-roomed clubhouse to the peripheral pitches used by other sports, the comfort of the members and visitors is paramount.

The club were formed a year after the Great War and played friendlies until joining the Spartan League in 1928. The Imber Court sports ground was acquired in 1919 and a year later the clubhouse was built. It has since been extended many times.

The football side was not really developed until around thirty years ago when the canvas sheet which enclosed the ground, enabling them to take a gate, was replaced by

a wooden fence. This was subsequently replaced in 1973 by a 6'6" concrete wall which completely closed off the playing area. In 1971, in readiness for the Southern League, three floodlight pylons were erected, but due to the proximity of a cricket square a fourth could not be put in place. It was fully 22 years before the problem was rectified. In 1984, five turnstiles were constructed and placed at opposite ends of the ground, while substantial terracing went down around three sides at the same time. The first major change to the layout came in 1988 when the terrace at the Mounted Branch End was covered by a concrete cantilever stand to cater for 1,800 spectators.

The focal point of Imber Court almost from the outset was the delightful timber and steel main stand which was constructed around 1923 and doubled in size in 1934 for the princely sum of £265. After the Bradford fire disaster, she was on borrowed time, and despite much work to make it less hazardous the club regrettably had no choice but to replace it.

Demolition, and reconstruction of the new, slightly smaller stand which holds 284 people was completed in 14 weeks during the close season of 1994. In contrast to the work on the original, the cost of the new stand was in the region of £123,000.

WALTON ROAD
Molesey FC

The Walton Road ground was already equipped with a small stand when Molesey St Pauls became Molesey FC in 1953. Although the club acknowledge this as their founding date, there had been previous Molesey sides in junior football since the turn of the century.

The ground was originally at 45 degrees to its present position and by 1960 had a covered area opposite the stand. It was soon all to change when the shape of the ground completely altered following promotion to the Spartan League. The covered stand was moved to the new pitch site and an orchard which once stood behind the cover, now housed half the pitch. The turnstile entrance stayed more or less in the same place with the splendid galleried stand and clubhouse complex straddling the half way line. Floodlights followed ten years later and as the Athenian and Isthmian Leagues beckoned things began to get very tight at the club. A financial crisis was averted in the late eighties and a new set-up saw a radical improvement at the ground which corresponded with promotion to Division One of the Isthmian League. A new perimeter fence went up and the seating in the stand was converted from bench to modern tip-ups. Terracing went down around the ground and a new tea bar was installed.

With promotion to the Premier Division a new covered area was erected behind the far goal and a new turnstile complex put up as Walton Road benefited from a lively management committee.

Imber Court, the immaculate home of the Metropolitan Police FC.

RICHMOND ROAD and KINGSMEADOW STADIUM
Kingstonian FC

Above: Richmond Road, Kingstonian, now sadly gone. Below: Kingstonian's new home.

Kingsmeadow Stadium is one of a group of new grounds built to a standard design by those who simply cannot have had much experience of bigger crowds at smaller venues. The contrast between the two grounds could not be more marked, as Richmond Road has steep-sloped terraces and a classic twenties style main stand, capable of seating 1,200 people, whilst the Kingsmeadow Stadium has virtually no adequate terrace and only half the seats.

The much lamented Richmond Road sports ground was in fact the third venue used by the club in the same road, the original site being close by at what was to become the East Surrey Barracks sports ground. By 1919, the club had crossed the road and were playing on the second ground which boasted a pavilion. The land had previously been used for allotments and so much effort was required to improve the pitch. All the hard work appeared to have been in vain at the end of the 1919-20 season when the ground was leased to Leyland Motors, after rumours abounded that Kingstonian had folded. A ground-share agreement ensued which was not successful, and eventually the club bought the field next door, and latterly the former ground, for a combined sum of £5,000.

On the third of the neighbouring grounds work soon began to transform it into a venue capable of hosting crowds of 5,000 plus. A timber stand was erected, and opened by the Lord Mayor in January 1922, and soon after a wooden perimeter fence went up around the pitch. The banking which was later to be converted into concrete terracing was fashioned, and dressing rooms and an addition to the stand were in place by 1926. The latter was purchased from a Horse Show Society in the County and built on the end of the main stand, where it remained until the end.

After the war, the permanent terracing was gradually put down, and a small covered enclosure opposite the stand erected. By the mid-sixties floodlights had been in use some while, and new dressing rooms were in place for the match officials. The final structure of any significance to go up was Kingstonian's third clubhouse, the forebears of which had all been on the same site. The developments were never in vain, for crowds of 4-5,000 were regular. The ground record was 11,000 for an Amateur Cup tie against Bishop Auckland in 1955, and even up to the end, the capacity was set at 6,500.

With the ground beginning to show its age, and with the prospect of a financial windfall on its sale, Richmond Road followed its two predecessors, and succumbed to the bulldozer. The new ground was built on the site of the old Norbiton Road Sports Ground, half a mile away, and was opened with a league match against Slough Town in August 1989. In a similar, and no less sad way to those at Aylesbury, Ashford Town, Raunds Town, Thatcham Town etc, the designers have produced a ground which caters superbly for officials, players, and visiting dignitaries, whilst providing the bare minimum for those paying through the gates. The stand, which houses most of the club rooms, bars, restaurants, changing rooms etc. is in itself a splendid structure, and is virtually identical to that at Buckingham Road. The rest of the ground is very flat with the bare minimum of elevation to the terracing, making it extremely uncomfortable if faced with a large crowd.

Unfortunately, almost all new grounds in the current era suffer poorly in comparison to much loved grounds of many years standing, and Kingsmeadow Stadium is no exeption.

THE ARENA
Feltham and Hounslow Borough FC

The original Feltham Football Club played on basic pitches at the Glebelands, next door to the current ground, and then at Rectory Fields, an Army depot in Lower Feltham. When the new Arena was opened by the Council in 1962 the club moved in and have remained ever since.

It was built as a running track and had a pavilion with changing rooms as the only facility until the huge 1300-seater stand was added in 1966. The rest of the ground was slightly banked to give an elevated view all around. It remained virtually unchanged until fire regulations forced a drastic reduction in the capacity, with half the seating being removed, although it is still possible for 600 people to either sit or stand should the capacity ever be needed. The Arena lost its running track when it was decided to lay an artificial surface a few years ago and the club continued playing on it in the Isthmian League until 1995 when regulations instructed them to add another 300-seater stand on the opposite side of the ground as well as replace the perimeter fencing. As the ground is council-owned and with an average crowd of around only 60, it was not considered feasible and the club have dropped into the Combined Counties League.

Ashford Town FC

SHORT LANE
Ashford Town FC

Short Lane is slowly but surely bringing the club nearer their ultimate goal of Isthmian League football. It has only been home to Ashford Town for nine years since they moved from Clockhouse Lane Rec, but has been transformed from an area of waste land into a dual purpose ground with football one side of the approach road and cricket the other.

There is only a small covered area with a post and rail around the ground at present but the installation of floodlights in the autumn of 1995 complete with a thriving clubhouse should see the club continue forward. Three cup finals, and a first and second place in the league inside two seasons has seen the club enjoy its finest hour and Isthmian League football may not be too far away.

M25 Inner East

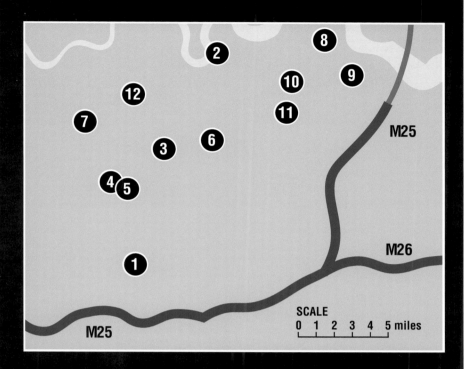

SCALE
0 1 2 3 4 5 miles

M25
M26
M25

1 **Whyteleafe FC**

2 **Greenwich Borough FC**

3 **Beckenham Town FC**

4 **Croydon FC**

5 **Croydon Athletic FC**

6 **Bromley FC**

7 **Tooting & Mitcham FC**

8 **Erith & Belvedere FC**

9 **Slade Green FC**

10 **Welling United FC**

11 **Cray Wanderers FC**

12 **Dulwich Hamlet FC**

Above: Croydon Athletic FC.

Right: Church Road, Whyteleafe.

Photos in this section by: Gavin Ellis-Neville, Mike Floate, Kentish Times, V.J. Robertson, Richard Wall, Dave West

IN marked contrast, this area is less well served with established clubs, although it does include Cray Wanderers, the second oldest football club in the world. WHYTELEAFE's Church Road ground is believed to have been home since the club were founded just after the war. They only entered the Athenian League in 1981 and have developed their ground to Isthmian League standards since then.

Greenwich Borough similarly only entered the Spartan League from amateur football in 1981, and had two pitches at Harrow Meadow, one floodlit and the other with a small covered area, before settling on the far pitch. South of Greenwich is Beckenham Town, who also have a recent pedigree on their current ground, moving to Eden Park from Stanhope Grove in 1981. The railed off pitch and small 100-seater stand with clubhouse is sufficient for the requirements of the Kent League that they joined from the Spartan League in 1982.

CROYDON SPORTS ARENA
Croydon FC

Croydon Football Club have always had the same problems as those suffered by the likes of Harlow, Sandwell Borough, Billingham Synthonia and on a much larger scale Gateshead, in that although the facilities are excellent, the presence of a running track and ancillary athletics equipment means a distinct lack of atmosphere.

They have played at the Arena since their formation in 1953, when the ground was formally opened before a game with Pegasus FC. The stand was available from the start and has been modified several times. Now it can hold 450 who have a good elevated view, if some distance from the play. Over the years the

club have suffered their fair share of vandalism, the clubhouses in particular have been badly hit; the first was built in 1964 and a new one followed which was opened by the ever-willing Sir Stanley Rous in 1981.

Floodlighting came early, in 1970, and was switched on before a match with Crystal Palace, but it wasn't until 1989 that major work on the installation of a new athletics track meant the club were homeless and seriously jeopardised their existence. The Arena stayed vacant for some time whilst new perimeter walls, concrete fences, floodlights and seating went in before Croydon returned. The last two seasons have not been easy for the club but they are still in there pitching, and whilst the Arena may not be everyone's cup of tea, it is still home.

NFC SPORTS GROUND
Croydon Athletic FC

The other Croydon club are an amalgam of Wandsworth FC and Norwood FC who were formed within months of each other just after the war. They merged in 1986 taking both titles before becoming Croydon Athletic in 1990.

Norwood played at the ground for four years before the merger and in the relatively short period of the club's existence, facilities have been developed to an impressive degree, with floodlights in 1990 and a 100-seater stand which incorporated material from an earlier piece of cover. Since then further cover has gone in and the ground is now completely fenced off as the club attack their goal of Isthmian League football. It's all a long way from Wisley Gardens or Lloyds Park of only a dozen years ago!

HAYES LANE
Bromley FC

There is a school of thought that some of Bromley FC's very early games at the turn of the century were played at Widmore Road and the White Hart Field Cricket Club, although it may well be that an older outfit, Bromley Assistance Club used the grounds. Bromley's inaugural season of 1892 was spent at the Queensmead Recreation Ground before transferring the following year to the Glebe Road site where they remained for seven years until it was required for housing.

This ground had an entrance off Station Road and the footballers and cricketers of Bromley Town FC had a pavilion each, while the football pitch also had the benefit of a members' stand. They then moved a few hundred yards to the vacant Plaistow Cricket Ground, which backed on to the other site and was, along with the cricket club, separated by a hawthorn hedge.

This was home until 1904 when they fell foul of the planners again who wanted the

Top: The old wooden stand at Bromley, pictured in 1986. Centre: How it looked six years later. Bottom: Another year on and a new stand takes its place.

ground for more housing. Following talks involving members of the football, tennis, cricket and bowls clubs, and the Norman family who were large landowners, they were all offered facilities on a long lease in Hayes Lane, just a hundred yards from the present ground. The official opening was on September 3rd 1904 by the Mayor of Bromley, but at that stage there were no changing rooms or clubhouse, just a roped off field. Changing rooms however, soon followed.

This sports ground lasted until 1938 when, besides the Council requiring the site for more housing, a new road was set to bisect it. The landowners again offered the clubs another site just 100 yards away, and although the Bromley FC and the bowls club

agreed, the tennis club died and the cricket club went elsewhere. The sports ground was partly built on, but the rest reverted to agriculture. The new Hayes Lane stadium was already in progress and available for the start of the 1938-39 season when it was opened by Stanley Rous on September 3rd prior to a 6-1 defeat by Walthamstow Avenue. The club's superb timber main stand had around 2,000 seats, and the banked up perimeter was sufficient to assemble a crowd of 10,789 to watch a match against a Nigerian XI on September 24th 1949. Bromley FC switched on their first floodlights on 27th September 1960 when an Isthmian League XI played Japan's National side at Hayes Lane. With the help of the lights to ease fixture congestions the club took the league title that season.

The banking eventually became terracing and the ground one of the more homely of the London area grounds not swallowed up by developers. A massive fire in October 1992 completely destroyed the main stand and dressing rooms, putting Hayes Lane out of action until the new modern 320-seater stand was built. This was used for the first time on September 11th 1993 for an FA Cup tie with Dulwich Hamlet.

SANDY LANE
Tooting and Mitcham United FC

The vast open spaces of the Sandy Lane ground are an echo of many other senior grounds in the London area which once saw massive crowds but are unlikely to again. When viewing the ground in its entirety, Champion Hill at Dulwich, Church Road Hayes and Claremont Road Hendon all come to mind.

Surprisingly for a ground that is over 70 years old, the only significant structure built has been the huge grandstand which was originally much smaller, but was later lengthened at either end to provide close on 2,000 seats. The 60's and 70's saw regular attendances of 10,000 or more during the club's cup runs and their decision to create the banked terracing so early was always vindicated.

Tooting Graveney FC was formed in 1887 by a group of local lads and after much levelling work was done, a pitch at Figges Marsh was used. Two other clubs, Tooting Bec and St. Johns amalgamated to form a strong side which challenged for honours. Mitcham Vestry gave the club notice to quit their ground and they moved to the Lonesome Ground in Streatham which proved most unsatisfactory as it was under water for most of the winter. 1907-08 season saw the club playing at the North Surrey Poultry Farm at Gorringe Park and they stayed there winning the Suburban League before moving again to a field beside the railway on what is now the Ridgeway.

When the Great War ended none of the original men were around to re-float the club

and the home-based players had been turning out for Darracq in the Munitions League. The natural progression was to form Tooting Town from this base playing at Tyrrell Poultry Farm which had two pitches, one of which was sub-let at a tidy profit. It soon became apparent that a permanent home was required, and a successful new ground scheme brought in over £1,000 which was enough to negotiate the purchase of an unfenced agricultural field in Sandy Lane which was swiftly enclosed. A local firm of contractors designed and erected the wooden stand which cost £600 and seated 360, quite adequate for the club's needs at the time.

The main competition came from Mitcham Wanderers who dated from 1912 and first played on Cranmer Green and later at grounds at Park Place and Streatham Lane, the latter now covered by a housing estate. With both clubs in the same league a merger was logical and took place in 1932 with the new club playing at Sandy Lane. Almost immediately the existing stand was extended by adding four more bays to increase the seating to 600 which is how the ground remained until the Second World War. Bomb damage was minimal and the stand was repaired with the adjacent Nomads Tennis Club being written off and subsequently turned into a car-park.

Terracing first appeared at the Sandy Lane end in 1946 along with a new fence and turnstile, while the terrace was extended right around the side in time for an Amateur Cup tie with Leytonstone which attracted over 10,000 fans. 1950 saw the provision of what were described as possibly the finest dressing-rooms in amateur football which cost £3,500 and were opened by Sir Stanley Rous in December of that year. Up until then players had been forced to use two former

army huts after the original dressing rooms perished in the war.

During the summer of 1957 much attention was focused on ground improvements, and at one stage the club considered buying one of the massive stands at the doomed 40,000 capacity Mitcham Stadium, but this was eventually aborted and the stand found its way to the Eyrie at Bedford Town.

1958-59 saw the greatest season in the club's history with record crowds flocking to Sandy Lane as the famous FA Cup run took off. The qualifying rounds were safely negotiated before 10,000 saw visitors Bournemouth beaten, and Northampton Town went the same way in front of 10,200 in the second round. Nottingham Forest attracted 14,300 to Sandy Lane on a frozen January day where Tooting took them all the way before a late penalty sent them back to the City Ground, where the dream ended in a 3-0 replay defeat. These attendances were dwarfed the following year when over 17,000 saw the championship decider against Dulwich, and this era of success heralded more ground improvements, including a new £3,000 clubhouse and in March 1962 floodlights, celebrated with a game against Arsenal.

The sixties were quiet on the ground front, and it wasn't until 1974 that a huge crowd again packed into Sandy Lane for an FA Cup tie against Crystal Palace, and the following season saw the club's run to the Fourth Round of the Cup including a tie with Swindon watched by 7,500 people.

Those halcyon days soon faded and very little change occurred at the ground until 1985 when new lighting was installed which proved to be the last major development at the ground. Along with virtually every other club in non-League football

Two views of Sandy Lane, a ground which has hosted a 17,000 crowd for a championship decider.

Tooting and Mitcham United have suffered from a serious decline in interest, and the ground has deteriorated, with the terraces crumbling and weed-strewn. Ground regulations and restrictions now place the capacity at 8,000 although it is unlikely that any more than half that number would be permitted, should the club have another long-overdue FA Cup run.

PARK VIEW STADIUM
Erith and Belvedere FC

Belvedere and District FC were formed in 1919, having been prevented from calling themselves Erith FC due to a dispute with members of an insolvent club of that name. There were many clubs in the area that had sprung up around the engineering trade but eventually Belvedere emerged to play on a ground believed to be in Newman Road. The club then moved to Park View in 1922, changed their name and played the first game in August of that year.

A remarkable snap of Park View, Erith and Belvedere FC, taken from the main road following terrible floods in the early 1950s.

They were very successful, and reached a peak when getting to the 1924 Amateur Cup final, the proceeds of which went towards construction of a splendid brick and timber main stand which seated 800 people on benches and provided changing facilities underneath.

Until then the players changed in the Belvedere Hotel before walking to the ground. A small shelter stood opposite the stand until the sixties when the whole of the side was covered by the corrugated iron enclosure which runs the length of the ground. In 1956 the club sold an area of land which enabled them to build the changing rooms used today plus the ancillary rooms, which now are used for hospitality and meetings. Gradually the banking around the ground gave way to concrete terracing and much later regulations meant the outer walling changed substantially.

More recently the construction of a fly-over behind one end of the ground, has meant the loss of one entrance and the driveway, but to compensate a separate entrance from the railway station and small car-park have been built.

Park View is a throw-back to the days when a shop-worn, slightly weather-beaten old ground was not looked upon as an embarrassment to the league, but was loved as an old aunt and cherished. There is no doubt that the old girl is hovering somewhere around her sell-by date as the crumbling terraces and dodgy-looking covered enclosure will bear out. However, the main stand with its proud fascia name board is a treasure and is looking strong and healthy. The club's ground-share agreement with the rejuvenated Dartford FC has breathed new life into a ground which in its pomp groaned under the combined mass of 8,000 spectators who gathered to watch the FA Cup tie with Coventry City in 1932.

PARK VIEW ROAD
Welling United FC

Although Welling United's remarkable rise through the leagues is well-documented, and the ground's previous inhabitants Bexley United and Bexleyheath and Welling used Park View Road since before the Second World War, the chronology of the place is rather difficult to piece together. It is not commonly known when football was first played there, some indications suggest around 1925, but what is known is that by the late thirties there was a substantial grandstand on the ground with dressing rooms underneath, which suffered bomb damage during the blitz and was eventually pulled down.

Although football had ceased, there was the odd junior game played on the ground by Welling Civic and immediately after the war by Upton Athletic and Phoenix Sports. During this time players were forced to change over the road in a dairy until Bexleyheath and Welling came back. The club had failed to survive the war and for five years the ground was virtually derelict, as the stand was demolished and the rest of the ground became strewn with glass and debris. In 1951 a campaign was launched to reform the club in the Kent League. Two ex-Nissen huts were hastily erected for dressing rooms and crowds on the banked ground numbered 2,000 plus. A new grandstand was built and cover went up opposite as Park View Road came alive again. Sadly, as the 60s came, the club's ambitions got the better of them and the money spent on developing the ground eventually broke the club. The directors saw Football League membership as a possibility and despite polling no votes on two occasions the existing stand was enlarged, the whole of the opposite side was covered and the slope reduced on the pitch. The crowds were still coming in, 3-4,000 were the norm in the sixties, but the club, by now called Bexley United played their last home game in April 1976 in front of 222 spectators.

Meanwhile Welling United had been playing parks football before moving to

SMALL GLEN
Slade Green FC

Slade Green is an area a couple of miles from Erith but not necessarily in the shadow of that club. They played their early football in the Dartford, Kent Amateur and Greater London Leagues before joining the Kent League in the mid-sixties. The Small Glen was opened in 1946 and had changing rooms and a grandstand built seven years later. From then on extensive ground improvements were not particularly relevant until ground grading nudged the club into action in the eighties.

In 1984 the changing rooms were re-vamped with a physio room built and the pitch improved and surrounded by a post and rail. Three years on the multi-purpose training area was built and the main pitch floodlit soon after.

As the nineties arrived the Small Glen continued to improve with a new clubhouse and extra changing rooms put in and seats installed in the stand which was joined by another, bringing the seating capacity up to 150 with around 400 standing under cover.

To date the highest attendance was for a friendly with Millwall in July 1992 when an estimated 3,000 were present.

Butterfly Lane in Eltham, and they were one of ten clubs interested in taking over the ground. Although moves were made to try to reform Bexley, nothing came of it and in January 1977 Welling were granted a 15 year lease. Again the ground had been left to rot and a fire had damaged the stand, but when access was gained in April work commenced to reclaim Park View Road. The first match was on August 26th 1977 and it heralded the start of a climb to the Conference that has seen the ground capacity set at 5,500, of which 1,500 are under cover and 500 seated. New boundary walls, perimeter fences, turnstiles and terracing have all been installed to comply with the various leagues as they progressed and Park View Road remains a ground with more history than most buried beneath its concrete.

OXFORD ROAD GROUND
Cray Wanderers FC

To simply describe Oxford Road as being a pleasant, 20-year-old typically rural Kentish ground would be completely pointless without describing the previous 115 years of football which led up to it. For Cray Wanderers are the second oldest football club in the world and have a history which goes back to 1860, when a group of labourers got together and played on a field in Star Lane whilst employed building the embankments for the Chatham Railway.

With no facilities players changed in the Coffee Tavern, which is now a listed building next to the railway viaduct in St. Mary Cray High Street. At first, rugby was played, but when Sidcup Swifts came to play a friendly and found the opposition had 15 players to their 11, football was played, and from then on the club switched codes.

DERRY DOWNS
In the 1890's Cray played on open land near Grassmeade, which had a ricketty wooden stand built to the classic design seen throughout the country much later. They were not permitted to take gate money at Derry Downs, and so in 1898 rented an enclosed field from a Mr. Joynson and transported the stand down to the new ground on one of his trailers.

FORDCROFT
The old stand at Fordcroft was the scene of a tragedy on Easter Monday 1900, when during an `A' team match against Morden Swifts from Deptford, lightning struck the ground. A flash travelled down the flagstaff, splitting

it in two, and then through the stand's iron roof and into the dressing rooms beneath, where many spectators were sheltering. One young man was killed and over 30 were seriously injured. Fordcroft was used until 1936, when Mr. Joynson sold his paper mill, and his house and land, including the football ground, and moved away. The site is now covered by the Tip-Top factory in Cray Avenue, another listed building.

TWYSDEN'S
Wanderers moved to Footscray, to a ground with a pavilion which was unready for use when the first match was played against Margate, on November 28th 1936. The pitch had a curious hump in the middle caused by a water-pipe lying just beneath the surface.

The war put paid to football on a national scale, and Cray Wanderers name did not appear again until 1944, when they began playing at Grassmeade, just a field away from Derry Downs. This was eventually to be their permanent home for nearly twenty years, but several other grounds were used by the club after the war, as they hit a period of crisis and uncertainty. Grassmeade was owned by St. Philomena's School, and was rented jointly by Cray and the local gas company's sports guild. In 1947 they were both asked to vacate the ground, as the owners wished to use it for other purposes, but shortly after, a change of policy meant that another local club leased the ground. The following seasons saw Wanderers playing at St. Mary Cray Recreation Ground, in junior football and at their lowest ebb. The AGM of

A splendid photo of the old stand at Fordcroft, one of the many homes of Cray Wanderers FC.

1950 brought the club its first good news in years, that the Gas Board Guild had negotiated a lease on a ground at Northfields Farm, an oval-shaped field next to Grassmeade, and were willing to share it with them. After much re-turfing and tidying up, the first match took place against Foots

Cray Social on September 16th 1950. The lease was for one year only, but problems with lack a of support at the ground, and an absence of co-operation from the local farmer, meant yet another move was planned, this time to a muddy site, close to the river, and adjacent to the old Fordcroft at Tothills. This spot is now covered by the Roman Catholic Church.

Just prior to the move to Northfields, a group of local men, including Mr. Mick Slater agreed to form a limited company to run the club, with Slater acting as secretary, and it was he who set up the experiment of playing floodlit friendlies back at Grassmeade. Although primitive they continued for over two years, with the club playing league games at Fordcroft, as Bromley and Bexleyheath and Welling both used the ground. A heavy storm eventually destroyed the lights and they were not replaced until 1968.

GRASSMEADE
From 1955 the ground was rented permanently, and for the first time the club were able to make some long term plans for improving facilities. Within a decade, a pitch length stand, some covered and some seated, was in use, and low terracing had been laid behind each goal, with an open railed touch - line bordering the school. A clubhouse and a new lighting system meant the club were honoured with many representative matches held at the attractive tree-lined ground. For some time before the final eviction, and the last game at Grassmeade on 21st April 1973, the club had known that they were in trouble again. The school trustees had once again evicted Cray, this time as the ground was sold for housing, and their next home, at Oxford Road, was not ready due to planning problems.

OXFORD ROAD
The committee negotiated a lease with Sidcup Conservative Club, and levelled a site which was soon replete with a small covered stand named after Mick Slater, and a clubhouse, which sadly burned down in 1976, and was then rebuilt. In 1992, 100 seats were installed in the stand, and the following year a bus shelter type cover went up opposite. The ground is partially fenced off with wooden panelling, and until 1994 was shared by Dartford FC.

Cray Wanderers Football Club have spent 135 years living up to their name, and it is rumoured that when finances allow, a further move could be on the cards.

CHAMPION HILL
Dulwich Hamlet FC

The question of whether the modern Champion Hill is a new ground or the old one rebuilt is not really the important issue. Today's splendid ground is indeed built on the site of the famous old one, give or take fifteen yards, although there is now no trace of it or the approach road, as all the area fronting the ground has been swamped by a huge superstore. In this instance however, for once a club appears to have benefited from the interference of a chain-store which normally spells either a move to a remote concrete irrelevance or, at the very worst, extinction.

A 1930s view of the old Champion Hill ground.

Dulwich Hamlet have played in and around the Champion Hill area since their inception in 1893, following the cricket club members' decision to form a football club. A piece of ground in Woodwarde Road was used for practice games at the start of that season and as there were no facilities of any kind the players changed in the Reading Room in Dulwich Village carrying the posts and flags with them as they walked to the ground. The pitch often became unplayable and whenever possible pitches in Dulwich Park were sought.

After two seasons a new ground at College Farm in Burbage Road was used, but soon after Hamlet were on the move again to Sunray Avenue where they stayed for nine years.

For the 1902-03 season the club were in the enviable position of having two grounds, the reserves playing at Sunray Avenue whilst the senior side moved to the Freeman's ground in Champion Hill. During the summer of 1906 a stand was built capable of holding 250 people, all of whom paid a further 3d for the privilege of staying dry, and on the Constance Road side some three tiered standing boards, an early form of terracing, were laid down. It all proved short-lived, for in 1912 Hamlet moved to Champion Hill for the first time. By the start of the Great War there were dressing rooms and a stand at the ground which was barriered off all round and continued to be used all through the hos-

tilities. By 1919 new dressing rooms were constructed with a new pitch barrier, and rough terracing was cut into the banking around the ground. Between the wars crowds were huge, and to solve the considerable problem new seating was installed in the enclosure and the terracing on the north side was completed, with six more steps created opposite in 1920. A year later the covered accommodation was increased at the cost of £1,000 'in thanks to the club's loyal supporters who have stuck by them'.

By the late twenties the forward thinking committee had plans well in hand for a brand new ground close by capable of holding 20,000 or more, and as the thirties approached fund raising was under way and work had commenced to raise the ground level, create banking and lay paths. Even with this going on the club's old ground was still considered good enough to stage an Amateur Cup semi-final replay in 1929.

The new ground was finally ready in October 1931, and the Secretary of the FA Sir Frederick Wall performed the opening ceremony. A vast covered enclosure which held 2,000 and a seated stand which held 2,400 graced the new ground whose capacity was put at 30,000 and some 16,200 people saw the first game against Nunhead on the 10th of that month. The receipts from the first couple

of seasons meant further improvements were made, including increasing the banking, adding crush barriers and replacing the wooden fences around the pitch with iron railings. As the Second War came and went the halcyon days of regular five-figure crowds and Amateur Cup finals waned, although Champion Hill continued to be used for important representative matches.

It wasn't until 1964 that the next major structure went up, in the form of the clubhouse and six months later, on October 28th Chelsea came to officially switch on the floodlights in front of a crowd of 4,000. Throughout the next twenty years the massive terracing and end to end stand began to show signs of wear and tear. Part of the stand was condemned as unsafe as were large areas of the terrace which led to them being declared unusable. With gates down to a couple of hundred Champion Hill had become a millstone, and when the chance came to demolish the old girl and start again it was welcomed with open arms.

The new home has none of the characteristics of the previous grounds but is attractively designed with a capacity of 3,000, a far cry from the 20,500 that saw the 1933 Amateur Cup final, but quite adequate for the modern day.

The attractively designed new home of Dulwich Hamlet FC.

Middlesex and its borders

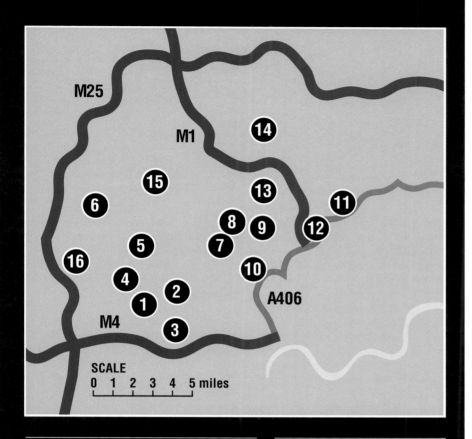

SCALE
0 1 2 3 4 5 miles

1	Hayes FC
2	Yeading FC
3	Southall FC
4	Hillingdon Borough FC
5	Ruislip Manor FC
6	Harefield United FC
7	Harrow Borough FC
8	Wealdstone FC
9	Kingsbury Town FC
10	Wembley FC
11	Finchley FC
12	Hendon FC
13	Edgware Town FC
14	Boreham Wood FC
15	Northwood FC
16	Uxbridge FC

Photos in this section by: Gavin Ellis-Neville, Richard Wall, Dean Walton and James Wright.

THE area around the M25 which is, in the main, in Middlesex has had its fair share of grief with Southall, Hillingdon Borough and Wealdstone all losing long established grounds within the last ten years. Both Edgware and Wembley have suffered serious fires and Harrow Borough have had their old stand condemned.

Middlesex is a contrasting county which is in many eyes more lazily referred to as London, and the grounds contrast greatly too. Southall's cavernous Western Road ground is now derelict whereas Boreham Wood and Yeading have both altered their compact little grounds, the latter to stage Southern League football courtesy of ground sharers Wealdstone. Edgware are the club's new landlords, but Southern League football will not come to the White Lion Ground as the Stones have switched across the pyramid to the Isthmian League.

CHURCH ROAD
Hayes FC

In 1942, the clubhouse at Church Road, Hayes suffered a direct hit during an air raid, which completely destroyed it, and the club's records to boot. As a result, pre-war information on the club tends to be somewhat sketchy. Certainly Hayes played from their formation in 1908 at a ground sited roughly where Pump Lane meets Station Road, at the end of Coldharbour Lane. This was known as Botwell Common, and the club were called Botwell Mission, not changing their name to Hayes FC until 1924.

The move to the new ground in Church Road, which was then known as Cox's Meadow came in 1920, and the *Middlesex and Bucks Advertiser* announced the opening by saying ".. a new ground has been secured by Botwell Mission for the coming season, which it is be hoped will be a great improvement on the old Coldharbour Lane enclosure. A pavilion is to be erected on the ground...

Below: The covered terrace at Hayes FC

and it is expected that an up to date enclosure will result."

Cox's Meadow opened on August 26th with a Whites v Stripes trial, and the first competitive match was against 2nd Scots Guards in the Great Western Suburban League.

The first structure of any significance was a grandstand, which was erected in 1925, shortly after the Mission became Hayes FC. The main stand now at the ground is primarily brick built and can seat 450, whereas the covered terrace opposite holds a further 1,000 or so. The banked ground was terraced slowly after the Second World War and has remained more or less unchanged since. Its development can be gauged by the record crowd which gathered for an Amateur Cup match in 1951 when 15,370 crammed onto the terraces to watch Hayes take on Bromley.

Western Road, Southall, is now a grim sight, but once held 20,000 people for an FA Cup tie.

THE WARREN
Yeading FC

The Warren finally opened after what seemed an eternity for the club, with a league game against Crown and Manor on September 22nd 1984.

It was as long ago as 1978 that talks first began with the Council to find a permanent home for the rising club, as they had spent the years since formation in 1961 on grounds at Brookside Recreation Ground until a move four years later to Warren Park. Briefly in 1976 the club were forced to play back at Brookside but eventually, after a long search, negotiations for a site in Beaconsfield Road began in 1981. Work took a year to complete and Yeading proudly displayed their new double decker clubhouse to coincide with gaining senior status.

The pitch was post and railed off and a stand erected down one side. The following year floodlights went up, and the switching on was celebrated against Tottenham Hotspur when 3,200 people saw the match, a record to this day.

Since then, Queens Park Rangers have used the ground for their Combination games and Wealdstone also shared the Warren before moving on to Edgware. Isthmian League football has meant changes and improvements, and a covered terrace

now stands behind the near goal while the original stand has had 250 seats installed. The Willie Barrett stand also provides shelter under the boardroom with the whole complex fenced off to a high standard. The floodlights of Southall's former Western Road ground are visible from the touchline which graphically illustrates how the fortunes of two neighbouring clubs can change so suddenly. Both have been to the FA Vase Final within the last ten years, and whereas The Warren goes from strength to strength, Western Road is merely going to seed, with the club playing home games two counties away.

WESTERN ROAD
Southall FC

The slow and painful demise of one of the biggest and most impressive of the post-Great War football grounds is one of the major sadnesses of the last few years amid the many evacuations affecting clubs all around the country. Whereas some grounds, now covered by superstores or houses are not especially mourned, others such as the Huish, St Joseph's Road and the Cross Keys most certainly are.

The problem with Western Road is that it

lingered on, slowly overtaken by vegetation and neglect until it became a huge anomaly amidst a sea of suburbia.

It is not known when football began at the ground, but is widely accepted that the boom time for club and ground was in the twenties and thirties, when success in Amateur Cup and Athenian League led to massive support. The ground changed in size and shape in the mid thirties when the club merged with Park Royal, and many of the new players were skilled labourers who set about creating the vast concrete terracing on what until then had been substantial grass banks. A wooden grandstand was built on the far side with changing rooms, and such was the success of the work and the size of the ground, that when Watford journeyed for an FA Cup Third Round tie in 1936, it attracted a crowd of between 17,000 and 20,000 .

The grandstand was eventually gutted by fire, and a new stand with dressing rooms underneath was built on the opposite side. But Southall suffered from a severe lack of interest other than for one special season which culminated in a visit to Wembley for the FA Vase Final.

The last season at Western Road was spent with the reserves, and anybody else who fancied it, using the ground which by this stage was weed-strewn and the fencing dilapidated. The first team had moved to Harefield, and on latterly to Tring Town, abandoning Western Road to the inevitable fate of more housing in what is already a densely populated area.

The shift to a predominantly Asian population traditionally not a football orientated group, may have had an effect, but in truth the club suffered from a decline in interest which is mirrored in most areas. It is only a shame that such a vast ground is not now in the Council hands as a hockey centre. Making full use of the vast terracing would be infinitely preferable to yet more housing.

Yeading's Warren.

MIDDLESEX STADIUM
Hillingdon Borough FC, Ruislip Town FC, Ruislip FC, Bromley Park Rangers FC

The name of Hillingdon Borough often seems as historic as Clapton and Corinthian Casuals, when one recalls their Cup exploits and FA Trophy final in 1971.

However, the name graced football circles for less than 20 years, the club playing at their Leas Stadium home from 1954 to 1963 as Yiewsley and eventually in 1983 as Hillingdon F.C., until their demise with the sudden and over-hasty sale and eventual demolition of the Leas in 1987.

Until 1954, Yiewsley played on a ground close by, called Evelyns. The Leas Stadium site was a rubbish tip and was turned into an impressive football ground through finance provided by the club chairman of the time.

At its end it still boasted a capacity of around 14,000, with 1,000 seats and cover for 8-9,000, with a clubhouse and car-park used latterly as a lorry park. The record gate at the Leas was over 9,000 for the FA Cup tie against Luton Town. In what appears to be a desperate effort to stay alive, the club merged with Burnham F.C. in the Southern League, but the name was soon deleted from the front of the programme.

A few miles away in Ruislip, a small club named Ruislip Town had scratched about in various leagues including the Hellenic and were struggling in the Middlesex League when an ambitious

project took off on the field next door, as Lovell Homes built a brand new ground with banking on two sides, a seated stand and a large clubhouse as part of a housing deal on Brakespeare Road. The suddenly-revived Ruislip dropped the Town and entered the Southern League, hopping over the fence and abandoning the old ground.

It was not a success and soon financial problems engulfed the set-up, and a merger took place with Bromley Park Rangers enabling a new board to take over. This was also short-lived, and when the vast majority of the new people left, football again had a bleak future at the grandly named Middlesex Stadium.

On the arrival of a new benefactor, the club were re-incarnated yet again as Hillingdon Borough. The club's playing side has revived in the Spartan League and they remain at the neat, if a touch barren, ground.

Next door, the former home remains with the goals now around six foot high rather than the conventional eight foot. The weed infested car-park, changing rooms, clubhouse, and store-rooms all in various states of decay, stand quietly by as if with an ear cocked to the comings and goings next door. The original driveway into the ground, which once had a bright welcome board, is gated and overgrown. More recently, the pitch on the new ground has been turned around, so the concrete stand is now situated on a bank behind one goal.

The name of Hillingdon Borough has risen, fallen, and been resurrected. Ruislip however, have done the precise opposite.

GROSVENOR VALE
Ruislip Manor FC

The Manor are a marvellous example of how a club can utilise assets to the full, without losing the essential ingredient of a homely ground.

The entrance, at the end of a cul-de-sac, set amongst a huge post-war housing scheme doesn't inspire confidence, but once through the new brick-built gateway into the ground, the almost rustic charm of the place is easy to appreciate.

A group of large wooden sheds seemingly bonded together with 6ft panel fences, are clustered around the entrance, and house the changing rooms. A further shed stands, complete with overhang and leaning posts, the plaque on it reading "This shelter was erect-

ed by the Supporters' Club for the comfort of their patrons." This group of buildings appear to date from before the war but was in fact built in the early sixties.

On the far side, the main stand, a wobbly looking structure made of corrugated iron and wood, continues to defy the elements and provide more 'comfort for the patrons'. It is to be hoped that is so for a long time to come, as to replace it with a more solid but soulless building would be very sad. The clubhouse, situated in the car-park, is tight against the ground and another overhang, giving cover to extra seating, protrudes from it. The far end of the ground is enclosed by a concrete outer wall, with the pitch enclosed by a smart new wooden fence.

In the far corner of the ground is surely one of the most unusual buildings to be seen

in sporting circles. A Second World War gun turret, huge, bleak and brooding, stands, still guarding Northolt Aerodrome as it has done for 50 odd years. In those intervening times a massive housing estate has been built between it and the R.A.F. site, but the turret remains and it seems always will. In past times it has been used as dressing room, and tea-bar, as well as a courtesy area for officials but for the present remains dormant.

The club originally played on a ground in Sidmouth Drive, a stone's throw away, but after the war moved to Grosvenor Vale and soon segregated the playing area from the rest of the park. The record crowd to date is for an FA Amateur Cup tie with Tooting and Mitcham United in 1962 when over 2,000 attended.

EARLSMEAD
Harrow Borough FC

Harrow Borough were formed, as Roxonian FC in 1933 and played their first match on 9th September at a new ground on the Earlsmead Estate, fronting onto Northolt Road. The ground had a pavilion, the materials for which were provided free by a local builder, a former player with the defunct Roxeth United. Members of the new club erected the pavilion themselves and the ground was opened and the club flag hoisted by the Rev. E. Stogdon.

The club had been in residence less than four months when informed the ground would have to be relinquished at the end of the season and they would have to move to another part of the estate. The second ground was priced at £1,625, which included provi-

PRESTON PARK
Harefield United FC

Harefield, near the famous hospital, is possibly the most rural of all the villages in the old County of Middlesex, being within a mile or so of both Buckinghamshire and Hertfordshire. It once boasted two clubs, North Harefield, who until 1976 played in the Middlesex League on an enclosed ground which was eventually turned into a show jumping arena, and Harefield United.

The Hares played from 1930 on an open field called Taylor's Meadow, which is still used for football today, before moving to their new ground in Brakespeare Road in 1963, in time for their move to the Parthenon League.

They have been there ever since, building a small shelter which was furnished with portable chairs and laying down post and rails and later floodlighting as they went through the Middlesex and Athenian Leagues up to the Isthmian League.

Harefield played in the last ever Athenian League game, the League Cup Final at Berkhamsted against Wolverton Town, before joining the expanded Isthmians where their ground has been improved with exterior fencing and a further small stand opposite the original.

LOWER MEAD
Wealdstone FC

Wealdstone have gone from the absolute peak of non-League football, achieving the double of Alliance League and FA Trophy in 1985 to the sadness of suffering two relegations, followed by a voluntary drop into Division Three of the Isthmian League ten years later. But the hardest pill to swallow for their vociferous supporters was the loss of Lower Mead in 1991 to yet another Tesco superstore, with all the subsequent financial chaos which ensued thereafter.

The Stones have since played at Vicarage Road, Watford and the Warren at Yeading before moving in 1995 to Edgware, but with little immediate chance of a new ground of their own. Lower Mead has become history. It was not one of the prettiest football grounds, shoe-horned into a space behind a row of shops and a cinema with little car-parking, but it had character and atmosphere by the bucket load.

The area around the ground was entirely different 75 years ago when Lower Mead was opened, as it was rural land behind a farm and much bigger than its modern shape. The first building was a small wooden stand, placed where the open terrace was laid after the war, and and dressing rooms soon followed at the near end. Opposite, a timber terraced area was dedicated to an old clubman and named the Elmslie End, and this was later covered, as was the Cinema End during the sixties. The large open terrace to the north was created after the war when the land behind it was sold for housing. Opposite was the seated stand purchased in 1928 which survived until the ground's sad demise. It originally stood at Summerstown FC until they were forced to fold, and gave sterling service to the end.

Lower Mead saw some startling crowds, its banked terrace giving access to 13,500 for an Amateur Cup match against Leytonstone in 1949. Today, a couple of hundred amble around the frozen food counter where the pitch once was, while another couple of hundred still fervently support the Stones at their new but temporary home in Edgware.

sion for a football pitch, two cricket teams, and a quarter mile cinder track in addition to tennis courts and a pavilion. An appeal was set up to try to raise funds for this mammoth project.

Within nine months Roxonian moved to the new ground in Carlyon Avenue, on the site that Harrow Borough now occupy. A new pavilion was started with an all-round verandah, dressing rooms, baths and showers, a kitchen and lounge. The first game on the new ground was a practice match on 18th August 1934 with a Spartan League game the week after. By 1938 the purchase of the site was complete, as was the pavilion, described as "the best of its kind in the neighbourhood."

At the AGM for that season the club was re-named Harrow Town, and it was announced that surveying had begun for the rest of the proposed amenities. Already several tons of earth had been dumped at the

pitch side to create banking for the spectators, and soon after a fine covered stand was presented to the club by a member of the Champniss family who were local landowners in the area. The new stand had seating for 250, with standing room for 100. Indeed the fine old stand is still holding court the best part of sixty years later. In its infancy it regularly saw crowds of 2,000 at Earlsmead, but now it is deemed not adequate for crowds of 300 in the Isthmian League.

The club continued to play friendlies throughout the war, and indeed just prior to it further work was done to drain the pitch, and more dressing rooms were added. September 1948 saw the Supporters' Club granted a licence to build a steel and concrete pavilion for indoor training, the cost of which was borne by themselves, and in 1950 more cover was erected.

In 1965 the club President announced that the club's facilities were "an embarrass-

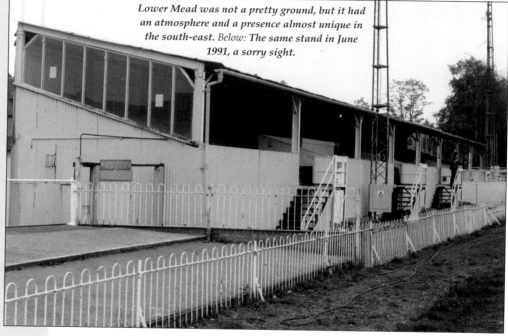

Lower Mead was not a pretty ground, but it had an atmosphere and a presence almost unique in the south-east. Below: The same stand in June 1991, a sorry sight.

ment and a bad image for the Borough of Harrow". He also announced another change of name, this time to Harrow Borough. The main pitch was moved and levelled in 1969, and concrete posts and steel tubing surrounded the pitch. The ground remained relatively untouched until a deal was struck in 1974 between the football club and the council, whereby the area at the lower end of the ground which contained the second pitch would be sold off. The funds were then used to redevelop Earlsmead to an approximation of what it is now. All matches were played away that year whilst work went on to erect floodlights, concrete terrace all four sides of the ground with one and a half sides covered, plus a fine new clubhouse behind the goal.

Happily the stand, and the Anderson shelter next to it remained amongst all the newness. The ground re-opened for the start of the 1974-75 season, and since then extensions have been built onto the car-park, and the Anderson shelter has lost its roof to the Lord Justice Taylor report.

With the sad demise of Lower Mead, Earlsmead has become the premier football ground in the area, although with the freshness of the twenty year old alterations now well and truly gone, as is the old main stand, it has a character hard to define in a heavily urbanised district such as South Harrow.

Summers Lane, Finchley, showing the dual purpose stand. Much work has rejuvenated the old ground in the last year.

BILL MASTERS STADIUM, SUMMERS LANE
Wingate and Finchley FC

Finchley Football Club was formed in 1874 when it had its headquarters and changing rooms at the Railway Hotel in Ballards Lane. A selection of pitches were rented at the time in Long Lane which remained the club's home for some ten years until they moved to a well-appointed ground at the back of the Green Man pub in Whetstone.

This was home for a further ten years until their next move to the Woodhouse Lane ground, which was on the corner of Woodhouse Lane and the Great North Road. The changing rooms were then at the Park Hotel, later known as the Tallyho Hotel. In 1899 the club moved again, this time to a new ground at the Swan and Pyramids, playing their first game on 19th September.

It is documented that this ground had wooden palings enclosing the pitch but it only lasted two years as it was required for building land and again the club moved on, this time to Cobleys Farm, on the corner of the Great North Road and Granville Road, close to Finchley Memorial Hospital. This ground was known as Fallow Corner and was home for just one season before a move up the road to a pitch just to the north, also known as Fallow Corner, and on the edge of Cobley's Farm. This historic place is where Charles Dickens lodged in 1843 before writing Martin Chuzzlewit. Many years later part of the ground was incorporated into the Holloway Grammar School sports ground.

Fallow Corner remained home until the First World War when the club closed down, and when football restarted it was no longer available. It was not until June 1921 that a ground was finally located for the club by the Council and the team re-formed. Long Hill was home for a season until the club moved to Gun Station Meadow, former home of Saracens Rugby Club. This was by far the most advanced ground on which the club had played and boasted wooden huts left

SILVER JUBILEE PARK
Kingsbury Town FC

The surprisingly rural home of Kingsbury Town is like an oasis in a sea of urbanisation deep in Metroland. The Silver Jubilee Park stretches all around the playing area which is fenced or hedged off and has all of its facilities along one side.

It is not known precisely when the club first moved to the ground but it is believed to have been shortly after the Second World War as the area was used as an anti-aircraft station and the Nissen huts left over were used for changing in until one of them burnt down.

The ground itself had a small amount of cover which eventually blew down in the seventies and was subsequently rebuilt and lengthened in 1978. Partially behind the stand which now has 200 seats, is the brick built clubhouse, around thirty years old and the focal point of the ground.

The playing surface is enclosed by a post and rail which since Isthmian League insistence decreed so, is infilled by a rather ugly red fence. Behind it, the grassy banks are sufficiently sloped to have allowed a crowd of 1,500 plus to watch a friendly with Tottenham Hotspur in 1980 which remains the ground attendance record and quite possibly helped to finance the erecting of the floodlights which went up the following year.

Silver Jubilee Park, Kingsbury.

behind after the war with an old copper boiler for the bath. There was a large wooden stand with seating and a hedge bordering the ground and the main road. For an FA Cup tie in the early twenties, the club obtained some old aircraft wings and corrugated sheeting which secured the hedge and prevented free entry. The Gun Meadow remained home until 1929 when, with promotion back to the Athenian League, work began at Summers Lane.

The ground was part of land bought from the Ecclesiastical Commissioners and some 60 acres had been turned into sports fields. The concrete stand was opened on December 20th 1930, some two years before the ground itself was declared open. It had nearly 600 seats and presided over the football, yet within a year had been converted to a two-sided stand to accommodate rugby on the adjoining ground - a task it still performs to this day. Summers Lane began hosting all

manner of events such as boxing, baseball and summer fetes and soon major cup finals and representative matches were held there in front of crowds of 4,000 and 5,000. The ground record was broken in 1950 when Bishop Auckland came to town in the quarter-final of the FA Amateur Cup and 9,555 crammed in to watch the Finches go out. Two years later Crystal Palace were the visitors for an FA Cup tie which officially attracted 7,000 although many got in free, which may well have swelled the crowd to 10,000.

The banking around the ground was soon turned into terracing and by 1960 it was complete with new entrances, all financed by the thriving Supporters' Club. Two years later West Ham United were the visitors when on October 10th 1962 the floodlights were switched on at Summers Lane. The ground has since undergone a couple of name changes, not least since the merger with Wingate FC which brought about the

Wingate-Leyton Stadium, the Abrahams Stadium and latterly the Bill Masters Stadium. In recent times it has undergone something of a facelift with the pitch moved nearer the stand and a new rail system installed. The lights have been upgraded and an all weather pitch, weight training room and new bar have given the place a fresh lease of life.

WHITE LION GROUND
Edgware Town FC

The White Lion Ground has been staging Isthmian League football every week from August 1995 since Wealdstone moved in to share, ending a nomadic temporary trail via Vicarage Road and Yeading forced by the demise of their own Lower Mead.

Edgware Town (or just Edgware as they once were) have played at the ground from their first days just prior to the Second World

The main stand at Vale Farm in 1986. Fire destroyed it six years later.

Fire wrecks stand

THOUSANDS of pounds worth of damage was caused to the Wembley FC ground at Vale Farm on Tuesday when a mystery fire destroyed the club's 240-seater stand just before 4pm.

Fire crews, who had to smash through the club's locked metal gates, quickly brought the blaze under control after it spread to the nearby clubhouse and changing rooms.

Harrow fire chief, David Bonner, said the dry weather and brisk wind helped drive the fire towards the clubhouse.

He said: "We don't know how the fire started. It quickly spread across the roof of the clubhouse, mainly because the stands were constructed of timber and it's very dry and the fire had a bit of a wind behind it."

Club vice chairman, Eric Stringer, said "The officers said there could be suspicious circumstances surrounding the fire, but who the hell would want to do anything like this?"

Fire investigators are probing the cause of the blaze.

War. It is believed that the ground belonged to Moss Bros. and was initially destined to be a rugby ground but, following the full resumption of sport after the war, it quickly became popular for football in the Corinthian League. The grandstand, which burned down in the early 1980's dated from around 1946 and the banked areas were also in place when the record crowd at the White Lion of 8,500 saw an FA Cup tie, ironically against Wealdstone. Club histories state the date as 1948 but the clubs met in 1948 and 1949, both times at White Lion, so it's one or the other! The terracing opposite the main stand was covered around this time and the area behind the goal nearest the pub was also terraced, although in later years it reverted to grass banking, until new hard surfaces were demanded by the ground gradings.

For many years during the seventies the place decayed and in 1982 the old stand burnt to the ground. The replacement is of an identical size, as per the insurers' demands, and has seating for 220 with the cover opposite holding around 1,000. Recent times have seen a change of fortunes, and with Wealdstone in residence as well, 1995-96 could be a lively season at the White Lion.

The Grounds of Hendon FC

Thanks to sterling work by clubman Graham Etchell, the story of Hendon Football Club's homes is well documented.

Formed as Hampstead Town in 1908, they began playing at the grandly named National Athletic Stadium in College Road, Kensal Rise. It had been in existence since 1890 and was the home of Queens Park Rangers for two spells around the turn of the century. The club initially attempted to buy the ground, which had a pavilion on one side, but failed although they still planned to erect an uncovered stand opposite. They left in April 1901 but were back the following year paying a staggering £240 per annum rent. This should not have been a major problem to a club that had attracted an attendance of 15,000 but it still proved too much and they moved on again to Park Royal.

Hampstead did not move in until some three years later and it is not established whether they played on the main pitch which was equipped with grass banking all around, or whether a secondary pitch was in use. Certainly no junior club at the time needed a ground of that size, nor indeed could they afford the rent, although it is known that the owners, All Saints College, wanted the Council to take over the running

WEMBLEY FOOTBALL
& ATHLETIC CLUB   No. A
MANY THANKS FOR YOUR
DONATION OF
3D
GROUND   TOWARDS OUR
IMPROVE
FUND

Farm with new lights in 1981, a concrete walk-way five years later and new pitch railings in 1987. One negative note was the removal of the picturesque trees following Dutch-elm disease in 1977. This, together with the demolition of the nursery and tennis courts, since replaced by an indoor leisure centre and traffic proficiency centre has meant the perimeter of the ground has changed as much as the interior.

A 30 year lease was secured and the club appeared to be stable until a fire threatened the whole club's existence. The blaze gutted the main stand while the covered terrace on the Wasp's side was condemned as unsafe to further increase problems. The two stands had provided cover for 40 years and the club were suddenly left with none at all.

Fortune, however favoured the club and a local builder Mr Brian Gumm, the club chairman, worked tirelessly to re-build the ground. The remaining terrace was raised and covered with a new roof, beneath which 450 seats were added. The old main stand site was concreted over and the work completed in just four months. Prior to the 1993-94 season new toilets, turnstiles and a tea bar were constructed in the near corner of the ground, which has only bits of terrace plus the Ron Clarke Memorial Gate as remnants of the development work in the 1950's

During the 1995 close season, with extra turnstiles required and a boundary fence needed, yet more renovations went ahead, the most interesting being the installation of a bank of former British Rail ticket booths as turnstiles.

VALE FARM
Wembley FC

Wembley FC was formed in 1946 when two local junior sides, Sudbury Ratepayers Association and Sudbury Rangers amalgamated, and began playing in the Middlesex League on an unfenced roped off pitch at Vale Farm, an area purchased by Wembley Urban District Council for recreational purposes back in 1928.

Tall elm trees bordered one side of the pitch and in the far corner behind the goal was a tennis court. The remainder of the playing field backed onto housing although the area behind the other goal near the main entrance was open and later became a nursery. A wooden pavilion, near the entrance housed the dressing rooms. Due to cricket, the club had to vacate the premises promptly at the end of the season and any remaining home games were played at the Glacier Sports Ground two miles away in Alperton. As a result a petition was presented to the council for an enclosed ground.

It was suggested that Wembley should share Vale Farm with the Borough's other senior club Kingsbury Town, but they withdrew from the plan and eventually the council relented and offered a three year lease from October 1948 at a rent of £400. With the ground enclosed, the club were now able to take a gate but their future was never assured and the turning point finally came in 1951 when the lease came up for renewal

At first the council attempted to raise the rent to an exorbitant level, but in protest the officials of the club prepared and presented a document outlining the club's ambitions which impressed the powers that be to such an extent they offered the club a 21 year lease with the option to develop the ground. They wasted no time and terracing and a small enclosure were erected on the Wasp's side of the ground for the start of the 1951-2 season, along with grassed embankments around the pitch. On New Year's Day 1955, the first section of the elevated wooden main stand was opened, and over £1,000 was spent replacing the small enclosure with covered accommodation which ran from one penalty area to the other. This stand was opened with a game against Grays Athletic on 18th August 1956.

The following season the pitch was properly enclosed and railed off, the main stand was doubled in size, and more terrace was laid down in front of the pavilion. The funding for these improvements came from the Supporters' Club and also the Chairman, as well as via gate money from crowds which regularly passed the 1,000 mark, with the record gate posted against Wealdstone in the London Senior Cup in January 1953.

In 1961 the pavilion was re-vamped, with the bar and dressing-rooms also improved, and as the club progressed floodlights were used for the first time on the 16th March during a game against Erith and Belvedere. To celebrate the club's 21st anniversary a new clubhouse was built adjacent to the main stand with part of the pavilion being demolished, and a larger entrance provided. A small hut was also put up for visiting guests which later became a tea hut but is now a storeroom.

On the playing front during the late 60's and early 70's the club struggled and when the Isthmian League expanded, Wembley failed in their bid for election. However, the club were determined to press on and with financial aid from Brent Council, the old dressing-rooms were demolished and a new £20,000 complex was built behind the main stand in 1974. Election to the Isthmian finally arrived in 1975. More changes came at Vale

Above: An excellent view of Hendon's Claremont Road ground. The exterior has changed considerably although inside, happily, it is virtually untouched.

Right: The only known picture in existence of Hendon's former Farm Avenue ground.

of the ground, which at first did not happen, although may well have done later.

The ground was used by Hampstead until 1912, when they moved to the new Avenue Ground. Kensal Rise was again used briefly by Queens Park Rangers during the Great War when the Army took over their ground in Park Royal but by 1917 it had been turned into allotments for the War effort and by 1921 was housed over.

Today, the entrance to the ground is covered by numbers 78, 80 and 82 College Road with 72-86 Liddell Gardens now built where the pavilion was, while part of Clifford Gardens stands on the site of another entrance and pathway which led from the railway station.

The Avenue ground was located five minutes drive from Claremont Road and was built on land belonging to a Mr Dickers who owned Cowenlaw Farm. It was surrounded by tennis courts and had an entrance from Cricklewood Lane with one side running parallel with Farm Avenue. Town opened the ground on Saturday September 21st when

they beat local rivals Kilburn in a London League game. It is known there was a stand on the ground and that Civil Service FC also used the pitch for Isthmian League games.

On May 7th 1926 the club were told that the Hendon UDC had offered the club a piece of land for an annual rent of £255 per year. By June of that year work had already begun on the new stadium which covered four and a half acres of grass land that once formed part of Clitterhouse Farm. The farm house and outbuildings have, remarkably, survived, the former now converted into flats and the latter used for storage by the council.

William Harbrow Ltd constructed the stand with glass screen ends for possible extension at a later date. Nearly seventy years later the stand is virtually unchanged, with most of the original bench seats only being replaced with bucket seats from Vicarage Road, Watford in 1993 which reduced the capacity to 387. The dressing

rooms are under the stand along with the physio room which was originally a hospitality area.

As the new ground took shape a wood paling fence surrounded the pitch and a six foot high fence went around it. The pavilion at the Avenue Ground was transported to Claremont Road and the interior modernised, while soon after the massive covered terrace was built and named the Gordon Raymond Stand in memory of the club chairman who was mainly responsible for it. Until the Second World War the old club name of Golders Green, as the club had been known since 1933, was painted on the roof but was removed when classed as a landmark to enemy bombers. The banking was terraced with railway sleepers and Claremont Road was officially opened on Saturday September 18th before an FA Cup tie with Berkhamsted. The attendance was almost 3,500, paying receipts of £83 17s.

Gradually the banking was converted into concrete terracing and much later a wooden hut for supporters was replaced by a brick built one behind the southern end. This is now used to store pitch equipment. The tea bar and supporters' club shop stand on what was the old wooden clubhouse, demolished when a modern version was built just outside the ground.

The first floodlighting system at the ground was switched on when Wolverhampton Wanderers visited Hendon on September 25th 1962, attracting a crowd of 4,500. The match programme talked of how the four high level towers would alleviate the problems caused to players losing the ball in the glare given out by lights set lower and facing each other across the ground. The first match under them was actually a week earlier for a Mithras Cup game against Finchley.

The original pylons still stand although eight lamps now power the system which was upgraded in 1971 and again celebrated with a match, this time against Luton Town on October 4th.

Claremont Road has seen gates of 3,000 plus for Rugby League and Gaelic Football matches in recent years, but the highest recorded attendance for football is the 9,000 who watched the FA Cup 1st Round tie with Northampton Town in 1952. Despite the current capacity of 8,000 with over 5,000 under cover that record will probably now stand for ever.

Left: Northwood's new stand under construction.

M25 North East

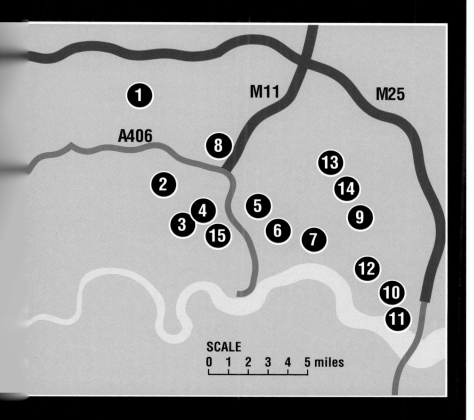

M11

M25

A406

① ⑧ ⑬ ⑭ ② ⑤ ⑨ ④ ③ ⑮ ⑥ ⑦ ⑫ ⑩ ⑪

SCALE
0 1 2 3 4 5 miles

THE AREA covered by north-east London and parts of Essex is a veritable football graveyard of once famous non-League sides with grounds to match.

Romford, Ilford, Walthamstow Avenue, Leytonstone, Barking, Rainham, and very soon, Leyton, have all seen famous old grounds swept away by either financial misfortune, lack of interest or simply old fashioned asset stripping. Woodford Town's old Snakes Lane ground was unused for some time when the club went under, but a new club called Woodford FC now play there in the Spartan League.

A brief rundown of the grounds that have disappeared from the map during the last twenty years makes depressing reading indeed.

GREEN POND ROAD
Walthamstow Avenue FC

When over-run by the Leytonstone juggernaut in 1989, Green Pond Road was consigned to the same file that contained Ilford and would also ultimately list Dagenham and Redbridge Forest.

The ground was impressive to the end, with covered terracing on all sides with the 900 seater stand dominating. The capacity of around 10,000 was only just short of the record attendance which saw the FA Cup tie with Stockport County in 1939, when 12,500 turned up.

The Avenue's proud history should never have been allowed to fade away as it

1	Enfield FC
2	Walthamstow Avenue FC
3	Leyton FC
4	Leytonstone FC
5	Ilford FC
6	Barking FC
7	Dagenham & Redbridge FC
8	Woodford Town FC
9	Hornchurch FC
10	Aveley FC
11	Purfleet FC
12	Rainham Town FC
13	Collier Row FC
14	Romford FC
15	Clapton FC

Green Pond Road at its opening in 1921.

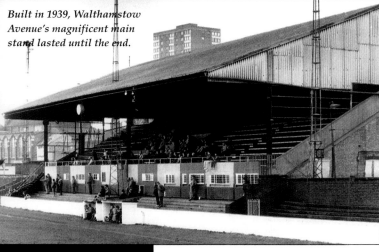

Built in 1939, Walthamstow Avenue's magnificent main stand lasted until the end.

did, first smothered by a club with money and no ground and then by developers who wiped it away for housing.

Walthamstow Avenue Football Club was formed out of the Pretoria Avenue school team which stayed together when they left and played as Pretoria Avenue OB's and then Avenue United before becoming Walthamstow Avenue in 1903. They played on a pitch within the Barclay Estate in Whipps Cross and then in Lloyd Park for a number of years before the Great War. With the limited number of grounds available, Avenue gladly accepted a ground-share deal with Walthamstow Grange before, in 1920, they were given a rough field with a stream running through it which had formerly been allotments in Green Pond Road.

Appeals were launched in an effort to buy the land, and due mainly to a bakery owner who loaned the club £400, it was bought freehold for £625.

First the ground was enclosed by a six foot fence and pipes were laid by the council to divert the stream. Players and supporters worked to lay hundreds of tons of clinker, hard core, soil, sand and top dressing and after weeks of work, the ground was opened on December 21st 1921. It had a sizeable wooden stand with a clubhouse for training and social purposes at the back, and was post and wired off. There were dressing rooms with baths and the crowds soon flocked as 3,000 saw the first league game against Slough. Green Pond Road slowly was

banked up with sleeper terracing during the twenties and thirties and reached a peak in 1938 when the club achieved an FA Cup Second Round replay against Stockport County which attracted 12,500. It was the last big game at Walthamstow before fire swept through the ground destroying the clubhouse and stand. Again club men got to work and the new grandstand which survived to the end and could seat close on 1,000 people, was opened on August 26th 1939 by Stanley Rous. It was 40 feet high, 135 feet long and had a members' enclosure as well as one for VIP's. There was a new club room, twice the size of the old, two large dressing rooms, a referee's room, secretary's office, board room and Supporters' Club. The whole lot cost a staggering £6,000.

The club played through the war years and in the fifties the terracing and improving of the ground began again, with the covered areas, set back from the pitch, put into place. Some 6,000 people could be covered at the ground, but much of it began to show its age and as interest waned, as indeed it did throughout football in the sixties and seventies, then the old place became unwieldy, and when Leytonstone and Ilford came in to ground-share with the struggling club, its demise was perhaps then only a matter of time.

BROOKLANDS
Romford FC

Brooklands is without question one of the most talked about lost grounds of the post-war era, still lamented by those who visited it and even those who did not. Romford FC had use of the ground from 1929 until its demise in April 1977 in desperate circumstances. Although it didn't in the end reach its projected goal of a 40,000 capacity, it saw a crowd of close to half that figure in 1951 before it was fully developed.

Various clubs existed in Romford before the Great War including the original Romford FC who played on a pitch at Great Mawneys. Victoria played on a pitch at Brooklands when it was part of a much larger sports set up with hockey, cricket and tennis. In 1929 the new club took over Brooklands and enclosed one pitch which was turned 45 degrees, and then built a small seated stand with the opposite side opening out on to a cricket pitch. Just prior to the Second World War the ground was fully enclosed and banking was formed all around with a covered area opposite the grandstand while after the war a further area of cover went up.

The grass banking was large enough to accommodate 18,237 in 1951 when Southall visited for an FA Amateur Cup match and when it was eventually concreted all around and the impressive 1,500 seater brick built main stand went up, the capacity rose to around 25,000.

Despite this Brooklands was living on borrowed time and, with massive debts, the club were forced to sell in 1975. The money raised did not allow the club to proceed with the proposed new site at Oldchurch Park and despite firstly attempting to re-erect the stand at the new site and then offering it to Dagenham FC for sale the whole thing fell through and Havering Council withdrew the offer of the site. The last game was played at Brooklands in April 1977, ironically between Hornchurch, whose Athletics track ground was unavailable on the day, and Chesham.

There has since been a club by the same name playing relatively successfully in the Essex Senior League on the very ground that was unavailable when the last game was played at Brooklands, namely Hornchurch.

GRANLEIGH ROAD
Leytonstone FC

Granleigh Road football ground disappeared in 1986 when the home club moved off to engulf Walthamstow Avenue at Green Pond Road. It was one of the most compact grounds in the south, tucked almost underneath a high level railway station and squashed against gardens which in effect rendered it a three-sided ground.

It was first used in 1894 and was home until April 1986, which was the club's centenary year. They too had success in the FA Amateur Cup, winning it for the third time in 1968 at Wembley, but it was in the FA Cup that the Stones posted their all time record crowd of 10,500, against Newport County in 1951. To those who watched football at Granleigh Road, it seems incredible that such a crowd could assemble at such a cramped venue, but the terracing which stretched behind both goals and in front of the grandstand was deceptively spacious.

Within a year the site had been cleared and a small complex of housing now gives no hint it was ever a ground at all.

LYNN ROAD
Ilford FC

Ilford were the first to be taken over, amalgamating with Leytonstone in 1979 having played at Granleigh Road for two seasons when their proposed ambitious new complex near Barkingside failed to materialise.

Their history was as impressive as that of the Avenue, with Amateur Cup Finals and Isthmian League championships, and their old ground was well kept too, having been home since around 1903. It had a large 1,000 seater stand with a paddock in front which was covered by a peculiar extended roof to the stand, and its banked surrounds were partly terraced with one end covered as well as part of the side opposite the stand. When forced to vacate, the ground fell into disrepair and was eventually built on, with no trace left of what once was a venue which could hold 10,000 spectators.

MAYESBROOK PARK
Barking FC

Barking Football Club has existed in various forms since 1880, which is the present club's official formation year. Barking Rovers first used the town's name in their title, playing matches on the Vicarage Field until forced to vacate it after damage to the cricket square. Shortly after, they folded, but almost immediately a new club, Barking Woodville were founded, and although successful, they too folded shortly afterwards.

The old Vicarage Fields ground at Barking.

SUNGOLD
Collier Row FC

The village of Collier Row in Essex, although so close to the East London sprawl has somehow managed to maintain a semblance of its rural identity and as a a result the ground overlooks some pleasant countryside. Sungold is typical of so many Isthmian League grounds which have their perimeters fenced in by garish corrugated sheeting courtesy of the league's insistence on fully enclosed grounds.

Although the ends are bordered by a nursery and a car lot, the far side has a pristine wall with fir trees behind. These replaced a line of mature elms which had given the ground a more rustic feel until disease hastened their demise. A primitive form of floodlighting once hung suspended in the trees, draped around them for training purposes back in the fifties.

The site was bought by the club as a farmer's field in 1948 when they moved from their previous ground in White Hart Lane in the village. At first it was nothing more than an open field with a railway carriage for dressing rooms and baths placed outside. Later a wooden pavilion was built but destroyed by fire in the fifties and the club were forced to rebuild, making their own bricks in the process. The new pavilion has since been incorporated into the modern version which opened 20 years ago and being on a higher level to the playing surface dominates the ground. Entry into the Isthmian League saw the building of the seated stand on the far side, which contains seats rescued from a cinema at Butlin's in Clacton. There is a tale they were originally once part of the old ocean liner Queen Mary, but that may be just legend. What is true, however, is that the pitch was grazed by cattle until the 1970's when a goat took over the job, and injury was often risked before matches by courageous clubmen forced to move the beast which had an alarming tendency to attack and butt people rather than be disturbed! Discretion being the better part of valour, the goat was finally dispensed with and the pitch is now tended in the conventional manner.

Towards the end of the century a team known as Barking Working Men's Institute appeared and they too quickly won recognition, eventually winning the London Senior Cup in 1912. In 1919 the club became known as Barking Town, and Vicarage Field was the scene of much success, until circumstances forced them to vacate and move to a purpose-built ground on the edge of Mayesbrook Park, an open space surrounded by dense housing.

Today, the ground is not wildly different from its beginnings 20 years ago, with a long low covered seated stand down one side, with the other three sides open standing. Behind the near goal is the clubhouse, which houses the Cockatoo Disco, with a car-park behind. In the early days of Mayesbrook Park, new visitors often took a detour in the town to try and catch a glimpse of the old ground, which stood alone and forlorn for many years. It was heavily fortified and only by balancing precariously on dustbins or car-roofs was it possible to pay last respects.

It would be difficult to find a more centralised ground than the old Vicarage Field, just across the road from the railway station and between the town's two main shopping streets. Rail travellers could not miss seeing the faded letters of Barking Football Club on the back of the covered terrace, opposite the main stand. The entrance, just big enough for a visiting team coach,was at the end of a

Mayesbrook Park, Barking.

driveway adjacent to the library. The dressing rooms and social club were housed under the main stand which straddled the half-way line on the town side, and the other three sides consisted of concrete terrace with rather unkempt grass beyond. After remaining sadly derelict for some years, it was finally put out of its misery when the Vicarage Field Shopping Centre was built on the site.

VICTORIA ROAD
Dagenham & Redbridge FC

Dagenham and Redbridge is the latest configuration to come out of the take over saga, playing at the Victoria Road home of the old Dagenham FC. They were not the first to use the ground, however, for Brigg Sports played there until 1955.

Deri Park (seen here and below) is now in a sorry state.

DERI PARK
Rainham Town FC

Deri Park died as a football ground some three years before Rainham Town FC conceded defeat in 1994. It succumbed to the worst elements and is now a dreadfully vandalised, overgrown bomb site, where what cannot be stolen has been destroyed and what cannot be ripped apart has been set alight.

Deri Park was built during the post-war boom time and was as old as the club itself. It had a corrugated asbestos and concrete stand with bench seating and a low covered standing area opposite. A concrete wall surrounded the pitch with a post and rail in front and this was reached down a track between houses, a factor that put paid to any hopes of selling the land for development, as it would mean relocating neighbouring dwellings to build a wide enough access road for contractors' vehicles. Almost as a final straw, noxious methane emissions wafted from underground and as the value of the land diminished daily and the chances of selling became virtually nil, Deri Park and Rainham Town collapsed within three years of each other.

Briggs moved to their new ground in Rush Green Road, merging with Ford Sports to become Ford United, whereas Dagenham had been playing on Dagenham Arena, situated within Old Dagenham Park, which had a running track, a large grandstand and substantial terracing.

Victoria Road was not so developed with a small covered area and grass banking partly terraced with sleepers, and it was not until the late fifties that the first full sized grandstand was built along the clubhouse side of the ground with a covered area erected over terracing opposite. That side has since been extended virtually the full length of the ground and the two ends which were grass banks until league rulings forbade it, are now terraced.

Although comfortable, Victoria Road is a modest ground which has a capacity of around 5,000, approximately the figure posted for the FA Cup tie in 1992 against Leyton Orient.

SOUTHBURY ROAD
Enfield FC

Of all the major non-League clubs in the South-East, Enfield FC probably suffer more than most from their geographical location, just a short bus ride away from Highbury and White Hart Lane. Despite the alleged attractions of Premiership football, Enfield have held their own in the higher ranks of the amateur game, and Southbury Road, and indeed their previous grounds, reflect that success.

The earliest days of football in Enfield saw a group of youngsters form Enfield Spartans as an option to the already established Enfield FC, North Enfield and Tottenham Hotspur. The first match, a friendly, took place on September 23rd 1893, and home matches for that season were played at Bailey's Field, situated behind the Jolly Butchers pub in Baker Street. The stables were used by the players as changing rooms. The following year they entered the Tottenham and District League, playing on a basic field at Canonbury Road which was roped off and at one time was home to Stamford Hill FC. Before the war a field was used at the Southbury Road end of Cherry Orchard Lane which was the previous home of the old Enfield FC who had merged with North Enfield by then and subsequently folded. Changing facilities were at the George Hotel and players were forced to walk through the adjoining streets to the ground.

When football re-commenced after the Great War, work began to develop the ground. Now named Enfield FC the club erected with volunteer labour a small wooden stand complete with a few rows of planking for seats and some weather boarding for protection, and put down duck-boards around the pitch. At the Baker Street end a form of wooden terracing was created which gave an elevated view, and at the far end of the field near the stand were the dressing rooms. Cherry Orchard Lane was merely a muddy unmade road in those days which ended in a path which led past the old ground in Bailey's Field and through a rusting iron gate which had an old hut to keep the gateman dry. A screen was put up along the alley by the pitch to prevent a free view. Close to the ground were tennis courts and on an adjoining field Nesta Cricket Club played.

Not surprisingly, bearing in mind the almost total urbanisation of the district, the much loved Cherry Orchard Lane ground was built on, but on 5th July 1936, Enfield Urban Council began work on a new ground within Enfield Playing Fields.

It was anticipated that it would take eight weeks, but it was not ready until the October. Tenancy for the first season cost the club £200, and various fund-raising exercises met the cost.

The contractors were Ceans of Stratford who had amongst their earlier clients, Arsenal, Chelsea, Ilford and Dagenham and when work finally finished and the ground opened before an FA Cup tie with Golders Green on 31st October, it had an impressive 120ft long stand with 750 seats and an further covered area for 400 standing spectators. Dressing rooms and offices, plus a large club room were incorporated and were in use when the ground was formerly opened the following week before an Athenian League game with Walthamstow Avenue. At the time the rest of the ground was flat standing and the pitch was not fenced off but the club were confident that it would ultimately accommodate between 20,000 and 30,000 spectators.

Little of note then occurred at Southbury Road until 1958 when a new lounge bar was opened before a friendly with Arsenal, and four years later a record crowd of over 8,000 saw Tottenham Hotspur play an inaugural floodlit match on the ground.

As the 80's beckoned further upgrading was embarked upon when crash barriers were installed and the stand-side terracing was extended while new floodlights and a club shop soon followed. More terracing was

laid along the Gayer Road side with barriers including the inevitable segregation and both ends were re-surfaced.

More recently the stand has had more seating installed as Southbury Road attempts to keep up with the ever spiralling ground regulations involved with membership of the Isthmian and Conference Leagues.

SHIP LANE
Purfleet FC

Purfleet's Ship Lane ground is a perfect example of what can be achieved with forward planning and patience. The club was founded as recently as 1985, and played then at the existing site, but on pitches running at ninety degrees to the current playing area and backing on to a leisure centre that is now the Thurrock Hotel.

The whole site was originally Aveley Technical College until permission was granted to create a leisure centre from its redundant shell. Huge amounts of earth were removed and replaced to level off a playing area which by now had been reduced to one pitch running parallel to the hotel complex.

Within a year, an impressive 300-seater

stand was built along with new changing facilities and floodlights. As the club progressed to the Isthmian League, the requisite 'A' grade was achieved when a covered enclosure was erected behind the western goal. The far (northern) side of the ground is open, but dominated by the brick 'dug-out'. To call it a 'dug-out' is a disservice as, with its slate roof, the structure is eight feet high and twenty five feet long - i.e. bigger than some main stands! Behind the far (eastern) goal are the dressing rooms and tea bar, all housed in a pleasant brick-built building fronted by a small flower bed.

The stand, replete with intermittent yellow and green plastic seats, is superbly designed and set into the bank leading up to the hotel. No stanchions impede the view, there are matching stairways on each flank, and interior lighting adds to the effect.

The small entrance, situated in the hotel car park, leads to a wooden stairway running down into the ground, which is ideally situated to expand as the club progresses. Purfleet have enjoyed uninterrupted success since their formation when two junior clubs, Rainham W.M. and Fondu, merged, and this comfortable compact ground is a tribute to the leadership of Chairman Harry South and General Manager Tommy South, owners of the Thurrock Hotel.

MILL FIELD
Aveley FC

The Mill Field ground has never really attracted the support it deserves in an area where there is so much competition. The banked ground was opened in November 1953 when a select Grays XI popped down the road to play a commemorative match. The impressive terracing around the ground was put down in spells between the opening and 1956 while a year later the brick-built main stand was built with changing rooms and more than 300 seats.

Around the same time Grays Athletic did the club another favour when they sold them the small stand situated on the east side of the ground. Known as the Pepper Stand at Grays, it was surplus to demands and cost Aveley £100. Inevitably, when the club's floodlights were installed their neighbours once again duly obliged to celebrate the occasion on 27th November 1967.

Almost all the building work that went on at Mill Field was voluntary but it has meant the ground is capable of holding 8,000 although the biggest crowd to date is the 3,741 which saw an FA Amateur Cup match against Slough Town on February 27th 1971. As the Isthmian League requirements change the Mill Field keeps pace with them, and in recent times more terracing has been laid, the perimeter fence infilled, and turnstiles installed at what is one of the more interesting Essex grounds.

*Above: **A 1921 news photo of Cherry Orchard Lane in Enfield.** Here: Enfield's Southbury Road ground.*

The Hornchurch stadium.

THE STADIUM, BRIDGE AVENUE
Hornchurch FC

The Stadium was built as a council-owned athletics track on the site of an old rubbish tip during 1952 and opened on November 1st of that year when Brentwood and Warley were the visitors to Upminster FC. It has changed little since then with the original dressing rooms now converted into an area devoted to officials.

The club originally played in the Romford League before the war and then the Spartan League after it, appearing on the Recreation Ground now known as Upminster Park. The dressing rooms stood where the library is now and the ground had entrances along a pavement lined by hedges. Problems with authorisation to take gate money led the club to move to the new stadium where they remain. Due to the banking which surrounds the ground the capacity is fixed at 3,000, attained when the current record crowd attended an FA Cup tie with Chelmsford City in 1966.

OLD SPOTTED DOG GROUND
Clapton FC

Clapton are one of the oldest clubs in existence with an impressive early history, winning the Amateur Cup three times before the Great War and twice again after it. The Spotted Dog has been home since 1888 when the club moved from playing on an enclosed ground in Elm Farm.

Originally the land was used by St Barts Hospital, but the club negotiated with the owner, a Mrs Vause who charged a high rent of £35 per year for its use. At that time the area was rural with the ground reached down Upton Lane. Cricket was played there right up to the Great War, with players of both sports changing in an old barn.

Clapton's popularity was immense and crowds of 3,000 or more would gather for friendlies until they joined the Southern League when 4,000 or more became the norm. To house the 12,000 which turned up to see a match with Tottenham at the turn of the century, temporary stands were hired to elevate some of the crowd. The Spotted Dog began to develop between the wars, but in truth never reached any great heights with a corrugated iron fence around the by now enclosed ground and a small changing hut. There were two small stands, one with seats for around three hundred, and not much else, but with the ground changing hands regularly (the council bought it before selling on to a brewery), there was only a general agreement to allow the club to stay.

As Clapton settled into mediocrity, the ground fell into disrepair and the stands were eventually condemned. A small modern stand was built to allow them to continue in the Isthmian League, but in recent seasons the old ground has been in danger of becoming an all-weather sports centre. In truth there is little or nothing left of the Old Spotted Dog other than memories in print.

Photos in this section by: Gavin Ellis-Neville, Mike Floate, Terry Horgan, V.J.Robertson, Richard Wall and courtesy of the Enfield Gazette.

The Old Spotted Dog ground is one of London's most famous grounds, but has been tailored to today's needs and is changed beyond recognition.

South and West Essex

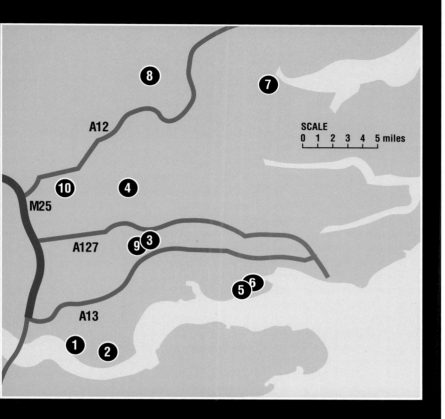

1 **Grays Athletic FC**

2 **Tilbury FC**

3 **Basildon United FC**

4 **Billericay Town FC**

5 **Canvey Island FC**

6 **Concord Rangers FC**

7 **Heybridge Swifts FC**

8 **Chelmsford City FC**

9 **Bowers United FC**

10 **Brentwood FC**

Photos in this section by: Pat Brunning, Gavin Ellis-Neville, Mike Floate and Colin Peel.

THE area to the north of the Thames in Essex has a mixture of former Essex Senior League clubs in the Isthmian League plus one or two who would like to make the move. Chelmsford City are the lone Southern League club in the area but continued speculation regarding the sale of their ground has meant a period of uncertainty, although it appears they have got two further seasons at New Writtle Street.

RECREATION GROUND
Grays Athletic FC

In 1890 a gentleman by the name of H.J. Carter leased 8.5 acres of land which became Grays Recreation Ground, and although only half the size it once was, the ground is today home to Grays Athletic. In its infancy, the Rec had timber-built dressing rooms and was also home to Grays Cricket Club and staged cycling, greyhound racing and fairs. Grays Town were the first club to call it home, with Athletic playing on the Hoppit, a field opposite The Bull pub in Little Thurrock.

The pitch then ran from east to west with the changing rooms and pavilion on the Prospect Place side. After the Great War, the ground was secured by a trust and improvements made, with the pitch turned round, railway sleeper terracing put down behind the goals and a post and rail put around the pitch.

Loans and donations were called for and received soon after, as the main stand was built for £1,225. During the thirties the west side was fenced off permanently and used mainly for greyhounds, but with athletics falling in popularity, the land was sold. The

Grays F.C. showing the houses built on land formerly used for athletics.

Grange Road houses now stand on the site, having been built in 1934, and that side was soon covered by a 120 foot wooden stand on the proceeds.

After the war the pitch wall was built and the sleepers removed and replaced with concrete terracing giving the ground its bowl shape. There were six turnstiles at the entrances and a press box which once saw service as a ship's bridge was installed. In 1952, a much-admired club man was honoured when a new covered enclosure on the west side was named in his memory. The Smallcombe Stand was named after Teddy Smallcombe, who played for the club at the start and was then instrumental in securing the ground. Aveley Football Club purchased the old tin stand which stood there before and re-erected it at their ground, naming it the Pepper Stand.

In 1958 the club entered the prestigious Athenian League, and built a clubhouse with a bar and board room and ten years later they bought the old floodlights from Millwall FC and switched them on before a game with Charlton Athletic. As the sixties and seventies came and went, the ground began to show signs of age. It was eventually sold to the club patron, after the council declared it could only be used for sporting or leisure activities. The saddest moment came a year later when a fire destroyed the main stand and dressing rooms, taking all the club's kit with it.

The stand was never replaced, but the Smallcombe Stand now has adequate seating and on the site of the old stand are the Bridge Court Flats, built over the new dressing rooms, offices and refreshment bar. The club's long awaited ball court was also opened soon after as the Recreation Ground was given a new lease of life, and not a moment too soon. The capacity now stands at around 4,500 which is less than half the record crowd of 9,500 who watched the FA Cup match with Chelmsford City in 1959.

CROWN AVENUE
Bowers United FC

Bowers were formed in 1947 and played in the Southend and District League on a ground at the rear of the Railway Hotel in Pitsea. They moved to the Thurrock and Essex Olympian Leagues playing at the Gun Meadow, adjacent to the old Pitsea United ground at Gun Inn. Both grounds were later taken with the building of the by-pass which sliced through the middle.

They now play at a compact ground in Crown Avenue with a pre-cast stand which seats 200, and very recently installed floodlighting. A thriving Social Club has been a boon and the ground record attendance is a healthy 1,800 which saw an FA Vase match with Billericay Town.

Tilbury in 1990 showing signs of wear and tear.

ST CHAD'S ROAD
Tilbury FC

The Isthmian League ground grading appears to have had a positive effect on the home of Tilbury Football Club. The last dozen or so years have seen the ground slowly deteriorate with much of the covered terracing in a poor state of repair and a general air of decay which has transferred itself on to the pitch.

However, the 1995 close season has seen massive change with a new 220 seater stand going up opposite the old stand and two new areas of cover either side of it. The boundary wall has been replaced, as has the perimeter around the pitch and new turnstiles have been installed. There are also plans to extend the old main stand and raise the roof to enable the existing seating to be set at a steeper angle to give better lines of sight.

All this is a far cry from the dereliction which greeted the club when they returned to football after the war. Their previous home, the Orient field, was next door, but the Ministry of Defence commissioned it and the current ground, which had been in use as a greyhound track, for an anti-aircraft site to guard the docks. The Orient field was owned by a director of that club who let Tilbury use it virtually rent free, but after the war he stipulated that to continue, they would have to become a nursery side to the League club, an offer they declined.

Moving into the greyhound stadium was not an easy task for it had become badly derelict during the war years. It had two old covered areas of shale banking and it took a year before the efforts of supporters, dockers and locals bore fruit and the ground re-opened. A small grandstand with 300 bench seats had been built and a small wooden hut installed for changing, with terracing of sorts laid opposite the stand. The ground was originally leased, but the club's extraordinary FA Cup run in 1949, which took in ten matches, paid for the ground and the adjacent Northfield, which is still used today. The

Fourth Qualifying Round tie against Gorleston attracted a crowd of 5,500 to St Chad's Road which is still a record.

During the 1950's a new covered area was built and in 1956 a boardroom and tea-bar went up, followed closely by the first clubhouse in 1958. 1960 saw the brick-built dressing rooms and in 1966, the ground was floodlit for the first time.

By 1970 the original grandstand was in need of replacing and a new rather stark concrete stand with a collection of stanchions in front was built to seat 200.

Whilst the seventies are seen as a successful time at the club, culminating in an even more extraordinary FA Cup run to the 3rd Round and a trip to Stoke City, the overspending was to have a major effect on Tilbury and after building the new clubhouse behind the goal in 1973 and extending the dressing rooms in 1978 the debts began to bite and no more improvements could be made. Having survived, the club are now positive that the future is rosy and once again St Chad's Road has been saved from possible obscurity.

SCRALEY ROAD
Heybridge Swifts FC

The Scraley Road ground has come a long way since it was transformed from a carrot field in 1966. The Swifts were forced to move there after sharing a ground with Sadds Athletic for a couple of seasons. This ground-share transpired because of the demise of the Bentalls Sports Ground which was the main focal point for sport and recreation in the area and had been their home from the very early days.

The ground was also home to Bentalls Cricket Club and was the scene of the Heybridge Fete an attraction thousands flocked to each year. When the parent club were taken over by Acrow Ltd the ground was sold and Heybridge Swifts were unceremoniously kicked out. Many of the club's belongings were lost during the move and they came perilously close to closure. Happily, the carrot field was acquired and slowly but surely a football pitch was developed. A low brick-built seated stand appeared to one side of the half-way line and the pitch was roped off and later barriered.

A small area of cover was put up opposite the stand and this was added to much later when the club had progressed into the Isthmian League and were forced to drastically improve their ground. Hard standing all around the pitch was laid and in 1994 two small areas of cover were built at either end to provide shelter at what is a comfortable and accessible country ground. The long-lamented Bentalls Sports Ground is now-buried by a shopping precinct with just one small building left as a poignant reminder.

New Lodge, Billericay.

NEW LODGE
Billericay Town FC

Billericay Town enjoyed unparalleled success during the late seventies in the Essex Senior and Athenian Leagues which launched them on a run of three Wembley visits to FA Vase finals in four years. It was around this time that New Lodge began to take shape having barely altered since the club moved there from the Archer Ground in Laindon in 1971.

At the time there were two football pitches separated by a cricket square and the council-owned ground was used by a junior club, Outwell Common FC.

The old wooden building which had served as a changing room was transported to New Lodge where it still stands, now used as a buffet bar. The clubhouse was opened in its original format at the same time and was the only other building on the ground for ten years. A fence was soon put up to enclose the ground, although there remains another pitch just outside which is still in use.

For big matches, including the Vase games, temporary wooden terracing was drafted in from the County Cricket Ground at Chelmsford which enabled the club to post

a record gate of 3,193 for the semi-final first leg against Farnborough Town in 1976 and nearly 4,000 for the floodlight opener against West Ham United some 18 months later.

The main stand, a rather clumsy looking steel structure was built around 1980 and five years later the Supporters' Club erected a smaller stand on the opposite side. An area of covered terrace is to the left of the main stand and brings the total covered capacity to just over 1,000. A fine brick-built viewing gallery to the right of the stand is around nine years old. A selection of sheds and outbuildings are dotted around the ground and in places the terracing is beginning to look a touch second-hand but it is not difficult to envisage the huge crowds at New Lodge only 16 years ago.

PARK LANE
Canvey Island FC

Canvey Island have had a long and, on one desperate occasion, tragic climb to the heights of the Isthmian League and FA Vase semi-finals. All of the club records were lost in 1953 when devastating floods

GARDINERS CLOSE
Basildon United FC

The club were formed in 1963 as Armada Sports and played at the Gun Ground in Pitsea, the former home of Bowers United, now sliced in half by the A13.

In 1967 they changed their name to Basildon United, and played in the Greater London League on a pitch in Grosvenor Park which has also now been built on. They moved to new site in Gardiners Close which was open land set aside by the New Town Commission as blue belt land for recreation and leisure, playing the first game in August 1970 against West Ham United in front of 4,000, which remains a record. The first installment was a post and rail but dressing rooms followed shortly and an L-shaped clubhouse was built. The early seventies saw two stands either side of the dressing room which still remain, one now with seats. A pay box came along some time later.

Ten years on Crystal Palace were the visitors to open the floodlights and in 1985 before an FA Cup tie with Alvechurch the stand opposite was opened although never finished. A newer model eventually took its place complete with 120 seats.

As the Isthmian League came, then terracing behind the goals did too, and although Gardiners Close is up to league standards, it is likely that the club will be on the move within the next twelve months.

Basildon United FC

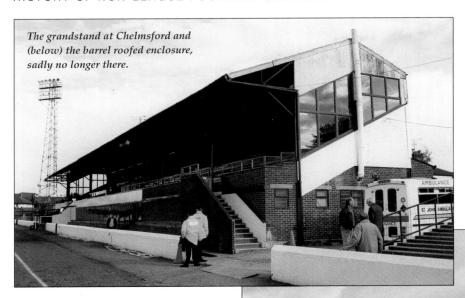

The grandstand at Chelmsford and (below) the barrel roofed enclosure, sadly no longer there.

Chelmsford FC moved from what was an impressive ground complete with grandstand but prone to the wet, at King's Head Meadow, into a new home described in the *Essex Weekly News* as being "...in such capital order. The playing pitch is quite level with the exception of one corner...A substantial post and rail fence surrounds the enclosure, and a cinder path has been laid all round. On the New Writtle Street side of the ground a temporary stand, capable of holding over 400 people, has been erected. Eventually there will be a thoroughly up to date stand with dressing rooms, offices etc. beneath it, and the present structure will be transferred to the opposite side of the pitch..."

The opening ceremony was performed by Mr. Hugh Wright, President of the club who later explained that the Meadow was no longer fit for football, and the new home was imperative. King's Head Meadow had been used since 1897, and when the move finally came, a lease was agreed for 7, 14, and 21 years, with the hope that the club would eventually purchase it.

New Writtle Street got its 'up to date stand', with a huge barrel-roofed covered enclosure opposite, but the demolishing of that side completely transformed the ground and directly or indirectly led to the chaos which has surrounded the club. During the summer of 1994 it was announced that the ground had been bought by an unnamed purchaser, many believe it to be Essex County Cricket Club whose ground is next door. Although Chelmsford City are to continue there for another two seasons, the whole sorry saga has many similarities with that of another well-supported Southern League club, Wealdstone. Both sets of fans deserve far better than they are getting.

destroyed them whilst taking countless lives as waters engulfed the British Isles. It was a month before a semblance of normality returned to the place with the club continuing their season in the Thurrock Combination on their ground at Redcroft Paddocks.

They were formed in 1926, it is believed through Naval connections, and played for many years in the Southend and District League before joining the Thurrock Combination for that ill-fated 1953 season. The earliest known ground was at Furtherwick School before moving to the Paddocks and then in 1955 King George V Fields in Poplar Road. The club always had an ambition to play on an enclosed ground and when senior status and a move to the London League came in 1962, so did the move to Park Lane, Leigh Beck, quite possibly the only football ground in the country that is below sea level.

Permission to turn three and a half acres of the Leigh Beck Recreation Ground, as it was known, into a football ground was finally given after protracted talks with the Trustees of the Estate and the Council and much activity made the ground ready for the start of the 1962-63 season. The ground was enclosed by a close-boarded fence and the dressing rooms were on site. Soon after a covered enclosure was built along one side.

There were other improvements, but it was not until 1983 that a reorganisation saw the ground and club become eligible for the FA Vase and in 1988 the FA Cup again after a lapse of sixteen years.

The last decade has seen the ground upgraded to Isthmian League standard, the capacity now 2,500 with seating and standing cover on both sides. With promotion in mind a 'B' grade was achieved in 1994, helped by the profits of three fine FA Vase runs in as many years. The semi-final tie with Tiverton Town on 27th March 1993 brought in a record crowd of 3,250 which will take some beating at this tight and intimidating little ground.

NEW WRITTLE STREET
Chelmsford City FC

New Writtle Street has witnessed more than its fair share of turmoil since the grand opening in 1922. The original club folded, and a new club were formed just before the Second World War, playing on the same ground. Many years later City merged with Brentwood FC, and in the nineties a disastrous scheme which involved knocking down the massive covered side and turning the pitch around 90 degrees was aborted, leaving the ground looking half-built.

Finally, in the summer of 1994, a merger with Braintree Town almost took place which would have seen the end of football at New Writtle Street. All this is a far cry from the optimism and pomp which greeted the opening of the ground.

THE HIVE
Brentwood Town FC

There is currently a team called Brentwood playing at the Brentwood Centre in the Essex Senior League, but they have no connection with Brentwood Town who played at a ground called the Hive before a rather hasty merger with Chelmsford City saw them disappear along with the ground which was sold off for housing.

The Hive, in Ongar Road, was the first home of Brentwood and Warley, who transformed it from an open field, to a ground which had cover on one side with a small wooden stand opposite. This stand was replaced by one much larger with 500 seats, in 1958 and the standing cover was extended as the club progressed.

In 1965 the club turned professional as Brentwood Town and played for three years in the Southern League reaching the Second Round of the FA Cup in 1968-69 and the Third Round a year later before the sudden and dubious merger with Chelmsford.

Chiltern Hills and the Thames Valley

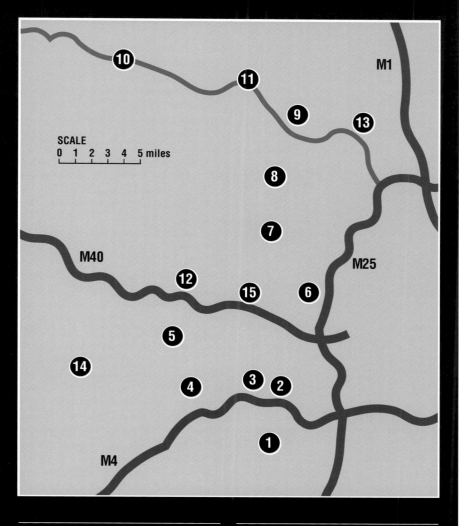

1	Windsor & Eton FC	11	Tring Town FC
2	Slough Town FC	12	Flackwell Heath FC
3	Burnham FC	13	Hemel Hempstead Town FC
4	Maidenhead Utd FC		
5	Marlow FC	14	Henley Town FC
6	Chalfont St. Peter FC	15	Beaconsfield FC
7	Amersham Town FC		
8	Chesham United FC		
9	Berkhamsted T. FC		
10	Aylesbury Utd FC		

WITH the loss of Wycombe Wanderers to the Football League, and the relegation of both Chesham United and Marlow, the domain of top dog in this part of England belongs to Slough Town.

Although there is no shortage of interesting and elderly grounds in the area, many of the clubs are struggling to make an impact on their respective leagues and feeling the pinch of the ground gradings. Burnham found themselves in the Hellenic League for 1995-96 season with a batch of other clubs settling in the lower reaches of the Isthmian.

STAG MEADOW
Windsor and Eton FC

The Stag Meadow, situated on the edge of Windsor Great Park and surrounded by broad oaks is over 80 years old, although the current structures on the ground are all post-war. The main stand replaced an earlier timber version which was burnt down during the Second World War by an intruder although the official word seemed to blame enemy action!

The club were originally formed in 1892 and played on an open field known as Windsor Recreation Ground, the precise whereabouts of which are unknown. Four seasons later they moved to another field behind The Swan pub known as Balloon Meadow which is now part of the racecourse just off Maidenhead Road.

There were other fields used on a one-off basis until the Royal Commission gave the club full use of the field known as Stag Meadow for a peppercorn rent with free rein to expand at any time. For some years the ground remained undeveloped with players using pubs to change until the first timber-built grandstand was built on the site of the present one. It had dressing rooms underneath and stood for around twenty years until destroyed in 1943.

The ground as seen today began to take shape in 1948 when the current main stand was built which now seats 320 people. Although a substantial size it had but two small rooms underneath used primarily for storage and it wasn't until 1952 that adequate changing rooms were built alongside. These are still in use today, albeit in extended form.

The following year saw the opening of the long awaited clubhouse which again is still in use, and a further year saw the covered enclosure built on the far side which lasted precisely one night as it was blown down, and had to be rebuilt. Over the years it has been patched and slightly lengthened and during the summer months tends to be over-run with vegetation, but it still holds over 600 people on the rare occasion that it needs to. The banking at the Park end came about after debris and rubbish accumulated and the club fashioned a bank rather than

Windsor's Stag Meadow in June 1994 - clearly in need of some weed killer.

Top: The main stand at Windsor.

clear it away back in the mid-seventies. A similar bank appeared at the entrance end around the same time and both were put to full use when AFC Bournemouth were the visitors in the Second Round of the FA Cup in 1983, the Royals having battled through five rounds to get there. Floodlighting arrived at the ground in 1976 after a struggle for planning permission, and Ipswich Town were the visitors for the match to commemorate the occasion. As hard standing and turnstiles became relevant with the club's promotion, then further work was done soon after. Other than minor cosmetic surgery these were the last significant changes at Stag Meadow.

Today, the ground slumbers quietly, the massive oak tree to the left of the near goal just waiting for the club to hit another golden spell. But, as at St. Albans City not so long ago, the club are in fact held back by the rules surrounding the tree's continued presence.

SLOUGH CENTRE, DOLPHIN, WEXHAM PARK
Slough Town FC

Slough Football Club came about after the merger of Slough Albion and the Young Men's Friendly Society in 1890. They played for over 50 years with a quite breath-taking lack of success, and it was only when a merger with the more prominent Slough Centre FC took place, to form Slough United, that the club began to blossom.

Slough FC played their early football on basic pitches until procuring the use of the Slough Stadium, known as the Dolphin, which they shared with greyhound racing. The war years saw the Dolphin out of use for football. The club had previously been offered the chance to buy it from the owner of the Dolphin Hotel next door, but it was declined and the Greyhound Racing Authority purchased it instead. They were forced by the blackout regulations to race on Saturday afternoons and so the club had to look elsewhere. A move to the cricket ground in Chalvey Road followed, which was not popular, nor was a ground-share at York

Road, Maidenhead. However, in 1943 a merger took place with the new club playing at the Centre Stadium in Belfast Avenue.

Slough Centre had formed in 1937, after a generous gift from the Slough Estates Limited provided for a new ground in Edinburgh Avenue. Despite this outlay, the ground only lasted six years, for in 1943 they moved to the new Centre Stadium, which was opened by the ever present Hon. Sec. Mr. Stanley Rous, before a game with a Dutch Naval XI. Edinburgh Avenue is now buried under an industrial estate. The clubs merged in June 1943 and played at the Centre Stadium until the state of the pitch became such that they were forced to return to the Dolphin. By now there were internal wranglings between officials from the old Slough club and those from the Centre, and these weren't helped when it was decided to stay at the Dolphin, with the reserves playing at the Centre.

In June 1947, the Slough Centre Football Club broke away and re-formed, and shortly after Slough United changed their name to Slough Town, playing at the Dolphin. The fortunes of the two clubs were markedly different, for large crowds were watching the Centre, and the ground was slowly being improved to accommodate them. United were having problems again with the greyhounds and were losing money. By 1950, the Centre had built a covered area opposite the main building, and were attracting many spectators to their well-appointed ground, which has a record attendance figure of 6,000 for a friendly with Queens Park Rangers. This soon changed, and despite Belfast Avenue by now having over 800 seats under cover, interest in the club waned, and when a change in the system of rates meant a staggering bill that the parent club were not prepared to pay, it was the final straw for Slough Centre FC.

At its peak, the Slough Centre stadium was impressive. A large brick-built administration block stretching virtually the length of the pitch, with a verandah along the top, was fronted to two seated areas, some covered. Directly opposite stood, from 1953, a covered area, and either side of the main stand were various small buildings for refreshment and storage. The pitch was surrounded by a large banked cycle track. The ground still exists although it is no longer impressive. To the uninitiated, it is a sports field with a large changing room complex now variously used by youth clubs and the like. The seated areas and the cover have all gone, as has the cycle track which was flattened a dozen years ago. Football is still played on the ground where it is difficult to imagine that an FA Cup 1st Round match took place in front of over 4,000 people in 1945.

Slough Town took advantage of the situation and, still playing at the Dolphin,

Slough Town's ever-changing Wexham Park.

YORK ROAD
Maidenhead United FC

Maidenhead's town centre ground is remarkable for the fact that it has occupied a prime spot between the town and the railway since 1871, and despite arson and vandalism is still a pleasure to visit. However, it could have ended very differently, for the club were severely stretched financially by an ambitious new clubhouse project and having slowly recovered were rocked by a fire which completely destroyed the 64-year-old main stand along with the dressing-rooms. However, the club have admirably bounced back, tidied up, and carried on.

In the very early days Maidenhead's matches were played at Kidwells Park, which eventually became the home of the town's other club Norfolkians, until the move to York Road in 1871. At that time the site was much larger, with the pitch facing north-south with one goal close to the railway line. A pavilion was provided in one corner, and club records show it being re-thatched in the 1880's

After the Great War, the clubs merged to become Maidenhead United F.C., and in 1922 the 500-seater wooden, black and white main stand was opened on the north side of the ground (the pitch having been re-laid east-west). The banked terracing utilised many discarded railway sleepers around the four sides of the ground. The railway side saw a covered enclosure erected to cater for 1,000 spectators in 1935, with funds generously provided by the Supporters' Club, and a

became one of the top amateur teams in the country. A move to the Isthmian League was followed by the news that they would have to vacate the Dolphin, as it was to be demolished, and a supermarket built in its place. In 1974 Slough Town were re-located to a rural site at Wexham Park. Already in its 20-year history the new ground has changed beyond recognition. What was, in its infancy a bland, flat-looking ground, with a main stand which gave the impression of being thrown up in a hurry, is now a very fine stadium, built with the Football League in mind. The flat standing open ends, which were backed by wire fencing are now completely

enclosed, and the cover which stands opposite the stand has been moved back, as the pitch was shifted to accommodate the new structures. The offices and entertainment areas are far in advance of the everyday clubhouse, and give the impression of a corporate hospitality suite, rather than anything to do with football. Outside, a large car-park is protected from the club's golf driving-range by a massive net umbrella, behind which stand the home and away entrances. The whole set-up is a million miles away from the Dolphin, although there are many enthusiasts who wish that was still in use.

WYMERS WOOD ROAD
Burnham FC

A visit to the Gore Cricket Ground in the affluent Burnham area of Berkshire during the summer would give little clue to the fact that until very recently it was the venue of Southern League football. Other than the small concrete stand on the half way line there are no other visible signs of football on what is a well-kept sports ground which has been home to Burnham since the twenties.

1930's maps show the Gore marked as simply `Recreation Ground', and also show the club's former ground at Baldwins Meadow, which was located off the High Street close to The George public house. Around that time the club were playing junior football in the Maidenhead, and Windsor, Slough and District Leagues. After the War, the club joined the Great Western Combination and three years later built the small stand. In 1970 the smart clubhouse went up, in time for the club's elevation from Combination football to the Hellenic League, and as that

league was followed by the Athenian and Spartan Leagues, then the clubhouse was also improved.

The three-sided nature of the ground and the flat standing limits the capacity to around 2,500, a total almost reached for the FA Vase tie with Halesowen Town in 1983, and has meant the possibility of the cricket

club moving away, leaving the Gore to be split between housing and football. A decision on that scheme is imminent although the club's relegation to the Hellenic League may mean there is not such a hurry after all.

Supporters' Club members laying terracing on the popular side at Maidenhead, circa 1950.

Right: **The old stand at York Road, destroyed in 1986.**

Next to the stand was a modern clubhouse, built in 1973 to replace a much older, small timber affair.

In 1983, the club took over the cricket clubhouse and began laying out a new ground at Broadwater. The stand, clubhouse and terrace were soon removed and in their place is now a selection of flats on the football pitch with the new pitch on the other part of the former cricket out-field. New dressing rooms were erected along with a main stand and floodlights as the club played for the first time in the Athenian League during its final season. Originally the stand was used as covered terracing, but in 1987, bench seating was installed in part of it. In 1988, with the assistance of the FA, a hard surface training area was added at the ground and when Berko were promoted to Division One of the Isthmian League in 1993, terracing was laid down behind both goals to enable the main stand to be filled both sides with individual seating.

SPRATLEYS MEADOW
Amersham Town FC

The 75th anniversary of the opening of the football ground at Spratleys Meadow was celebrated in 1995. It has never reached any dizzy heights, but has over-seen the club's ups and downs since a move from their first pitch at Barn Meadow in 1920. The club were formed amid great excitement in 1890, and began using a pitch, which is now a recreation ground behind the High Street. There were no changing rooms, and the players used St. Mary's School for dressing, or walked to the ground ready for action.

In 1920, the club leased Spratleys from the local squire for £10 per year, but it wasn't until 1933 that dressing rooms were built on the ground. Two years later the wooden stand was erected on the top side of the ground overlooking the town. During the war, the dressing rooms were converted into a makeshift mortuary in preparation for air attacks, but mercifully were never required. However, the authorities of the time had agreed to pay the club for hiring out the

further 15 years elapsed until extensive development began when the resurgence in football's popularity after the war years required better facilities.

The sleepers slowly made way for concrete terracing, the south-west area being first to benefit, complete with tea-bar, which is now the club shop. The north-west part of the ground was then terraced and covered, and the club's continued success on and off the pitch meant that the work was virtually completed by the early 60's. The area to the south-east was the only one not developed. This was rectified in 1994. The north-east part of the ground is again undeveloped, after the terrace was levelled to build a clubhouse, which got no further than the skeletal remains seen today. It is now used as a covered car-park, and certainly does nothing to enhance the attractiveness of the rest of the ground. The site of the ill-fated main stand was concreted and permanent porta-cabins installed in 1986. To comply with ground rules, 100 seats were provided under the south enclosure, with a further 120 added once purchased from Millwall's demolished Den in 1993.

The two large covered areas behind the west goal have been re-furbished with a mural painting depicting various historical dates pertinent to the club on the perimeter wall. The east end of the ground which once backed on to allotments is now the site of a church and the St. Johns H.Q., and is beginning to decay. In 1986 part of it was bricked up as a safety measure, although again work was sympathetic to the ground and did not effect the overall appearance.

BROADWATER
Berkhamsted Town FC

When the first Berkhamsted Town side was formed exactly 100 years ago, they took over an existing ground that the Sunnyside club had used until their demise. It was called Sunnyside Enclosure and was situated near the church of the same name. The current Berko club were called The Comrades, as were so many newly re-formed clubs on returning from the Great War.

They played on the town cricket ground in Lower Kings Road, which was sandwiched between the Grand Union Canal and the London to Euston railway line. The pitch ran parallel to the current one, but 70 yards nearer the road on the opposite side of the cricket ground to the pavilion.

There was an old wooden stand and dressing room complex that was built in 1924 and an area of terracing which was laid by supporters just after the Second World War.

The new ground at Berkhamsted Town.

rooms, and at the end of the war, the club informed them that no payment had ever been received. They retorted the club had not paid out the £250 for the completion of the stand in 1935, and it was decided to call it quits.

In 1968, a girls private school made available a portable classroom which was no longer required, and Amersham Town re-erected it on the ground as a clubhouse. It was extended in 1983 to include board rooms, kitchen and lounge. Floodlighting was installed in 1977, but it is not currently up to standard and is used only for training.

In January 1990, a tremendous gale ripped the old stand apart, blew it several hundred yards and destroyed it forever. The focal point of what had been a seldom-changing ground was gone. There appear to be no plans to replace it, and so Spratleys Meadow is again a railed-off pitch.

Chesham's well-appointed ground with a squash club behind the popular side.

PLAYING FIELDS, AMERSHAM ROAD
Chalfont St Peter FC

Chalfont Football Club is situated in the attractive Buckinghamshire countryside but any development is held back by its placement in a tightly-guarded green-belt area of natural beauty. At some point in the near future green-belt and ground grading may clash, but until then the Playing Fields are destined to remain unchanged.

The club have played there since 1952, having at first been on a pitch on Gold Hill Common and around the time of the Second World War on a field at Welch's Farm, off Lovel Close. The ground forms part of Mill Meadow public amenities area and is surrounded by a Community Centre, tennis club, scout and Red Cross rooms and a playground. In 1952 the club immediately enclosed the playing area on obtaining senior status, and in 1956 a 200-seater stand was erected by voluntary labour and included dressing rooms underneath. As with many clubs at that level, the ground remained virtually unchanged until floodlights and a training area were installed in 1979 as they progressed in the Athenian League. Later, in 1985 the impressive clubhouse was built and a year after that, now playing their football in the Isthmian League, the stand was re-roofed which deprived the public of the sight of the club name emblazoned across the fascia which, much as at Warminster, could be seen from some distance.

In 1988, two small areas of terracing were laid down behind each goal and the dressing rooms were later extended and a car-park laid.

Further development is unlikely, but with the close proximity of Watford, Wycombe Wanderers and Slough Town the ground is unlikely to exceed the record crowd of 2,500 posted in April 1985 when the then First Division Hornets played a benefit game for the victims of the Harrods bomb blast.

MEADOW PARK
Chesham United FC

The home of Chesham United Football Club has seen many changes since its inception as a football ground just after the Great War. An amalgamation of Chesham Town and Chesham Generals in 1919 brought about the formation of United, and for a while the new club continued to play on the cricket ground home of the Town, believed at the time to have been known locally as the Pig's Trough!

The cricket club still play on the same site, which is next to the Meadow but on a lower level, and reached by the same narrow lane. On moving into the next field, the club took with them their old wooden pavilion type stand and re-erected it straddling the half-way line, where it stood for a further 63 years, until it was sadly destroyed in a blaze. It was a typically ornate structure, vaguely reminiscent of the stand that met a similar fate at York Road, Maidenhead.

In the early thirties, the club added a substantial amount of cover down the opposite side to the stand, and this in due course had

Chalfont St Peter FC.
Below: Volunteers building the stand and dressing rooms in 1956.

ALFRED DAVIS MEMORIAL GROUND
Marlow FC

Marlow Football Club is one of the oldest in the country, being founded in 1870 as Great Marlow. They were one of the original 15 entrants to the FA Cup in 1871, and are the only club to have entered the competition every year since its inception.

The club's early years were spent firstly at Aldermeadow and then in 1898 the Crown Meadow, which was home until the First World War. At some point during this period, the club purchased from Southampton Football Club, after much haggling, a massive ornate wooden pavilion which stood on the Saints' ground which at the time was the County Cricket H.Q. in Northlands Road. The club dignitaries managed to agree a price of £100 provided they dismantled and transported it.

It is not known precisely how and when this was achieved, but the club were not able to enjoy the fruits of their labour for very long, for the Crown Meadow was sold to a Mr. Riley during the Great War and the club moved briefly to Star Meadow, close to today's ground. The Star was a much more basic setting, which was unfenced and had no facilities and as a result the club suffered demotion to the Reading League from the Great Western Suburban. This proved to be the catalyst for today's modern club, for the Honorary Secretary at the time, Alfred Davis, appealed for funding, and indeed contributed much himself, and the club were successful in purchasing a ground in Oak Tree Road. Sadly Mr. Davis died before the ground opened in 1924, but the club dedicated the ground to his memory, and to this day it carries his name.

An interesting story concerns the old ground at Riley Rec. Although newspapers told of the old cricket pavilion (below) being bought, it has never been established just how much of it was re-erected. The site today (right) shows a clump of bushes where the building stood, but just how much of a building remains a mystery - unless this book provokes a response!

Marlow's ground is one of the most photogenic in the country. The main stand, now a sprightly 65 years old, is a delight from any angle.

The Crown Meadow grandstand was sold for £87.10s.0d. and the ground is now known as the Riley Recreation Ground, and is used as a children's pitch. The area where the stand was situated is now covered by trees and bushes. The Star Meadow is now under the Spring Gardens Estate.

Marlow soon began to develop their new home, having returned to the Spartan League and taken the Division Two Championship. The main stand, still looking a picture today was built in 1930, and after the Second World War the cover on the Green Verges side was erected. The club continued in the Spartan League until 1965 when they joined the Athenian League, promotion being achieved in 1971. Just prior to this the floodlighting system was installed in 1970, but a further 14 years elapsed before the Isthmian League took them on board.

Thus began the most remarkable decade in the history of club and ground. After a dismal couple of seasons the club started to climb the league and the ground began to change to satisfy the ground gradings, firstly with concrete terracing added in 1985 and again in 1991 at the Oak Tree Road end. More terrace was added at the Trinity End as Marlow prospered in league and cups, and recently turnstiles were put up, which were used to the full when Plymouth Argyle were the visitors in the FA Cup.

Today the Alfred Davis Memorial Ground is delightfully well kept, the entrance to which is uncluttered by ugly walling, unlike so many other grounds whose aesthetic qualities have been ruined by league requirements. A small car-park is to the left of the changing rooms, tucked away in a concrete building which adjoins

the pitch by way of a small area of synthetic grass. A caravan houses the club shop at the back of the car-park next to the main stand, built in 1930. This marvellous structure is best viewed from the opposite terrace where its elevation is evident on a similar par to the surviving stand at Harwich and Parkeston. It has to be said that the overall appearance is almost spoilt by a surfeit of advertising hoardings, but it is just holding its own.

To the side of this is a small terrace with an area of cut grass behind. It would be so easy to disregard this part of the ground and pretend it is a nature reserve, but great care is taken to preserve its attractiveness. The Trinity end now boasts a covered enclosure built in 1992, which blends in nicely with the surroundings. On the Green Verges side the covered stand, a 1950's vintage, is still looking good but is heavily decorated with colourful advertising. On either side of it, identical sections of terrace provide hard standing. Behind the Oak Tree Road end, an all weather training area has been installed with two rows of terrace between it and the pitch, all of which were added in 1991.

The whole playing surface is barriered off with chain-link fencing acting as a filler rather than the ugly breeze-block effect which is now common.

For those who can fully appreciate the site of a former football ground without the need for acres of crumbling terracing and rusting turnstiles then a visit to the Riley Recreation ground, five minutes from the Alfred Davis is highly recommended.

Absolutely nothing exists to suggest that a major football ground was ever there, but to be armed with the faded photo of the huge old pavilion and to simply stand and imagine the scene 80 years ago is a must.

Of all the unanswered questions posed during the research for this book, the most intriguing were concerning the stand.

● How was it transported from Southampton to Marlow?
● Who was it sold to after the war?
● And how long did it survive?

Many people at the club believe that only a small part of the pavilion was bought if at all, but it is a fascinating story.

terracing put under it, and in recent years was covered again after sections became dangerous and of little use. Behind the goal at the cricket end stands a solid squared-off concreted bank, which was used as a car-park until the ground was fenced off for league regulation purposes a few years ago, and at the other end for many years there was apparently nothing but a grass bank. However, in preparation for an FA Cup tie with Cambridge United in 1979, the grass bank was found to be covering several rows of terracing that the club had forgotten existed. This was hastily unearthed and is again in use today. To the left of the 200-seater stand built to replace the original, is a steep terraced area, replete with barriers, which has changed little over the years, and is still a popular spot.

The Meadow, now called Meadow Park, has witnessed many large crowds in its 75 year history. The famous Amateur Cup run which took in over a dozen games and culminated in a narrow defeat at Wembley brought tractors and trailers down the valley and hills which stretch out behind the ground, and these were parked behind the goal to provide better viewing for some. In 1979, a crowd of 5,000 packed in to see the Generals take on Cambridge United in the Third Round of the FA Cup, and this remains a record, although plans are afoot to radically improve the ground, which will make this capacity feasible again. Whatever happens to Meadow Park, it has to be hoped that this most rustic of town grounds does not alter to its detriment. Although it has been spruced up in recent years, the feeling of the ground, and its shape are happily unaltered.

VAUXHALL ROAD
Hemel Hempstead FC

Founded in 1885 as Apsley FC, the club played its early football in the West Herts League, on various pitches around the town. The pre-war history of the club is sketchy, but their permanent home up to 1972 was at Crabtree Lane, which they took over in the early thirties. The record attendance at that ground was 3,500 for an Amateur Cup match against Tooting and Mitcham United in 1962. The club changed its name to Hemel Hempstead Town around the time of the Second World War, and eventually merged with South Midland League side United to form the current club.

In 1972, the Crabtree Lane ground was sold for yet more development in the already widely-expanding town, and the club relocated to a purpose-built ground in Adeyfield which has held 2,500 for a centenary celebration match against Watford. In November 1992, the football club was rocked by a fire which wrecked the dressing rooms and clubhouse and forced the club to play some matches away until temporary accommodation could be arranged.

BUCKINGHAM ROAD GROUND
Aylesbury United FC

In 1986 Aylesbury United vacated their weather-worn but homely Turnfurlong Lane ground which had been base since 1935 and moved to a brand new purpose-built stadium which set a trend for the likes of Kingstonian, Ashford Town and Witton Albion.

As is the norm with so many grounds new on the scene, the facilities for players, officials, directors, committee men and guests are superb, whereas the paying public are less well served. The terracing around the three sides of the ground is total but very shallow, which is a problem whenever a half decent crowd gathers and the standard cover opposite the stand is capable of holding 500. In some ways the tidiness of the ground compensates for the blandness and viewing problems, and the entrance and administration areas are without question beautifully designed. However, Buckingham Road and, it has to be said, its offspring, have been somewhat harshly likened to a `roofless warehouse' by one or two traditionalists who miss the rust and weeds of Turnfurlong Lane.

Aylesbury United started in 1897 when a club from the local night school merged with the Printing Works side and began playing at the Works itself.

They remained there until 1935 when a pitch became available in Turnfurlong Lane and this was home for fifty years, witnessing a record crowd of 7,500 for an FA Cup tie with Watford in 1951.

WILKS PARK
Flackwell Heath FC

The small village of Flackwell Heath near High Wycombe has seen football since 1907 when the present club were formed. Home was the Recreation Ground until the Second World War when Wilks Park was prepared and made available. It has always been an enclosed ground, the adjacent housing ensuring that, and for many years the only structure on the ground was the changing room building which has since been modernised but is still the original.

The change to the current state came as recently as 1984 when they were successful in gaining membership of the Isthmian League. The 150-seater stand was built straddling the half-way line, opposite the old changing rooms which have an overhang that until then provided the only cover at the ground. The perimeter was walled or fenced in all around, the bottom part being wire mesh as the pitch slopes away and it was feared that at full tilt players would often be unable to stop in time!

Soon after they began their tenure in the league the lighting went up and so far the record crowd has been 700 when the re-formed Aldershot Town brought their support along in 1992. The largest crowd for any match at Wilks Park assembled in 1986 when an estimated 4,500 crammed in to watch a Charity match against Oxford United.

THE TRIANGLE
Henley Town FC

Although Henley Town are currently operating in the modest Chiltonian League, they are 125 years old and have played in the Spartan and Hellenic Leagues as well as the FA Cup, on a number of sites around the town.

The first few years were spent on pitches at Dry Leas, on the Marlow Road, now occupied by Henley Rugby Club and 'Mr Jones's Meadow' in Remenham Lane. The Marlow Road ground was later shared with Friar Park FC and a dressing room was erected which was described as "closely resembling a rabbit hutch". For the 1898-99 season the club moved to another pitch in Remenham Lane which is now occupied by the Henley Cricket Club.

Finally, in 1900, Henley transferred to a field in Reading Road where they remained for over 70 years. Before the Second World War a small stand was erected with dressing rooms, but they were taken down and never replaced when the ground was requisitioned for the war effort. Although when football re-started in 1945 the club were given permission to use the Nissen hut and felt-roofed building that had been left behind.

The Nissen hut became changing rooms and the other building eventually a small clubhouse. Sadly, in 1971 the landlord regained possession of the ground and in the club's Centenary season they were homeless. The grandstand which was erected in 1967 by a neighbouring firm in recognition of the club relinquishing a piece of land from its lease, was taken down and the ground is now used for storage and parking.

Since then, the club played on a pitch at the Triangle and then at the Sports Centre, but happily have obtained a 21-year lease at the Triangle and built a clubhouse and dressing rooms which were opened in 1993.

HOLLOWAYS PARK
Beaconsfield SYCOB FC

The current Holloways Park has been in existence since 1971, when the club were forced to move as the M40 motorway was built over their old ground, which was known by the same name and owned by the club's patron Lord Burnham.

Prior to that, a number of pitches were used, the first being on White Hart Meadow before the Great War.

Senior status was gained in 1980 when a small brick built cover went up to add to the clubhouse, and in 1990 floodlights were erected. The record crowd at the 2,000 capacity ground stands at around 600 for a Berks & Bucks Cup tie with Chesham United in 1985. 1994 saw the merger with Slough SYCOB who played for eight years at the Haymill Centre after moving from Farnham Road.

Photos in this section by:
Pat Brunning, Gavin Ellis-Neville, Mal Keenan, Kerry Miller, Dave West, James Wright and Middlesex County Press.

PENDLEY SPORTS CENTRE
Tring Town FC

Tring Town played on the Cricket Club ground for some forty years before being offered a piece of land on the estate owned by the showjumping broadcaster Dorian Williams. Players changed in the boiler room of nearby Pendley Manor until changing rooms were built at the back of the strangely-shaped wooden stand which dates from the early fifties.

Redundant classrooms were obtained from Rothchild Mansion School in 1974 and these were converted into changing rooms.

The small ground has only seen a crowd of 2,000 or more twice, firstly for a friendly with West Ham United, and secondly for the FA Cup tie between Aylesbury United and Slough Town in 1985 when Aylesbury were in the process of moving.

One of the quainter stands in senior non-league football, at Tring Town.

Oxford and the Berkshire Downs

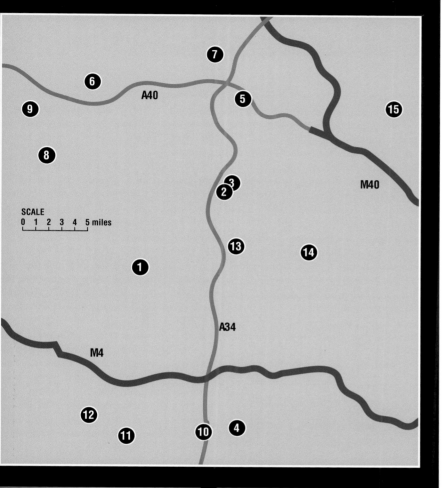

1	**Wantage Town FC**	**12**	**Hungerford Town FC**
2	**Abingdon Town FC**	**13**	**Didcot Town FC**
3	**Abingdon Utd. FC**	**14**	**AFC Wallingford**
4	**Thatcham Town FC**	**15**	**Thame United FC**
5	**Oxford City FC**		
6	**Witney Town FC**		
7	**Kidlington FC**		
8	**Clanfield FC**		
9	**Carterton Town FC**		
10	**Newbury Town FC**		
11	**Kintbury Rangers FC**		

THE re-emergence of Oxford City with their new ground and FA Vase Final appearance has overshadowed the strides made by one or two other clubs in the area. Thatcham Town have also developed a new ground and come close to Wessex League honours, while Thame United and Newbury Town both spent heavily on upgrading their grounds.

ALFREDIAN PARK
Wantage Town FC

Alfredian Park has been the home of Wantage Town Football Club since 1922, when they purchased the ground in Manor Road for £400, thanks to loans from local traders in the town.

The ground was called Alfredian Park via a competition run by the committee of the time, and the loan was paid off at the rate of £40 per annum over the following ten years. Thus Wantage Town became the first junior amateur club to own its own ground after previously playing at Challow Park in Wantage since their affiliation in 1892.

A small changing hut was erected in 1929, but in 1933 the club built a new pavilion containing separate dressing rooms for the teams and officials, a bathroom and a pay box at a cost of £105 11s. These changing facilities were in use, with a variety of improvements, until the current building was first used in 1987. The old pavilion still stands as a reminder of more Corinthian days, and is used as the groundsman's hut.

In 1938 a shelter was built for spectators, including bench seating for officials. This still stands next to the larger cover which was erected in the mid-fifties, and apart from losing ten feet to storm damage is virtually unchanged. By 1949 mains water had been installed for showers and baths where previously water had been drawn from a well standing close to the dressing rooms. A Nissen hut was also put up and used for extra changing accommodation and equipment storage.

Until 1969 the club had used various pubs in the town as a headquarters, but then at a cost of £4,000, a new wooden clubhouse was built, which has had new changing rooms and kitchen added to it and the front of the club is now re-built in brick. Training

Alfredian Park, Wantage.

floodlights were erected in 1984 though plans are afoot to construct match standard lights for the near future.

The Alfredian Park ground is very picturesque with a variety of trees on all sides and the backdrop of the Ridgeway Hills at the far end from the clubhouse. It almost seems a crime that such a delightfully maintained ground has a highest attendance of only 496, versus Newbury Town in 1956.

Abingdon United FC.

CULHAM ROAD
Abingdon Town FC

Culham Road first saw football played on it in 1899, when Abingdon FC merged with St. Michaels to form the current club, which then moved from its town centre ground, to today's site which has the flood plain of the River Thames, just 120 yards behind one goal.

In the early days the ground was simply an unenclosed pitch which was shared with the cricket club, and sat at right angles to its present position. Where the car-park is now positioned, there were tennis courts up until the Second World War.

The first buildings on the ground were some old wooden dressing rooms which were situated between the current entrance and dressing rooms; these were replaced in 1967. The first stand was built in the 1920's and was roughly behind where the small stand is on the clubhouse side of the ground. This burnt down in 1947, and was replaced two years later by a part concrete stand which in turn was gutted and turned into a lounge bar in 1984.

In 1950 the club entered the Spartan League and erected a cow-shed on the far side which is more or less still intact although it did lose a few yards off the end when the new stand was built. The ground stayed dormant for around 17 years until the new dressing room complex was opened, and this was followed five years later with the building of the clubhouse. Prior to this a small room near the dressing rooms had been used. During the last ten years major work has gone on to turn Culham Road into a comfortable ground capable of staging top grade football. In 1985, the first hard standing was put down, and two years later the floodlights were finally turned on with a Berks & Bucks Cup match against Burnham.

The following season work continued unabated with the completion of the hard standing and the enclosure of the ground with chain link fencing. A temporary stand was built in 1989 to allow the club to gain access to the Isthmian League, the seats coming from Oxford City's old White House ground.

As the club have gained promotion the amount of cover has steadily increased, with the main stand and cover down to the River End being built in 1991. The stand contains over 230 seats which were bought from Wembley Stadium in a similar manner to those at fellow Isthmian Leaguers Marlow.

In one corner of the ground stands the old clock which was also a legacy from the White House ground. Now having a ground of their own once again, Oxford City have more than once requested the return of their clock, only to be met with a polite refusal!

On entering the ground at Culham Road, the casual visitor is struck by the very greenness of it. Not only is it situated in a pleasantly rural area but most of the structures appear green too. It can never be described as simply an ordinary ground, as between each visit something always seems to have either been built, painted or moved. The forward-thinking people within must be congratulated on turning Culham Road into a stadium which, like good wine, improves with age.

*Above: **Culham Road, home of Abingdon Town since 1899.** Below: **The clubhouse.***

NORTHCOURT ROAD
Abingdon United FC

The junior of the two Abingdon clubs was formed in 1946 and shared the ground at Northcourt Road with North Abingdon Cricket Club until 1992 and as a result it has never been fully enclosed. The dressing rooms date from the founding of the club and the playing area was just an open space until it was fenced in the early 1970's. It remained much the same until a set of training lights was installed in 1980 which enabled the record crowd of 1,200 to see Oxford United play a fund-raising game.

In 1986 the club entered the FA Cup for the first time, drawing with Stourbridge and electing to replay the following day at Northcourt Road. The cricket club were also at home that afternoon and the stray balls from both games caused immense problems, something that would never be allowed nowadays.

In 1988 a 52-seater stand was built on the half-way line and prior to this the only cover was a canvas stand occasionally erected for FA Cup ties and other big games. The seats came from the Marlborough Road stand at the sadly defunct White House Ground at Oxford City. The clubhouse was extended in 1989 and now runs the width of the pitch behind the top goal.

In 1992 North Abingdon CC merged with Abingdon CC and the joint club now play most games at Culham Road next door to Abingdon Town FC. The old pitch is now just used for the odd junior game. For a number of years the club has struggled to get proper floodlights but due to the ground being in a conservation area a long battle ensued which was only won in 1994 when retractable lights, such as those at Moor Green and Felixstowe were installed. They were inevitably opened against Oxford United in late 1994 before a crowd of 800.

WATERSIDE PARK
Thatcham Town FC

Thatcham Town have had their fair share of grounds over the years since formation 100 years ago. The first recorded game was in early 1895, when the team played Newbury on a pitch on Dunstan Green, which is still an open space today.

Between then and the outbreak of the Second World War, this, and another ground in Park Lane were home, although there is little information available on either ground. During the War, the club moved to a field owned by Mr. Robert Brown, which was also just off Park Lane, until 1947. Brown's Field is now the home of Thatcham Cricket Club.

The first Supporters' Club was formed around this time, when they moved, with permission of local farmer Vic Tostavine, to the Turnery Works, where supporters helped prepare the pitch by collecting buckets full of stones. The move was fairly short-lived, for negotiations began to purchase land in Lancaster Close around 1950, and it was ready for the first game on 6th September 1951 when Royal Ascot were the visitors for a Reading League game. The dressing rooms were already in place in what was to develop into a fine ground in its 41-year history, with a capacity of some 3,000 and seating for 300. The record attendance at Lancaster Close was for the floodlit opening game against Fulham on January 25th 1982.

Town aspired to a higher standard of football, and in December 1992, they moved to their purpose-built ground at Waterside Park, on a ten acre site, with a ground capacity of 2,000, including 293 seats. Built with the Southern League in mind, it has superb dressing and social facilities to match the club's ambitions. The seating area is set

THE WHITE HOUSE and COURT PLACE FARM
Oxford City FC

The fact that Oxford City's spiritual home, the White House ground was so cruelly taken away by their landlords is one of the great sadnesses of recent non-League football. Whilst it can be argued that a spanking new ground on the main A40 at Marston is easily accessible and ideal for expansion as the club progresses, the White House had charm and history in abundance. Tucked away amongst back streets near the City Centre, the old ground had a character and atmosphere about it that Court Place Farm will take a great many years to equal, if ever.

That is not to say that the new ground is unattractive. The long approach road from the car-park possesses a sports complex situated alongside, and on entry, the first impression is of spaciousness, with the huge administration and dressing room complex set back from behind the goal, complete with a vibrant clubhouse. Two stands, similar in size but not symmetrical, stand each side with the ends open. The club name is proudly displayed above the stand and the mass of advertising hoardings bear testimony to the hard working commercial department. The capacity of the ground when opened was 2,000 with 150 seats, although the club are ambitious and have further plans. After leaving the White House, City were forced to field youth teams to keep the club alive, until joining the South Midlands League as a senior side again, playing for one season at Cutteslowe Park, and until the move at Roman Way, former home of Pressed Steel F.C. and Headington Amateurs FC.

The White House at its demise had an official capacity of 9,000, although it is unlikely the club would ever have been allowed to fill it, as they did for an Amateur Cup tie against Leytonstone when 9,500 crammed in. In those days, with far fewer cars, the tightness of the ground was not a major problem.

The sturdy, proud-looking main stand at one time suffered the indignity of having its roof skewered by two poorly-designed floodlight pylons. These were removed when the ground closed, leaving gaping holes in the asbestos. The rear portion of the stand was fenced off, and in its twilight years bushes threatened to engulf it.

Almost as if in an act of defiance, the stand remained whilst development went on all around it, only succumbing to the bulldozer around the time that the new ground was opened.

slightly back from the pitch at ground level, which means the view is not all it might be, but this is only a minor irritant at a very tidy ground.

MARRIOTTS CLOSE and OAKEY PARK
Witney Town FC

Witney Town's move to their out-of-town stadium at Curbridge named after the former Chairman Aubrey Oakey has not been without its problems. Terrible drainage difficulties meant much of the first couple of seasons' action became bogged down but improvement eventually came.

Witney celebrated their centenary back in 1985 and for most of that time played their football on what was latterly known as Marriotts Close but in early days was Mr Marriott's Field. Officially the club records state that the ground was first used just after the First World War, but it could well have been much earlier than that, although for many years the field was undeveloped with just a small corrugated shelter put up during the early thirties. The players changed in the Red Lion Hotel at the top of Corn Street.

During the World War Two the ground was used variously as a prisoner of war reception area and a training ground for the Home Guard. As a result, the Leys Recreation Ground was temporarily used while Marriott's Close was made playable again. In 1961 the club successfully obtained a long wooden hut from Kidlington airfield and transported it to the ground where it was re-erected and opened in September of that year as a clubhouse.

It did steadfast service, being extended in 1968 with a lounge area, until November 1974 when the club's Trophy Room was built followed by a two-storey clubhouse on the site of the old hut. The ground was purchased in 1968 by a committee led by Mr. Oakey and soon after the first floodlights went up, opened before a match with Swindon Town.

One of the last significant changes at the ground was in 1974 when the old cover was replaced by a new stand. A projected idea for

Clanfield's dressing rooms and cover, built on the cricket square when football took over.

RADCOT ROAD
Clanfield FC

The Radcot Road ground has had football played on it since at least 1890 when the original club was formed. The village nestles in the Thames Valley twelve miles south of Witney, and supported football and cricket teams until the mid 1960s before interest in cricket waned and the football club was able to take over the site unencumbered by the overlap of seasons.

At the time, the ground was circular as it is today but, with no football facilities at all, the players had to change in the village hall. An old wooden cricket pavilion stood just to the left of where the far goal is today, and the concrete footings can still be seen. The square was situated roughly between today's centre circle and the stand.

The dressing rooms were first built in 1965, with the clubhouse and cover going up three years later. Further improvements and additions have been made since including the entrance, car park, and the planting of conifers to eventually act as a much needed wind-break in this low-lying area. The club competed in the Witney & District and North Berkshire Leagues before promotion to the Hellenic League necessitated the ground taking its current form.

a similar stand opposite never got off the ground despite much publicity.

Towards the end Marriotts Close was looking tatty, with the cover along the road side of the ground in need of repair and the tennis courts, later used as a car-park, in a similar state. Around 1991 plans were put in motion to move out of town, selling Marriotts Close for development. Oakey Park was built on land within an industrial park and boasts a large grandstand complex

with changing rooms and luxurious function rooms all incorporated. It has just over 200 seats with a covered area capable of holding a further 1,000.

YARNTON ROAD
Kidlington FC

Kidlington were formed in 1909 and played on various fields before settling at a pitch in Lyne Road now covered by a housing estate. Their next ground was in Exeter Close which was undeveloped apart from a changing hut which still exists, but only as a tractor shed for the cricket club that play alongside on what was the old ground but is now covered by a medical centre.

The club moved to their current home in 1969. Farm land was transformed into a pitch and the original clubhouse was soon built having earlier seen service on a local airfield. It was subsequently re-built into its modern state in 1980 and looks out over a ground which has really not developed much further, possibly due to the club's 30 year membership of the Hellenic League who do not have such severe ground requirements.

Witney Town's former home at Marriott's Close.

KILKENNY LANE
Carterton Town FC

Carterton FC were formed in 1922, and played in the Witney and District League right through to 1982, when the club was re-formed with the merging of Carterton Boys FC, and the Town suffix was added.

The recreation ground in the centre of the former village was home until the council offered, at a peppercorn rent, a derelict site in Kilkenny Lane which was soon transformed with the building of an impressive clubhouse across the front of the ground. For a while, as the club settled in the Hellenic League, the ground was no more than a pitch with a barrier and dug-outs, but in 1989 temporary floodlights were installed. The car-park was soon enlarged and the entrance re-designed, and in 1994 the new lights and some temporary seating were installed to cater for promotion to the Premier Division.

RECREATION GROUND
Kintbury Rangers FC

The Recreation Ground has been in use since around 1926, when it was left by William Gladstone in trust to the people of the area for the exclusive use of sportsmen. The small pagoda-shaped pavilion has been extended since it was built at the time of opening, and now houses a small bar, as well as the dressing rooms.

Floodlights were installed three years ago, and a small stand was also planned for the near future. The original club was founded in 1890 and, amongst others, played on a ground on an estate called Wallingtons. The present club were formed during the war, in 1943.

STATION ROAD
Didcot Town FC

Didcot's modest home has undergone major pruning of late which has reduced it to a bare railed-off pitch and a small cover to comply with Hellenic League rules. The original pitch was 20 yards or so further up the ground, with a small covered area down half of one side and another behind the goal.

Before the land was sold and 23 houses built on it, the pitch was shifted down, although the clubhouse, a former Nissen hut with an extension, remains intact.

The Town club first played on a pitch still used today by Didcot Casuals, at Brasenose Park before moving to Station Road between the wars. A later scheme to sell the ground and move to a site on the other side of the railway owned by South Oxfordshire DC was put on ice, but may well be resurrected as the club attempt to sell what is left of the old place to expand elsewhere.

HITHERCROFT SPORTS CENTRE
AFC Wallingford

The two clubs in the town, United, who played in the Chiltonian League, and Town from the Hellenic League were playing in 1995 as AFC WALLINGFORD, in the Chiltonian. The decision to amalgamate is an obvious one, although there is some surprise at the drop down in status, as Wallingford are pretty much central in the Hellenic catchment area.

Their home at Hithercroft Sports Centre was opened in 1977, catering for many sports. The football ground has a stand and is fully enclosed with dressing rooms which were added in 1982. Prior to moving on to Hithercroft, Town played at the Bull Croft, latterly the home of United. It has a post and railed-off pitch with a small covered standing area by the dressing rooms. It will continue to be used by the new club's reserve and junior teams.

WINDMILL GROUND
Thame United FC

Thame have always played on the Windmill Ground and took part in local football until 1959, when they joined the Hellenic League. At that time the ground was just an open field with two pitches, open countryside on three sides and a dressing room block which was still used right up to 1994. In the late 60's a cover for 300 to 400 people was put up on the side near the clubhouse which was opened by Ron Springett in 1969. It has since had many extensions although is now due for demolition.

Thame were one of the first sides in Oxfordshire to have floodlights which were up and running by 1980 and soon after the ground began to become enclosed when houses were built behind one goal. Prior to this the land was used for grazing ponies. As Thame progressed to the Isthmian League the Windmill became fully enclosed and the training pitch was sold for more housing, ironically to Beazer Homes whose signboards were prominent on the ground for some time! The covered area gained seats slowly but surely and could accommodate 230 spectators while the ground became fenced off with hard standing all around.

With promotion to the Second Division the club embarked on their largest project to date. The cover on the clubhouse side was replaced by a large stand and social area which eventually will include bars, a restaurant and new dressing rooms, not unlike those at Witney Town. When this is complete the old clubhouse will be demolished and the area made into a car-park as Thame continue their quest to be the top non-league club in the county.

BULPIT LANE
Hungerford Town FC

Hungerford Town's ground in Bulpit Lane has existed, more or less on the same site, since the club were formed in 1886. The area where the football, rugby and cricket clubs all play within close proximity to each other is common land and was known as the Downs when the Town first started.

Between the wars the playing area was enclosed with a wooden fence and dressing rooms built, but these disappeared during the Second World War. A new dressing room with a verandah was erected in 1947 and again the ground was fenced, this time using corrugated iron. The first grandstand of note was built in 1950, using concrete and asbestos, on the west side of the ground, and this is still in use, complete with seats from an old cinema at an army base.

In 1972 the club bought a redundant pre-cast concrete building previously used by the local British Legion which was converted into a clubhouse and soon after at the bottom of the ground, a newer brick-built changing complex was built, thus demoting the old 1947 version to life as a storage room.

The clubhouse was extended with a function room in 1975 and the old iron fence suffered severe damage around the same

Hungerford Town's Bulpit Lane ground.

time and was partly replaced with a solid concrete panel fence.

Further changes have occurred since, the main one being the erection of a covered enclosure opposite the old stand, which went up around fifteen years ago and has now also been given seating.

The perimeter post and rail is now infilled as to requirements and Bulpit Lane has been given a capacity of 3,000, almost twice the current record gate which saw the FA Vase Semi-Final with Sudbury Town in 1989.

FARADAY ROAD
Newbury Town FC

Newbury Town's 108-year history is as peppered with ground problems as their neighbours Hungerford's have been smooth running. Newbury seem to have had a virtually constant battle against short leases, town planners, swampy pitches and relief roads ever since they kicked off on the cricket ground over 100 years ago.

The club were formed at a meeting on September 13th 1887 and quickly agreed to accept the offer of a pitch at the cricket ground at two guineas a season. The marriage was not a happy one, for more than once the cricket club gave notice for the footballers to go and finally the Corporation gave

Newbury some land at Greenham Dairy Farm. Again it was not a success and the poor state of affairs was having an adverse effect so a ground-share agreement was sought with Standard FC who played on the Rectory Ground at Pinniger Park. The site was found to be not central enough which affected gates and Newbury moved back to the cricket ground 1905.

They stayed, then as Newbury Town, for five years until moving to the first Town ground, which soon acquired a pavilion. After the Great War, negotiations were made with a view to buying a stand from Maiden Erleigh race course, and this went ahead during 1919, the capacity being recorded as "400 or more".

As early as 1936, the club were told of plans to route a new road through the ground which put any future planning on hold, but when war broke out again these plans were forgotten. Indeed, in 1946 when applying to resume playing, the club were given a three-year lease. The pavilion had been vandalised and Town were obliged to put it right under the terms, and the agreement continued into 1949 when Reading FC agreed to play their A team matches at the Town ground.

The club entered the prestigious Metropolitan League in 1952 but within a year revised plans for a relief road had been

published which meant the club would have to move to a site next door. This did not occur in the end for a further ten years, by which time a 50-year lease had been agreed and a 120ft long shelter erected by the Supporters' Club. During 1962 fencing went round the new ground which was next door to the old one and work began on the clubhouse in April of that year. In 1963 the club were notified that work was about to go ahead on the road, and extra effort was made to enable the new ground to be opened in the presence of the Mayor, on August 24th before a game with Stokenchurch. Almost immediately the new pitch gave major problems and matches were arranged away from home. Also, the club were without a stand for the first time in dozens of years. This ground was home for barely seventeen years before again negotiations began to re-locate to a site next door, which would cost in the region of £100,000.

After a further season the new ground in what is now Faraday Road was opened on August 30th 1980 before an FA Cup tie with Pagham. Three months later Southampton switched on the new floodlights before a disappointing crowd of 402 but it was another two years before permission was given to build a stand which opened in November 1983 during the club's first season in the Isthmian League.

As fortunes have since changed, the ground has been progressively improved but, true to form, it suffered closure for some time as the ground regulations laid down had not been strictly adhered to. Part of the 1994-95 season was played on away grounds as problems occurred with fencing and a new stand.

Being part of an industrial area and having been on the same ground for twelve years, Town may feel a little apprehensive that it might soon be time to move on again.

Photos in this section by: Gavin Ellis-Neville, John Haines, Andy Molden and Dean Walton.

The extremes of non-league football in the Oxford area...

Above: Osberton Radiators, ex Oxford Senior League side and FA Cup entrants, immortalised on Radio 5 by John Inverdale.

Right: A modern structure at the university sports ground in Iffley Road, Oxford where Roger Bannister ran the first four-minute mile. Non-league football is occasionally played here.

North Oxon and Buckinghamshire

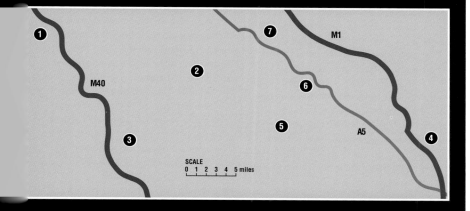

SCALE
0 1 2 3 4 5 miles

1 **Banbury United FC**

2 **Buckingham Town FC**

3 **Bicester Town FC**

4 **Dunstable FC**

5 **Leighton Town FC**

6 **Milton Keynes City FC**

7 **Wolverton Town FC**

8 **Newport Pagnell Town FC**

Below: A packed main stand at Buckingham Town for an FA Vase match with Tiverton.

THIS area covers the northern part of the Cotswolds and stretches across to the ever-expanding city of Milton Keynes including a small part of Bedfordshire.

By far the most interesting ground, Wolverton Park, is now, sadly, no longer a non-League venue - although it is used by Wolverton Ladies as well as for junior football - being merely a shadow of its former impressive self.

Brackley Town moved from Buckingham Road to their current ground in Churchill Way just over twenty years ago, and have built a covered standing area as well as seating in front of the clubhouse and changing room complex. A time of turmoil saw the club voluntarily drop from the United Counties into the Hellenic League in 1994.

In modern times, Banbury United, Dunstable and Milton Keynes have all dropped out of the Southern League which leaves Buckingham Town as the top club in the area.

FORD MEADOW
Buckingham Town FC

In 1883 a meeting was called in the White Hart Hotel in the small market town of Buckingham with the idea of starting a football club. The Rev. Stewart was instrumental in forming the club which began playing on an area of meadow land close to the River Ouse in 1883 and has done so ever since.

Local papers indicate that the first match was against a Banbury side and ended 0-0. As was usual the players used a hostelry to change in, normally the New Inn, and it

wasn't until during the Second World War that the first stand and dressing rooms were erected at the ground by Messrs Pollard and Sons. Until then Ford Meadow had been nothing more than a pitch roped-off through wooden stakes which regularly became submerged by the infant River Ouse. As the club made its way through the fifties, at one point dropping out of the Hellenic League into the Aylesbury and District, the ground remained more or less unchanged.

The South Midlands League brought a new challenge and a primitive form of floodlighting was perched along a series of telegraph poles, which had been acquired from Coventry City's training ground in the early sixties. The current clubhouse began to see light in 1968 although it was not officially opened until 1970 and in 1980 the lights were re-vamped to comply with regulations.

The modernised Southern League ground now has a new seated stand opposite the original one, which has had new sides and a new roof in recent times but still retains its initial interior and so qualifies as being the original!

Perhaps because Ford Meadow has rarely seen large crowds, it has never needed to be substantially altered and indeed the modern housing all around gives the ground a new enough look. The record crowd to date is 2,451 which saw the FA Cup tie with Orient in 1984 and although the capacity of the ground is officially 4,000, in its present form it is unlikely that police would allow a larger crowd than that to congregate on what is a pleasant unassuming ground in a residential area.

THE STADIUM
Banbury United FC

One of the great tragedies in football is when a once proud stadium is allowed to deteriorate to such an extent it gives the impression of having given up on itself and lost all self respect. Whilst the ground,

home since 1933 of Banbury United, previously Banbury Spencer, still has the vestiges of its past, it was until very recently allowed to go completely to pot and has only just received a new lease of life.

The Stadium is reached by way of a long narrow, badly-rutted lane alongside the railway sidings, an approach forever under water due to the potholes. The ground entrance still sports a hoarding for the Beazer Homes League, which they sadly left in 1990, and leads to an open area which at one point housed a press box, and to the left a covered cow shed behind which were a group of huts selling refreshments and souvenirs. These were all removed around 1980, and the area has remained open . The long covered terrace behind the town goal is intact apart from a portion of the roof on the side, where it curves around in a manner recalling Southport's Haig Avenue in its league days. In the opposite corner is a breeze-blocked area with bench seats to cater for officials. The far side of the ground, bordered by trees, is now badly neglected, with a gaping hole where the main stand once stood. A large pile of heavily weed-strewn rubbishy material lies dumped on the site of the stand which was condemned in 1985 as unsafe, and stood boarded up until its demise in 1990.

Behind the open-end goal the terracing remains but the skeleton of the 20ft. high fence is askew and rusting. The railings and advertising hoardings which surround the pitch are in an advanced state of vandalised decay. However, the club, continue to play, despite threats from the ground's owners to wind them up, and indeed upgraded the floodlighting when they purchased some of Oxford City's old system from the dismantled White House stadium.

Behind all these problems is a still proud club who, it must be hoped, can yet recover from too many years on a downward slide and become a force once more in Oxfordshire football, even if it means vacating the Stadium and moving out of town.

WILLEN ROAD SPORTS GROUND
Newport Pagnell Town FC

Newport Pagnell Town are relative novices, formed as recently as 1963 as Newport Pagnell Wanderers by a group of lads in the town. Their first games were in youth football on a pitch next to the cricket square on Bury Field with players changing at the back of the Cannon pub in Union Street. Very soon, after an influx of players from the disbanded Aston Martin works side, the club took off and success led to a move to the new ground at Willen Road in 1972 after a short period using the youth club in Wolverton Road.

The opening game, in April of that year came against Bletchley Town with Wanderers having changed their name to Town.

The brick built stand was initially erected as a standing cover, but promotion to the United Counties Premier Division brought a need for seating and so 100 were installed. Many more improvements have been made in recent years as the club and ground progressed. A function room was added in 1982 with new changing rooms, while a fence and some 300 fast-growing conifer trees now surround the playing area. After much heartache and several rejections, approval for floodlighting was finally granted and the first match under the new system took place on 22nd April 1991.

BELL CLOSE
Leighton Town FC

The Bell Close ground has only been segregated off from the other activities for around ten years. Up until then the site was always shared with cricket, tennis and hockey. Although the other sports continue at the ground which is run by a sports association, the football has expanded since 1992 when the club entered the Isthmian League from the South Midlands League.

Bell Close was the original home of Leighton United who played in the South Midland and Spartan Leagues and was developed around ten years ago when a stand was built. New dressing rooms have followed to replace those at the back of the clubhouse, and fencing and terracing at the top end, along with floodlights, have completely changed the ground which is aiming for a B grade to qualify for continued Isthmian League status.

Banbury's condemned stand, complete with mural, now demolished.

SPORTS GROUND, OXFORD ROAD
Bicester Town FC

Early 1930's action at Bicester.

The nomadic existence of the Town club makes it all the more remarkable that it has survived and prospered, bearing in mind that for most of the time since its formation (an amalgamation of Bicester Rovers and Bicester Harriers), the club has played second fiddle to cricket at the Sports Ground.

Both original clubs date to before 1874 and shared the Station Road ground, for friendly matches until the new club began playing at the cricket field in 1896 for a few seasons until offered a field on the Banbury Road owned by a Mr Busby. Although a little out of town it was becoming more difficult to find pitches to play on and it was not until they were evicted following damage to surrounding fences that they returned to Station Road, using the adjacent St Edburg's Hall to change in.

This continued for a few seasons until building work began in Prior Road and consumed part of the ground making it too small for football whereupon Town played until the Great War on a pitch in London Road near the level crossing.

In the twenties they reverted to the cricket field and a pitch along Oxford Road, both belonging to a Major Coker who also owned the golf course and was a keen sportsman. With the golf poorly patronised it was suggested the cricket and football clubs should play at the links, which would be wound-up and levelled. Major Coker agreed, but it was not until 1929 that the ground was finally bought for £900 by a group of eleven businessmen from the town. It was soon enclosed with a galvanised tin fence and the cricket club pavilion re-erected and used as changing rooms. Outside the ground where a footpath ran, a roadway was created which now leads to the car-park. The old wooden stand was built soon after. The current changing rooms date from around 1960 and were built alongside the old pavilion which had by that time sprouted wing-style extensions which housed showers. The stand had also been extended by then as the ground began to grow.

Due to the continued presence of cricket, the club has been unable to expand further, but it appears the cricket and hockey clubs are to relocate to a site in Chesterton which will allow the Foxhunters to enclose the ground for the first time, without the neighbouring rugby club posing a problem. The club certainly deserve this spot of luck.

CREASEY PARK
Dunstable FC

Creasey Park is another fairly contemporary ground which has tended to attract more than its fair share of ill-fortune. Built in the early sixties following the formation of a Limited Company by the then Deputy Mayor of Dunstable, Walter Creasey, the ground's emergence was primarily due to Mr Creasey falling out with Luton Town FC over the allocation of Cup-Final tickets.

Prior to that Dunstable FC had played on local pitches in the area before being re-formed in 1950 and using a private ground on a vacant field owned by Bagshaw's Foundry. It was later taken over by Thomas Tillings and is now covered by The Mall, a housing complex next to Dunstable College.

The new site on Brewers Hill was at the end of an unmade road and at first consisted of nothing but two small huts, one for dressing rooms and another a small club room.

The banking around the pitch was created by surplus earth from the levelling of the ground and the impressive brick stand and offices were built around 1963-64 with a small area of terracing in front and opposite, while a wooden fence surrounded the ground. There was originally a 60ft long cow-shed type enclosure opposite the stand some but this was replaced by the Harold Stew stand in 1978 which blew down to be in turn followed by the Andrew Downey stand which also blew down - although it was re-erected straight away. Finally in 1993 it was replaced by the John Stanford stand which was extended by 50ft. The wooden fence was removed and replaced by a concrete one as Creasey Park improved in the sixties to accommodate Southern League football. A crowd of some 6,000 saw Manchester United play there in 1974 as the Board of the time brought the likes of Jeff Astle and George Best to the ground; but the inevitable crash occurred two years later and Dunstable Town folded to be succeeded by Dunstable FC. They too struggled under a wave of apathy in the town, compounded by the nearness of Luton, and did not emerge for the 1994-95 season.

Dunstable OB's moved into the ground, playing in the South Midlands League but they lasted less than half a season before folding and their fixtures were taken over by a new club, Dunstable United.

MANOR FIELDS
Milton Keynes FC

Manor Fields was opened by the Duke of Edinburgh in conjunction with the Playing Fields Association back in 1952. Then it was the home of Bletchley FC who had just moved into the Spartan League and the ground consisted of a small wooden stand on the half way line with a long shack running all down the opposite side, with ash as hard standing.

Creasey Park, Dunstable.

The top goal nearest the A5 had a steep grass bank behind it with an entrance through a car-park. Since those days, Bletchley became Milton Keynes City and in 1971 found themselves in the Southern League but sadly soon folded and the ground was taken over, firstly by Milton Keynes Borough, and later Milton Keynes FC who are currently in the South Midlands League. Very little has changed the basic shape of Manor Fields other than general wear and tear. The main difference is the replacement of the tin shed with a sturdy corrugated cover with concrete terracing and the installation of floodlights. The clubhouse in the far corner of the ground has been upgraded more than once, the small area of land behind the goal having been sold for development to help with finances. The record crowd on the ground was in 1967 when 1,997 saw the United Counties League Cup Final against local rivals Wolverton BR.

Manor Fields suffers most from simply being situated where it is. Milton Keynes is in the main made up of a population which originated from elsewhere and as such has no real allegiance to the club or the area. The site, next to the A5 trunk road has not realised the potential it showed when the Duke of Edinburgh opened it 43 years ago but is still doing a job, although possibly not in front of the crowds it deserves.

Photos in this section by: Pat Brunning, Eric Marsh, Andy Molden, Chas Rawlings and Dean Walton.

Above: An early 1890's picture of the Whitsun Sports at Wolverton Park.

Below: A view from the same angle some 100 years later.

WOLVERTON PARK
Wolverton Town

The former home of Wolverton Town Football Club is now in a sorry state and used only on a day to day basis by junior clubs as well as Wolverton Ladies FC. It is difficult to imagine the ground packed with the many thousands who would throng to the Whitsun Works Sports Days or cycling tournaments which proved even more popular than the football.

The Park was built and opened for the benefit of employees at the London and North-Western Railway Company who had their works next door. Known as the Wolverton Park and Recreation Ground, it was opened by "The Chairman of the company accompanied by the directors, nobility and gentry of the neighbourhood" on August 3rd 1885. The seven acre site had a cycle track, running track, football pitch, tennis courts and a bowling green, and over 15,000 people assembled in Wolverton before some 5,000 marched to the ground for the grand opening. All staff were given a day's holiday and a commemorative medal was struck for those attending the first sports day.

Wolverton (L & NW Railway) FC joined the Southern League in 1895, won the Second Division at the first attempt, but were relegated two years later and went into Northampton football. Much later they were known as Wolverton & BR before finishing their days firstly as Wolverton Town and then, slightly more bizarrely as either MK (Wolverton) or a variation on that theme as they sought for some reason to incorporate Milton Keynes into the name of a club which no longer had any connections with the railway. The Park was instrumental in launching the careers of several Olympiads in either track and field or cycling and it wasn't until the Great War that the Whitsun Sports were discontinued, although later re-instated. The lay-out of the park was virtually unchanged until the fifties and sixties when it began to fall into disrepair. It was the subject of much wrangling as to who owned it. Some believed it had been given to the town, although that was denied in other quarters. What is known for sure is that the banked areas around the track were

The seated stand, shown to the right of the word 'Shop' on the 1899 plan below, is believed to be the oldest football stand in the country.

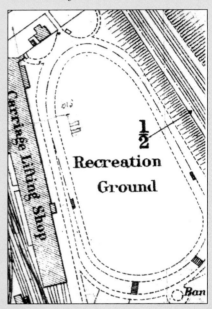

partially covered by stands on the bends nearest the entrance, and the little green wooden stand which is still in situ today was built sometime between opening and 1900, when it is shown on maps. These could possibly date it as the oldest football stand in the country, even older than those at Denaby and Gravesend. The seats inside it however, are relatively modern, having come from Loftus Road, home of Queens Park Rangers FC.

The adjacent covered terrace is much younger, having been erected in 1947-48 and licensed to hold 1,000. Although bearing little relation to the splendid ground it once was, the Park continued to stage senior football through the eighties and it had a moment of glory in 1987 when over 4,000 saw the Berks & Bucks Cup Final between Aylesbury and Wycombe Wanderers. The future for a ground wedged up against the railway looks uncertain, especially as successive generations seem all too eager to wash their hands of it.

Hertfordshire

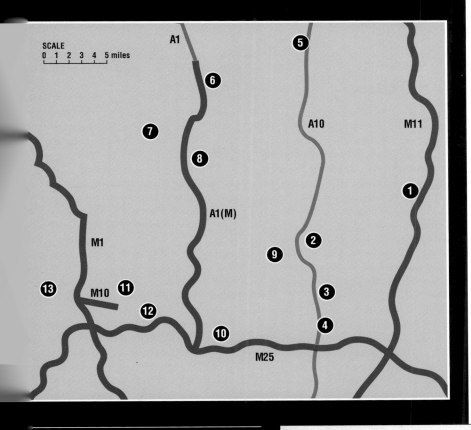

SCALE
0 1 2 3 4 5 miles

A1

5

6

A10

M11

7

8

A1(M)

1

M1

2

9

3

13

M10

11

4

12

10

M25

H ERTFORDSHIRE is a sprawling county with the open flatlands of Cambridgeshire to its north contrasting with the outer London suburbia of Potters Bar in the south. Its grounds are just as polarised, with historic Clarence Park and the Top Field being the oldest, whilst Ware are in the process of watching Wodson Park created for them following the sad loss of Buryfield.

With the elevation of Barnet to the Football League, the rejuvenated Stevenage Borough rule the roost in the Conference as premier non-League club in Hertfordshire.

GEORGE WILSON STADIUM
Bishop's Stortford FC

Bishop's Stortford Football Club moved to its present home in 1919, having previously played at the Laundry Field, a ground which local historians believe was located roughly where the 18th hole is now at Bishop's Stortford Golf Club, just off Dunmow Road, on the eastern side of the town.

Their new ground, just off South Road in an area known as Havers Park, was opened and first used on Saturday October 4th 1919 when Ware were the visitors in front of 400 spectators. After the penultimate game of that season, a presentation to the club of a

1	Bishop's Stortford FC
2	Ware FC
3	Hoddesdon Town FC
4	Cheshunt FC
5	Royston Town FC
6	Baldock Town FC
7	Hitchin Town FC
8	Stevenage Borough FC
9	Hertford Town FC
10	Potters Bar Town FC
11	St Albans City FC
12	London Colney FC
13	Hemel Hempstead FC

Above: Bishop's Stortford in 1974, before alterations and terracing.

Right: The main stand 20 years later with glass viewing area.

Photos in this section by: Eric Marsh, VJ Robertson, Colin Sinden, Gareth Stephens, Martin Wray, James Wright.

pavilion which was formerly in use by the Polo Club at Silver Leys was announced. It was also revealed the Town Ground had been bought by a Joe Brazier who would provide "a good and level ground".

In the early days the Town Ground was little more than a field, where spectators were separated from the players by a heavy rope propped up on posts. The only cover was in the polo pavilion, while in the rear was a changing room so small there was no way all 22 could get in at once and the teams had to change separately.

The mid-thirties saw a small wooden stand and a tannoy system erected while refreshments were sold from a kiosk. As the boom times arrived just after the war crowds soared and in 1947 2,820 saw the Herts Senior Cup semi-final against Cheshunt. It was around this time that the club purchased an old Nissen hut which served both as a clubhouse and a training area in bad weather.

In 1961 the new main stand with seating for nearly 250 people was opened, but it had taken an age to complete due to the shortage of brick. It had a segregated area for directors and guests plus dressing rooms, a boardroom and a bar with social facilities upstairs.

A new ground record was posted in 1967 when 4,500 saw Stortford beat West Ham United in a celebration match to switch on the recently acquired floodlights and a covered terrace was put up at the Thorley End which is popular today with home fans.

The following year a new tea bar, office and concrete terracing next to the main stand were constructed as the ground and the club enjoyed success with crowds of 1,000 or more for each game. It was around this time that it was renamed the George Wilson Stadium in honour of the club Chairman who had been on the committee since 1929.

Two years later the ground record went again as 6,000 saw the Blues hold Peterborough United to a 2-2 draw in the FA Cup 2nd round.

The rear of the main stand was refurbished in the late 1970's to provide a glazed viewing area accessible from the club room and in 1981 the financial windfall, which came from winning the FA Trophy, saw work on the impressive area of terracing opposite the main stand.

Previously it was only partly terraced with a large grass bank behind it leading to a small car-park. The new terrace was put to the test in January 1983 when, having drawn at Ayresome Park, Stortford took on Middlesbrough in the FA Cup 3rd round in front of over 9,500 spectators.

The summer of 1988 saw the club sell off part of this area for housing and a smaller car-park was built along with new turnstiles. The club room and viewing areas were also modernised and a porta-cabin was brought in to house the Supporters' Club shop and Commercial Department.

The Rhodes Avenue End, or Town End as it is popularly known, was refurbished in 1992 when a large exit gate and new turnstiles were put in, and more recently still a close-boarded fence has tidied up the south side of the ground. This has cordoned it off from the ditch which still claims its fair share of matchballs.

BURYFIELD
Ware FC

Buryfield's fate was sealed in May 1995 when work began on a 28-week programme to build Ware Football Club a new ground at Wodson Park, on the northern edge of the town. The new ground will have the standard clubhouse, changing rooms and seated stand combination on one side with covered terracing opposite, all complying with Diadora League regulations. The owners of Buryfield plan to convert all or part of it into a car-park for the works next door and the ground will disappear after nearly 70 years of football.

Ware Football Club, or Ware Town as they were known in the early days, began on a pitch at Presdales in November 1892. The ground had already been used to stage the 1890 Herts Senior Cup Final and was popular, although in truth it was nothing more than a flat field on land owned by a Mr. Cox, a local football man whose sons played in that final. Mr Cox was invited to act as President and naturally allowed the club to play at Presdales until they moved to a pitch at Highfields along Hoe Lane, now home to Hertford Rugby Club. In 1894 the club appealed for funds to help erect a pavilion on a ground that seemed a permanent base, and by November it had been built. Sadly, Ware were forced off Highfields and played next in Canons Park which is roughly where Canons Road is now. The pavilion and fencing were moved to the new ground but this, and the new rent of £7 10s a year put the club in debt. By 1902 they were again on the move, this

time to a ground now under Marsh Lane Industrial Estate in London Road. Here they stayed until 1921 when Presdales Lower Park was made available and accepted after the Canons Park ground was sold. Three years later came another move, this time to Page's Field - now covered by Fanshawe Crescent. This ground proved far from satisfactory with no facilities of any kind. A transfer to Park Road came in 1926 on to a pitch used previously by Ware Engineers. It was soon roped off, but there were no changing facilities and players used the Millstream pub for many years until the Ware Swimming Pool opened and their rooms were then utilised.

In 1935 the pitch was turned around to run east to west and the Council re-sited the grandstand, but 12 years later the pitch was back on its original site. The boom years after the war saw crowds of 3,000 or more for derby matches, and the ground was improved significantly. A new covered stand went up near the halfway line and changing rooms in the shape of old Nissen huts were bought as Army surplus and erected in 1949. A new brick-built stand replaced the old wooden one in 1961, and this contained dressing rooms underneath and seating for 250 people. A small area of corrugated cover had stood nearby but this was moved to the opposite side of the pitch where it still stands, and replaced by a club room. A dozen years later Buryfield saw floodlit football for the first time when, on September 4th 1973, Arsenal played Ware to celebrate the switch-on. Today the shabby-looking ground is on death row. It is nothing a stay of execution and a wash and brush up would not put right, but the outlook is bleak. The covered enclosures on either side of the pitch are rusting and weed strewn while the main stand has seen better days. Despite all this, it was an interesting ground where little had changed until the fateful future plans were unveiled.

Buryfield is soon to become an expensive car park for Glaxo.

Hoddesdon's stand used to be on the halfway line but, as the aerial view (below) shows, the pitch has been moved down away from the cricket square.

LOWFIELD
Hoddesdon Town FC

Twenty years after their formation in 1879, Hoddesdon Football Club moved from an original site on Mancers Field to Lowfield which is still home today. Situated on the west side of town, Lowfield is flanked by Park View and the High Street to the east and Barclay Park to the west.

The seven acres of ground, originally owned by the Barclay family, have been shared by both football and cricket for nearly one hundred years, but it wasn't until 1924 that the arrangement was put on a formal footing. The deeds stated that the ground was conveyed to the council who were empowered to let any part of it to the two clubs. One stipulation was the ground had to be made available to the people of the town for one day each year for an annual fair.

In 1982, both clubs signed a 50-year lease, thus providing security, and under the new arrangement the football club would have sole use of Lowfield for 32 weeks of the year. This however prevented Town from entering the Isthmian League in 1984. The original pitch backed on to Beech Walk at the northern end and as a result covered most of the cricket area including the square. In the mid 1950's the pitch was moved 40 yards south, away from the square, and at the same time the club built the covered enclosure which straddled the half-way line, but now fills one half of the ground. This replaced the much older pavilion which stood on the site close to where the clubhouse now is.

The seventies saw more improvements to Lowfield when, firstly, after a long battle with the Urban District Council and then with the tenants, floodlighting was erected and the switch-on was celebrated with a match against West Ham United on March 7th 1973. The game attracted a record crowd of 3,500.

A pay-box was erected at the main entrance to Lowfield around the same time, and eighteen months later for the first time, a solid timber rail went up around the pitch, replacing the ropes which were often a problem when wet. The wooden rail did sterling service for twenty years until a grant from the Football Trust allowed for a new metal version.

As the years went by the problem of dual use was never resolved, and so the pitch was moved a further 30 yards south, utilising the scrubland behind the goal. The drainage of the area was a major problem for a while, as was the fact that moving the pitch meant the lights were now out of line, and two of the pylons had to be moved from one end to the other.

Permanent seating and enclosures for club officials were added to the stand in 1978 at the request of the Athenian League, and dug-outs built at the end of it, which were added to in 1993.

GARDEN WALK
Royston Town FC

Garden Walk saw just ten years of Isthmian League football before the ground grading requirements and the possibility of a move to a new site convinced the club that a return to the South Midlands League for a third time would be the right course of action.

Despite surviving on gates of two figures on occasions, the club were instructed to erect another stand opposite the existing one which would have cost in excess of £20,000. Not being prepared to spend that kind of money for what may only have been a couple of years' use, they resigned from the league.

Royston Town are 120 years old and played on at least three grounds previous to Garden Walk - at Newmarket Road, Baldock Road and Mackerell Hall. All three were no more than open fields with small huts for changing and they eventually moved to their current home, which they now own, in 1923. An old timber stand stood roughly where the current one is now. The present structure was put up in 1984, along with the re-vamped dressing rooms, when the club were accepted into the Isthmian League.

The clubhouse dates from 1974 and the floodlights were switched on in September 1981.

Although tightly hemmed-in by housing, Garden Walk has a homely look about it and is now one of the better grounds in that league having recently succumbed to the Isthmian regulations with hard standing and pitch perimeter fences infilled. It remains to be seen whether they aim to go forward once again at a new ground or plod along for a while at Garden Walk.

NORTON ROAD
Baldock Town FC

The club's current ground at Norton Road has existed for only thirteen years, following a decision to accept the council's offer of land for a new ground. Their previous home at Bakers Close was first played on before the turn of the century, but at that time was only 100 yards long, and hampered by a pair of trees.

When the club entered a local league they began playing at Pinnocks Lane, and then for a short while on what is now the cricket ground. Around this time, Bakers

SPORTING NEWS, NOVEMBER 5, 1949

Three

VICTORY OPENING

11-GOAL SMILE

The face that launched 11 goals belongs to smiling Christine Norden, who kicked off at Cheshunt Football Club's new stadium on Saturday. Here you see her meeting members of the Cheshunt team.

XXXX:oc:ou:X **Cheshunt 11, Hastings Utd. 1**

CHESHUNT celebrated the opening of their new stadium in no uncertain fashion. They trounced Hastings (including their five professionals) to the tune of 11 goals to one. Cheshunt were at full strength, both Jack Freeman and Bert Rayner returning to the side following injuries.

The Cheshunt forwards completely monopolised the play, being particularly good in front of goal. They missed very few opportunities to score. Keeping the ball on the floor, the team moved with the reliability of a machine, so precise and accurate was their passing.

Ralph Wetton improves with every game and is rapidly becoming a top class wing-half. Forwards Ray Spiller and Arthur Ault are serving up some delightful football, plying the other forwards with a flow of good passes.

The defence was never under any real pressure and had a comfortable afternoon watching the forwards riddle holes in Hastings.

The game opened with Cheshunt attacking, and Spiller was only inches wide with a good effort. Within five minutes the home team opened the score, a fine pass from Ferguson to Arthur Ault allowing him to run on unopposed and coolly shoot past the goalkeeper. Hastings attacked for a spell and, after forcing several corners, equalised when Ward came too far out of goal. The ball was lobbed over his head, and in the scrimmage, Harry Freeman had the misfortune to put the ball into his own goal.

A period of ...

could not break through the Cheshunt defence where Fred Pointing ...pletely blocked...

Cheshunt's stadium never entirely lived up to expectations, but remains home to the club.

THEOBALDS LANE
Cheshunt FC

The first game at the new stadium at Theobalds Lane was played on Saturday October 29th 1949, against Hastings United in the London Premier League. It was a momentous day for more than one reason as it also brought the club's record victory of 11-1, and the entire opening ceremony was performed in the company of one of Britain's most pneumatic film stars of the day, Christine Norden.

The small stand at the ground today is the original; the cover opposite and the floodlights did not follow until 1963. The vastness of what is one of the biggest grounds in the area is accentuated by the modest development which has taken place. The souvenir programme of the day tells of plans for a cycling track which would attract "the world's greatest stars, with athletics meetings and good class cricket matches". Cheshunt Stadium never really reached the heights that it aspired to, but there again not many grounds in that era did, although to its credit, it still hosts senior football today, with Cheshunt FC making plans to return to the Isthmian League.

The early days of the club when it re-formed after the war were spent playing mainly away games, with the 1947-48 season seeing them at a ground in College Road. They stayed there for just over a year until the stadium was ready for use, although not complete, as the programme regrets. It was finished enough, however on January 28th 1959 when over 6,000 spectators saw Cheshunt take on and beat the Amateur Cup holders Bromley, 2-1. Not long afterwards the club were forced to move from the ground due to the poor state of the new pitch and they played the remainder of the season at Brookfield Lane until returning the following August, and it was around that time that the main stand was built.

Close was acquired from the local brewers and the offending trees removed, but by 1921 the club were playing at Willian Road, and later at the Park, now covered by Tesco's, before a final move back to Bakers Close in 1925, when they entered the South Midland League.

Up to the Second World War Baldock consolidated their position, erecting the clubhouse pavilion in 1936. This served them until 1958 when a new brick-built club was opened by Sir Stanley Rous, the secretary of the F.A.

Almost 25 years on Sir Stanley re-visited Baldock to open the new ground in Norton Road. A move to the United Counties League bought immediate ground improvements, which included floodlights.

Today with the club at their highest-ever position, the ground has been bought up to Southern League standards.

TOP FIELD
Hitchin Town FC

The first Hitchin football club dates back 130 years and played a very unorganised form of the sport on Payne's Park, just south of Top Field. Soon after Top Field was used for the first time, and indeed one of the first-ever FA Cup ties took place there, in 1871.

The land was held as part of the Cow Trust, run by the Cow Commoners, who were allowed to run their cattle or sheep along Bedford Road and across the field once a year. It is this trust that has been a bugbear to the club who are technically not allowed to erect permanent buildings at the ground. Presumably this accounts for the wonderfully old-fashioned terracing that arcs its way around Hitchin's delightful rural home.

Rather than being fashioned into an earth bank, the planks are arranged as steps complete with struts and supports at the back, not unlike the inside of an old wooden grandstand. Much of this terrace still exists behind the Fishponds Road goal and all down the side opposite the main stand, whereas the Ickleford end is now conventionally terraced in concrete.

The ground first began to take shape in the late 1890's when a wooden grandstand, larger than the current structure, was put up, and the first of the terracing appeared. The players changed in The Cricketers pub, which stood where the Firs Hotel is now, and walked the short distance to the ground. The move to turn professional proved ill-judged; the club struggled and, when the grandstand was burnt to the ground just before the Great War, the heart went with it and they folded. Hitchin Town did not reform until 1928 when they immediately began playing at Top Field which once again started to develop. A smaller wood and iron stand complete with 450 seats was built on the site of the previous one, with dressing rooms below and the ter-

The superbly archaic wooden terracing at Hitchin.

racing was completed as was the corrugated cover along the side. Such was the success of the development that the record crowd of 7,878 was set in 1956, when Wycombe Wanderers visited in the FA Amateur Cup.

Since those days the ground has changed remarkably little with the floodlighting the major construction, switched on before a match with Arsenal in 1962. The dreaded Isthmian League regulations have meant a new wooden fence has gone up just inside the turnstiles but, bypassing that, the terrace curves around to what is known as Windy Corner. This at one time housed a couple of huts for a tea bar and the groundsman's equipment. The stand covers most of the Bedford Road side and has behind it the dressing rooms with the old boardroom - now a hospitality room - alongside. The Ickleford End is now open concrete standing, although briefly in the eighties it sported a cover which was removed by one of the great storms of the time and never seen again. League rules, which forbid any grass banking in the top division, have meant the fencing has been brought forward, thus scarring this lovely ground unnecessarily. The majority of the club's possibly unique terrace runs all down the side opposite the main stand, and is covered now only in the middle third, after the two outer thirds were destroyed in storms. The club shop and match day office occupy a gap where the terrace was removed a few years back.

Top Field is another ground seemingly trapped in a time warp, and long may it remain so. Somehow it appears to have survived intact for 65 years in its current state despite storms and vandalism, both official and unofficial, and is part of our footballing heritage to be cherished.

BROADHALL WAY
Stevenage Borough FC

In some ways the recent history of football in Stevenage is mirrored by events which occurred a dozen or so miles west, at Dunstable. In common with their Bedfordshire neighbours, the town of Stevenage has had three different clubs playing at Broadhall Way within the last 25 years, each at some stage in the Southern League.

And, to link the two grounds together a little more, when Stevenage Town moved to Broadhall Way from London Road they also brought their covered stand along, erected it for a while and then gave it to Dunstable to put up at Creasey Park.

The London Road ground stood in the town, next to the railway station, and had a wooden stand with a post and rail around the pitch. The stand had dressing rooms underneath and opposite stood the old lean-to, which ended up at Dunstable. Eventually the site was cleared and is now covered by the Leisure Centre.

The new site was farmland until in 1960 work began to develop it and by 1961 the club moved in to a ground with a post and wire surrounding the pitch and a little lean-to. It was 1964 before the new stand was built - a 450 seater which stood for 30 years - until the new regime and promotion to the Conference saw it swept away and replaced. Terracing was laid down using old concrete fence posts and tarmac and a wooden clubhouse went up in the top corner but, despite the initial enthusiasm, problems were around the corner. Stevenage Town ceased trading in 1968 to be replaced almost immediately by Stevenage Athletic, who played in the Metropolitan League before entering the Southern League.

The ground had by then gained a small stand opposite the main one but was still very undeveloped and was to remain so, as Athletic lasted until 1976 before going the way of Town.

Broadhall Way has undergone many changes and is now a Conference club trying to emulate Barnet and Watford, the Hertfordshire clubs in the Football League.

Broadhall Way was sold by the council to a local businessman and lay dormant and partly derelict for two years. With the embryonic Stevenage Borough, then just called Stevenage FC, playing on park pitches as a youth team, representations were made to be allowed back. Indeed, a number of matches were played there until the owner sent in machinery and destroyed the pitch. Eventually, with the clubhouse gutted by fire, the pitch ripped up by JCB's and the stands wrecked by vandals, the council repurchased the eyesore and in 1978 Borough moved in. The stands were soon renovated, the pitch re-laid and a whole club rebuilt as Borough began the long haul to their current position in the Conference.

That promotion alone forced the demolition of the main stand, and the installation of new changing rooms and offices within the self contained area of the new 450-seater stand. Terracing has been laid all round the pitch and covered areas now stretch behind both goals with the old standing covered area still in situ for the time being. The £1million development is not finished however, for the club are embarking on an extension to the covered ends and the doubling of the terrace capacity in an attempt to gain Football League status. Maybe the curse of Broadhall Way has gone at last!

HERTINGFORDBURY PARK
Hertford Town FC

The shape and structure of Hertford Town's home has not changed significantly since the late 50's when the main stand was erected and terracing was put down under the covered area opposite on the River Lea side. The ground itself, although straightforward and typically Isthmian, is situated in a delightful area some way from the town along a lane which leads over the River Lea from the main road.

Hertingfordbury Park showing signs of maturity.

The enclosing concrete wall is still in good shape, nearly forty years after it was erected, and inside the entrance stands the porta-cabin which has served as a clubhouse since January 1992, when fire destroyed the second of the club's social rooms, built in 1974 to replace the original wooden building dating from the late 50's.

On the half-way line and facing the river is the main stand, built in 1959, with 300 seats and a boardroom and changing rooms underneath. This replaced an earlier building put up when the ground was first developed after the Great War, and burnt down in 1946. Opposite the stand is an area of cover, originally erected in 1950 and extended and completed the following year, and a similar structure stands behind the car-park goal which is a few years' younger. Hertingfordbury Park first saw floodlit football in 1956, but the current pylons date from 1965.

PARKFIELD
Potters Bar Town FC

The site of the ground of Potters Bar Town FC has a fascinating past well-documented by the local Historical Society in the town.

Parkfield started life as part of a larger estate called Cathale on which Cathale House was built in 1603. The 1837 deeds show a house on land between what is now the stand and the south east corner of the pitch. The house was re-named Parkfield before it was converted into a girls' school and eventually pulled down in 1935. A year earlier the land had been bought by the

A floodlit Potters Bar Town FC

County Council and in 1938 a new school, now known as Oaklands College was built close by. During the war years the area where the clubhouse now stands supported a number of air raid shelters and the whole site first saw football in the early fifties when Potters Bar Crusaders used it for three years.

The Town, under their original name of Mount Grace Old Scholars, began playing there in 1960 on a pitch which ran east to west. It was not until 1983 that the clubhouse with its changing rooms, showers, kitchen and bar was built and further development came when the club took the step up from the Herts County League. Since then a barrier was put around the pitch, in 1990, and dug-outs and temporary cover followed a year later. 1992 saw the small stand with 25 seats and in 1993 the floodlighting was turned on when Barnet were the visitors on December 8th.

Potters Bar Town have created a fine home in what is a pleasant area with more than its share of history.

CLARENCE PARK
St Albans City FC

The council owned sports and recreational ground known as Clarence Park was given to the people of the city in 1894, and recently celebrated its centenary. Before the City were formed in 1908, Old Albanians played on a pitch laid out on the cricket ground, which at that time was surrounded by a cycle track. The cricket pavilion was used for dressing rooms, and when City moved into Clarence Park they brought with them a set of goalposts and nets donated by the defunct St.Albans Abbey FC.

The first match was on 12th September, with a friendly against Clove, and the initial season was spent in the Spartan League Eastern Division and the Herts County League Western Division. As time went on the ground developed and in 1922 the wooden low-slung main stand was built down virtually the whole of one side, at a cost of £1,400. The banking, which stayed in place more or less until the late 50's when it was replaced with concrete terracing all around the ground, was fashioned from old railway sleepers. In 1963 a further section of covered terrace was added opposite the main stand and soon after the club installed floodlights which, other than the odd embellishment here and there, was the last major change at the ground.

Today's Clarence Park is a delight to visit, and is a vibrant place all year round due to the various sports activities on offer. Top quality hockey and cricket take place as well as the football in a beautifully-kept tree-lined area. The main stand is now well into its seventies but displays no outward sign of ageing. Peeping over the roof is the tall recently-refurbished clubhouse which is reached via a flight of stairs, and opposite

St Albans City F.C. and (right) the tree which caused the grief at Clarence Park.

stands the covered terrace which has also had a spruce-up and now sports a vandal-proof Coca-Cola advertisement along its inside wall.

Both ends are open as they always have been, with the now infamous tree safely protected by a preservation order, bursting through the terracing behind one goal. It is that lone tree which has prevented City from taking their place in the Conference, and forced them to consider moving to a new purpose-built ground in or near the city. The mere utterance of the words 'purpose-built ground' are enough to send any lover of football architecture into a blind panic, and when spoken in the same breath as Clarence Park, then they only double the grief. Unless there is a change of heart or of policy, then Clarence Park will not see Conference football as long as the tree stays healthy. It may seem cruel but as far as St. Albans City fans are concerned, it's a shame it's not a diseased elm!

VAUXHALL ROAD
Hemel Hempstead FC

Founded in 1885 as Apsley FC, the club played its early football in the West Herts League, on various pitches around the town. The pre-war history of the club is rather sketchy, but permanent home up to 1972 was at Crabtree Lane, which they took over in the early thirties. The record attendance at that ground was 3,500 for an Amateur Cup match against Tooting and Mitcham United in 1962. The club changed its name to Hemel Hempstead Town around the time of the Second World War, and eventually merged with South Midland League side United to form the current club.

In 1972, the Crabtree Lane ground was sold for yet more development in the already widely-expanding town, and the club relocated to a purpose-built ground in Adeyfield which has held 2,500 for a centenary celebration match against Watford. In November 1992, the football club was rocked by a fire

which wrecked the dressing rooms and clubhouse and forced some matches to be played away until temporary accommodation could be arranged.

COTLANDSWICK
London Colney FC

Cotlandswick Playing Fields have seen a high standard of football over the years as, before London Colney moved there in 1975, the ground was home to Marconi Instruments, of the Herts County League. When that club disbanded, the site remained semi-derelict, until Colney moved from Whitehorse Lane Recreation Ground, home since 1907.

The old, doddery-looking pavilion, which served both football and cricket was originally fronted with a pleasant flower bed, and small wooden fence, but it has now been boarded up and is only used for storage since the club built a brand new clubhouse and changing rooms on to it. A small breeze-block stand was erected around ten years ago, and this has since been moved closer to the pitch and had seating arranged inside it.

1	Harlow Town FC
2	Saffron Walden Town FC
3	Witham Town FC
4	Braintree Town FC
5	Halstead Town FC
6	Coggeshall Town FC
7	Wivenhoe Town FC
8	Brightlingsea FC
9	Clacton Town FC
10	Harwich & Parkeston FC
11	Great Wakering Rovers FC
12	Tiptree United FC

The steeply angled seating in the main stand at the Royal Oak, one of the best documented grounds anywhere in the country.

RURAL ESSEX covers most of the north and east of the county which has two of the most fascinating grounds in the country, at Harwich and Braintree. The Eastern Counties, Essex Senior, Isthmian, Southern and Essex and Suffolk Border Leagues are all represented here with Braintree Town, although suffering from internal strife and the possibility of having Chelmsford City move in with them, are the top club in the area.

ROYAL OAK GROUND
Harwich and Parkeston FC

The history of the Royal Oak ground is without doubt the most thoroughly researched and documented of all major non-League venues in this country. Its life story is as fascinating as the ground itself, despite its slightly weather-worn look nowadays.

At the club AGM in July 1898, it was announced they would be hiring the meadow at the Royal Oak to enable play on an enclosed ground at which they could take a gate. A lease was negotiated for £25 per year for seven years and the ground, such as it was, was opened on September 10th. The local press reported that the old cart-way which crossed the meadow had been removed, the pitch re-turfed and a straggling hawthorn bush which bordered the main road had been replaced by a 6'6" corrugated iron fence. A further fence was erected from

the Royd House to the Farm House and on the east side a platform, 180 feet in length, was constructed to cover a ditch and create enough room for an enclosure. The official opening took place with a game against the Coldstream Guards and the first-ever goal on the ground was scored by one Archibald Snodgrass!

Soon the ground was hosting important games and in 1899, 5,000 saw the Amateur Cup quarter-final against the Royal Artillery with thousands more watching from a vantage point known as Jews Hill. The first grandstand had by then been built at a cost of £98, a wooden structure which survived until the Second World War, and this was joined by an uncovered stand built by the same man, which went up when the club were honoured to stage the Amateur Cup Final of 1901.

Just prior to the Great War a small stand was put up for storing bicycles at a cost of 1d per game, which seemed a strange thing to do as the ground had no changing rooms at the time, players having use of the pub.

The club reformed after the war and in 1922 bought the ground for £500 which allayed fears that it would be sold off for development, and ten years later a new covered stand had been built on the popular side for 1,000 spectators with a fence put up and a pavilion built by the supporter' club at the Dunns End. The pavilion is still in splendid fettle today housing the dressing rooms - the first ever to be built at the Oak. In an effort to entice in more spectators (who could still get a free view from outside) the club bought 40 old school desks which were arranged around the ground as seats with built in foot-rests.

This was only a temporary measure, for a grandstand was a priority but it was early in 1936 before work was completed on the 80 foot section of the stand on the popular side. The east side still had a large ditch running alongside it, and in 1937 the Corporation filled it in enabling the club to put up more cover. Two months later the ground record was broken when 5,469 paid to watch the Amateur Cup match against Romford but despite this, the club were worried crowds were not big enough, and so re-constructed the entrance to negate the problem of queueing. Within a week the work proved fruitless as war broke out. The club closed down although a few matches were played for recreation.

The war years were not kind to the ground and a former player wrote in the press, "the ground is in a shocking state, no pavilion, no dressing rooms, no stands fit to sit in, no ticket boxes and no football gear". Work to repair and replace went on, while negotiations for compensation got underway and friendlies were played on Barrack Field and Hamilton Park, home of Parkeston Railway. The Royal Oak was closed for re-seeding and opened again in September

1946, by which time they had learned of an award of more than £2,000 compensation by the War Department.

By November 1948 the 50-year-old stand had been replaced by a 560-seater on the same site. Made of steel and concrete, with wooden slats as benches, it was built to allow people to stand in a paddock in front. More fencing work had been done on the isolation hospital side and terracing was improved at the Dunns End. The new stand was opened by the indefatigable Mr Stanley Rous on November 13th 1948.

Four years later, a 90 mph gale tore the roof off the popular side stand, hurling it onto the tops of some adjoining houses. A 'raise the roof' appeal was launched which was not a success, but at the eleventh hour the insurers came to the rescue. The first Social Club was built in time for Easter 1957 from materials re-cycled off bomb sites and various ground improvements continued throughout the fifties, including the leasing of the land behind the stand for a car-park. The old corrugated fence at the front of the ground was finally replaced in 1961 with a smart new wall complete with information board and coat of arms, while a tea bar was also built at a cost of £2,000.

As the sixties went on interest started to wane and gates began to fall so little was done to the old ground. However, a flood-light appeal provided the impetus for the first system which was switched on by Geoff Hurst on October 16th 1968. The next major change was a sad one for, in 1979, the old wooden stand erected just before the war was pulled down, having been reduced to a bare skeleton by the sea breezes. It was never replaced, and indeed no major work took place until the late eighties when £30,000 was spent on repainting the stand, installing 220 plastic seats, a new turnstile entrance and decoration of the dressing rooms.

More recently hard standing has been laid around the pitch and doubtless more will follow to keep in line with league policies. The way the Royal Oak ground has evolved, from a meadow with a cart track across it to a stadium with three stands crammed with umpteen thousand fans for Amateur Cup ties, and then back to its present position of struggling to entice a few dozen people to watch an FA Vase tie is a poignant tale. The casual visitor cannot feel anything but saddened that the legacies left to this generation by years of dedication are now largely ignored.

CATONS LANE
Saffron Walden Town FC

The original club are believed to have been formed in 1872, playing in friendlies and cup matches at the Friends School and the Common but they lasted only until 1889, although three other clubs were active at the time in the town.

They were dormant for less than a year and by October 1890 the Hon. Secretary Mr Arthur Smith had re-formed the club and negotiated a lease at £3 per year for a field in Loft's Lane from Lord Braybrooke. The lane soon became known as Caton's Lane, after William Caton who lived in the big house further down. The ground was bounded by a hedge behind one goal and at the church end was a timber fence, the south side open. Brown canvas sheeting was hung on posts along this side to allow admission money to be taken. A rope would be stretched around the pitch and duck-boards put down as there was no shelter of any kind at that time.

The Great War came and went and a new ground was proposed behind the Gas Works, but finance dictated the club remain at Caton's Lane as fund raising had not progressed far enough. Instead the cash collected went towards improving the ground, starting with a corrugated iron fence enclosing it. Club members erected it during 1927 and shortly after, a covered enclosure went up on the top side. Dressing rooms appeared during the following summer and were opened on November 28th 1929, and within another year a further shelter behind the Caton's Lane goal went up as the club strove to have the best ground in the county. The club progressed through the Herts and Essex

Border and North Essex Leagues to the Spartan League, which demanded the building of changing rooms for the referee and linesmen, near the entrance to the ground which were ready in 1933. Success in this league and the Amateur Cup prompted the club to carry on with developments backed by the Supporters' Club, and a 200-seater grandstand was opened on Boxing Day 1937 at half time in a game against Polytechnic.

The post-war years were a struggle for the club and 1953 saw them £276 in deficit, although they found funds to pull down the old stand at the top of the ground and replace it with a new timber and corrugated iron shelter. In the summer of 1954 work began on new changing rooms behind the main stand, with the help of grants from the Playing Field Fund and the Council but, despite volunteer labour, the job took the best part of four years to complete.

Little changed at Caton's Lane until 1966 when the old timber pay box, referees' room and store at the entrance were demolished to make way for a groundsman's concrete shed, but this was just a taster as major ground improvements were planned. First to go was the ugly iron fence along the top of the ground and then, once the idea of converting the old changing rooms into a clubhouse had been rejected, an ex-RAF hut was erected and

converted, standing next to the supporters' hut, all the work carried out by volunteers. It was eventually completed and opened in December 1972 by Martin Peters of Tottenham Hotspur and England.

The club entered the Eastern Counties League in 1974, and during that summer embarked on a further series of improvements to bring Catons Lane in line with other clubs. A concrete path was laid from the main stand to the entrance and the Catons Lane end fence was pulled down and replaced with a concrete wall. A terraced enclosure was built in front of it soon after. Four years later members completed the concrete fencing at the Church End and the top end stand was rebuilt in brick and concrete. A floodlight fund was started which came to fruition on October 9th 1979 when Royston Town were the opposition for the first evening game, in the East Anglian Cup. Norwich City officially opened the floodlights the following week in front of over 1,500 people before a friendly which they won 10-1.

Catons Lane has changed little since then, merely keeping in line with Isthmian League regulations and mercifully is still a pleasantly rural ground, a rarity in the south-east of England.

The Grounds of Harlow Town FC

Harlow Town FC came to national prominence in 1979 when their incredible FA Cup run finally came to a halt in a seven-goal thriller at Vicarage Road, Watford in a fourth round tie. Nearly 10,000 packed into the Sports Ground to see the third round replay with Leicester City which was won memorably, 1-0, a ground record which will never remotely be in danger.

The ground has been home to Harlow Town since it was built in 1960, but has caused no little grief in recent years. It was used for the first time in August of that year when a game was staged between an Essex XI and a London League XI, and Harlow played their first game a week later. The ever-present Mr Stanley Rous opened the ground before the club's Amateur Cup game with Saffron Walden.

On January 13th 1970, the floodlights, having been bought from the recently defunct Brentwood Town FC, were officially opened by West Ham United. A crowd of some 8,000 saw the match.

The ground from the start had been given an old chicken-run type cover, but this was replaced in 1972 with a new £15,000, 500-seater grandstand which Tottenham Hotspur opened in front of another 8,000 gate. At that time the ground had huge grass banks around three sides

Harlow Sports Centre

with the clubhouse, stand and dressing rooms and other ancillary buildings all down one side. The attendant athletics track and field apparatus are scattered about which does nothing to help the sight lines, but the stand itself is huge with perspex sides and 450 steeply terraced seats. During 1978 the clubhouse was modernised and used to full advantage during the club's historic Cup run.

During the eighties it was generally assumed Harlow would be relocating to a more functional, purpose-built ground on the edge of town. In 1985 the club announced the move to Roydon Road and as the time wore on the facilities were

allowed to deteriorate at the Sports Ground. It took fully six years for planning permission to be granted, but in 1991 work began. Pre-season friendlies and reserve games were played there before work started as the club's headquarters had already moved over. The shell of the main stand, perimeter fencing, and a fully-functioning clubhouse were all in place when the funds dried up.

The sister company, Harlow Town Arenas were forced into liquidation and without a ground Harlow Town did not compete in 1992-93. The stadium has since remained unused, although the new owners have attempted to re-open as a

SPA ROAD
Witham FC

The large sprawling Essex town of Witham lies between Chelmsford and Colchester on the A12, and has had a football team in some form or other since the late 1800's. The town enjoyed its best days either side of the Great War, until interest waned in the 30's and they disbanded at the outbreak of World War Two.

In 1948 a small band of men re-formed the club once again, and it was instantly successful, moving a year later to the Park, home of Crittall Athletic. A Supporters' Club soon formed, and the club progressed in intermediate football, until the six year search for a new ground, and with it senior status, culminated in the club being offered the Spa Road site.

However, five years elapsed before, in 1975, the club moved into a ground that had previously been open land.

Today it is neat and tidy, and presumably holds the minimum grading for Isthmian League requirements. A long winding approach road leads to the ground, perched on a sloping area of grassland close to a housing estate. Inside, the clubhouse, dressing rooms, and a refreshment hut in the form of an old caravan painted in the club colours

greyhound stadium, but cannot gain planning permission.

In the summer of 1993 the club were resurrected and a new clubhouse was built which included three bars and two function halls. The dressing rooms were built to Conference standard and the main stand tidied up with a small covered area in front for spectators.

All the chaos of the last three years is in stark contrast to the early history of the club which was spent at Marigolds, current home of the cricket and hockey clubs, and at Harlow College, a private school which existed before the New Town was built but was demolished in the 50's.

In 1922 the club moved to the Green Man Fields, playing in the East Herts League. This ground was famous for its slope and had a stand with dressing rooms as early as 1931, when the club were still junior. Three years later the stand doubled in size and was used for many County Rep games before the war. In 1952 the stand was extended down the whole of one side with seating added and some covered standing room was also in place at this time on the opposite side. In 1955, training lights were erected at the ground behind The Green Man Hotel, which was the club headquarters and is still there today, although the old ground is now covered in housing.

occupy the corner nearest the car-park. The only other building is the small seated stand, situated astride the half-way line on the far side. The ends are both open although iron struts have been erected behind the left hand goal indicating the possibility of some standing cover in the near future.

CRESSING ROAD
Braintree Town FC

With the possible exception of the Royal Oak ground in Dovercourt, Braintree's home for the last 72 years is the most fascinating and well researched of all Essex non-League grounds.

Keen to provide recreational facilities for its workers, the Crittal Window Company built the Cressing Road sports ground in Clockhouse Way which the football club, then called Crittall Athletic, moved into in time for the start of the 1923-24 season. Founded as Manor Works FC they played for five years on the Fair Field in the town centre, just behind where the old Town Hall and Library now stand. In 1903 they moved to Spaldings Meadow in Panfield Lane where they stayed for 20 years. There was a wooden pay hut by the main road, but the only facility was a stand which was erected each year for the agricultural show.

The new sports ground boasted a 400-seater stand on the Cressing Road side which had a sloping roof supported by 12 uprights, bench seats, glass screen ends and a wooden picket fence along the front, the latter surviving until the 50's. The other three sides were banked up and part of this is still visible at the ground to the right of the club entrance. The ground was officially opened by Mrs F.H. Crittall on August 25th 1923 in front of the 6,000 people who attended the 4th

Annual Sports Day, but the first football match was on 15th September when the reserves played Great Leighs. Two years later the Sports Day crowd had grown to 8,000 and a year later 6,000 saw the Essex Junior Trophy Final, still a record for a football match. A new pavilion with changing rooms, baths, an entertainment area and bar was opened in August 1926 and this survived until replaced by the existing clubhouse. It stood overlooking the cricket ground outside the banking, and the overgrown site is still visible. In the mid-thirties a second grandstand, which had a pitched roof and five rows of bench seating to seat 400, was built opposite the first. Sadly, it was simply known as Number Two stand. Number One stand had an elevated tower behind it supplied by the Supporters' Club in 1946 to house broadcasting equipment, and in later years, until knocked down in 1974, it contained the floodlighting controls. Later in 1946 No.2 stand was dismantled, cut in half and grafted onto each end of No.1 stand to increase seating capacity. There was then cover all along the Cressing Road side, but opposite was barren. Building constrictions saw that the club's plans to build a double sided stand with dressing rooms and a boardroom never saw light.

During the mid-fifties an FA directive stated that all FA Cup games must be played on enclosed grounds and so the present green fence was erected. The remaining aluminium fence went up in the sixties to effectively cut off the rest of the ground. Floodlights were installed in 1967, and a Trevor Brooking-inspired West Ham United were the first visitors. This was to be the ground's peak, for the increasingly unsafe left hand side of No.1 stand was in an advanced state of disrepair, and was demol-

A rare photo of the paybox and entrance to Spaldings Meadow, taken in 1905. Braintree played there as Manor Works until 1923.

A sports meeting at the Cressing Road ground in 1928 and (below) a fascinating comparison picture taken over 65 years later with track remains clearly visible.

race with the shell going up in the summer of 1993. A yellow and blue roof was added during the season. At around the same time, the popular far end, known as the Quag End, was covered. An all-weather training area was laid behind this over another part of the track and during 1994-95 further terracing was added to the uncovered areas.

In early 1995 the club re-purchased the ground from the council and at the same time secured a lease for the remainder of the now over-grown Crittall Sports Ground. Two football pitches are to be developed with separate cover and changing rooms. New changing rooms behind the main stand will create further space as the club move toward their centenary. Cressing Road has possibly seen more change in its 60-odd years than any other ground in the country but, even now, a visit will still reveal the original shape and outline of the sports ground, with portions of the cinder track still in place.

ROSEMARY LANE
Halstead Town FC

Halstead Town were founded as far back as 1879, but did not acquire a permanent home in the town until the beginning of the 1948/49 season.

The club played their early football on Coggeshall Pieces, a ground now covered by Ramsey School, and the Three Gates which, although used as a football pitch for over 50 years, was never given the benefit of any facilities of note, and during the war reverted back to agricultural use, as it remains today.

The club soon re-formed after the war, the County Association declaring their pleasure at this fact. They also stated that over 400 clubs were already registered compared with over 600 in 1939. The aim was for every village to have a football club, but many grounds, Halstead's included, had been taken by the R.A.F. for food production, and also the shortage of manpower meant a dearth of referees.

The first thoughts of trying to find a new home for the football club came about in October 1946 at a dinner at the local Co-op hall. The committee at the time inspected several sites, and expressed a hope in the press that the public would support the club financially, and within ten days had agreed on a site by the Tortoise Bowling Green. Four months later a Supporters' Club was formed primarily to assist with the new ground, and the club further endeared themselves to the public by winning the Essex Junior Cup.

By August negotiations were complete and work began on the new ground. Hedges and fences were bull-dozed and the town sand-pit filled in as well as a large ditch. The club meanwhile had moved from their temporary home at Courtaulds Sports Club, which is still used for football, and were forced to play at Coggeshall Pieces for the 1947/48 season. Work continued throughout

ished. Worse was to follow for a severe gale in January 1974 destroyed the roof of the rest of No.2 stand and contractors completed the job with the back wall. In the weeks that followed the rest of the stand was taken down. By the summer of 1975, the ground had fallen way below senior standard and with crowds of only 40-50 there was no funding to re-build the stands. By then the council had purchased the ground from Crittalls who had little or nothing to do with the club, and they changed the name to Braintree Town FC. The start of the 1975-6 season was spent elsewhere as the ground was closed, but hard work and determination saw the club pull through and Cressing Road slowly began to develop once again. A small lean-to was erected in 1977 where the main stand is now but it lasted barely a year before wind struck again. It was replaced and doubled in length in 1985 after the club retained the Eastern Counties League. The majority of the uncovered seats from the old No.1 stand survived through all of this until the late eighties when additional improvements were made. Terracing replaced the rough banking and at the same time the present cover was erected at the clubhouse end with the wire roping replaced with a metal barrier around the

pitch.

Earlier, one half of a portable building had been brought over from Witham and was due to become a new clubhouse, but the funds were not forthcoming and the footings grew over. Part of the shell was used to erect the lean-to. The other half of the building went to Witham Town FC.

The first ever turnstile at the ground was provided courtesy of Stowmarket Town's old Cricket Meadow, which had previously acquired it from Portman Road, Ipswich in the 1930's. Sadly, it was replaced in 1994. The next major change came in 1990 when the small stand was replaced by the present 296-seater structure, in all the fifth different stand on that side.

The ground once again began to take on a welcoming appearance, with the old cinder track gradually disappearing as further developments took place. Following the success of the new stand, both Wisbech and Bedworth had stands built by the newly-formed company that marketed them, and part of the deal saw half of Bedworth's old enclosure brought to Cressing Road and erected in front of the site of the former No.1 stand, over the old track. The roof was broken up and used for hardcore for the new ter-

Halstead's New Football Stand Opened

Mr. S. A. Courtauld, President of Halstead Town Football Club, cutting the black and white ribbons and declaring the new stand open.

Halstead's grandstand has changed little since it was opened.

on the new ground, with some 300 posts put up and 500 sheets of galvanised metal erected around the ground. Hardcore from demolished air-raid shelters was used for the entrance and car-park, with all the work done by volunteers.

Some 1,800 witnessed the opening match against Eton Manor, with the Haverhill Silver Prize Band marching to the ground against a backdrop of flags and bunting. During the pre-match speeches it was hoped that the proposed new stand and club-room would come to fruition.

Within a year, the club room was opened after another memorable all-hands-to-the-pumps effort. Initially, with the involvement of the Ministries of Supply and Education and the Hon. R.A. Butler M.P., a price was agreed for removal and re-erection of a building from the local aerodrome. When they arrived at the site, officials found the building had vanished!

Accordingly the club agreed to build a club room from scratch and this they did for the sum of £900, and it was officially opened with a friendly against Cleveland O.B'S, of Ilford on August 20th 1949. Exactly a year later, the club's long-awaited stand was opened for the first game of the 1950/51 season. The concrete and steel structure was built to accommodate 500 people and is much the same now as it was then, albeit a touch pale around the gills but it looks out over a ground which has changed remarkably little in forty odd years.

The entrance is now modernised although still recognisable as the original and the perimeter fence is new, but Rosemary Lane is so far untouched by over-zealous gradings. The town sand-pit occasionally makes a re-appearance in dry weather and can be seen as a darker area near one of the goal mouths.

Coggeshall Town and Youth FC

The original Town date back to 1878, but were reformed just nine years later in 1887. Records of the club, including mementoes and club shirts are proudly displayed in the town.

The current ground until five years ago shared facilities with the cricket club, the old, well cared-for pavilion being used as changing rooms for both, although the football pitch was on the lower level. On the cricket club's move a second pitch was laid permanently, for the reformed club's minor teams. The parent club suffered horrendously from over ambition and folded, losing senior status in the 80's. Happily the ground did not suffer and the sturdy green corrugated iron covered stand built into the separating bank continues to serve, 35 years after it was built, when the club moved from the Highfields site, which still is occasionally used for training by the club.

RUSH GREEN BOWL
Clacton Town FC

Clacton Town are another club who have suffered from losing a long-established ground to council planning with their Old Road stadium, home since 1906, gobbled up and replaced with Safeway, Iceland, Harveys, Halfords and Texas. None of your simple knock 'em down and put up a Tesco's here; all signs have been obliterated. The ground in the early fifties could well have developed into something much larger, as it already had a seated stand either side with terracing which raised the capacity to around 5,000.

The Supporters' Club planned for a new stand on the south side with covered terracing all round, a far cry from times just before the war when players changed in an old railway carriage emblazoned with the legend First Class. Amusingly, the referee's accommodation was labelled Third Class!

The stadium remained home until the club were forced to vacate in 1987, the last game being against Lowestoft Town on February 21st.

The new ground was a reclaimed rubbish tip. The land had previously been earmarked for a football stadium in the 70's but with the club reluctant to relocate it had remained undeveloped. The move was not without its problems, the projected clubhouse having to be re-planned as a single storey building when the foundations proved inadequate. The pitch was re-turfed and new floodlights were bought and erected which also drained the coffers. However, the

CHAPEL ROAD
Tiptree United FC

Tiptree's pleasant ground is hemmed in on three sides by housing and surrounded by netting to avoid aggravating the neighbours. The ground has only developed to its current degree during the last ten years or so as the club have moved up from Essex Senior League football.

The clubhouse stands between the car-park and the pitch with an extension on the front and the canteen has a pointless-looking wall built in front of it covered in advertising. The recently rebuilt stand has a new roof (pictured above) after strong winds destroyed it and has the club initials picked out in the brickwork, not dissimilar to that at Chatteris Town.

Hard standing has also gone down within the last few years and the dressing rooms have been replaced as Chapel Road slowly moves on as best it can.

first game went ahead on November 7th of the same year, against Soham Town Rangers, but did not finish as a floodlight failure put paid to it with 20 minutes to go. At the end of the season the local council decided the drainage was insufficient and put in four more channels, a week before the start of the new season. The first stand was erected during that term with the seating following twelve months later. In May 1989 the council were at it again when, agreeing to infill an area of the pitch that had subsided, they provided top soil riddled with stones and flints. They refused to accept liability and despite efforts to sift the stones the club were forced to postpone a match and fined, an action which finally prompted the council to right their handiwork. 1993 saw the ground surrounds completely concreted as Clacton Town slowly brought the Rush Green Bowl up to the heights attained by the late-lamented Clacton Stadium.

OLD ROAD — A VISION OF THE FUTURE

It will be like this in 195-(?)

ACCOMMODATION for 5,000 spectators, all under cover, is the ultimate aim of Clacton Town Supporters' Club. James McClure, "East Essex Gazette" staff artist, has drawn this sketch of the ground as he imagines the spectators of the future will see it when the Supporters' Club's improvements are complete.

A new stand to replace the present wooden structure is planned for the south side. It will be raised six feet above ground level to allow for dressing rooms and administrative offices underneath.

****

EAST ESSEX GAZETTE
September 22, 1950

Clacton's Old Road ground as it was envisaged in 1950. Sadly it is now under a collection of superstores.

NORTH ROAD
Brightlingsea United FC

From the original formation of Bright-lingsea Town in 1902, up to its amalgamation with the athletic club and the purchase of five acres of land for £400, two different venues were used each year. The recreation ground was home until March when, to prepare for its summer use, it was closed and the club had to transfer to Red Barn Farm for the most important part of each season.

The decision to purchase was made following the offer of the acreage by Mr. Reg Girling, who owned a cornfield at the top of North Road. An offer of £100 also came in from an acquaintance of the President. A number of small loans over and above the mortgage were taken out to finance the building of a stand and dressing rooms, the total cost of which came to £825.6s.1d. A press box, also used in the early days as dressing rooms for the referee and linesmen, was erected courtesy of the local newspaper. The ground opened on September 7th 1929, with a game against Parkstone Railway.

The club progressed through the leagues, although little was done at the ground until 1972, when new changing rooms and a bar were built, replacing the old structures via a grant from the Playing Fields Association. Two years later a function hall was added, financed by the club. But bad times were ahead and in the mid-eighties a new committee was formed to repay debts and improve the ground. Floodlights were installed in 1988 at a cost of £16,000, a post and hand rail erected around the pitch, and a concrete path laid with new trainers' dug-outs. As the club progressed, so the dressing rooms were extended and a further area of cover was put up, with fifty seats installed at a cost of £2,600. The Regent End of the ground is now fenced with a large catchment net, following the sad destruction of the mature elm trees which stood at one end until disease wiped them out.

BORROUGHS PARK
Great Wakering Rovers FC

The football club and its ground have both come to prominence within the last ten years, thanks largely to the efforts of club men and women who have transformed what was a semi-derelict allotment just off the High Street into a football ground capable of staging Essex Senior League matches and possibly more besides.

The club was founded in 1919, and is thought to have first played on a ground within a gypsy encampment, before using the recreation ground which now backs on to Burroughs Park. The club continue to utilise the ground through their various youth teams, who are able to use the club facilities as Burroughs Park adjoins it. The whole area was once parish council allotments, with many plots vacant. The club suggested grouping the occupied ones together, which was agreed, and a long lease was taken out on 104 plots to create a football pitch, clubhouse and car-park.

With a pitch playable, and porta-cabins in place, the first game came in September 1987, and within two years the clubhouse was open for business. In 1992, having improved the dressing rooms and extended the pitch by five yards, the club were granted senior status, a much sought-after award which is more difficult to attain than in many parts of the country. During the summer of 1994, floodlights were erected, a stand was begun, and the ground was partially enclosed.

It was named Burroughs Park in honour of the club's President, Mr. Roger Burroughs, who gave so much to help create the ground.

BROAD LANE
Wivenhoe Town FC

The Dragons of Wivenhoe came to prominence in 1978 when they left the Essex and Suffolk Border League, and the King George V Playing Fields, to move into senior football at their new ground on an old carrot field in Broad Lane.

For over 50 years they had played on a variety of pitches without any changing facilities, on venues such as Claude Watchman's Meadow, the Spion Kop, Vine Farm and Broomfield. When the new site was bought for £2,500 it signalled the start of a trip to the top flight of the Isthmian League and a subsequent financial problem which all but put them back to square one.

The clubhouse with changing rooms was built at the time the new ground was laid out to enter the Essex Senior League, and a 120-seater stand was eventually built in time for promotion to the Isthmian's. Two further promotions saw the club in the Premier Division with a race to gain the necessary grade the following year. Both ends of the ground were concreted and covered and the second grandstand was started which gives 250 seats altogether. However, some four years on the middle section is finished but the flanks are skeletal and half-built and, with a long-running problem regarding a covenant on the adjacent land preventing building work, it looks set to remain that way.

Wivenhoe have returned to Division Two but enjoyed glory with league success and runs in both Vase and Trophy, and can look back on a record crowd of 1,912 for an FA Trophy match with Runcorn in 1990, before the ground was improved to its current standard. The capacity is set due to safety regulations at 2,685 although, in truth, Broad Lane is big enough to hold 5,000.

Photos in this section by: Gavin Ellis-Neville, Kerry Miller, Nigel Upson and Jon Weaver.

The home of Essex Senior League side Burnham Ramblers FC.

Ipswich & West Suffolk

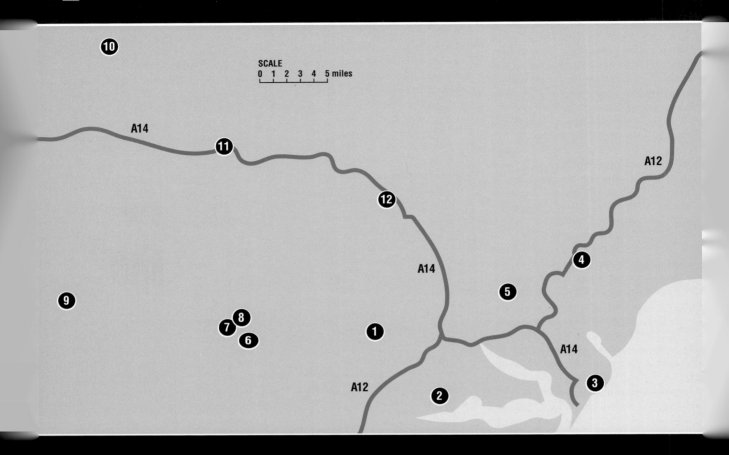

SCALE
0 1 2 3 4 5 miles

1   **Hadleigh United FC**
2   **Brantham Athletic FC**
3   **Felixstowe Town FC**
4   **Woodbridge Town FC**
5   **Ipswich Wanderers FC**
6   **Cornard United FC**
7   **Sudbury Wanderers FC**
8   **Sudbury Town FC**
9   **Haverhill Rovers FC**
10   **Mildenhall Town FC**
11   **Bury Town FC**
12   **Stowmarket Town FC**

The stand at Felixstowe (right) has recently been re-opened, but the view from inside doesn't get any better. It once faced the cricket pitch behind and was remodelled by taking the back off and putting it on the front, and then reversing the seating within. The old cricket pavilion (above) is still in fine shape.

THIS area, which takes in Ipswich and most of the south west of Suffolk, is dominated by the town of Sudbury, which has Town, Wanderers and Cornard Utd for the public to chose from. Town are the senior side, playing in the Southern League, whereas their reserves, plus the other two are all in the Eastern Counties League. Although the Priory is by far the most advanced ground, there are much older homes; Felixstowe and Haverhill play on well established sites.

The feeder leagues in the area, the Essex & Suffolk and Suffolk & Ipswich Leagues are fortunate to have members in such stunning countryside and many smaller grounds such as those at Leiston and Long Melford are worthy of note.

MILLFIELD
Hadleigh United FC

Situated on the banks of the River Brett, ten miles west of Ipswich, the pleasant town of Hadleigh, in Suffolk, is fortunate to have a thriving sporting scene, tucked away on the meadows below the town, which comes alive on a winter's Saturday afternoon with football, tennis, bowls, rugby, and hockey all catered for within a square quarter of a mile.

Hadleigh United have had a base there since 1955, having previously relied on farmers and landowners to rent pitches on a temporary basis. During the war the site was used for army manoeuvres, and was not ready for football until the Hadleigh Town

Council created a ground. The original dressing rooms still stand, just inside the car-park, and in their early days provided washing facilities in the form of tin baths filled from the River Brett. The rooms are now used as a store. The clubhouse was erected by volunteers in 1978, and extended in 1983. The front, with its overhang, provides cover and is very popular, with an additional back-less covered area, erected in 1993, to its left.

Tight up against the river is a smaller training pitch adjoining the main one, and

Hadleigh United have come on in leaps and bounds since 1979 when this photo (left) was taken of the entrance. Above: United's Millfield ground 16 years later.

behind the far goal are the alternative sporting venues on offer. The whole area is now allegedly safe from flooding due to creation of a new weir, and the club can take comfort from the knowledge that the clubhouse will not be flooded for a third time!

B.A.S. CLUB, NEW VILLAGE
Brantham Athletic FC

Very little is known of the early history of the Brantham football club. They have played in New Village for much of their existence if not all of it, and been members of the Eastern Counties League since 1977 having been members of the S.E. Anglian, Colchester and District, Ipswich and District and Essex and Suffolk Border Leagues. Their ground has always been shared with cricket, and is also home to a tennis and bowls club.

DELLWOOD AVENUE
Felixstowe Port and Town FC

At first glance the Town Ground at Felixstowe could be described as pleasant and uncomplicated but not particularly outstanding. The background to the place is, however, fascinating.

The Town Ground has been played on since the turn of the century, when it was surrounded by open fields and reached along a dirt track.

Facilities were non-existent until the classic Edwardian pavilion was built for the cricket club around 1920. This eventually had changing rooms added to it which were used by both clubs. The football club was formed in 1890 and played their early matches on pitches behind the Felixstowe Lawn Tennis Club and near the golf course on Ferry Road. The original club folded in 1911 and did not reappear until 1923 when a certain Canon Cocks re-formed it, the team playing on the Town Ground just to the right in front of the pavilion.

After the Second World War, Town did not appear until Felixstowe United merged with Walton United to form the current club which eventually out-grew the Ipswich League and joined the Border League where they remained until the club entered the Eastern Counties League in the mid-seventies. To comply with league ground rulings the pitch had to be enclosed which was impossible with the cricket club still in attendance. To get round this problem the main pitch was abandoned and the second team pitch behind the stand was used. The club's wooden stand which faced the cricket pitch and separated it from the second pitch was ingeniously remodelled by taking the back off and putting it on the front, and then reversing the seating arrangements within. A perimeter wall was built, a line of trees were planted in front and a path made from the dressing rooms which were, and still are, some distance from the pitch. An old hockey changing room was moved over and is now in use as a board room for entertaining at half time. The most recent changes have been the installation of floodlights after several applications for planning permission were initially turned down, and the sad decision by the council to close the stand on safety

grounds which has meant the additional expense of providing temporary cover to allow the club to stay in the league. The floodlights were opened on 25th January 1991 with a game against neighbours Ipswich Town which brought a record attendance of over 1,500. The lights are of a similar collapsible style to those at Moor Green to comply with the planning regulations and the heads are encased in large ugly but secure boxes when at ground level, one of which is clumsily placed right in front of the stand.

The cricket pavilion was abandoned in 1977 when a new one was built further to the left and was eventually offered to the club and re-opened purely as a football clubhouse in 1985. It is still the club's HQ although moves are afoot to somehow alter or replace it to extend the facilities further. Directly across the ground from the club next to the tennis courts lie the ruins of an ancient old manor house called Walton Hall which was excavated many years ago. Felixstowe have suffered from council bureaucracy but are still battling away.

Brantham Athletic's old stand before it was destroyed by fire and replaced.

and in 1972, after many setbacks, 10 acres of farmland were purchased, and what was little more than a water meadow was turned into two football pitches and a cricket square.

The club's elevation to the Eastern Counties League has been mirrored in the activities on the ground. A clubhouse was opened for business in December 1985, and in the last five years new dressing rooms have been built. Floodlights were installed in 1992 and duly opened with a visit from Ipswich Town. Later, in 1993, a new 200-seater stand was built, a path laid all around the pitch and a new toilet and refreshment block added. Finally the area of hard standing behind the top goal was covered as the ground continued to be all that the club had wished for on its debut 37 years ago.

Just after the Great War a timber and corrugated iron stand was erected by players and members of the club, and remained in use until 1991 when it was destroyed by fire. The remainder of the ground is undeveloped with a barrier around the pitch. A new stand is now in place which can seat 100 and floodlights have been installed. There is also a social club that is used by the whole community. Sadly, it wasn't used by the football club in 1995, for as this book was being compiled it was announced they had folded. It is to be hoped that it is only a temporary measure.

NOTCUTTS PARK
Woodbridge Town FC

Woodbridge Town have, within the last ten years, regained their senior status, entered the Eastern Counties League and after 105 years finally moved to a purpose-built ground of their own.

Notcutts Park is, hopefully for them, the last in a long line of grounds used since the club were formed in 1885. The first recorded match was played at Farlingaye Hall, but between then and the fifties there were numerous fields pressed into use, including Peterhouse Field and later the Kingston Playing Field. This remained home during the 70s and 80s until, having entered the Eastern Counties League, the club began negotiations for a new ground to Premier Division standard. Work began on Nutcutts Park in March 1990 and the ground was opened the following October with a game against Arsenal which attracted a capacity 3,000 crowd. The small stand which holds 200 now has an area of seating and the hard standing and post and rail around the pitch all set the new ground off pleasantly.

HUMBER DOUCEY LANE
Ipswich Wanderers FC

The club came out of Sunday football as Loadwell Ipswich and were founder members of Division One of the Eastern Counties League in 1988. They rent the ground which has only been developed in the last couple of seasons to comply with league rules.

The floodlighting system which was installed in March 1994 is the brightest in the league with the exception of the two reserve sides of Cambridge and Sudbury and was followed by the erection of two small stands which can accommodate 500 at a squeeze. New dressing rooms and a hospitality room in the shape of a porta-cabin went in towards the end of the 1994-95 season as Wanderers made slow but steady progress.

BRUNDON LANE
Sudbury Wanderers FC

The Wanderers were formed in 1958, and for the first 18 years of their existence played at Peoples Park, often used to graze cattle, with changing facilities in either the Horse and Groom or the Black Horse. From the start the club strove to buy its own land,

PRIORY STADIUM
Sudbury Town FC

With the presence of the club's marvellous 60 year-old wooden main stand and large covered terrace, the overall impression of Sudbury Town's neat home is that it is much older than its 44 years.

However, the ground was laid out and purchased in 1951, the surface having been raised some 5ft. to combat the threat of flooding from the nearby River Stour. It is said that a large percentage of the hard core came from a demolished police station, although the evidence is only hearsay!

The story of Sudbury Football Club started in the 1880's, when the club's forerunners played at a ground called Bellevue. Shortly afterwards, a field owned by a Mr. Canham was used and then, just prior to the turn of century, the Friars Street Sports Ground, home, then as now, of Sudbury Cricket Club, became their base.

The pavilion, still in use and recently extended by the cricket club was the changing room and no other permanent facilities were provided until 1934, when a grandstand was given to the club by the Sudbury Gala Committee, who had no further use for it at the Peoples Park in Waldingfield Road.

Sudbury Wanderers FC

The picturesque wooden main stand at Sudbury Town.

A public appeal for funds to put a roof on the stand was successful, and the finished article was re-erected, backing onto Quay Lane. On matchdays, tarpaulins were erected around the ground on the railings, and pay-boxes were situated to allow a gate to be taken.

The town were ambitious to move upwards and onwards and formed a Limited Company with £1 shares. They purchased a large acreage of water meadow for £800, and set about turning it into a football stadium. Once again the glorious old grandstand was on the move, this time just a few yards away to the Priory where it proudly sits, in its dotage, 45 years on.

Today, part of the original acreage has been sold off for development behind one goal, and the local rowing club were recipients of another plot, donated by the club. The clubhouse, a huge rambling friendly place sits to the right of the steep covered Orchard Stand with the canteen block and changing rooms between it and another area of open terrace which may well be covered by the time you read this.

BLACKHOUSE LANE
Cornard United FC

Blackhouse Lane is another of East Anglia's newly-developed grounds, the club having only moved there in 1983 after starting life as a Sunday side in 1964 at Cornard Recreation Ground. When the Upper School was built in 1974 the club began using the grounds, whilst playing in the Colchester, and later Border Leagues before moving to Blackhouse Lane in 1982.

It was a very basic ground which was shared with cricket and to enable them to enclose the ground from the cricket square the pitch was turned round 180 degrees, allowing them to gain promotion to the Eastern Counties League. The Division One championship followed, as did the building of the brick stands, changing rooms and floodlights which give the club and the town of Great Cornard a ground to be proud of.

HAMLET CROFT
Haverhill Rovers FC

Hamlet Croft is an unusual arena which has echoes of Halesowen Harriers, in that it has a large bank running along one side, overlooks the immediate locale from an elevated position and is reached via a lane.

It has seen football since before the Great War, indeed a Haverhill side first rented the ground for £10 per season from the owner, Mr. D.M. Gurteen, who owned most of the town at the time. Prior to moving to Hamlet Croft the club played on a ground called Seven Acres which was bordered by Wratting Road on one side, with the railway line at right angles to it. It was owned by the local Co-operative Society and had a main entrance via a railway bridge. The ground is no more, as is the railway, the latter a victim of Dr. Beeching in 1964.

In 1926 Rovers again found themselves tenants of the Co-op when they purchased the ground from the Gurteen family who began charging a rent of £25. Ten years later, in the summer of 1935 the Haverhill Rovers Helpers' Committee began collecting money for a grandstand. The sum of £250 was duly raised and soon after the wooden stand was erected and described as being a 'de-luxe stand, a credit to the club, and the best for miles around'. When completed it was handed over as the property of the football club and is still in position, although in an advanced state of decay with the corrugated sheeting rusting away and the timber interior partially sectioned off. Either side of the stand are the dressing rooms which, although they look reasonably modern, are believed to have been put up in the fifties, while the clubhouse is of seventies vintage. One aspect of Hamlet Croft that always proved a problem was the pronounced slope, which was alleged to be even more spectacular than that at Huish in Yeovil. It was finally removed around 1962 when the club were forced to play for one season at the Town Rec close by while the new pitch was laid, and the evidence is clear today with the stand and ancillary buildings all situated on what is now a steep grass bank. It was around this time that the club declined the opportunity to buy Hamlet Croft, a decision that they

doubtless regret, for it is now a council-owned ground on which they have a long lease.

RECREATION WAY
Mildenhall Town FC

Mildenhall FC have been in existence since the 1890's and have had several pitches around the town, including Bridal Way and Sheldricks Meadow, neither of which were anything more than fields.

During the war the current site which was a recreation ground was given to the town by the Bunbury family. It had a large hawthorn hedge all around and was used for football and cricket. The pitch ran at right angles to its present position with one goal under what is now the swimming pool. In 1970 when the pool was built, the pitch was turned round and shortly after the cricket club departed for pastures new leaving a small hut which both clubs had used for changing purposes. This was destroyed by fire and new dressing facilities in the shape of the current prefabricated buildings were erected inside the ground. However, they didn't stay inside for long, as the building of a new estate just behind the ground meant an access path had to be constructed across the corner of the old cricket pitch and between it and the changing rooms. This eventually lead to the ground being altered significantly with the removal of much of the hedgerow and the fencing in of the playing area.

Entry into the Eastern Counties League saw further improvements with a small covered area put up in 1989 and, in 1992, a splendid new brick built clubhouse with the club name picked out in the brickwork (similar to Tiptree United and Chatteris Town). The floodlighting system came at the start of the 1994-95 season.

CRICKET MEADOW and GREEN'S MEADOW
Stowmarket Town FC

Stowmarket Town was formed in 1883, following the amalgamation of two local sides, St. Peters and the Ironworks, and immediately began playing at the Cricket Meadow.

As the name suggests, the ground was always shared with cricket, and in the formative years the playing area was no more than a roped-off pitch, and the precise date of the building of the small wooden stand is not known. The White Hart pub, situated behind Knight's Sale Yard at the Town End of the ground became the club headquarters, and provided changing rooms for visiting teams, who had to run the gauntlet of the crowd after the game, especially if they had won.

The early thirties saw success both on and off the pitch, with big crowds thronging to the Meadow, but that all changed in the latter part of the decade to such an extent that in 1938 the club ceased playing altogether. During this time, two clubs shared the ground, Nobels (later named ICI), and Stowmarket United. When football recommenced after the war, the club played as Stowupland Corinthians, and later as Stowmarket Corinthians, but by 1947 Stowmarket Town were back. Within four years the club had attracted their record crowd at the Cricket Meadow, when 3,800 watched an FA Amateur Cup tie against Romford. Such was the interest in the game, that extra viewing areas had to be created by parking eleven lorry trailers along the Finborough Road side of the pitch.

It was around this time that the club purchased, from Ipswich Town for the sum of £175, wooden terracing which was to serve so long at the ground and, indeed, for a further nine years at the new ground. The club were never able to radically improve the Cricket Meadow, and by the eighties it had become somewhat ramshackle, and was coveted by the council, who wished to re-locate the club and build a supermarket and car-park. 100 years of football at the ground came to an end on May 17th 1984, when Stow beat Gorleston 4-1.

The council moved the old wooden terracing, and some of the turf to start creating the new ground at Green's Meadow. A covered standing area was built, plus a stand with 200 seats, and floodlights were installed. Several porta-cabins were provided for changing rooms, and a clubhouse. The first game at the start of the following season was against Sudbury Town, but the official ground opening came in December when Sir Alf Ramsey turned on the lights before a match with Norwich City. The first ten years at Green's Meadow were completed when the council formally handed over the ground to the club as its own.

The Cricket Meadow had a pronounced slope, and three small lights at the bottom of the ground which lit up the tiny training area. Three sides were open, the allotment end had a few boards missing behind the goal and the wall at Knights Sale Yard was a popular spot where spectators could lean against the wall to watch the match. A small

The classic Cricket Meadow at Stowbridge and (below) the spanking new Green's Meadow.

wooden standing area was on one side of the seats, with the other side covered and this created a good atmosphere when full.

The stand had 100 seats, and was built to the design of a cricket pavilion with changing rooms underneath. By the players entrance stood a PA hut. There were two turnstiles at the old ground, one of which found its way to Braintree Town's Cressing Road ground whilst the other followed the club to Green's Meadow.

Green's Meadow is in some ways similar in shape to the former ground, having a seated stand with a covered area next to it, albeit slightly shorter, and a PA hut in the corner. The other three sides are open standing, but unlike the cricket ground, the playing area is railed off with hard standing all round.

The contrast between the two grounds however, comes with their respective settings. The old site was pleasantly rural, with a weather-beaten timber fence surrounding it, whilst the new one has the elevated Stow by-pass hurtling through directly behind the 15 foot tall chain link fence. The entrance to the ground is at the back of a spacious car-park, which was utilised to the full when the record attendance was set in July 1994, an Ipswich Town

side playing a friendly which attracted over 1,200 spectators to Green's Meadow.

Photos in this section by: Pat Brunning, Bill Dixon, Colin Lamb and Richard Wall.

KINGS ROAD and RAM MEADOW
Bury Town FC

The town club from Bury St Edmunds are going through a torrid time at the moment and the move from the Kings Road in the late seventies has not triggered off the long term success the club were perhaps hoping for.

The Kings Road ground was home for over 100 years and was a characterful ground with a number of stands and terracing which once held nearly 5,000 for a match with Kings Lynn in 1950. There were two entrances with covered areas to the east of the grandstand and to the west of the changing rooms with, at one time, covered terracing at both ends, although latterly the east end was open.

The seated stand had bench seating with cushions available

while another stand next to it stretched down to the corner flag.

The ground was lost in 1976 when a road and a car park were built across it, and the Supporters' Club hut was the only artefact to follow them to Ram Meadow. Now, nearly twenty years later, Bury are in danger of returning to the Eastern Counties League which they left in 1987. Their ground has a capacity for around 3,000, with half those under cover and has seen a crowd of 2,500 for an FA Cup tie with Enfield in 1986.

Nowadays, the attendances are somewhat less and the contrast between neighbours Sudbury Town and Bury is marked. Indeed, a sign of the apathy surrounding the club came a couple of seasons ago when the two met for a league game, and an official took the phone off the hook an hour before the start of a rain-drenched match, complaining that she was fed up of telling people the game was on!

Cambridge

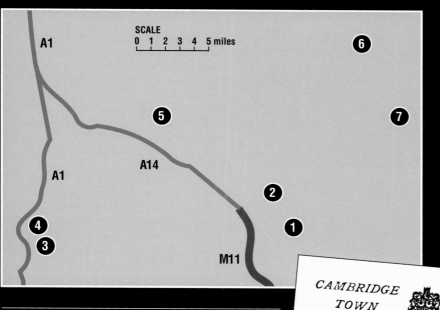

SCALE
0 1 2 3 4 5 miles

A1

A1

A14

M11

1   **Cambridge City FC**

2   **Histon FC**

3   **Eynesbury Rovers FC**

4   **St Neots Town FC**

5   **St Ives Town FC**

6   **Ely City FC**

7   **Soham Town Rangers FC**

Photos in this section by: Pat Brunning, Gavin Ellis-Neville, Neil Harvey, Mal Keenan, Richard Wall and Martin Wray.

CAMBRIDGE TOWN FOOTBALL CLUB.

OPENING CEREMONY
of the
New Ground, Milton Road,
on
Saturday, April 29th, 1922.

THE MAYOR (G. P. Hawkins, Esq.) will formally open the Ground, supported by members of the Corporation, the University and Patrons of the Club, who will be photographed by Messrs. Starr and Rignall.

The Cambridge Town Silver Band
WILL PROVIDE THE MUSIC.

Match: TOWN v. MERTON.

An aerial view of the original ground at Milton Road, opened in 1922.

CAMBRIDGE basked in the glory of having two professional clubs from 1958 when City joined United in the paid ranks. City's Milton Road ground was the more developed of the two and although the original ground was demolished, the new ground is built on part of the old site. United left the non-League ranks in 1970 for the Football League.

The oldest ground in Cambridgeshire belongs to Newmarket Town, whose wonderful old wooden grandstand is in danger of disappearing.

CITY GROUND, MILTON RD
Cambridge City FC

For those who meticulously record each ground visited, the City Ground caused a dilemma in 1985, when the new site was opened, the original having been demolished the year before. The debate as to whether to classify it as a new ground, or rather as a re-built old one, is down to the individual. Unlike the impressive development at Champion Hill, Dulwich, which is virtually on the same spot as the famous old original, the new City Ground lies at right angles to its predecessor, with one goal encroaching onto what was the old pitch.

Whilst not as yet reaching the heights of the old ground, it is adequate and accessible, in what is a very densely developed area of Cambridge.

Cambridge Town, as they were then known, were formed in 1908, and until their move to the Town Ground, used a number of sports grounds, many of which are still in use. For the first three years a pitch close to the railway in Purbeck Road was home, and the highest recorded attendance there was 1,500 against Ipswich Town 'A'. The odd game during this period was played at Perse School, until the club relocated to a ground which is now the site of the Cattle Market in Hills Road, by the railway bridge. This ground was quite advanced with a grandstand and duck-boards all around the pitch, and hosted a friendly against Racing Club de France which was watched by over 5,000 people. However, when the club re-formed after the war, they played at Trinity New Field, before using the sports grounds at Jesus College, Grange Road, Corpus Christi

Two rare action shots at the Purbeck Road ground around 1909.
The pitch still exists as do the pine trees.

College, Magdalene College, St. Johns College, the Amalgamation Ground and the Old County Ground. Most of these still exist, and all had reasonable facilities as was expected from the inhabitants of those seats of learning.

The nomadic life changed dramatically when Town purchased a site and began creating a football ground. The pitch was dug, levelled and turfed, and a grandstand was built along with a pavilion opposite. Banking was formed around the pitch, and the work was completed in time for the opening ceremony before the game against Merton in the Southern Olympian League on April 29th 1922.

The programme for the day lists the expenditure at £2,769, and estimates that the club would owe Lloyds Bank £1,100 at the end of the season. Nine years after the opening, Town built a new seated stand for 750 and, soon after the last war, terracing began to appear on the popular side which was extended and then covered by the late fifties. The record crowd at the old Town ground assembled to see an FA Amateur Cup tie against Leytonstone in 1950, and the club must have welcomed the new terrace, the figure being put at 12,078. A further 12,000 crowd saw the local derby with United in the FA Cup in 1953, by which time more hard

standing had been laid at what was now called the City Ground, the club having also changed their name to City. A remarkable 11,000 watched the floodlight opener against West Ham United on February 25th 1959, which also saw the temporary installation of terracing at the school end to accommodate the crowd.

The City Ground was at its peak in the early sixties. In a club brochure issued to support an application to join the Football League, described it as follows: "Covering approximately 9 acres. The grandstand has seats for 750, with a standing paddock in front for 800. The popular side accommodates 8,000 with most under cover....and has ample room for expansion and a capacity of 50,000..."

During this period the site included a full size second pitch, a bowling green, and large premises for supporters as crowds of 4,000 to 5,000 were regular. The City Ground had hosted cycling and athletics meetings up until the late 50's, and in 1967 the club embarked on a new venture, when introducing greyhound racing. In a similar way to that at Holker Street, Barrow, this proved to be the downfall of what was a splendid ground. The ugly, intrusive paraphernalia which accompanies dog racing took away the ground's grandeur, and when the chance came to demolish it and re-build, there were few tears shed for it in its final state.

The 1984-85 season was played on opposition soil, apart from three home matches staged at the Abbey Ground, and those of Royston and Soham Town. When the new City Ground was opened with a Southern League game against Corinthian, it had the stand sitting in the middle of what was the second pitch. An extensive car-park covers the rest, and a new development has wiped out any trace of the old ground. Further improvements have been made, with an area of cover opposite the stand and terracing extending around the ground. The only links with the past are the turnstiles and the shape of the land itself, which appears not to have changed. City have used the opportunity to create a modest ground tailored to the kind of crowds which they can expect to see, and unlike some, have given careful thought to planning and for that deserve credit.

The front entrance is superb with a massive car-park and, although not easy to spot from the main road, the new City Ground, once found, is an acceptable venue for senior non-League football.

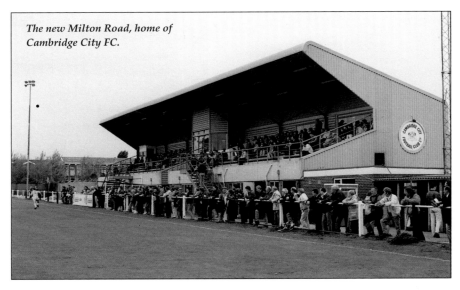

The new Milton Road, home of Cambridge City FC.

SHORTLANDS and ROWLEY PARK
St Neots Town FC

Until 1899 St Neots FC had played their matches on the top area of the local common. Growing crowds and a lack of facilities for taking gate money forced them to look elsewhere. A director of Paine and Co. Ltd, a Mr McNish, offered the club use of the extensive lawn at his home, Shortlands House and they remained there until 1987 when the site was sold for development.

Little was done at the ground for 30 years or more until a well-furnished hut was erected just by the entrance as changing rooms, all paid for by Paine and Co. It had separate rooms plus lighting and washing facilities. A year later the first grandstand went up, a wooden structure with a corrugated iron roof and glass sides covered with wire netting. Sited on the railway side of the ground, it held 250 and was built by Wrycrofts for £172 10s and opened on December 29th 1933. Twenty-three years later the club planned for a second bigger stand opposite the existing one and next to the changing hut. It eventually opened around 1960 and was brick-built with changing rooms, committee room and toilets. There were at various times matches played under floodlights during the fifties but the illumination was never more than training standard.

When Paines sold the land in 1987 the bulldozers moved in immediately but the ground was left derelict for some four years before any work began.

The club were dormant for two years until returning in junior football on a pitch at Priory Park whilst a new ground was prepared on the old A45 and named Rowley Park after Mr. Peter Rowley, the generous benefactor who has rented it to them at a peppercorn sum.

BRIDGE ROAD
Histon FC

Histon were founded in 1904 and it is believed have played at the Recreation Ground from that time. In its original state, the ground ran parallel to the railway line and in 1934 had a grandstand opened which stood backing onto the track. Entrance was through the woods next to the line at a level crossing.

The record attendance on the ground was the 3,400 who saw the 2-2 draw with Kings Lynn in the FA Cup in 1949, when the club was known as Histon Institute. They dropped the tag in 1952 and ten years later road works led to a re-positioning of the pitch and the demolition of the old stand, as the B1049 was built across the old recreation ground.

The pitch was re-laid at a angle to the old one, and a new complex including elevated seating was opened in 1964. Floodlights were installed and switched on before a match with Arsenal in December 1984, and since then, the bar has been modernised and an all-weather training area laid down.

Histon's new stand on the old ground in 1934.

Two views of the now demolished ground at Shortlands, St Neots.

WESTWOOD ROAD
St Ives Town FC

St Ives Town have, during the past 34 years, lost one splendidly old-fashioned ground in Meadow Lane but now have a home to be proud of, tucked away next to a sports centre at the end of Westwood Road. The current ground is reached down a driveway to the side of what is now a car-park but was once the second team pitch. To the left is the main building, the majority of which dates from 1981 and has the changing rooms and a clubhouse with a small covered terraced area in front, stood back from the pitch. Opposite is an impressive new stand which is soon to be filled with seats.

When ARC decided they required the site of the Meadow Lane ground for quarrying, the club were offered and accepted a parcel of land which once was the car-park for the local school. They left behind a ground, which had over 200 seats and a marvellous old timber stand proudly displaying the club name. The small changing rooms were off to the side in a hut. The end of Meadow Lane came when the farmer whose land St Ives had leased, decided to sell up, and ARC bought it to sound the death knell of a fine ground.

ALFRED HALL MEMORIAL FIELD
Eynesbury Rovers FC

Eynesbury is a village in Huntingdonshire which has been all but swallowed up by St Neots, yet has managed to retain its identity, as has the football team which has played on the same pitch for just over 60 years. The early days of the club were spent on Priory Park Rec and Cemetery Lane, with a very brief spell at Shortlands, the then home of St Neots.

The ground and surrounding area was completely different to the present day, being very rural and isolated. The pitch was reached by walking through a farmyard gate, roughly where Hardwick Road is now. The club soon put in a turnstile, and after the war when football returned to Mr. Walton's Field as it was then known, they began to plan improvements, and in 1952 the stand was built with two areas of covered terrace either side. Dressing rooms were installed underneath which meant an end to changing in The Plough public house in the village.

Rovers won Division One of the UCL in 1977 and celebrated by building the present clubhouse which necessitated knocking down one half of the cover, and ten years later floodlights were installed and celebrated with a game against Luton Town. The other half of the cover was also taken down leaving the skeletal framework and terrace only to the right of the stand.

The ground was donated by the family of

Ely's new home.

PARADISE GROUND and UNWIN SPORTS GROUND
Ely City FC

The spiritual home of Ely City Football Club will always be the Paradise Ground although for some nine years now they have played at the Unwin Sports Ground, a 12 acre out of town site fashioned from a playing field after the continual blocking of progress at the Paradise made it impossible to remain there.

City had shared the council-owned ground with cricket, hockey and rugby clubs over the years and themselves began there in 1890. It had a 400-seater steel-framed stand with asbestos roof, and railway sleeper terracing behind one goal and along the road side which was laid in 1956. The original changing rooms were in the wooden cricket pavilion but in 1970 a new timber building was put up behind the goal opposite the stand. The football club built a small bar in the later years. The capacity was tested to the full in 1956 when over 4,000 crammed in to watch City lose 6-2 to Torquay United in the first round of the FA Cup after the club had beaten the cream of Cambridgeshire football in previous rounds. Cambridge United, Cambridge City, Histon and March Town United were all defeated before Sudbury went down 1-0 at the Paradise to set up the Torquay tie.

On leaving Paradise, the out-buildings were found to be sufficiently decayed to warrant demolition, and although the ground is still used for Sunday football and cricket, no trace of the football artifacts exists.

The move was made in 1986 when the ground was virtually as it is now. It had been developed from a basic playing field with a pre-fabricated dressing room building, and boasted floodlights, (something that was never possible at the Paradise), and a clubhouse. In 1993 a new 200-seater stand was erected and the ground further enclosed, with the remainder fenced in by a hedge.

Mr Alfred Hall in his memory to ensure football would always be played there It is now owned and run by the trustees.

In 1989 the club built a new gateway at the only entrance to the ground and the following year re-furbished the clubhouse and dressing room extension.

The record crowd at this pleasant and unpretentious ground is 5,000 for a friendly with Fulham in 1953.

JULIUS MARTIN LANE
Soham Town Rangers FC

Soham's once modest ground has been transformed in the last two years and is now undoubtedly one of the most comfortable venues in its league.

The club were formed following the amalgamation of Rangers and Town in 1947, Rangers having played until the war at a ground in Brook Street, which is now partly covered by the Brook House Hotel. Town had played, since their inception in 1920, at the current ground which was purchased as agricultural land. After the war a small shelter was built on the half-way line with a wooden stand and dressing rooms, which are believed to have come from Abbey United (now Cambridge United), going up around 1949.

These lasted until 1989 when the old stand was knocked down and replaced with the splendid brick-built 200-seater structure now gracing the ground. The new dressing room block is in fact 20 years old and was erected next to the embryonic clubhouse which was first opened in 1968 but has since been extended.

Eynesbury Rovers FC.

Soham Town Rangers have transformed their ground in recent seasons... although happily some of the older artefacts remain.

The vast majority of the newer developments were completed in 1993, when both ends were covered and protection was built to the left of the main stand. The floodlighting system was opened by Arsenal in 1983. Soham Town Rangers can now feel justifiably proud of their fine ground.

Elsewhere in the town are Soham United who play in the Cambridgeshire League on Qua Fen Common. In the fifties they were on a par with Rangers, but have since been somewhat overtaken. Their ground is showing its age, although the old enclosure which enjoyed a previous life as a Tote Stand at Newmarket Races still hangs on while portacabins have replaced the derelict changing rooms.

TOWN GROUND, CRICKETFIELD ROAD
Newmarket Town FC

According to some records there was a football club of sorts in Newmarket in 1877, and that date is officially recognised by the club as their formation. For the first season the club played at the Severals, moving to Sefton Lodge for a period until the Town Ground was opened in 1885.

It had taken two years of planning by the committee, which included champion jockey Fred Archer, to form the new recreation club and acquire seven acres of a field next to the railway and fashion a sports ground. It was fenced in for the sum of £153.14s. and a rental of £12 per annum was agreed with Mr. Slater who, in turn, let the field from the Duke of Rutland.

The football and cricket clubs were combined at this stage, although they were to split three years later, and both games were played on the ground for 100 years, until the cricket club moved away in 1985.

The new recreation ground was initially used on Easter Monday 1885 for an athletics meeting, and the first football match, against Bury St. Edmunds Grammar School was played on 21st October of that year. At that time the pitch ran perpendicular to the railway, and the men changed in tents pitched roughly where the new houses are now. All this altered at the turn of the century when a stand, which had a small changing room, was built adjacent to the half way line. This timber construction lasted for thirty years until replaced by the larger stand which is in good health to this day. For the start of the 1905-06 season the pitch was turned to its present position, and the Town Ground, as it was then known, remained in that form until after the Great War, when it was bought by the Jockey Club. Within a year, it was pur-

chased for £400 by the cricket club and, soon after, a timber refreshment hut was built next to the old stand, and this, too, remains, although used as a store for marking equipment.

During the 1928-29 season the new stand went up, built to accommodate 150 spectators, and including a central access tunnel, changing rooms with baths and toilets. Such was the workmanship of the day, that the stand is still in good order, although the present day club have provisions to replace it with a brick structure. As in World War One, the Town Ground was used for friendly matches throughout the hostilities, and when competitive football returned a covered corrugated enclosure was built behind the goal at the western end of the ground, commonly known as the 'cow shed', but this lasted only four years before being demolished.

In October 1949, an FA Cup tie between Newmarket Town and Abbey United was watched by 2,701 spectators which has been taken as a club record, although 12 years earlier the club played the other Cambridge side, Town, in the Amateur Cup in front of a crowd unofficially put at 3,000, although this has never been verified.

The football club were always on the look-out for ways to improve the ground in the cheapest possible manner, and in 1956 they acquired two huts from Stradishall air force base which were re-assembled as covered enclosures either side of the stand. A further asbestos and timber building was placed next to the stand, but once re-roofed it was later re-sited as a clubhouse. One of the enclosures was demolished in 1970, and the other, with the clubhouse, went in 1985. In January of 1958 Newmarket Cricket Club, who owned the ground at the time, applied to both the Urban and the Rural District Councils for permission to convert it to light agricultural use. Their application was rejected, but by December of that year the cricket club had completed the sale of the ground to the football club for £800. However they continued using it in tandem for a further 27 years. Very little changed at the Town Ground until the eighties, when a strip of land was sold for a bungalow development, and on the proceeds work commenced on demolishing the enclosure and clubhouse, a new rail around the pitch (not previously possible due to the cricket), and floodlights. The new clubhouse and enclosure were used on the first occasion in November 1985, and ten days later the lights went on for the first time against Ely City.

Some ten years on from those major changes, the club are considering replacing the stand and the pay-hut with more modern buildings. It could be that the old girl may well be pensioned-off at the age of 66 but it would be nice if she could be left to watch over the Town Ground in her dotage.

Bedford and District

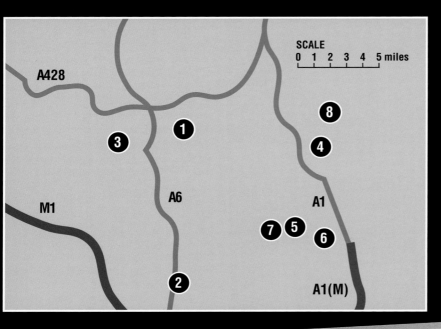

SCALE
0 1 2 3 4 5 miles

A428

M1

A6

A1

A1(M)

1 Bedford Town FC
2 Barton Rovers FC
3 Kempston Rovers FC
4 Biggleswade Town FC
5 Langford FC
6 Stotfold FC
7 Arlesey Town FC
8 Potton United FC

Right: A match programme showing Biggleswade's Fairfield Road ground.

Below: Barton Rovers FC.

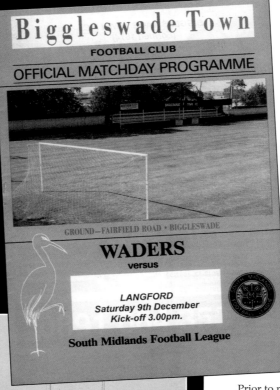

Biggleswade Town
FOOTBALL CLUB
OFFICIAL MATCHDAY PROGRAMME

GROUND—FAIRFIELD ROAD · BIGGLESWADE

WADERS
versus

LANGFORD
Saturday 9th December
Kick-off 3.00pm.

South Midlands Football League

BEDFORD TOWN's Eyrie was one of the most imposing and impenetrable homes yet hosted some astonishing matches before its terminal slide into becoming an annexe for a brewery. The reformed club have fought back, have a new out of town home. Technically the club are back at status forefront, although Arlesey Town are the FA Vase and South Midland League champions and their Lamb Meadow is of a high standard.

The area is primarily South Midlands League country with a sprinkling of United Counties thrown in plus a couple from the Isthmian League, and is dotted with a number of clubs whose grounds have yet to develop or have fallen away in recent years. However the days of Bedford being home to half a dozen or more senior clubs is long gone.

SHARPENHOE ROAD
Barton Rovers FC

Barton are the nearly men of the South Midlands, coming so desperately close to landing the FA Vase during the late seventies and early eighties. The glory days coincided with the move up from the South Midlands to the Isthmian League and a relocation to Sharpenhoe Road in 1975. They reached the quarter-finals in 1976 and 1979, the semi-finals in 1977 and 1982 and the Final itself in 1978.

Throughout all this they began developing their ground which is now capable of holding 4,000 and it was, possibly, the continued distraction of the Vase runs which prevented the club moving up the league.

It has not prevented them from improving the ground however, and the 120-seater stand is now complemented by a 1,000 capacity covered standing area which, with the infilled perimeter fence, refurbished dressing rooms and terracing around the ground, has allowed the club to compete in Division Two of the Isthmian League.

Prior to moving to Sharpenhoe Road, the club played on basic pitches at Church Pitch, Barton Cutting and Sharpenhoe Road before the war, before spending 30 years on Barton-Le-Clay Recreation Ground. Within a year of moving, the club had seen their record crowd of 1,900 posted against Nuneaton Borough in the FA Cup - a fourth qualifying round tie which they lost 3-2 in their very first year of entry.

THE EYRIE, RALEIGH STREET and THE EYRIE in MEADOW LANE
Bedford Town FC

The town of Bedford has, up until the early 1980's, been well off for senior football and a glance at the FA Cup history books will reveal that since the war alone Bedford Avenue, Bedford Corinthians, Bedford Queens Works and Bedford St Cuthberts have all competed alongside Bedford Town. The first two have since played in local junior football but the other three subsequently folded.

The loss of the original Bedford Town and its massive Eyrie tucked away in a heavily suburbanised area of the town was a major blow to the area and to non-League football in general. For, along with the loss of Brooklands at Romford and St Joseph's Road, Guildford, it began to dawn on many people that even the major footballing venues were not safe, particularly in the south.

Bedford Town FC re-formed in 1908 but little is known of the original club. They began playing on a field in London Road and later on the Queens Park ground which was subsequently used by Bedford Avenue. They moved to a field close to the site of the Eyrie and by 1923 Ford End Road had become home. It was an enclosed ground without facilities, owned by the Charles Wells Brewery next door. The club soon put in entrances and dressing rooms, and a small timber grandstand on the site of the ones that followed much later.

Such was the degree of the banked wooden terracing that more than 5,000 were able to watch the Beds Premier Cup match with Luton Town Reserves in 1934 and almost 6,000 attended the FA Cup match versus Dartford in the same year.

The Eyrie was well-maintained during the war and soon after a 2,000 capacity covered enclosure went up over the banking on the brewery side with a further stand built at the Raleigh Street end. The banking was terraced in concrete and the stand re-built to hold 1,000 people as the Eyrie, as it was then known, took shape in preparation for the massive crowds that were to come.

1953 saw Kettering Town attract a Good Friday crowd of over

10,000 and in 1955 13,150 crammed in to watch the Eagles beat Watford in the FA Cup to set up a date with Arsenal. Eight years later glory returned in the Cup and, having beaten Newcastle at St James' Park, Carlisle United attracted 18,000 to the impressive stadium.

Two seasons later the crowd record was smashed again as 18,407 saw Everton beat the Eagles in the fourth round of the Cup. From there, although further success was to follow, the crowds dwindled and the ground was soon in danger as the lease on it was running out. Greyhound racing arrived in 1971 but eleven years later, with the club still expecting to be re-housed by the council, the axe fell when the brewery lease expired and the owners took control of the site in order to extend the brewery. The last match at the Eyrie was in April 1982 and although greyhounds continued until the following January the ground was almost immediately torn down and turned into a storage area. Parts of the perimeter wall still exist and recently a couple of the outbuildings were being used but the huge stand which looked out over two splendid stadia at Mitcham and Bedford disappeared along with the club.

The name of Bedford Town was but a memory until in 1989 a group of supporters re-launched the club which began playing on a public pitch in Allen Park, ironically close to Ford End Road, with the first game on September 7th 1991.

Promotion was sought, and a five and a half acre site in Cardington was found and, with council backing, the ground was under way culminating in an opening match against Peterborough United on August 6th 1993.

Since then the new Eagles have entered the Isthmian League, the ground having gained a small stand with 100 seats and a covered area of terrace behind the goal for another 250. The whole site is fenced off and a thriving social club stands at the entrance. It is strange that one council could effectively allow the club to die, yet another, not seven years later put their full weight behind a re-launch. It has to be said that the old Eyrie and the club were stagnating, but no more so than 80% of other clubs at the time, and the new club have breathed fresh life into the area which was served by Bedford United and Kempston Rovers until the rebirth.

Bedford Avenue FC were another senior club in the area who had a chequered history, playing on enclosed grounds as Bedford Queens Park Rangers before going to Newnham Avenue until the site was acquired for an athletics track. Although it had a stand with concrete terracing in front, the pitch was not the required size and so the club moved to an unfenced ground next door where they sadly faded away, merging with Bedford North End.
This club had played at Astell's Meadow in Cardington Road but at the time of the amalgamation were playing on a pitch opposite the Athletics Stadium.

The much lamented Eyrie.

FAIRFIELD ROAD
Biggleswade Town FC

The football pitch at Fairfield is only part of a huge sports ground incorporating cricket and hockey. The left hand side is designed solely for football and a semi-permanent barrier runs down the cricket side.

The timber main stand with attendant advertising boards is flanked by two enclosures, both with curved corrugated roofs. Stretching across behind the town end goal is a low timber clubhouse and next to that is a weather-boarded score box with adjacent changing rooms. A hanging plaque on the

wall reveals that the Lindsell Memorial Pavilion, which overlooks the pitch, was re-erected courtesy of Wells and Winch brewers in 1954, replacing the one gutted by fire in May 1948.

Just how old the football stands are is not known, but they must surely have been there since the war years. More common knowledge is that the floodlights, which were switched on in 1989, were originally at Charlton Athletic's Valley Ground before it was closed and subsequently modernised.

FORDE PARK
Langford FC

Forde Park has come a long way in the 11 years since the club played their first competitive game there against Milton Keynes Borough in August 1984. Until then home had been King George V Playing Fields in the village which were opened in 1952. Before the war the club played on a field on Bulls Meadow at the bottom of the village close to the river and at the Leys, which is now covered by council houses.

The new ground is almost in the neighbouring village of Henlow and was fashioned out of a rubbish tip when a lease was granted by Mid-Beds District Council in 1981. After three years the ground was levelled, seeded and landscaped and dressing rooms were built with a small clubhouse and two small areas of cover down the side. Forde Park was finally christened on 22nd August 1985 with a game against Queens Park Rangers which attracted the highest attendance to date of over 450. Later, seats were added to one of the covers and in 1988 the floodlights appeared. A year later an extension went on to the clubhouse; the original structure once did duty as an office at an equestrian centre in Huntingdon.

In 1992 the ground was bought outright and progress continued with the laying of hard standing around part of the pitch.

ROKER PARK
Stotfold FC

The present ground was first used in 1911 by a team called Stotfold Athletic who played on a meadow named 'Roker'. For the first 20 years or so the re-formed club played in local leagues before elevation to the South Midlands League in 1952. It is believed the long low stand which stretches along most of one side of the ground was put up around that time. It has a small number of seats but can cover 300 people in a capacity crowd of 5,000.

The focal point is the modern clubhouse and changing room complex which stands on the corner of the ground.

HILLGROUNDS ROAD
Kempston Rovers FC

Kempston Rovers were formed in 1884, predating the Football League by four years. Their home in the early years was a pitch in Newells Lane which staged matches in front of crowds of 1,000 or more on a regular basis.

It was not until 1929 that, with the financial aid of a local businessman, Mr. Horace Hill, Rovers acquired a new ground and clubhouse at Hillgrounds, which secured their future. It was opened on October 1st 1929 with a friendly against local rivals Wootton Blue Cross.

The club had always been in the shadow of their massively-supported neighbours Bedford Town but had achieved stability, remaining at the first Hillgrounds until 1973, when they transferred a few hundred yards down the road to make way for a road junction onto the new estate.

The original ground had a clubhouse which extended towards the pitch and was barriered off; that site is now covered by the junction of Bedford Road and Hillgrounds Road. The second ground which lasted less than fifteen years was similar, with a clubhouse and dressing rooms combined, and a small overhang creating cover. Again the

playing area was barriered off, with advertising hoardings all around, and was still more or less intact until the early nineties, when it had become derelict and overgrown. It is now covered by houses. The Rovers moved to the latest Hillgrounds pitch in 1986 and have developed a splendid clubhouse, with a 100-seat extension plus an area of covered terrace.

LAMB MEADOW
Arlesey Town FC

Arlesey's early years were spent on various farmers' fields used as and when required. The first game was on November 14th 1891 when the visitors to Mr. Papworth's field were Biggleswade Red Cross, and the next game on the same pitch saw Arlesey play Hitchin Blue Cross.

Other venues included a field near Three Counties Station, Long Meadow, Lamb Meadow and the Common, followed the next season by games at the Bury Meadow, owned at the time by Colonel Fyler. The club finally settled at Lamb Meadow until the landlord of the Lamb Inn evicted them in 1912. Without a ground the club lay dormant for a year as many of the players went to Arlesey Juniors who were playing at Bury Meadow which had changing facilities in the Bury House itself. The advent of war put paid to football in Arlesey and when it recommenced it was Arlesey Town who had taken over at Bury Meadow where they remained throughout the between-war years. With no changing rooms at the ground and the Bury House no longer available, the club was forced to use the White Horse pub to dress in from 1934. However, war again loomed and on the resumption the Bury Meadow belonged to a brick company who had plans to build a sports complex, and so once again Arlesey Town were homeless. The existing landlord of the Lamb Inn was approached with the idea of moving back to Lamb Meadow, and enthusiastically he offered it rent free for the first few seasons. Many hours were needed to transform the field, which had a pavilion as changing rooms, back into a football ground but it was achieved and with the sterling work of the Supporters' Club the ground was completely altered. The Supporters' Club purchased the land from the brewers Wells and Winch as well as the area where the clubhouse is now. A brick shelter for 300 people was put up in 1953, and a 7ft high chain link fence enclosed the ground. In 1954 new changing rooms and a committee room were built and during the summer the pitch was levelled. Three years later a new entrance and car-park were constructed - these are now under the clubhouse.

A protracted problem with planning permission meant that the club purchased, from Biggs Wall who were developing nearby, a building to use as a clubhouse but could not site it or work on it until 1969, and two years

later it was finally opened. Ten further years passed before the long-awaited floodlights were switched on with a game against Luton Town in 1981 and another decade went by before the unveiling of the club's new stand on the clubhouse side.

Arlesey put themselves firmly on the map in 1995 when, having already won the South Midland League, they went to Wembley and beat much fancied Oxford City. The Lamb Meadow may well see the fruits of that success in the coming months.

THE HOLLOW
Potton United FC

Potton were formed in 1943 and obtained use of the Recreation Ground in Sandy Road, owned and maintained by the Parish Council. The existing pavilion was repaired and made acceptable for changing and later bathing, but it soon became apparent new facilities were required as the club went forward. Large crowds often assembled, and the club could only take a gate on a limited number of occasions, which meant a collection was their only income.

In 1946 negotiations began with the Land Settlement Association for the club to rent an area of land in Biggleswade Road to turn into a football ground and by mid-1947 final terms were agreed and work began. The pitch area was levelled, seeded and enclosed and a wooden framed building 54' by 24' was obtained from the Ministry of Works for use as dressing and committee rooms.

The Hollow was officially opened in January 1949 when Wisbech Town were the visitors. Concrete posts had been put around the pitch with wire threaded through but it was some years before the steel tubing they were designed for was available. Covered accommodation in the form of ammunition huts sliced in two stretched down half the pitch length and some years later bench seats were installed in two rows of fifty. Since those early days many improvements have been made, not least a second pitch for a Sunday side which continued until the cricket club who had previously used Sandy Road Rec moved in. The dressing rooms were extended to provide a small clubhouse and floodlighting was installed.

In 1984 the ground was fully modernised when a brand new dressing room and clubhouse replaced the rapidly deteriorating old building. This impressive structure now caters for both football and cricket clubs. An enclosed floodlit five-a-side pitch was opened in 1987. Another of the relics from the past which had served the club so well, the old shed type cover, was removed in 1990 and replaced with a new 200-seater stand, and a third tower of lighting on each side added to bring the lux value in line with requirements.

Northants & East Warwicks

THIS area which stretches from Warwick in the west across to Raunds in the east is rich in historic grounds, many legacies of the strong Northampton League which became the United Counties League.

The jewel in this particular crown is the reasonably newly-formed Rushden and

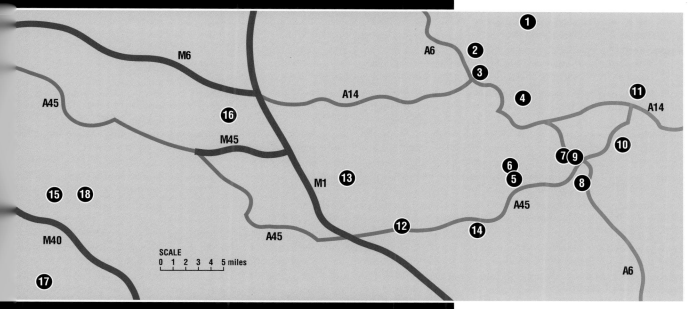

Diamonds, an amalgamation of Irthlingborough Diamonds, a post-war club who had no little success in the FA Vase, and Rushden Town who dated from the last century and had played at Haydon Road since 1922. The modern ground built to house the new team is stunning, and easily the most advanced non-League ground in the country, comfortably beating Yeovil's three-quarter finished ground and Dorchester's aesthetically very pleasing, yet more modest stadium.

1	Corby Town FC
2	Desborough Town FC
3	Rothwell Town FC
4	Kettering Town FC
5	Wellingborough Town FC
6	Wellingborough Whitworths FC
7	Irthlingborough Diamonds FC
8	Rushden Town FC
9	Rushden and Diamonds FC
10	Raunds Town FC
11	Thrapston Venturas FC
12	Northampton Spencer FC
13	Long Buckby FC
14	Cogenhoe Town FC
15	Racing Club Warwick FC
16	VS Rugby FC
17	Wellesbourne FC
18	AP Leamington FC

The modest Nene Park, home of Irthlingborough Diamonds has been transformed into the finest new non-league stadium in the country for Rushden and Diamonds.

ROCKINGHAM TRIANGLE and OCCUPATION ROAD
Corby Town FC
and Stewarts and Lloyds FC

It has to be said that Corby Town's move out to the Rockingham Triangle Sports Stadium has done them few favours. Their former ground in Occupation Road may well have seen better days but had its own identity and was sufficiently developed for them to apply for Football League membership several times in the sixties. At its demise in 1985 it still had an official capacity of 14,000, with cover for some 6,000 on the terraces, and seats in the main stand for 600.

Corby Town was formed in 1948, when a split occurred within the ranks of Stewart and Lloyds FC and the new committee decided to turn professional, moved next door into Occupation Road and immediately began developing the ground. Meanwhile Stewart and Lloyds re-formed to continue playing on their works ground. The Corby Town ground soon boasted a wooden main stand with dressing rooms and a full length covered enclosure down the opposite side. Both ends were banked and later terraced as the club began to attract huge gates. October 1949 saw 7,200 pack in to see the club defeat Peterborough United and a year later Kettering Town's visit attracted over 9,000, a record that was broken twice in a fortnight in 1952. In FA Cup ties against the same two sides, the latter drew in 10,239, posting an attendance which was never bettered at Occupation Road and certainly won't be at the Triangle.

Stewarts and Lloyds original ground is still used by the United Counties League side, and has not changed dramatically since it opened in 1935, although a number of buildings have come and gone since then. It is part of a huge British Steel-owned sporting venue which incorporates rugby, cricket and bowls as well as football, and each organisation has its own social club.

The football ground is now segregated from the rest by a clumsy metal fence made necessary by the club's elevation to the Premier Division of their league. At the same time, the current stand with its 100 seats was built to replace the small bus-shelter type which stood on the same spot. Much larger and more impressive was the club's original grandstand which stretched along three-quarters of the pitch until it was removed and sold. Various locations have been suggested as to its new home, with Desborough Town being one, although the date coincides with the building of Town's new ground next door, so it may be that it only travelled a couple of hundred yards.

More recently the single tier red-brick clubhouse behind the goal has become two-tiered, with the dressing rooms still underneath. Prior to this arrangement the massive former Works Social Club, which looks over the whole site, housed changing facilities, as did the small hut which stood behind the goal for many years.

In 1985 Corby Town's Occupation Road home succumbed to developers, and they moved to the brand new £800,000 council sports complex out of town at Rockingham Triangle. Opened on September 6th 1985 by the Rt. Hon. Neil Kinnock, the Stadium is splendidly designed for athletics, although it is not and never will be a football ground. Whether by choice or due to some disagreement between club and owner, at the time of writing there is not a single mention on or near the ground of Corby Town Football Club. The signs say 'Rockingham Triangle Stadium' and the neighbouring cricket, rugby and tennis clubs all have welcoming boards but the casual visitor would have no idea that a semi-professional football club were in attendance. In truth the 1,150 seats in the stand give a good view if the spectator can cope with watching from a distance, as the seats are elevated in a similar fashion to those at Cwmbran. But, not unlike Sandwell Borough's uninspiring home, those watching at ground level are less well served. Nearly 30 years after applying to the Football League, Corby Town are playing in front of less than a hundred in a stadium that doesn't appear to want them.

WATERWORKS FIELD
Desborough Town FC

The first Desborough club to play competitive football was Unity who were founded in 1884 and changed their name the following year to Desborough Town. The early history is not fully documented but it is known the club played on a field adjacent to the present site, and changed in various pubs in the town as was the norm. The main grandstand was built in 1922 and in February of that year officially opened by Mr. W.J. Westmoreland, chairman of the Northamptonshire Football Association. It cost £300 and was financed by public subscription, individuals purchasing 10 shilling shares for which they were repaid during the next few seasons. After the Second World War, the ground developed further, with cover erected in 1946, and pitch barriers installed.

The clubhouse, built in 1967, has been extended several times since, and when the club purchased the ground from the council in 1973, the main priority was installation of floodlights, but these did not arrive until July 1981, when the huge pylons, visible from miles away, were obtained from the old Corby Steel Works.

CECIL STREET
Rothwell Town FC

Roughly equidistant from Corby and Kettering and also with a Stewarts and Lloyds connection is Cecil Street, home for 100 years of Rothwell Town FC.

The ground has been in use since 1896, although until around the Great War the pitch ran at right angles to its present position, with one goal roughly where the houses are now at the back of the main stand. The first structure was a wooden grandstand, which stood opposite the current one; it was built in 1924 and opened before a game against Peterborough United Reserves. Shortly after, twin covered shelters went up which stood until 1960.

A year earlier a fire had wrecked the stand and, rather than rebuild on the same site, the club took down the shelters, re-erecting one of them opposite on the site of the burned stand. With the financial help of many including near-neighbours Kettering Town a replacement was built which is still in use today. Underneath are the dressing rooms which replaced the old ones sited in a hut which can still be seen at the back, and even to this day has the sunken bath that was the envy of many.

The six-pyloned floodlighting system was purchased in 1982 and came from a building site owned by McAlpine's close to the town. This proved to be the last major change of any kind until 1994 when promotion to the Southern League meant the provision of more cover behind the clubhouse goal, the steelwork for which came from Irthlingborough Diamonds' re-built Nene Park ground.

Waterworks Field, Desborough

Rothwell's gravelly car-park leads to the entrance and the clubhouse which was built in 1972. An old railway carriage stands guard at the gate, on the right of which is an open piece of land which used to house a tennis court and pavilion. The square-shaped stand has a wooden interior and an almost flat roof. The fact that there are three lighting pylons each side of the ground means that, annoyingly, the middle one is quietly rusting smack in front of the seats, but other than that the view is good. Opposite, the ground is bordered by hedges which protect a school and behind the far goal a green sheet is now in place to further enclose the ground.

Cecil Street has character and, despite its antiquity, appears to have been well looked after as it approaches the arrival of its birthday telegram from the Queen!

ROCKINGHAM ROAD
Kettering Town FC

The chronology of the development of the Rockingham Road ground is not easy to follow, but is made somewhat easier by club historian Mel Hopkins' excellent newspaper research.

The club's first games were played on what was known as George Eldred's Field which was in Green Lane close to where the Police Station is now. Twenty-two years later they moved to North Park, which is still there, until 1897 when they transferred to Rockingham Road. The ground was already in use for football, but had a pronounced slope from end to end although the early days were spent playing parallel to where Cowper Road is now.

There was a grandstand from early on, but by 1930 the club had a new stand which the active Supporters' Club raised £166 to pay for. Despite this, they were obliged to rent it until it was officially handed over to them. The covered enclosure to the right of the stand took the brunt of a terrible storm in 1935 and was completely demolished, although 50 yards or so was eventually rebuilt. A small area found its way down to Cossham Street in Mangotsfield where it stood for a short while until found to be unsafe.

At this time the players changed in an old barn which stood some distance from the pitch in the corner of what is now the car-park, and walked through the crowds.

The Second World War came and went with the threat of losing the ground to the effort averted. However, it was badly damaged by vandals, with dressing rooms, grandstand, social club, and tea huts all suffering. Surprisingly, despite the shortages, a new stand went up with dressing rooms closer to the pitch in 1944, but again the ground was cursed as the building blew down soon after.

The primary concern after the war was to rectify the severe 1 in 48 slope, done by

Kettering's Tin Hat (above), now gone, and the stunning cantilevered main stand (below).

removing 11,000 tonnes of earth from the Cowper Street end and banking up the Rockingham Road end. Further banking was added and railings put in around the pitch; a new car-park and fence along the Brittania Road side all appeared in the immediate post-war enthusiasm. Concrete slabs from demolished air-raid shelters at Corby and Wellingborough were laid down as hard standing, and in June 1947 another grandstand was erected, courtesy of Kettering Cricket Club, who sold it to the Poppies after it was blown down in yet another gale.

As work went on, more fencing was put around the ground which became completely enclosed by the end of 1947 and the far end and Brittania Road side were covered. Cricket was still being played at this time, as the main stand was set further back, flanked by twin covered enclosures, and for a while dog racing was tried.

In the summer of 1950 the far side was completely terraced and new turnstiles were put in place in the Cowper Street corner and new dressing rooms added - wooden, with a brick base. The terrace was further covered in 1952 from the fund-raising efforts of the Supporters' Club, but soon after part of the roof was blown off. The following year saw the replacement of the railway sleepers with concrete and in 1957 the Rockingham Road stand was built along with more fencing, a manager's office and a boardroom as the club prepared for the ground's Diamond Jubilee.

The progress made through the early sixties, with the first floodlights and the 8ft brick wall down Cowper Street as well as the canteen, ended with a lull in developments and little of significance happened until 1972 when major changes were announced which would alter the face of Rockingham Road for all time.

The dressing rooms, covered enclosures, and grandstand were all wiped away and a stunning 2,500 seater cantilever stand with office space and dressing rooms was erected covering two thirds of the side. This superb structure, one of the biggest anywhere in non-League football now dominates the ground completely.

The rest is now a mixture of open and covered terracing, currently spoiled by an ugly boarding type of fence which acts as a wall at the back of the Rockingham Road end, now that the 'Tin Hat' has disappeared. The covered side is now restored to full working order after the middle section was damaged and removed a few years ago. The Cowper Street end is still open and terraced at the front with the shallower rear part as loose banking. The corner to the left of the stand is taken up by a single storey, rather unattractive Social Club with the slightly older canteen and offices at an angle next to it.

The ground has been given the nod of approval from the Football League and is one of the more pleasing of the top grade grounds in non-League football today.

HAYDEN ROAD and NENE PARK
Rushden Town, Irthlingborough Diamonds FC and
Rushden & Diamonds FC

Hayden Road was given to the town for sport in 1922 as a ten acre plot to be shared between cricket and football. The main stand which is still hanging on was built when it opened and provided seating and changing accommodation.

Later a small area of tin cover went up opposite the stand as the cricket area was fenced off, and when the club sold Gordon Inwood to West Bromwich Albion the fee was used to concrete the remaining

Hayden Road, Rushden. A former Southern League ground vacated when Town merged with Diamonds.

three sides of the ground. An old Nissen hut was employed as a clubhouse in 1965 but altered to a brick building in the 70's. Floodlights were erected around the 1975-76 season.

Hayden Road eventually became a stumbling block for the town club for although impressive in its early days, it had not changed significantly enough and the Southern League rejected it.

After the merger with Irthlingborough Diamonds in 1992 the ground was occasionally used for evening matches by Higham Town, and is now home to Rushden Rangers junior side. The old stand, now 73 years old is still there and until recently bore the club name on the roof fascia.

NENE PARK
Nene Park was originally constructed on a piece of overgrown wasteland in 1969 after the club had spent its first 20-odd seasons on council pitches as a youth team. The ground quickly developed with long low stands capable of seating 350 either side of the pitch with room for another thousand under cover. Floodlights were turned on by Ipswich Town manager Bobby Robson in November 1978 and were replaced in 1989.

The record crowd at the old Nene Park was over 2,400 who saw Dagenham sneak away from an FA Cup replay with a win in 1978, and that remained until the ground was completely re-built to Football League requirements upon the merger of the two clubs in 1992. The original stands and changing rooms were swept away to

DOG AND DUCK GROUND
Wellingborough Town FC

The Dog and Duck is a marvellous throw back to the recent past when football grounds were allowed to fester quietly without being garishly ponced up in the name of pyramid progress. Although part of the ground may be knocked down, or possibly already has been, and the medieval perimeter fencing has seen better days, the Dog and Duck has survived in its current form chiefly due to the club dropping out of the Southern League into the less demanding United Counties.

A short lane running next to the pub which gives the ground its name leads to the huge rambling arena, the shape of which indicates that it was formerly a cricket ground.

A worn jet black corrugated iron fence encloses two sides of the ground with a less historic greyer variety behind the pub end goal. The wooden-faced clubhouse, until 20 years ago the property of the Silver Band Club of Earls Barton, stands next to a horribly stark white-washed single-storey dressing room built around 1963 on the main road side. Both are set back at an angle away from the pitch which confirms that the Dog and Duck was a dual-purpose ground. Cricket continued there until the 50's and tennis and athletics until much later, all fitting in around the football. The tennis club had its own pavilion and two courts, situated where the training pitch is now. Opposite the changing rooms are three fascinating buildings, all of differing ages which have experienced diverse fortunes. The crumbling remains of an ancient timber stand, replete with brewery adverts on the fascia awaits its cremation.

The interior has been removed leaving bare skeletal forms where the seating once was. The stanchions are now twisted and buckled with a clutch of advertising boards in front attempting to keep out unwanted guests. Behind, amongst the dereliction, is a small building which was used as dressing rooms until 30 years ago but is now barricaded up awaiting its fate. Next to it stands an altogether more secure grandstand, built in 1965 and open-sided with colourful seating, a breeze block and timber front and a corrugated asbestos roof.

The third building is an intriguing pavilion, very old but well cared for with an extension acting as spectator cover and now converted into a refreshment room. Surprisingly, this building is not connected to cricket, but dates right back to Wellingborough's previous ground near the Gas Works, and was transported and re-erected when the club began playing at the Dog and Duck in 1901. At that time the pub and the land were owned by Praeds Brewery and the ground was surrounded by a fence which had a canopy attached to it to act as a cover. It stretched along most of the main road side of the ground, before eventually giving way when that side of the ground was developed in the early sixties.

Directly behind the Dog and Duck ground is the home of **WHITWORTHS FC**, also in the United Counties League. Their lane leads to a square-shaped changing room block built around ten years ago when the club reached the UCL. The pitch was originally hemmed in by hedges which dictated the narrowness of the playing surface, and when the football club approached the parent club for permission to expand the field, they agreed. The small cover behind the far

goal was once on the half way line when the pitch ran left to right before it settled on the angle it now stands. Another area of cover was built on the half way line as the ground was transformed for the promotion. The old changing hut was removed and for a while the players changed in a permanent-looking porta-cabin building which is attached to the works next door.

THE BERRISTERS and KILN PARK
Raunds Town FC

Raunds Town Football Club were preparing for their Centenary celebrations in 1996 on a ground which is only five years old. They vacated the Berristers which had been home for 43 years to move to a purpose-built ground on an out of town site in 1991, and 1,500 saw the opening match against Crystal Palace on July 23rd of that year.

All the facilities are situated down one side, with the dressing rooms, club room, seated stand and covered enclosure all together. The seats are at ground level and set back from the pitch, giving a very moderate view indeed. The other three sides are on open hard standing and again some distance from the pitch with the dug-outs intruding. The entrance and car-park, close to a roundabout are eye-catching with the rear of the club building backing on to it.

From the start Raunds played on the Greenhouse Field, which was situated off Thorpe Street close to where the Smiths Container entrance is today. There were no facilities at the field and the players changed 300 yards away at the Globe Inn. They were there until just after the war when the owner was looking for money and turfed off the be replaced in stages by firstly, twin single decker cantilever constructions, each curving to enclose the ground on all corners. A further triple decker stand was opened at the far end in January 1995, with the final part of the jigsaw in the planning stage during 1995/96. The superb Diamond Centre, complete with bars, hospitality suites, restaurants and lounges is situated behind the right hand side stand facing the large car-park - once the second pitch on the old ground. A batch of porta-cabins stand guard over the open end of what has turned into possibly the finest modern non-League ground in the country. What has made the modern Nene Park a success, as opposed to the many other new stadia that have sprung up in recent years, is the way the ground and the facilities have borne the spectator in mind. Without running away with the idea that the corporate guest is all that counts, Diamonds have provided comfort and style inside the ground. Nene Park is now a very long way from Hayden Road. Clearly the ultimate aim is elevation to full FL status.

An aerial view of Nene Park with the Diamond Centre at the bottom of the picture. A new stand behind the goal on the left was opened in January 1995.

---

recently re-formed club. For a while they used Joe Elliott's Field which is now covered with housing, before moving to the Manor School as the search for a permanent home continued.

Berrister's was farmland but when the club heard it was on the market for £900, a collection was held in the factories around the town to make the asking price. Once the deal was completed an old wooden army hut was purchased at Brigstock for £75 with a communal bath built in, and later two dressing rooms, a committee room and a tea room were built along the side of the ground where the old Social Club was situated. All around the pitch were oak posts with wire passed through. In the late sixties the social club was bought and leased out. Eventually the club opened it themselves and it lasted until the move when it was sold to Long Buckby.

In 1981 a new covered stand was built

next to the dressing rooms, the zinc sheets coming from Kimbolton Airport while Esstee Ltd provided the timber. When promotion came the stand was converted into seating and the pitch barrier changed to iron poles as Berristers prepared for eight more years of United Counties League football before its eventual demise in 1991.

CHANCERY LANE
Thrapston Venturas FC

Thrapston's council-owned playing field has housed football since it was laid out and opened in 1950. Thrapston Institute used the pitch until Venturas came about in 1960.

The original wooden dressing rooms still lurk quietly by the side of the newer version which is also used by the cricket club. A post and rail runs around half of the pitch, with a small breeze-block stand replete with club

name to the side. The clubhouse, opened in 1974 stands back from the pitch and was built by club members, as was the stand, opened around seven years ago. The remains of a castle mound are to be found close by in the landscaped grounds.

KINGSTHORPE MILL
Northampton Spencer FC

Northampton Spencer are a team that have come to prominence only in the last few years, becoming a major force in the United Counties League in the 1990s. Their early days were spent at an undeveloped ground at Dallington Park before they moved briefly to Duston High School for two years.

In 1972, the club were offered and accepted the chance to shift to a private ground owned by Plessey. The site was very basic with only a pathway through the adjacent allotments, no vehicular access, and poor player facilities. However, some old church rooms were acquired and sited on a brick platform to form changing rooms. An extended frontage had benches making a small stand. A clubhouse, opened in 1979, now stands next to the old changing rooms and this has a low cover which is welcome on wet days.

More recently, a somewhat acrimonious court battle resulted in the club winning the right to buy the ground for a nominal sum after the Plessey Sports Club's interest in the site waned. The legal hurdles cleared, the club continued on their upward spiral both on and off the pitch by creating a driveway into the ground and, in 1993, a new canteen and dressing room extension.

The approach to Kingsthorpe Mill,

The Berristers, former home of Raunds Town FC.

through a semi-derelict industrial estate and allotments, is depressing and the vista across from the car park is no better with a hotch-potch of white railings, in need of repair, and an ugly barbed wire-topped chain link fence separating the ground from adjacent railway land. However, from the railway side the character changes, with the old stand, club rooms and new dressing room complex all in different styles, but somehow gelling into a fine unit of which this very homely club are justly proud.

STATION ROAD
Long Buckby FC

Long Buckby have played at the Station Road sports ground since the war, the original club having led a nomadic existence in the 1930's. They have made several moves, all within the same complex in the last 25 years. The original pitch was situated lengthwise alongside the site of the current function room with a small wooden stand roughly where the path runs today.

It did not survive for very long, being removed a few years later when the pitch was relocated in preparation for United Counties League football. The stand that exists today dates from around 1970 but was originally longer, roughly half of it having been lopped when the pitch was lengthened to comply with FA Vase regulations. At that time the players used wooden changing rooms where the modern block now is, and a wooden fence enclosed the pitch. A section of this with one floodlight pylon had to be removed every spring for the cricket.

Further progress was made in 1978 with construction of the dressing rooms and clubhouse and some fifteen years later, chiefly to escape from the annual springtime disruption, trustees purchased the land on which the pitch now lies and built a fine new stand, the third to be erected in 25 years. Use of the second pitch still continues, however, the old stand is used for storage.

COMPTON PARK
Cogenhoe United FC

The early days of football in the village are not documented, but the first game on the village playing field was against Northampton Yeomanry in 1950. Up until then various pitches in and around Cogenhoe and Whiston had been used whenever possible. The club stopped playing sometime after 1958, but within ten years were back at the playing field. Facilities had always been basic with just a small pavilion housing two changing rooms, neither of which had washing facilities. Around 1976, the club extended the pavilion to incorporate showers, and three years later erected a shelter at the side of the pitch.

It soon became apparent that a new ground was needed to move the club forward, and a site was selected on part of a permanent pasture belonging to the estates of Lord Northampton on the edge of the village. Initially, 5.6 acres, sufficient for two pitches, a car-park and a clubhouse were negotiated. The main pitch was surrounded by moveable posts linked by a rope, and the second pitch had ten floodlights to aid training mounted on three old telegraph poles. The clubhouse was built courtesy of a brewery loan, and a small breeze-block stand soon followed. As success moved the club on, then a perimeter wall or fence had to be erected around the main pitch to enable Cogenhoe to gain promotion. The total acreage at the ground is currently 10.5, which has expanded due to the youth team policy. Possibly the most ambitious project, was the challenge of raising £26,000 for the floodlights at Compton Park.

The ground in its first phase was opened in 1985 by Ron Atkinson, then manager of Manchester United.

LOXLEY ROAD SPORTS GROUND
Wellesbourne FC

Wellesbourne's council-owned ground, as with so many lower league clubs, is shared by cricket and bowls. The pitch is surrounded on three sides by a low post and rail, with two dug-outs curiously positioned together, twenty yards or so from the goal line on the cricket pitch side.

A superb clubhouse proudly sporting the football and social club name stands behind one goal, and to the left, almost as an after-thought, a green-painted basic iron stand housing a few seats which was erected, against the club's wishes but to comply with League rules, on reaching the Midland Combination Premier Division.

Until 1979 the club used the cricket pavilion for changing and it was the only real feature on a ground which sadly is ham-strung by a church decree which forbids the charging of admission.

WINDMILL GROUND
Leamington FC

There are moves afoot to resurrect football in the town of Leamington, some eight years after the last game was played on the old Windmill Ground.

It had been a venue for football since around 1890 and was used by more than one club from that town until 1937 when, due to poor gates and a financial crisis, it was sold to Coventry City for their A team matches.

After the war, the Lockheed Company, which was situated opposite the ground, purchased it from Coventry and installed their own club who joined the Central Amateur League. By this time the Windmill already boasted substantial covered accommodation down one side which later had bench seats installed and over the years, as the Lockheed club progressed, covered terracing went up behind the town goal and along the opposite side.

As AP Leamington the club competed in the Alliance Premier League before suffering relegation in 1982. A year later they had won the Southern League title, but were refused entry back to the Alliance. This was compounded by the sale of the ground to a building firm, and with it the threat that the Windmill would disappear after 100 years. Leamington, unable to progress, and only able to exist from year to year disassociated themselves from Automotive Products (AP) and slowly faded away.

The Windmill soon became a housing

The new stand at Long Buckby. The old ground is just behind it, next to the cricket pitch.

estate, but a good portion of the buildings were salvaged and put to good use at Stratford Town's ground as offices and a boardroom. But due to cash flow problems, not everything was re-erected and to this day a large pile of rusting ironwork complete with fading advertising hoardings, - all once the main stand at the Windmill - lies in the long grass at Masons Road.

An early shot of Butlin Road, VS Rugby.

TOWNSEND MEADOW
Racing Club Warwick FC

The name Racing Club did not come into existence until the late sixties by which time the old Saltisford Rovers were settled having had a number of homes. The club first played by the Dun Cow pub on a pitch so close to the road-side that spectators watched from the pathway.

The players changed in a nearby washhouse amongst other places and this lasted until a move to St. Nicholas Park in 1958. This was a council park where the players changed at a shed in the confines of a nearby laundry as there were no facilities available. Eventually the club moved to a pitch on the Coventry Road, now covered by the Woodlowes Estate, where officials erected a Nissen hut which was used for changing.

Finally a transfer was sought to land close to the racecourse and there was a choice of moving to the ground now used by Warwick Rugby Club or their present one. They chose Townsend Meadow which was racecourse land and had been used by the militia in early times. Another Nissen hut, this time from RAF Gaydon was acquired and baths were installed which are still used by the players today. The pitch was levelled and a clubhouse constructed in 1967 while a changing room building was brought across from the old cricket ground at AP

Leamington. A small area of corrugated cover stood roughly where the racecourse side stand is now and the referees' changing rooms were in the converted stables which are still in use and stand just inside the entrance. In the mid-eighties twin breeze-block and corrugated iron stands were built on either side of the pitch and a perimeter fence put up, not dissimilar to the racecourse rails. Floodlighting only reached Hampton Road in 1990 by which time they had climbed to the Southern League and laid hard standing at the ground.

Today, Townsend Meadow is a slightly scruffy but homely place and one of the less developed of Southern League grounds. The assortment of buildings are functional without being particularly attractive but are redeemed to some degree by the presence of several fine oak trees around the ground and the fact that Warwick Racecourse wraps itself around the place.

BUTLIN ROAD
VS Rugby FC

Valley Sports home has seen more than its fair share of ups and downs in its short life. Progressing up through the leagues as a natural successor to the defunct Rugby Town, the club built the ground up to Southern League standards only to come within hours of folding in 1993.

The future is again bright for VS and Butlin Road has survived. The approach to the ground past other municipal pitches is pleasant with a small car-park is behind the large clubhouse. Inside the block of turnstiles the terracing is split by an ugly and unnecessary caged walkway, imposed on the ground by league regulations in a similar manner to that at St. John's Lane, Worcester. A bank of terracing stretches along one side of the ground towards a covered terrace at the far end, brick-built but open to the elements. On the far side is a modern 240-seater stand, built to replace the original on the same site. Two clumsy extensions either side erected during the brief reign of a former chairman give some protection. The end nearest the club is part-covered terrace backed by fir trees.

VS moved in to Butlin Road in 1973 taking over what was part of an allotment and within a dozen seasons created a ground which was suitable for the Southern League and that had seen a record crowd of nearly 4,000 for an FA Cup tie with Northampton Town.

Photos in this section by: Pat Brunning, Andy Dakin, Colin Peel and Dean Walton.

Racing Club Warwick FC.

Worcestershire and surrounds

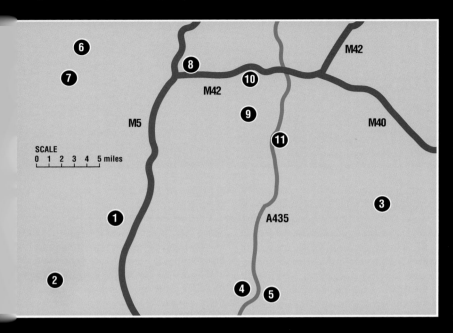

SCALE
0 1 2 3 4 5 miles

1	**Worcester City FC**	7	**Stourport Swifts FC**
2	**Malvern Town FC**	8	**Bromsgrove Rovers FC**
3	**Stratford Town FC**	9	**Redditch United FC**
4	**Evesham United FC**	10	**Alvechurch Villa FC**
5	**Badsey Rangers FC**	11	**Studley BKL FC**
6	**Kidderminster Harriers FC**		

WORCESTERSHIRE is rich in senior football with a number of top notch grounds, the jewel being at Aggborough. The City club have struggled, dropping out of the Alliance, but the area still boasts two clubs in that league plus three Southern League outfits and a rejuvenated new club in Alvechurch Villa. The main bulk of clubs are a legacy of the strong Birmingham League.

ST GEORGE'S LANE
Worcester City FC

At the main entrance to Worcester City's home, the striking first aspect is the obvious eagerness to welcome visitors, with three separate signs inscribed "Welcome to Worcester City". Once inside the ornate iron gates, flanked by a strong brick wall and turnstiles, the rear of the `New Stand' comes into view, with the impressive club rooms built into it. To the right are the administration offices, and to the left, at an angle to the ground, a white-washed two-storey dressing room building, built in 1939.

In its original state this grand-looking building was perfectly symmetrical, but it has since had a small extension added nearest the gates, and further more recent alterations to the upstairs V.I.P. lounge have given it a lop-sided look. However, with a coat of paint and the removal of the unsightly garish cage attached to the players' door as a security measure imposed by the league, this building could look almost as good as new.

The New Stand, built by Metal Construction Co. of Worcester for £23,000, is outwardly in fine fettle. It boasts close on 1,200 wooden seats, and its high corrugated roof and partially glass-backed rear is remarkably roomy and well cared for. Sadly, directly opposite, the much smaller

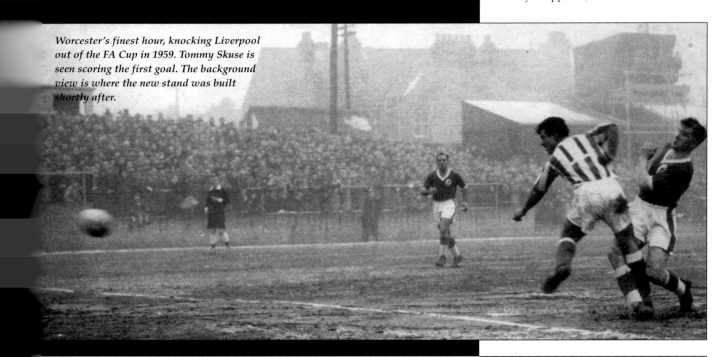

Worcester's finest hour, knocking Liverpool out of the FA Cup in 1959. Tommy Skuse is seen scoring the first goal. The background view is where the new stand was built shortly after.

St George's Lane. The stand in the centre is now condemned and City expect to move to a brand new ground in due course.

AGGBOROUGH
Kidderminster Harriers FC

Aggborough became the most talked-about ground in non-League football at the end of 1993/94 when, having won the Conference title and embarked on an astonishing run in the FA Cup which ended in a narrow 5th Round home defeat by West Ham United, Harriers were denied their rightful entry into the Football League.

Only when Macclesfield suffered the same fate a year later did Aggborough fade slightly from the public eye. The cause of all the grief was the 60 year old main stand which once declared unsafe was set to be replaced with a full length cantilever structure in the close season. Unfortunately, that wasn't soon enough andLeague rules denied them promotion.

Kidderminster Harriers began life as a running club in 1877, started a rugby team three years later and finally switched to football in 1886 after a period when some matches were played under both codes at the same time. The rugby club played on the Lakes ground, later known as White Wickets Recreation Ground, before moving to the Chester Road cricket ground which was eventually used for football. With several teams fielded each week, a breakaway club formed called Kidderminster Olympic and for three years the pair vied for the healthy support in the town, both commanding several thousand for each game. There were problems with the football encroaching onto the cricket square and the club moved to Old Aggborough, a ground formerly used by United Choirs Rugby Club. This ground was little more than a pitch with a rope around it and the site is now covered by the College of Further Education.

The new Aggborough was opened in May 1890, although there had been a grandstand on the ground for a couple of years before that, and the recently-amalgamated club formed by Olympic and Harriers played Walsall. The very early Aggborough was enclosed in an oval shape with a wooden stand which tapered in at the side and a banked athletics track around the pitch. The grandstand had bench seats and a wicker fence, with a post and wire around the pitch. The ground had a capacity of 15,000 even then and with teams in the Midland and Birmingham Leagues, the outlook was rosy, but the club had over-stretched itself and folded in 1891. Harriers reformed almost immediately and with athletics also at the ground it was very popular in the post Great War years. After the war the ground was purchased by the Kidderminster Harriers Ground Co. Ltd who charged the football club rental to play, and this problem was not fully resolved until the council bought the ground in 1945. By then, the grandstand had gone, replaced in the twenties by a corrugated iron cowshed, so named because it was

Brookside Stand, bought before the war, is now unused; its decaying seating led to it being condemned and boarded up, and it now functions as storage space. A sad end to a structure which gave over 50 years service. Next to it is the massive sloping-roofed Cowshed, which can comfortably keep 500 people dry in wet weather. On the canal side of the New Stand an area of concrete terrace replaced wooden sleepers in 1980, and it was here the original dressing rooms were situated until they were demolished and replaced in 1947, by the building which now houses them.

Worcester City FC were founded in 1902 following the merging of Worcester Rovers and Berwick Rangers. They inherited the latter's ground in Severn Terrace, next to the racecourse and near a street bearing the same name which still exists. The first match for the new club was against Stafford Rangers on September 20th 1902.

The following season was spent at Thorneloe, the old home of Worcester Rovers, a ground which was in all probability at the northern end of Pitchcroft, as a road of the same name can be found there today. The third move in as many seasons came when City became tenants of the Royal Grammar School grounds at Flagge Meadow, still in use as a sports field and just a few hundred yards from St George's Lane.

In 1905 the club successfully appealed to the public for help with donations to pay for the laying out of the new ground, estimates for which were around £300. It was opened by the Mayor on October 25th 1905, again against Stafford Rangers but this time in an FA Cup tie in front of 2,000 spectators. By the start of 1907-08, the enclosure had a stand on the St George's Lane side with banking on the other three plus turnstiles, courtesy of Worcester Racecourse, and remained more or less unchanged until 1929.

The Brookside Stand was built in 1929, and ten years later, just prior to the Second World War, the dressing rooms by the

entrance were put up. After 1947, when materials became available again, the free-hold on the ground was bought and facilities were further improved. The brick facade went up in 1948 and a small area of cover was erected over the terracing at the canal end, although it only lasted a few years. The brook which runs behind the Brookside was culverted in 1950 allowing the bottle-neck in the top corner to be widened along with the pitch itself, and the first floodlighting appeared in 1951. St George's Lane was by now developing into one of the biggest non-League grounds in the Midlands. In 1953 the Brookside Stand was moved a few yards and in 1956 the current Cowshed was added when the canal end cover was removed. 1963 saw the biggest changes by far at the ground when the massive new main stand was built entirely through the funding efforts of the Supporters' Club. The social club and skittle alley housed underneath went in around ten years later.

The Southern League championship of 1979 financed more major changes, including new floodlights - the third set to grace the ground - modern turnstiles and exits, a Vice-President's Lounge and fresh terracing on the Brookside and canal end.

Since those days it is fair to say that the ground has become slightly seedy as the parent club struggle to gain a foothold on the ladder once again. Although hard standing now covers the entire ground, the Brookside Stand was condemned following the Popplewell Report and one or two other areas are in need of repair. It is a 'Catch 22' situation as the club are desperate to move away to a ground with more room. As it is, there is virtually no parking at a ground in a heavily residential area, and any attempt to gain Conference standing would be futile. Sadly, progress looks sure to account for this marvellous old ground in the same way it has done for Hednesford, Gresley, Yeovil and countless others.

Aggborough: An historical outside view as the main stand , now demolished , was replaced in 1994.

made by Dales of Leominster who manufactured sheds for farms. A long curving covered enclosure stood at the Hoobrook end between the wars and this survived until it was blown down. The new grandstand which was to cause so much heartache nearly sixty years later was opened on August 31st 1935 before a match with Stourbridge. It had 460 seats and was described as one of the best stands in the Midlands. After the Second World War the area in front of it was terraced in concrete and the old, little-used ash track was replaced by a tarmac cycle track. Sadly, this too was rarely utilised and remained an anomaly until the oval shape of the ground was changed in the eighties.

The original post and wire was replaced by a concrete wall and the club entered the revered Southern League in 1948, having been members for a matter of days at the start of the 1939-40 season before war broke out.

Aggborough made the headlines in 1951 when in December Kidderminster played Aston Villa under floodlights, one of the first to do so. Thirty-two lamps were mounted on 14 pylons and although it was not a great success due to difficulties following the play, it heralded a breakthrough. A new system was installed in 1966 but nine years later a major problem hit the ground when the middle section of the cowshed roof was demolished in a gale. It was repaired but the old structure was subsequently replaced in April 1979 by the Bill Greaves Memorial Stand, named in tribute to the late chairman. As the club moved into the Alliance Premier League the floodlights were once again updated and in 1983 substantial terracing was laid around what was still at that time an oval-shaped ground.

During the last dozen years, as the club has seen its most productive period ever, Aggborough has been completely trans-

formed. The track has all but gone, a new covered terrace now stands behind the near goal squaring off that end, and the new stand has put paid to the area in front of what was the old stand. Indeed, it was renovated and extended with new dressing rooms, VIP rooms and a players' lounge as recently as 1983 but all was swept away 11 years later.

Aggborough, with its professional approach, club shops, newly-built entrances and superb new main stand is a million years away from one or two of the humdrum grounds which saw Alliance Premier League football at its outset. If not for a technicality it would have been hosting League football as effortlessly as it did FA Cup football when West Ham came to town in 1994.

MASONS ROAD
Stratford Town FC

On approaching Masons Road, the surrounding area and ground are reminiscent of Northampton Spencer's Kingsthorpe Mill. To reach it involves negotiating a rather gloomy industrial estate and, once inside, the nearside of the ground is so far the only part to be developed.

To add to the similarities, the ground is hemmed in by a railway and waterway, in this case the man-made Stratford Canal which, unlike the River Nene at Northampton Spencer, is unlikely to flood the place. An imposing new Safeway complex is now built on the adjoining site which has led to preliminary talks with the club to fence in and improve that side of the ground. Certainly the raw materials are there with large piles of metal work, corrugated iron, floodlight pylons and even second-hand advertising hoardings all patiently waiting to

Kidderminster's main stand with its later extension covering the paddock.

Stratford Town FC. The building to the left came from Leamington's Windmill ground.

BEEHIVE
Studley BKL FC

Studley BKL are a works team for BKL Fittings, and have been around since 1971. Their ground has recently undergone quite major surgery, as a new by-pass has meant moving the pitch onto land previously occupied by Abbeyfields Hospital.

The clubhouse and dressing rooms were constructed in 1980, and also cater for further pitches within the complex which house the reserves amongst others.

Since reaching the Midland Combination, the club have laid hard standing and erected a tiny stand which will have to either be knocked down or transferred when the move is completed.

be re-assembled.

In a town whose name is synonymous with English history it is a touch surprising that the only real antique artifacts at the ground are those aforementioned heaps of iron debris. These are the dismantled sections from two sides of the old Windmill Ground - former home of AP Leamington - which were purchased when, sadly, the Windmill was sold by the owners and built on. The portable wooden triangular shed, erected next to the stand, in current use as a committee room, and the solid black building (formerly changing rooms but now housing snooker tables), tucked into the corner of the ground, are also both from the Windmill. The main stand, a long low structure built in 1960, has unusual brick supports which hold the struts in place and has a selection of seating in place including some which previously adorned Molineux. The club have played on the ground since 1953, having moved a few hundred yards from Alcester Road.

COMMON ROAD
Evesham United FC

Evesham's 27 year old home is built, as many are, on an old rubbish tip. It is often prone to suffering extremes of the weather, and waterlogging is a problem the club have endured since moving from the Crown Meadow in 1968. When the upheaval came, the old stand went with them having stood at the Meadow since its grand opening in 1953. It had changing rooms behind it and cost £1,533 when new, most of which came from donations, among them £487 from the Evesham Horse Show and £20 from the Allotment Society.

In 1975 the clubhouse was erected, bringing much needed revenue to a club playing in the Midland Combination, but it wasn't until 1992, when they won the league and were accepted into the Southern League that floodlights were installed and hard standing was put down around the ground.

A small area of cover behind one goal dates back around six years and the new dressing room complex was completed in time for the club's much-acclaimed promotion. The huge railway embankment which runs alongside the ground gives a splendid, though strictly illegal, view of the game at what is a young and as yet relatively undeveloped ground in an extremely attractive riverside town.

WALSHES MEADOW
Stourport Swifts FC

The Swifts' attractive riverside ground, tucked away behind the new sports centre was, surprisingly, deemed unacceptable by those who drew up the starting twenty for the inaugural Midland Football Alliance. It would appear the main area of concern was the lack of proper seating in the 45 year old green-painted shed which does a perfectly good job keeping people dry just as it was intended to do when grandly opened with a match against Aston Villa in 1950.

This little scenario neatly encapsulates the mentality of those who would rather see a uniform, soulless, concrete box with garish plastic bucket seats than something which, though it might be somewhat frayed around the edges, has become an integral part of a football ground.

Swifts have an official founding date of 1882, since when several Stourport teams have been in existence, notably Stourport Unity who played for a while on Cross Meadow before moving to Olive Grove, and a team based at Harrison's carpet works, who left the area at the turn of the century. The first Swifts practised on a field near the Station Hotel and played their initial games on Bewdley Road near the New Inn.

The club changed its ground several times, firstly to part of Moor Hall Park, and then Feathers Farm which seems to have been a particularly dangerous site as the

Evesham's stand which went with them from Crown Meadow in 1968.

Kidderminster Shuttle observed "several collarbones got broken and shins were cracked".

Many of the Swifts players migrated to the Harrison's club who also played on the Olive Grove, and Swifts folded, but when the works club went under too Unity were left as the only team in the town. They lasted until 1906, when they too folded and another club called Town briefly emerged. A second generation of Swifts were born around this time; playing at Olive Grove and winning the Worcester and Bromsgrove Charity Cups, they continued until the outbreak of the Great War. When hostilities ended, steps were taken to re-instate the club who played up until the late thirties at The Hawthorns, on a ground now covered by the Parson Chain Company. Soon after the Second World War the club moved to Walshes Meadow, and changed in a building which stills exists in the neighbouring Bewdley Rugby Club. The new shelter was built in 1950, and other than the small extension to the wooden clubhouse remains the only structure on the ground. The clubhouse was

Stourport Swifts and Aston Villa players in front of the new shelter at its official opening.
Below: The same Walshes Meadow stand, 45 years on.

first built in the early seventies, and in 1993 was further extended towards the pitch. Two thirds of the ground is sectioned off from the rest of the sports ground by a concrete block fence built some two feet off the floor to allow for possible flooding of the nearby

River Stour. As it has not flooded the pitch since the late forties, that bureaucratic touch seems a little over the top. Immature trees and a fence run along the river side of the ground which is reminiscent of Hadleigh's similarly situated ground, and has a pleasant backdrop of elegant dwellings in this most agreeable of Worcestershire towns.

RECREATION GROUND
Badsey Rangers FC

Badsey Recreation Ground is somewhat unusual in that it is blessed with two stands and a changing room building, but does not have a barrier around the pitch due to preventative council regulations. The club's relatively lowly position in footballing circles is surprising bearing in mind the facilities on offer, indeed the first stand in its original form was built back in the late twenties with a second smaller stand following complete with changing rooms.

The Recreation Ground was opened amidst much pomp on 15th May 1920 and Rangers moved from their original home at

The two quaint old stands at Badsey have been there for decades, yet the club cannot get permission to post and rail the pitch.

Aldington Pastures the following season. The Pastures once packed in some 3,000 spectators for a Hospital Cup match against Evesham with a line of brewery drays providing an elevated view around the ground. It had no buildings on it and soon reverted back to farmland, which it remains.

The new ground has changed little since opening, unlike the village which has expanded greatly. However, it is still surrounded by open land, and the two stands remain although one is currently out of bounds and the other is now in a different format having been blown down many years ago, and re-built using the same materials. A new changing block now separates the two, a far cry from the days back in the thirties when the players had to walk from The Wheatsheaf pub.

VICTORIA GROUND
Bromsgrove Rovers FC

In the 'Story of Bromsgrove', a historical reference to a town renowned a hundred years ago for its nail-making, Reverend Leadbetter states that "It is not until the eighties that Association football was introduced to Bromsgrove. The present Rovers Club originated as a Boys' Club, and there is a record of a match on 5th December 1888."

In fact the club were playing friendlies three years earlier, on a field along Old Station Road, and then in 1887 on the Recreation Ground in Market Street. It was around this time the club began its long association with the Roebuck Inn, which was to be the club's headquarters for over 50 years. In 1889 the club moved to a ground which had several names, Churchfields, Jefferies Field, or the Meadows, and is now the grounds of Parkside School.

In 1892 the club joined the Studley and District League, and relocated, this time to Well Lane, which they used for 18 years until their final move to the Victoria Ground in 1910. Well Lane ground was where the North Bromsgrove High School now is, and had an entrance down a footpath via Well Lane. Despite the fact there were no spectator facilities whatsoever, the crowds would often top 1,000. At that time the players would change at the back of the Roebuck and walk to the

VALLEY STADIUM
Redditch United FC

Redditch United Football Club moved to an area of waste ground off Bromsgrove Road in 1948 having previously played on a works ground in Millsborough Road. The site was soon brought up to playing standard with a surrounding fence and a wooden stand where the current building is now. A long covered area went up opposite which stretched along most of the pitch with rough banking at either end. The entrance was a little further up the lane to its current position, with changing rooms and a small social club eventually going up roughly where the turnstiles are today.

The cover only lasted a dozen or so years for it was destroyed in gales and was not replaced until the ground was completely modernised in time for the club's elevation to the Southern League. Ground grading was nowhere near as stringent as it is today, but everything was re-built as a result of a partnership between the club and the town development corporation and was adequate enough for them albeit briefly, to be members of the Alliance Premier League, or Conference as it is now known. The old stand was removed and replaced with the curious multi-purpose structure which is a social club, function room, board room, dressing room, directors' and sponsors' area and seated accommodation all rolled into one with room for 300 seats. Opposite now stands a terraced and banked area with cover for around 1,000 which went up at the same time and the car-park end has a cover which brings the capacity officially to 9,000 although in reality the club would never be allowed to admit even half that amount. The record crowd at the old version of the ground is 5,500 which saw a West Midlands League match with local rivals Bromsgrove Rovers in 1955.

The oval shape to what is a very large ground gives rise to the possibility that something other than football has been played at the Valley, but apart from ideas for greyhounds at one point, it has remained a football ground with much potential.

ground, a trip often fraught with danger from irate followers. A change of league to the Birmingham Combination meant a change of ground, and at the start of the

1909-10 season, the club moved to the Victoria Ground. The land was owned by a club member named Joe Tilt, who rented it to the club. There was an entrance on to the Birmingham Road, and the ground fronted on to Victoria Road. As there were no changing rooms, the Roebuck continued to be used. After the first war, the club was posting average gates of 2,000, and often more would watch, as there was little but a hedge acting as a barrier along one side. Despite team struggles on the pitch, a small wooden stand was erected, and officially opened on Boxing Day, 1924.

Little was done to Victoria Park until after the Second World War. During the time that American servicemen were in the area, the pitch was used as a baseball diamond

Bromsgrove Rovers, pictured in 1990.

but, despite this, remained in good condition, and soon after organised football swung into action again, the crowds began to flock back in their thousands. For one Senior Cup Final ten lorries were driven onto the ground as emergency stands as a crowd of 5,768 watched Rovers beat Wellington 4-3, and in 1948 new turnstiles were provided in time for the FA Cup tie with Hereford United, which attracted a crowd of 5,219.

Victoria Park began to be transformed as the old wooden stand, so grandly opened in 1924, was replaced by the current colourful structure, and the banking to the left of it was covered over with what is known as the 'Cow-shed'. Finally, in 1953 new dressing rooms were built opposite the stand, a sturdy brick-built structure which has since been extended to include modern clubhouse facilities. The current floodlights date from 1971, when they were erected costing £4,000, to replace the original set which had been in use since 1953, when Aston Villa were the visitors for the special occasion.

As has been the case with all the grounds that house successful clubs, recent times have seen dramatic changes, with additional stands, segregation, turnstiles and so forth. Victoria Ground is no exception, although happily it retains a pleasant appearance and provides a comfortable view from any spot. The whole area is terraced, with the cowshed stretching back some distance, vaguely reminiscent of Stonebridge Road. In the area between the covered end and the stand, the back gardens of the adjoining dwellings are fenced off, but the corner flag is not that far from the nearest back door, and on matchdays there cannot be much privacy. The dressing rooms are now situated behind the stand, which is emblazoned with the club name across the roof, and has steps up into it at each end and from the middle. The South End was terraced to prepare for promotion to the Conference, and is soon to be covered. All along the Birmingham Road side are situated a long low collection of buildings, housing offices and club rooms, part of which were the old dressing rooms.

Above: A wonderful '50's shot of Langlands with the old wooden dressing rooms and cover... Later the clubhouse (seen here) was built alongside it...

...and later still a stand was attached to the front of the clubhouse.

LANGLANDS STADIUM
Malvern Town FC

Langlands Stadium is a slightly misleading name for the home of Malvern Town, as it is more modest than the name suggests, having a concrete main stand and clubhouse on the near side, with flat standing on the other three.

Briefly, when entering the car-park, the clubhouse with its water tower looks for all the world like a greyhound tote and gives the impression of a stadium from the outside, but the expanse of land on the far side of the pitch has only been used by the Malvern Athletic Club in the past.

The club were formed after the Second World War and played at Victoria Park, on the ground presently used by Colletts Green FC, a former Sunday League club who now play in the Midland Combination. On purchasing the land, which was part of the Madresfield Estate, for the new ground, Malvern began work on a wooden hut which was used for changing and later converted into a clubhouse.

A new block for changing was built by

club men in the early sixties and a small lean-to was added to the hut. The ground was altered significantly at the end of the seventies when a stand with seating for 140 was built in front of the changing rooms. An extension and floodlights went in and these were used for the first time when Worcester City visited for an FA Cup First Qualifying Round game in September 1980. This match also attracted the record gate at the ground of 1,221. The old wooden hut has been replaced by a more modern clubhouse, but this has encountered its problems and much work is going on to repair it.

The widespread past use of the ground for athletics is confirmed during very dry weather when the site of an old sand pit for long-jumping can be seen on the pitch, similarly to that at Halstead.

VICTORIA PARK is currently the home of Colletts Green, although they are looking to move on. The council-owned ground has had a small covered stand for many years, possibly even when used by Malvern, and many local cup finals have been staged there. Its openness is a problem for any ambitious club, and there are rumours it may end up becoming a rugby ground in the not too distant future.

LYE MEADOW
Alvechurch Villa FC

The original Alvechurch side was formed in 1929 and played on a pitch at the Meadows, in Meadow Lane with changing rooms in the Red Lion pub. Later they moved on to an area called The Gaunts, off Bear Hill which is now built on, before moving to an open meadow on the Redditch Road in 1957.

The first building at the ground was a long green hut which stood near the bottom end and was used for changing and had a bar installed. From there the meadow was transformed, as banking was developed and a main stand built on the half way line, followed by a covered enclosure at the north end. In the early seventies as the club were in the middle of an almost uninterrupted run of success in the Midland Combination and West Midland Leagues, a cafeteria and dressing room complex was built. This stood back from the half way line and was later extended with the addition of a function hall.

The small village club reached its peak in 1981 by winning the Southern League when it was split into two equal sections, but despite its development the Alliance Premier League deemed the ground unacceptable and denied promotion. The following year they were runners-up and won the League Cup the season after but soon the great days faded and Alvechurch rejoined the pack on a ground which did not change to any great degree from then on. In 1992, following a series of financial problems, the club folded and despite re-forming almost straight away it was not enough. The detachable parts of the main stand and the covered enclosure were removed and taken to Bloxwich Town and brick rubble was strewn all over the

pitch with many of the hoardings and rails damaged. The club noticeboard outside which normally announced the next match, simply stated with desperate poignancy, `The End'.

Happily, it was not, for a new club, Alvechurch Villa were formed and set about putting together a side and rebuilding the ground. The main stand has been re-roofed and Lye Meadow has been tidied up as a new wave of enthusiasm comes to Alvechurch. The former club are in the record books for all time after playing the longest FA Cup match ever which, due to competition rule changes, will never be beaten. In 1971, after beating Moor Green, Darlaston and Atherstone Town, Alvechurch drew 2-2 with Oxford City at Lye Meadow. The replay at the White Horse was drawn 1-1 after extra time, and the second replay at St Andrews also finished 1-1 after extra time. They then tried again at Oxford United's ground twice, drawing 0-0 on both occasions before Church finally scraped through 1-0 at Aston Villa in the fifth replay. The exhausted team's reward was a trip to Aldershot where they lost 4-2.

Photos in this section by: Pat Brunning, Andy Dakin, Paul Dennis, Gavin Ellis-Neville, Kerry Miller, Dean Walton and James Wright.

The stand at Lye Meadow was reduced to rubble and taken away to Bloxwich Town. The end came in 1993, but happily Alvechurch Villa have begun to rebuild the ground.

Birmingham and the Black Country

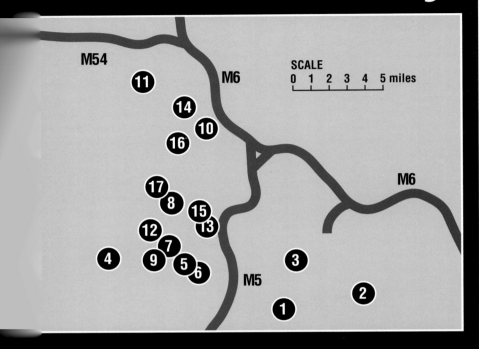

SCALE
0 1 2 3 4 5 miles

1 **Northfield Town FC**

2 **Moor Green FC**

3 **West Midlands Police FC**

4 **Stourbridge FC**

5 **Halesowen Town FC**

6 **Halesowen Harriers FC**

7 **Cradley Town FC**

8 **Dudley Town FC**

9 **Lye Town FC**

10 **Darlaston FC**

11 **Wednesfield FC**

12 **Brierley Hill FC**

13 **Oldbury United FC**

14 **Willenhall Town FC**

15 **Tividale FC**

16 **Bilston Town FC**

17 **Gornal Athletic FC**

The listed pavilion at the Cadbury Sports Ground in Bournville, Birmingham.

THIS huge conurbation houses a whole range of grounds which stretch to a Midland section of the Southern League, the Midland Alliance, Midland Combination and the West Midlands League. There is no club within the top tier of non-League football, indeed only Halesowen Town play in the Premier Division of the Southern League, and they have struggled recently.

It could be argued that the sheer volume of clubs is diluting the standards with too many chasing too few players, but clubs such as Highgate United, Willenhall Town, Stourbridge and Halesowen Town have all been successful in the past although with ground grading getting sharper each year the chances of more and more clubs progressing gets slimmer, with in some cases their only hope being the unearthing of a rich and many would say foolish benefactor.

SHENLEY LANE
Northfield Town FC

It is a very pleasant surprise to find such an attractive setting for a football ground so close to the city. A little local knowledge soon reveals the reason, for the area is administered by the Bournville Trust who, over the years, have maintained this vital green oasis, and were instrumental in the first tentative steps towards providing sporting facilities for the newly-formed Allens Cross Community Association.

Responding to a highly successful set-up at nearby Kingstanding, Mr. Christopher Cadbury helped raise the money to lease 22 acres from the Village Trust, to provide a sports ground for the local people in Allens Cross, a huge municipal housing estate built in the early 1930's where, until the formation of the ACCA, folk had no recreational outlet of any kind.

The field was declared open in 1935, the Silver Jubilee of King George V and Queen Mary, and to mark the event the Playing Fields Fund was set up. Finance was also provided from various other sources, and via these benefactors in 1938 a clubhouse pavilion, tennis court and caretakers house were built and duly opened by Mr George Cadbury.

The ground was laid out for cricket, plus two football pitches with a small wooden stand on the side of the main pitch. At first there was criticism that the facilities were too far from the residential areas, but this proved unfounded and the sports ground was a great success and soon became home to Allens Cross FC. In later years that club merged with Castle FC to become Cross Castle, before adopting the more formal Northfield Town FC in 1966.

During those years the ground was used for baseball, which was popular during the war, and also staged many gala sports days. The ground is still supported by the Bournville Trust and the Cadbury family and, since the amicable split from the ACCA by the more localised Community Association, the ground has improved immensely. Spectator facilities in the form of a covered stand behind the near goal, later with seats added, was built with superbly designed dressing rooms and administration areas. Railway sleepers are still in position either side of the small lean-to stand on the half-way line and the rest of the ground is open as it is still shared with Allens Cross Cricket Club.

The great sadness at Shenley Lane is the club's inability to progress due to a lack of floodlights. The close proximity of residential flats, plus the fact it is trust land has meant planning permission is unlikely; rather than the club climbing the pyramid ladder, the opposite could be the case. Whatever the outcome, football will always be played at Shenley Lane.

THE MOORLANDS
Moor Green FC
and Solihull Borough FC

Few grounds in the country can have changed so completely in shape and design as the Moorlands since the club entered the Southern League in 1983. The whole playing area was turned around 90 degrees making two sections of terrace redundant, while the 60 year old main stand found itself positioned behind one goal.

The club moved to their present ground in 1930, having had five previous grounds in the intervening 30 years since the club's inception. Formed in 1901, Moor Green used a farmer's field on the corner of Moor Green Lane and Russell Road at a cost of £2 per season, until an increase in rent led to the club moving on. That ground is now built on, with the new Reddings Road occupying the

*Above: **The Sherwood Road end under construction at the Moorlands in 1947. It is now grassed over and isolated in the car park (below) since the pitch was moved.***

This terrace at the Moorlands also became redundant and was eventually flattened in 1993.

pitch site. Moseley Rugby Club now have a ground very close by.

The following season the club moved to a very unsatisfactory ground on All Saints Road in Kings Heath, which had changing rooms some distance away down the Birmingham to Evesham Road. One season later Moor Green found themselves at The Woodlands, in Moseley, which also had changing rooms some way away and was on the corner of Wake Green and College Road, adjacent to Moseley Grammar School, and

now built on. Again after only one season the club were on the move, this time to the uninvitingly titled Coldbath Road, Moseley. The pitch was laid out on part of Moseley Ashfield Cricket Club's home which remains to this day. Then in 1908 came a transfer to Windermere Road, which proved an excellent choice as it had several pitches which drained very well. The privately owned ground was offered to Moor Green Football Club for £2,000, a figure beyond their means, and eventually sold to the National Playing

Fields Association. The ground is still in use today, with a hockey club utilising part of it, and various junior sides the rest. Up until a few years ago Moor Green played third team matches there. In 1930 part of Old House Farm was offered for development. The then Moor Green secretary, George Fisher, who was an estate agent, bought the farm, and then sold it to a builder, retaining seven acres for the football club. The original lay out of the ground began to take shape soon after it opened, when the stand was built at a cost of £1,000, with a separate pitch on the far side of the ground, and a cricket square in between the two. At this time the stand straddled the half-way line, and the pitch was roped off through wooden stakes. Birmingham City used the ground for training from 1936 to 1941, and also played their reserve matches there which meant spectators could often see two matches in a day for 6d. After the war, concrete terracing was built on either side of the stand, and at both ends, while the School End was covered. The capacity at that time was estimated at 6,500, but it was never reached, although an Amateur Cup-tie in 1951 against Romford brought in 5,000.

The ground then changed little until 1983 when a decision was made to join the Southern League. To provide the necessary car-parking and floodlighting, the ground was completely altered. With the pitch moved 90 degrees and the second pitch being taken out, the two terraced ends found themselves redundant, along with the Sherwood Road end at the back of the car-park, and the School End cover now some distance from the pitch, and only used in extremes of weather. To compensate, a 1,000 covered area was built at the Petersfield Road end and flat standing provided along the sides, which also houses the floodlighting system, an ingenious device that lowers the pylons when not in use, to comply with planning regulations. The crumbling covered terrace was finally knocked down in 1993, and the area flattened in readiness for future use.

SOLIHULL BOROUGH have been ground-sharing with Moor Green since selling their Widney Stadium in Solihull in 1988. It was a modest ground with a capacity of 1,500 and had been home since the mid-sixties. There was cover for 200 with flat rough standing, but its real value to the club was the fact that it was in the Birmingham commuter belt, prime country for housing. The sale figure was earmarked for a new purpose-built stadium in the borough but the club have met with much resistance and continue at Moor Green for the foreseeable future. Their reserves play on a former works ground which has a barriered-off pitch and a clubhouse but its location close to an expensive residential area has all but killed off any hopes of further development.

TALLY HO GROUND
West Midlands Police FC

The Tally Ho ground has been a field hosting sports since well before the Second World War and eventually became the sporting and training ground for Birmingham City Police in the fifties. The main football pitch ran along the side of the main road next to a row of pre-fabricated buildings which were removed and the land grassed over. A small wooden pavilion was primarily used for cricket and football until the more modern complex, which has been much altered in recent years, was built.

The whole ground is completely visible from the main A34 which runs past it in the shadow of Edgbaston Cricket Ground central to Birmingham's sprawl. The huge administration and hospitality building dwarfs the large stable complex which is close by and a newly-built glasshouse type extension resembling something out of Kew Gardens now looks out over the football pitch where a small lean-to used to suffice.

A permanent barrier stretches along the front of the ground with the other sides making do with thick mesh fencing supported on concrete slabs which are removable for the cricket season. In the absence of any seating the club have use of a temporary stand on wheels like those occasionally seen at county fairs and this is tucked away in the corner. The impressive lighting system arrived in 1994 allowing the club to compete in the newly-formed Midland Alliance.

WAR MEMORIAL ATHLETIC GROUND
Stourbridge FC

A visit to the Amblecote home of Stourbridge Football Club is an exercise in attempting to picture the ground as it was in its pomp rather than the sad state of decline that now envelops it. Originally opened in 1888, the Athletic Ground staged football and cricket in tandem as well as athletics until around the Second World War.

The ground is still used by Stourbridge Cricket Club, and as a result the football area is rendered three-sided, or more accurately two-sided now the old wooden stand has been demolished. Entry is through the War Memorial gates, where the walls are permanently decorated with next match posters for the Saturday and Sunday sides. Once past the bank of turnstiles, the vista is of the three-gabled cricket pavilion, closed up for winter, while positioned to the far left, the clubhouse stands heavily fortified against the light-fingered.

Behind that again are a line of old red painted turnstiles, now visible due to the stand's demise. Perched on the top of the banking are a group of wooden huts which house refreshments and a souvenir shop. The business part of the ground is situated furthest from the entrance, and covers the length of the playing area with matching covered terraces and a curiously roofed stand perched in the middle, providing a small amount of seating. Somewhat incongruously, the seated areas are separated from the rest by a thick wire-type fence, which appears to serve no purpose and impairs the view of those watching around the half-way line.

Mid-sixties action at Stourbridge showing the main stand with its wings, built in 1948.

The small stand behind the near goal at Stourbridge shortly before it was demolished.

The sturdy-looking terrace cover behind the far goal is quietly rusting but still provides some protection and indeed some acoustic qualities for the noisier home fans. The football side of the ground began to develop between the wars. Until then the only structure had been the small wooden stand with its simple bench seating which is believed to date from around 1890.

The middle portion of the current main stand, and the cover at the far end were both erected in the mid thirties after the pitch reverted to its current position, having been turned at right angles for a few seasons. Soon after the last war the two wing stands were added to the existing one and two years later a new brick built social club and boardroom went up.

The wing stands proved to be the last spectator facilities to be built, for since then the ground has changed little, other than the sad demolition of the 100 year old main road end stand in 1990. 1963 saw the first floodlights go up at Amblecote at a cost of £4,500 and between 1964 and 1969 the social club, board room and dressing rooms were all re-built on the site of the old ones.

On the bend between the two stands stood an old black half-time scoreboard and this saw service until 1970 when it was pulled down, and two years later the site was covered by the club shop.

Through no real fault of its own Amblecote is trapped in a bit of a time warp, hamstrung by the continued presence of the cricket club. Talks have been held sporadically over the years to try to overcome this problem but to date the three-sided nature of the ground has prevented the club from gaining entry into the top division of the Southern League. The logic of that decision goes against the grain when considering Northampton Town who, until recently, played on a ground of equally limited shape in the Third Division of the Football League.

THE GROVE
Halesowen Town FC

The Grove is as old as the football club; Town were formed in 1873 and played at The Grove from the start. The ground has always been full of character with various assorted shacks and stands but within the last fifteen years, since the club began its domination of the FA Vase and enjoyed a subsequent move into the Southern League, it has blossomed into one of the best non-league grounds in the Midlands.

The very early days of the ground are not well-documented, but it is known that at some point the three open sides of The Grove were banked up to form viewing areas, possibly with shale or ash as was the case in many other industrial areas. The first changing rooms were in a small wooden hut which stood roughly where the second set were built, on the other side of what was the cricket ground, now part-covered by the open terracing.

The Stourbridge Road end had a corrugated tin cover over part of it and was a grass bank until terracing was formed by adding wooden railway sleepers in eight or nine rows. Opposite the open side was another banked area, eventually given a low timber stand which stretched along a good portion of that side and was painted in the club colours of blue and white. This was built by the council in the early thirties and survived until the splendid new cantilevered, 420-seater Harry Rudge Stand - named after an old club stalwart - was built in its place in 1987.

The smart looking Hawne Lane stand is actually 1952 vintage having been put up by the club over the banking. More recently it was given a thorough overhaul, with its interior terraced in concrete, and complements the Harry Rudge Stand perfectly. Around this time the pitch was levelled and this becomes obvious when comparing the two versions of the Hawne Lane end.

Right up until 1985, the players changed in the old dressing rooms, walked across the cricket area and entered through the crowd, the club having obtained permission to close off the recreation ground for one hour before the game to allow this to happen. That side was eventually cordoned-off with a post and rail, and in the seventies, when cricket ceased, the ground was enclosed with a corrugated fence, the players entering through a gate. Later still a concrete fence was added as the whole of that side was built up with concrete terracing and crash barriers.

Whilst the dressing rooms were being built in 1952 players were forced to change in The Waggon and Horses pub, a quarter of a mile away, but even when they were ready the walk through the crowd could be tricky at times. Now, the changing rooms are situated behind the Hawne Lane end stand on the site of an old tennis court which was part of the recreation grounds, and the players enter through a caged walkway.

Above: **The old cover at Halesowen Town.**
Below: **A similar view but with the new Harry Rudge stand in its place.**

As the ground regulations have become stricter and the club have enjoyed promotion to the Premier Division, more improvements have been made. Two new turnstile blocks went up in 1990 with a new boardroom, and the following year the rest of the ground was terraced giving an impressive capacity of 5,000 with 1,500 under cover, precisely the gate that saw an FA Cup tie with Hendon in 1954 which created the unbeaten ground record.

HAYES PARK
Halesowen Harriers FC

Hayes Park is a remarkable place - the direct result of one man's dream becoming a reality. Until the mid-eighties Harriers were a Sunday side playing, from their inception in 1961, in Birmingham parks football, then latterly in the more prestigious Festival League. Their home ground was The Grove, Halesowen Town, where they played until the club decided to go it alone, and try Saturday football.

The Chairman had the finance available to purchase several acres of land which were then made up of a steep sloping bushy area, used mostly by picnickers and dog-walkers, and this stretched to a plateau near the site of a long-forgotten mine-working. An impressive feat of engineering was needed to transform the area into firstly, a flat surface and secondly, an accessible ground. A long winding roadway was cut from Park Road up to the site and thousands of tonnes of earth transferred from one area to another to create the steeply sloping bank which surrounds the ground.

Specialist help was enlisted in the shape of the chief groundsman from Wembley Stadium, who provided the know-how to lay the pitch. Since the opening, a seated stand has gone up, initially to comply with league rulings, but it is proving difficult to obtain permission for further expansion.

BEECHES VIEW
Cradley Town FC

Cradley Town are a young club formed as a result of a merger between Albion Rovers and Haden Rangers in 1970. Albion Rovers were responsible for the beginnings of the new ground, which urgently needed to be upgraded as the club were immediately successful and gained entry to the Midland Combination. However, it was found the pitch was too narrow and much remedial work was necessary.

A licensed bar was the next step with a small stand erected to allow the club to take their place in the Premier Division. As Cradley settled in after a switch to the West Midlands League, a new stand was built and floodlights added in 1991.

Above: A Cradley programme cover showing aerial views of the ground and a picture of that well-known Black Country lad, Marco Van Basten!!

Below: Halesowen Harriers FC.

Dudley's Round Oak ground.

ROUND OAK and the SPORTS GROUND
Dudley Town FC

Dudley Town have done exceptionally well to recover from the despair at losing their famous Sports Ground almost overnight in June 1985. The football and cricket grounds were both closed following a major collapse of the limestone workings underneath. This resulted in gaping holes appearing in the outfield of the cricket pitch and the whole complex was abandoned.

The cricket ground had been home to Dudley Town since their move from Shavers End in 1912 which had been the club's first pitch of any kind. During the late 1920's the Sports Centre football ground was built as a project to provide work for the unemployed. The vastness of the banked ground was emphasised by the crowd of 16,500 who witnessed the opening game, a figure which was never beaten. The huge brooding main stand was capable of holding 1,800 people in its heyday and just four years before its demise was refurbished and had a new VIP room, Press box and public address system installed. Floodlights with a lux level up to Football League standard were erected in November of the same year and the ground was set fair for many years to come. The Southern League Midland Division Championship was won in May 1985 but just a month later came the wholesale abandonment of the grounds. Eventually the club were allowed in to recover some fixtures and fittings, including the lights, but the clubhouse had to be left along with the permanent fixtures.

Almost immediately negotiations began to purchase the Round Oak Stadium, originally built for Round Oak Steelworks but then owned by British Steel. The sale was completed in April 1986 but it was to be two years before the ground would be ready for Southern League football. Those seasons were spent on various grounds, including Stourbridge's Memorial Ground, until August 1988 when Round Oak finally opened. The stadium was used primarily for cricket, bowls and tennis and clues to the original shape can still be seen today in the

Dudley's former home which was condemned overnight following mining subsidence.

outside wall. Cricket was soon disposed off and the pitch moved over to make room for the perimeter rail and main stand which can accommodate 300. Four of the eight floodlight pylons rescued from the Sports Ground were put up and a concrete walkway laid down to satisfy the league regulations.

The Round Oak may never rival the Sports Ground as an atmospheric venue, but it is a permanent home that the club can be proud to have acquired in the face of potential disaster.

NOOSE LANE
Willenhall Town FC

The current Willenhall team is a relative infant, being spawned in 1953 from the amalgamation of RAF Association FC and Aston Road Villa. Prior to this there had been a number of sides bearing the town name, by far the most successful being Willenhall Pickwicks.

They began in the mid-1880's and played on a pitch by the Portobello Bridge near the

GARDEN WALK
Gornall Athletic FC

The Garden Walk at Gornall Athletic is a splendid example of how a ground can be tailored to the needs of its regular crowds without going overboard on the ubiquitous 'improvements' that are neither relevant nor affordable.

The vast concrete terracing in front of the clubhouse and dressing rooms is split into two halves, the furthest away the most recent, having been laid in 1983. Immediately in front of the club is the original terrace which was put down when the ground was opened in November 1950. Its 45-year vintage is all too evident now but it still provides a superb view of the pitch and surrounding areas. In between the two is a small area set aside for bench seating, provided in 1986, which is adequate for today's meagre attendances. Gornall Athletic were formed in 1945 and played their early football on a field at the back of The Fountain public house just a few hundred yards up the hill from Garden Walk. Club members got together to purchase their sloping acreage from local industry and set about hewing out the pitch to create a large bank, only one-third of which was terraced. An old RAF building was purchased from Stourbridge Tennis Club and stood where the newer clubhouse is now. On the opposite side is a low iron cover inside of which are the skeletal remains of bench seating. This replaced the first cover which, before it gradually died a death, stretched along the length of the ground.

STOURBRIDGE ROAD
Lye Town FC

Founded in 1930, when they began playing at Stourbridge Road, home of Lye Cricket Club, the Town have used the ground ever since. In the first years before the war, the pitch ran at right angles to its present position, but once turned round, the three-sided ground began to take shape.

A stand was erected behind the end nearest to the clubhouse just after the war, and the players changed in dressing rooms which stood on the site of the current clubhouse. Prior to this, The George public house was used for changing and socialising. The stand had seating added in the early fifties, and these seats eventually found their way into the stand which stretches along the touch line, and has done so since 1967. The third version of the cover behind the goal is more recent, and has been filled in at the back. The clubhouse, situated just in front of the entrance to the sports ground, was built in 1975.

railway, changing in a bedroom at the local pub, The Shakespeare. The ground was unenclosed and therefore collecting entrance money was not easy, but provision was made in 1911 when the club drew Stockport County in the FA Cup. Between 3,000 and 5,000 spectators crammed into the Portobello to watch the Picks lose 2-0. The Union Lock Sports Ground is now built on the site of that famous match.

Around the turn of the century Willenhall Swifts came into being playing on the Wakes Ground by St. Giles Church before moving to the Spring Bank ground in Temple Road, later the site of Willenhall Greyhound Stadium. Both clubs continued until the outbreak of the Great War when, with most able-bodied men away, they folded. A works side, Vaughan Bros. took over the Portobello and a new Willenhall club was formed by the remaining members of the Picks and the Swifts, and they played at the Spring Bank until 1930 when mounting debts and the depression forced them to close. Vaughans, however, had continued and took over tenancy of the Spring Bank, while another team, Union Locks played at the Portobello.

In 1952 the new Willenhall Town began playing in the Wolverhampton League with little success, on a council-owned pitch at the Memorial Ground until the club purchased

six acres of land in Noose Lane and began to create a ground. It was not until April 1975 that ex-Wolves star and manager Stan Cullis opened the new ground for the club's entry into the West Midlands League. It had a permanent barrier and a small amount of cover on one side that came from Hall Green Greyhound Stadium and within six years was followed by a two-tier clubhouse and floodlit training area. September 30th 1980 saw Stan Cullis again at the ground to switch on the club's floodlights which heralded a new era. Success followed, including a trip to Wembley for the FA Vase final against Whickham. The semi-final home leg had attracted a crowd of 2,900 to Noose Lane, a record at the time but since bettered by the visit of Crewe Alexandra in the FA Cup 1st round tie the following November.

Noose Lane has been improved a number of times since then, primarily with the addition of a seated stand opposite the original structure, although since losing their place in the Southern League the ground has changed little. The training area is now chiefly used as a car-park and a wall has gone up in front of it. The club are founder members of the new Midland Alliance League which could well be the springboard to a resurgence at Noose Lane

Lye Town, shared with cricket, has a certain charm.

Bilston Town FC.

QUEEN STREET
Bilston Town FC

Quite possibly the only time that Bilston FC has not suffered from its proximity to Wolverhampton Wanderers and West Bromwich Albion is when the former came to Queen Street to play a friendly to commemorate the switching on of the new floodlights back in 1953. Some 7,500 spectators crammed in that day to a ground which has altered a number of times since and is now undergoing a further face-lift with a new stand being built at the Trinity Road end.

Bilston United were formed 100 years ago and played their first season on a pitch in Prouds Lane where they changed either in a public house in the town or simply walked to the ground already in kit. It is not certain which of the green areas still in existence today along the lane were home to United, but what is known is that for one season they played on a ground along the Willenhall Road, before reverting to Prouds Lane until the outbreak of the First World War. When football resumed the local council housed the club at their new home in Queen Street which was banked-up and roped-off, the opening game being against Tamworth Castle on 27th September 1919. Not long after, the main stand, which still exists in modernised form, was erected with dressing accommodation underneath. This stand plus the small area of cover at the Trinity end appear to be the only structures of note until floodlighting was installed in 1953. The club house on the stand side of the ground dates from the mid-fifties. Queen Street was sufficiently large enough to accommodate 7,000 fans back in 1968 when Halifax Town were the visitors for an FA Cup 1st Round tie after the club had battled through from the first qualifying round. They were then simply known as Bilston FC, the United tag having long since been discarded. Since these times Queen Street has had its ups and downs and in 1985 wholesale changes occurred when the club was elected to the Southern League.

Much of the banking was terraced and the stand spruced up; in 1989 the Trinity Road cover was condemned and removed. More recently, after a gap of six years, the ageing floodlights were renewed along with the replacement cover, and hard standing was put down to comply with Southern League regulations

DELL SPORTS GROUND
Brierley Hill Town FC

The Dell has recently had a major overhaul which was contracted to take 26 weeks, but in fact took 116, which meant the tenant club, then called Oldswinford were forced to play away and suffered greatly. The Dell was originally opened in 1960 as a football ground used by schools sides and it wasn't until three years later that the athletics track was built, which now somewhat dwarfs the footballing side.

Oldswinford were formed in 1955 and played at Field Lane, Wollescote Park, Swinford Common and South Road, before moving in with the famous Brierley Hill Alliance at Cottage Street in 1975. Just two years later both clubs were forced off the ground when Dudley Council sold it to ASDA, and they moved to The Dell. Due to continuing financial problems Alliance folded in 1981 and Oldswinford became sole tenants. During the 1994 close season the club changed its name to Brierley Hill Town F.C. in the hope that it might give them the impetus to emulate their famous near namesakes.

THE CRICKETTS
Oldbury United FC

Oldbury have played at The Cricketts ground in Rowley Regis since 1978 when they sensibly vacated the ground in Newbury Lane which later became Oldbury Stadium, home of Sandwell Borough. For four years from founding in 1958 the club played in Brittania Park before moving to Newbury Lane.

The site was originally a clay quarry

until the council bought and used it as a tip before selling on to the club for £3,000, half of which came from the Sports Council through a grant. The five and a quarter acre site was levelled and dressing rooms were built by Kencast who created a problem by overstaying their welcome and delaying the building, thereby sentencing the players to change in a shed for half a season, and to wash in a makeshift bath made out of polythene stretched over railway sleepers!

The £16,000 clubhouse followed and the covered standing behind the goal was added to the small seated stand. For a brief period from 1982-1986 The Cricketts saw Southern League football and it was at the start of that period that the ground record of 2,200 was set for the Walsall Senior Cup match with Walsall Wood. Today, the ground sports a huge fence to block off the adjacent M5 and for the start of the 1995 season there were four areas of cover around what is one of the better grounds in the Midland Alliance.

THE BEECHES
Tividale FC

Tividale were immortalised some years ago by the feature 'From Tividale to Wembley' which chronicled a season in the FA Cup from one club to another. They have had little claim to fame before or since but must be commended for continuing in an area not short of League and non-League football. Their Beeches Ground is also commendable, with covered terracing for around 1,000 with a further 200 seated all down one side. Tividale's humble beginnings were down to the enterprise of one man, Ted Jones, who formed Tividale Hall Youth Club - the forerunner of the current team - in 1952.

COTTAGE GROUND
Wednesfield FC

Formed as Wednesfield Social in 1961 the club played their first fifteen seasons on the St George's Playing Fields. On entering the West Midlands League in 1976 they moved to the former sports ground of James Gibbon's, which had a wooden pavilion with dressing rooms and little else. A post and rail was put in place and two years later, after promotion to the Premier Division, a small stand was built at a cost of £7,500 which, since 1992, can seat 148 people.

The original wooden building has since been replaced by new dressing rooms and a VIP room. Floodlights were installed in 1991 at this modest little ground which has a record attendance of 480 for the FA Cup tie with Burton Albion in 1981.

As his youth team grew up, they were formed into Tividale FC in 1954, playing at the old Revo Ground in City Road, joining the West Midland Alliance in 1964, the same time that Staffs County Council bought the ground, and made it their headquarters. The following year Tividale faced hardship when a fire destroyed the pavilion and they lost equipment valued at £750. They immediately moved back to the Tividale Hall School where it had all started, and Warley took over the Revo. In 1968 the club applied to the British Waterways for a lease on ground they had at Tividale. The Board's estates officer, Mr Beech was so helpful the club named the ground after him! Whilst work was underway, matches were played at 'Dank's Ground', and later at Dudley Sports Centre. The new clubhouse was opened in May 1973 and fifteen months later Stourbridge were the first visitors for the opening match at the Beeches in August 1974.

CITY GROUND
Darlaston FC

The 90-odd year old City Ground, stuck in the middle of virtually impenetrable Black Country suburbia, is teetering on the edge of dereliction, but has a charm and a fascination not easily defined.

The view from the outside does not fill the visitor with confidence, for although the main frontage to the ground is marked with a sign board, that is about the only item left standing of its own accord. The fencing is of various makes and ages, all propped up by a series of posts, some of which are lashed to scaffolding to stop them from falling over. A war-time ex-Government building is bricked and boarded up to such a degree that the spray canned graffiti almost improves it, and only after venturing further does it become apparent that the players' entrance was once tucked away in the corner. There is a turnstile which is currently unused, leaving the only entrance through a gap between terraced houses. Once inside, the antiquity of the place is immediately apparent as is the fact that despite outward appearances, the club and ground are still cared for. A wonderfully evocative old wooden stand straddles the half-way line as it has done since the early thirties when it is believed to have been transported from Aggborough, home of Kidderminster Harriers. Opposite is a small and hastily repaired covered area which until a few years ago was much longer before gales took care of it.

The derelict government building turns out to be only partially so, for at either end are the changing rooms, built in 1942 as part of the deal which saw the erection of a building for a youth club on top of the slope behind one goal. This is now in use as the social club. The long government building was built during the war as a de-contamination and ARP unit for £300 and had changing rooms included which the club have used ever since. Later the rest of it became a Housing Department and Social Services centre until left to rot some years ago. There were originally four turnstiles, two next to each other in the entrance with one at either end of the famous fenced end. One was taken away in 1986 as it was dangerous with the other going out of business in 1994.

The end to end slope is similar to that at Chard Town in Somerset and was even more pronounced until the 1970's when it was partially levelled.

The City Ground was once in open land with not a house to be seen and is believed to have been inside the grounds of nearby Darlaston Hall. It was also the site of a fair ground, but was bought on behalf of the club by a Mr. Pritchard and left to the council as trustees thus guaranteeing football on it. The first building was a shack for changing in which came after the players had been using a room at The British Queen pub, and this was in use until the war-time buildings went up. Previous ground information is very patchy, but the club had at least three earlier homes, one possibly now covered by a school in Salisbury Street and another in Bauld Street, now Stafford Road.

Photos in this section by: Pat Brunning, Andy Dakin, Gavin Ellis-Neville, Kerry Miller, Dean Walton and James Wright.

Darlaston's splendid sloping ground.

Herefordshire & Shropshire

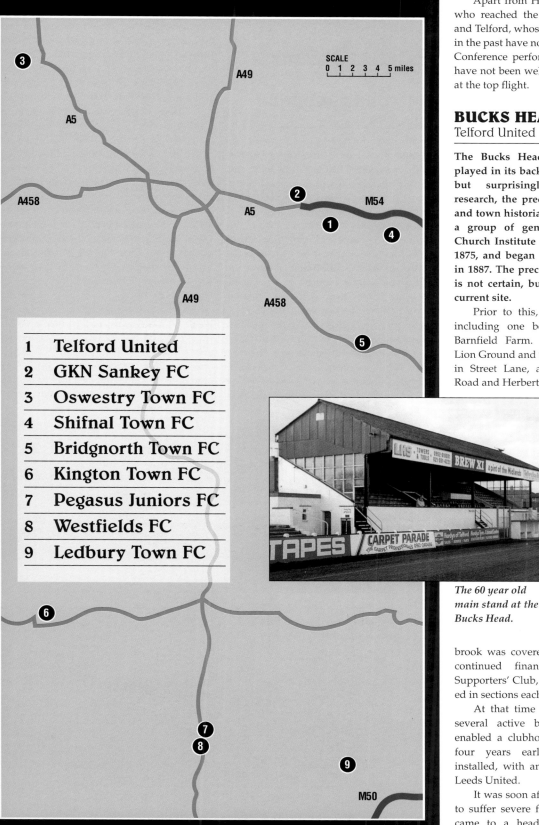

1	Telford United
2	GKN Sankey FC
3	Oswestry Town FC
4	Shifnal Town FC
5	Bridgnorth Town FC
6	Kington Town FC
7	Pegasus Juniors FC
8	Westfields FC
9	Ledbury Town FC

SOME of the most beautiful and unspoilt parts of the country can be found in the two counties which form part of the Marches with Wales. Both have county leagues more along the lines of those in Somerset and Hampshire with village clubs playing in the main on relatively undeveloped grounds.

Apart from Hereford United themselves who reached the Football League in 1972, and Telford, whose fabulous FA Cup exploits in the past have not yet been fully reflected in Conference performances, the two counties have not been well-blessed with non-League at the top flight.

BUCKS HEAD
Telford United FC

The Bucks Head pub has had football played in its backyard since the late 1800's, but surprisingly, despite substantial research, the precise date has eluded club and town historians. What is known is that a group of gentlemen from the Parish Church Institute formed a football club in 1875, and began playing in Watling Street in 1887. The precise location of the ground is not certain, but it is assumed to be the current site.

Prior to this, several fields were used including one believed to have been at Barnfield Farm. Haygate Admaston, Red Lion Ground and Spraggs Recreation ground in Street Lane, an area between Haygate Road and Herbert Avenue are others.

The first structures on the ground were wooden changing rooms, situated close to the gates on top of the Watling Street bank. They survived until replaced in 1949 with new ones built under the West Stand.

Slowly the ground took shape with a cow-shed type cover erected in stages on the east side. To build the cover and terracing at the Regent Street end, a small brook was covered over in 1948, and with continued financial support from the Supporters' Club, the terracing was completed in sections each season.

The 60 year old main stand at the Bucks Head.

At that time the Supporters' Club had several active branches, and their help enabled a clubhouse to open in 1969, and four years earlier floodlighting to be installed, with an opening friendly against Leeds United.

It was soon after this that the club began to suffer severe financial difficulties, which came to a head when the Development Corporation bought the ground from

Telford's council inspired stand which effectively nullifies most of the terracing either side.

Wellington Town, with the option of buying it back in stages for the same amount

However, the most controversial clause in this otherwise generous offer was that the club change its name to Telford United, to identify with the rapidly growing new town. The council also announced they would build a new stand to assist in the club's push for Football League status, and the East Stand made its debut replacing the old cow sheds in 1973.

Unfortunately, it appears too little thought went into the planning of the stand, which was built on top of the east terrace and situated in such a way as to completely nullify a large chunk of terrace on either side of it. To this day the view of anyone 25 yards either side of the stand is of only half the pitch.

The club successfully bought back the ground and have, in the last 20 years, updated it to cater for the requirements of League and Cup football. Today it is a curious mixture of the delightful, the clumsy, the vibrant, and the downright gruesome.

The focal point is the delightful West Stand, nearly 60 years old and now housing the club administration offices and changing rooms. It backs on to the car-park in a similar manner to that at Twerton Park. Strangely, although the rest of the ground is predomininently black and white, the new seating in the East Stand is blue with T.U.F.C. which somehow confirms the general clumsiness of that area, originally prompted by the Development Corporation. The mass of neatly-painted advertising hoardings give a vibrancy to the ground, being both colourful and attention grabbing but not overdone as is sometimes the case elsewhere.

The mere fact that the club are just one step away from the Football League, and have enjoyed many cup runs in the past has forced the old girl to suffer high barbed wire fences, seemingly pointless 8ft. metal gates at various intervals and a 12ft. tall corrugated fence sweeping around the Watling Street end, completely hiding the adjoining Bucks Head pub!

Despite all this it remains a comfortable, interesting ground, tantalisingly close to being one of the very best.

THE WORKS GROUND
GKN Sankey FC

Sankey of Wellington FC were formed in 1910 and played on a number of pitches within the factory complex. In 1960 the company opened a new ground which had a covered enclosure down one side with around thirty narrow struts holding up the roof, as per Chorley and Morecambe.

The club entered the prestigious Cheshire League and built a main stand in 1960 to similar specifications as those at Cheltenham, Chorley and Kings Lynn with the square port holes at the front. For five years they played professionally until reverting to amateur status in the Shropshire County League. In 1988, now called GKN Sankey, they sadly disbanded and the two stands were demolished. The grandstand disappeared, but the covered enclosure eventually went to Pelsall Villa where it has been erected behind one goal.

VICTORIA PARK and PARK HALL STADIUM
Oswestry Town FC

When Oswestry Town played their last match, in 1988, on what had become a sadly run-down but still homely ground there were many who waved farewell to the club which had been playing since around 1860, expecting it to fade away. But although it was a number of years between the last NPL game and Oswestry's return in Welsh football, the club never died. The old Victoria Park ground was sold and is no more, but there is fresh hope; Town are playing on the Park Hall Stadium, within the confines of what was a National Service Centre.

A few of the old military buildings are still in situ, as is the athletics stadium within, built into a bowl which gives a fine viewing area. A stand was built by the council back in 1968 complete with dressing rooms and the site has been used over the years by schools, athletic clubs and the like. Town have salvaged the floodlights and the most modern of the stands from Victoria Road, and are hopeful of re-erecting them to give more cover as they strive to reach the League of Wales.

Oswestry have been full members of the Welsh FA from the start and played on what was known as the cricket field. This in fact was where the football ground was developed, but until the Second World War it was used for both games, but then the cricket side was requisitioned to build a munitions factory and the ground became enclosed.

Two views of the disused GKN Sankey works ground circa 1990.

The cavernous interior at Oswestry Town, just prior to the end.

By 1950, a grandstand had been built and standing areas formed, the record crowd of 5,500 attending a match with Hereford that year. From then on as the club moved from Welsh to English football, and from Birmingham League to the Northern Premier and Southern Leagues, the ground slowly developed with a further covered area and dressing rooms at the road end and a social club to the right. One stand was condemned following the Bradford Fire Disaster and replaced, only to be taken down again and put into storage for the new ground.

Houses now cover the whole playing area with no trace at all of the old but interesting Victoria Park.

PARK ROAD
Kington Town FC

The lovely old market town of Kington is based in Herefordshire, although the club have always played in Welsh football. Park Road perfectly mirrors the town, comfortable, old-fashioned and gloriously untouched by English football's draconian ground criteria.

Despite looking vaguely Edwardian, the

Kington Town's stand was paid for by the Supporters' Club and built by volunteers.

ground only dates from around the Second World War, and did not have dressing rooms until 1950. In 1955 the site was bought from a committee man who owned the garage next door, and a group of ten people paid £100 each, which was refunded within two years. In 1961 the Kington Town Supporters' Club paid for the black and gold main stand which was built by club volunteers and opened in October of that year. It remains the only cover on the ground. The post and rail system went in soon after and in 1981, members again volunteered their labour and built the clubhouse which was opened by John Toshack.

The 1950's and 60's were the golden age for the club and ground, the early developments co-inciding with a season when the club won six senior trophies.

Even today, local derbies and evening matches on Kington Fair Day pull in the crowds at what is a rare, untouched corner of English football, played exclusively in Wales.

NEW STREET
Ledbury Town FC

Ledbury play on what is a small but neatly-formed ground a stone's throw from the High Street and next to a cemetery. The site was purchased by trustees in 1923 and by 1926 the first grandstand had been built. It still remains today, albeit in altered form. It had a timber frame with corrugated iron and was put up by a local man for the princely sum of £63. Dressing rooms were a hut by the cemetery wall but in 1960 new dressing rooms went up behind the near goal. Three years later volunteers built the original clubhouse with bricks recycled from a demolished local gasworks.

When digging the foundations for the toilets back in the sixties, the remains were found of what was once a row of cottages on the ground, and these are now under a modern block.

PHOENIX PARK
Shifnal Town FC

The Shropshire club were first formed back in 1964 as Shifnal Youth Club, playing in the Wellington League at Idsall School. In 1969 the name changed to Shifnal Juniors and again in 1972 to Town as the club went through the Wellington League and into Senior Football.

The first proper ground was built from scratch on what was a ploughed field after years of trying to get council backing for the club. Admirals Park was opened in 1979 with the club by that time in the Premier Division of the West Midlands League. Having obtained a 15-year lease and raised some £8,000, a new grandstand was opened in 1981 and within two years a social club joined it as the football went from strength to strength with successive league titles. Volunteer work from club members saw the dressing rooms first go up, and again the stand was erected in the same fashion, with those hard at work oblivious to the fact that within four years they would lose their home to Bridgnorth District Council for housing. It was a devastating blow and the club were forced to leave the league as a temporary ground at Idsall Sports Centre was not up to standard. The last game at Admirals Park was on May 17th 1985 when Wolverhampton United visited for a league match.

Dropping into the County League the club floundered for some years until purchasing Phoenix Park in 1988. Much work was needed to transform the site into a football ground but by 1992 their splendid new home, not dissimilar to that at Dudley Town, was open. Since then the cantilever stand and clubhouse have followed with dressing

Shifnal Town programme showing the fine new ground.

rooms and floodlights in 1994 and with recent elevation to the Midland Alliance League, Phoenix Park is aptly named.

ROTHERWAS
Westfields FC

The Westfields ground, tucked away at the back of a sprawling industrial estate dominated by Thorn Lighting, has an interesting history which began when it was initially used in the fifties for cricket by AEI, a company taken over by Thorn.

Cricket ceased in the mid-sixties although the old green pavilion is still in situ and used in its extended form as changing rooms. Westfields moved to the ground in 1974, having played on council pitches on Widemarsh Common, and as the West Midlands League loomed a pitch barrier was erected. The tiny stand in front of the changing rooms dates from 1984, and the larger seated stand was bought with the prize money awarded for winning Division One of the league in 1987. The boardroom has stood since 1989 some way from the pitch which was once used by Hereford United as a training ground.

CROWN MEADOW
Bridgnorth Town FC

When football resumed in 1946 after World War Two, many clubs were hastily formed or re-formed at around the same time. St. Leonards FC became Bridgnorth Town FC and played on a basic ground further down

The garish but homely stand at Ledbury.

Innage Lane, which although now buried under a municipal car-park, was just a few hundred yards away from Crown Meadow.

Around 1958, the council moved the Town to a newly prepared pitch with no facilities, which at that time was surrounded by fields. Players changed in The Hen and Chickens in the town and walked up to the pitch. It is reputed those who played well qualified for a lift back, while the rest walked!

Some three years later, with the aid of a grant from the National Playing Fields Association, the council built the changing rooms next to the entrance, but it wasn't until the late 1960's that the covered standing area behind the goal was erected, along with the permanent pitch barrier.

During these years the town expanded and two sides of the Meadow were covered with housing, which gives the ground a more enclosed feel. A clubhouse was built in 1978 as Bridgnorth continued to grow in stature and this was added to in 1985 to celebrate the rise to the Southern League.

By then the long-awaited floodlights had arrived, as had a line of conifers, to give a more compact feel to the open side of the ground. The last major construction to date was the splendid new stand, which was opened in September 1993 and which along the touchline in front of the now established conifers.

Until that time, the club had had to get by with just the covered end, and seats put in directly behind the net. But the building of the seated stand with its futuristic-looking roof has completely transformed this homely little ground.

The new stand at Bridgnorth Town.

The entrance and turnstiles are situated behind the old stand on a lower level, with the changing rooms adjacent, quite some way from the playing area. A number of thoughtfully-provided park benches, each dedicated to the memory of supporters are a nice touch, placed near to the corner where the tiny club shop stands

Due to the close proximity of neighbouring bungalows, many of whose well tended gardens are constantly in peril from wayward footballs, it is unlikely Town's home can improve much more than it has already. However, having survived happily in the Southern League for a dozen years, there is no reason why they should not continue to do so.

PEGASUS JUNIORS FC

Pegasus Juniors are 40 years old, and played in the Hereford League before joining the Hellenic League. They have had more than one home pitch, the first the old police ground at the Essex Arms, which at one time was resplendent with a pavilion until it was destroyed by fire.

The club also played on a railed-off pitch with no cover at the Leisure Centre in Holmer Road. For some time they were fortunate enough to have the use of Edgar Street whenever Hereford United were not at home, but that seems to have gone by the wayside, particularly as United now have a youth team playing there on a Saturday morning.

Also in Hereford, very close to all three of those grounds is the County Ground, venue for all major County matches that are not staged up the road.

In 1985 it was leased by the council to Hereford Lads FC, who have a clubhouse within the vast school-like building next door, and although the ground was eventually purchased by the HFA, the Lads' Club continued there.

In 1987 a timber building which formerly did service as an office of the Welsh Water Board was acquired and re-erected with dressing rooms and showers. This was extended in 1993 and fitted out with plush offices and a council chamber, all opened by Sir Bert Millichip on June 2nd 1994.

A record Bucks Head crowd of 12,500 for a Shropshire Senior Cup match between Wellington and Shrewsbury Town in 1936.

Photos in this section by: Pat Brunning, Andy Dakin, Glyn Davies, Colin Peel and James Wright.

Stafford and North Birmingham

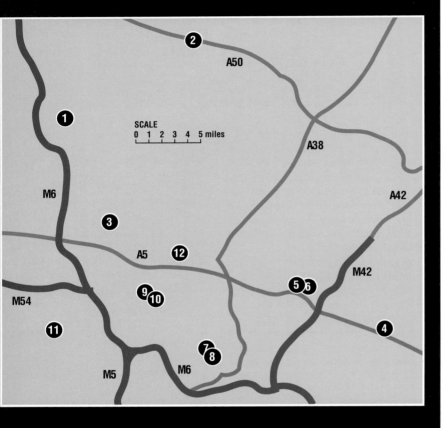

SCALE
0 1 2 3 4 5 miles

1. **Stafford Rangers FC**
2. **Rocester FC**
3. **Hednesford Town FC**
4. **Atherstone United FC**
5. **Tamworth FC**
6. **Bolehall Swifts FC**
7. **Sutton Coldfield Town FC**
8. **Paget Rangers FC**
9. **Pelsall Villa FC**
10. **Walsall Wood FC**
11. **Blakenall FC**
12. **Chasetown FC**

The Bass Stand at Marston Road, Stafford.

WITH their recent resurgence and move from Southern League football at Cross Keys to Conference football at Keys Park, the Pitmen of Hednesford have wrestled the top club mantle away from Stafford Rangers who are making the opposite move to the Southern League. The area is strong in West Midlands League clubs as well as a sprinkling of Southern League Midland Division homes.

The town of Tamworth is well served as, apart from the main club, Bolehall Swifts, the former Southern League club Mile Oak Rovers, now playing in local football, and Polesworth NW are all close by.

MARSTON ROAD
Stafford Rangers FC

During Stafford Rangers' early history it is known the team played on a pitch near The Antelope pub off Stone Road in 1884 but soon moved to Newtown in Doxey and used a ground near Bagnall's Bridge. Marston Road was first used for a competitive match on Saturday 5th September 1896 when Dresden United Reserves from Longton were the visitors for a North Staffordshire League game.

Players changed in an upstairs club room at the Albion Hotel before crossing the road to what was referred to as the Albion Ground in those days. During 1920 the ground was purchased when Rangers became a limited company and soon banking appeared around the pitch and four huts were bought from Cannock Chase War Training Group. The first Supporters' Club built a stand on the Lotus site which is quite possibly the structure in use today, and work also commenced on dressing rooms, offices and turnstiles ready for the 1921 season. Two years later the club hit financial difficulties and the ground was mortgaged for £500 but worse

followed for in 1929 fire destroyed part of it.

During the war Marston Road fell into disrepair but was lovingly renovated by Supporters Club members ready for the first season back in peace time, and remained more or less unchanged until a surge of ambition, brought on by an upturn in playing fortunes saw the launch of a floodlighting fund.

£6,000 was raised and on Monday 8th September 1969 a crowd of 3,045 watched the official opener against Port Vale. The seventies saw the ground develop to its current status with a new seated stand to replace the ramshackle old girl which stood along the Marston Road side. Considerable delays were experienced following planning permission for the 450-seater and the old stand was still in place when Rotherham United's visit in the FA Cup 3rd Round on January 4th 1975 brought in the record gate of 8,532. The stand was used for the last time the following month and volunteer work helped create the new one in time for the start of the following season.

The last significant work at Marston Road was the building of the new dressing room block and office complex which was officially opened in December 1977 following a match with Stoke City. Today the ground is a spacious and comfortable place with easy access but a reduced capacity of 3,500. A new perimeter fence has tidied up the edges and with a ten year plan for improvements underway Marston Road may well not have seen its last facelift.

RIVERS FIELD
Rocester FC

The ground at Rivers Field is very new, having been built on the site of a Roman fort in 1987. It is a vast improvement on the previous ground, Mill Field just across the road, which had a small hut in what is now a farmer's field.

Rocester are believed to have used the old ground from their inception in 1890, although virtually nothing is known of those days as club records are long gone and the local press did not cover their matches. The only structure of note on the ground was the changing hut, a weather-boarded building built in 1919 which served the club well right up to the move in 1987.

Continued success in League and Cup

Cross Keys was demolished during the summer of '95. The new Keys Park is just up the road.

was the catalyst for Rocester's decision to create a new well-developed ground and leave the Staffs Senior League for the West Midlands League. Once an archeological dig had been completed on the site, work began to transform it into a football ground. A grandstand was built, the pitch barriered-off, and in 1989 floodlights were installed as was a small covered stand which had come from the demolished Fellows Park at Walsall. Rivers Field was soon enclosed and with a capacity of 4,000 the new ground is a far cry from the Mill Field which was home for over 90 years.

CROSS KEYS GROUND and KEYS PARK
Hednesford Town FC

After what seemed an eternity, the old and much-loved Cross Keys Ground was vacated in favour of a brand new stadium, purpose-built for life in the Conference with Football League status firmly in mind.

The old Cross Keys has already been flattened and there is now no trace of what had been a football ground since the turn of the century. Just 200 yards up the road is Keys Park, with a capacity for 3,500, seating for 700 and cover for 1,000. It has a two-storey main stand with dressing rooms and offices underneath and a kitchen, function room and boardroom upstairs. Both ends of the terraced ground are covered with the area opposite the stand open, as the club aim to build another stand to bring the ground up to a 6,000 capacity for the Football League. The first game at Keys Park was on August 1st 1995 when neighbours Walsall were the visitors.

The Cross Keys ground was as quaint as the new one is functional and tidy, but it had simply outgrown its useful purpose at such an ambitious club. For eighty per cent of clubs around the country, it would still be perfectly adequate, but the jump to the Conference is a massive leap, and often a new ground is the only answer.

There were a number of teams in the Hednesford area as early as the 1870's, with many pitches laid out on colliery ground as football became the main form of recreation for the pitmen. Two teams joined forces in 1880 forming a club called Hednesford Town who were based at the Anglesey Hotel. The ground at the Anglesey was known as the 'Tins' because of the sheeting erected around the ground. 1903 saw the club in debt to the tune of £40, and a local councillor agreed to meet the deficit providing the club left the Tins and moved to the Cross Keys. From the very early days a large wooden stand graced the ground with banking sufficient to comfortably hold 5,000. Little changed during the wars until the early fifties when the popular side stand was erected and on March 24th 1953 a celebration match between Wolves and West Bromwich Albion officially switched on the club's first floodlights, watched by some 7,000 spectators. The 1960-61 season was marked by a pair of unfortunate setbacks as a stand was blown down and the refreshment rooms were burnt out. The following year the stand was replaced.

Over the passing years structures either fell or were pulled down, but to the end it was a fascinating football ground, which had a capacity of around 4,000 many of whom were under cover. The record crowd at the Keys was 10,000, for an FA Cup tie with local rivals Walsall in 1919, all made possible by ash banks which were fashioned out of waste from the local pit.

With its unusual entrance, the old stables from the pub and its wooden stand perched on top of a bank, the Cross Keys was a unique ground which made it all the more difficult to accept when it was just wiped away inside a matter of days.

The new stand at Rocester.

LAMB GROUND
Tamworth FC

Tamworth's Lamb Ground is a prime example of a stadium which is ideally situated close to the town, yet with ample space for expansion despite its proximity to the road system. This being the case, it has surprisingly not fulfilled its true potential during its 60-odd year history as a senior ground.

Early football in the town was played primarily by Tamworth Castle FC who used the field behind the Lamb Inn before it was laid out in the thirties. The current club were forced to use a field behind the Jolly Sailor pub for one season as the rent for The Lamb proved exorbitant. Supporters created banking around the ground which had no amenities, the players changing in the pub; but within a year a more realistic rent was negotiated and the supporters began a similar task of banking the ground in readiness for football.

The first significant building to go up just after the war was the stand on the Cross Street side along with wooden huts for dressing rooms. Two years later came the seated stand opposite with wooden sleeper terracing also put into place. The entrance to the ground, long before the road from the pub was considered, was at the end of Meadow Street where, at the time, there were allotments.

The ground began to change during the sixties, when floodlights bought from Scarborough Football Club were introduced and the Meadow Street entrance was closed. The clubhouse which originally stood in the car-park, and came from Bradleys where it was a works canteen, was demolished and an old office converted into a bar. The original changing rooms were finally replaced when the clubhouse was extended in 1993, while the Meadow Street end gained a neat covered terrace a year earlier.

With the old enclosure looking sprightly, the original sleepers spruced up with a more modern cover and a prospective new stand

Atherstone United has changed within the last four years to keep in line with league rules.

in the pipeline with changing rooms and function hall, the future looks bright for The Lamb. The proposed stand will stretch along the car-park side removing the unattractive tottering wooden fence.

SHEEPY ROAD
Atherstone United FC

Atherstone Rovers first played in Sheepy Road back in 1887, on a field adjoining the current ground. Their successors, Town, used the cricket field in Ratcliffe Road for the following season. The football part of the ground was roped-off for most matches and in 1897 a stand was erected to seat 80 people, but the landlord was not a football fan and the club were forced to look elsewhere.

The landlord of the Red Lion public house encouraged the club to move to a field in Sheepy Road and at Christmas 1900, with the old stand transported by hand-cart to the new ground, the first game was played. Little else occurred at the ground for some time (other than the pitch being widened in 1908 to conform to Amateur Cup rules), until after the Great War when a new 500-seater stand with refreshment rooms replaced the old one.

It was a further dozen years before changing rooms were provided at Sheepy Road, as up to then players had used the Angel Inn the best part of a mile away.

Just prior to the Second World War the club erected a brick built stand to replace the wooden one, and in 1948 the popular side cover was begun and completed in time for the Birmingham Senior Cup Final in 1949. The cover lasted a mere four years before a gale destroyed it. It was replaced in 1954 by a 120 foot long structure using reinforced concrete pillars and an asbestos roof.

The supporters were given permission to build a clubhouse on the Sheepy Road side in 1956, and the wooden building was eventually finished in 1959. It did service until 1970 when a modern brick unit, including a function room, changing rooms and baths replaced it. A further bar and office block was built by the Sheepy Road entrance the following year. The ground continued to improve through the sixties, with the old wire fence around the pitch replaced by a post and rail, while railway sleepers were laid for terracing at the Gypsy Lane end. Derby County visited in 1968 to officially open the new floodlights which proved to be the last major change at the ground for Town as in 1979, having narrowly missed out on becoming founder members of the new

A fine 1993 view of the Lamb Ground, Tamworth.

RENE ROAD
Bolehall Swifts FC

The ground in Rene Road has been home since 1961, when it was undeveloped. It was made into a sports club in 1975 when the covered enclosure with the club name emblazoned on the roof was built.

It was post and railed but changed little until 1994 when new floodlights were installed with a smart new stand behind one goal, all opened by then Manchester United and Welsh star Mark Hughes.

Alliance League, the club collapsed with huge debts.

Happily for the people of Atherstone, a new club, United, were formed and entered the West Midlands League, eventually bringing Southern League football back to Sheepy Road in 1987. The Supporters' Club was sadly closed and changing rooms, which had to suffice for five years until new ones were built alongside the main stand in 1984, were hurriedly provided in a tea room behind the stand.

In more recent times, as ground regulations demand, the pitch fencing was infilled, more cover was erected to bring the capacity up to scratch, and the fence enclosing the ground was replaced, all making Sheepy Road fit to host Premier Division football.

COLES LANE
Sutton Coldfield Town FC

There have been two separate football grounds in Coles Lane. The first is now covered by the local ambulance depot, while the second and current ground has been home since 1920, and can now celebrate its 75th anniversary.

The club was founded on January 2nd 1879, when a meeting at the Town Hall passed a resolution to form a body known as the Sutton Coldfield Football Club. The first match was played on the Meadow Plat in Sutton Park on February 1st, and the players changed at the Station Hotel, and were taken to the ground in horse-drawn carriages. This state of affairs continued until 1900 when,

having affiliated to the Birmingham FA, the club moved to the first Coles Lane ground which they occupied throughout the First World War. Sutton took over the present ground when they entered the Sutton and District League in 1920.

Due in part to a continued exodus of the club's best players to professional sides, the pre-Second World War period was barren on and off the pitch. The ground had been partly developed with a wooden stand that bore a fascia with the legend Sutton Town FC painted on, and had several tannoy speakers arranged along inside. It was capable of holding 300 people with room for more in front, and stood on the site of the present stand until October 15th 1955, when fire tore through its 80 foot length completely destroying it.

The pitch sloped away some seven feet in one corner, and was surrounded by posts and rope, while the ground was fenced in all around. Improvement schemes had to be shelved on the outbreak of war and when the club re-formed in 1945, Coles Lane was desolate, needing far more work than the club had first expected. The playing area had been ruined, with huge holes dug by children, while vegetation some two feet high covered the entire pitch. The stand was being used to house

Sutton's lofty main stand in the '90s and (below) how it was in 1956, having come from Manchester City.

pigs and had been badly damaged, and the fencing had been torn down. All the club's equipment was also lost. At one point the council had even rented out the ground to a man giving donkey rides to children.

Four months of hard labour by committee men and supporters followed while the council, who owned the ground, repaired the stand. Three years later the Supporters' Club gifted a crash barrier, and a car-park was completed at the Coles Lane end. The next major work came in 1953, when the ground was re-vamped with drains laid, the pitch levelled and re-turfed, and concrete paths laid down.

Coles Lane took on a new lease of life, but this was shattered by the fire which swept away the stand. A successful appeal to raise £4,000 was launched, and in 1956 work began on the new stand, a concrete and brick structure with a corrugated back and roof. The sides were open to the elements but had changing rooms underneath and a wooden staircase at the side. It was purchased from Manchester City, and is still in use today, although changed slightly in appearance. The ends have been enclosed, and the legend

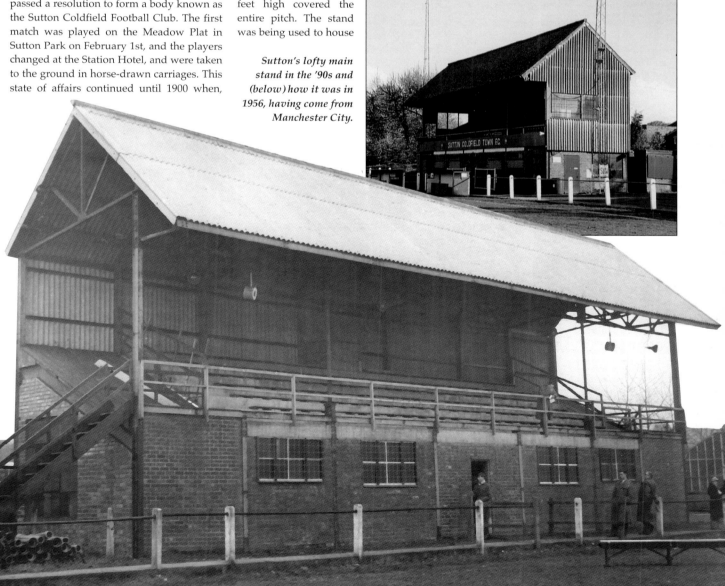

on the front now reads Sutton Coldfield Town FC, the 'Coldfield' having been added within the last few years. The rough banking which surrounded much of the ground was replaced by concrete terracing in the mid seventies, and a large clubhouse was opened in 1972. A corrugated cover now reaches down the side opposite to the main stand.

PAGET RANGERS have shared Coles Lane for two seasons after financial pressure cost them their Springfield Road home.

After a prolonged stay of execution, Rangers' pleasant ground was finally lost in 1995. It had been home since just after the war, when they bought the site for £550, having previously rented at £15 a year. By the end of its playing days, it had gained an open 200-seat stand, and a box-like directors' stand just to the left of the changing rooms. There was a barriered walkway all round the ground and it was fenced-off with concrete walling in the areas that weren't naturally shielded by trees and bushes. Most of the modern improvements came about after the club finished as runners-up in the Midland Combination, and played for just one season in the Southern League. A mass walk-out of players and staff virtually consigned Paget to relegation and in truth, the ground, although pleasant and comfortable, would not have come close to meeting the much stricter criteria laid down by that league in the intervening years. Paget moved in with Sutton Coldfield Town, their near neighbours, but even in the opening days of the 1994-95 season, friendlies were still being played at Springfield Road, as the old girl hung on in there.

THE BUSH GROUND
Pelsall Villa FC

The current Pelsall club dates from 1961, although football was played in the village

A leafy Pelsall Villa.

at the turn of the century. The Bush is a long-established sports ground known chiefly as a venue for cricket, and was leased from a brewery when the club moved in, with changing facilities in the nearby Red Cow pub. Later, after they linked with the cricket club, changing rooms and a proper headquarters went up.

It was in 1978 that major work began at the Bush, with the construction of the present dressing rooms, a new fence to enclose the ground and entrances and exits. Promotion to the West Midlands League Premier Division in 1984 brought further improvements, with a 100-seater stand built at the Bush End and a directors' box adjacent to the cricket club.

In 1991 Aston Villa were the guests when Pelsall unveiled their new floodlights and, with the advent of the Midland Alliance in 1993, The Bush was again upgraded when the old 550-seater stand from GKN Sankey's much-lamented ground was re-constructed in place of the old cover at the Bush End.

RED LION GROUND
Blakenall FC & Bloxwich Strollers FC

To the casual observer the Red Lion is a pleasant unpretentious Black Country ground which looks for all the world as if it has been in place for 30 years or so and inhabited by a few dozen locals on alternative Saturdays.

Happily, the truth is different (though the attendance estimate is close!). The ground in its original form dates from the 1890s, and was the home of Bloxwich Strollers for the best part of thirty years. Strollers eventually gave up the tenancy around 1958 and, after the ground had stood unused for two years, Blakenall took over the lease from Walsall Council and moved in. At that time the ground had one entrance - through an archway in the pub car park, and down an eighty yard long path. The players took to the pitch in the corner to the right of the stand. The roadway alongside that part of the ground was then a cul-de-sac, and the changing rooms and match-board huts, bought from an R.A.F. camp on Cannock Chase for £325, were situated at its end. An old wooden stand once provided halfway line cover on the clubhouse side, but at the outbreak of World War Two was put into storage by the council and never did find its way back to the Red Lion. It has graced the pastures of Walsall Rugby Club's Delves Road ground ever since. The archway entrance became redundant when the impressive clubhouse and dressing room complex was built in 1967, and the area was banked up. Prior to that, in 1959, wooden cover costing £600 was erected behind the goal. This has since been refurbished with the more recent addition of bench seating. When viewed under lights, the blue-painted front of the stand gives off an almost unreal iridescent aqua glow. The original entrance walkway area has now been built upon and the cul-de-sac opened out, but the archway at the pub still remains. Happily, so does the

Action at Paget Rangers' Springfield Road home. Paget now share with Sutton Coldfield.

The Red Lion ground, Blakenall.

name of the ground despite the fact that it is now totally isolated and unconnected with the pub itself. Blakenall's home for thirty-odd years is now shared - and here's an irony - by Bloxwich Strollers who, having experienced a resurgence in fortune, are playing football once again at their spiritual home, the Red Lion.

THE SCHOLARS
Chasetown FC

The Scholars ground has come a long way in the dozen or so years of its existence. The football club spent in the region of £50,000, converting what was a council refuse tip into a highly regarded sports ground which is now hosting senior non-league football.

Chasetown FC were originally formed as Chase Terrace Old Scholars, hence the name of the ground, and played from the outset at the Burntwood Recreation Centre, previously known as the Cannock Chase Colliery Sports Ground. Although it was only a parks pitch, it boasted a 300-seater stand which sadly was razed to the floor in 1983. The ground still remains and until recently was used for rugby, and is now occasionally utilised on Sundays.

The move to The Scholars came in the same year as the fire and the clubhouse, changing rooms, and areas of hard standing were all provided at that time. In 1987, a roof was added to the hard standing adjoining the clubhouse, and 112 seats installed. In 1990 the club erected floodlights, which were first used for a league match against Harrison's on March 20th 1990.

Since then essential work has continued to allow the ground to keep up with league requirements, with hard standing all around the pitch and a complete perimeter fence segregating the ground from woods at the rear. Unlike so many new grounds, The Scholars

OAK PARK
Walsall Wood FC

Although it shows no signs of it now, Oak Park was originally laid out back in 1928 as the Welfare Ground for the Walsall Wood Coppice Colliery. It was of standard design with a pavilion and a railed-off football pitch and within four years the new club had built the splendid wooden grandstand which, remarkably, has survived to this day, despite extensive vandalism elsewhere on the ground.

The pavilion was burnt down during the Second World War and was replaced by another which was extended with a brick building alongside for tea rooms. Part of this too was destroyed by fire a few years ago.

There was a small area of covered standing where the second pavilion stood, but this was pulled down to make way and although footings were laid behind one goal to replace the cover, it was never built, although the footings are still visible.

has an element of character about it, and it is to be hoped future developments by this progressive club do not take that soul away.

Photos in this section by: Paul Barber, Pat Brunning and Dean Walton.

The Scholars at Chasetown before much renovation for grading purposes.

Nuneaton to Leicester

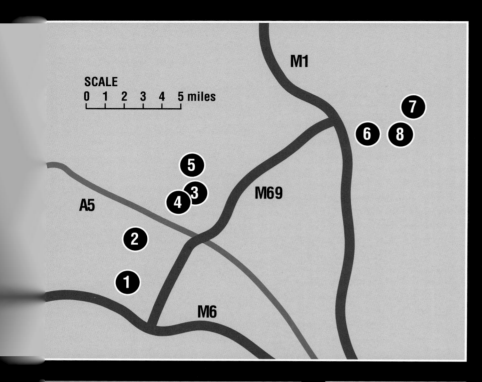

SCALE
0 1 2 3 4 5 miles

M1

M69

A5

M6

7
6 8
5
4 3
2
1

1   **Bedworth United FC**

2   **Nuneaton Borough FC**

3   **Hinckley Town FC**

4   **Hinckley Athletic FC**

5   **Barwell FC**

6   **Leicester United FC**

7   **Oadby Town FC**

8   **Leicestershire FA Ground**

Photos in this section by:
Pat Brunning, Reg Bull,
Keith Clayton, Gavin Ellis-Neville,
Dean Walton and Martin Wray.

The old stand at Bedworth can be seen in the 1955 action photo on the facing page. The same stand is shown (below left) as it was in the early '90s. A new brick-built stand (below right) was erected on the same site in 1993.

CLOSE proximity to the catchment area for the old Birmingham Combination League, the Leicester Senior League and the West Midlands League has led to a strong contingent of clubs with established grounds.

Nuneaton Borough have seemingly ridden the storms of recent years and are regrouping with a modernised ground whilst Hinckley Athletic are a well supported side with a fine ground. The Senior League has a host of clubs with enclosed grounds including established outfits such as Anstey Nomads, where 4,500 spectators once watched an FA Amateur Cup tie in the fifties, and Friar Lane Old Boys whose Knighton Lane East ground saw an FA Vase semi final in 1975.

THE OVAL, MINERS WELFARE GROUND and THE BRITISH QUEEN GROUND
Football in Bedworth

There have been a number of clubs with the prefix 'Bedworth', but according to the club's history they are all one and the same hence the formation date of 1895. In fact the first club, Bedworth Town, was formed in June 1896, playing on a ground at the rear of the Conservative Club with dressing facilities at Mr. Shortridge's Tramway Refreshment Rooms. They folded around the turn of the century. In 1905 Bedworth ECS changed their name to Town and played at the Welfare Ground until 1923 when they too went under.

The third Town club was formed two years later when Collycroft United adopted the old name whilst playing at the British Queen ground in King Street. They changed the name to Bedworth Central in 1938 and back to Town the following year, but during 1940 they too folded.

The fourth Town club were created after the war, playing at The Oval until they were wound up in 1968, whereupon Bedworth United were formed.

Bedworth 1 Nuneaton 1, August 1955. The old double-decker bus was used as Supporters' Club offices by Bedworth.

The British Queen was a fascinating ground which saw not only football but cricket, boxing, flower shows, fetes, fairs and brass band concerts. It was the work of one man, Billy Goodyear, the publican of the adjoining British Queen Inn who transformed what was once a tip into a sports ground with changing rooms used throughout the year. For a while Birmingham City's 'A' team hired the ground, which had been opened in the early twenties and was owned by the brewers Lucas's of Leamington. Soon after the war with the Miners' Welfare Ground being used more and more, the Queen began to fall into disrepair and was eventually sold by the brewery to the owner of the fair who in turn sold it for development. Kings Gardens housing estate now stands on the site.

The Welfare Ground has had its shares of ups and downs. Over the years the shape of the ground has remained oval, although with various changes, such as the building of a canteen and dressing room, some areas are no longer available as vantage points. The huge banking to the side of the canteen, with its winding path down from the turnstile, was full to bursting point on February 23rd 1982 when 5,127 people watched a crucial local derby with Nuneaton Borough, but today it is neatly trimmed but virtually unused.

In recent times The Oval has changed for the better, in a similar, but less dramatic, way

to Kidderminster Harriers ground at Aggborough. The cinder track which ran around the outside of the pitch meant crowds behind the goal were many yards away. This track was removed in recent times and the pitch-side fencing re-sited, squaring off the playing area. A new £150,000 main stand was built two years ago on the site of a long low structure which had given service for many years once an earlier pavilion was demolished.

The banking behind the goals still curves around in its original shape giving an insight into the ground's recent past. A low brick-built structure housing the dressing-rooms, clubhouse and V.I.P. lounge is, from a distance, purely functional in appearance, but does provide a splendid view from the flat roof which joins on to the boardroom. Unusually for this league, cars are parked inside the ground at pitch-side in a similar manner to Salisbury.

MANOR PARK
Nuneaton Borough FC

Nuneaton Borough's Manor Park ground has altered significantly since its inception in 1919, mirroring the ups and downs of the various Nuneaton clubs that have been based there. The current state of the ground is favourable, with the totally refurbished main stand sporting new seating, and a new covered Canal Side Terrace in prospect, to

replace the condemned area which vanished in 1987.

However, in the desperately difficult years of the late 1980's, with the club perilously close to folding and no money for repairs, the Manor fell into disrepair, with the huge Cock and Bear Terrace suffering the indignity of being declared out of bounds, as did the Canal Side. Since enduring back-to-back relegations the club has been reconstituted and is busy restoring the Manor to its former glory.

The original club, Nuneaton St Nicholas, first saw light of day in 1889, playing on a field in Higham Lane, before moving firstly to Coton Road, and then two seasons later to Daffern's Field, opposite Mount Street. In 1894 they became Nuneaton Town and played on two other fields both close to the Rose Inn but by the turn of the century were back on Daffern's Field. A year later debts sent the club under but within a season another club emerged named Nuneaton Juniors but reverted back to Town after a year. They played on the Rose Inn pitch at a guinea per annum until 1905 when they moved again, this time back to Daffern's Field in Arbury Road. Inside a season the club had taken off, and a small stand had gone up, the pitch was levelled, and a corrugated fence with a pay box erected. Sadly, the ground owner had other ideas and in 1908 they were on the move again, successfully obtaining the Newdegate Arms ground

The huge covered terrace at the Cock and Bear end of Nuneaton's Manor Park.

which had previously been used for rugby and cricket. The club ousted the rugby club by the simple expedient of paying more rent money, and took tenancy until the Great War. This ground was situated roughly on the site of the bus station, and consisted of a cinder track with a covered stand to the side.

During the war, the club lost the use of the ground and so at the end of the hostilities bought a site at Wash Lane Farm for £2,300 which could be developed for the Birmingham League. The ground initially was laid at 90 degrees to its present position, but after one season the pitch was turned around, with grass banks and a Dutch Barn type stand with seats provided. This stand was to give service for the next 70 years at Manor Park.

In the early days the pitch suffered from having a footpath across it, and it is recounted how they also had to cover a small duck pond with boards before playing! Soon, the club provided a barrel-roof stand on the Canal Side, built by local firm Parsons and Sherwin, and this survived until it was condemned and de-roofed in 1987. Little in the way of development occurred until the early 1960's when the huge covered terrace was built at the Cock and Bear end on a bank which elevates it to well above the level of the crossbar.

Nowadays the end looks magnificent, dwarfing all other areas in the ground, and provides a splendid view even though set a little way back from pitch-side. The turnstiles lead to an area which has been extensively tidied up since the dismal 1980's, complete with a car-park area and a large clubhouse, stark on the outside but lively inside. The club's new main stand unusually features seating starting at ground level with no frontage and was built into the shell of the original stand in 1989. Beyond that the open terraced end remains in its original state, the club prevented from developing it further due to the housing behind. Along the side, and on the site of the condemned cover, it is hoped to build a replacement which will add another dimension to the rise, fall, and rise again of Manor Park.

Whippet racing, boxing, cricket, and rugby have all been staged there over the years, but it is pleasing to note that the club's nightmare of the eighties is over and football is flourishing again, under some of the best floodlighting around. The original lights were erected in 1965 and replaced in 1978. Then in 1993 the club embarked on a marvellous FA Cup run beating Swansea City at home in a replay, before being edged out in another replay by A.F.C. Bournemouth. To enable the game to be televised, the lighting was upgraded at a cost to the television company of £20,000. Nuneaton Borough have come a long way in four years.

LEICESTER ROAD
Hinckley Town FC

Formed as a school team called Westfield Rovers in 1959, the club played at the school before moving to the Granville Road Recreation Ground. This still exists today but is much smaller and no longer used for football. The Leicester Road sports complex was created in the sixties when the cricket and rugby clubs vacated a site in town and moved to the new area.

The football pitch today is built on what was a secondary rugby pitch until Hinckley Town moved in during the late sixties. A post and rail went in and the ground was fenced off before a grant was obtained for half the £3,000 cost of erecting the main stand.

At this time the players were changing in the sports complex and walking down to the ground, but this was soon unacceptable as the club moved from Nuneaton Amateur, Leicestershire Senior League and Central Midland Alliance to the West Midlands League, and eventually the Southern League. For the West Midlands League porta-cabins were installed and they were used until a new changing block went up along with the clubhouse which has an overhang providing cover. The ground attendance record is the 2,000 who saw the friendly with Real Sociedad in 1986 which was staged to commemorate the switching on of the floodlights.

MIDDLEFIELD LANE GROUND
Hinckley Athletic FC

On the formation of the original Hinckley AFC in 1889, the Holywell Ground on London Road was immediately used by the club. The players changed at the Holywell Inn which stood at the back of the ground behind the Ease End goal.

The pitch sloped from end to end and was used right through to the start of the Second World War. Little is known of the facilities in those days other than the fact there was a Spion Kop, a stand and dressing rooms. The Workhouse stood at the top, and although it, and the pub still stand, the ground is gone without trace, covered by the Hinckley College of Further Education.

In June 1945 Hinckley United, as they were then, were without a ground as the brewery owners of the Holywell no longer wished it to be used for sport. The Middlefield Lane site, having some years previously been used as a dog track, was secured in August 1946, and cost the club £500.

A month later the club changed their name to Athletic and within a year were back in the Birmingham Combination. A cinder track was laid for dry standing and also to provide for athletics fixtures. Temporary dressing rooms were constructed using wood from the old Holywell Stand and a substantial Kop was created before a stand was built, smaller than the old one but more durable. In early 1947 the approaches to the ground were improved with many tons of ash. When the pitch was bull-dozed in the close season, the debris was used to create raised terracing around the ground. Concrete posts were sunk ready for a wire cable to surround the pitch as the ground quickly took shape.

By August 1947 there was dressing room accommodation for both teams and an embankment along one side, but a lack of cash and timber prevented the main stand from going ahead until 1950 when, after an appeal raised £750, it was built. The stand remains today, without its wooden slats as these were replaced with tip up seats from Leicester City's Filbert Street in 1993.

On Boxing Day 1949 some 5,410 people crammed into the ground for a league game with Nuneaton Borough and this remains the biggest crowd ever to watch a football match in Hinckley.

In 1955 a new clubhouse was built near the entrance and two years later new dressing rooms were opened, which stand today but in modified form with offices and a canteen. With the election of the club to the Southern League in 1959, concrete slabs were laid behind the near goal to provide terracing; the ground at this time also offered covered accommodation in the Chicken Shed opposite the main stand.

A full main stand at Hinckley Athletic.

Little happened at the ground for some while as the club struggled and eventually left the Southern League. Then in 1977 the present clubhouse was erected behind the Middlefield Lane goal replacing the old one built 22 years before. Two years later floodlighting arrived and Leicester City did the honours on October 1st 1979 in front of over 1,500 people.

In 1985 high winds demolished the old rusting Chicken Shed, but within ten weeks a smart new terraced covered side had been built and was named the Ron Holtham Stand in memory of a former Director at the club. A new set of lights, installed at a cost of £20,000 but easily up to Conference standard, were switched on at a match with Coventry City in 1991.

Work has continued to enclose the ground with concrete panelling and plans are in hand to terrace and cover the grass bank at the Richmond Park end as Middlefield Lane recovers from its mid-life crisis and goes from strength to strength.

INVICTA PARK
Oadby Town FC

Oadby's Wigston Road ground is one of the better Leicestershire Senior League homes and has been in existence since around 1948. Its original clubhouse came from an old Prisoner of War camp in Leicester and was added to in the seventies when the pre-fabricated bar was installed.

The ground was bought from the adjacent farmer back in the sixties and the pitch was roped or wired off until the permanent post and rail system went in. In 1990 the new clubhouse, which gives a small amount of cover on the overhang, was opened before a game with Newcastle United but as yet Invicta Park has not been blessed with any seated accommodation.

Invicta Park, Oadby.

KIRBY ROAD SPORTS GROUND
Barwell FC

Football has been played in Barwell since the 1890's, but the current side only date from 1991 when Barwell Athletic merged with the third Hinckley side, Hinckley FC, who until then had played on Hinckley Athletic's home ground.

Before this alliance, the basic facilities within the nevertheless attractive sports ground had sufficed, with a permanently barriered pitch segregated from the cricket club by changing room facilities built in 1978.

The two sports had previously shared a double-sided pavilion until it was demolished. In the between times players changed in what is now the clubhouse by the entrance to the ground. On entering the Midland Combination the club erected a yellow and green painted covered area, as an extension to the changing rooms, and installed seats from G Block of the dismantled Leicester City Members' Stand. Floodlighting was also purchased and erected in September 1992, having previously seen service at Harrison Park in East Leicester, and prior to that at Enderby Town FC.

A further covered area of hard standing was completed in 1994 as the club continued to consolidate their newly-found position in senior non-League football. Behind the left hand goal the Sports Association have provided an indoor bowls club for the area. From the outside, it looks like a warehouse, and the side which runs behind the goal could possibly benefit from an advertising hoarding or two. However, inside it is quite magnificent, with a full-size bowls green, and restaurant, fully-lit and imaginatively adorned with sponsors' boards.

GEORGE STREET and UNITED PARK
Enderby Town FC and Leicester United FC

The name of Enderby Town did not die in 1985 with the birth of Leicester United, but was merely shunted to one side to be used for business purposes rather than on fixture lists. Their enforced move from George Street to the old Leicester Cricket Club ground in Blaby meant the end for a ground that opened as recently as September 4th 1959 amidst much celebration before a match with the FA Cup holders Aston Villa.

The original clubhouse cost £50, and was constructed from old wooden bungalows on the 14 acre site which was formerly farm land. In 1963 a new clubhouse with six changing rooms, a board room and office accommodation was built at one end of the ground at a cost of £5,000. The pitch by then had been impressively fenced off with chain link and concrete posts and very soon a covered stand was completed. This followed the club to Blaby when George Street was lost. September 1971 saw the floodlights switched on in front of 700 people for a game against Irthlingborough Diamonds and two years later the 420-seater stand was built opposite the covered area. It was all to no avail, for the ground is now completely gone. The floodlights now shine over Barwell FC and the stand is re-sited in the middle of the newer version at United Park. The open nature of the right-hand side of the ground and the general shape with its circular boundary wall gives the casual visitor a clue to the ground's cricketing past. Leicester United have not had it easy in their first ten years and the ghost of Enderby Town has not yet been exorcised.

HOLMES PARK
Leicestershire FA

Holmes Park was bought from the now defunct Wigston Town by the L.F.A. in 1980. It had staged Leicester Senior League football for many years under the club's original name of Midland Athletic.

New changing rooms were built in a bungalow style in 1990, which replaced the old ones, now lurking at the back of the clubhouse, opened in 1981. With the added help of the local council, perimeter rails and a stand have been put-up to make Holmes Park the permanent home of all Leicestershire County Cup Finals. In recent times Oadby Town have staged an important FA Vase tie there when their own ground was waterlogged.

Burton, Derby and Matlock

THIS area in the heart of the East Midlands coal fields either has, or had, many Welfare Grounds, some of which exist without senior football while others reverted back to the Welfare organisation when the pit closed and are no more. One of the most fascinating of all non-League grounds is situated within this region at Gresley Rovers, but sadly for lovers of traditional working class football grounds, the Moat will soon be no more.

HOLBROOK, MOIRA, and KILBURN are just three Welfares that still exist apart from the others mentioned. Former membership of the Midland League and the Midland Counties League is reflected in some of the established and well-developed grounds such as HEANOR and ALFRETON.

ETON PARK
Burton Albion FC

The club and the ground of Burton Albion carry on a rich footballing tradition which started with three clubs all of which played in the Football League, Wanderers, Swifts and United. When the Second World War ended there were none, and it wasn't until 1950 when at a meeting of over 700 local people Burton Albion were born and immediately given use of the Lloyds Foundry ground in Wellington Street.

On August 5th the club staged its first practise match watched by 1,400 spectators, and 12 days later Wellington Street was filled with 5,000 people for the first Birmingham League game against Gloucester City.

Albion enjoyed almost eight years at Wellington Street which was spartan by the standards of the day, and when part of Eatoughs sports ground in Derby Road became available the Supporters' Club were able to finance the purchase for £2,000. The club switched to Southern League football and immediately began work on a 300-seater stand which cost the club £6,000 brand new.

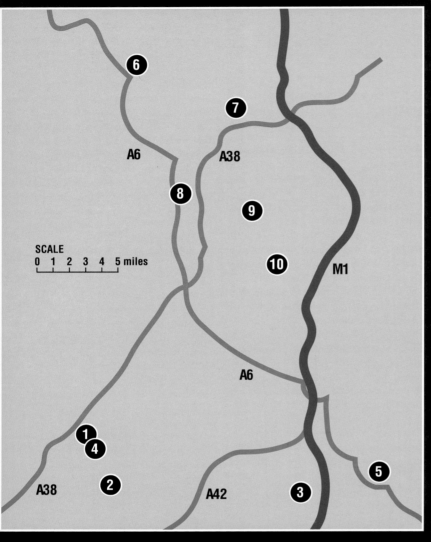

1	**Burton Albion FC**
2	**Gresley Rovers FC**
3	**Shepshed Dynamo FC**
4	**Stapenhill FC**
5	**Loughborough and the Collieries**
6	**Matlock Town FC**
7	**Alfreton Town FC**
8	**Belper Town FC**
9	**Heanor Town FC**
10	**Ilkeston Town FC**

Eton Park, Burton.

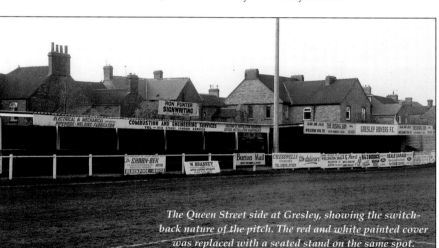

Right: The Bass Stand at Gresley Rovers, opened in 1990, with the white-painted cricket pavilion behind. Above: A 1960's view taken from the same spot. The surrounding housing has changed little. The cricket pavilion can be seen backing on to the old stand, as can the committee room, cover and benches, all of which were removed to make way for the clubhouse in 1979.

The season started at Wellington Street even though construction of the terracing and dressing rooms had fallen behind, but by September Eton Park was ready and on the 20th Nuneaton Borough were the first opposition in the FA Cup in front of 5,527 - the second biggest crowd ever at the ground. After an uncertain spell when club finances were stretched to the limit, the ground was improved with the addition of covered terracing and in September 1965 the unwanted floodlights from Ashton Gate found their way to Eton Park, the £2,000 required raised by public appeal. Then with more financial trouble looming the club accepted £2,000 for a small plot of land on which the Supporters' Club erected their clubhouse.

By the early seventies Eton Park was a substantial football ground, with an array of advertising hoardings brightening the place, but despite success and a sound home with a capacity for 4,500 with 2,000 under cover, the club again suffered desperate financial problems and during 1995 began negotiations to sell Eton Park and move out of town, in an effort to reduce increasing debts. It is ironic that Burton's ground is surrounded by all the room they could possibly need, yet they are forced to sell and move, doubtless to a cramped and purpose-built stadium with no elevation at all, whereas Gresley are forced to leave because their historic old home is not big enough to cater for the club's ambitions.

MOAT GROUND
Gresley Rovers FC

It is to be hoped that this book appears before the club's proposed move to a new ground in Bridge Street, on the edge of the village, goes ahead for the Moat Ground in Church Gresley should be visited and admired while it is still possible.

The ground has never had any pretence at being pretty, indeed its lack of certain facilities caused the club to continue in the West Midlands League, when rejected out of hand by the Southern League. However, it is, and has been since 1909, the essence of what non-League football grounds are all about.

For the neutral, it is in a perverse way a shame the club has progressed on the field to such an extent that the Moat will be redundant.

The club was founded in 1882, and first played in Albert Village, only half a mile away, but in Leicestershire. The ground was shared with cricket and it is believed the players utilised the pavilion to change in, although it is possible The Albert Inn, the club's H.Q. at the time, may well have been used. No trace of the ground remains today as coal and clay workings have obliterated the area. After thirteen seasons at Mushroom Lane, the club moved into the village on to a ground in Church Street, a stone's throw away from today's Moat.

The Queen Street side at Gresley, showing the switchback nature of the pitch. The red and white painted cover was replaced with a seated stand on the same spot. Below: Remove the advertising hoardings and benches and most of the ground is unchanged in 35 years.

THE GROUNDS OF LOUGHBOROUGH AND DISTRICT OVER THE YEARS

1995 saw the 100th anniversary of League football in the town with various exhibitions and celebrations to mark the centenary. Loughborough Town only survived five years, as League football proved too much, but the game lived on with Corinthians and United making their mark in local football before fading slowly away. Only recently have a new club emerged, Loughborough Dynamo, who will take on the mantle left by United.

As far back as the 1870's, football was taking hold in the area, and behind The Greyhound Inn was the **Athletic Ground**, known as Bromhead's Cricket Ground (after the landlord) until the 1880's. During the next twenty years the ground was developed to incorporate a pavilion and a grandstand and was staging League soccer. But with the demise of the Town club the ground was taken over by Loughborough Corinthians Club until 1908 when the council redeveloped the area and the ground was lost. Nothing remains except the main entrance which is situated between Putts the Painters and the pub and shows two cemented holes high on the wall which once held the sign board welcoming people to the Athletic Ground.

Loughborough Corinthians moved to a new site in **Glebe Street** which was home for thirteen years. The opening of the ground took place on September 5th 1908 before a game against Leicester Imperial. It had a small pavilion but no changing facilities, that task being performed in The Lonsdale public house.

Crowds of 2,000 and more were not uncommon at Glebe Street but at the end of the 1920-21 season the club moved to their **Browns Lane** ground, a site still much-lamented by the football-watching public of the town. The first game took place on August 27th 1921 against Hucknall Byron in the Central Alliance, and attracted a crowd of over 3,000. In its 52 year history, Browns Lane gained a large wooden stand and the grass banking around the pitch at one time boasted three covered stands - a three-quarter length opposite the main stand, another behind the far goal and a third next to the tea bar by the main stand.

The changing rooms eventually went in under the stand, but prior to that the players used a nearby pub. The banking around the ground allowed huge crowds to watch matches, especially in the twenties and thirties and 7,000 once watched Leicester City play Birmingham City in aid of Loughborough Hospital in 1929.

Over the years the ground was used by Corinthians, Loughborough Rugby Club, Leicestershire Nomads, Brush Sports and Loughborough United before the last-ever game, against Bridlington Trinity, another doomed club, in April 1973.

By then Browns Lane had been allowed to deteriorate. The main stand was still there, but the other two sides were bare, and just the cover by the tea bar, and the Supporters' Club hut remained. The ground was flattened by the council and a Leisure Centre built on part of the site. It was to be over 20 years before Dynamos were to form at Nanpantan Sports Centre.

The area to the east of the town was dominated by the coal workings which threw up many clubs, based at the Colliery Welfares. Ibstock Welfare had their own **Welfare Ground**, and the **Hastings Ground**, just behind The Hastings Arms in the village, was home to the Colliers until the twenties when Penistone Rovers took over for some sixty years. The ground had a covered enclosure, erected in the mid-sixties and had hard standing and railings around the pitch about the same time. Earlier, spectators stood on railway-sleeper-type terracing. The ground was chiefly known for holding large crowds for the prestigious Coalville Charity Cup Finals. At the time of writing the ground still exists but seems likely to be built on shortly.

Another substantial ground now long since gone in the area was the **Mantle Lane Ground**, home of Whitwick Colliery during their time in the Birmingham League. When Coalville Town folded in 1954, the Colliers took the grandstand from their Waggon and Horses ground and re-erected it at Mantle Lane. There was shale banking around the ground, part of which was covered and the players changed at the pithead baths before crossing the road through the brickworks to the ground. The club reached the third qualifying round of the FA Cup three times after the war, but as the pits closed and football faded away in the area then so did Whitwick. The pitch is now part of a golf course.

The **Waggon and Horses Ground** is still in existence, although no more than a pitch nowadays, but is possibly the most famous of all the grounds in the area. Coalville Town were in occupation from the early thirties until 1954 when they folded. The ground, which was opened before a game with Bolton Wanderers, had a grandstand built in the late thirties from the proceeds of the sale of a player to Leicester City. It had around 250 bench seats and was eventually transported to Whitwick. As was the norm in the area, pit waste was used to create banking around the ground and attendances of 6,000 in the 1930s and 1940s for Coalville Charity Cup Finals were standard. Pegsons FC used the pitch after Coalville and much later a local junior team, West End United, until recently used what is a famous Leicestershire ground.

The town of Shepshed, near Loughborough, was known in the 1800's as Sheepshed, and it has seen a number of clubs since the very first match at **Kirkhill** on November 27th 1879, when Sheepshed

The much lamented Browns Lane ground in Loughborough

Ibstock Welfare FC.

Institute Athletic played Loughborough Rising Star. The ground was not popular and was considered to be "totally unfit to play upon" and so the club moved on. The gateway which led to the ground from the changing rooms at the Institute (now the White House) can still be seen still but the pitch is now covered by Beresford Court.

The next stop was a field on **Charnwood Avenue**, opposite what is presently the Police Station and during their eight year stay the club, now known as Shepshed Town played Nottingham Forest, amongst others. Shepshed were so successful that a new ground was needed for the 1888 season and a flat pitch on **Ashby Road** was colonised for a further nine years. Problems with crowd control caused the ground to be closed more than once and with the pitch being some distance from the town and more local support sought, they moved again to **Little Haw Lane**, an enclosure nearer the centre. This was still some fifteen minutes walk from the town and crowds dwindled before the final move was made to the Dovecote in 1899.

Shepshed Albion took over from the ailing Town not long after and the crowds returned with 1,000 watching regularly and for some years the ground was trouble-free. Again, though, there were closure problems in 1909, but this time for pitch repairs. A notorious hump had been awkward from the start but its removal would mean **The Dovecote** could be used for cricket and athletics as well as football. By the turn of the twenties Albion had gone the way of Town, and the Parish Church FC used the ground for a while. It was not until after the Second World War that another Albion side took up residence. In 1958 attempts were made to buy what was still an undeveloped ground from the brewery landlords, but this was unsuccessful and it was not until 1975 that significant changes occurred, with the club now called Shepshed Charterhouse after the sponsors. A clubhouse was erected and stands and floodlights transformed The Dovecote into a thriving football ground which went on to stage Southern League and Northern Premier League football before they again became Albion and once more went into decline. The latest club is called Shepshed Dynamo and their membership of the Midland Alliance has meant a new seven foot high concrete wall around a ground which has seen its fair share of turmoil in close on 100 years.

The ground was surrounded by a high boarded fence, and had a turnstile at one end, although there were no amenities and the players changed at the new H.Q., the appropriately named Boot Inn. This was to be home for a further 14 seasons before the ground's owner, Mrs. Woodward sold the land for development. Sadly, this ground is untraceable.

Gresley's next move across the road to the Moat ground for the 1909/10 season, proved successful, but there was much to accomplish before the surface could be played upon. The northern end of the ground was a derelict, waste site after clay extraction a few years previously and the southern a works cricket ground for a local pottery firm. On the waste ground there was for many years a large mound of rubble which, when surrounded by water, resembled a moat, and it is believed from here that the ground's name is derived.

The Moat soon began to take shape, with various basic areas of cover erected around the ground where the cricket pavilion and canteen were the only other structures. At this time, and until the dressing rooms were opened in September 1930, the players changed at the Boot Inn. Remarkably, the dressing rooms, cricket pavilion and canteen are all still in full use, smartened up and still going strong. A small wooden press box was built in the late 1930's, and stood until re-sited under the stand in 1979. The covered terrace alongside the press box originally dated from the 1920's, but it disappeared around wartime before being re-built about 1950. This area was very popular with supporters during the halcyon days of massive crowds, and the terrace was eventually removed along with the press box and asbestos committee room when work began on the clubhouse in 1979.

On the other sides of the ground, the original covered areas were gradually replaced, and bench seating was installed, bought from Lancaster City, who had purchased previously from either Manchester United, or Morecambe open air swimming baths, depending on whose club history you read! The introduction of advertising boards soon transformed the ground from a dour, yet homely place into a colourful vibrant home, which seemed complete when flood-lighting was bought from Burton Rugby Club in 1985. However, the club continued to improve, concreting the area in front of the old stand, and improving the clubhouse, which had begun life as a site hut for extensive roadworks near Peterborough.

Finally, in 1990, to ensure Southern League football, the old stand was removed, complete with ancient chapel benches, and replaced with the long low red-roofed Bass Stand, which serves today. The new structure is complimentary to the rest of the ground, which has retained much the same appearance throughout its life. Being hemmed in as it is, the Moat ground is in a similar predicament to that suffered by Rossett Park, Marine, another ground which cannot expand any further than it has already.

For a village the size of Church Gresley to have nurtured a football club for over a hundred years, and continue to support it in such numbers, there is bound to be pride in abundance. It does seem certain that, should the Moat go the same way as the Walled Meadow, Granleigh Road and many other much-loved grounds, the club will continue to prosper. Let us hope that the dressing rooms, canteen, and cricket pavilion can somehow be safely transported and incorporated into the new ground.

EDGE HILL
Stapenhill FC

The summer of 1947 saw the birth of the somewhat unwieldy titled Stapenhill Waterside Community Centre Football Club who played on a pitch adjoining the railway and Drakelow Park. There were no facilities and so changing was done at the Freehold Tavern, nearly two miles away.

The ground was soon required for roads and railway sidings and from 1949 a pitch **on**

Stapenhill FC.

the other side of the railway was used. Although facilities were good, the pitch was terrible and so the club transferred again after one season, to a field next door to the original ground in Drakelow Park. This was a vast improvement with dressing rooms and a refreshment bar and there were often crowds of 1,000 or more at matches, but it did not last as the British Electricity Authority wanted the land and the club were forced to play on Heath Road Recreation Ground, changing in the concert room of the Plough Inn and selling refreshments from Mrs Plant's back garden!

The 1953-54 season saw the promise of a lease on a field adjoining the Edge Hill estate, and while work commenced to transform it into a football pitch the club played on the frequently waterlogged Stapenhill Fields until the new ground was ready for the start of the following season.

The playing surface was surrounded by a post and rail and a small timber pavilion was in place for changing. A long covered area ran alongside which has since been modernised and had 50 seats and concrete steps added to it.

Edge Hill stayed more or less the same until a social club was built in the mid seventies, but as the eighties closed wholesale alterations took place when the club entered the Midland Combination. Along with the work on the stand, the ground was fully enclosed by a concrete fence at a cost of £15,000, and after purchasing the site from the council an elevated viewing area was put up behind the car-park end goal. A secretary's office and hospitality lounge were installed, and the long-awaited floodlights switched on at a match with neighbours Gresley Rovers although the very first game was against Kings Heath in August 1994.

Recently the ground gradings have meant the addition of a further area of cover and a new referee's room. Club members dreamed of all this back in the fifties but it did not become reality until the 1990's.

CAUSEWAY LANE
Matlock Town FC

If Matlock's Causeway Lane ground was unfortunate enough to be based in a depressing inner-city site or indeed anywhere moderately urbanised, then to most it would surely appear seedy, decayed and summarily unattractive. Happily, it is situated in one of the most beautiful parts of the country and its rather crumpled appearance is primarily due to the council condemning the dear old main stand, which has been left discarded and uncared for. At the time of writing however there are plans afoot to re-vamp the ground and demolish the old stand.

Nobody is quite sure when Matlock Town began playing at Causeway Lane; estimates suggested range from 1895 to 1920. What is known is that the previous ground was in Hall Leys, and in the early days the club played in the Midland Counties, and later the Matlock and District Leagues.

The grandstand in question at Causeway Lane dates from the mid-twenties and has Y-shaped stanchions running along the front which bring Sudbury's Priory Stadium stand to mind. The fact that the Sudbury stand formerly stood on a shared cricket ground, and Matlock's still does, adds to the similarities.

Little happened to alter the ground until 1959 when a covered extension, which stretched along towards the town end and incorporated new dressing rooms, was added at a similar height to the stand.

The club's sporadic Cup runs seem to have played a part in shaping the ground's development , as the 1959 work coincided with an FA Cup run to the First Round, where they lost in a replay to Crook Town. Ten years later seating was installed in front of the dressing rooms around the time of the next Cup run, when they disappointingly lost at Bilston in the 4th Qualifying Round after knocking out Alfreton, Sutton Town and rivals Buxton.

More seats were added in that area in 1975, the year of Matlock's FA Trophy victory at Wembley which also included the all-time record crowd of 5,123 against Burton Albion. The terracing on the same side dates from 1974 and was put in place in preparation for the FA Cup First Round tie with Blackburn Rovers which the Gladiators lost 4-1.

The original floodlighting system went up in 1970, although it has been updated and replaced at least twice since then, and in 1973 a smart new entrance block was built followed four years later by the Social Club.

The post and rail system around the ground lasted until 1979, when the wall around the three usable sides of the ground was put in place. The fourth had to remain roped as it encroached on the cricket field. The Town End of the ground was developed around 12 years ago, when covered terracing was put down which gave more of an enclosed look and once the office block was constructed in 1989 it signalled the end of ground changes, other than the simply cosmetic for quite some time.

Causeway Lane, like so many other three-sided grounds, is forever in danger of falling foul of league regulations and cannot host football at any higher level than it does now. There were suggestions the cricket club may well consider moving off enabling the fourth side to be closed in and developed, but this idea appears to be a non-starter.

The superb setting of Matlock Town, overlooked by the castle.

TOWN GROUND, NORTH STREET
Alfreton Town FC

Alfreton Town in 1995.

Alfreton Town Football Club were re-formed in 1959 and began playing on the newly-created Town ground provided by the Urban District Council. The previous club which ceased playing between the wars, had used the Welfare Ground next door as home.

Within a year, covered standing was erected along the full length of the Welfare side of the ground which had been banked up sufficiently to allow a crowd of 5,000 to see a Central Alliance match with Matlock Town in 1960 - a record to this day. The following year saw seating in place for 180 spectators as Midland League football came to Alfreton.

In 1963 the small covered stand at the Alma Street end was put up, the grass banking having been cut away half way up to accommodate it. This was the last major change at the ground until 1971 when the original seated stand on the Welfare side was removed and replaced with covered terracing and seats for 150. Floodlights arrived in 1972, and a year later the dressing rooms, situated just outside the ground became redundant as the new sturdy-looking building which straddles the half way line was erected. The ground passed into the hands of the Amber Valley Borough Council in 1974 but they agreed to the club sub-letting the ground when a new innovation hit town in 1985. Mansfield Marksmen Rugby League Club played a challenge match in October that year - the first ever professional Rugby League to be staged in Derbyshire - and for over two years used the ground, posting a record crowd of 1,579 against Hull for a Challenge Cup tie in February 1987.

Around this time, the dressing rooms were adorned with a 44 seat directors' box and this was roofed a year later as a players' lounge bar was opened in a renovated part of the dressing room complex.

It was a busy time at the ground, for Town had been elected into the Northern Premier League which meant a host of changes including re-furbishment of the Alma Street end cover as well as the floodlight pylons and extensions to the lounge bar and boardroom.

1994 saw possibly the biggest change at the Town Ground when the main stand, though only 1981 vintage, had begun to deteriorate and was replaced by a new covered terrace with seating increased to 200. The pitch perimeter, which Trevor Delaney described in his excellent *Grounds of Rugby League* as "a rickety rail fence" was renewed, as was the wall around the ground. Additional hard standing went down and the main entrance was re-built. The council's £12,000 grant went a long way towards the cost.

1995 saw more changes as the club aimed for the top division of the NPL, with concrete terracing behind each goal and an extension of the main stand to pitch length. North Street has gone from being a homely yet spartan place to a functional and accessible ground which has a capacity of 5,000 at present - more than adequate for today's 200 or so regulars.

Action at Alfreton in 1969 with the old covered enclosure in the background.

THE TOWN GROUND
Heanor Town FC

The dual-purpose ground on Mayfield Avenue in Heanor has seen football for over 100 years and cricket for even longer. Records reveal Heanor began around 1883 and within ten years had been accepted into the prestigious Midland League where they drew large crowds, including an estimated 10,000 supporters to watch an FA Cup tie with Bury.

The ground was given to the people of Heanor by the Miller-Mundy family around 1910 and it was in 1924 that the massive corrugated covered terrace was put up which still stands today, glowering down on the spectators below. The stand had to be licensed at a cost of 2/6d per year during its early days. Terracing was formed using railway sleepers from the Midland Road Station prior to this and the banking, now concreted, is still in use today. The original club went bankrupt in 1907 and did not reappear until four years later when they began working their way up again. Sadly, in 1937 the club again found itself overstretched and went under, this time for fourteen years until the current Heanor was formed. During these enforced absences the ground was still used from time to time, during the summer for cricket and in the winter by local junior sides. On returning to football Heanor played for a short while at the Sir John Warren Ground and the Midland Road Ground before returning to the Town Ground in 1953 where they have remained.

The Supporters' Club were instrumental in building the tea bar behind the Broadway goal in 1955 and this was used until 1994 when the canteen was transferred into the Social Club. At around the same time they also built the concrete terraced stand behind the Wilmot Street goal which gave cover to 1,500 until, following a landslip, the council removed the stand and replaced it with open grass banking and a scoreboard in a vain attempt to entice Derbyshire County Cricket Club to Heanor.

The current dressing rooms were opened on 7th March 1959 prior to the County Senior Cup semi-final with Ironville Amateurs. Being a shared ground, substantial improvements are limited although it was deemed good enough for the Northern Premier League to invite them to join as founder members; despite pressure from the Supporters' Club, they declined.

Since entering the Northern Counties (East) League there have been changes on the ground. A social club was built, the proceeds from which have helped finance the seating under the old stand, as well as re-furbishments to the dressing and boardrooms. But most importantly it helped to pay for the floodlights which were switched on by Bobby Charlton in 1985. Two years later the club moved to the Central Midland League.

Today, although both Heanor Town Cricket and Football Clubs are prospering they are holding each other back. The cricket club side of the ground is delightful, and beautifully manicured, even in deepest winter. The football side likewise; its entrance built into the vast brick wall which sweeps down The Broadway. The slightly rusting but quite wonderful 70-year old stand now has wooden seats installed, believed to be from Nottingham Forest, but the concrete cover at the Wilmot Street End has gone and is now open grass banking. If future plans go ahead, then the stand will be replaced by a modern complex with dressing rooms and board room, while the children's small play area will become a car-park. The cricket club would re-locate allowing the club to pursue promotion, currently unattainable due to the three-sided nature of the ground. Of the dual purpose sports grounds still in use in the higher echelons of the pyramid, the Town Ground must vie with Kingsway in Bishop Auckland as being the most scenic although, due to ground gradings, neither would get anywhere near the Conference, and more is the pity.

Below: A glorious view of Christchurch Meadows in Belper, taken from the neighbouring mill.

CHRISTCHURCH MEADOWS
Belper Town FC

The development of Belper's centrally-sited ground has been determined somewhat by natural events beyond their control, rather than by those serving the club in the 44 years since its re-formation. The Meadows, which include the local cricket club plus bowls and tennis is situated on a flood plain, which makes the building of anything substantial a tricky prospect to say the least. This has had a beneficial effect for those whose pleasures are gained by admiring what is a simple, yet beautiful, ground unspoilt by progress.

The early Belper side faded away, having played most, if not all their football, at the Acorn Ground, an undeveloped field with a fearsome slope which still exists as a boys' pitch. On reforming in 1951 Town moved into Christchurch Meadows which had previously been the home of a junior club Field Head FC. Although the cricket club next door was long-established, the football pitch was just that - a junior ground - and players were obliged to change in The Talbot pub.

The first structure was a wood and iron main stand which stretched two-thirds of the pitch length on the Mill Side of the ground. It was twice as deep as the current stand but was demolished in the early sixties when the mill was extended, and removed part of the land on which it stood. Some of the original stand was re-used in the building of the current main stand which runs from the halfway line to the corner flag and can seat 200 with perhaps a further 1,000 standing.

The first dressing rooms were erected in 1961 behind the stand and are still in use today, next to the small clubhouse which came along seven years later. The floodlights were switched on in 1980 and once the perimeter fencing was installed soon after, Belper Town had put themselves into a strong position. The closing in of the far end however has posed problems due to the river, but it is a small price to pay for continuing at The Meadows. The backdrop of Christchurch just to the left of the near goal, and the huge mill looking down on the pitch make it one of the best examples of an unspoilt town centre ground still in existence.

Ilkeston's Manor Ground near the end.

MANOR GROUND
Ilkeston Town FC

The saddest thing about the recent demise of Ilkeston's town centre ground is that it was never allowed to fulfill its potential in the way it deserved. Having survived for close on 100 years, like Church Litten, it gave way to a supermarket and the club departed to a flat-looking arena made up of a series of permanent porta-cabins.

Undoubtedly it appeared tatty with its assorted collection of fencing styles, rough unmade banking and glaring lack of flood-lighting, but it had a soul and that was ultimately snuffed out after the last game played there against mighty Great Wyrley in 1992.

The Manor Ground was originally built in 1893 with the help of miners during a strike. It initially had a cycle track around it which meant the corners were raised and indeed stayed that way right through to the 1960's. Various Ilkeston sides, including Town, United and plain FC, all used the ground which, throughout its life, was never able to have a clubhouse on site due to a covenant prohibiting the sale of alcohol. So much for being owned by the public house next door!

An old wooden stand eventually went up and survived until just before the Second World War when condemned and it was not replaced until 1957 by a brick and timber construction. Just prior to this a small shelter, soon extended and capable of covering 1,000 spectators, was erected opposite it on the bank. Sadly, gales took away part of this and the council completed the job in the 1970's leaving just the footings which intrigued new visitors right to the end. The mid-sixties saw the construction of an area of cover just to the side of the pub end goal and there were plans to terrace the whole ground soon after, although these never came to fruition. The biggest game ever seen at the Manor Ground

The entrance, constructed in 1951 for an FA Cup tie with Rochdale.

was an FA Cup 1st Round tie with Rochdale which attracted a ground record of 9,800, giving some indication of its size and potential. A new staircase and wooden entrance gate with turnstile was constructed in the pub car-park to allow easier access for the game, but to add to the problems the players were forced to change in the Welfare Club outside the ground as the changing rooms were deemed unacceptable by the opposition.

Certainly the lack of lights proved the ground's downfall and when the club left for pastures new the area was swiftly converted into a supermarket although the shape of the ground and the stairway from the pub still exists albeit without the need to go through a turnstile to get in!

The New Manor Ground in Awsworth Road will undoubtedly benefit the club immensely for its space and floodlighting render it acceptable for the Southern League in which the club currently play. It is built on the site of an old council rubbish dump and is concreted throughout, with an area of

cover at each end strangely designed like modern bicycle sheds, although youngsters are unlikely to be caught canoodling behind these as they have no back or sides. The seated area has room for 200 and the administration offices and club room are situated in a selection of permanently sited and brightly coloured red porta-cabins, which stretch all down the opposite side. Certainly plenty of space has been allowed to provide for expansion within the ground which is as neat and tidy as the old Manor was scruffy. Such is the affection still held for the old ground that two framed photographs of her hang on the walls of the boardroom and clubhouse emphasising the point that you can't have your cake and eat it.

Photos in this section by: James Bell, Pat Brunning, Andy Dakin, David Kirby, Dean Walton, James Wright and courtesy of Belper FC.

Nottingham

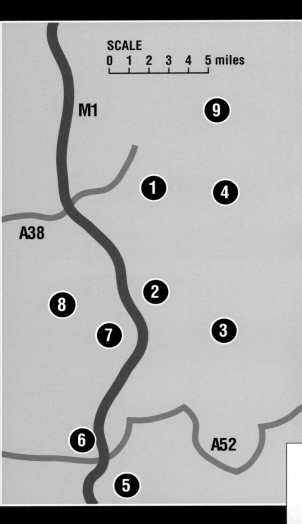

1	Ashfield United FC
2	Hucknall Town FC
3	Arnold Town FC
4	Blidworth Welfare FC
5	Long Eaton United FC
6	Sandiacre Town FC
7	Kimberley Town FC
8	Eastwood Town FC
9	Clipstone Welfare FC

THE THREE GROUNDS OF SUTTON TOWN...

Top: The race track, or Avenue Ground, pictured in 1947.

Middle: Priestic Road, sadly lost to a supermarket in the 1970s.

Bottom: Lowmoor Road, current home of Ashfield United as they are now known.

MUCH of Nottinghamshire was dominated by the coal industry with any number of Welfare schemes producing football grounds and clubs which survived until their pits closed. A number of others, Rainworth, Linby, Cotgrave, Thoresby, Bestwood, Bilsthorpe, Gedling, Ollerton, Welbeck and Calverton, all play in the strong Notts Alliance on former Welfare grounds.

There are three clubs in the Northern Counties (East), but only one in the higher grade of Northern Premier League since Ashfield United pulled out.

LOWMOOR ROAD
Ashfield United FC

Ashfield United are more universally recognised as Sutton Town, having been known by that name for over 100 years. They currently play on the old East Kirkby Miners Welfare Ground in Lowmoor Road which lay derelict for many years until resurrected by the club in 1978.

Prior to that move the club played on a number of grounds starting on a field by the Dog and Duck pub in the centre of Sutton-in-Ashfield close to Priestic Road. Next port of call was the New Cross Ground, also very close by and believed to have been no more than a pitch without facilities. In the time between the wars the club played on the Avenue Ground which stood in what was known as Cow Pasture Lane near the Potmakers Arms.

The first significant move in the club's long history came in 1951 when a ground in Priestic Road became available after Town had spent a couple of years at the Skegby Miners Welfare. At the time they enjoyed the help of a very active Supporters' Club who helped with maintenance and fund raising to get the ground up and running. Skegby Miners' Welfare had a large timber stand with separate dressing rooms and was banked all around to the extent that 6,000 people saw a game against Peterborough United in 1958 which was a record there. Sadly, the owner of the land cashed in and sold it to Fine Fare who built the inevitable supermarket, now owned by Asda.

In 1978 the club took over the ground owned by Portland Estates and once run as a Colliery Welfare. Its continued lack of use had rendered it derelict and much work was done to clear vegetation and prepare it for football. The wall which enclosed Priestic Road ground was re-erected and turnstiles put in place. Within three years the first stand was up and dressing rooms replaced those which stood in the old brick building just outside the ground.

In 1980 a record crowd at Lowmoor Road of nearly 2,000 saw Leeds United play a match to commemorate the new floodlights.

Since 1993 the club have been known as Ashfield United but, along with plans to cover the far side of the ground, they also ai, to revert to the name Sutton Town in a similar way that Forest Green Rovers backtracked, after a disastrous flirt with their alter ego Stroud FC.

WATNALL ROAD
Hucknall Town FC

Hucknall Football Club owes its existence to the miners who formed the club in 1946 through the Welfare Scheme, and began playing on a pitch in Wigwam Lane which had just a small hut for cover while the players changed in the No.2 Pit baths.

When the area was required for tipping, the Welfare moved to the current spot opposite what was No.1 Pit. Again the pit baths, situated where the adjacent petrol station is now, were used for changing with the pitch running parallel to the road, roughly where the clubhouse and car-park are today. After a couple of seasons the pitch was moved to its current position, with a second pitch separated from it by a cricket square. This arrangement continued until the by-pass took away a chunk of the grounds, brought the second pitch closer to the first, and spelt the end of the cricket.

The dual-purpose pavilion housing the tea bar and dressing rooms was put in place around 1962, while the little wooden stand which once perched precariously on the halfway line was removed when the impressive pitch-long covered terrace was built in 1990. As the club progressed from the Notts Alliance, the pitch was fenced off and a turnstile was installed, which came from the dismantled Fellows Park ground at Walsall. Notts County provided the seats which are now situated in the new stand.

Despite the work put in over recent years, there is a strong possibility the club may move across the road to the pit site - depending on what the underground investigations reveal - as the current ground is required for the obligatory supermarket. It may yet be the case that the ATC hut, which is now the club bar, will return from whence it originally came.

GRANGE PARK
Long Eaton FC

Grange Park gives the impression of being a lot older than it is, with bricked-up dressing rooms each end of the covered terrace on one side, and on the other, the current red brick structure with its more recent changing facilities underneath. But appearances can be deceptive as the ground was only developed as a senior football venue in 1957.

Previous Long Eaton clubs had played elsewhere, in particular Town, the forerunners of United who played just across the road on the now semi-derelict but still open speedway stadium. The entrance to the ground is past an indoor bowling green which was once a lido and the site of the original gateway. A long approach road circles the ground past a covered terrace with the original changing rooms at either end. Opposite this is a curious building with a high roof and loose standing underneath which looks for all the world as though it used to have seating at one time but apparently never has. Built three years after opening it has a small tea-bar on the side nearest a third construction which is shaped like half a Nissen hut and gives cover to 100 or so spectators. Slightly banked ends give a pleasing view should the spectator not be in need of cover at this unusual former Midland Counties League ground.

ST GILES PARK
Sandiacre Town FC

Sandiacre Town were formed as a youth team as recently as 1978. The senior side was established a year later and the ground at St Giles Park took shape soon after. Work started on the red brick club headquarters in 1982, and when the £40,000 project was completed it contained a function room with bar and dressing rooms. It was opened by Roy McFarland and the late Peter Taylor on 28th March 1984. The lack of pitch facilities held the club back at one stage and after missing a season they merged with Lace Web United.

Again in 1993 the ground was deemed unsuitable for the Central Midlands League and the club played for one season at Kilburn Welfare, which was not a success. However, with the building of the 300 capacity terraced cover and pitch barrier with hard standing, St Giles Park is again fir for this level of football.

Action from Hucknall showing the small stand which made way for a impressive covered terrace in 1990.

Arnold Town FC.

KING GEORGE V PLAYING FIELD
Arnold Town FC

The development of the main sports ground in Arnold since senior football was first played there in 1962 has been very gradual. It has always shared with cricket which adjoins the ground at the top end and, since the football club moved into the council-owned ground, the improvements have always been commensurate with whichever league the club has been in.

The story of football in Arnold is slightly complex and begins with Arnold St. Marys and Arnold Town who both played around the time of the First World War. They seem to have faded away, although St. Marys were reformed in 1928. They played in the Notts Alliance and later the Midland Counties League, where they were obliged to drop the St. Marys tag and become Arnold FC in 1963. A year earlier Arnold Kingswell were formed, playing their matches on a pitch in Church Lane before moving to another basic ground in Nottingham Road which is now used by Arnold Boys FC, and was about 300 yards from Gedling Road. Arnold FC played at the Calverton Road Rec from 1928 until 1957, and on Church Road ground for five years before moving to their current ground. The two teams merged in 1989.

Floodlighting came to the ground in 1981 by which time it was capable of holding nearly 4,000 people, as was proved in December 1967 when Bristol Rovers came to town in the First Round of the FA Cup.

WELFARE GROUND
Blidworth Welfare FC

Blidworth Welfare was first set up between the wars, but the current team only date from around 1980. The modern club re-built the ground in 1989 with a large shelter on the banking behind one goal and a seated stand for around 100 down one side. Floodlights were installed in 1990 just after the pit closed, a blow which also shut the huge Welfare building outside the ground.

A trust was set up in 1993 to run the new set-up as Blidworth consolidated on their bright start and, with the high banking that stretches around much of the old ground, there is plenty of scope, but this area has been badly hit by the destruction of the mining industry and crowds are unlikely to warrant any more wholesale changes.

CORONATION PARK
Eastwood Town FC

The delightful grounds of Coronation Park house the homely and old-fashioned ground of Eastwood Town FC. Formed in the year of the Coronation, Town played on a pitch which is now a bowling green just behind the bottom goal.

The newly re-named Coronation Park had an old farm-house within its grounds and this was used for changing until the relocation in the mid-sixties. The pitch had a steep grass bank around part of it, which still exists and a covered area all down one side, which went with the club when they moved a few yards up the hill in the mid-sixtie. The 1963-64 season saw the club move from the Notts Alliance to the Central Midlands League, and in 1971 a low wooden stand with seats was constructed down one side of the ground. Only part of that stand is still there, the rest succumbing to gale damage. Opposite the stand are the dressing rooms which are originals from the sixties and a clubhouse which has been steadily extended and altered since it first made an appearance in 1971 as a small shed. Terracing has been put down all around the pitch, and in 1993 part of it was covered when a new stand, which is a modern version of the old bowling green stand, was put up.

Coronation Park ground is classically simple, with plenty of cover and enough seating to accommodate an average crowd. With the ground criteria becoming stricter through as each season passes, it is unlikely that Eastwood Town will ever attain a greater height than the top division of the Northern Premier League without taking away the character that has developed in only thirty years.

Below: Eastwood Town's covered end.
Left: Just behind it in the park is the banking from the site of the old ground.

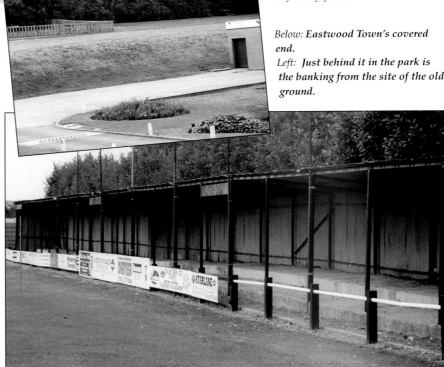

THE STAG GROUND
Kimberley Town FC

For some years Kimberley Town have been the younger brother to Eastwood Town and in a strange way the ground mirrors that. Today's Stag Ground is much the same as it always was, but now is fenced off from the rest of the park by chain-link topped by ugly barbed wire. Behind the near goal in a similar manner to Coronation Park is the town bowling green with a heavily fenced car-park nearby.

Surprisingly, for a football ground that is nearly seventy years old, the small section of cover in front of the bowling green is believed to be the only spectator facility there has ever been on The Stag. The remainder is post and railed off with a slight grass bank which slopes up to the pleasant gardens of the adjoining residences.

The ground was first opened in 1926 and used by Kimberley YMCA from 1947, although it was previously used by several minor clubs. The dressing rooms are vintage 1930's and before then players changed in the Stag Inn close by. The YMCA became Town in 1956 and are currently playing in the Central Midlands League.

LIDO GROUND
Clipstone Welfare FC

The mining village of Clipstone has been more fortunate than some, in that its pit was taken over by private enterprise and both it, and the Welfare, are thriving.

The football club echo the positive attitude and have recently moved up into the Central Midlands League after a highly successful last few seasons. The Lido Ground has been home to the Welfare Football Club since 1937 when they moved from their pit side pitch in Baulker Lane which was eventually used for tipping pit waste. The early days of the club, formed in 1928 as Clipstone Combine, were spent on a pitch at Bellfield's Farm, on the Mansfield Road, where the players changed in a barn. From there they moved first to Baulkers Lane where the changing rooms were in a stable, and then to the Welfare Ground.

They played on a pitch now home to rugby, using the adjacent cricket pavilion, and after the war, when the colliery created a football pitch by levelling the ground nearest the main road and adding a small shelter, they moved over. In the mid fifties, local people built a Lido to the left of the football ground which attracted huge crowds in the summer months and lasted until around 1990 when wear and tear demanded its closure and it was eventually filled in. The site now awaits use as a training area for the football club. Today's changing room building was built around 17 years ago for the Lido, but was taken over and converted, first into a canteen and then changing rooms.

Fenland

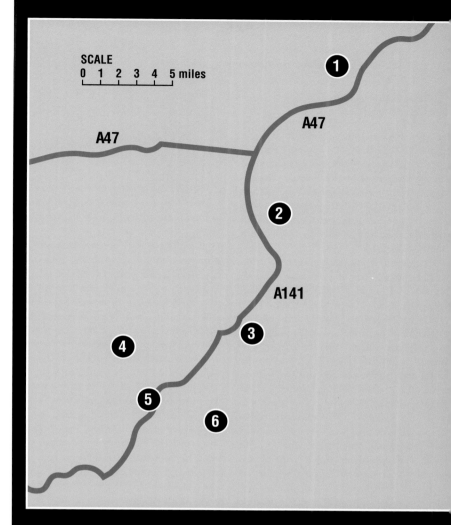

SCALE
0 1 2 3 4 5 miles

A47

A47

A141

1	Wisbech Town FC	4	Ramsey Town FC
2	March Town Utd FC	5	Warboys Town FC
3	Chatteris Town FC	6	Somersham Town FC

March Town United's gloriously garish old grandstand is very awkward to watch football from but wonderful to look at!

THE windswept flatlands of the Cambridgeshire Fens house a cluster of fascinating little football grounds dominated by the superb Fenland Park home of Wisbech. They are the only club to have played Southern League football, for twelve years up to 1970, and are well equipped to return, should they win the Eastern Counties League again to qualify.

FENLAND PARK
Wisbech Town FC

Fenland Park hosted Southern League football back in the 1960's and most certainly could do so now. With one or two neighbouring clubs under-achieving, Wisbech should easily have established themselves as the most senior club in East Anglia as far as playing status goes, but have elected to maintain their status quo in the Eastern Counties League.

Their ground, without question the finest in their league, has not been allowed to stagnate and boasts a smart modern stand that replaced the old structure in 1992.

The entrance to the ground at the back of a car-park is pure 1950's, with the bank of turnstiles and welcome sign prominent. The club's administration block, situated to the left on entering, is wooden and painted red as are all the other buildings dotted around the ground, which house club shops, tea-bars, and suchlike. The covered terrace behind the near goal was re-roofed recently, and is mirrored opposite by the far end cover. The cavernous Dutch barn which stretches down most of the far touchline has been used in the past to train under, and surely is unique in football with the possible exception of the cover at Christie Park, Morecambe, which is similar in shape but not quite as vast.

The ground, part of a four acre orchard purchased from a Mr. Bolton, was opened in 1947 with a match against Leicester City 'A', which Wisbech lost 3-2. The old stand from the club's previous ground at Harecroft Road and the hut which housed the dressing rooms were re-erected on the site of the new

Wisbech's huge cow-shed was, in fact, one of a pair of Dutch barns bought by a director for his farm in the fifties. As only one was required he donated this one to the club.

stand and have only been condemned and demolished within the last five years. The remainder of the ground consisted of grass banking for a year until the first cover, which still stands although now boasting a brick-built back and a new roof, was erected at the Learowe End. Two years later the opposite end cover was erected, and in 1957 the dressing rooms used today were built to the right of the Learowe End. The Dutch barn which is undoubtedly the focal point of the ground was purchased by a club director as one of a pair. As the director only required one, he donated the other to Fenland Park, where it was erected, the banking having been removed from that side of the ground. The canteen was originally a pigeon loft but is now a store room, and the boardroom came from a local aerodrome.

The ground has an official capacity of 7,500 but it is unlikely to be filled with anything approaching that number again although, in 1957, when Wisbech played Peterborough United in the Midland League, there was a record crowd of 8,044.

Wisbech have had three previous grounds. From 1920 they played at Wisbech Park, which still exists and where football continues to be staged, and then for a short

period at Walsoken Rectory field which is now a surgery, having once been the Turnpike Inn. The last ground before Fenland Park was at Harecroft Road, rented from a Mr. Overland and frequently water-logged. This ground boasted a stand and dressing rooms, both of which found their way to the new ground. After some years of non-use, however, that site has now been covered by a sports centre and swimming pool

GER SPORTS GROUND
March Town United FC

Just north of Chatteris is the larger town of March, which at one time was home to two senior clubs Town and G.E.R. United. The Railwaymen did not re-form after the war, and in 1946 March Town moved on to the ground, changing their name to March Town United in 1950.

March Town were formed some time in the 1880's, the official founding date is 1885, although there may be earlier records. Initially their football was played on pitches at Estover Road, Gaul Drove and Burrowmoor Road, until a Mr. Morton bequeathed the Avenue Ground for sport in 1923. It is still used by March Cricket Club. Town continued there until the first season back after the war when, with the GER ground vacant following the demise of the parent club, they moved in and have remained there ever since.

March GER United were playing on the GER ground in the early twenties when they bought it from the Grammar School by floating shares of £1 each. They had started life in 1911, playing at Elm Road, before moving to the sports ground, which was once known as Shepperson Fields. It regularly hosted sports days, which included tennis, bowls, cycling and, right up to 1960, cricket. Football commenced regularly in 1923 and shortly after the club built the still magnificent grandstand.

The old main stand at Fenland Park, Wisbech, was demolished around 1990.

Almost entirely wooden, and painted in bright yellow and blue, it is appreciated rather more by standing and looking than sitting in it and looking out! A maze of poles, pylons, and tannoys obstruct the view of the pitch which is some 15 yards from the stand due to the fact greyhound racing, and earlier sports events were held there until the track was grassed over leaving the pitch somewhat marooned in 1980.

The chicken-run on the far side of the ground dates from just after the war, and has been much altered by man and weather. The corrugated iron fence, complete with railway sleepers for fence posts, has also seen better days although it just about does a job. However, the old finishing line box has been upgraded and converted into a sponsors' lounge, a long low canteen building standing between it and the stand. The G.E.R. club itself stands just outside the ground by the entrance but is not connected to the football club. Approaching the ground from the town, the huge perimeter wall and rear of the stand look not unlike one or two of the old Northern Division Four grounds before they were spruced up or knocked down. Of all the non-League or sports grounds generally in use today, the GER ground must surely have been one of the most widely used.

Apart from more or less continuous football since the twenties, school sports days, galas, boxing, cycling, tennis, bowls, roller-skating, cricket, and greyhound racing have all been seen at Robingoodfellows Lane. It is sad that a ground with such a history is now host to football crowds of a hundred or less - maybe once a week - when 7,500 people crammed in to see an FA Cup tie with Kings Lynn in 1956. The positive side is that the sports ground and the marvellous main stand are still there to visit, admire and for all enthusiasts to enjoy.

WEST STREET
Chatteris Town FC

The fenland town of Chatteris has boasted a football club since 1920, when the Town side played their early games at Chatteris Park and Chatteris Recreation Ground, both of which are still in existence.

The current ground, just off the town's by-pass to the south, is a credit to the club, considering their desperate playing record of the early 1990s.

The main stand is a square-shaped building with steeply-tiered seats straddling the half-way line, and is vaguely similar to Devizes Town's stand which sadly bit the dust in 1994, although much newer looking. The rest of that side of the ground is open and somewhat windswept, with other pitches and a training ground behind the stand. Adjacent to the main stand is a smaller, much older-looking covered area, containing various benches and kitchen chairs with one step of terracing. The clubhouse and changing

Ramsey Town FC.

rooms to the left of the Town End goal are well designed and at first glance the building could easily be taken for sheltered accommodation, such is the architecture. An overhang provides more cover and a pleasing C.T.F.C, is picked out in light-coloured brick in the walling. The ground was first used sometime between the wars and during the Second World War was West Ham United's base when away from London. The main stand is believed to have been built around 1951, as was the small cover opposite, and the footings of the original changing rooms can be still be seen in the car-park just inside the gate. They were wooden, one per team, with a tea hut next door but were swept away when the dressing room and clubhouse went up in the mid-'70s. The field behind the main stand, originally segregated from the pitch by a hedge which was removed when the stand was built, was bought by the club in the early sixties from the Shepherds Society and transformed into pitches.

FORGE WAY
Warboys Town FC

The neighbouring towns of Ramsey and Warboys have football grounds which have many similarities, although the two sides play in different leagues.

The sports field in Forge Way has always been home to the football club, although cricket has been played there post-war, after the original field was almost doubled in size. The entrance has always been roughly where it is now, although Forge Way was originally fields with a pub called the Ship Inn, where the players changed. Around 1948, an old War Department hut from a local aerodrome was put in for changing, and is still used today, although vastly modified with a brick shell and extensions for social functions.

Although they had a spell in the United Counties League in the fifties, the club were playing in the Peterborough League until the late eighties, with the result that vast ground improvements were not necessary. The only main change was the small shelter on the half-way line made from iron and railway sleepers which had cost £100 when built in 1960. Currently there seems a grave danger the old girl may be swept away to be replaced by a brick structure, although another school of thought is that she may be re-sited behind one goal. The ground is shared with cricket which means one side is

open while the other three sides received a permanent barrier as recently as 1993 when the ground was floodlit for the second time, the first set going up for training purposes in the fifties.

CRICKETFIELD LANE
Ramsey Town FC

Ramsey share their ground with the cricket club as they have done since the thirties. Their early days were spent on a basic pitch marked out on the golf links before a move to Mill Lane between the wars.

The dual purpose ground they have now is delightful, with a cricket pavilion at the far end and the football clubhouse in one corner. A small covered area for a few dozen souls is flanked by dug-outs either side of the half way line and is of indeterminate age. A new post and rail system, floodlights, and advertising hoardings all give the ground a more football-like feel. With no hard standing and a 1,000 capacity, the Cricketfield Lane ground is never going to go very far up the pyramid, but is a pleasant home for all that.

WEST END GROUND
Somersham Town FC

Somersham's current ground was bought and transformed from farm land around 1960 after the club had played on a recreation ground close by. The early changing facilities in a pre-fabricated hut were spartan, and it wasn't until the early 70's that the first small stand was built, the pitch having been turned 45 degrees from its original site.

The main improvements have occurred since 1981 when the ground was purchased and the clubhouse opened. Since then a new changing room block has been added, a kitchen installed in 1985, and a post and rail fence erected four years later.

The 1990's have seen further developments with new stands either side of the half-way line and floodlights erected. These were first used during a Hinchingbrooke Cup match against Potton United on April 9th 1991 and officially opened the following November with a match against Norwich City which attracted the record attendance at the ground to date of 538.

Photos in this section by: Gavin Ellis-Neville.

Lincolnshire

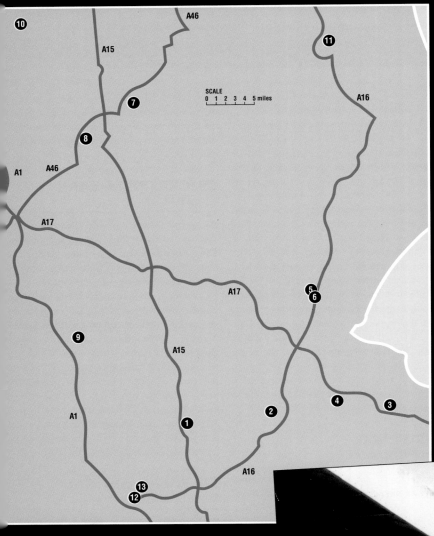

THE sprawling county of Lincolnshire is home to the best of the traditional non-League football grounds, at York Street, Boston. Whilst there have been a number of newer grounds which are more advanced, mainly in out of town areas where space is not a problem, and one or two which are historically of more interest, York Street is far and away the finest of the town centre grounds that have been developed without the aid of millionaires or finances generated by selling off bits from here and there.

Apart from Boston, whose under-achievement has meant the club have never reached the Football League although they should have done, the county does have a former League side in Gainsborough.

YORK STREET
Boston United FC

York Street is without question the finest traditional non-league ground in the country and has been since the club embarked on their radical re-building of the ground after failing to gain admission to the Football League behind Wigan Athletic.

The name of Boston United first appeared in 1934, but football had been established since the late 1800's when there were two clubs operating in the town. Swifts had their headquarters and dressing rooms at the Coach and Horses public house just opposite the pitch, whereas Town used a different pub, The Indian Queen, which was

1	Bourne Town FC
2	Spalding United FC
3	Long Sutton Athletic FC
4	Holbeach United FC
5	Boston Town FC
6	Boston United FC
7	Nettleham FC
8	Lincoln United FC
9	Grantham Town FC
10	Gainsborough Trinity FC
11	Louth United FC
12	Stamford AFC
13	Mirrlees Blackstone FC

much further away from the Main Ridge Ground.

The two pitches were in fact end to end and out of town, but by the early 1900's the Town boasted a small grandstand and had a rope around the pitch.

After the Great War the Swifts did not re-form and their ground reverted back to meadow land which vanished under a housing development in the late 1960's. The 1930's saw the club struggle, but following a public meeting it was re-formed under the leadership of Ernest Malkinson who stayed for over 50 years.

The ground by then had gained entrances and dressing rooms at the west end and was known as Shodfriars Lane, as indeed it still is in some quarters. Around this time the original long wooden main stand was built complete with eight sets of seats and a paddock in front. Opposite was a roughly asphalted terrace which was covered a little later and stretches right along Spayne Road. The changing rooms were situated behind the Town End which had its own entrance in Shodfriars Lane, and these were in use until the mid-sixties when new ones were built under the York Street stand. Most of Shodfriars Lane has been engulfed by the by-pass and the old dressing rooms and entrance are now under the adjacent Gliderdrome. The York Street stand went up around the mid-fifties and other than interior changes has altered little. The club's first floodlights were installed and played under in 1955 when some 10,000 saw the initial evening game against Corby Town

After a brief period when financial hardship meant a return to local football, improvements were gradually made throughout the sixties, and when the Northern Premier League was founded in

1968 York Street was deemed good enough for the club to become founder members. Sadly, when the Football League beckoned the reverse was true and, determined not to miss out again, the directors launched various fund raising schemes designed to generate the cash to completely re-build the ground and work started in 1978. The team continued playing whilst the building went on around them, starting with the Spayne Road side which was re-built and covered. The superb Town End covered terrace was next followed by the full length main stand in 1981. Indeed United's FA Cup run the previous year had culminated in a home match against Rotherham United being played in front of a building site where the main stand was going to be.

With new lights, turnstiles, toilet blocks, refreshment buildings and terracing, York Street had been transformed. It took the best part of ten years and drained the coffers to the detriment of the playing strength, but today's ground is the envy of virtually all the pyramid clubs and many League clubs. Its relative closeness to the town centre has not proved a problem, unlike many grounds whose proximity has spelled an impasse.

The oldest part of the ground is the York Street stand which has seats above a paddock and houses the changing rooms which lead onto the pitch through an unobtrusive cage by the side of the goal. The Spayne Road side terrace is around 15 steps deep, is fully covered for the whole length and stretches around to the Town End terrace, a superb steep covered kop which replaced a slightly smaller banked but uncovered kop in the early eighties.

The classic simplicity of the Main Stand complements the rest of the ground with its unobstructed views and steeply-set seating.

What sets York Street above most others is that the complete re-building was undertaken on the original site, with no grant-aided help and without selling it off and moving to some soulless industrial estate five miles away.

The one tiny blemish at an otherwise delightful venue is the 1982-vintage security fence which was put in place for the FA Cup tie with Sheffield United. Mercifully it only stretches along the Town End and, unlike the monstrosities at places such as Merthyr, Bangor and, to a lesser extent Telford, does not intrude a great deal.

Boston United is undoubtedly the finest of the town centre non-league grounds. It is a shame that it has, as yet, not hosted League football.

TATTERSHALL ROAD
Boston Town FC

The junior of the two Boston clubs has had an interesting last two or three years, with a run to the FA Vase semi-final which brought one of the biggest ever gates at Tattershall Road, a change of name from Boston FC to Boston Town (quite possibly due to the club persistently being mistaken for United just up the road), and the building of a third stand to further upgrade their 32 year old ground.

The club was formed in 1963 following a breakaway of personnel from Boston United and they began playing on a park pitch in Roseberry Avenue before moving to what was a farmer's field in 1963. A boundary fence was erected and an old stand was bought and transported from Heckington Agricultural Show Ground and placed along side the pitch which, for the first season, ran at right angles to its present position. The clubhouse was built soon after the move and, having turned the pitch, a further stand of similar design was built two years later.

More recently the clubhouse has been extended and dressing rooms re-built on the same site.

Today, the ground is surrounded by open land and is reached via a large car-park. The clubhouse and dressing rooms are all behind one goal and the new stand is to the left. Behind the far goal is the show ground stand which is possibly one of the most ricketty structures anywhere in football, but nevertheless quite delightful. It should have a preservation order slapped on it at once before Lord Justice Taylor remembers the whereabouts of Boston! The slightly younger, but almost equally gnarled, main stand has a clock (the hands of which at the time of writing had stuck at twenty minutes past two) precariously balanced on the roof. On the basis that it is right twice a day, it is therefore better than no clock at all.

CARTER PARK
Holbeach United FC

Carter Park, home of Holbeach United is just a small part of a large, beautifully-kept municipal park, bequeathed to the town by a Mr. Carter and used as a centre for cricket, tennis and football ever since. In the early days the pitch ran lengthways, but it was soon switched to its present position. The superb old wooden stand now hidden from the main road by the various club rooms, was erected at the time the park was laid out around 70 years ago and has given sterling service ever since.

Today the ground is little changed in shape, with only the modern changing rooms and clubhouse added. The whole area is verdant with trees and bushes behind one goal and a high hedge shielding tennis courts behind the other. The far side is open due to the continued presence of cricket and this has been a major factor in the club's investigation of the possibility of acquiring an enclosed ground to facilitate progress.

The joy here, should the club be successful, is that Carter Park would remain in situ for the club runs several sides, and the agreement of Mr. Carter's many years ago which demanded that sport must be played there, means there will be no supermarkets built on Carter Park.

ABBEY LAWN
Bourne Town FC

Bourne Town's only two grounds in their long history stand next to each other separated by a tarmac pathway. The club played on the cricket ground until just after the Second World War, using a local pub called the Black Bull to change in, before moving across to an adjacent strip of land next to the embankment of the railway line which went to Spalding.

The new ground took some while to develop as the club came out of the Peterborough League and into the United Counties, but eventually a clubhouse made of timber and brick was built. It contained changing rooms and was behind a small wooden enclosure on the half-way line. The larger modern stand was built in 1979, the original having been gutted by fire, and another enclosure was built alongside it. Behind the railway end goal is a grass bank which gave enough elevation for some 3,000 people to see the FA Trophy match in 1970 with Chelmsford City.

LONDON ROAD
Long Sutton Athletic FC

The London Road home of Long Sutton Athletic has had football of varying standards played on it since the park was opened in 1911. The current club, formed in the eighties proved to be the most successful until surprisingly returning to the Peterborough and District League during the summer of 1995. They dominated that league, joined the Eastern Counties set-up when the Second Division was created and appeared to have taken over the mantle of 'small village made good' from Parson Drove United, who started an irreversible downward slide around the time Athletic came to prominence.

Surprisingly, the ground had never enjoyed spectator facilities until the tiny stand was constructed to comply with league rules in 1988. The large wooden building behind it formed the original changing room complex, and is now used as a store. The clubhouse was first built around 1990 and has been extended more recently. At the time of writing the pitch is enclosed by temporary crowd control barriers. The left-hand boundary has a high chain link fence and an impressive line of mature trees skirting the driveway next door. The largest project so far undertaken by the club was the installation of floodlighting in 1990.

MULSANNE PARK
Nettleham FC

Nettleham were first formed in 1905 and played on a pitch in the neighbouring village of Grange de Lings, changing in the local pub. After the Second World War the club began playing on Bill Bailey's Field, in Scothern Road, at first using the White Hart to change in before rudimentary dressing rooms were knocked up.

As the village expanded during the seventies, a new playing field was called for, and eventually Mulsanne Park was created, being

Boston FC, now Boston Town, on the day of their FA Vase semi-final with Taunton Town. The stand came from Heckington Agricultural Show ground.

Nettleham FC with the club initials picked out in the brickwork.

comfortable ground, built from scratch in just ten years, improved again the following season when a 280-seater stand was erected opposite the existing one, bringing the seated capacity close to the club's next aim, which was the Northern Premier League. At the same time, came a moment in the ground's history when the old wooden cover, then known as the Roberts Stand, was pulled down and replaced by a new structure which stretches the width of the playing area and can keep over 1,000 people dry. With the concreting of areas all around the entrance and the provision of terracing, Ashby Avenue continues to develop without over-stretching itself and is a credit to those who have worked so hard during the last dozen years.

named after the French town with which Nettleham is twinned. Three pitches were laid out and a clubhouse with dressing rooms opened, catering for cricket and tennis as well. On leaving the Lincolnshire League for the Central Midlands League, the roped-off pitch was inadequate and so a post and rail was put around the bottom pitch of the three with hard standing.

On promotion two years later the ground was enclosed and a small stand with 120 seats built. Floodlighting has since gone in, acquired from Gresley Rovers FC.

ASHBY AVENUE
Lincoln United FC

Lincoln United Football Club were formed just prior to the Second World War as Lincoln Amateurs and this remained their name until an ex-professional was signed in 1954. The first season was spent at the Skew Bridge ground, a barren outpost devoid of any facilities and regularly waterlogged.

The site is now partly taken by a corporation tip and partly by a new loop-line for the railway. After the war the club moved to the beautifully kept Co-operative ground in Skellingthorpe Road which was home until United moved out of local league football

and into the Yorkshire League. The Co-op was shared with cricket and had a large pavilion at one end which was used by both. Sadly, it is now under Tritton Road.

As Lincoln had no ground for the new season, the Hartsholme Cricket Club generously gave their permission to play on the outfield which they used for some fifteen years, changing in the cricket pavilion. The pitch ran lengthways on the far side of the ground and had a small wooden shelter behind one goal. On securing the use of one of the corporation pitches next door in 1982, the club took the stand with them and erected it behind the far goal at their new ground which was swiftly segregated from the rest of the area. Continuing to change in the pavilion they then, with extensive help through loans and grants, erected floodlighting and added another small brick stand which straddles the half-way line.

A post and rail went round the pitch and in 1991, after their epic trip to the First Round of the FA Cup, they were able to build the impressive new dressing room complex which stands behind the near goal. Within a year it had been extended with a boardroom and secretary's office and these were officially opened in August 1992.

What was already an impressive and

SOUTH KESTEVEN SPORTS CENTRE
Grantham Town FC

It has become something of a sporting cliche to deride a club's new ground, and brand it as a soulless concrete city, or a hastily thrown-together set of goals with a few seats under sheets of corrugated iron. Certainly several grounds built in the last decade have not been over-burdened with architectural brilliance, nor indeed with a great deal to placate the regular supporter by way of viewing comfort. If the casual visitor also has to suffer an eight-lane running track with field event equipment thrown in, most initial reactions would be to avoid it like the plague.

It is therefore most pleasing to report that Grantham Town Football Club's new home has successfully managed to merge the aforementioned athletics with the football, without the latter looking uncomfortable and out of place.

The stadium was opened in October 1991, having been built on The Meres, a council playing field in Trent Road, to the south of the town. It is an impressive venue, with a large car-park in front of the turnstiles. To the left of these is situated the main entrance with the stadium's administrative offices, club shop and changing rooms under the stand and the splendidly lively clubhouse on the next level.

Inside the ground, as befits a new arena, everything is brightly-coloured and spick and span, with stairways going in all directions leading to the terracing, up to the back of the stand and down to track-side. On each side of the stand, steeply-angled terracing has been provided and, to the front, the enclosure is also seated. The rows of seats provided for the judges on the athletics finishing line are curiously popular, as is the large covered terrace opposite to the stand, which is reminiscent of many French stadia. Initially, the terrace was to be uncovered but the football club, who had a major say in the outcome, won their case, and that one battle possibly saved the stadium from being an

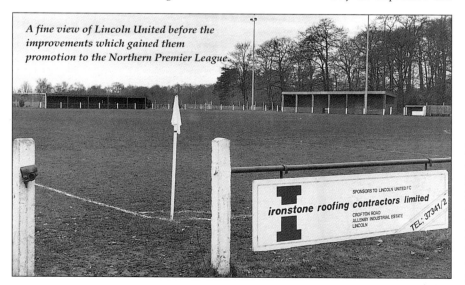

A fine view of Lincoln United before the improvements which gained them promotion to the Northern Premier League.

Above: The wide open spaces of Grantham's old London Road ground.
Right: The new stadium, thoughtfully provided with a steep covered terrace.

athletics track with a pitch in the middle, as is Cwmbran, and transformed it into an all-purpose ground to be enjoyed by all factions.

Grantham's vacated London Road ground was as far removed from the South Kesteven Sports Centre as it is possible to get, but nevertheless it was homely, if a touch shop-soiled on its demise. Owned by Buckmaster Estates, it was leased to the cricket club who sub-let it to the football club. They, in turn, were safe in the knowledge that the ground would not be developed until a site had been found for them. The ground had been a sporting venue long before football arrived as the cricket club had tenancy and soccer was a much later introduction on the northern side.

The early days before the club briefly folded, were spent on the ground, and a rival Grantham Avenue, took over at London Road. However, a re-formed Grantham FC returned to the fold, vacating their only other home, which stood tight against the mainline railway, and is now the site of a school in Hunting Tower Road. To this day banking can be seen by the side of the railway, where there was an excellent vantage point.

The London Road ground remained undeveloped, with cricket, bowls, and football all sharing the site which at the time was much larger, the bowls eventually becoming segregated. Facilities arrived in the form of a dual-purpose seated stand, to the right of the London Road goal, and a long chicken run extended down the north touch-line, not dissimilar to that at Gresley Rovers' Moat Ground. A rough area then led to a large covered terrace behind the far goal which looked out to open spaces on its left, where the cricket outfield began, in a similar way to that at Stourbridge's War Memorial ground.

The administration offices close to the entrance, were formerly stables for a local brewery and the back wall is the only surviving remnant of a sports ground which has existed in one form or another for over 150 years.

WOTHORNE ROAD
Stamford AFC

The endearing aspect of Stamford's fine, unpretentious ground is its determination to hang on to the past without completely ignoring the present.

A stunning Georgian market town, Stamford boasts seven church spires, most of which are visible from the pitch. Wothorne Road's ancient wooden main stand, even older stone walls and magnificent views across the valley, suitably complement it.

It is Stamford AFC's only ground, and 100 years old, being one of several sporting venues owned by Lord Burghley and protected as such. The focal point is the main stand, wooden with a breeze-block and brick frontage and a deckle-edged fascia, believed to date from around the turn of the century. It is one of the oldest stands still in existence. The original dressing rooms behind it are still in use, as are the bench seats arranged on small concrete blocks. Around twenty years ago it was extended to accommodate standing spectators, and mercifully the extension is in the same design and blends perfectly with the old girl who still does a sterling job protecting customers from the biting winds that can sweep across the valley.

Both ends are open and have a slightly sloping grass bank which may well have been somewhat steeper in the early days, while the railway side has a covered enclosure stretching from the half-way line to the goal line. Many moons ago this covered the whole of the side, but one half was taken down as a safety precaution. The clubhouse, opened in 1975, looks out over the pitch as does the club shop which was once the boardroom. The floodlights were bought and erected in 1981, primarily on the proceeds of the second of the club's three visits to FA Vase finals at Wembley. The record attendance at Wothorne Road is around 4,200 to see the FA Cup 3rd Qualifying Round tie against Kettering Town which ended 3-3. The Daniels must have rued the result, for the replay was lost 12-0!

PARK AVENUE
Louth United FC

The current Louth side dates back to 1947, when two Louth sides, Nats and Town, merged prompted by the formation of the Lincolnshire Football League.

The seven acres of land on which Park Avenue stands were purchased by public subscription from the people of the town. It has a concrete, glass-fronted pavilion, with covered standing in front and was formerly a seated stand, complete with three tiers of cinema seats until, in 1982, it was vandalised and the club converted the building into a new clubroom which overlooks the pitch. An extremely plush amenity, it looks out over two pitches, the main one with full strength lights and an adjacent training pitch.

In its original state, the stand was opened by Nat Lofthouse in the early sixties. The ground record attendance at Park Avenue was set in 1990 when 3,200 saw the team take on Derby County in a friendly.

NORTHOLME
Gainsborough Trinity FC

The Northolme is one of the oldest dual sports grounds in the country, having staged cricket, and later football, since the 1850's. During the early 1860's, several cricket clubs were formed who also chose to take up football during the winter .

Pringle Hill and the Moreton Terrace Ground, as well as Trentbridge were all used for both games, and were later occupied as temporary homes by Trinity, when the Northolme was unavailable. The new game of Association Football caught the imagination of the public and, as early as 1884, 4,000 packed in to watch the Lincolnshire Cup tie with Grimsby. At the end of that season, a few games were played at the Middlefield Ground, and soon after extensive improvements were made to Northolme which was already an enclosed ground. Within a dozen years the club had progressed to the Midland League and, to their surprise, in the 1896-97 season their hopeful application to join the Football League was accepted. Their top flight tenure was not smooth, further hindered by having to vacate the ground in August and May for the cricket. On one occasion the last home game was transferred to the Bowling Green Ground in Ropery Road, and sheeting had to be erected, courtesy of the Agricultural Society, in order to enclose the playing area and take a gate.

1910-11 season was the last at the Northolme in the Football League, and the club returned to the Midland League. Throughout the Great War the ground was used by a side called Trinity Institute, until

LINCOLN ROAD GROUND
Mirrlees Blackstone FC

The club and ground owe their existence to the Rutland Engineering Works, formerly in Broad Street, who bought the site in 1920. It was then laid out to provide for two football pitches and a cricket square but the football side had little or no facilities until around fifteen years ago when the current wooden stand was built.

The first major change at the ground was the demise of organised cricket in the late seventies which eventually allowed the owners to sell off the land behind the far goal - where the second team pitch was - for housing. A new clubhouse was built in 1965, around the same time as the old cricket pavilion was removed; it used to be sited just down from where the stand is now. As the club progressed and became Blackstone and later Mirrlees, a further extension to the clubhouse was planned and went ahead in 1984. Floodlights were installed in 1989 along with a perimeter fence, various tea huts and referees' rooms and these have all added to the development of Lincoln Road.

The loss of the land behind the far goal has benefited the ground, giving it a more enclosed feel. With a symmetrical line of trees either side, and the clubhouse and bowling green opposite, it is a comfortable site, although possibly lacking in some hard standing. The parent company pulled out of the town and the ground is now leased from BTR Ltd. Although the immediate future of the site is not threatened, there is muted a possible name change to Stamford Stones FC.

the club re-formed and took over again. At this time, Northolme was an imposing sports ground, oval-shaped and entirely fenced in. At first there was nothing more than a small shelter to keep the elements at bay, and with no changing rooms, the players had to make use of the Sun Inn. Many alterations occurred at the ground before the turn of the century, not least a 200-seater grandstand on the south side of the ground, and a post and rail surrounding the playing area. Much later a standing covered enclosure was added opposite, at the cessation of cricket. For their last season in the league a new stand was erected which replaced the first one, and these

remained until the Second World War when both were burnt down by vandals. In September 1930 the Supporters' Club terraced the Gasworks End, which was under a covered enclosure at the time, and soon after the War the Victory Stand, capable of holding 300 spectators, was built on the north side, on what had been the cricket outfield. The club by now had abandoned any plans to return to the Football League and had settled in the strong Midland League, slowly terracing the ground, and erecting a concrete perimeter fence.

Nowadays, the outside wall has been re-aligned behind the grandstand, and it is difficult to visualise the Northolme as a former cricket ground. The present capacity is put at 7,500, a far cry from the more liberal days when there was allegedly room for 20,000, should that many ever attend. It is unlikely that the record crowd of over 9,500 which turned up to see a Midland League game against Scunthorpe United in 1948 will ever be even remotely threatened. More sinister however, is the worry that this historic old ground is coveted by that old enemy the developers. It may not be the prettiest ground in the country, but it is one of the most interesting historically, and should be enjoyed for all that.

Gainsborough Trinity's Northolme.

Photos in this section by:
Gavin Ellis-Neville, Dean Walton, Dave West, James Wright and courtesy of the Grantham & Melton Trader.

Norfolk & North Suffolk

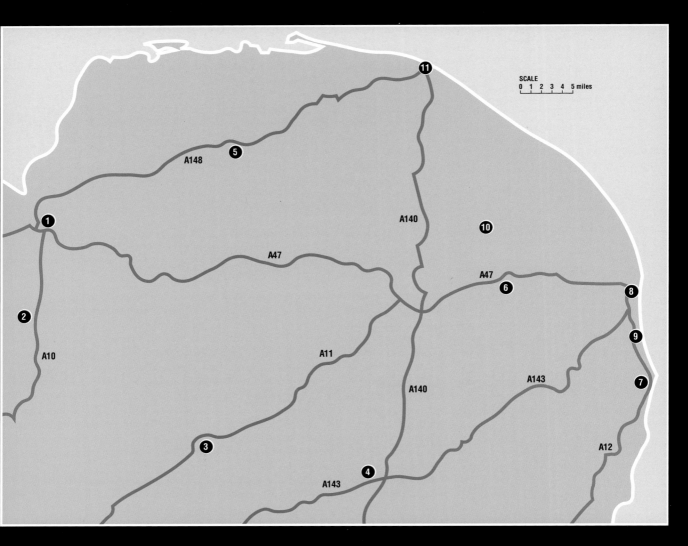

1 **Kings Lynn FC**
2 **Downham Town FC**
3 **Thetford Town FC**
4 **Diss Town FC**
5 **Fakenham Town FC**
6 **Norwich United FC**
7 **Lowestoft Town FC**
8 **Great Yarmouth Town FC**
9 **Gorleston FC**
10 **Wroxham FC**
11 **Cromer Town FC**

The popular Shed End at Fakenham's tight ground.

THE northern part of East Anglia is awash with a multitude of small villages, many of whom have clubs playing in the Anglian Combination and the less well-known North East Norfolk League. Geographical problems dictate that only a sprinkling seriously hanker after Eastern Counties, and ultimately Southern League, football. Those already there are in the main on old grounds, apart from Diss Town who moved in the eighties, and Norwich United.

THE WALKS
Kings Lynn FC

Although the capacity of the Walks Stadium is listed as being over 8,000 it is unlikely any more than half that number would be allowed into Kings Lynn's next big game. This is a deep contrast to the biggest crowd ever seen there when, in 1951 a massive 13,500 saw the Linnets lose an FA Cup tie to Exeter City, having put out four East Anglian sides in the qualifying rounds. The club celebrated this the following season by erecting the covered enclosure opposite the old wooden main stand which seated nearly 500 people.

At that point the Walks was at its most developed stage, having been the home of Kings Lynn Football Club since 1879 and of football in general for around ten years before that. The ground was first fenced off after Lynn's FA Cup tie at Aston Villa which they lost 11-0, but which brought in the sum of £260, back in 1907. The changing facilities were spartan and eventually consisted of a hut in a field by the Tennyson Road End which survived until the old wooden stand was rebuilt in 1956 complete with dressing rooms and clubhouse. The stand is virtually unchanged today and is on similar lines to those at Cheltenham, Chorley and Morecambe but without the portholes looking out from the front wall. The smaller stand opposite was stripped of its seats in the late sixties when they were sold to Hereford United and is now a covered enclosure. Both ends have been re-fenced in recent years with the Tennyson End completed in 1989 and the Hospital End three years later.

One of the more unusual matches at the Walks occurred just over 100 years ago when Lynn played a home fixture against Wisbech under lights to raise money for an old people's party. Over 1,000 people turned up to see the game which was illuminated by four bulbs placed in each corner and run by a kind of generator. The brown ball was whitewashed but was only visible when close up, and the experiment was not tried again. Some 70 years later the club installed its first full lighting system and celebrated by beating Cambridge City 4-0 in the first game. The lights were re-vamped in 1992.

In some curious way, The Walks mirrors the football club itself as being a bit of an

Above: Action from The Walks around 1950 showing the open terraces.
Below: The main stand at Kings Lynn, similar in design to those at Cheltenham, Morecambe and Chorley but without the portholes.

under-achiever. The prospects for both are good and with a little more ambition both could progress to the standard they deserve.

For a while after the Second World War Kings Lynn were joined in senior football by a team called South Lynn who played in the Peterborough League on an undeveloped ground on Pullover Road, just off the Wisbech Road, an area now covered primarily by housing. They entered the FA Cup for two seasons beating Wimblington Old Boys in their only win in three matches, but are now defunct.

BARONS HALL LAWN
Fakenham Town FC

The dual-purpose sports ground at Barons Hall was already in use when Fakenham Town moved there in 1907. They had been playing since their inception in 1884 at Hempton Green which saw a crowd top 2,000 for a Good Friday game with Holt FC before a move in 1889 to the more enclosed and central Star Meadow ground.

Barons Hall has always been shared with cricket, and the pitch at one time faced at right angles to its current position which meant the wicket was in the centre circle. This was obviously unsatisfactory and it was eventually re-sited lengthwise along the road, involving the sad destruction of an avenue of mature trees. The cricket club pavilion stood in the bottom right hand corner of the ground to the left of the current one and sufficed as changing facilities until the club built their own, roughly where the modern ones are today. When the two clubs pooled resources and raised £30,000 for a new pavilion it was believed to be the beginning of great things for the club. However, in order to comply with more stringent ground regulations as progress was made on the pitch, they needed to completely renovate the wooden building which stood where the old dressing rooms were, the pavilion being sited too far away from the pitch.

Since promotion to the Premier of the Eastern Counties League more changes have been made with the addition of two small stands. Both have seating courtesy of the nearby Sculthorpe Air Force base with one containing skeleton-type arrangement for children on the side which once overlooked the baseball diamond at the same establishment.

Nowadays the ground comes alive on matchdays with a noisy home crowd gathered under the shed behind the town end goal. Sadly, as is the case at so many grounds, in particular the Town Ground at Heanor, the cricket and football clubs are restricting each other. So much so that Barons Hall Lawn's days are numbered. The sale of the ground and the splitting of the proceeds is imminent and a move to two as yet undisclosed sites in the town to enable the football club to expand is inevitable.

When Barons Hall goes, a uniquely atmospheric little ground will be lost for good.

WAR MEMORIAL GROUND
Downham Town FC

The sports ground at Downham Market was created in 1947 as a permanent memorial to those who fell in the Second World War. The club's modest standing at the time dictated that no more than a pitch and a small cover were needed, and this remained the case for many years with players changing in an asbestos hut situated on the site of today's tennis courts.

The splendid RB Haynes pavilion was opened in April 1979 and now houses changing rooms and club bar. Behind the far goal is the municipal swimming bath which encloses that end. The field is very open and difficult to administer when collecting gate money and was even more so until a fence was built alongside the stand to segregate the adjoining rugby pitch. Promotion from the Peterborough League meant the pitch being barriered-off around three sides with the fourth roped due to the cricket square. In 1990 floodlights appeared, and these were officially switched on some three years later with a visit from Arsenal who won 14-1 in front of the record attendance at the ground.

Downham's early days were spent at a ground in Rouses Lane, now the site of a youth club, and around the turn of the century at the Howdale ground which was, and still is, common land.

During daylight the ground is pleasant but unexciting, but at night is transformed under one of the best lighting systems at this level of the pyramid. When the attendant mature trees overlooking the playing area are illuminated it gives the ground a most compact feel.

MUNDFORD ROAD
Thetford Town FC

The Recreation Ground has been home since 1905, Thetford Town having originally played on pitches at Abbey Heath until 1900, and alongside the river on meadow land for five years. The ground is part of a large sports complex, but is fully enclosed by a vast chain link fence which slews drunkenly in areas where it has been in receipt of unwanted attention.

There are two stands; the main stand, which looks the younger of the two, was built in 1946 and can seat 400 whilst the other, a wonderful old corrugated tin affair, is of uncertain age but has certainly done sterling service. To the right of the main stand is what looks like an old cricket pavilion, possibly a throw-back to when the ground was jointly used and the football was not segregated.

The floodlights were first installed in 1988 and have since been updated, to a lux value of 214. Mundford Road is a fascinating place which has enjoyed precious little good fortune in recent times but deserves plenty.

BREWERS GREEN LANE
Diss Town FC

Having played at a shared sports ground since 1888, Diss finally found a home of their own when they purchased seven acres of land which was formerly a sugar beet field in Brewers Green Lane.

With grants from various councils, work began on the new ground and clubhouse, and these were opened in 1983. An extension was added and a stand with seating for 270 spectators was built in 1992. The new ground is benefiting from success on the pitch, and is a pleasant spot, reached by a long lane off the main road.

The cricket ground in Roydon Road is sadly no more, having been developed, and the site is owned by Gaze's Estate Agents and Auctioneers, whose predecessors permitted the club to play on the ground more than 100 years ago.

PLANTATION PARK
Norwich United FC

One of the newest grounds in East Anglia is Plantation Park, the home of Norwich United, on the outskirts of the village of Blofield.

Situated close to the A47 ring road, it is the kind of ground that a casual passer-by could easily miss. Surrounded by acres of cultivated land, it is not immediately apparent who plays there unless the name board is glimpsed. As with any new ground, Plantation Park is spick and span and very comfortable, with hard standing and a fixed yellow rail around the pitch. A long functional stand, straddling the half-way line and with panelling at the back, provides cover and some seating. The clubhouse and dressing-room complex stands directly behind the goal.

The football club was founded way back in 1903 as Poringland & District FC and played at Poringland Memorial Playing Field. With continued success, in 1985 they were forced to seek pastures new as a senior club and played at the Heartsease Lane ground of Gothic FC until it was sold. Thus began the building of the new home which undoubtedly has room for expansion. On the 11 acre site there is a bowling green, and hopefully facilities for tennis will soon arrive.

Since 1980, when the club won the Norfolk Junior Cup, they have gone from strength to strength, moving through the Anglian Combination to the Eastern Counties League, and have reached the Norfolk Senior Cup Final on three occasions. Any future promotions would certainly not be hindered by lack of space for expansion at this remote but pleasant ground.

Lowestoft's Crown Meadow has been extensively rebuilt in recent years. Note the lettering in the wall, a regular feature in the Eastern Counties League.

CROWN MEADOW
Lowestoft Town FC

Lowestoft Town Football Club was formed in 1890, and has played virtually all its home games at the Crown Meadow since then, apart from a few early matches which were held at the Denes Oval, just 50 yards from the North Sea and still the home of Lowestoft Town Cricket Club.

The first real development at the Crown Meadow occurred just after the turn of the century when Town purchased the clubhouse of the former Royal Norfolk and Suffolk Yacht Club. After careful dismantling it was transported approximately one mile and re-erected to form administration offices and dressing rooms behind one goal. This splendid building remained in use until 1989 when it finally gave up the ghost and was replaced by a new complex behind the other goal. The modern project was financed by selling the land on which the old building had stood. Between the wars a small area of covered terracing and a wooden grandstand with bench seating were constructed down both touchlines; the covered terrace is still in use but both the stands have gone.

With an improvement in the club's fortunes during the early 1960's, floodlighting was installed, and three years later, in 1967, temporary wooden railway sleeper-type terracing was put down to accommodate the crowd which numbered over 5,000 at an FA Cup First Round tie with Watford - still the club's record attendance. This temporary structure remained in place until 1985.

Following further successes on the field, the old wooden stand on the east side was demolished and replaced by a brick-built cantilever stand containing 466 tip-up seats. A few years later the other grandstand on the west side was badly damaged by fire, boarded up and eventually demolished.

In 1985, when the old sleepers were finally taken up, an all-weather playing area was constructed during the season and the floodlights also upgraded. The remaining area behind the north goal, together with the site of the demolished stand on the west side were then fenced off to form an enclosure for the storage of new cars.

EMERALD PARK
Gorleston FC

Gorleston Football Club are something of a rarity in the non-League game in that they have managed to move from their spiritual home into a new ground which is both comfortable and efficient and does not resemble an oversized coal-bunker.

Emerald Park was built from scratch in the early 1980's and is situated on the edge of a sprawling estate. The ground is fully enclosed with cover on three sides and in recent times has had a new dressing room complex added behind one goal which replaced the portakabins stretching along the undeveloped side of the ground. A fence now completes the segregation until a planned new stand is built in 1996 along with a modern clubhouse.

Exorbitant rent demands hastened the move from the Recreation Ground in Church Lane which had been home for the best part of 100 years and was affectionately known as the `Recca'. The land was originally left to the children of Gorleston by around the turn of the century by a benefactor and by 1920 it had acquired an impressive grandstand with bench seating and a central dais for the presentation of cups and medals. The changing rooms were underneath and the playing area was surrounded by an oval-shaped grass bank with a huge perimeter wall running down the back of the stand. In 1929 the chicken-run which stretched the full length of the opposite side and could shelter 2,000 souls was erected. The shape of the Recca remained unchanged until the fifties when a section of open terrace was laid next to the stand and assorted canteen and equipment rooms were built. It was in 1951 that the record crowd packed into the Recca for a replayed FA Cup tie with Leyton Orient.

As was so often the case in those days the attendance figures were somewhat embellished, and have increased in the interim; the record is officially 4,473, although in many circles it is quoted as over 6,000.

Since Gorleston moved out, the Recca has changed dramatically although football is still played there. Town Hall FC, an Anglian Combination side, used it for a while but, within the last five years, all the structures - other than the clubhouse which is now used as a Scout hut - have been destroyed by vandals or the Council. The wall has been replaced by railings and the place now houses local junior matches, a far cry from an FA Cup First Round tie.

The old stand at Gorleston, now sadly demolished, although the pitch is still there.

TRAFFORD PARK
Wroxham FC

The pleasant Norfolk village of Wroxham has seen football at several venues since the club was formed in 1892. At least three pitches were leased at various times, all from the Trafford family who own significant tracts of land in the area and after whom the current ground is named.

The first pitch was just off the Norwich Road with subsequent grounds at The Avenue and Keys Hill. The Avenue Ground has reverted back to agricultural use whereas the others are now built upon.

Around the time of the Second World War the club moved to a field close to the railway in Skinners Lane taking with them an old timber pavilion which was erected and used as a primitive form of clubhouse. It lasted until around fifteen years ago and was replaced by a group of pre-fabricated buildings which, in turn, did the job until being flattened when the splendid new clubhouse was opened in 1994.

Although the ground is leased from the Trafford Estate, the area on which the clubhouse stands was obtained from British Rail, whose tracks are as close to the ground on one side as any in the country. The current main stand is a low part-timber affair built in 1990, replacing an earlier structure which had stood for around ten years on the same spot. Many of the improvements now being enjoyed at Trafford Park date from around five years ago with floodlights and the new post and rail system adding to the upgrading. The capacity currently stands at around 2,000 which is yet to be tested, despite continued on-pitch success in recent years. The visit of Wisbech in March 1993 posted the biggest crowd to date at Trafford Park, some 1,011 ringing the ground for an Eastern Counties League game.

CABBELL PARK
Cromer Town FC

There can be little doubt that Cabbell Park has seen better days. It was originally opened as Bond-Cabbell Park by Mrs Benjamin B. Bond-Cabbell of Cromer Hall on 8th September 1922. She presented the ground to the town of Cromer in grateful remembrance of the inhabitants who gave their lives in the Great War.

The original inscribed flagstone is still in evidence at the entrance to the ground, as is the wonderful grandstand built in 1922 although that is now in a very sorry state, with most of the roof missing or rotted. It has been condemned as unsafe for the past three years but remains a classic example of 1920's ground architecture which is sadly becoming all too rare in the 1990's. The legend 'Cromer Football Club' still stands out on the back wall and on the fascia.

Back in the thirties, Cromer enjoyed a

The remains of the old stand at Cromer may well have been replaced by the time this book is published.

brief spell in the Eastern Counties League, and after the war, until 1955, the club competed in the FA Cup reaching the Third Qualifying Round in 1953. Those times however seem a long way off as they currently play in Division Three of the Anglian Combination.

In the past few years Cabbell Park has had a bit of a face lift, with a new clubhouse and bar behind one goal, permanent railings around the pitch, new dug-outs, a tea-bar and a pay-hut. Floodlights are also in the pipeline when finances permit and so, too, is a replacement for the club's one jewel, that magnificent stand. Although in a desperate state it should be admired whilst still in existence, for any replacement, however modern and comfortable, will not be able to compensate for the loss of seventy-odd years' worth of history.

WELLESLEY RECREATION GROUND
Great Yarmouth Town FC

The Town club was formed in 1897 and began playing at the Old Recreation Ground before moving to the new enclosure on Wellesley Road, which according to the local press of the time was quickly improved: "posts and barriers have been put up to prevent encroachment on the field of play, and on the sixpenny side footboards are plentiful and should prove a boon in wet weather". One interesting point is that the formation of the Town club was blamed for a number of local sides 'dying a natural death'.

The Old Rec became the New Rec for the start of the 1897-98 season with the Mayor, H.E. Buxton, kicking off the first game in front of 1,300 spectators. By 1899 the club had erected what was locally known as the Pew Shelter and were in the process of starting a

One of the classic buildings still around on the non-League circuit today, at Great Yarmouth.

fund raising effort to build a bigger and more appropriate stand as a substitute for 'the present apology for one'.

Improvements to the ground progressed swiftly and by 1904 it was fully enclosed with a post and rail and banking which afforded a good view for the large crowds who gathered. Two years later, the magnificently ornate grandstand with its carved roof struts and deckle-edged fascia was completed. Capable of seating over 1,000, it has survived two World Wars and today is one of the most photographed of all grandstands throughout non-League football. It had dressing rooms with running water and its brick frontage was interspersed with a series of portholes for windows, possibly the prototype for those fifties vintage stands at Morecambe and Cheltenham. Between the wars, the Wellesley had developed further

with a cinder running-track in regular use and a long covered enclosure stretching along the side opposite the stand.

Yarmouth's successful exploits of the early fifties saw the ground struggle to accommodate the crowds which gathered for FA Cup games against Crystal Palace and Wrexham. For the Palace game the club shipped in lorry-loads of heavy duty fish containers which were arranged at each end of the ground as a form of terracing having first been tested by the club's heaviest supporter! The nearby racecourse loaned the club their garden seats to arrange around the pitch and 'fish-box room' was sold at 2/6d each. The labour proved worthwhile for a club record crowd of nearly 9,000 - although somewhat less than the hoped-for 20,000 - saw Yarmouth beat Palace 1-0.

It may be due to the fact that the ground

has always been hemmed in by tall elegant town houses or that the grandstand is virtually the same as when constructed 90 years ago, but Wellesley almost seems stuck in a time warp. The addition of floodlights in 1983 and a new all-weather running track have done nothing to alter that. Happily, the stand is again back to full working order after a run-in with a council 'Jobsworth' who closed it down on the basis that it required three trained fire stewards to be on duty throughout the game, and these they were generously prepared to supply at £90 each per match! Mercifully that nonsense has passed and the Wellesley can hopefully look forward to another 100 years of football on the East Coast.

Photos in this section by:
Paul Dennis and Gavin Ellis-Neville.

Humberside and the North Yorkshire Moors

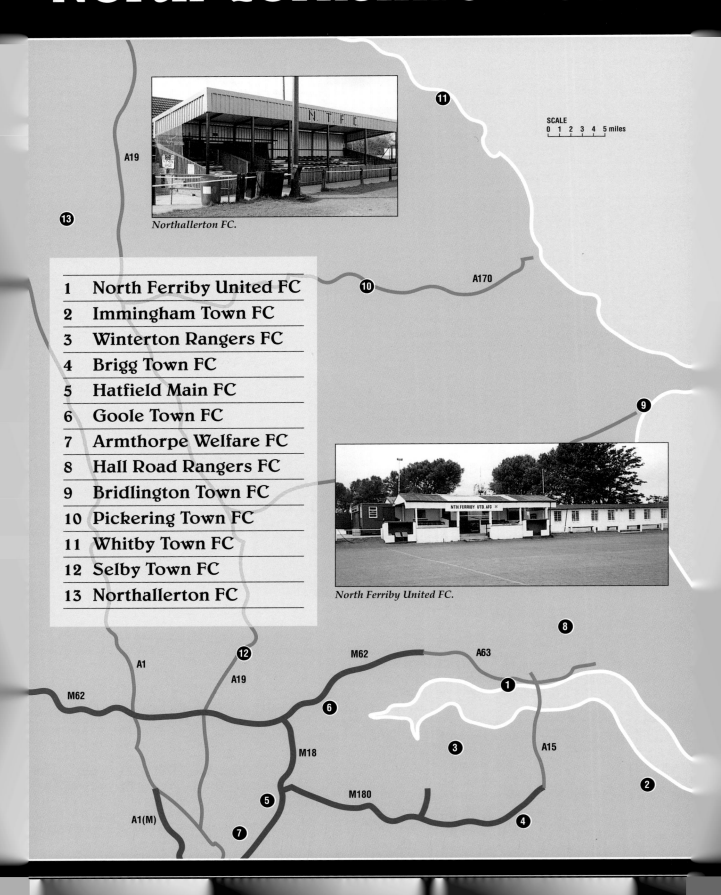

Northallerton FC.

SCALE
0 1 2 3 4 5 miles

A19

A170

1	North Ferriby United FC
2	Immingham Town FC
3	Winterton Rangers FC
4	Brigg Town FC
5	Hatfield Main FC
6	Goole Town FC
7	Armthorpe Welfare FC
8	Hall Road Rangers FC
9	Bridlington Town FC
10	Pickering Town FC
11	Whitby Town FC
12	Selby Town FC
13	Northallerton FC

North Ferriby United FC.

A1
A19
M62
M18
M180
A1(M)
M62
A63
A15

THE area south of the Humber down to Lincolnshire is sparsely populated with few large towns to support football on a major scale and with Goole Town having made the drop last year, all the premier non-League clubs are in the Northern Counties (East) League, attempting to feed into the Northern Premier League.

The north is as thinly populated with only the cities of Hull and York of any great size and neither of these has a pedigree in senior non-League football, the former being a traditional Rugby League town supporting Hull FC and Kingston Rovers, as well as Hull City FC.

The new stand at Grange Lane, North Ferriby.

GRANGE LANE
North Ferriby United FC

Grange Lane ground was initially fashioned out of a wilderness that had been allotments many years earlier. In 1969, North Ferriby were accepted into the Yorkshire League and set about building a ground suitable for that competition. Until then the club had played on council pitches whilst in junior football, in particular on the Playing Fields between the cricket pitch and the poplar trees. For their first season in the Yorkshire League, while Grange Lane was being built, wooden posts and rope, temporary trainers' boxes, goals and nets all had to be put up.

The new ground began to take shape after all the weeds and shrubs had been bulldozed to one end to form the upraised carpark, and the post and rails from the defunct Hull Brunswick's ground were bought for £50 and erected around the pitch. For a number of seasons the players continued changing at the Playing Fields before walking down to the ground but, after much graft and endeavour, a pair of pre-fabricated buildings - formerly numbers 8 and 10 Goths Lane in the village - were erected on the ground, having lain in storage for two years.

The original main stand, a pleasant, colourful structure was sadly demolished in 1993, and replaced by a more modern seated version vaguely reminiscent of the new structure at Long Buckby. The quaint little stand attached to the dressing rooms, which housed the V.I.P. area, was built in 1984 and was opened by former Manchester United player Stuart Pearson. In the summer of 1984 the seats were removed to give more covered standing for approximately 200 people. Since those early days a clubhouse has been built, and new changing rooms, floodlights, hard standing all around the ground and an office added, all helping make Grange Road the pleasant place it is today.

WOODLANDS AVENUE
Immingham Town FC

The latest incarnation of Immingham Town dates from 1969 when football returned to the town after an absence of 17 years.

The first Immingham was founded in 1912, and were original members of the old Lincolnshire League, playing until the start of the Great War but, when most of the playing staff joined up, the club had little alternative but to disband and it was not until the end of the Second World War in 1945 that a new Town were formed. They played on the Pelham Road ground which was little more than a gated field surrounded by dykes. They lasted just seven years until personnel problems again forced the club to disband, although the owner of the land, the Earl of Yarborough, had also refused them permission to continue playing there.

A further 17 years elapsed before the Town reformed once again with the help of a substantial grant from the local council. One of the first moves the club made was to obtain a building from Market Rasen racecourse and this was soon converted into a clubhouse. Opposite they erected a covered stand some 40 feet long, although the plan had been for one three times that size. This structure was damaged by gales in 1974 and subsequently taken down. The NCEL accepted the club in 1986 and, to adhere to ground regulations, new pathways, railings and toilets were introduced, with a small covered stand added two years later. This was extended in 1993 to its current 70 feet length.

In April 1992 a Sheffield United XI provided the opposition for the opening of the club's first floodlights in front of a ground record crowd of over 950. It has always been a rocky ride for the football people of Immingham, but Woodlands Avenue has as good a chance as any of surviving, unlike the ground at Pelham Road which has become a lorry park.

WEST STREET
Winterton Rangers FC

The village of Winterton lies just south of the Humber Estuary midway between Hull and Scunthorpe, and is home to Winterton Rangers. Founded in 1936 as a youth team, they played on a rough field in Sewers Lane before moving to Watery Lane just after the war. When a field became available for purchase, Rangers bought the land for £700, installing an ex-Army hut from a POW camp in Winteringham for changing rooms. Prior to this players changed in the Butchers Arms, 10 minutes walk away.

The pitch was little more than a hedged field at first but eventually acquired a small tin stand on the half way line which cost spectators 2d to enter. Cricket, on a matting wicket, was regularly played at the ground until around the time the first clubhouse was started in 1963; this took some three years to complete, all with voluntary help.

From then on West Street began to develop both outside and inside the ground. Housing sprang up close by while perimeter fencing and a 150-seater stand, along with an extension to the clubhouse and new dressing rooms all appeared within.

In 1978 the club won their floodlighting system in a national competition and celebrated by once again extending their clubhouse. Sheffield United provided the opposition at the opening of the lights and the crowd of 1,200 remains the ground record attendance. Since then turnstiles have been put in, a wall erected and hard standing completed all around a ground which has progressed slowly but sensibly during the last 25 years.

THE HAWTHORNS
Brigg Town FC

The town of Brigg lies to the east of Scunthorpe and, until that club's entry into the Football League, was virtually on a par with its Midland League neighbours. The Brocklesby Ox ground was well established with a grandstand on one side and a full length cover opposite, all created by local tradespeople keen to see football flourish in the town.

The Brocklesby Ox ground belonged to

VICTORIA PLEASURE GROUNDS
Goole Town FC

The Pleasure Grounds have been home to Goole Town Football Club since its formation in 1900. At that time the ground was already well established as a sports venue, having been used occasionally by Yorkshire County Cricket Club for various non-competitive matches.

It was opened for public viewing on 6th August 1888, and officially declared open on 8th September when a grand football match (in effect a rugby match) was played between a Goole fifteen and an eighteen-man team of locals! In the early days it was the home of Goole Rugby Union and has since staged Rugby League intermittently as well as becoming the major venue in the town for galas, wrestling matches, sports days and heavy horse shows. Rugby League has never really taken off at Goole despite a little success, a case in point being in 1937 when Goole RLFC won through six rounds of the Challenge Cup and faced Broughton Park Rangers; 2,500 people paid £500 to watch Goole lose 14-2 but the following week's match brought in less than £5 and at the end of the season the club folded.

It is extremely difficult for the casual visitor to the Pleasure Grounds to relate today's scene to that of its heyday. Certainly the town end of the ground had a Spion Kop which in later years was no more than crumbling terrace but was nevertheless very popular and always full. In between the wars the roofless wooden enclosure which had stood on the bank was taken down and eventually, when the running track was laid, the terracing disappeared altogether as the interior shape of the ground was altered. At the time of the Kop's enclosure, a low wooden stand with bench seating was erected opposite where the changing rooms are now, but this in turn was taken down and replaced by a slightly more modern structure, destroyed two years ago during a fierce gale. The area is now open with a couple of steps of rudimentary terrace. It is planned that a third stand be built there, which will doubtless be better able than its predecessors to withstand the constant battering of winds howling in off the North Sea. The far end of the ground overlooked by the docks and a huge timber yard is completely open with unused land between the pitch and the perimeter fence. The main stand is built on to a fairly substantial bank of concrete terracing and stretches some distance either side of the half way line. The interior has seating installed in around a third of its length and, unusually, a pair of steps leading to a huge directors' box designed for the presentation of trophies to various winners of competitive sport at the ground. This stand, as the remains of the foundations poking out of the terrace clearly show, replaced a longer one on the same site which also succumbed to high winds in the sixties. The new stand houses dressing rooms and a clubhouse, and it was on the opening of the stand that the old dressing rooms, which were situated in the corner between the Kop and the opposite side terrace, became redundant .

The overall impression is not of neglect in allowing the main sporting arena - which should be the focal point of the town - become as barren as it has, but of possible Town Hall apathy. Goole Town FC have enjoyed a very high standard of non-League football for many years, the ground holding nearly 9,000 for a match against Scunthorpe United in the Midland League some forty-odd years ago. However, by installing a four lane running-track that very few people use the council have effectively hammered a nail into the coffin of the Pleasure Grounds.

The Pleasure Grounds have seen better days.

Hull Brewery and was situated behind a pub of the same name. Sadly, the owners decided that more money was to be made by renting the land as a caravan park and in 1959 the ground was dismantled and to this day remains as a park behind the pub.

The Hawthorns was created on a children's play area and it is believed metalwork from the old stand was utilised to build the new one. A pair of wooden huts were erected and in 1965 a clubhouse built. This was extended with a bar a few years later. At around the same time the stand was rebuilt and in the late sixties two areas of cover were installed opposite.

Since then, new dressing rooms have gone up nearer the pitch and floodlights enable the club to play in the Premier Division of the Northern Counties (East).

The capacity at The Hawthorns is a healthy 4,000, although the record crowd was in fact set at the Brocklesby Ox when Boston United journeyed for an FA Cup First Qualifying Round tie in September 1954. Prior to the Second World War, Brigg played on a less salubrious spot close to the railway station, in the grounds of the Manor House Convent, where a small hut was barely adequate for changing and buckets of water were provided to wash off the mud. The club left there at the outbreak of the war and the ground and convent were built on long ago.

DUNSCROFT WELFARE
Hatfield Main FC

The club were formed in 1936 and played at the Stainforth Miners Welfare until after the war when the current ground became available. The Stainforth ground is now used primarily as a running track.

Dunscroft was little more than a railed-off pitch with changing rooms until the clubhouse came about in 1979. Since then a new 6ft. steel fence has been erected around the ground and hard standing put in on three sides. Two small areas of cover stand either side of the clubhouse, and the original CISWO-built changing rooms are still there, albeit re-roofed. Floodlights were erected around 1990, and extensive work done on the changing rooms and tea-bar. Plans are in hand for a further seated stand as the club prepare for football at a higher level.

WELFARE GROUND
Armthorpe Welfare FC

Armthorpe is just one of a number of Welfare Grounds around the Doncaster area that sprang up in the 1920's. Armthorpe's original colliery team dates from 1926 although the current outfit is only twenty years old, the previous club having disbanded in 1974. There is nothing left now of the old ground as it was originally set out, with a pavilion and a railed off pitch, but in place today there is a breeze-block

Pickering's pleasant Mill Lane home.

stand to seat 200 with a small amount of standing cover to satisfy the league's needs.

For many years the club played in the Doncaster Senior League, as did a host of other colliery sides, including Askern, Thorne, Hemsworth and South Kirkby.

Armthorpe Welfare's ground currently has a capacity of approximately 2,500 and has held close to that number within recent times when Doncaster Rovers played a charity match there in 1986.

DENE PARK
Hall Road Rangers FC

Rangers started life as a Boys' Club in 1959. They swiftly joined the East Riding League and later the Yorkshire League where they began developing their current ground at Dunswell.

The early days were spent at Spooners Ground in Inglemire Lane and the Hull Co-Operative ground in Beresford Avenue which boasted a pavilion and changing rooms.

In 1968 the club bought a plot of arable land and transported a long wooden pavilion from Blackburn Aerodrome in Brough, erecting it for use as a bar and changing rooms.

The modern brick-built facilities, housing bars, saunas and living quarters for the steward, are around fifteen years old and were the beginnings of the ground as it is now, up to the standards set by the Northern Counties (East) League. During the last five years, covered standing, a seated stand and floodlighting have all appeared.

MILL LANE
Pickering Town FC

Pickering Town have played on their delightful Mill Lane ground which is shared with cricket and bowls, since 1920. The North Yorkshire town has seen football since 1888 when the club played on a field at Westgate Back. Stories are told that players changed behind a hedge then, regard-

less of the weather, as it is believed there were no buildings on the ground.

In 1920 they moved to Mill Lane, erecting a small wooden pavilion which was shared by both cricket and football. At first there was no electricity or water but improvements were made in the early thirties, both inside and out, to the benefit of the players.

Supporters of the Pikes erected a new stand in 1956 with structural steel and corrugated sheeting. This provided standing cover for around 150 people and in 1963 a new clubhouse, which was a joint venture between the three sporting clubs, was built. Between then and 1987 various extensions and improvements were made to refurbish the bar and changing rooms and in 1990 the pitch was surrounded on three sides by hard standing with a permanent barrier added. The floodlighting system, complete with five pylons and a 190 lux value, was installed in 1992, while a new stand catering for 300 standing customers went up a year later. Plans are in hand to build a further seated stand in the near future to improve the current capacity and to keep in line with ground criteria.

QUEENSGATE
Bridlington Town FC

Queensgate has been a very sad place for the last couple of seasons ever since a court action, involving the leaseholder of the ground and the council, saw Bridlington move 60 miles to Doncaster Rovers' Belle Vue ground. It was not a success and eventually the club dropped out of senior football. A pub team called The Greyhound began playing as Bridlington in the Driffield and District League at Queensgate and moved into the East Riding County League for the 1995 season.

Queensgate has been a football ground since well before the Second World War, and had an early low wooden stand which was extensively repaired in the seventies, only for the council to condemn it overnight follow-

ing the Bradford fire. The ground was shared with Bridlington Trinity who were in the Midland League when Town were in the Yorkshire League and they stayed until a dispute involving unpaid rent saw them barred from playing at home. Arbitrators ruled they could carry on playing, but without use of the floodlights, and as the league rules stated lights were compulsory, Trinity folded in May 1990.

Four years earlier the new leaseholder had transformed the ground by building a main stand with 700 seats, and installing floodlights. It was hoped the modern clubhouse would boost finances for the club, and good runs in Cup and Vase briefly brought success. Despite this, the support was not forthcoming, the neighbouring rugby club being far better patronised, and Bridlington's Vase triumph over Tiverton Town turned out to be merely a swansong, .

AINDERBY ROAD
Northallerton FC

The Town have been at Ainderby Road for twenty years, only a year longer than at their previous home, the Bluestone Ground. When the council decided to extend County Hall in 1975, they offered Northallerton the inducement of a piece of land and some money to move out. As the Bluestone was fairly undeveloped, they accepted. The irony is the ground was never built upon and remains an open space, with Town continuing to develop Ainderby Road for Northern League football.

Bluestone had double changing rooms with baths, and a small covered stand with a plaque dedicating it to the memory of a young man who was killed locally. The new ground, opened on August 21st 1976, has two pitches, a clubhouse and car park and at the start had a small covered area. This has since expanded, the ground having been fenced off and a stand with 150 seats added. The other sides are terraced giving a capacity of 3,000.

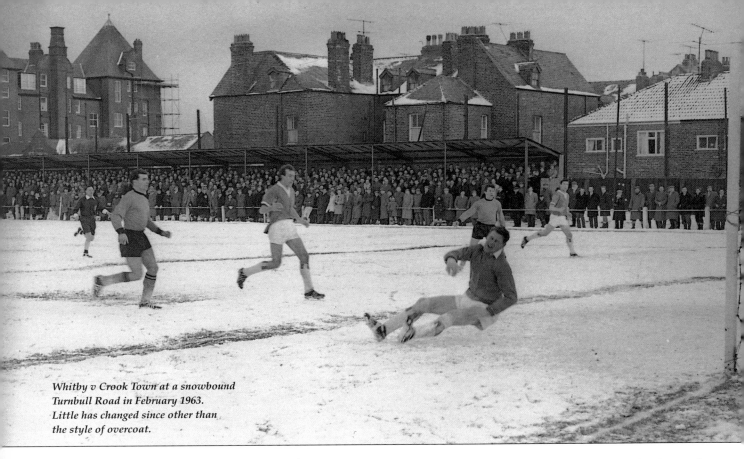

Whitby v Crook Town at a snowbound Turnbull Road in February 1963. Little has changed since other than the style of overcoat.

TURNBULL GROUND
Whitby Town FC

The story of football in the North Yorkshire coastal town of Whitby is fascinating, if a touch complicated. Local history appears to indicate that a church Temperance group played a friendly in 1880, and there is some suggestion that Whitby AFC were in existence before the first known fixture list in 1882.

Their initial ground was on Stakesby Fields where the club played friendlies, not entering the Cleveland Amateur League until 1891. The Northern League soon followed, as did a new ground at Upgang Lane. This was adjacent to the present Turnbull Ground, but at 45 degrees to it with one end known as the Upgang End and the other as the Laundry End. The club left the Northern League three years later and also parted company with the cricket club. In the turmoil that followed the club left league football although they carried on entering the FA and Amateur Cups. They returned to the Northern League in 1899 but once again travelling and cost saw the AGM voting to revert to Cleveland League football.

Two years on, the club went back to playing friendlies but were swamped by the emergence of two new sides, Whitehill Swifts and Whitby Shamrocks, eventually folding some time around the Great War.

By 1908, Shamrocks were playing at Upgang Lane and were the senior club in the town. After the First World War that mantle passed to the Swifts, who shared the pitch with a new club, Whitby Town FC, both playing in the Scarborough and District League.

On the 6th March 1926 delegates from both clubs met to discuss the possibility of a merger to bring more senior football to the town and a successful application was made to the Northern League for the new club, Whitby United, to be admitted. The club has remained members of the league ever since, changing their name to Town in 1949.

Swifts and Town shared the Upgang Lane pitch with the cricket club until 1926. It had originally been acquired in 1883, levelled at a cost of £177.10s.0d. and was ready for the clubs in 1885. When the football section went their own way in 1897 they had to give £17.10s, half the rental, to the cricket club who had to pay landlords Elliott Estates.

In 1926 United started by sharing the cricket ground, the pitch being roped off for Northern League games, but the land was sold to developers that year and the landlords gave notice to the cricket club to quit. A wealthy shipowner, Wilfred Turnbull, intervened and solved the problem. He purchased the land, although the developers retained a portion on the northern side which in itself created a problem as the cricket pitch then had to re-site slightl, leaving insufficient room for the football pitch. Undaunted, Turnbull bought an adjoining field which was to become the present Turnbull Ground. While that area was levelled and seeded United moved to Stakesby Road for two seasons before returning to the brand new ground which was officially opened on 31st August 1929 by Turnbull himself, plus many dignitaries, before a friendly match with Stockton.

The present main stand dates from the opening and had a long covered enclosure which ran all the way to the Upgang Lane end, on the site of the present supporters' kiosk and committee buildings. The new ground had been well equipped by Mr Turnbull who funded extensive fencing and netting to catch wayward balls, as well as the stand and dressing rooms, bathrooms, a referee's room, an ambulance hut and a motor cutter!

The ground survived the war years and in 1951 the 'Scratching Shed' was erected which covers around 600 people on the estate side. No one knows exactly why the cover is not parallel to the pitch. The new supporters' clubhouse was opened for an FA Cup tie with Scarborough on October 9th 1971 although the official ceremony did not take place until the following March. Tow Law were the first visitors to play under floodlights on March 23rd 1983.

Four years later a new dressing room block was built, encompassing offices, kitchen and a committee room. Finally, to date, a smart turnstile entrance was built by the reigning Northern League champions and 250 new seats installed in the stand.

Strangely, the record attendance at the Turnbull - which is given variously as 4,000, 4,500 or 5,000 depending on your source - was posted for the North Riding Cup Final against Scarborough in the same season that the club reached the FA Amateur Cup Final, where they lost to Hendon. The record had been broken that season when Harwich and Parkeston were visitors for a 4th Round replay but a further 1,000 saw the Scarborough match amidst wild excitement.

FOOTBALL IN SELBY

Situated east of Leeds and a dozen or more miles away from the nearest footballing town of any relevance, Selby is ideally placed to be a stronghold of Yorkshire football. The fact that the single senior club left in the town are only just climbing out of a major slump is something of a surprise. Over the 70 or so years since the birth of the Yorkshire League, Selby has been home to a number of clubs, all of whom have come and gone with their own grounds, apart from Selby Town who have played at Flaxley Road since 1951.

The club's previous ground was known as the Bowling Green, although its official title was the James Street Recreation Ground. It had the regulation wooden stand and was previously home to Selby FC and Selby Mizpah who competed in the FA Cup and the West Yorkshire League around the turn of the century. Selby resided there from 1919 until moving to Flaxley Road where they played their first game, a local derby against Goole Town in August 1951, which attracted a crowd of over 4,000. The Bowling Green is still used today by local sides although the stand was destroyed by fire in 1960 and never replaced.

In the early days Flaxley Road was covered behind one goal and, although re-roofed, this still exists. There were also two small stands, similar in shape to Nissen huts sliced in two, with curved corrugated iron roofs. Between these were the dressing rooms. There were two entrances, one to the left of the goal which has since been closed off, and another behind banking at the uncovered end. Some of this was removed when the ground was fully enclosed.

The clubhouse was opened in the late sixties and the dressing rooms re-built soon after. Floodlights were erected in 1994 and, other than training lights, are the first set to be played under at Flaxley Road. There have been two other major grounds in the town including that of Selby Shipyards FC who played briefly in the Yorkshire League in the mid-twenties near East Common. Their ground is now part of Abbots Road opposite the Rigid Paper Products site.

Yet another Selby side to play in the Yorkshire League and the FA Cup were Selby Olympia whose works ground for the Olympic Cake and Oil company still exists for cricket and football. Indeed a club of the same name still play in the York and District League on the ground now owned by BOCM PAUL Ltd. There was once a little wooden enclosure .... but of much more historical importance is the fact the renowned manager of both Huddersfield Town and Arsenal, Herbert Chapman, worked at the company and played for the club.

Photos in this section by: Gavin Ellis-Neville, Jeff Frank, Dean Walton, Kerry Miller and Chas. Woodward.

Sheffield area

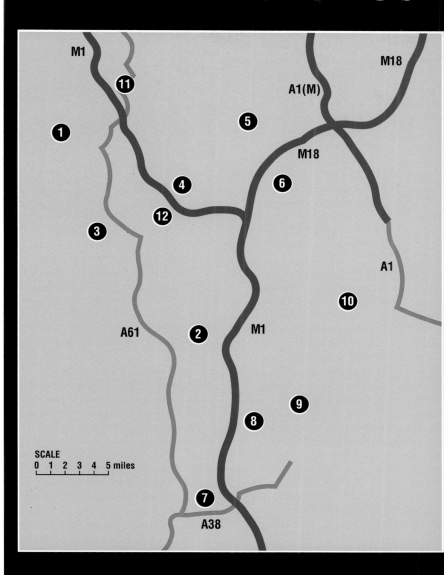

1	Stocksbridge Park Steels FC
2	Staveley Miners Welfare FC
3	Hallam FC
4	Sheffield Aurora FC
5	Denaby United FC
6	Maltby Miners Welfare FC
7	South Normanton Athletic FC
8	Glapwell FC
9	Shirebrook FC
10	Worksop Town FC
11	Worsbrough Bridge Miners Welfare FC
12	Sheffield FC

THE area immediately to the north and east of Sheffield is another former mining area where many of the clubs are, or were, connected with the Miners' Welfare. A glimpse through the FA Cup club-by-club records will show many colliery teams that have disappeared along with the pit and the Welfare, and plenty of others that still survive, independently of the pit.

Langwith, Beighton and Kilnhurst are just three, with Beighton reaching the First Round proper in 1952 before losing to Wrexham. Kiveton Park play in the Central Midlands League, whereas Goldthorpe, Treeton, Grimethorpe and Yorkshire Main all still play in the County Senior League.

Of the more senior clubs, Sheffield is blessed with the oldest club in the world, the oldest ground in the world and one of the best three-sided grounds in this country.

Stocksbridge, one of the best three-sided grounds.

BRACKEN MOOR
Stocksbridge Park Steels FC

Bracken Moor is another glorious football ground which suffers from the new wave of antipathy towards three-sided arenas. Only a technicality, and a dubious one at that, prevented the club taking their place in the Northern Premier League in August 1994, and they continue in the Northern Counties (East).

The club is actually an amalgam of Stocksbridge Works FC, who had a huge and crumbling ground, and Oxley Park FC. The merger took place in 1985 when the former

INGERSALL ROAD
Staveley Miners Welfare FC

The present Staveley Welfare club dates back only seven years, coming out of the local Chesterfield League. A Sunday side has used the Welfare for around a dozen years, but the original colliery team has long since gone. Ingersall Road was a Welfare Ground with a standard pavilion and a football pitch, but fortunately not encumbered by cricket, so it was always enclosed.

It is not readily known what, other than the pavilion, was built from the start, but the ground as it is now, with its banked sides, has changed within the last fifteen years or so since the pavilion burnt down.

For a while the players changed in the Welfare itself before walking down to the ground, but eventually new dressing rooms were built from an old school building in the town, with a boardroom and tea bar. One side now has a 200-seater stand, there are floodlights and Ingersall Road can boast a ground capacity of 5,000.

were struggling, having joined the NCEL on the demise of the Yorkshire League. The latter, however, were a successful local side with a basic park pitch and a vibrant committee and the two came together to form the club as it is known today.

Bracken Moor, and the field above it which is home to Stocksbridge Old Cricket Club, have been sports grounds since the early part of the century, the area which now houses the football pitch having been a severely sloping cricket ground, with two football pitches marked out, right up to the Second War.

It was bought by the Social Services section of Samuel Fox Steelmakers whose cricket and football clubs transformed it. They levelled the ground around 1950 in a massive engineering venture, the scale of which may be seen by the grass banking they created and the way the stand is built into what looks like a hill. While the work was in progress and until the pitch could settle, the old club moved to a farmer's field further up the lane at Stonemoor, where a large hut was transported for changing in. The hut is now used by the rugby club nearby, but the pitch site has reverted to farmland.

At Bracken Moor the players changed in a small green hut which stood where the stone-built changing rooms are today. These were erected in 1964, along with the 500-seater stand and the terracing which runs along the side and behind both goals. In 1990 floodlights were installed, and in 1994 the near end was covered as per the instructions of the League only for the club to be refused promotion. With a re-furbished grandstand, press box, snack bar and toilet facilities the ground, still shared with Stocksbridge Works Cricket Club, is as good as any in the league. But with the two cricket clubs either side of them in effect holding the club back, is it beyond the bounds of possibility that they might one day merge, playing as they do in the same league, and allow the Steelmen to develop the fourth side of Bracken Moor?

OSBORN ASTRO ARENA
Sheffield Aurora FC

The Arena can be included as a non-League football ground perhaps because of what it was, rather than what it now is. Aurora were formerly known as Crookes FC and played on conventional grass with a small stand on the half way line and a barriered-off pitch.

All this changed when the owners converted the pitch into an artificial surface, moving the stand a dozen yards in to accommodate extra car-parking and erecting a ten foot fence around the whole thing, thus removing its status as a football ground and changing it into a multi-purpose arena which houses competitive football once a week.

Hockey, American football and five-a-sides all have their markings painted onto the surface which makes things awkward for players and spectators alike, but one consolation is that the only postponements likely are for heavy snow drifts!

Sadly, the club folded during the summer of 1995, but the ground will remain.

HALL CORNER
Glapwell FC

On entering the home of Glapwell Football Club, there are several clues on display which point to the site being of some significance in the recent past.

A pair of solid-looking gate-posts, minus gates, stand guard at the corner of the ground, which is surrounded by an equally solid boundary wall. Mature trees grow just inside, and on the part now bounded by a nursery there is a bricked-up doorway in the wall. These are all that remain of Old Glapwell Hall which stood on the exact spot of the current changing rooms and clubhouse. The pitch was originally fashioned from the gardens of the Hall which fell into disrepair during the pre-war years and was demolished around 1950. Assorted trees and

SANDYGATE
Hallam FC

As befits a club ground which is possibly the oldest in the world, much has been researched and reported since its inception in 1860. Indeed, cricket had been played there since 1805. The first mention of a football match on the ground was in a local paper, reporting on a game between Hallam and Sheffield Club on Boxing Day 1860, while during the following season matches were regularly reported.

At this time and for many years to follow, the players changed in the Plough Inn, just across the road from the ground. The landlord of the Plough also owned the ground. It is believed that football was played across the bottom of the field at the start, as opposed to on the current playing area, for in 1865 the shape of the ground was altered when various walls were demolished and ponds drained in order for the pitch to be extended clear of the cricket square. During the latter years of the century, Sandygate was used for rugby and the Hallam Annual Sports which attracted crowds in excess of 20,000. The early 1900's saw a number of important cup matches take place, the enclosed nature of the ground allowing admission money to be collected.

During 1929 the old Plough Inn was demolished and re-opened the following April. It had a large meeting room which was used by both clubs and the landlord charged a rent of £18 per season for the ground. During 1932 a Thursday League side called Alliance began renting Sandygate but as they made no contribution to the maintenance of the ground this caused Hallam some concern. More worrying was the fact the landlord let the ground to other clubs for the following season, citing his reason as a lack of bar takings due to poor attendances. Hallam were suddenly homeless but continued to register with the local FA while Crookes WMC and St Phillips CI used the ground. Crookes eventually moved out and Fullwood FC took their place until 1940 when the RASC entered a local league and took over tenancy. In 1946 the club secretary approached the new landlord of the Plough with a view to the club once again using Sandygate and, happily, they were once more able to play there, sharing the ground with Fullwood.

Two years later the clubs approached the present owners of the ground, Tennants Brewery, regarding the building of a toilet block with three coin-in-the-slot locks. On modernisation in 1985 the locks were

SHEFFIELD FOOTBALL CLUB v. HALLAM AND STUMPERLOW CLUBS.—This match was played on Wednesday upon the Hallam cricket ground in the presence of a large number of spectators. Owing to the severe weather several players were absent from each side, but the spirit exhibited by those who were present prevented the game from flagging or becoming uninteresting to the observers, who were extremely liberal with their plaudits on the successful charge or quiet "dodge," and equally unsparing in their sarcasm and country "chaff" on the unfortunate victims of the slippery ground or the "pure" scientific. The day was beautiful and the "uniform" of the men contrasting with each other and the pure snow had a most picturesque appearance. The Sheffielders turned out in their usual scarlet and white, whilst most of the country players wore the blue garment of the Stumperlow club. It would be invidious to single out the play of any particular gentleman when all did well, but we must give the palm to the Sheffield players as being the most scientific and also more alive to the advantage of upsetting their opponents. No serious accidents however occurred—the game was conducted with good temper and in a friendly spirit—and when darkness closed upon the scene the Sheffield club, notwithstanding their inferior numbers, counted two goals to nothing, and went home fully satisfied with their victory.

Where it all started... a report of the first ever match on what is believed to be the oldest football ground in the world.
Below: Hallam FC 130 years later.

removed and found to contain no pennies dated later than 1951. Incredibly, for a ground which had been used for football for nearly 90 years, this was the first structure of any kind to go up.

In 1951 Fullwood moved out and Hallam obtained a proper lease from the brewery having agreed to their terms that a grandstand be built on the ground. This was completed in 1954 and opened on December 18th before an FA Amateur Cup match against Ferryhill Athletic. At this time players were still changing in the Plough, but in 1956 the club acquired a large wooden building that was used at half-time and as a tea room. Further

improvements followed, with a post and railed fence going up around three sides of the ground and a dugout built for the trainers. The 'new' ground accommodated its record crowd of 2,000 when Hendon were the visitors for an Amateur Cup match in 1959. Completing the bulk of the work needed to progress four years later, the club's pavilion was built and opened on April 21st 1964 before a match against Sheffield Wednesday. 1972 saw a real threat to the ancient old ground when Whitbreads, who had taken over as landlords, wrote to the club advising that they intended to dispose of surplus assets, which included Sandygate. Mercifully nothing came of this plan as the brewery were unable to obtain planning permission for housing and nothing more was heard. Indeed, when gales damaged the buildings and stand roof, Whitbreads were forthcoming with a donation enabling repairs to go ahead.

Lengthy discussions involving both clubs eventually secured a 99-year lease at Sandygate for the sum of £50,000 with a peppercorn rent, if demanded, thus ensuring football would still be played. By now Hallam were in the upper reaches of the pyramid and were obliged to provide lighting at the old ground, the funds for which were provided by local businesses.

The first game under lights was a Sheffield Senior Cup game against Frickley Athletic on November 18th 1992 with Hallam winning 4-3. At the end of the following season promotion was gained, but not before 100 seats has been installed in the stand, courtesy of Sheffield United who donated them after rebuilding one of their own stands at Bramall Lane.

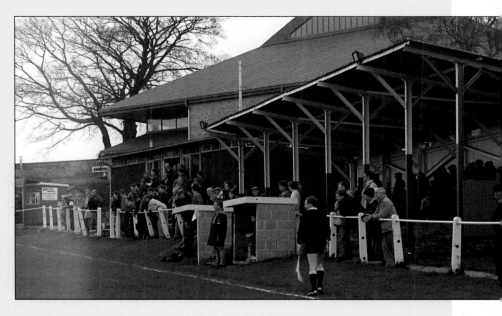

Worsbrough Bridge Miners Welfare... sadly not acceptable for promotion.

PARK ROAD GROUND
Worsbrough Bridge Miners Welfare and Athletic FC

The grass banking which stretches around two sides of the Park Road pitch gives an excellent view of the game and comes in very handy on big occasions such as the day Blyth Spartans attracted 2,300 for an Amateur Cup tie in 1971.

Although the Miners' Welfare club play on it, Park Road has never been a Welfare Ground, having been bought by the Athletic club from a local land owner in 1953. Football was played on the ground well before the Second World War, but the re-formed club moved onto it in 1947, entering into an agreement with the Miners' Welfare to fund the taking of a lease in 1959. This influx of cash and personnel saw the building of the changing rooms and Welfare Hall at the start of the sixties. Some ten years or so later the sturdy-looking brick-built stand, complete with 200 seats, was built into the bank.

The keyhole-shaped ground is shared with cricket with the square situated behind the far goal in a similar way to that at Matlock Town and Arnold. This allows the club to have hard standing down the side just in front of the River Dove and there is a projected scheme to cover part of that side.

Floodlighting was installed in 1993 to allow the club to keep in touch with the ground gradings as this tidy little home develops slowly but surely.

its name to Shirebrook Town FC, thus resurrecting the lost name. Today the old Welfare is not a patch on its former self, but the club have managed to inject some life into the place, erecting floodlights and creating banking around the pitch.

All down one side is a low, cantilevered enclosure with a cinder path and the remains of railway sleeper terracing underneath, which dates back to the fifties. The post and rail enclosing the pitch is seriously buckled but performs its intended job, and a rough grass bank, created as an afterthought five years ago, now surrounds the other three sides. At the rear of one goal is a mesh tunnel leading to the changing rooms situated in the Education Centre behind, and the overgrown

footings of some long-forgotten tennis courts can be seen behind the far goal. A desperately forlorn, semi-derelict bandstand, waist deep in undergrowth, looks mournfully over the rest of what was once a proud Welfare ground. The brick entrance and wall have now gone, but football happily is flourishing at the ground. The third ground in Shirebrook is currently just a field with a set of goal-posts, but in earlier days the Model Village ground also had a low enclosure built on similar lines to that at the Welfare, and was used by, amongst others, Shirebrook Villa, Vics and Rangers.

Photos in this section by: Andy Dakin, Gavin Ellis-Neville, Kerry Miller and Steven Taylor.

OWLERTON STADIUM
Sheffield FC

Sheffield FC are universally known as the oldest football club in the world, a statistic many have tried in vain to disprove although it has prompted a number to ask who indeed their opponents were, if the second oldest club are Cray Wanderers in Kent.

Football, in those days, was a rough mixture of several codes often with any number of players taking part on both sides and many different fields and meadows were used by Sheffield FC. Some very early games took place at Bramall Lane, until they began playing on Abbeydale Park. The park is now a multi-purpose sports complex which houses rugby, hockey and county cricket as well as football. Originally the facilities were quite basic with only a rudimentary area of cover with dressing rooms some distance away and when the club entered the Northern Counties (East) League they were forced to look elsewhere.

In 1989 they began playing on Hillsborough Park, an old athletics track next to Sheffield Wednesday's home which was adequate for seating but had no floodlights. When promotion was gained it became obvious that lighting could never be installed due to complaints from residents - the same residents who live next door to Hillsborough which boasted the best lighting in the country 40 years ago!

In 1991 the club moved to the space-age Don Valley Stadium. Built and completed in 1990 for the World Student Games at a cost of £25 million it covers the site of the former Brown & Bayley Steelworks. The high banking was created by hollowing out the site and using the spoil, which was banked and then covered with the main 10,000-seater grandstand. The actual seated capacity is 25,000, more than half of which is under cover, but for Sheffield FC matches just a small area was opened and games were played out in an eery atmosphere. The stadium is currently home to the Sheffield Eagles Rugby League Club as well as being a major athletics venue.

Amazingly, the most advanced stadium to have been built in this country was deemed unsuitable for the league and in 1994 Sheffield were forced to leave for the less well-advanced and far older Owlerton Stadium. Owlerton was originally built on waste ground as a speedway stadium and opened in 1929.

Greyhound-racing was started three years later and, much later still, stock-car racing was introduced to an oval-shaped stadium which is not well-suited to football. The terracing and stands were closed for safety reasons in 1989 but, after much remedial work, re-opened and Sheffield FC now play there with matting laid across the track for corner kicks. The rugby league side also used the ground for five years from 1984, their residency prompting the council to install lights in 1986.

THE HOMES OF WORKSOP TOWN FC

When Worksop Cricket Club sold the football section of their Central Avenue ground to make way for an extension to a town centre car-park, it signalled the start of a nightmare for the club and its supporters. Interminable wrangles meant three years elapsed before the club finally returned home to Worksop after sharing Northolme with Gainsborough Trinity.

At one stage negotiations with Worksop Rugby Club were ongoing until problems with planning permission put paid to that. In February 1989, however, with the club in danger of having to resign from the NPL, it was announced that a site had been found at Claylands, which was owned by the Greater Notts Co-operative Society and in use as a football and cricket field. The existing stand at Central Avenue would have been re-sited behind one goal, with cover all down one side and the present cricket pavilion was to have been replaced by a brick-built changing room with provision for a boardroom. The idea again ran into problems, chiefly due to lack of access and the three-sided nature of the ground which had always been a problem at Central Avenue. The project went no further.

Later that year the council came to the rescue by making available a playing field on Sandy Lane. This was once a rubbish tip and much remedial work was needed to raise the level of the pitch before work could commence. It was a long and nerve-wracking wait but when the dressing accommodation went up it enabled the club to remain in business. In August 1992 the new ground was finally opened and the Tigers moved back from Gainsborough who had generously shared with them for three years.

The ground at this time had an almost complete social club and three small covered terraces, and the following season more terracing was added and the grandstand and boardroom opened. 1994 saw a new sponsors' lounge, secretary's office and club shop as Sandy Lane came alive with a successful season on their return to their home town.

CENTRAL AVENUE and before.

Old minute books indicate that the club were founded in 1861 and played on a field off Netherton Road which later became the Portland Campus Playing Field and Holy Family RC Church. The players changed in the old White Swan on Cheapside.

In 1891 the President of the club obtained a lease on land owned by the Duke of Newcastle who was selling off his estate. It was in the centre of town and bounded by Hardy Street, King Street, Allen Street and the River Ryton. Known as Bridge Meadow, the ground was fenced off and football was played on the eastern side and cricket on the west with a quarter-mile cycling track around the whole site. In granting the lease the Duke also

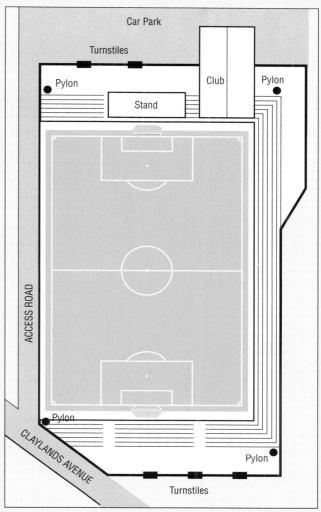

The ground that never was... Claylands as it was planned in 1989. The main problems proved to be lack of access and the fact that it was a three-sided ground.

gave the club £50 and this enabled them to transfer the two pavilions from Netherton Road. Players at this time changed at the Queen's Head or Cattle Market Hotel in town. Worksop played at Bridge Meadow for just two years before the President, realising the lease was expiring, bought the neighbouring land on Central Avenue. As he was also President of the cricket club, the ground was shared by the two sporting bodies, while the Newcastle Avenue Sports Ground, Bridge Meadow, soon reverted to grazing land and was eventually swallowed up by housing.

Dressing rooms were built to a basic standard shortly after the move and were situated in the corner where years after the old Tigers Club stood. Much later a wooden grandstand was built along the full length of the Netherholm side of the ground which suffered damage on a number of occasions. The Canal End terracing was developed from banking in the late 50's with cover and the River End was also terraced but remained open. In the late 70's the arrival of a fresh Chairman saw Central Avenue improve dramatically with new changing rooms built on the half-way line where a large part of the old stand had been missing, and the Tigers Club built in one corner in place of the derelict changing rooms. With the installation of lights Central Avenue remained a Northern Premier League ground until 1989 and the sale of the land for a car-park. Today, the pitch is under tarmac although one terrace is still in situ, albeit only just. The cricket club area remains unaffected.

Worksop's old Central Avenue home. The cricket ground is still there but the football pitch is now under a car park.

The Potteries and the Peaks

THE Potteries and the Peaks cover parts of Staffordshire, Cheshire and Derbyshire and have a number of extremely old grounds, one of which has claims to be the highest in the country. Also Macclesfield's fine home should by rights be hosting League football, but more of the debatable goal-post moving which plagued Kidderminster got the better of the Conference champions.

The closeness of Manchester and Stoke is almost certain to have an effect on the development of the clubs in this area, with only Macclesfield and Leek attracting substantial gates.

JACKSON AVENUE
Nantwich Town FC

The history of the football ground at the bottom of Jackson Avenue can be traced right back to the original club's inception in 1884. There had been football played in the town for several years prior, but evidence in local papers suggests that the club as it is known now (but without the 'Town') was formed in the summer of 1884, quite possibly by the merger of existing smaller clubs.

One of the biggest crowds to cram in to the ground - at that time known as London Road - was the 2,000 which witnessed the English FA Cup 1st Qualifying Round game against Irish champions Linfield Athletic, back in 1891. There was little or nothing in the way of facilities then, and the players changed in two small rooms measuring six yards by four in the Leopard Inn, a short walk away across the fields which now house Jackson Avenue.

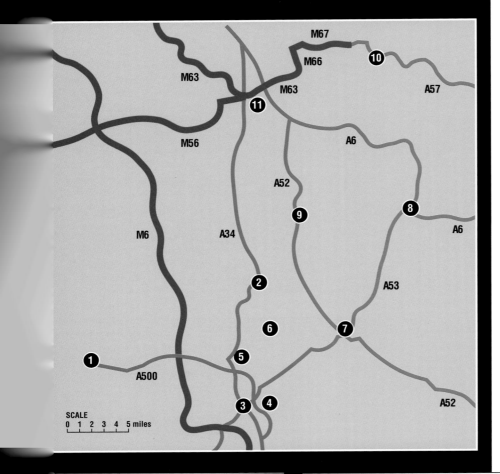

SCALE
0 1 2 3 4 5 miles

1 **Nantwich Town FC**
2 **Congleton Town FC**
3 **Newcastle Town FC**
4 **Eastwood Hanley FC**
5 **Kidsgrove Athletic FC**
6 **Knypersley Victoria FC**
7 **Leek Town FC**
8 **Buxton FC**
9 **Macclesfield Town FC**
10 **Glossop North End FC**
11 **Cheadle Town FC**

Two old grounds in the Crewe area... Yockings Park at Whitchurch (top) and the LMR ground (right).

Jackson Avenue, Nantwich.

Subsequently, dressing room were provided at the ground on the opposite end to the present ones.

Club records show the first grandstand constructed on the ground was paid for on the strength of some exceptional gate receipts taken around the time when the club was enjoying a successful period on the pitch, around 1901-02. This old stand survived both wars, and periods of disuse at the ground and was only replaced in the seventies by the current structure.

For six years between 1915 and 1921 the London Road ground lay dormant. During the hostilities the club had ceased playing and the pitch had been sown with oats. As a result, when the club re-formed in 1919, they applied to play at the cricket ground in Kingsley Fields. Permission was granted and a wooden stand was erected for 500 people, and within two years a record crowd at that ground of 5,121 paid to watch a Cheshire Senior Cup replay against Winsford.

The tenancy at the cricket ground was to be short lived. Overlapping seasons coupled

with encroachment causing damage to the square prompted the club's return to London Road for the 1921-22 season, which is where they stayed until the Second World War broke out and they temporarily disbanded again in 1940. On re-forming, the club was forced to start playing on Barony Park, but even that was not ready, and the first few games in the Crewe Combination were played at the Grammar School, with one fixture even fulfilled on the King George V fields at Crewe. Playing on the Barony was not a success; the teams were forced to change in the nearby Baronia Works (only demolished in the last five years or so), and many matches were postponed due to ground conditions.

As a result the club took out a loan from the FA and purchased the old ground in London Road for £750 from Jackson's the Builders who had been renting it to a man named Gerald Fox, who used it as a chicken run, keeping hens in the dressing rooms and turkeys in the referees hut! At first the club were unable to get Mr Fox off the land, and as a result the pitch had to be swept clean of hen and geese droppings before each match. The teams at that stage changed in the Bull's Head bowling green pavilion, which was opposite The Leopard. A few years later as the club flourished a Supporters' Club was formed and money found to buy and erect a refreshment hut on the site of the present canteen. In the early sixties, two of the mainstays of Nantwich football, Jack Lindop and Eddie Lockyer, were chiefly responsible for acquiring the present dressing rooms which replaced those at the other end of the ground, and later, in 1972 they initiated construction of a new stand built to replace the old wooden one.

In more recent times, a small clubhouse was erected in 1989, followed two years later by floodlights which were ceremoniously opened with a game against Liverpool.

BOOTH STREET
Congleton Town FC

Sadly, there is very little in the way of written archive material on Congleton and its ground, home since well before the Great War. What is known is that the field was extremely rough and was eventually fenced off through wooden posts using strong haulage wire from a nearby coalmine.

Railway sleepers were laid to terrace the ground which had no cover until the square wooden stand complete with changing rooms was built some time in the twenties by a Mr James Standeven. Prior to that players changed in the Wheatsheaf Pub (now a Chinese chip shop) in Booth Street. As happened at a number of grounds during the War, including St Austell and Yeovil, American servicemen took over the place and immediately offered to correct the existing 9ft. slope, but permission could not be granted and so it remained.

In the sixties a further area of covered terrace was erected and more recently the old stand was taken down and replaced by a modern cantilever structure. An Army hut, originally from a station in Oswestry, and used as a clubhouse was flattened to make way for the new stand. A brand new clubhouse was soon put up and Booth Street is again a functional ground with a capacity of 5,000, some 2,000 short of the record crowd which attended a League match with Macclesfield in 1954.

LYME VALLEY PARKWAY
Newcastle Town FC

Newcastle Town club as they are known today were formed in 1964 as Parkway Hanley, and played on several pitches within Hanley Park, changing at The Hawksmoor pub. Pitches at Keele University were also used on occasions. On transferring to Sunday football the club moved to a new ground at Northwood Lane which had on-site dressing rooms and a railed off pitch and there they remained until 1985.

Meanwhile, another Newcastle Town had been playing since 1982 on the old Lilleshall Road sports ground and when the two clubs merged soon after, keeping the same name, they began to make an impression on the local scene.

The old and the new at Booth Street, Congleton.

Newcastle Town, showing the cycle track and new stand.

The Northwood Lane ground is presently used by Redgate Clayton, and the sports ground, now named the Lyme Valley Parkway Stadium, has changed significantly in recent years. It was originally built in the mid-fifties as part of a much larger complex involving rugby and cricket, and for many years was used as Stoke City's training ground. The banked velodrome around the ground was redundant for some time but is now back in action for cycle trials - its natural curve and elevation creating some useful vantage points around the pitch. The wooden dressing room and clubhouse set back from the half way line was the only structure of note until the council owners erected the 200-seater stand alongside it. Opposite this there is a new covered terraced area which can hold 700 and stretches along most of that side, further enclosing what in its early days was a basic undeveloped ground, but is now much more comfortable and capable of holding 4,000 as it nearly did in 1991 when the record crowd of 3,500 turned up to see a pre-season friendly with Stoke City.

TRENTMILL ROAD
Eastwood Hanley FC

The site of Eastwood Hanley's ground is a depressing indictment of the modern morals and lawlessness which pervade the country. The club have been forced to concede defeat to vandals and thieves who have plagued the ground and the clubhouse for so long. Continued attacks have rendered the ground unusable, its remoteness making security almost impossible, and Hanley are now sharing with neighbours Kidsgrove Athletic.

It all seems light years away from the optimism of only a decade ago when pitch-length stands were mooted and a transit van made an 800-mile round trip to buy 96 lamps from Arbroath's old floodlights. The clubhouse was opened in 1984, and new cover went up in 1991 with dressing rooms following, but Trentmill Road is derelict now, and the club, formed in the boom era of 1946 are eking out their existence elsewhere.

Kidsgrove Athletic, now also the home of Eastwood Hanley.

CLOUGH HALL
Kidsgrove Athletic FC

Kidsgrove Athletic finally found a permanent home around 1960, some eight years after their formation. Council land was acquired and fenced off with green corrugated tin, and a pavilion costing around £2,000 was built. Players changed for some time in the Clough Hall Cricket Ground pavilion until their own changing rooms were built a few years later. The first cover of any description was erected around 1970 opposite where the Ernest Langford Stand is today, but it was rarely used and later destroyed in a storm.

Since then the pavilion has been extended and the main stand built on the halfway line with two other smaller covered areas either side of it, one of which has since been relocated behind the goal. Another covered area stands where the first used to be and new dressing rooms complete what is a pleasant ground which attained North-west Counties League standard in 1991.

TUNSTALL ROAD
Knypersley Victoria FC

Football is but a young whipper-snapper at Knypersley, having only been played on the ground since 1933. Miners from the local Victoria Colliery originally made a cricket pitch there back in 1877. The colliery was owned by Sir Robert Heath who sold the ground as part of a Welfare scheme for the men who eventually erected a clubhouse in 1912 which is still there and now used as a play-school.

Football arrived in 1933 as Knypersley FC, and progressed until the club moved to Biddulph Moor. That club eventually folded and Knypersley Vics were the natural progression. The ground is three-sided, sharing still with the local cricket club and there is a covered stand for 200 people, opened in 1990 and replacing a much earlier tin shed on the same site.

Until 1988 the cricket pavilion was used as changing rooms but as the ground developed, so did the facilities and, with the floodlights in for the 1993-94 season, Tunstall Road is moving slowly with the times in this pleasant part of Staffordshire.

HARRISON PARK
Leek Town FC

Harrison Park should have been staging Conference football in 1995. The fact it did not was recorded officially as being due to financial problems, but unofficially there were allegations of sharp practice from influential people on boards elsewhere.

To rub salt into a gaping wound Leek found themselves playing in the Southern League for a season with 'local derbies' against Dover Athletic, Chelmsford City,

Dorchester and Hastings on the fixture list and all this whilst near-neighbours Macclesfield Town romped away with the league Leek believe they should rightfully be in. How ironic too that the club allegedly deemed the main architect of Leek's problems were relegated a year later.

All this, after strident efforts to bring the ground up to acceptable levels in the last few years which has seen a complete transformation of what was a homely, if slightly untidy, residence.

The club were formed during the Second World War by a group of lads from the Lowe Hamil area who played friendlies on the White Lion Field as Abbey Green Rovers.

They eventually joined the Staffs County League as Leek Lowe Hamil and played on a narrow pitch on Millwards Field, now covered by a garage. The Chairman of the club bought the field that now houses Harrison Park for £1,250 and named it Hamil Park.

The club name was changed to Leek Town in 1951 and they entered the Manchester League. The ground at the time was little more than a field with a hawthorn hedge surrounding it and a large natural bank at the back.

The players changed at the Blue Ball pub some 600 yards away until dressing rooms were built in the mid-fifties. On discovering the pitch was encroaching on land belonging to others it was decided to turn it around, which meant excavating the bank to make room. (The bank behind the far goal today was many yards nearer the main road before the alterations of 1953.)

The first dressing rooms were put up shortly after, complete with an overhang for shelter, and a small covered area opposite also went up to house around 400 but rapidly went down again when destroyed in a storm.

When Chairman Geoff Harrison died the club honoured his memory by re-naming the ground Harrison Park. In 1972 with the sad demise of Rugby Town and their Bilton Road ground, Leek purchased the floodlights in

time for their debut in the Cheshire League. At that time the small stand on the car-park side provided the only seating and this was renovated, along with the dressing rooms, in 1987 when the modern ground began to take shape. More terracing was put down in 1989 and in 1992 the splendid cantilever stand was begun.

Within the last two years both ends of the ground were completely covered - there are now two seated stands and cover on all four sides - as Harrison Park prepared for Conference football. With a capacity of 3,800 it is possible the club may yet post a new record attendance to beat the official one of 3,512 which assembled in 1973 for an FA Cup tie with Macclesfield Town although, in 1950, a crowd of over 5,000 watched a Staffs Junior Cup semi-final between Ball Haye Green and Port Vale A.

SILVERLANDS
Buxton FC

Silverlands seems to have had three main periods in its lifetime as a football ground. It was first used when the land owner, a Mr Drewry, lent the field for a Derbyshire Challenge Cup match against Bakewell on November 1st, 1884. It was by no means the club's first home, for since the founding they had used a number of venues, often battling against the elements in what is one of the most elevated towns in the country.

The club was born from players at the cricket club and records show the first game was on October 27th 1877 on a pitch near the old barn at The Park, the home then and now of the cricket club. As was the case with so many of the early football clubs, virtually any field would do for a game. In Buxton's case, grounds at the Wyelands, Macclesfield Road and Cote Heath, the latter on a field belonging to the landlord of the Eagle Hotel, a Mr Jackson, were used. This was believed to have been in London Road and was home on and off for some time from 1879.

A wintery Leek Town before the new stand was built on the extreme left.

When Silverlands became available steps were taken to ensure a free view was not possible at what was then an unenclosed site. It was roped and staked and as early as 1885 there were plans for a cover to encourage ladies to the ground, but this was not built until 1890, along with dressing rooms.

There was then talk of another pavilion for the "working class supporters", the first being used by members, visitors and ladies.

The second major period for the ground commenced after the World War Two when, in order to add to the old wooden grandstand which stood where the current one is now, terracing began to go down. The stand was replete with bench seating in front and eventually made way for the 600-seater in place since around 1965. Opposite the stand, a long enclosure covered the full length of the ground and has only been replaced during the last few seasons. The old wooden changing rooms were on the corner opposite the entrance, next to a tea hut, but this bottleneck was swept away during the eighties when the new dressing rooms were built under the main stand, along with office accommodation, all of which cost somewhere close to £11,000.

The final chapter at Silverlands concerns the selling of land behind the left hand goal, which entailed removing the banked terrace to enable a road to be built to access a new housing development on allotment land behind the ground. This has resulted in a much narrower flat standing area which gives the old ground a lop-sided feel, with the opposite end and the popular side still fully covered.

Buxton claim Silverlands to be the highest ground in the country, although Tow Law Town must run it very close.

Silverlands at Buxton, one of the highest grounds in England.

MOSS ROSE
Macclesfield Town FC

Three years ago the Moss Rose hosted League football when Chester City shared the ground, having vacated Sealand Road while the Deva Stadium was built. The 40-odd mile trip each way meant attendances were even lower than they used to be at Sealand Road, including arguably one of the smallest crowds ever for an FA Cup 3rd Round tie when 1,500 turned up for the match against AFC Bournemouth in January 1991.

Even so the League guidelines were acceptable at the time with only minimum alterations to the old ground. Having helped Chester City survive it must have been a bitter pill to swallow when told their massive lead at the top of the Conference throughout most of the 1994-95 season would count for nothing as the guidelines had changed and Moss Rose was no longer fit to stage League football.

The story of football in Macclesfield has never been fully documented but it is known that the club began, possibly playing rugby in 1874 at Bowfield Lane and later at the Macclesfield Cricket Club in Victoria Road. They played a couple of seasons on Rostron's Field, near Coare Street in the town before returning to Bowfield Lane. In September 1891, the club began playing at the Moss Rose but by 1897 were bankrupt and the ground was taken over by Hallfield FC, who conveniently changed their name to Macclesfield in 1904.

The ground began to take shape around 1906 when the timber stand was erected on the main road side of the ground which at that stage had a grass bank all around. It is not known when the old garishly-painted dressing rooms were built in the pub corner of the ground, but certainly quite early in the life of the place two areas of cover were put up along most of the terrace opposite the stand. The Cheshire Senior Cup always brought in huge crowds virtually wherever the matches were played, and with interest at its peak just after the war over 10,500 saw the final between Winsford United and Northwich Victoria in 1947, emphasising the potential of the ground even then. The first floodlighting system was installed for the start of the 1965-66 season and Northwich Vics were the first visitors in front of 3,200 spectators. Possibly the biggest single transformation at the Moss Rose was in 1968 when the old grandstand which had served the club for over 60 years gave up the ghost and was replaced by the impressive cantilever structure which is on the same site today. It has a 650 seat capacity and has since been developed at the back with various offices and also houses the dressing rooms, the old ones disappearing around 1979.

The old stand at Moss Rose, as it was in the 1960s.

The ground gained further terracing at one end and around the stand in 1988 removing the grass banking in the process while a Social Club was opened in 1990. As League football beckoned with Chester's sojourn, a number of cosmetic changes occurred; perimeter walls were strengthened and fences put up to segregate the crowds, and doubtless the parent club were happily appreciative knowing that all the improvements were to their benefit. Sadly, the falling masonry from the pyramid has crumbled all around them and damaged the club's aspirations. It must be hoped that they do not fall by the wayside, as Altrincham did for a number of years after getting so close to the old Fourth Division.

ARTHUR GOLDTHORPE STADIUM
Glossop North End FC

The grandly named ground in Surrey Street has been home to the Glossop club since 1955 when they finally settled on land which, during the war, had been a stores depot and an admiralty tip.

Their past includes some 21 years as a Football League club, with one season in the First Division at the turn of the century. Those years were spent at the North Road ground which is still used by Glossop Cricket Club to this day. When they left, it was the start of a nomadic existence, using pitches at Pygrove, Silk Street, Water Lane and Cemetery Road for their Manchester League games before finally settling at Surrey Street when they gained promotion to the Lancs Combination.

The scratching shed with its wooden terracing was erected around the time the ground opened, and had a rudimentary corrugated building for changing rooms at one end and a small stand on the half way line. The original fencing was replaced by more solid but uglier concrete panelling and in 1980 dressing rooms and a clubhouse were built on the site of the first ones.

Macclesfield's main stand.

The grandstand survived until the seventies when it was burnt down, and was only replaced around five years ago. The council-owned ground has been floodlit since 1992 and has seats for 200 with cover for 300. Whilst not the prettiest ground in the country, Surrey Stadium - named after an old benefactor who helped secure the ground - does not attract vast crowds any more but is perfectly adequate for North-West Counties League football. The North Road ground, primarily a cricket arena, was successfully adapted for football in 1914 when 10,736 saw an FA Cup tie with Preston North End, North End then themselves a Football League club.

Photos in this section by: Andy Dakin, Paul Dennis, Kerry Miller James Wright and Clive Westbury.

PARK ROAD STADIUM
Cheadle Town FC

The Park Road ground is probably better known for being used by teams other than Cheadle Town, or Grasmere Rovers as they were known until 1983. For some sixteen years, between 1966 and 1982, it was Manchester City's training ground, before they moved to Platt Lane. Then briefly, Stockport County used the second pitch for youth games in the late eighties. Rather more exotic is the fact that Eusebio, Simoes, Torres and crew used Park Road as a training camp along with the rest of the Portuguese World Cup squad during the 1966 World Cup Finals.

The main feature of Cheadle's home is the square-shaped main stand which dates from 1959, and originally had 300 seats, the tip-up variety being added in 1988. Alongside it stands the 11 year-old club-house, with the floodlit all weather five-a-side pitch to its right.

The covered terrace at Glossop.

North Cheshire

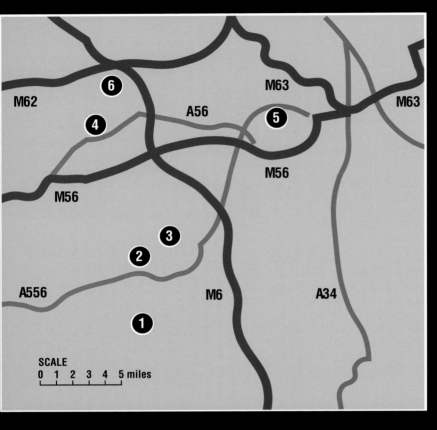

M62

6

4

M63

A56

5

M63

M56

M56

3

2

A556

M6

A34

1

SCALE

0 1 2 3 4 5 miles

1	Winsford United FC
2	Northwich Victoria FC
3	Witton Albion FC
4	Warrington Town FC
5	Altrincham FC
6	Tetley Walker FC

THE area stretching from the salt towns of the south up to the edge of Manchester's commuter belt has three teams which have reached the top flight in recent years, with Altrincham and Northwich currently flying the flag. The old Cheshire League was a fine breeding ground for the established clubs in the area and the Northern Premier League has carried on the tradition.

Lower down the pyramid, there are a number of clubs which have, or did have, substantial grounds. Lostock Gralam, Wilmslow, Linotype, Grove United and Knutsford are all in the Mid-Cheshire League with all but Grove having at some stage entered the FA Cup. Middlewich joined the NWCL in 1995.

DRILL FIELD
Northwich Victoria FC

Without question the Drill Field is the most celebrated and well-known non-League football ground in the country. It has been in existence since 1875, which makes it the oldest continuously-used football ground in the world. In recent times its very future has been in serious doubt on more than one occasion, but happily those financial boarders have been repelled, and the club and the ground are back on an even keel, mainly due to the unswerving dedication of many who wish to see this former Football League club return to the top level.

The Dane Bank at Northwich, and (below) the main stand.

As might be imagined with a ground of such antiquity, it has undergone several overhauls, minor disasters, and been altered to such an extent that its chronological history has been catalogued in order to give an indication of just how much change has taken place.

The field on which the ground took shape was the drill area of the 22nd Company 3rd Battalion Cheshire Rifle Volunteers. On tenancy, the club fenced off the pitch with iron stakes and ropes, and by 1890 a new grandstand had been constructed

A Northwich team photo with the original stand, replaced in 1968, in the background.

Crewe back in 1965, and these did service until 1979, when a new system was installed at a cost of £12,000 .

It has been 120 years of constant change at the Drill Field, mostly for the better, although in truth it has degenerated in recent years. However, plans are in hand to erect a stand at the terminus end, which cannot fail to brighten that part of the ground and, with the continued work of the Drill Field Trust Fund, the future looks a lot rosier than it did. Some 11,290 packed into the ground on Good Friday in 1977 to watch the local derby with Witton Albion, and a similar number witnessed the Vics' marvellous FA Cup win over Watford in the same year. Surely the Drill Field will one day witness those sort of crowds again.

BARTON STADIUM
Winsford United FC

Winsford have played on the site of the Barton Stadium since their founding in 1883 as Over Wanderers. It was originally no more than a field with little in the way of facilities and the players changed in the adjacent pub called the North-Western which gave the ground its early name.

In 1921 the club purchased the land from a Mrs Newall with the help of Chairman Reg Barton and public subscriptions, naming the new stadium after him. The pitch was moved twenty-odd yards and a small wooden stand put up around that time lasted until the Second World War when it was taken down as unsafe, eventually finding its way to Foden's Cricket Ground in Sandbach.

Soon after the war ended work started on developing the stadium, the land having been open and neglected for six years. The local council built the brick dressing rooms opposite what is now the popular side and the sloping-sided stand was also erected at the same time. Terracing was put down around the ground which had banking and a metal perimeter fence added as it took shape. Both ends were given rudimentary covers

costing the princely sum of £70, and holding 600 people. The stand was opened in October 4th but lasted less than two months as it was blown down in a gale. It was re-erected in January of the following year, this time costing £104.2s.10d!

The Drill Field soon became popular for staging important matches, such as the Cheshire Cup-Final which regularly drew crowds of several thousand. The club briefly dallied in the Football League from 1892-94, and on their return to more local football continued to be successful, which led to the ground developing quickly. A new pavilion costing £130 was opened on February 13th 1909; it contained dressing rooms, verandah and a paddock. Two and a half years later an uncovered stand seating 350 people was erected in front of the pavilion. In 1912 a new covered stand on the Town side (now the Dane Bank) was constructed for 500 spectators, and extended a year later for a further 1,000 people. By this time, the majority of the spectating area had raised banking, thus enabling the club to accommodate ever-increasing gates.

After the war, Northwich Vics purchased the ground from The Volunteers for £1,000 and celebrated by moving the town side stand from one side of the pitch to the other, and there it stayed until replaced in 1968 by the present main stand. The Dane Bank was then re-covered in 1928.

After the Second War, Drill Field was in need of some major repair work, part of which involved building a standing cover at the bus terminus end of the ground which ran the width of the pitch. In 1950 the Dane Bank was terraced under the cover which had been damaged in the war, and this protection was replaced in 1959 - the third structure to stand on the Dane Bank since the ground opened. Much earlier, on a date not known, a shelter had been erected at the Water Street end and this lasted until a freak storm demolished it during the 1966-67 season, and it was replaced soon after with a bus-shelter cover.

Still the changes continued and in May 1968, the old wooden stand which originally stood on the Dane Bank was taken down and its successor was completed within three months to oversee the first-ever match in the Northern Premier League against Bangor City. After the Bradford fire many clubs were forced by safety authorities to remove potentially hazardous structures, and so in the late eighties the bus terminus cover was removed and is now a rather ugly flat standing area backed by a concrete slab wall.

Northwich Victoria were fortunate to be gifted the old floodlights from Gresty Road,

Winsford's Barton Stadium changed dramatically when the greyhounds were introduced.

and it was then that Witton Albion attracted the highest crowd ever to attend a game at Barton Stadium when some 7,000 saw a Cheshire County League game at the newly-appointed ground.

The next major alterations came in 1969 when greyhound racing arrived. To accommodate the sport, the terraced ends were removed and the regulation track laid down. Soon after the substantial covered side was erected, capable of holding 2,500 people. This cover came from unwanted market stalls that were cobbled together so successfully it is still there today.

In 1973 the outgoing council assisted the club by erecting floodlights and building a new concrete fence around the ground which still stages greyhound racing at present. The original dressing-rooms have now been extended and altered and currently house a clubhouse, offices and a lounge. Although the ground is looking a touch shop-soiled and is much altered from the heady days of 1947 it is not alone in that, and unlike many it still retains a certain character.

Wincham Park.

WINCHAM PARK
Witton Albion FC

In thirty years time Wincham Park will still be known as Witton Albion's new ground. The distinction between the two grounds used by the club in the last 85 years has come about since their decision to vacate the old Central Ground in 1989. Although a perfectly functional and accessible venue, Wincham Park suffers from having no individual character, in much the same way as Kingstonian, Aylesbury United, and Oxford City. In the case of these four clubs, all have moved from much-loved grounds full of character - albeit of the slightly rusting variety - into bland concrete venues all seemingly designed by the same people.

Wincham Park is situated some way out of the town of Northwich, in a large industrial complex. Surrounded by huge car-parks, it

has unlimited scope for expansion should the club take off in the anticipated manner. Two similar-looking stands stretch down each side of the pitch with small fairly flat standing areas covering both ends. The openness around the ground is accentuated by the low design of the stands, the seated areas of which resemble Adams Park at Wycombe and Deva Stadium at Chester.

An impressive 1,600 can be kept dry stood up, with a further 640-plus seated. The ground was opened in 1989, after the club had vacated the Central Ground at the end of the previous season, the last game being a 1-1 draw against Frickley Athletic.

Prior to the move to Central Ground, Witton played their very early football on a pitch at the back of Witton Vicarage for a while before moving to a ground called Penny Lane off the Middlewich Road. This was substantial enough to stage the Cheshire Cup which attracted a local derby crowd of over 5,000 for the final between Northwich and Winsford United around the turn of the century.

In 1910 the club was offered a plot of land for rent with the proviso that they fenced it off and, being situated out of town

at a ground where free spectating was possible, they transferred to the more centralised area which had been drained and turfed and was ready for the first game in the autumn of 1910.

In 1921 the ground was purchased for £750, and six years later the first major structure went up in the form of a seated stand nearest to the road which served its purpose well until the ground's demise 62 years later.

It originally cost £500, and had 1,000 seats, but did not contain offices or changing rooms until later. At that time the players used a wooden building to change in, situated roughly where the clubhouse was eventually built.

In 1934 modern brick dressing rooms were put up, the old ones became a refreshment hut, and until after the war Central Ground remained unchanged. In a manner similar throughout the well-established football grounds of the time, the grass banking soon became terracing, with a concrete wall and walkways around the pitch. The massive wall at the Tabley end of the ground cost the club £3,700 and was built in 1964, a year after the social club and five years before the first set of lights went up in 1968.

Don Revie formally opened these with a match against Leeds United. To gauge the size of the Central Ground, a crowd of nearly 10,000 saw the derby with Northwich in 1948, and this is believed to be the record attendance.

CANTILEVER PARK
Warrington Town FC

Cantilever Park is named after the huge Cantilever Bridge which looms close to the ground. Previously it had been known, less glamorously, as Loushers Lane.

It has been home to Stockton Heath Football Club, now called Warrington Town, since around 1956. They played on pitches in Stockton Lane in Grappenhall and at London Road before settling at their current ground where an iron and timber main stand was soon built. Playing in the mid-Cheshire

The last hours of Witton Albion's old Central Ground.

League, they began slowly to develop the ground with the Cheshire League in mind, and in 1960 a clubhouse containing dressing rooms, a central hall, bar and a verandah to seat 150 was erected.

Their efforts were in vain, for Cheshire League football eluded them until 1978 when it expanded and took them into the Second Division. The name Warrington Town was taken at the AGM in June 1961, but it was not until the late eighties that the club put themselves on the map, reaching the Final of the FA Vase at Wembley, after managing the semi-finals the year before.

They then reached the Third Qualifying Round of the FA Cup before going all the way to the quarter-final of the FA Trophy in 1993. With promotion to the Northern Premier League, Loushers Lane has improved considerably, now enjoying a covered stand on one side with a seated stand opposite, the ground and the pitch being enclosed in a sturdy concrete wall. Whilst the club and the ground may never reach the stardom of their neighbours in the Rugby League, Town have quietly built Cantilever Park perfectly in line with today's needs.

New North Terrace with 1683 seating

New Golf Road terrace with 1871 standing

Existing main stand to be newly renovated with new entrance & internal areas 1006 seating

Existing East Terrace to be renovated 1327 standing

Moss Lane and the plans which lay ahead.

twenties, and in the sixties the present main stand, a large, square-shaped building, was opened, complete with 850 seats. The east terrace was built in 1979 ready for the new Alliance League and with the club going so tantalisingly close to Football League membership on more than one occasion, Moss Lane has continued to improve, although not sufficiently for the League at the moment.

MOSS LANE
Altrincham FC

Moss Lane will always be known as the home of one of the unluckiest non-League sides in the country. No club has got nearer Football League status without achieving it, and it is all the more sad to see Altrincham struggling with a ground which, although adequate to stage a whole host of FA Cup ties in the past, is now deemed nowhere near good enough for the League.

Moss Lane was originally part of a 60 acre area of common land called Hale Moss. The club moved there in 1910 having used Pollitt's Field, a stone's throw from the cur-

rent ground. Originally known as the Athletic Grounds, it had a small stand on the Moss Lane side with a changing hut at the Chequers end. Just before the Second War, the supporters raised over £2,000 for a new stand and dressing rooms with covered standing on both sides, which provided protection for 3,500 people.

Concrete terracing came early to the ground which had once hosted a crowd of 10,000 for a schoolboys' match in the

Photos in this section by: Andy Dakin, Paul Dennis, Cliff Hase and Alan Watson.

LONG LANE
Tetley Walker FC

The club are only just over 20 years old, yet they have comfortably outgrown the Warrington and District League and are now coming towards the end of a development plan that sees them in the NWCL with even higher aspirations.

Long Lane has been home since day one and has an 8ft concrete fence all around the ground with conifers and mesh screens to keep the ball and the noise inside. In 1994, in preparation for the new league, hard standing and a pitch barrier were installed, and a small 60-seater stand and covered terracing built along with pay booths and a tea bar. Floodlights were expected by the start of the 1995-96 season as was a further stand which would bring seated and standing capacities up to 250 each.

Altrincham FC.

Merseyside and the coast

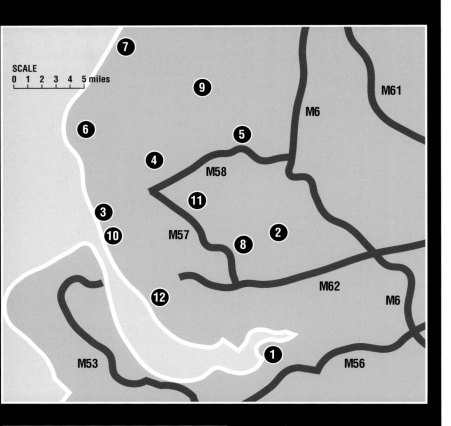

1	Runcorn FC
2	St Helens Town FC
3	Marine FC
4	Maghull FC
5	Skelmersdale Utd. FC
6	Formby Town FC
7	Southport FC
8	Prescot AFC
9	Burscough FC
10	Bootle FC
11	Knowsley United FC
12	South Liverpool FC

The continued stint in the top flight of English football by Everton and Liverpool has not had a detrimental effect on all Merseyside football by any means. Although attendances are poor in many cases, the same is true throughout football, and not just in the major footballing cities.

The area has seen a number of strong clubs, with Skelmersdale, Runcorn and St Helens all reaching Wembley in Amateur Cup, Vase or Trophy with Marine going close once or twice. It also has two former Football League clubs if one counts Bootle FC which is a third generation club. Southport have done wonders in rescuing Haig Avenue in recent years and are not a million miles away from fulfilling their dream of League football once again.

CANAL STREET
Runcorn FC

Surprisingly for a club of the stature of Runcorn FC, there is precious little documented history on the development of the Canal Street ground since it was converted for football on the formation of Runcorn FC in 1919.

It was originally laid out for Rugby Union, ran at right angles to its present position and was enclosed. Such was the size and shape of the ground then, that around 15,000 crammed in to watch a rugby match in 1900. There were changing rooms away from the ground in Wilson's Hotel, until just before the First World War. Following incidents with the crowd, the club were instructed to build dressing rooms at Canal Street.

During the summer of 1914, the ground was changed around to run north to south. and, following its sale, the new owner would allow only association football to be played and Runcorn FC were born.

Below: Canal Street, Runcorn.

After the Second War a burgeoning Supporters' Club transformed parts of the ground, laying concrete terracing where previously there had been railway sleepers on ash and cinders. A timber stand straddled the half-way line from the early twenties and soon acquired a covered enclosure next to it which over the years has been re-roofed and had barriers installed as the demands of the respective leagues have decreed.

The terracing opposite the new main stand has taken a battering from the winds which howl across the estuary and, although it is now open standing, a wooden stand occupied the space until the early seventies when it was severely damaged in a storm and subsequently dismantled. Further along towards the town end there are two further stands of contrasting designs which replaced an earlier one also de-roofed by gales. The newer of the two was put in place following the club's appearance at Wembley for the FA Trophy final of 1993 and has brought the covered capacity back up to acceptable proportions.

By far the most catastrophic time for the club and the ground came, ironically, during one of the best seasons in their history. Firstly a section of perimeter fence gave way during an FA Cup tie with Hull City which closed the bottom end and the corner of the ground nearest the river and secondly, the remaining section of terracing lost its roof to another big wind. Finally and most spectacularly, the wooden main stand which was the only remaining link with the old days was destroyed in a huge fire effectively rendering the ground unusable from March 1993 onwards. Home matches were played at Witton Albion, Chester City and Northwich Victoria whilst negotiations went on regarding a possible move across the water to Widnes Rugby League ground. When these fell through work began to again bring Canal Street up to Conference standards and eventually a new steel stand with 490 seats replaced the burnt structure. Part of the adjacent covered enclosure was removed to make way for it and new crash barriers were put in place around the river end.

The club's return to the ground midway through the 1994-95 season was not without a final twist; their first game back was postponed when drainage problems flooded part of the pitch.

HOGHTON ROAD
St Helens Town FC

The original St Helens Town club were formed in 1903 and played at the old St Helens Greyhound Stadium which stood in Park Road for twenty years until recently folding.

After the Second War a group of businessmen purchased the Hoghton Road site which was covered in allotments at the time. It had originally been the home of Sutton Cricket Club but they vacated the site in the early 1900's and the land had latterly been used in the war effort. In 1948 the Supporters' Club purchased a wooden building from RAF Haydock. This was re-sited on the ground and used as a tea bar and in 1949 they raised £1,000 for the building of the small, 250-seater stand, still in use today. In 1950 a crowd estimated at around 5,000 saw a match against Manchester City which marked the transfer of Bert Trautmann to that club. The whole area was put up for sale in 1953 and for one season the club played at the City Road ground of Pilkington's Glass, the former home of St Helens Recreation who played Rugby League until 1939 on a ground which once held 23,397 for a mid-week Challenge Cup replay against Huddersfield in 1920. In later years amateur Rugby League was played on the ground that in the eighties had been reduced to a standard pitch by removal of the stands.

Town moved back to Hoghton Road after pressure from the Supporters' Club to take it off the market and after Sutton Rose Vale ARLFC had played a few games there. In 1962 John Connelly, Burnley's former Town winger, opened a 200-seater social club which was built on the old training pitch. The original timber clubhouse, built in 1958, was knocked down in 1966 when the club was extended and between then and 1977 it was extended twice more. The final improvements in that period came when cover went up over the Hoghton Road end refreshment bar in 1982, with a directors' box erected the following year.

The floodlights, purchased with the profits made from Town's success in beating Warrington in the FA Vase final at Wembley in 1987, were opened by Everton in October 1988. Since then, to comply with North-West Counties rulings there has been further terracing laid down and cover for 550 is now in place. Whilst it must be said that Hoghton Road is looking a touch run-down, it has a certain character, undoubtedly originating from its being home to cricket, allotments, Rugby League and a FA Vase semi-final since its inception around the turn of the century.

ROSSETT PARK
Marine FC

Marine FC from Crosby are another well-established club who have fallen foul of ground grading criteria in recent years. Despite having a ground large enough to accommodate the modest crowds they would attract in the Conference - bearing in mind the close proximity of the Merseyside teams - Rossett Park is deemed unacceptable, having only three sides available to the public.

The fourth side is hemmed in by the rear gardens of houses but had a narrow strip of land open to spectators until 1979 when the Northern Premier League made it a provision of entry that it was removed, due to the tight and possibly dangerous nature of the perimeter barrier. Ironically, the NPL have, by ordering this to be done, ensured Marine stay in their league as the Conference will have none of it.

Although Marine play at College Road in Crosby they were originally based half a mile away in Waterloo Park, and resided there from 1894, the year they were formed. When the club split with the breakaway Waterloo Melville in 1903 they moved to Rossett Park which was bought by a consortium of members who called themselves the Rossett Park Land Company, which still exists today.

The compact little ground is wedged in between Jubilee Road and Rossett Road with Crossender Road running along the back where rear gardens form a backdrop to the lovely old timber stand which has seated 400 people since 1922. Before the houses in Crossender Road were built there was a second pitch which ran across the top of the main one behind the stand and was used by the reserves. On either side of the stand are terraces fashioned from railway sleepers although on the popular side they were replaced by concrete in 1986. The Jubilee Road side was covered way back in 1925 but after frequent storm damage it was finally replaced in 1991 by a sturdier structure, which covers two-thirds of the side and is vaguely similar to the new cover at

Marine's cosy Rossett Park is about to change dramatically.

Whaddon Road, Cheltenham. A year later two steps of terracing were laid down in just three weeks by a club supporter and around 800 people can fit in there. The College Road end is one of the more fascinating ends in non-League football with a small covered terrace, known as "The Shed" behind the goal not dissimilar to that at the other end where there is a sloping gravel area. On either side are two small terraces, one of which was partly covered in 1991 with help from the club's Hon. Life President Ellis Jones when he was 84 years old!

The changing rooms, dating from 1972, are in the corner next to The Shed and replaced the original building which was situated where the garden area is in front of the clubhouse. There is a small press box to the right of The Shed and a club shop and medical room just in front. The main entrance to the ground is at this end where there has been a club room and snooker hall since the mid-twenties. A concert hall was built there in 1969, now refurbished as a function room, and in 1975 a members' lounge was also built, but this was completely destroyed when part of the roof collapsed in 1992. It has since been re-built at a cost of £25,000.

In 1994 Marine's floodlights, originally installed in 1977, were upgraded to 210 lux making them, somewhat erroneously, perfectly adequate for Conference football.

The club are on record as saying that a move to an out of town ground is not feasible and have had plans for £250,000 worth of development, accepted by Sefton Council. The plans include replacement of the old stand at the Crossender end with a cover, and removal of the other Shed and terraced areas to make way for side to side terracing behind both goals. There will be two grandstands, one for visiting supporters, and the capacity will be 4,000, to be allowed on up to five occasions per season. Until now the club has been forced into the onerous task of playing big games at Anfield but the newly-developed ground will give out a clear message to the powers that be, summed up by the words of one defiant club man who vows Marine are "not going to commit financial suicide and bankruptcy just to satisfy the whims of certain people."

With the site worth around £500,000 and a new ground sure to cost three times that amount, the decision must be the right one, even if it means losing the last vestiges of the old Rossett Park.

OLD HALL FIELD
Maghull FC

The Merseyside club celebrate 75 years in existence in 1996, and are delighted to be able to do so following a fire which destroyed the clubhouse and dressing rooms in 1990. Happily, a new brick-built headquarters has gone up on the ground shared with Maghull Cricket Club.

They have played at Old Hall Field since the early fifties, having previously used a ground at Days Lane High School with other matches being played at Pimbley Recreation Ground. A stand which formerly stood at the old ground was transported to the new and stood in the corner by the canal for many years. The original building which housed the dressing rooms and bar came from Skelmersdale, and, ironically, had once been the office of a firework company!

WHITE MOSS PARK
Skelmersdale United FC

Skelmersdale is widely assumed to be a `New Town' after the mass building which went on in the late 1950's, but the reverse is true, with the town even mentioned in the Domesday Book.

The football club played in the middle of the old town virtually from their beginning in the 1890's right through to 1958 when the New Town Corporation bought the land to expand their headquarters.

BROWS LANE
Formby FC

Brows Lane is one of a select few grounds in the country that had a grandstand built behind the goal rather than more conventionally on the half way line. It still stands today, and is almost as old as the ground itself which dates from 1920. It is timber built with around 200 seats and from the start was blessed with dressing rooms underneath. Along one side of the ground until a few years ago, the equally ancient covered area, then bowed and rickety, was removed and replaced by covered terrace.

Grass banking around part of the pitch enabled the club to post a record crowd of 2,500 in 1973, when they played Oldham Athletic in the first round of the FA Cup. In 1965 Formby opened their new wood and brick clubhouse, and this was in place until September 1990 when an arson attack destroyed both it and the club offices. It has not been replaced. More developments seem unlikely as there are plans to move to a new site in Hogs Hill Lane.

The ground had an ash bank all round with an old shelter and a timber fence around the pitch. There were huge advertising hoardings down one side with a single entrance at the top of Sandy Lane. Dressing rooms were basic, not much more than a wooden hut.

When the club moved off, the ground, and indeed the whole town, were swamped by development and there is no trace of it. White Moss Park was the sports ground for the Skelmersdale Shoe Company, less than half a mile away, with old wooden dressing rooms but no other buildings of note. It remained that way for some years until the early sixties when Skem entered a golden era which was to catapult them to the top of amateur football and lead to the development of White Moss Park.

The club reached the Amateur Cup Final in 1967 and have won the Cheshire League twice since 1968. An FA Cup run in 1968 saw them beat Droylsden, Darwen, St Helens, Stalybridge and Northwich before finally losing to Chesterfield. With a win in the 1971 Amateur Cup Final, funds were available to continue building up the ground.

The old dressing rooms were phased out and a 350-seater stand built down one side of the ground, with terracing either side on a banked-up area. Both ends were covered, one small area and one on a steeper bank being much larger. The banking was built up with hard core and waste and the pitch is now surrounded by hard standing. The club turned full circle from the mid-'70s when, having built up the ground and reached the Northern Premier League, they then went down to the Lancashire Combination before joining the Cheshire League and then the North West Counties.

In that time the two end stands decayed to a point where they had to be removed and that left just the main stand with three open banked sides. The record crowd at White Moss Park is the 7,500 which saw the Amateur Cup replay with Slough Town in 1967. The current capacity is 10,000 although, in real terms, maybe only a third of that total would be allowed today.

Formby boasts one of the very few grandstands built behind the goal.

The main stand at Southport (above) is the only surviving area from Football League days. The crumbling terracing has been replaced by sectioned covered areas (below), steeply banked for good viewing.

HAIG AVENUE
Southport FC

In a similar way to that at Broadhall Way, Stevenage, and the Brewery Field at Spennymoor, Haig Avenue has undergone a complete transformation within the last few years, following the club's re-emergence in the Northern Premier League and the Conference.

In the years following Southport's relegation from the Football League, Haig Avenue suffered a gradual decline, culminating in the condemning, and later demolition, of the covered terraces. Only the magnificent 2,000-seater stand remained from the lay-out of the ground as it was in League days.

The stand had been opened by Chairman of Burnley FC and Football League Management Committee member Mr. Bob Lord in 1967, following a tragic fire on Boxing Day 1966 which completely destroyed the old grandstand along with the offices, dressing rooms and all the club's playing equipment and records.

Southport Football Club, previously Southport Central, have played on the Haig Avenue ground since 1905, when they moved from their Scarisbrick New Road ground. The road and ground were then known as Ash Lane, but it became a home from home when the grandstand which had stood at the old ground was re-erected at the new one. Once elected to the Football League in 1921, the stand was extended to accommodate 2,000 spectators, and a small wooden cover, known as the scratching shed went up opposite. In 1923, this was replaced by what the local paper naively described as "A much loftier and decidedly superior erection". It lasted but five years, having been badly damaged by a gale in October 1927 and was totally destroyed four months later. A Stand Fund Committee was formed to raise cash to replace it, and in November 1929 a new structure was opened to the right of the Scarisbrick Road End, at a cost of over £1,000. During 1931, the landlords, Southport Corporation, made a grant towards a new stand at the Blowick End of the popular side. In addition, cover was provided behind the Scarisbrick New Road end, leaving only the Blowick End without cover.

It was claimed at the time that 12,000

could be accommodated under cover, making Haig Avenue the most modern ground in the Third Division. The fireproof stands were built with much assistance from the Supporters' Club, and were constructed with steel framing, covered by galvanised corrugated iron sheeting. The work was rewarded when in 1932, a record crowd of over 20,000 watched the FA Cup Fourth Round Replay against Newcastle United.

The ground had reached its peak, and the curving terraces, half covered and reminiscent of those at Borough Park, Workington, remained in place for 55 years until the modern day council declared them unsafe. Meanwhile the new stand had arrived. For too many years it kept watch over the crumbling ground and in 1992 looked on as the terraces were destroyed. The club were informed that £350,000 worth of work was needed to transform Haig Avenue into a Conference ground. A share issue was floated and with help coming from many areas, the club forged ahead. In just three months the terracing had been completely renewed, using kit form pre-cast concrete moulds. Once in place the cover was erected and new turnstiles and entrances put in. Toilets, refreshment bars, and walkways followed, and the floodlights were upgraded. By May 1993 Haig Avenue had been re-built, and the grandstand could once again gaze out over the rest of the ground without feeling somewhat out of place.

HOPE STREET
Prescot FC

In recent times Hope Street has become Sandra Park, but it will always be known as the home of Prescot Cables who rose to fame by winning the Lancs Combination and twice reaching the first round of the FA Cup, back in the fifties.

The original Prescot team played, as did many of that era, on the local cricket ground, in their case in Warrington Road, alongside the railway and opposite where the Leisure Centre was built a hundred years on. After a season a separate pitch was laid out at the back and the club played with varying degrees of success until 1902, when the cricket club turned down the suggestion to form a recreation club and banned the footballers from the ground. Unsurprisingly, the club came to an end.

There were several other clubs in the town at the time, but the one which came to the fore was the Wire Works side who used Warrington Road for a while after the original Prescot, before meeting with a similar fate. However, a local MP helped the club secure a piece of ground at the junction of Eaton Street and Hope Street and this was laid out for cycling, football and athletics and opened in September 1906, with the renamed Prescot Athletic playing there. Players changed in the Hope and Anchor,

150 yards away, until a barn was converted to dressing rooms at a later date. Hope Street continued to be used for sports until the Great War when, with interest waning, it was left to the footballers. By then they were known simply as Prescot, with a re-formed Wire Works side sharing the ground for a while. With the running and cycling tracks gone, improvements were made to the ground with cinder bankings created and a fence erected. The newly-formed Supporters' Club covered over the Hope Street end banking, and dressing rooms were built there, allowing the barn to be demolished. The ground was lengthened and widened, new turnstiles were built and the directors of the Wire Works were invited to the opening ceremony - the first of many visits which culminated in the change of name to Prescot Cables in 1928. By the summer a new grandstand had been built on the west side of the ground and an entrance made from Eaton Street. A covered paddock was also built as was an extension to the grandstand which increased seating to 1,000. Such was the enthusiasm for the club, that by 1930 they had applied to join the Football League. They were unsuccessful, and consoled themselves by building a gym and tea room under the stand and installing seating for directors at the Eaton Street end.

Hope Street survived the war and changed little until August 1960 when a huge fire devastated the club, destroying the main stand. The catastrophe took the heart out of the club and support, which had begun to wane, dropped off even further. Although a brand new main stand was built, on almost identical lines to those of Cheltenham, Kings Lynn, Morecambe, etc, with a thriving social club underneath, the club struggled and it is said, never fully recovered from their loss. Their name changed to Prescot Town and back again but little happened to the ground as the club dropped into the Mid-Cheshire League before joining the Cheshire County League in 1980. The stand was renovated and dressing rooms put underneath and later, when the NWCL was formed, further work brought the ground up to a B grading.

In recent times, floodlights have at last shone down on Hope Street and the cover has been renewed. Back in the thirties the ground once held over 8,000 on its banked terraces but the club, currently just known as Prescot FC exists, as do many nowadays on 100 or less.

VICTORIA PARK
Burscough FC

The current Burscough Football Club was formed in 1946 and have played continuously at Victoria Park since that time. Prior to the Second World War Burscough Rangers, a different and unconnected team, used the ground until they folded in March 1935 with heavy financial problems.

It was they who purchased the old grandstand from Everton Football Club in 1928, that had stood on the Stanley Road end since the turn of the century, transporting it to Mart Lane by rail and steam lorry and erecting it with the help of volunteer labour. The Bradford fire disaster and subsequent report spelled the end for the stand as it would have cost £100,000 to renovate, and the decision was made to pull it down and replace it, again using volunteer labour from within the club.

The ground was originally owned by James Martland Ltd, and was used for cricket from the turn of the century. Burscough Rangers played at Victoria Park until the Great War when it reverted to a cultivated field but returned thereafter playing at Travis's Field in the early twenties. Not long before they folded, Burscough Rangers persuaded the council to purchase the ground from James Martland Ltd with help from the Playing Fields Association, and the stand from themselves which they then rented to Rangers and Burscough Vics.

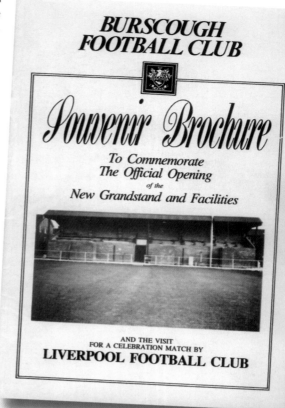

BURSCOUGH FOOTBALL CLUB

Souvenir Brochure

To Commemorate
The Official Opening
of the
New Grandstand and Facilities

AND THE VISIT
FOR A CELEBRATION MATCH BY
LIVERPOOL FOOTBALL CLUB

The ground was used for local finals during the Second War and in 1951 Burscough FC bought it for £400 following a public subscription fund. A covered enclosure was built at the Crabtree Lane End in the same year and six years later in September 1957 a small social club was opened beneath the grandstand. During the next fifteen years work was constantly carried out to improve Victoria Park. The Mart Lane end wall was re-built in 1959, and soon after a new canteen was provided, the old one becoming offices. In 1963 the revamped clubhouse was opened at a cost of some £6,000. At that time cricket was still played at the ground but in 1970 a wall was erected, segregating the football ground from the rest and thus ending cricket for ever. Two years later in March 1972 Oswestry Town became the first team to appear there under lights when Burscough played them in a Cheshire League fixture.

A further fifteen years went by with little of note happening at Victoria Park until the Bradford fire signalled the end for the old Everton Stand. Constructed mainly of wood, both it and the old canteen were taken down and replaced a year or so later by a new 250-seater structure which was opened before a celebration match against Liverpool. Around this time the floodlights were damaged in gales and a further concerted effort saw a new system installed.

Having provided hard standing all round the ground, the club then erected a cover for 500 people opposite the grandstand

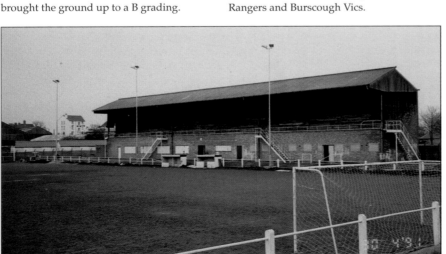

Prescot's main stand. Built to the standard late '50s design, this time with square port holes.

and refurbished the Crabtree End at what is now a tidy and comfortable little ground. Situated in the middle of the village, on the main Liverpool to Ormskirk Road, around ten miles from Southport, the terrain is such that on match evenings Southport's lights can be seen from Victoria Park.

The record attendance to date at the ground was back in 1949, when the club played Wigan Athletic in the first qualifying round of the F.A.Cup, in front of some 4,798 spectators.

Left: Burscough FC.

FOOTBALL IN BOOTLE

The current Bootle Football Club is the third to take that name and only did so when Langton FC, a dockers club, moved out of the Liverpool Shipping League and were obliged to vacate Edinburgh Park. It is now the home of Waterloo Dock who reached prominence in the FA Vase in recent years.

The original Bootle were formed in 1880 when a local church side, Bootle St Johns were persuaded to aim higher by the founder Robert Lythgoe, who later went on to instigate the Liverpool FA. Their first ground in Irlam Road was rented from, and shared with, Bootle Cricket Club, but the following year they played at Marsh Lane and stayed there entertaining the likes of Preston North End and Everton in cup competitions.

By 1886 they were again sharing a ground with the cricket club, this time at Hawthorne Road where, on October 23rd that year, an estimated 10,000 people saw a Liverpool Cup match against Everton - by far the biggest crowd to have witnessed a football match on Merseyside up to then.

The 1889 season saw formation of an unofficial Second Division and also the beginning of a breakaway club from Everton which became Liverpool FC. This sounded the death knell for Bootle who realised they could not compete with the big two and, folding, soon resigned from the League.

The ground and pavilion is still used today by Bootle Cricket Club and is better known as Wadham Road.

The second Bootle FC were not formed until 1948, joining the Lancashire County Combination and playing at Bootle Stadium in Stuart Road, a banked venue with an old timber stand which backed onto the Southport Road, and was better known for cycling meetings than for football.

With finance again a major problem - not being on a bus route, the crowds had difficulty in getting to Stuart Road - the club moved to Seaforth Greyhound Stadium. The old stand at Bootle was demolished in the sixties but Everton played their Central League games there for a while, and much later in the seventies Waterloo Dock used it. Things did not improve and, after two games in the 1953-54 season, Bootle FC folded.

Around that time Langton FC had begun playing and were dominant in amateur football for many years. In 1973 they left the Shipping League, changing their name to Bootle FC as many of the players and committee were from the area. They found a temporary ground at Orrell Mount, known locally as Silcocks, and once again a Bootle team joined the Liverpool Combination before moving into the Lancs Combination the following year when Bucks Park was ready.

Three years in the Cheshire League were followed by entry into the new North-West Counties League, somewhat fortuitously in view of the spartan facilities at what was not much more than a parks pitch. Since then the club have consolidated with Bucks Park gaining an area of terracing, seating accommodation for 400 and cover for a further 1,000. Although not the most scenic of venues the third Bootle have done well to survive in one of the great stronghold areas of English Football.

The seating at Bootle FC.

ALT PARK
Knowsley United FC

There has been more than one club called Kirkby Town over the years, and Knowsley United were one of them, forming in 1984 and playing on the Simonswood Lane ground of one of the former clubs for a couple of seasons before moving to Kirkby Sports Centre for a further two years.

Meanwhile, Huyton Rugby League Club were playing at Alt Park, as they had since 1969, when Lord Derby opened the ground before a match with Salford. Their home had taken shape from 1966 when they were given permission to create a rugby ground, the agreement alone costing £4,000. A 21-year lease saw them able to build a clubhouse behind one goal to add to the small cover down one side which later had seats. What was always a very basic ground was not improved by a wave of continued vandalism which threatened the very existence of the club, and eventually the stand was decreed unsafe, prompting the club to look elsewhere.

In 1983, the ground began to be developed but Huyton did not stop to see it come to fruition for they conceded defeat at Alt Park and moved to Runcorn.

Taking the name of the Borough, Kirkby Town became Knowsley United and moved into a revamped Alt Park in 1988. It now has seating for 350 with cover for several thousand in its total capacity of 9,000. However, the optimism which heralded the re-building has not transferred itself to the paying public and, despite success on the pitch, there were strong rumours during the summer of 1995 that the club may be forced to fold.

HOLLY PARK
South Liverpool FC

South Liverpool are another club whose ground fell foul of waves of vandalism and were finally battered into submission in 1990. For many years the club suffered relentless damage and theft and a combination of that, plus poor gates led to the club moving away from Holly Park to ground-share with Bootle for a year. It was not a success and when the club finished third from bottom of the Northern Premier League, they called it a day. Happily, the small band of supporters re-formed the club, merging with local Liverpool Combination side Cheshire Lines.

The merger, however, was fraught with problems and the club were asked to fend for themselves and so re-formed again, playing on a school pitch as South Liverpool once more.

Holly Park was a substantial ground which was opened in 1935 for the new South Liverpool club (a previous club having gone some years previously). By February of 1936 a new seated stand and covered enclosure were opened, and with the addition of concrete terracing either side of the grandstand and down the opposite side, a record crowd of some 13,000 crammed in to watch the Nigerian XI play a floodlit game in 1949. Some six years later, South Liverpool had their first major experience of vandalism when the stand was gutted by fire and from then on the spectre was never far away.

Today, there is little left of the ground which was flattened after the vandals had finished ruining it, and Holly Park is no more than a memory.

Photos in this section by: Andy Dakin, Stan Strickland and Dean Walton.

Two Liverpool area grounds which are no more. Simonswood Lane, Kirkby (above) and Holly Park, former home of South Liverpool (here).

Manchester

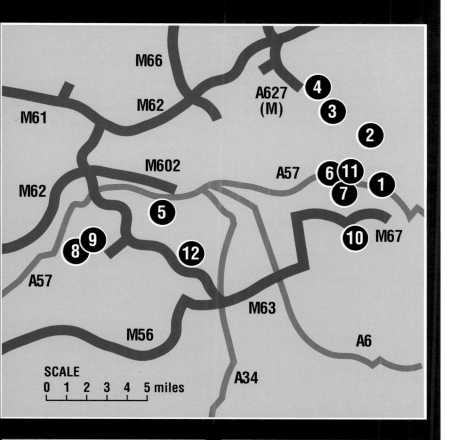

M66

M62

M61

A627 (M)

④

③

②

M602

A57

⑥ ⑪

M62

①

⑦

⑤

⑧ ⑨

⑩ M67

A57

⑫

M63

M56

A6

SCALE
0 1 2 3 4 5 miles

A34

1	Stalybridge Celtic FC	7	Droylsden FC
2	Mossley FC	8	Flixton FC
3	Oldham Town FC	9	Trafford FC
4	Chadderton FC	10	Hyde United FC
5	Salford City FC	11	Curzon Ashton FC
6	Ashton United FC	12	Maine Road FC

ANY club that is even remotely successful in attracting spectators in the city of Manchester is doing exceptionally well. With so many League clubs within easy reach by road and rail, the non-League scene is always stretched to entice the crowds. The sheer volume of clubs in the North-West Counties, Northern Premier and Conference Leagues as well as lower down the pyramid in the Manchester League means a constant struggle to build a competitive side on a limited budget.

The hoped-for improvement in gates when the public either cannot obtain tickets for the likes of Old Trafford or Maine Road or tire of paying a small fortune for them when they do, has not really come about. The upshot is that only Stalybridge Celtic are in the Conference at the moment, without seriously pushing for a return to the League after 73 years.

BOWER FOLD
Stalybridge Celtic FC

Bower Fold is, in theory, only one championship away from a return to staging League football which was last seen at the ground during two inglorious seasons more than seventy years ago.

It retains much of the character that it had then, albeit on a reduced level, and is possibly helped by being in a semi-rural area where little has changed in that period. Football was first staged there around 1909 when Bower Fold was a field, used by Stalybridge Christ Church and Stalybridge United, before a generous and prosperous player, Herbert Rhodes, paid £100 to have the ground levelled and fences erected for the first game in September 1909 against Xaverian College.

Just after the Great War the club built a 500-seater main stand which allowed honoured guests and ladies to escape the muddy banking which had been formed.

Bower Fold, Stalybridge, a former Football League ground.

Within three years the ground was suitable for Football League entry, the sloping areas having been strengthened with railway sleepers, and soon after a covered area was constructed behind the near goal and along the opposite side to the main stand. Such was the extent of the ground, that an estimated 12,000 packed into Bower Fold for a match involving Dick Kerr's Ladies XI in 1921. The more realistic attendance record is 9,753 some two years later against West Bromwich Albion.

As the original structures began to fall into disrepair they were gradually replaced, and the shape of the ground also changed slightly as perimeter walls and fences segregated old terracing. The main stand has been altered and added to, but appears to be just about the same building, with the covered areas now second generation at least, if not third. Modern criteria has dictated that Bower Fold become completely concreted, with new fencing around the ground and a pitch-side barrier. The main stand is still hanging on, and although there have been rumours of a brand new structure, they so far remain only that.

SEEL PARK
Mossley FC

Surprisingly little is known of the early days of Mossley FC other than its formation in 1903 as Park Villa. The site of the modern day Seel Park has been the club's ground since they moved from a farmer's field called Luzley just off the Mossley Road.

Seel Park began life as no more than a banked field but was large enough to accommodate crowds of several thousand during the post-war boom years and this culminated in the record crowd of some 7,000-plus which saw the Cheshire League match with Stalybridge Celtic in 1950. At that time Seel Park had a timber grandstand, believed to have been erected between the wars and the main viewing area was a large grass bank which ran behind the School End goal and around to the stand itself.

Sadly the bank was cleared away to enable hard standing to be put down three

years ago leaving the terracing surrounding the main stand, dating from 1968, as the only elevated area.

The club's great days of the late seventies and early eighties were well-catered for by extensive improvements to Seel Park. Just prior to their visit to Wembley for the FA Trophy final in 1980 an enclosure was put up at the Park End which can hold around 700 people and extensive terracing went down. An additional covered area was put in opposite the main stand which itself was removed and replaced with a neater brick-built structure in 1983.

WHITEBANK STADIUM
Oldham Town FC

Oldham Town's new ground, on the opposite side of the town to their old one, was once rather less exotically known as the Chamber Colliery Welfare Ground, having been home to colliers when they were playing in the Manchester League in the early eighties.

It has since been used by various junior sides, but when Town came off their ground in Nordens Road, the Welfare was renovated, the clubhouse restored and re-opened as the 'Two of Clubs', and a new stand built to seat 150. There is also a full length stand in the pipeline but that will be built in stages. Floodlights were also installed for the first time as Town's ambitions are slowly fulfilled.

The club started as a works side from the George Dew factory, playing on park pitches before moving to Nordens Road, a ground owned by J.J. Chadwicks, a subsidiary of the Courtaulds Group.

The ground was part of a complex with cricket and was reached through a mill which was eventually knocked down, leaving an eerie landscape which had to be traversed when going to matches towards the end. The club changed its name to Oldham Dew and then Oldham Town before moving away in 1994.

At the time of writing the site of the old ground has been cleared and land filled ready for housing on the site, with no trace of the club ever having been there.

ANDREW STREET
Chadderton FC

Chadderton's one and only home since their formation in 1947 has been at Andrew Street. It began life by being converted from an old rubbish tip and until 1960 had a cinder pitch, the grass one being a requirement for the Manchester League. The only building on the ground for many years was an old wooden hut which was used for changing and stood until 1993 when it was burnt down.

In the early sixties as the club and ground progressed the pitch was enclosed with post and rope, and a wooden perimeter fence was put up, replaced in 1979 by the concrete version. To replace the hut, portacabins were brought in as temporary office and dressing rooms and these sufficed until the brand new two-storey complex housing club bar, kitchen, treatment room and dressing rooms was completed in 1994.

In 1981 the middle section of the terracing was put down and covered, being improved five years later with provision for 200 bench seats. Four years later it was extended on both sides and now stretches the full length of that side.

1990 saw more terracing go down opposite the stand and the impressive floodlighting system followed. One major problem the club have with the Andrew Street ground is the ancient right of way which runs across it preventing the club from ever locking and securing the premises. The Oldham Municipal Borough Council who own the ground are powerless to do anything about what is a wholly unsatisfactory situation.

MOOR LANE
Salford City FC

Salford are in the unenviable position of running a football club under the nose of the most famous club of all just up the road at Old Trafford. Despite this and a constant battle against vandalism, City have continued in the North-West Counties League updating their ground even though each season brings fewer spectators but more demands to house them safely.

Salford were formed as Salford Central during the War and played on Littleton Road Rec, part of which is used today by Manchester United's 'B' team. From there they moved to the White City Stadium, which was not a success bearing in mind it was opposite Old Trafford. They then transferred to an old athletics track in The Crescent, a pitch laid out in a horseshoe bend on the River Irwell. This had been used as an anti-aircraft site during the war and a Nissen

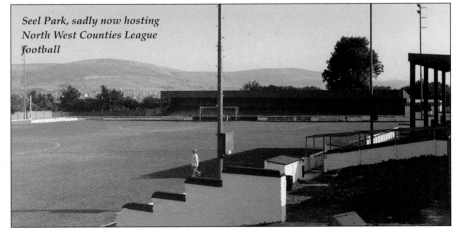

Seel Park, sadly now hosting North West Counties League football

The covered stand at Chadderton FC (above). In 1963 the Andrew Street was little more than a field (below).

SURREY STREET, HURST CROSS
Ashton United FC

Hurst Cross is nearly 110 years old, having been opened on September 18th 1886, but would have seen little action after the early 1990's were it not for the work of those running the club at the time. Hurst Cross had deteriorated to such an extent the club were refused entry to the Northern Premier League, and nothing less than a complete overhaul was required. It is now a colourful, vibrant ground, alive with advertising, new seating facilities, terracing, lounges, and refreshment areas.

The name Ashton United only surfaced in 1947, as until then the club were known as Hurst FC. There were several grounds used in the intervening years before the move to Hurst Cross, including Holebottom, Rose Hill and Robinson Lane. The original club

hut was converted and used as dressing rooms by the club. Finally in 1979, Salford moved to Moor Lane, the former home of Manchester Rugby Union FC. That club had moved on some time previously and the ground was then used by Langwithy ARLFC until around 1976, laying idle and vandalised after that time. There was a roofless open-backed stand and the ground was banked and part-terraced, but had no electricity, water or drains. The old dressing rooms opposite the stand had been burnt down, and it was many months before football could be staged there.

Since then the club have added City to their name and have built a small covered enclosure on one bank. The record crowd for a football match at Moor Lane is 3,000 which saw the FA Vase match with Whickham in 1981.

Salford City, a former Rugby League ground rescued from dereliction.

BUTCHERS ARMS
Droylsden FC

Dating back to the late 1800's, the remarkable history of the Butchers Arms is as chequered as any ground in the country. It has endured complete change at least three times, been home to several different clubs and even been left unused. The field had originally been a fairground and it was not until the tenant of the adjacent pub laid out a bowling green, put up out-buildings, and eventually became president of the new club, that football was staged.

The original club folded and re-formed several times in the post-War period, but by the 1920's the field was enclosed, with a wooden fence stretching around most of it. There were no spectator facilities until 1923 when, after raising 5,000 shillings, the pitch was railed off, duck-boards laid down and banking added, with a small stand going up soon after. Some five years later the shelter along Greenside Lane was built to hold around 400 and by 1933 there were three stands, and sunken baths installed in the dressing rooms. Blackpool 'A' team were sharing the ground whilst playing in the Manchester League and at the time the Butchers Arms could hold some 8,000 with over 2,500 under cover. Their first application to join the Cheshire League was accompanied by a promise to build a new 2,000-seater stand should they be elected. They were not accepted and so contented themselves with putting up new offices and turnstiles, lengthening and widening the pitch and building a new cover for 1,000 in time for entry to the Lancashire Combination.

Blackpool made way for Manchester City in 1937, and work continued with an exit made into Greenside Lane, a new covered stand behind the Market Street goal and more banking opposite with terracing. The stand from the previous year now had a glass-sided press box for protection from the elements. The stands were painted red and white and as War approached voluntary labour helped erect the impressive main gates.

Unusually, the club played through the

Above: The bright and cheerful home of Ashton United pictured in 1992.
Below: The ground had become almost derelict, as this comparison from the late '80s shows.

folded in the 1890's but was re-formed in 1908 by Alderman John Kenworthy, a local mill owner, who was also Patron of the Hurst Agricultural Show, which was held on the ground.

Almost at once Hurst Cross began to take shape and, to keep costs down to a minimum, the bulk of the work was performed by the committee. The *Ashton Reporter* told of £50 being spent, and soon after the pitch was levelled and new turnstiles built, and a concrete fence put around the ground. By 1913 the cost had risen to £2,000, with the opening of the main stand on July 6th 1912, in time for the Ashton Show.

Many felt the ground was comparable with Football League stadia of the day, a statement backed up by the fact that the stand boasted dressing-rooms with baths, a boardroom with telephone and a special glass-fronted area for VIP's. A covered area was later added, as was banking around the ground. But although capable of holding a crowd of over 11,000 for their FA Cup tie with Halifax Town in 1952, Hurst Cross was never going to become like the league grounds it once imitated and fell into a poor state of repair. Happily, in 1990 the original

stand was replaced by a modern structure on the same site, and the terracing re-vamped. A new covered area lies opposite the stand, which is surrounded by a cluster of brick buildings, all painted red and white, and housing a tea-bar and souvenir shop, and club room. Every available space is covered by advertising which gives the place a lively feeling, even when empty, in total contrast to the rather gloomy residential area in which the ground is situated.

Big plans at the Butchers Arms may see a complete rebuild similar to that of 1951.

War and as peace returned plans were made to transform the ground completely by switching it around by 45 degrees. The whole place by now was described as 'very shabby', and this hampered the club's forward planning, although crowds held up healthily at around the 2,000 mark. Then in 1948, rivals Droylsden United, who had started many years earlier as Belle Vue, announced they had bought the ground from the brewery. This provoked two years of bitter rivalry between the pair, with United gaining the upper hand and the old club moving out to play at Moorside Stadium, a disused trotting track in Sandy Lane, which had cover for 1,000 but no seats. Refreshment rooms and new dressing rooms were built and supporters remained loyal while work went on at the Butchers Arms with the main stand being dismantled and re-erected ten yards further back, while the terracing and pitch were both

SHAWE VIEW
Trafford FC

Although only developed to any great degree within the last five years, Shawe View has hosted both Rugby League and football and been home to a variety of clubs.

During the 50's and early sixties it was Manchester City's training ground and their 'A' and 'B' sides also played there. It had halogen lighting mounted on wooden posts and a grassed bank made of ash stretched along one side and behind the far goal with dressing rooms at the side. Salford Rugby League club are believed to have used it as have Altrincham's reserves and the Alliance side of Trafford Borough RLFC.

In between all this Urmston Town used the ground in their Manchester League days and played there until unable to continue in the NWCL as Shawe View was not up to standard. It lay unused and overgrown until a new club North Trafford took it over, renting it for two seasons before acquiring a lease.

Much work has gone on to transform the ground into something near to NPL standard with a concrete panel fence and numerous gates the first to go in.

It now has three areas of cover, all centralised with hard standing and a complete post and rail. Trafford Council have provided new changing rooms and portacabins now house a clubhouse and hospitality area. The North Stand contains a set of seats which formerly graced a nearby language laboratory and the opposite side has 184 seats which historically looked out over Leeds Road, Huddersfield.

enlarged. In April 1951 the Council announced they had purchased the ground to preserve it for the footballers of Droylsden, but equally importantly with United struggling to survive, the two clubs merged as Droylsden FC and played at Moorside Stadium during the first part of the season as more work went on prior to their return in December.

The long awaited transformation of the Butchers Arms began with the pitch turned around, one goal sited where the old bowling green had been. The popular side banking was then bulldozed and the sloping part of the old field levelled off. The stands were knocked down, offices demolished and only the dressing rooms remained. A new 200 seater stand was built with the old cover going up opposite and a fresh perimeter fence appeared around the ground. The work was completed in time for the opening match of the 1952-53 season against Morecambe Reserves.

In recent years the terracing at the far end was removed when it was discovered the pitch was too short for FA Cup football and for a while the ground was three-sided. That has since been rectified and further work will continue to drag the dear old Butchers Arms screaming into the realms of the Conference gradings. Plans are afoot to remove the old main stand and build a new 650-seater version, with another opposite the car-park end of the ground.

VALLEY ROAD
Flixton FC

Flixton Football Club are rightly proud of their home which has been transformed with the addition of a magnificent £320,000 clubhouse, incorporating various bars and function rooms, and boasts a viewing gallery on the second floor. A far cry indeed from the club's foundation in 1960, when they began playing in local junior leagues on council pitches at Urmston Meadows before taking over in 1973 what was no more than a farmer's field on the banks of the Manchester Ship Canal.

For the first season, before changing facilities in the shape of a small wooden hut were put in place, the players changed a few hundred yards down the road at the Woodsend Playing Fields. The hut eventually grew to incorporate a bar, and a year or so later this generated sufficient funds to fully enclose the ground with a concrete wall, with some hard standing and a perimeter fence.

The hut sufficed until 1980 when the pre-fabricated building to the right of the entrance was put up as a new clubhouse. This in turn produced further funding to build new changing rooms and covered standing down one side, which has since been extended. As the eighties came to an end two areas of cover went up on the canal side, followed by the strangely-angled floodlights which stand facing each other a few yards in from the corner flags. Behind the goal nearest the entrance, the car parking space has expanded every five years with an extra section being added in 1995 when the new club was opened. To necessitate this, a small area of cover, was taken down; a small price to pay for having one of the best facilities for miles. The clubhouse also advertises the football club name, which is visible from several hundred yards away across the Ship Canal.

BRANTINGHAM ROAD
Maine Road FC

Maine Road Football Club's home for the past fifteen years has been the Manchester County FA ground in Chorlton-cum-Hardy. The club was formed by a group of Manchester City fans back in 1955 and began playing on Hough End Playing Fields in Withington before moving to Ward Street OB's in Stockport in 1973. This was home for two years before further moves to the Tootal Sports Ground in Newton Heath and the Leesfield in Flixton.

Primarily they were a Sunday team and only made the switch on joining the Manchester League in 1972. From there the progression to North-West Counties League football and a developed ground took fifteen

Shawe View, former home of Manchester City 'A' and Urmston Town, now Trafford FC.

years. The first building was a small covered standing area holding 20 seats for officials and guests and this was followed a year later by another stand with 200 seats, a refreshment bar, and a new brick-built clubhouse. A further stand went up in 1989 for around 500 with a new toilet block and concrete hard standing all around the pitch. Finally floodlighting was installed as the ground was brought in line with Division One regulations. Not surprisingly in such an area of football, the 2,000 capacity has never really been threatened, the highest gate being 875 against Altrincham in the FA Cup in 1990.

EWEN FIELDS
Hyde United FC

Ten years ago, Hyde United Supporters' Club, who held the ground in trust, sold it to Tameside Council, who saw it as part of a much grander scheme. The sale heralded the start of a transformation at the ground which, to complete its humiliation was re-christened the `Tameside Leisure Park'.

There had been various school and church sides playing football prior to 1885 in the town, but in August of that year, at a meeting held at the White Lion, Hyde Football Club was formed. Early friendly matches were played at a ground previously used by Hyde Rugby Club, in Walker Fold, but two seasons later they were playing on a field close to the Bankfield Hotel, which may well have been where Ewen Fields is today. The club were successful, and to open the 1886-87 season, Blackburn Rovers, the triple FA Cup winners, played a game in front of over 2,000 spectators. A year later Bolton Wanderers were the visitors and in preparation for the match the ground was boarded all round, and an enclosure built along one side. The local press of the time heaped much praise on goalkeeper Bunyan who played in the Bolton game, but was to make headlines two months later in the first round of the FA Cup, when Preston North End, the best team in the world at the time, scraped past Hyde 26-0 at Deepdale.

In 1898, the club moved to Townend Street, and set up their headquarters at the Gardeners Pub in Lumn Road, then called Back Lane. This was home until May 1906, when a rival club Hyde St. Georges were swallowed up in a merger, and Hyde FC began playing on their ground, Ewen Fields. The early optimism and success of the pre-War years faded, and for two years during the hostilities, the club carried on but by February 1917 Hyde FC had folded, and Ewen Fields became a vegetable patch.

Following a prolonged campaign by the local newspaper, a new team, Hyde United were formed and played at Townend Street with a proviso from the new owner who was a butcher, that he be allowed to graze his cattle on the pitch. The teams changed at the Globe Inn, with the paper gloomily predict-

NATIONAL PARK
Curzon Ashton FC

The `Nash' has been around in one form or another since before the Great War. It was originally owned by St. Peter's Church whose football club first used it. Eventually it was sold to the National Gasoil and Engine Company and their club changed the rather unwieldy cognomen to Ashton National FC.

The pitch ran parallel to the railway line, and had two large wooden stands either side, both of which were destroyed in fires around 1938, believed to have originated from the timber yard which is still situated adjacent to the ground. Lancashire League side Dukinfield Town took over the ground for a while, and eventually a merger between Curzon Road Methodists and Ashton Amateurs created Curzon Amateurs, latterly Curzon Ashton.

The modern club dates from 1963, the National Park having been developed to Northern Premier League standards with the building of the 350-seater Branfoot Stand in 1982. The seats were acquired from the demolished Manchester White City Stadium. Two years previously the clubhouse had been obtained and transported to the ground in full, and a small covered area of terrace added.

The ground is dominated on one side by the huge expanse of a timber works and at one end by a row of terraced houses. The stand is basically breeze-block and iron, and the cover is similarly shaped but without the seats. The rest of the ground is functional if not spectacular, when compared to some of the other Tameside stadia.

ing that Ewen Fields had no chance of staging football again, and that it was to be used for housing within months.

In the summer of 1920, the club were elected into the Manchester League, and duly moved back to Ewen Fields. The close season saw dressing rooms and offices in place, and success continued. In 1922, tons of ash was spread around the pitch side to make life more bearable and less muddy, and new fencing installed. The following season a Supporters' Club was formed and a match programme issued, while soon after the first stand went up, which existed on the Walker Lane side until 1981. This was joined by another, larger stand, costing £575 and seating 400. It was officially opened by Councillor Hibbert before 3,000 people on August 25th 1928, prior to a game with Rochdale Reserves.

Hyde continued to be unbeatable in the league, and following two more Championships - making five in ten years - they joined the Cheshire League. Much work was necessary during the 1930 close season; new drains were laid, goals erected, and sleepers put down for terracing on the popular side; hoardings were put up near Tinker's Passage, and the Mottram Road end was banked. At this point the capacity of the ground was estimated at 10,000, and half that number watched the first game against Altrincham. Throughout the thirties the crowds flocked to Ewen Fields, and as War approached an ever-optimistic Hyde opened a Social Club.

Football continued until 1942, in a wartime league, but the club were dormant from then until July 1945, when a meeting reformed the club who went back into the Cheshire League as a limited company. In 1955, having weathered a cash crisis, it was decided to further improve Ewen Fields by

erecting a concrete and metal pitch surround and repairing the popular side terracing. The changes continued in the late fifties, with two covered areas at the Tinker's Passage end in place. In 1966 a new Social Club was built, and a year later the club took the bold step of entering the newly-formed Northern Premier League. At the end of 1968, Joe Mercer's Manchester City were the guests to open the £4,000 floodlights in front of 4,000 paying fans, but their flirtation with the league was short-lived, for they were on the brink of going under, and were forced to re-join the Cheshire League.

It was 1981 before Hyde United could return to the NPL, and to comply with the ground regulations of the time, the old Walker Lane stand was demolished, and a brand new perimeter fence erected around the ground. This was however the calm before the storm for, having purchased the ground, the Tameside Council decided to replace conventional grass with a synthetic Baspograss. This led to the revelation that the pitch had been on the skew, and as a result the Mottram Road stand is now at an angle to the pitch. The wooden stand was demolished, and replaced with a new structure which has a board room, first-aid room, toilets and tea-bar. The old secretary's office and tea-bar, which stood by the turnstiles went too. Grass mounds were left behind the Walker Lane goal, and to the left of the main stand, and the dressing rooms were moved to the girls' school next door, to enable American Football, which has a squad of 50, to be played.

Since then, the grass mounds have been levelled, the covered standing on the Leigh Street side removed and Ewen Fields is now the Tameside Leisure Park and unrecognisable from ten years ago.

South Lancs

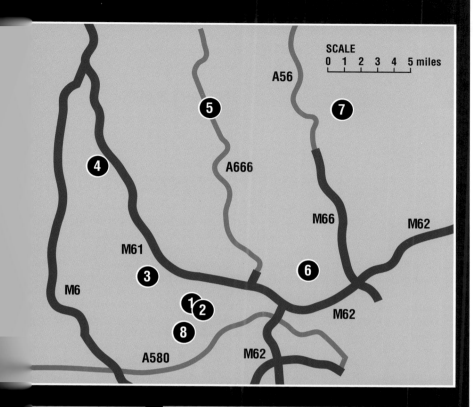

SCALE
0 1 2 3 4 5 miles

A56

A666

M66

M62

M61

M6

M62

A580

M62

1	Atherton Collieries FC
2	Atherton Laburnum Rovers FC
3	Daisy Hill FC
4	Chorley FC
5	Darwen FC
6	Radcliffe Borough FC
7	Rossendale United FC
8	Leigh RMI FC

Below: Two stands at Atherton Collieries hanging on for dear life.

THE North-West Counties and the Northern Premier Leagues dominate the area of South Lancashire immediately above the M62. Unlike the Tameside area to the east of Manchester, there have not been any representatives in the Conference and with the two senior clubs, Chorley and Horwich RMI both suffering various financial problems, it is left to Atherton LR who have carried out much work on their ground to reach the NPL, and fly the flag.

ALDER HOUSE
Atherton Collieries FC

Of the three senior clubs in Atherton, the "Colls" are by far the oldest and have a ground which, although now in a different format, is as old as the club.

In 1916, a group of miners representing the six pits within the district formed a club for the welfare of those at home involved in the war effort. The early days saw the pitch at right angles to its current position, but this changed when mine owners Fletcher Burrows built the community centre which still stands proudly by the entrance. When the pits were nationalised, the club was given to the people of the town.

Alder House has altered considerably over the years, the original changing room shack doing sterling service behind the near goal until the players began changing under the original clubhouse. On the half-way line the wonderful ricketty little stand with recently replaced roof and sides, seems to be leaning forward as if in prayer for its continued survival. Next to it, is its 10-year old big brother built on an area which was originally terraced using sleepers.

The current changing rooms are from timber merchants Mallinton and Derry who used the building as a trading centre, before the club bought them five years ago. The small clubhouse has been extended recently in a similar way to that at Welton Rovers, by building around it with breeze blocks and then gutting it. Seating has been provided in front of it, and another more temporary enclosure, re-roofed after it was partially destroyed by high winds in January 1993, has been erected behind the dug-outs on the half-way line. The club have continued to press forward with improvements, the floodlighting being erected in 1994, and a car park laid out on the site which in the past has seen bowls and a boxing ring.

CRILLY PARK
Atherton Laburnum Rovers FC

Atherton Laburnum Rovers have been in existence since 1954, taking their name from Laburnum Road Playing Fields where they began. After a couple of seasons they moved on to Hagfold Playing Fields, remaining there until a farmer's field

Atherton L.R.'s new Crilly Park stand.

became available in the shadow of the massive Laburnum Mill. The early days were spartan, and the players changed in air-raid shelters, previously used by the mill. To gain entrance to the ground, players and spectators had to negotiate a duck pond, roughly where the gates are today.

It wasn't long before the ground began to take shape, with a pitch-side fence fashioned by driving railway sleepers into the ground and suspending chains acquired from the local pits across them. In 1972 the club spent £3,500, investing in a new solid concrete perimeter fence which club officials claim has been the best financial move they have yet made. To this day it is as good as new.

The first structure to provide cover was the clubhouse which had a verandah, but eventually in 1983, the covered enclosure set some way back from the pitch behind the far goal was erected. Three years later, two small areas of cover appeared either side of the half-way line, being joined together by more cover in 1991 when the gap was filled, and seating provided.

Since then a new 200-seater stand has been built in front of the car-park to cater for the club's promotion to higher spheres.

On entering the ground, the enclosed feel of the surrounding houses makes it difficult to imagine that only 30 years ago the area was merely fields dominated by a massive mill with a set of goalposts in the middle.

A glance at the aerial photo in the clubhouse emphasises the difference.

Atherton Laburnum Rovers have tasted success during their residence at Crilly Park and it will be interesting to plot the continued growth of club and ground as time goes by.

NEW SIRS
Daisy Hill FC

Daisy Hill FC were originally founded 100 years ago and until the Second War played in Westhoughton and Bolton Leagues on a variety of pitches including one on Leigh Road near the railway station and another behind Kearsley Street.

The club reformed in peacetime and played for several years on the Recreation Ground adjacent to New Sirs until they obtained a lease for the land around 1958.

The site had seen football staged before the war but was never developed and it remained that way, players changing in the Daisy Hill Hotel above the stables until a Scout hut was bought and used for that purpose.

The impressive curved structure behind the near goal is made out of two separate 60ft by 20ft buildings laid end to end and incorporates changing rooms, a boardroom kitchens and a clubhouse. In front is the brick based timber stand containing over 200 seats originally at Ewood Park, Blackburn. Along one side a small covered area which can hold around 200 was built around ten years ago. Daisy Hill briefly changed their name to Westhoughton Town FC in an attempt to generate more interest in the town but happily have since reverted to the original name. The record crowd at New Sirs is believed to be for the Westhoughton Charity Cup final in

August 1980 when 2,000 saw the match with Horwich RMI evoking memories of pre-war finals at the old Red Lion Ground where up to 5,000 would pack around the natural slopes to watch the matches on the home of the now long gone Westhoughton FC. The Red Lion Ground was opposite the pub of the same name but was sliced in two by a road some years back.

VICTORY PARK
Chorley FC

Chorley's magnificent brooding ground stands within a stone's throw of the club's former home at St. Georges Park, which until quite recently was the home of Multipart FC.

On entering an empty Victory Park there is an unmistakably Lancastrian atmosphere about the place. The vast, solidly-built main stand has a mass of ironwork holding up the roof with two floodlight pylons bursting through it and a series of square port holes along the the brick front. The entire edifice has provided the model on which, in later years, Kings Lynn, Cheltenham Town and Morecambe designed their stands.

Behind the goal nearest the car-park is the huge covered end, the roof supported by over 30 stanchions embedded into concrete, and opposite, on the Pilling Lane end, a similarly supported newer-looking covered terrace behind the goal with only three stanchions. A safety barriered, unmade grass

A new stand at Chorley, in use in 1947 but not finished.
Below: A fine view of Victory Park.

STAINTON PARK
Radcliffe Borough FC

Stainton Park has only existed since 1970 when Bright Street, the club's home since their formation in 1949, was earmarked for development. At first there were no facilities of any description at the ground, and the players were forced to change in the home of the Radcliffe Times' editor, Mr Harry Spencer.

Bright Street lasted until 1968 when the club played at Crumpsall until a site on the opposite side of the town, almost adjacent to the cricket club was found in 1970. A local builder, Henry Stainton, gave his name to the ground which soon boasted a small stand along one side and was enclosed all around. The ground was heaving in 1982 when Borough played championship rivals Caernarfon in front of 1,500 spectators and it became apparent that improvements were needed. There was a successful floodlight appeal and in 1988 a covered stand was put up behind one goal.

The clubhouse which stands alongside the pitch was out of action from 1980 but with that re-opened and the oft-troublesome pitch now giving less grief than before, the fledgling Stainton Park is looking good.

bank stretches around to a small fenced car-park in front of the club-house.

Chorley Football Club has been in existence since 1875, although for the first eight or nine years the club played under the rugby code. An inaugural meeting took place at the Anchor Inn on October 15th 1875, and play began at the Dole Lane ground, later to become the Coronation Recreation Ground. In those early days, the ground was quite small, though subsequently enlarged by the addition of two further fields adjoining Mount Pleasant Gardens, when the club decided to change to the more scientific game of association.

Dole Lane was to remain the home of the Magpies for 25 years, until forced off by the Corporation who wished to transform the ground into a recreational area. At that time the club were experiencing severe financial problems, but supporters rallied round and held a bazaar in order to clear debts and raise money for a new ground. It transpired the club had a one year stay of execution, so they did not vacate until April 1901, by which time the search for another ground had been successful, with a lease obtained for the Rangletts Ground, between Duke Street and Pilling Lane. Although the field was in poor condition, having previously been a colliery, it was later re-laid and made serviceable, and the grandstand at Dole Lane was re-sited at Rangletts together with the dressing tents and two refreshment bars, the whole affair costing just over £100. The first match at Rangletts Park was on September 7th 1901, against local rivals Chorley St. George, who had a well-equipped ground next door at St. George's Park.

St. George's had made many improvements to their ground, including a fine new stand for over 500 people, but a series of misfortunes befell the club, and in February 1905 they asked to be released from their remaining league fixtures and disbanded. Quick off the mark, the Chorley management applied for tenancy of St. George's, not only because that ground was in better condition but also

because they were in danger of being evicted from their own. The application was granted and the club moved next door in September 1905, beating Bacup Borough in the first game, in front of 1,500 spectators.

Chorley entered a quiet phase leading up to the first war, but with the pre-war boom in football, they searched for fresh pastures. In September 1920, they opened a new ground in Duke Street, just yards away from the previous two. Much of the land had been used for a rubbish dump, and had to be levelled with banking shaped for the new season. In the same month Peel Park, home of Accrington Stanley, was opened in front of 10,000 spectators with a game against Chorley.

In August 1929 the first stage of covered terrace went up at the Pilling Lane end and three years later the club attendance record was set, and remains, when 9,679 paid £275 to watch an FA Cup tie with Darwen. Around this time, the club's ill-fated grandstand was built on the site of the present structure, but disaster struck in the form of a fierce gale which tore the roof off the Pilling Lane end and deposited it on a group of nearby greenhouses, causing some £800

worth of damage. A friendly match was played in 1944 to raise funds to pay the bill, and a Combined Services eleven took on Chorley in front of over 4,000. However, a far worse catastrophe was to occur, just hours after the club had defeated old rivals Accrington Stanley in the FA Cup on November 16th 1945, when the main stand caught fire. Before being brought under control, the seating accommodation, board-room, dressing rooms and equipment were all destroyed.

True to their spirit and within two years, a new, and even more impressive brick and wood stand was opened on the site of the original, and this signalled the start of the shaping of Victory Park as it is today. The low ricketty stand at the Pilling Lane end was replaced by a far sturdier grey-roofed terrace, and the opposite end gained an equally solid covered end, copied some years later by Morecambe. Surprisingly the rest of the ground has never been fully developed, although the grass banking is deep enough to have accommodated some hefty crowds in the past. When empty, Victory Park is one of the most awesome stadia in England, and curiously feels far more intimidating in that state, than when filled with hundreds of spectators on match day.

GRUNDY HILL and HILTON PARK
Horwich RMI FC (now Leigh RMI FC)

Although well past its prime and no longer acceptable to the NPL due to its switchback pitch, the loss of Grundy Hill to housing development is a major blow to the area and to non-League football. At the end the ground looked tired and ready to concede defeat to both the vandals and old Father Time. With so much work needed to spruce it up to league standards the trustees took the option of a ground share with Leigh Rugby League club a dozen or so miles away, and for good measure also accepted that town's name .

Grundy Hill, Horwich, now sadly demolished.

A grainy old photo from 1897 of Barley Bank, Darwen's Football League ground.

BARLEY BANK and THE ANCHOR GROUND
Darwen FC

The history of Darwen Football Club is such that many people believe the club's Football League days were spent at the Anchor, such is the antiquity of the place. The truth, however, is that their League ground was Barley Bank, demolished shortly after Darwen left the League and now buried under Avondale Primary School.

Barley Bank had a stand which was in poor repair when the club vacated in 1899, and it is not known precisely how much of it was used in erection of the Anchor Ground, although £140 was spent on provision of the seated stand. At the time the club were involved in a court action brought by a former player and this led to the disposal of all the equipment from Barley Bank including the dressing tents, and the railings around the pitch. The new ground, where the rent was £10 for the winter, was prepared solely by volunteers.

The Anchor has changed significantly within the last fifteen years; the large cantilever stand on the far side of the ground was removed leaving a couple of steps of terracing and an ugly concrete panel wall, while the Gracie Fields stand behind the car-park end goal was also demolished in 1993. This structure was erected on the proceeds of the club's FA Cup tie at Arsenal in 1932, which although lost 11-1, generated enough funds to enable the club to cover the terracing. It left just the cavernous enclosure, which has a couple of rows of wooden seating, and the remains of the old terrace, which stretches most of the length of the pitch, with only the newly re-built clubhouse and changing rooms between it and the corner flag. Nowadays the best view of the Anchor is from the open side as the remaining stand is still in good fettle and offers a tangible reminder of better days. All around the ground the old terracing is crumbling and weed strewn, the popular side being the only one used on a regular basis. There are a number of buildings of uncertain age dotted around the entrance which nowadays is faced by a huge paint factory complex, but the club have recently fought back against the elements in that area by relaying the terracing at the Gracie Fields end.

Grundy Hill was first opened in the early 1900's when the Railway Mechanics Institute moved their club from the old ground on what is locally known as The Racecourse. The football part of the Institute had originally begun as the Lancs and Yorks Railway FC in 1887 changing their name nine years later. On moving into Grundy Hill, joiners from the works helped create a covered enclosure on the railway station side, which straddled the half way line and stood next to an old railway carriage that gave service as a changing room until the huge blue-painted wooden building was erected in the corner nearest the cricket pitch. Men from the works also built the grandstand which was opened in the thirties and at the end could seat 500 in reasonable comfort, although the classic design of a roof supported at the front by eight struts and a centrally situated floodlight pylon did little to improve the view. In similar fashion to the GER Ground at March, the stand was appreciated more as an historical artefact - to look at rather than sit in. Inevitably, railway sleepers had been utilised for terracing and these were still evident in the final days under the cover opposite the stand and to the right and left of it.

In 1956 supporters of the club built the cover which stood at the east end of the ground until 1987 when a fierce storm destroyed it sending the roof crashing out of the ground. Much of the cover on the railway side was similarly damaged a year later, and in the final years only a small section remained, albeit with the side wall intact giving tangible evidence of the first structure on the ground 70 years earlier.

Grundy Hill was unique for its remarkable undulating pitch which gave the impression that play was uphill from whichever side it was viewed. Whereas the Huish at Yeovil and Loakes Park at Wycombe sloped side to side, and Zembard Lane at Chard has a gradient of around 1 in 5 end to end, Grundy Hill was like an inverted crown green bowling rink tipped at an angle for good measure.

The site may well have been built on by

Looking towards what was the Gracie Fields Stand at Darwen and (right) the opposite end, rudimentary terracing.

now, leaving the cricket ground next door and bowls club close by, to keep alive the RMI.

Hilton Park is better known as the home of Leigh Rugby League Club, and has been since its opening game in August 1947. It was first laid out when the rugby club were given the old stand from their previous ground in Mather Lane and three years later a huge 12,000 capacity Supporters' Club stand was built which allowed the ground record to be set in 1953 when some 31,326 saw a Challenge Cup-tie with St Helens. Both ends were terraced in 1964, and despite fire regulation work on the new old main stand, the current capacity for rugby is probably less than 10,000.

DARK LANE
Rossendale United FC

From around 1870, a Myrtle Grove team that was one of the fore-runners of Rossendale United, played on a works site near the Rossendale area of Cloughfold. Meanwhile a Rugby Union team had moved on to Dark Lane to play their code, but this did not last much past 1890 as many had taken up soccer. This allowed the lads from Myrtle Grove to take over Dark Lane, and change their name to Rossendale FC. They were admitted to the Lancashire League and in 1894 applied to join Division Two of the Football League, but came bottom of nine applicants.

The club's spirit ebbed away after this and the team disbanded in 1897. In the same year, Rawtenstall FC were demoted from the Lancashire Combination and for one year no senior football was staged in Rossendale. The next move came when The Bluebell pub

A 1941 Rossendale team group in front of the current main stand.

became the headquarters of a new team risen from the ashes of the previous clubs. They were called Rossendale United, and would play on Dark Lane in the centre of the Borough of Rawtenstall. Originally Bacup were offered the chance to join the new set-up but they declined, having their own team and ground. The club was officially launched on July 6th 1898, and the first match played at Dark Lane on September 3rd against Oswaldtwistle Rovers. However, the new club encountered financial problems and despite being elected to the Lancs. Combination in place of Darwen Reserves an emergency meeting was held at the local Liberal Club to decide whether or not to continue. The club struggled on and eventually support improved but the ground needed upgrading, and minor work was carried out to facilitate this. The first major work on the ground came in August 1928 when a new stand was opened for a game against Dick Kerr's XI and this marvellous structure, healthily refurbished, still looks good today in its smart coat of kingfisher blue and white. The first set of floodlighting was erected in 1959, Nelson being the first visitors, losing a League Cup tie 4-0. The floodlights were

eventually replaced by a new system in 1972 and opened with a game against Burnley

In November 1975 the ground attendance record was set when Shrewsbury Town attended for an FA Cup-tie. This proved to be the last big game at Dark Lane for some time as the ground had fallen into disrepair and needed a major overhaul. After securing a 99-year lease from the holding company the club have begun changing Dark Lane for the better. The boardroom and dressing-rooms were re-furbished in 1985, and two years later new terracing was laid at the Staghills Road end of the ground. A new hard standing area was created, the tea-hut given a complete overhaul and essential safety work carried out to enable the club to play in the Northern Premier League. New turnstiles were installed for the 1989-90 campaign and more work done on the stand. In 1991 a gymnasium was built and 1993 saw the lights updated again. With the exception of a handful of games in 1981-82 which were played elsewhere due to the holding company's decision to allow another club use of the ground, Rossendale United have used Dark Lane for nearly 100 years, and it has probably never looked better.

Dale's near neighbours Bacup Borough play on an exposed ground at COWFOOT LANE which has spectacular views over the moors and the Forest of Rossendale. Bacup FC have been around since 1875 and have played there for most of that time. It is not known precisely when the ground was first used, but Bacup joined the prestigious Lancs Combination in 1902 and it would be fair to say the ground was around for that. There are several areas of cover, attached to the boundary wall to give shelter and seating for around 500, with sufficient sloping standing areas for it to be comfortable. Just after the war, Nelson FC visited the ground attracting a crowd of nearly 5,000 for a League match, a record likely to stand.

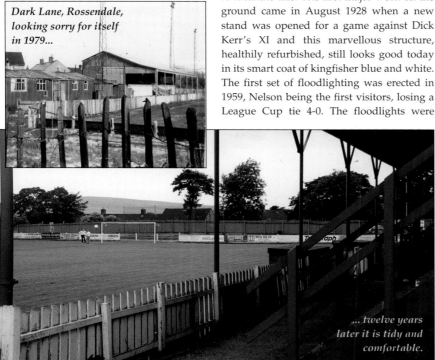

Dark Lane, Rossendale, looking sorry for itself in 1979...

...twelve years later it is tidy and comfortable.

Central Lancashire and the coast

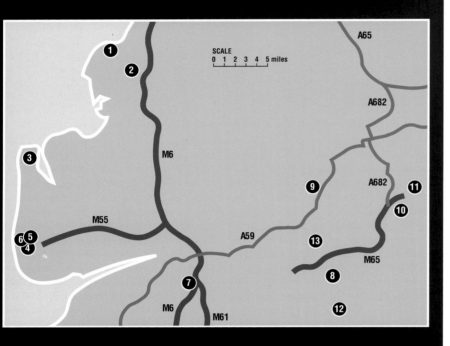

SCALE
0 1 2 3 4 5 miles

A65
A682
A682
M6
M55
A59
M65
M6
M61

1	Morecambe FC	7	Bamber Bridge FC
2	Lancaster City FC	8	Accrington Stanley FC
3	Fleetwood Town FC	9	Clitheroe FC
4	Blackpool Mechanics FC	10	Nelson FC
5	Squires Gate FC	11	Colne Dynamoes FC
6	Blackpool Wren Rovers FC	12	Haslingden FC
		13	Great Harwood FC

Christie Park, Morecambe.

CENTRAL LANCASHIRE, for the purposes of this book, is defined between the Ribble and Morecambe Bay and includes the ribbon of industrial towns from Preston to Burnley. It has a former League club in Nelson and the son of one in Accrington, plus the ghost of Colne Dynamoes, an ambitious club that could have gone all the way until the architect of their success became thoroughly disenchanted and folded the club virtually overnight.

Morecambe, in the north and Bamber Bridge in the south of the area have both radically altered their grounds very recently, the former having taken their place in the Conference during 1995.

CHRISTIE PARK
Morecambe FC

Christie Park in its more modern format was an amalgam of styles based on other well-known grounds which were developed around the same time. The covered Lancaster Road end, opened in September 1958 was built to the same design as Chorley's imposing structure which stands relatively unaltered at Victory Park, whilst the modern main stand, opened four years later was based on the main stand at Whaddon Road, Cheltenham. Behind the opposite goal, the massive covered barn-like structure which is occasionally used for training purposes is reminiscent of that at Fenland Park, Wisbech, although possibly by coincidence rather than design.

Morecambe's first season was spent at Woodhall Lane, then as now the home of the town cricket club, before Roseberry Park was built on council-owned land ready for the 1921-22 season, and was opened with a game against Fleetwood Town. Soon after, a wooden stand and dressing rooms were added to the ground which was already fenced-in thus enabling the club to take a gate at home games. The name Roseberry Park lasted only four years, for it was purchased by a local man Mr. J.B. Christie, who bequeathed the land in trust for the exclusive use of the football club, who responded by re-naming the ground Christie Park. It slowly developed, with a scratching shed appearing behind the far goal, covering the whole width of the playing area. As was common practice at the time, loose banking was provided around the pitch and this stayed relatively unmolested until the Lanky Road terrace was built, at a cost of £3,000. Two years later, the club invested in floodlighting, celebrated with a match against a Tom Finney XI, which Morecambe won 4-3, and two years on from that, the new stand replaced the original at a cost of £21,000. By this time the old scratching shed was showing its age. It eventually succumbed to a fierce gale in 1967, was blown away and replaced soon after by the current stand.

Since then, the ground has suffered a major setback when the covered terrace was declared unsafe, and the roof removed. The concrete bases of the pylons can still be seen embedded in the ground, as can the plaque built into the side of what was the stand wall which details the opening of that structure. The open side has lost most of its cinder bank, and is now part flat standing with portions of terraced grass providing an elevated view. In truth, the modern day Christie Park is clinging on to its self-respect in some areas, whereas in others it is quite splendid. The main stand is tidy and comfortable, and strangely provides a better view than does its brother at Whaddon Road, and although now shorn of its roof, the terrace is in good shape.

An updated floodlight system and a small stand to cater for disabled supporters have been added within the last three years, and plans are in hand to further develop the area in front of the Supporters' Club and squash club, as Morecambe look to update the ground to Conference standards.

GIANT AXE
Lancaster City FC

Apart from the first two games of the 1905/6 season, the Giant Axe has always been the home of Lancaster Football Club. The two opening games were played at Quay Meadow, which was also used for whippet racing when not in use by junior clubs and is situated some 400 yards from the present ground.

For many years the ground retained its Edwardian roots. The open field had the football pitch to the west, with space for another alongside before sloping gently upwards to a railway embankment.

On the west side were two 500-seater grandstands with conventional pitched roofs, and to the north was a directors' pavilion. The main pitch was surrounded by a cinder track with a rail on the inside for specta-

tors to lean on. Such was the scale of the ground that 7,500 packed in to watch an FA Cup-tie with Carlisle United in 1936. The only other form of cover was a scratching shed, the date of which is unknown.

On entry to the Northern Premier League at the beginning of the seventies the ground had to alter, the first major change being the shape of the Giant Axe. Originally, it had been oval with blue and white railings running inside the track, leaving two large grassy D-shaped areas, regularly filled by small boys, behind either goal. After squaring off the playing surface, a wooden fence was erected along the bank side which effectively cut the ground in two. Then in 1975, just prior to Wigan's visit in the FA Trophy, wooden pallets were delivered to the ground and stacked to form terracing. The pallets remained for a couple of seasons, giving sterling service as duck-boards or fence-fillers in emergencies. To provide cover for the standing faithful, a plan was drawn up to move the scratching shed to a position behind the goal, and eventually it was re-sited against the wall on the Long Marsh Lane end on a slope 25 yards from the pitch.

On the evening of November 22nd 1976 the two wooden grandstands burnt down. Despite the fact that when the pitch was moved nearer, the southern-most stand had a restricted view, the loss of these cavernous structures was immense and to compound the problem the directors' pavilion was condemned around the same time. There was now an urgent need to provide more cover at the Giant Axe, and the Long Marsh end was completed with the addition of some tubular bench seating bought from Morecambe open-air swimming baths. More of the same were sited on the opposite end, and some in front of the boardroom. The club built their new stand on the site of the old ones and immediately re-sited the benches inside until new ones became available.

To improve the view, banking with retaining walls was provided at both ends,

the north end cover was partly concreted and the rest filled with shale. At this stage the Axe began to take shape again, and the wooden fence was replaced with a sturdier concrete one giving the ground a more solid appearance. As needs changed, then the banking was removed leaving flat standing instead. The north-west corner of the ground is the only area which has so far escaped, as the old pavilion survived the fire and has been in use as changing rooms ever since. Sadly, the club have suffered other arson attacks which have nullified the clubhouse, and only recently has a replacement become available after protracted wranglings with the council. As the ground grading became more stringent then various minor changes have had to occur involving turnstiles, toilets and seating, which has had the effect of making the Giant Axe an ever-changing arena. The old girl deserves a period of calm and it must be hoped that she and the club soon get it.

HIGHBURY STADIUM
Fleetwood FC

The running of football clubs in the town of Fleetwood appears to have been fraught with financial danger ever since the formation of Fleetwood Rangers in 1887, who played at the Copse ground which was situated where the junction of Sidings Road and Station Road now stands. An Ordnance Survey map of the 1890's shows the ground to be shared with cricket and replete with a grandstand.

Within ten years the club had folded due to lack of interest, and a new club was formed around the same time, called Fleetwood Amateurs. To coincide with the formation of this club, directors of Fleetwood Estate Co. offered them facilities at the developing Warrenhurst Park, which is now the Memorial Park. A small stand was erected alongside the pitch on the north side of the park. The new club were very successful and by the 1908-09 season were in the West Lancs League, although by then they had been evicted from Warrenhurst Park by the Estate Co. who wanted to move in a local hockey club. For that season they rented a pitch at Old Fleetwood Road golf links close to where Broadwater now stands. The club had dropped the amateur tag from their name to enable them to play professionals, but all the players suffered that season with low-lying ground constantly flooding.

The committee approached the directors of the North Euston Hotel with a view to creating a new ground on land at the rear of the building. The hotel was formerly a barracks with a drill square, and work soon began on the site which necessitated the demolition of many buildings and the removal of a large open air swimming pool at the promenade end.

The club were penniless and totally

The Giant Axe

Fleetwood v Barrow Reserves at the old North Euston ground, 1934/35.

reliant on townspeople for help with the construction of the ground. An appeal brought forth a very positive response and the ground was ready for the start of the 1909-10 season at a cost of £100, which included a stand. Within five years Fleetwood had sold their stand to Blackpool Football Club, and it stood as the north west stand at Bloomfield Road between the kop and the main stand until demolished in the mid eighties.

North Euston ground was opened with a friendly against Preston North End on 8th September 1909. The club continued to grow before and after the Second War, but the ground's limited capacity brought problems, with unruly behaviour amongst home supporters causing it to be shut for two weeks. An order was made to construct dressing rooms for away teams and match officials, who had previously changed in tents. There was precious little room for expansion at North Euston, but fortunately the committee identified a piece of land opposite the Queens Hotel, a limited company was formed to finance the project, and the land bought for £2,370. The ground was quickly made available with a capacity of 30,000!

The total cost of the construction was around £10,000 and once more Preston played a friendly to open the new ground on September 1st 1920. The early twenties were fairly successful but attendances were always poor, with the Queens ground a mile out of town and regarded as being in a country area. Lack of support equalled lack of money, and the great floods of 1927 were the final nail in the coffin of a football club in serious decline. They went into voluntary liquidation and folded, but the ground was sold to another company to prevent developers from acquiring it. Fleetwood Rugby club used the ground until April 1930, when they too folded due to lack of interest. Ultimately the huge ground at Queens was swallowed up by Romney Avenue and Leighton Avenue (The back wall of houses in Romney Avenue is the original perimeter wall of Queens). An amateur outfit by the name of Windsor Villa became the senior club in the town from the mid twenties, playing at North Euston. They

changed their name to Fleetwood Football Club in a bid to attract better players and they were very successful in the thirties. A new grandstand was opened on 9th January 1932, and three consecutive Combination Cup wins and a Lancs Junior Cup followed. This seemed to be their peak for a decline set in and continuing restrictions at North Euston still caused problems.

In December 1936 Fleetwood Council purchased four acres of land adjoining the Memorial Park and fronting onto Highbury Avenue for conversion to a stadium for Fleetwood Football Club. The last match at North Euston was on 22nd April 1939, and the first game at Highbury on 26th August 1939. Five days later War broke out and the ground was subsequently left to rot, due to a shortage of materials and labour for the duration of hostilities. The summer of 1946 was spent erecting new cover to accommodate 3,000 on the popular side opposite the main stand, and the second game was played on August 31st 1946, some seven years after the first.

During March 1948 the Council, (the club's landlords) asked Fleetwood to allow speedway at the ground. It was a boom sport in post-war years, but meant demolition of the cover on the popular side to fit in the track, plus the removal of the corners of the playing surface and their return after each match. The shelter was re-built further back and speedway took off, but there was soon friction between directors of the football and speedway clubs as promises were made and not kept. The speedway company requested a fresh 21-year lease in 1949, but the football club refused, which seems to have been a wise move, for the sport declined badly and the club folded in 1952.

Speedway's legacy has been a deterioration of the ground; the cover on the park side was not re-built. Apart from three sets of floodlights being used and a clubhouse erected very little has since happened to the ground whose record attendance is currently 6,150 against Rochdale in an FA Cup tie thirty years ago.

JEPSON WAY
Blackpool Mechanics FC

The club were formed in 1947 as Blackpool Metal Mechanics and began playing on various pitches on Stanley Park in the town. Eventually a piece of land became available to rent at a playing field in Common Edge Road and the club relocated.

On joining the Lancashire Combination an old RAF hut was obtained from Weeton Army Camp, re-erected at the ground and used as a clubhouse in the early 1960's. At around the same time the ground was fenced off and soon after a small covered stand was put up which lasted until replaced in 1988. The first Lancs Combination match was against Morecambe where the record crowd of 1,200 was posted. Common Edge Road has changed dramatically in the last seven years with three areas of covered standing being erected and terracing added in 1993. The seats came from the old Derby Baths in the town where they were used in the spectators' gallery.

The original clubhouse gave sterling service until 1988 when the new one incorporating dressing rooms was built on the same site. Floodlighting was introduced in 1990, the pylons bought from a rival club who had been refused planning permission, and a concrete fence, replacing the original, has enclosed the ground with the last stretch partly financed by a grant.

Future plans include a multi-purpose indoor five-a-side pitch within a complex which would stand next to the clubhouse. When the dirt track to the ground was changed to a tarred road to allow access to a new industrial site nearby, it was re-named Jepson Way by the council at the club's request in honour of the late founder member and secretary Walter Jepson, hence the official ground address is no longer Common Edge Road.

SCHOOL ROAD
Squires Gate FC

Squires Gate and Wren Rovers play on adjoining grounds in School Road which were fashioned out of a corporation waste tip in 1960. Originally, the clubs played on adjacent pitches with nothing more than a rope separating them, but in time the two grounds were segregated.

Gate's ground is enclosed by a post and rail system which was given by their neighbours as were some of the seats in the stand. The club came out of the West Lancs League in 1991 to join their neighbours in the North-West Counties League.

BRUCE PARK
Blackpool Wren Rovers FC

Blackpool Rovers, or Wren Rovers as they are better known, make up the trio, all vying for the same support and players. Their Bruce Park ground next door to Squires Gate, has a bigger capacity and has been developed for much longer.

Membership of the Lancs Combination until it was enveloped in the NWCL meant the club gained a head start, although much effort was needed to create the present neat and tidy ground. There are a number of covered areas for around 500 with another 250 seated, and the ugly corrugated fence has been swept away and replaced with a concrete version.

Most of the work was done after 1991, and included hard standing and floodlights, opened in October of that year before a match with Manchester City in front of a record crowd of just over 1,000. For a brief period Rovers used the former home of Blackpool Borough Rugby League Club at Borough Park in the late eighties when their ground did not gain a grade for the league. It is unrecognisable now from those days being covered on all four sides with floodlights and as well developed as the Mechanics' ground, a few hundred yards up the road.

Three Blackpool grounds within a few hundred yards of each other. Squires Gate FC (top) - the floodlights facing the other way belong to next door neighbours Wren Rovers (centre). Just up the road is the home of Blackpool Mechanics (bottom).

IRONGATE
Bamber Bridge FC

The rise to prominence and the development of Irongate into a Northern Premier League ground has been meteoric to say the least. The club were formed in 1952, and played until five years ago in the Preston and District League. In 1983, a plot of land nothing more than waste ground and bordered by railway sidings and housing was purchased.

The King George V Ground in Higher Walton had been home until the new ground was first used on August 15th 1987, the clubhouse opening six months later. Irongate was officially opened by the Mayor and Mayoress before a friendly game with Preston North End which attracted what is the highest attendance to date of 2,241. Floodlighting was installed in 1991 which allowed the club to progress to the NPL, and their rise was confirmed when they reached the semi-final of the FA Vase in 1992, attracting a crowd of over 2,000 for the First Leg against Wimborne. The ground is reached via a track at the end of a cul-de-sac, and leads to a splendid red-brick clubhouse which fronts directly on to the pitch. Both the pitch and the ground are fully fenced in, and there is covered terracing along one side for 150 people. Further improvements including another stand were made recently to bring the covered capacity up to 650.

Aerial view of Bamber Bridge's Irongate in its early days.

SHAWBRIDGE
Clitheroe FC

In 1925 Clitheroe FC came to Shawbridge after much hard work to transform the former meadow below Pendle Hill where cows and sheep had grazed. Prior to then and since their inception back in 1877 the club had used a field in an area called Up Brooks. The new ground once had a public footpath running down the side of the ground where the touchline is now, and if football ever ceases to be played there, then the path will have to be re-instated.

Shawbridge boasted what was considered to be the best stand in the Lancashire Combination, built around 1930 and having over 300 seats and dressing rooms underneath. Unfortunately, due to poor support and lack of maintenance during the 60's and 70's, it fell into disrepair and was eventually condemned by the Council and removed. It has since been replaced by a smaller structure on the same site. Just prior to the war, the club erected a metal stand on the Pendle side. In use for barely six weeks before mysteriously disappearing overnight, subsequent detective work disproved the club's story that it had been requisitioned for the war effort when it was found to have been recovered by the contractors who had not been paid!

Many years of over-use, with medal matches, local league finals, donkey derbies, fetes and markets had seen the pitch reduced to a mud heap, made worse by the sheep who grazed the grassy areas and left their own deposits in due course. It was not until 1992 that the pitch was verti-drained at a cost of £3,000 which proved a great success.

The early sixties saw the club attempt to drum up enthusiasm for floodlighting but like so many other schemes at the time it came to nothing, more important issues having to be faced. As the mid-seventies approached, the club were on the brink of going under as Shawfield had become unacceptable to the league but fortunately the local railway sidings were being demolished and Clitheroe were presented with concrete posts and flagstones and these were used to

A panoramic view of Shawbridge, Clitheroe.

enclose the ground. It proved to be a god-send and the beginning of a resurgence which has seen Shawbridge transformed and awarded a B grade, a remarkable achievement for such a small club. A further covered area has been built over four steps of new terracing along one side and more cover is in place attached to the back wall at the School End. Shawbridge is now a vibrant and colourful ground, much improved, and is in line for a further stand to bring it up to NPL standards.

SEEDHILL and VICTORIA PARK
Nelson FC

Nelson played in the Football League for ten years from 1921 to 1931, rising to the Second Division in 1922. Their elevation from Lancashire Combination Football was not successful for very long, as they were replaced by Chester in 1931, returning to their original league before folding in the mid-thirties.

The club was formed in 1898 and played its early football on a basic pitch at the back of the Golden Ball pub on the Colne Road. The old Seedhill Ground became home some time around the Great War and had a small wooden stand with grass banking all around, and a scratching shed behind the Park End goal.

When the club were promoted to Division Two in 1922, various fund raising schemes brought in the finance to build the huge 2,000-seater stand on the Carr Road side which stood until the ground's demise when a major road was built across part of it. The old stand was dismantled and went to the Victory Park ground of Barnoldswick FC.

With the club folding and the Second World War intervening, Seedhill became derelict, and it was not until 1946 that it was brought back up to Lancashire Combination standards when Nelson re-formed. The stand was extensively repaired and a two-storey building, housing changing rooms and a board room was built at the Town end. The wall which separated Seedhill from the cricket ground next door was re-built and Nelson started again in the Lancs. Combination. Seedhill changed little until the early seventies when speedway racing was tried at the ground, followed by stock car racing which signalled the beginning of the end. Other than the area in front of the main stand being terraced, little had changed and it was looking somewhat the worse for wear. With the Blackburn to Colne Road taking off a large chunk and no room to turn the pitch around, Nelson relocated to a council pitch in Victoria Park, a few hundred yards away.

The more modest, but very pleasant, ground now has a small stand with cover for around 200 and is to North-West Counties League standards. The Seedhill ground was flattened, becoming a piece of waste land next to the motorway occasionally used for fairs.

EWOOD BRIDGE
Haslingden FC

Haslingden are relatively new to the senior scene, coming out of the West Lancs League in 1993. Their ground at Ewood Bridge has only been developed to its present standard in that time with a new post and rail and a huge clubhouse, dressing room and administration block built on the site and a small seated stand along the side.

The ground as a whole is hemmed in by two railway lines and a road built on an embankment, with a grass bank behind one goal and hard standing all around.

An outside view of Seedhill, former Football League ground at Nelson and (below) Nelson's 'new' home at Victoria Park.

Showground at Great Harwood.

SHOWGROUND
Great Harwood Town FC

The town of Great Harwood, known locally as 'Arrud', has had a showground on the site for over 100 years. The summer Agricultural Society Show attracted thousands in its heyday and was a focal point.

The original football club, Great Harwood FC played there in the Lancashire Combination on a pitch sub-let and at first un-enclosed from the war until the seventies when the present ground began to take shape.

Floodlights were erected in the early sixties and were switched on before a match with neighbours Blackburn Rovers. Around the same time a 200-seater stand was built on the north side of the ground and as the club progressed up to the Northern Premier League a 500 capacity covered enclosure was put up all along the south side of the ground, and opened by Mr Peter Swales, Chairman of Manchester City. A plaque commemorating the occasion is mounted by the turnstiles.

The old club folded amidst mounting debt in 1978, and Great Harwood Wellington FC, a club previously playing in the Lancashire Combination on a pitch adjacent to the Showground, took over and entered the North-West Counties League in 1982 as Great Harwood Town.

Around 12 years ago, the now heavily fortified clubhouse was built at the western end of the ground, and to accommodate this, the pitch was moved some 20 yards to the east, thus leaving a small portion of the covered terrace some way behind the goal and tucked away from the new lay-out of the ground. To comply with NPL rulings, in the summer of 1992 the ground was fully concreted all round.

The Showground has seen much turmoil in its lifetime, but still retains a gritty, Northern atmosphere which pervades the place, despite a battering from the lawless youth of the area.

HOLT HOUSE
Colne Dynamoes FC

The story of Colne Dynamoes Football Club is both happy and tragic but is splendidly told in Phil Terry's official history. Holt House saw the remarkable rise of a club which started in the Nelson and Colne Amateur League and finished as champions of the Northern Premier League whilst full time professionals.

Ultimately, success was their undoing, for although walking the NPL and visiting Wembley, the trappings of top flight modern football, with blanket policing, hooliganism and impenetrable League committees, saw the founder member and owner close the club down. Colne British Legion moved on to Holt House but they too resigned from the East Lancs League during the summer of 1995.

Holt House originally was a large area with a number of pitches, the third of which was home to the Dynamoes. They played there until promotion saw the club share Seedhill with Nelson FC, playing in the Burnley Combination. It proved short-lived, and they took the popular decision to move back to Holt House. The corporation granted the club permission to play on a different part of the site which had not previously

been used, and this was to remain home. In 1975 the club joined the Lancs Combination, and enclosed Holt House for the first time adding a small hut for refreshments. The ground was three sided, sharing part of the cricket outfield, but was soon widened and drained. As Lancs Combination became North-West Counties the club encountered difficulties as they were refused a grading, the main problems being the dressing rooms which were away from the pitch, and also the cricket area which meant early season home games were staged at the Rolls Royce ground in Barnoldswick.

The ball was well and truly rolling at Holt House, and new dressing rooms and a covered area were erected as promotion came and by 1985 floodlights had been installed with further covered areas put up behind both goals. The lights were switched on by Everton and England player Trevor Steven on December 15th 1985 before a cup game with Irlam Town.

The revenue the large crowds generated for the club provided a new stand built in 1986 and success continued into 1989 when Dynamoes reached the FA Vase Final beating Emley. They had reached the top of the NWCL and were elected into the Northern Premier League, which prompted further hectic improvements with enclosed terracing at the cricket field end. With full time professionalism arriving at Holt House, it was almost a foregone conclusion that the championship would come, and so it did, but with it came heartache, as the Conference committee declared the ground completely unsuitable. Talks were held with Burnley and Blackburn Rovers Football Clubs with a view to a ground-share but they came to nothing. As the new term approached pre-season friendlies were arranged including one against Newcastle Blue Star, but within days the press were informed that the club had ceased trading. A mixture of frustration and anger saw the end of Colne Dynamoes but, unlike many, their ground did not perish with them and Colne RBL used it until 1995.

Holt House, former home of Colne Dynamoes.

PEEL PARK and CROWN GROUND
Accrington Stanley FC

Much has been written about the demise of Peel Park since its sad end as a football ground when the original club went out of business in 1962 and it remains one of the most visited of all the tangible former grounds still around.

It was bought by the amateur club Stanley Villa, just after the Great War following the club's climb to power after the original Accrington FC folded in 1896. It grew to hold 20,000 in its prime and boasted a huge Spion Kop with seated stands either side and an impressive brick-built entrance and turnstile block which still exist. The ground stayed more or less intact for some years, indeed the newly-formed Accrington Stanley (1968) applied for permission to use it in their early days, but in 1972 a massive fire destroyed the main stand which led to the ground's partial clearance.

The site of the Kop is now a sloping grass bank with no sign of any internal buildings except for a solid structure perched on what was a terraced bank and served as a tea bar. It still carries a plaque indicating the building to have been a gift from the Supporters' Club. The entrance is still there, albeit bricked up and the Peel Park pub overlooking the ground has some fascinating photos of the good old days.

Accrington Cricket Club, home of the original Accrington Stanley, founder members of the Football League in 1888.

The Crown Ground, although nothing more than a pitch, was already in use when the new Stanley began playing there in the Lancashire Combination. It was a rough and ready place in the early days with wooden fencing enclosing the ground and a small cricket-style pavilion in use as a changing room and clubhouse. It had been built on the site of an old clay pit and used by junior club, Ewbanks, a works side. Soon it began to take shape with a covered area down one side and another a few years later on the Brickyard side. The pavilion was swept away when the new seated stand was erected in 1989, changing rooms having already gone up earlier.

Having progressed through the Cheshire League and the North-West Counties League, the Northern Premier League beckoned and its strict ground grading was reached by 1987 by which time the Crown Ground was enclosed by a concrete wall and the three areas of cover could keep 1,600 people dry. The clay pit has come a long way and the club now aim for the near future and the Conference.

Photos in this section by: Andy Dakin, Mike Floate, Andrew Mollitt, Ray Maule, Colin Stevens, Richard Wall and courtesy of Fleetwood Town History.

1992 programme cover showing the impressive alterations at Accrington Stanley.

West Yorkshire and Harrogate

WEST Yorkshire is the heartland of Rugby League with many thriving amateur clubs under the professional set-ups. With Leeds United and Huddersfield Town both attracting big followings, Yorkshire's non-League clubs also have a hard task to set in motion a successful team and bring in the crowds. Emley and Guiseley have both tasted success in recent times, but neither has a ground at this stage to allow them to progress, while former League sides Bradford Park Avenue and Halifax Town have similar problems in trying to climb back.

The lamented Yorkshire League was the long term home for many of the area's clubs, plenty of whom originated from colliery teams, and both Emley and Frickley play on old Welfare Grounds, with many more still used lower down the scale, at Grimethorpe, Woolley, Pontefract and Fryston to name but four.

WELFARE GROUND
Emley FC

Despite the club's 90 year history, Emley and their ground have only come to national prominence since leaving the Huddersfield League in 1969. A decision to apply for a move up to the Yorkshire League was made after four consecutive league titles had come to the Welfare Ground, and that proved the catalyst for all that has gone since.

The early history of sport in Emley is unclear. What is known is that rugby was played at the Welfare Ground in the last century, and perhaps as early as 1884, for a membership card inscribed as being from `Emley Cricket and Football Club' exists, although it is not obvious if the football referred to is soccer or rugby. It is assumed that the rugby club was disbanded in 1902, for Emley Clarence Association Football Club was formed in 1903. It is not clear how long the Welfare Ground was in use the first time around, but a photo reveals that ten of the 1909 side were miners from Park Mill and Emley Moor pits, which is a good indication

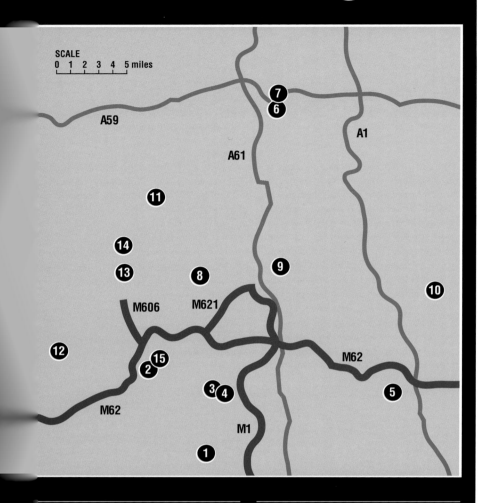

1	**Emley FC**
2	**Liversedge FC**
3	**Ossett Town FC**
4	**Ossett Albion FC**
5	**Frickley Athletic FC**
6	**Harrogate Town FC**
7	**Harrogate Railway FC**
8	**Farsley Celtic FC**
9	**Yorkshire Amateur FC**
10	**Garforth Town FC**
11	**Guiseley FC**
12	**Halifax Town FC**
13	**Bradford P.A. FC**
14	**Eccleshill United FC**
15	**Beck Lane Ground**

Photos in this section by: Pat Brunning, Andy Dakin, Gavin Ellis-Neville, Barry Lockwood, Ray Maule, Kerry Miller, Colin Stevens and James Wright.

Emley's Welfare Ground.

CLAYBORN
Liversedge FC

Money for Liversedge FC's home was provided by publicly-subscribed funds through a trust founded by a Mr Clayborn whose name the ground bears. For many years it had been used as a venue for various schools matches, but as need dwindled the ground and pavilion deteriorated.

The club took over Clayborn just after the war, playing in the West Riding County Amateur League before moving up to the Yorkshire League. The pavilion, which still stands on a grass bank created when levelling the area in the twenties, housed changing rooms. The pitch was roped off, and until the brick-built covered enclosure was erected in 1984 the ground changed little, although its immediate environs slowly encroached. New changing rooms have been built onto the back of the pavilion, and floodlights went up in 1991 before a second and larger seated stand was built along the side by the bank. Prior to the move to Clayborn, Liversedge played on a corporation pitch at Primrose Lane in Hightown where, in the absence of facilities, players changed alongside a stone wall or, in inclement weather, in the nearest inn.

The most significant improvement was the long-awaited opening of the stand and dressing room complex, first used on September 2nd 1989. The Northern Premier League had welcomed the club on the basis that the work would be ready, and so it proved. Transformation of the ground continued in 1993, when two covered shelters were brought from Denby Grange Colliery and erected with the permission of Kirklees Council, and later the toilets behind the old changing rooms were demolished to make way for a wall, allowing more car-parking.

The Welfare Ground now has a capacity for 3,000 with 800 under cover, and 250 seats in the stand which is similar in appearance to that at Paulton Rovers' Winterfield Road ground. The whole place is an excellent example of what can be achieved by the smallest of villages, despite proximity to much higher grades of football.

INGFIELD
Ossett Town FC

Formed in 1936, Town are the older of the two Ossett clubs. Their early games were played on Fern House ground behind the club of the same name, which lies now under an industrial estate. The area which became Ingfield was bought in 1957 and had a mill at one end and at the side a stone-built garage, first used as changing rooms, but later converted into a small social club. Some while later a portacabin from Denby Grange Colliery became available and this was pressed into use as changing rooms until very recently when new ones were built nearer the pitch.

Ingfield has never been developed to any great degree with only a small lean-to providing cover behind the goal, roughly where the new terraced enclosure is. There are still remnants of the grass banking that ringed part of the pitch but the area around the old dressing rooms is now roughly flattened for

that the club were still using it then. Prior to the war, Emley Clarence changed their name to Emley Juniors, and later 'United'. Their headquarters were at the Green Dragon or the White Horse. As the players were all villagers they changed and washed at home, there being no facilities at the ground, and that included no nets, corner flags or equipment to mark out the pitch. The lines were made by turning over narrow trenches, thus creating a brown soil line. As the Huddersfield League was suspended because of the war, Emley United played in the Wakefield League, their home venue being Albert Hills, an old cricket ground formerly used by the Wesleyan Chapel.

Following the war another team called Emley Juniors formed and Emley United folded, the majority of the players joining the Juniors. After a brief period when the club played youth football only, they moved to the ground at Chapel Lane, their former home, and in 1932 the club dropped the tag to become Emley AFC. Around this time they were forced to move headquarters to the Reading Room (now the Brownie hut). That year's budget had levied 1d on the price of a pint and, as a result of the increase, sales of beer at the pub they used dropped dramatically; the landlord ordered Elmley to leave as they were not drinking enough!

The White Horse later became the club's HQ again, but they continued to play on different fields, using Chapel House Farm field and Out Lane, the latter owned by a Mr. Gill who charged £12 per year rent. Changing rooms were still at the White Horse, half a mile away, but in August 1957 the club moved back to the Welfare Ground, which was re-opened on August 8th and by then blessed with a pavilion and facilities good enough for the league.

The late sixties were halcyon days for Emley, winning four league titles and only losing two matches during that time. Despite this, the average gate stayed at around 100, until the Amateur Cup run of 1968-69. By the time Emley had beaten Brook Sports,

Keighley Central, Harrogate Railway, Ossett Albion and Evenwood Town the crowds had reached over 1,300, and when Dulwich Hamlet were beaten, 4,662 packed into the Welfare. The last sixteen saw Barking travel to Yorkshire, and 5,134 fans saw the match abandoned after 55 minutes with the visitors leading 2-0. Two weeks later a further 2,928 watched Barking win through. Various improvements had been carried out by this time. The perimeter fence was made good, and railway sleepers obtained from the recently-closed Crigglestone Colliery. They were placed along one touchline then banked up with red shale. With help from the National Coal Board a shelter behind one goal was provided and with continued success on and off the pitch, a social club was drafted and opened on October 10th 1972.

Nine years later Huddersfield Town visited the Welfare to switch on the newly-installed £12,000 floodlights, and this proved a wise move for the eighties were just as engrossing with runs in the FA Vase culminating in a Final appearance at Wembley against Colne Dynamoes.

Ossett Town FC.

hard standing. The bank immediately behind the near goal was terraced and covered in 1988 and soon after a small breeze-block stand went up on the half-way line. Floodlighting was erected in 1987 allowing Manchester United to play a friendly the following year which attracted the current record crowd of 2,600 to Ingfield. Ossett Town plan to have further cover shortly as well as more seats to conform with League requirements.

DIMPLE WELLS GROUND
Ossett Albion FC

Ossett Albion FC was formed as a junior club in 1944, playing on the Church Street Recreation Ground which is currently used by Ossett Trinity Rugby League Club. The following season saw them playing at Beck Lane, but this proved unsatisfactory and after two years they decamped, moving to Kingsway. Plans were drawn up to develop the ground with new dressing rooms but when a better proposition appeared, the club moved on again. Both Beck Lane and Kingsway grounds have since been covered by housing.

An agreement was drawn up with Ossett Cricket Club to share the facilities at Queens Terrace. The land allocated was an old tip and whilst the ground was under preparation Albion ground-shared for five years with Ossett Town at their Fern House ground.

Just one game was played at the new ground, an FA Amateur Cup tie with Yorkshire Amateur in November 1955 while the pitch settled in readiness for the following season. The club built a basic grandstand on one side and also provided new changing accommodation next to the cricket pavilion. A row of poplars were planted to act as a wind break and later railway sleepers were used to create terracing alongside the cricket pitch. Other than a brick-built refreshment bar in 1968 (which has since been converted into a board room and office), little changed at the ground until 1980 when, beginning to

Frickley's main stand with gleaming new roof.

show signs of wear and tear, it was up-graded. The advent of the Northern Counties East League heralded a new era, and over the next decade the A grade was achieved. The first improvement saw the total enclosure of the pitch by a new perimeter wall, dug-outs and turnstiles with exit gates following on. The standing areas were then terraced, floodlights erected in 1986 and a year later new dressing rooms built close to the pitch. On completion of the concrete hard standing all around, covered enclosures were erected at either end the ground.

More recently, the original grandstand has been re-furbished and a sponsors' lounge built as the former tip completes its transformation.

Dimples Wells is a typically rugged, homely ground, comfortable and interesting and is reached through the cricket ground - the landlords of the site - in a similar way to that at Feethams in Darlington. The 3,000 capacity has yet to be tested to the full, with the record gate to date being 1,200 for a friendly against Leeds United in 1986.

WESTFIELD LANE
Frickley Athletic FC

The focal point of Frickley's former Colliery Welfare Ground is the sturdy 500-seater main stand which was built in 1926 by the miners during the strike of that year. It was complete with dressing rooms, but now has a boardroom and offices and until recent years was heated by coal fires. The rest of the ground was grass banking until after the war when the covered 2,500-capacity terracing opposite was put up.

The Welfare Ground for Frickley Colliery was first laid out in 1925, when three square acres were allocated and the pitch put down. A corrugated fence stretched around the site for many years, but nowadays it is more formidable concrete panelling which is required to placate the league.

During the 60's, when the colliery employed upwards of 3,000 men both it and the football ground were at their peak. Each man paid one shilling a week towards the Welfare, and Westfield Lane enjoyed regular improvements, including further areas of terracing and improved pitch fencing.

The record crowd was set around this time when some 6,500 saw the Colliers draw 2-2 with Rotherham United in the FA Cup 1st Round in 1971 before losing the replay. Since then, the club has risen from the Midland Counties, through the Northern Premier League and then up to the Alliance Premier League, before suffering relegation in 1987.

The club jettisoned the Colliery title back in the mid-seventies, becoming Frickley Athletic, and when the colliery itself closed, and the income from the men ceased, the club struggled, their plight not helped by the storms of February 1991, when a floodlight pylon crashed through the roof of the old stand. Not until October were new floodlights installed and it was December before the damaged stand could be repaired.

Ossett Albion FC.

WETHERBY ROAD
Harrogate Town FC

The first impression on entering Harrogate's ground, is how well it blends with the surrounding prosperous residences. The entrance and turnstiles front the main road and lead into an area apparently comprised of various parts from other grounds, but with a pleasant and welcoming result. Down the main road side, two areas of open terracing are separated by a covered portion, with a tea-bar in the corner. The far end is made up of a collection of connected buildings, some temporary looking, which stretch the width of the ground.

A clubhouse, old changing rooms, new changing rooms, club offices, toilets and a hospitality room all stand side by side, with covered seating tight behind the goal for good measure. Opposite the covered terrace is a raised car-park and a brand new seated stand set slightly back from the pitch, with an extra parking area on the other side. The whole is backed by trees separating the ground from the adjoining properties. The 350-seater stand was opened by the Secretary of the Northern Premier League Mr. Duncan Bayley, who described it as "One of the jewels of the League." The near end is flat standing, but has temporary buildings dotted around, in character with the rest of a cheerful-looking ground, heavily adorned by advertising hoardings.

The original club was formed in 1919 and played on a ground in Starbeck Lane, not far from Harrogate Railway's home. A year later the Corporation took the land for housing and created St Andrews Estate and so the club formed a limited company, buying six acres in Wetherby Lane funded by 3,000 shares at £1 each. The ground was officially opened by the Mayor of Harrogate on Saturday 28th August 1920 prior to a game against York YMCA. The euphoria lasted for twelve years until a disastrous season saw Harrogate finish bottom of the Northern League and disband, the ground being sold to the Council. Wetherby Road became home to various clubs during the next few years including Leeds United 'A' and Yorkshire Amateur. It wasn't until 1936 that Harrogate Hotspurs were formed, playing through the War in local leagues until becoming Harrogate Town in 1950 and rejoining the Yorkshire League.

More recent times have seen the development of the ground from its fairly basic set-up to the fine site it now is. The 350-seat cantilever stand was built in 1990 and opened on August 21st, and the terracing has been improved. The current capacity is close to 4,000, and as the record crowd is 3,208 against Starbeck Railway in 1948, Wetherby Road is one of a dwindling number of old grounds that is still capable of bettering its record.

Wetherby Road is still being upgraded and the club's development plans for the next two years include improving the floodlights, adding two extra turnstiles, extending the covered area on the main road side, and re-developing the old changing rooms and secretary's office as well as terracing the Stray End.

It is hoped that the work, with projected costings of over £160,000, simply for Harrogate to remain in their present position in the pyramid, does not detract from what is a fine ground.

Ricketty cover, now gone, at Harrogate Town.

STATION VIEW
Harrogate Railway Athletic FC

The railway club in Starbeck were formed in 1935 and have always played on the railway ground although that has lagged somewhat behind its cross-town neighbour in recent times. In the season immediately after the War, the club won the National Railway Cup prompting them to look for a ground of their own, but stayed when the parent company (LNER) lent the money to buy the ground provided the workers agreed to have a penny deducted from their wages to help repay the debt.

Station View has never been a picturesque venue, but it still has character, with its early fifties covered terrace in situ. The railway works closed in 1959 and the exodus of players and money led to the club falling on hard times, eventually dropping into the Harrogate and District League in 1970, leaving the ground to fall behind. Happily, there was a recovery through the late seventies and eighties which found the club in the Northern Counties (East). Sheffield United provided the opposition for the floodlight opening in 1991, and more recently a perimeter fence has gone in to completely enclose the ground which had no seating in 1995, although planning permission had been approved for a new stand.

NETHERMOOR
Guiseley AFC

Guiseley Football Club are currently the most successful of the non-League clubs in West Yorkshire, having progressed to two Wembley finals and two semi-finals in five years, as well as propelling themselves to the top of the NPL by winning league championships. However, Nethermoor has not been able to move with the times. Although comfortable and neat, it is small and unable to attain Conference standard at present.

The football and cricket grounds are side by side and were one field until firstly the pavilion then the new dressing room and covered stand were built between the two, there being sufficient space for both clubs.

Guiseley were formed in 1909 and began playing at Nethermoor where there were no facilities other than a pitch, the changing rooms being over a mile away in the Red Lion. Between the wars, an old scout hut was purchased from a church in Otley and converted into dressing rooms, thus negating the walk which by then had been reduced to half a mile on the club's move to the Station Hotel. It was the only building of note until 1935 when the club pulled off a master stroke, buying an old wooden grandstand which stood in the grounds of Harry Ramsden's fish and chip shop. It had been used by trippers when listening to brass bands but, being more use at Nethermoor, was purchased for £50. A roof was added and seats installed, and sixty years on it remains more or less unchanged.

Little altered until the seventies, when the single-storey clubhouse was opened as a joint effort with the cricket club, the dressing rooms being shared within their seasons. With funding from various quarters the footballers got their own dressing rooms in 1983, the work performed by the Manpower Services Commission. As the club moved out of the Yorkshire League and headed for the NWCL, it became obvious that much work was necessary to retain the level the club had reached and floodlighting was installed during the 1987-88 season, Scarborough journeying to play the inaugural match. The pylons had come from a British Rail goods yard in Bradford but had lain in storage as funds were not available. Once installed, they were followed by a perimeter fence, a training area fashioned from the old tennis courts and new turnstiles, over £60,000 being spent in all.

Despite all this, still more was needed for the NPL and in 1991 a covered standing area was built in front of the dressing rooms. Due, perhaps, to the tightness of the football side of the ground and the lack of steep banking, Nethermoor has a modest record crowd of 2,500 which saw the Vase semi-final with Bridlington Town in 1990.

THROSTLE NEST
Farsley Celtic FC

Farsley were formed in 1908 by a group of school leavers who began playing on the Rec at Red Lane. During the Great War the ground was ploughed up for the war effort and no football was seen there for some six years.

The Red Lane ground had no changing facilities and players used the Bay Horse Hotel in the village before walking to the ground. Nowadays it is still in use as home to Phoenix Park RUFC.

After the Second World War the club were re-formed and played briefly at Calveley Lane before purchasing six and a half acres of former council tip from R G Hainsworth and building the present

This extension to the clubhouse replaced the old main stand at Bracken Edge.

Throstle Nest ground. The first match played there was against Frickley Colliery on Saturday 28th August 1948, with Celtic winning 3-1. Two Nissen huts were placed near the top goal for changing in and a small area of cover put up alongside. A further couple of huts were used as a club room and a cafe-cum-tea bar and stood until the present clubhouse was constructed.

The club's FA Cup run to the first round in 1974 heralded some major changes at the Throstle Nest and funds were channelled into the building of new dressing rooms, the Nissen huts being taken down. The end was then covered, and has since been extended with some seating added, in 1984. The entrance was also re-built with two new ticket boxes, and the exterior fences improved by having the pitch railings replaced with advertising boards.

Also in the 80's the brick main stand capable of seating 300 with a small directors' box was built along the side where previously a terraced bank stood. More recently the Northern Premier League regulations have demanded further improvements which include turnstiles and a new toilet block both of which have enhanced the ground.

The Throstle Nest today is only part of an area catering for sports, with a cricket ground situated at the back of the stand and a council-run sports centre just outside near the entrance. Behind the far goal, a junior pitch is in regular use.

BRACKEN EDGE
Yorkshire Amateur FC

The famous Bracken Edge in the Harehills district of Leeds was originally built as a rugby ground and was used by the Roundhay Club until 1930 when they vacated, moving to Street Lane. Following a committee meeting in April 1930, the club took up the option of a lease, thus returning to Leeds. Having sold the lease on their Elland Road ground in 1920 to the newly-formed Leeds United, Amateur embarked on a tour of various grounds in the area, including one at Wetherby Road in Harrogate.

Bracken Edge was already equipped with a stand, and was fenced off and drained, the work coming to a staggering £3,500. Club officials believed the area was more attracted to soccer than to rugby, expressing their belief that the public would support the team. The first football match at Bracken Edge was on September 6th 1930 against Goole, and at the time the players changed in old wooden rooms situated where the housing developments are at the road end of the ground. There was a large bank which sloped down behind both goals and an even bigger one which ran the length of the pitch opposite the stand. The entrance to the ground was in the corner, nearest to the town and has long since been filled in and is now the end of a cul-de-sac.

The impressive grandstand stood unmolested until the aftermath of the Bradford fire when it was doomed and replaced by the scaffold and iron overhang which now juts out from the modern club rooms standing in its place. The grass mounds behind both goals still exist and the large bank on the side has now been sliced in two by the introduction of a floodlit training pitch. To the left of the cover, more banking has been lost to terracing in recent years.

Throstle Nest, Farsley.

BRIERLANDS LANE
Garforth Town FC

The name Garforth Town has only been in existence for ten years, whereas the club was formed as a Sunday side, Miners Arms, in 1964. Playing at the Welfare Grounds at Swillington and Micklefield they eventually changed to Saturday football in the West Yorkshire League.

The new ground at Brierlands Lane was reclaimed from a refuse tip and made good at a cost of around £3,000 which included the building of the present changing rooms and the small covered stand. In 1977 the club joined the Yorkshire League, who insisted on a change of name as they would not accept pub sides, and so Garforth Miners FC were born. Progress was made with an FA Vase run in 1982 and entry into the FA Cup in 1984. Unfortunately the law concerning floodlights denies the club entry at the moment.

Then playing in the Northern Counties (East) League, Garforth Miners became Garforth Town in 1985 and celebrated by reaching the Quarter-finals of the FA Vase before going out to Collier Row.

Brierlands Lane has been held back by the refusal of permission for floodlights and in order to alleviate this problem it has been suggested that the pitch be moved further from the homes allegedly affected by them.

Eccleshill United continue to improve their ground.

PLUMPTON PARK
Eccleshill United FC

Eccleshill United were formed as a sports club in 1948, after a previous club disbanded when most of the players went into the forces in 1939. The old club played on the recreation ground, as did the new, changing in the cellar of the Working Men's Club. The club moved to a pitch on Acres Fields until it went for building purposes, forcing another move, this time to a field on what is now the Kings Park Estate, with dressing rooms at the Bolton Hotel.

Playing in the Bradford Amateur League, they then went to Myers Lane, building their own dressing rooms and reaching the West Riding Amateur League. In 1963, with the club successful, a plot of land on Plumpton Park was purchased, and work began on transforming disused quarry land into a playing area. Two pitches were created, drainage laid and dressing rooms built and a clubhouse followed. As Eccleshill reached the Northern Counties (East), terraced areas went down, a covered enclosure was built, and in 1990 the ground was entirely enclosed. Seats were added the following year and since then a training area and further covered standing has been erected at this go-ahead little club.

Eccleshill's refusal to stand still off the pitch has yet to transfer onto it, but when it does Plumpton Park will be ready.

THE SHAY
Halifax Town FC

The Shay has, it seems, been under the Sword of Damocles for quite some time with the Council making noises about creating a new multi-purpose stadium for the football and Rugby League teams. The added problems of automatic relegation from the Football League have meant the club playing in a huge bowl of a ground, which would no longer satisfy the rabid thirst of the League's grading committee. It is to their credit that the club battled through and have held their own in the Conference.

Halifax began playing at a ground in Sandhall until it became the site of a munitions factory during the Great War. The Shay was first used when the club entered the League in 1921, having been fashioned from a council rubbish tip. A grandstand was obtained from Manchester City's Hyde Road ground, and the players changed in a hut. Opposite, was a small covered enclosure called the Patrons' Stand which had seats added in the late fifties. The banking behind the Tram-Shed End was shallow and perched on the speedway track wall, but has now been made into a tarred area and opposite, the steeply banked Trinity End has a terraced area

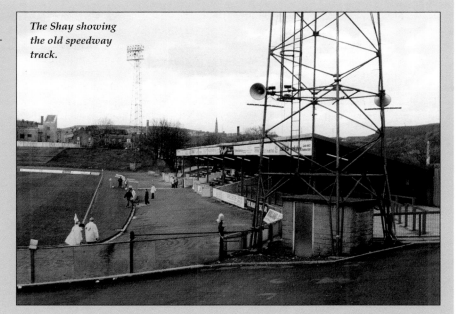

The Shay showing the old speedway track.

down the middle but in its League days seemed to have trees growing out at right angles to the pitch.

Remnants of the speedway track are still evident at the Shay. The sport was first brought to the ground in 1948 for three years and then re-introduced in 1965, and a number of old buildings around the place may well be relics from that time. Halifax are on a hiding to nothing if they attempt to bring the Shay in line with League gradings and the future must surely be a ground-share similar to Huddersfield. With the shape of the ground, a wealthy and enterprising Council could create a splendid stadium for rugby, speedway and football but the sport and leisure side of that body are possibly not on the same wavelength as those elsewhere.

PARK AVENUE, McLAREN FIELD, MOUNT PLEASANT
Bradford Park Avenue FC

When Park Avenue were voted out of the Football League in 1970 to be replaced by Cambridge United, their ground was sentenced to a lingering death made worse by the fact that some twenty years after the final game, and after the building of an indoor cricket school, there are still vestiges of the terraces and walls to remind Park Avenue folk of their loss.

When the club folded from the Northern Premier League in 1974, a Sunday side continued to keep the name going and they have progressed to a point where Northern Premier League football on a new ground is a distinct possibility in the near future.

Rugby League has always had an influence on Park Avenue, for the football club were born out of a rugby club who turned to soccer in 1907 after making heavy losses the previous year. The ground had been used for sport since it was officially opened as a cricket ground on July 20th 1880, with the rugby taking a section of the outfield. The enclosure which became the football ground was laid out in 1884 with a pavilion and stand catering for both sports. By 1907 when football was introduced the banking around the playing area had two large open stands behind the goals and a covered enclosure running the full length of the Horton Park side. This development enabled the club to immediately apply for a place in the Football League, but being unsuccessful they joined the Southern League before acceptance into the Football League the following year. Crowds of 27,000 and 28,000 saw Bradford as a rugby team, the highest-ever gate at the ground being in the thirties when 34,000 saw a match with Leeds.

The shape of the ground changed little right to the end and on the demise of the club - who had briefly shared Valley Parade - it was mooted that Bradford Northern RLFC were to move in following the Council's purchase of the ground. It did not happen and the ground was allowed to rot, the Archibald Leitch-designed main stand eventually coming down four or five years later by

which time trees and bushes had already colonised much of the terracing, eerily enveloping the turnstiles. Although the site is now used by the indoor school, there is enough left to satisfy the morbidly curious.

Happily, Park Avenue have moved on, and having played at Manningham Mills until it was deemed unacceptable to the league, they moved to McLaren Field, home of Bramley RLFC. The ground was built in 1966, Bramley having played next door on the Barley Mow ground which is partly covered now by the new ground. It has a capacity of around 4,000 and a main stand which is designed almost identically to those at Cheltenham, Kings Lynn and Morecambe football grounds. The cover at the Daisy Hill end came from the old ground.

In 1993 the club again moved, this time to Mount Pleasant, Batley, also home of the Rugby League side. Their ground has been home since 1880 and was originally shared with cricket, Yorkshire playing County championship matches on it. The Heritage Stand, opened in 1990, replaced a magnificent old barrel-roofed stand which had seating for 800, was built in 1913 and lasted until it was condemned following the Bradford fire.

Park Avenue hope to escape from playing their football on rugby grounds in another city, and return home to a site which can see them challenge again for Conference status at least.

The sad remains of Bradford Park Avenue.

BECK LANE, HECKMONDWHITE
Littletown and Huddersfield Town FC

Previously the home of Heckmondwike RFU and AFC in the early part of the century, Beck Lane is a gem of a ground which is swathed in history going back to the latter part of the 1800's when Heckmondwike Rugby Club formed and played the League code until switching to soccer in April 1903.

Since those days Beck Lane has been home to an assortment of clubs besides Heckmondwike who were successful and played in the FA Cup before the Great War. It was originally built with ash banks on three sides, and had railway sleeper terracing. Between the wars a stand with dressing rooms was built behind the goal nearest to the railway, but for some reason this was moved at the end of the Second World War to the side where the current large structure stands. Huddersfield Town have owned the ground since 1933, and have used it for

everything but Football League games. Other sides have been in residence with various degrees of success such as Norristhorpe Nipps, V.A.W., Heckmondwike Spen, Spenborough and Rendon's. Huddersfield vacated the ground for a while and it quickly went to seed, but happily it was rescued by the committee of Littletown FC who agreed a contra-deal with Town which meant that their juniors would once again play there. Possibly the most famous game to have been staged at Beck Lane was the semi-final of the FA Youth Cup in 1957, when a youngster named Denis Law played in front of a crowd of over 5,000.

Today Beck Lane is a splendid venue with a white painted fence surrounding the entire playing surface, which is akin to a bowling green. A newer grass bank now stands around part of the ground and the covered bank is replete with advertising hoardings. The entrance gives a clue as to the one time importance of the ground with solid brick buildings creating a gateway which at one time had a turnstile. To stand on the far side and view Beck Lane and its facilities is a must. The mere thought of 5,000 crammed in to watch Denis Law in action as a 16 year-old is awesome.

Beck Lane, home to Huddersfield Town's youth team for 60 years.

Durham Coalfields across to Teesside

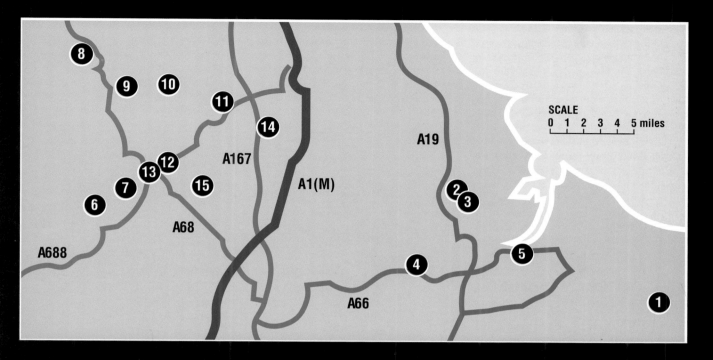

SCALE
0 1 2 3 4 5 miles

A19

A167

A1(M)

A68

A688

A66

1. Guisborough Town FC
2. Billingham Town FC
3. Billingham Synthonia FC
4. Stockton FC
5. South Bank FC
6. Cockfield FC
7. Evenwood Town FC
8. Tow Law Town FC
9. Crook Town FC
10. Willington FC
11. Spennymoor United FC
12. Bishop Auckland FC
13. West Auckland FC
14. Ferryhill Athletic FC
15. Shildon FC

Top: The old Catterick racecourse stand which survived at Spennymoor until the report following the Bradford fire.

Bottom: The new-look Spennymoor United.

To do justice to the north east and its wealth of historic football clubs both present and past would need a book of its own the size of this one. The area stretching from the exposed Welfare Grounds at Evenwood and Langley Park across to the grim Teesside towns of Hartlepool and Middlesbrough houses a mass of football grounds which have all seen their moment of glory.

The north-east was the epitome of success in the amateur game with huge crowds ·cess flocking to Bishop Auckland, Crook Town, Willington and Cockfield to watch the clubs fight for national glory. Many of those to the west are born of Welfare schemes, indeed the Durham area alone had over 130 pits in production after the war, many of which had football clubs within the Welfare. Most are long gone, but the names are still remembered in the annals of League and Cup. Ushaw Moor, Tanfield, Trimdon Grange and Usworth all played in the FA Cup, and a number of Welfare Grounds are still used in Teesside and local leagues as well as the more senior clubs in the Northern League.

KING GEORGE V GROUND
Guisborough Town FC

Town are the latest in a list of clubs that have represented Guisborough over the years. Awkwardly situated south of the main bulk of north-eastern sides, the club came to prominence in 1973 when they were formed to play in the Middlesbrough League, on a pitch at the playing fields now covered by a golf pitch and putt course.

Success in the Northern Alliance in the late seventies saw them embark on the creation of a ground from within the park, and a small stand and floodlighting, and a new post and rail system around the banked ground has made it one of the better in the Northern League.

Guisborough's greatest season to date was in 1980 when they were champions of the Northern Alliance and finalists in the FA Vase where they lost to Stamford. During that run, the record crowd of 3,112 was set up at the semi-final against Hungerford Town, and after a period in the Midland League, further ground improvements saw the club enter the Northern League.

CENTRAL AVENUE
Billingham Synthonia FC

The mere fact the Synners have for most of their playing life been connected with I.C.I. Billingham has meant their grounds have all been within what were the confines of chemical company land. The club were first formed in 1923, and played on a ground within the works a few hundred yards from Central Avenue.

Just before the war, with the factory expanding, an alternative ground was found in Belasis Lane, opposite the gates of today's ground and now covered by the car-park and an office block. Billingham's next and last

Above: The opening game at Central Avenue in 1958, a 2-2 draw between Billingham Synthonia and Bishop Auckland watched by a crowd of 4,200 - still a record for the ground. Below: Billingham v Pegasus three years earlier at the old Belasis Lane ground, just across the road from Central Avenue.

move to date was over the road to the newly-opened stadium. It boasted a massive 2,000-seater stand, banking all round the cinder track and was built on a former rugby pitch. The stadium's scale was such that in 1958, its opening year, it was selected to stage an England 'B' international. The first game was against Bishop Auckland in September of that year when the ground was opened by Lord Derby. That 4,200 match attendance remains the highest at Central Avenue. Nowadays, although the stand is still impressive, only a small area has seats, the wings being open for standing. In 1994 Synners played Woking in the replay of an FA Trophy tie but as the terracing within the stand was deemed too steep they were forced to close most of it for safety reasons. As no harm befell anyone in the preceding 26 years, it seemed a little perverse that the council should suddenly decide to impose this regulation on the club just two hours before possibly their biggest game for decades.

BEDFORD TERRACE
Billingham Town FC

Town are the younger of the neighbouring clubs in the Northern League, only having been formed in 1967. Their early football was played in the Stockton and District League on a pitch in Mill Lane, until a piece of derelict waste land was slowly converted into a neat and tidy football ground.

The club were known as Billingham Social Club in their Teesside League days, but were obliged to change to Town following their admittance to the Northern League. As well as the compact and functional main stand which seats 250, the ground can hold 3,000 should it ever need to, and in some ways is far more workable than Central Avenue, although much less spectacular.

NORMANBY ROAD
South Bank FC

One of the more pleasant surprises in the 1995 close season, was to see the name South Bank FC in the list of pre-season friendlies. They were founder members of the Northern League in 1889 and played on the same ground throughout until 1993 when after two years of constant attacks by vandals and other far more devious criminals, their old ground with its grass banking terraces, grandstand and clubhouse was totally destroyed.

A timber grandstand had been built at a cost of some £300 back in 1909 and replaced by a much later version destroyed in one of the fires. A new consortium took over the struggling club which, along with most others, was suffering in the midst of the recession through apathy and lack of finance, and this immediately fuelled rumours of a running-down and closing up of the club.

When the ground began to fall apart and

FOOTBALL IN STOCKTON

There have been a number of clubs over the years which have carried the title Stockton, but the oldest and most well-known was simply Stockton FC formed in 1882. Their Victoria Ground also dates from that time. It was enclosed and provided with a wooden pavilion along the eastern side nine years later.

Before the Great War, Victoria Park had gained a further stand opposite with one end banked and regularly attracted crowds of several thousand until the Second War. By then the ground had railway sleeper terracing although the original stand was lost in the war. Victoria Park continued as a fine ground until the club went into decline, finally folding in 1975 after a trip round some of the lesser leagues. The area was swiftly covered with housing, but the club's assets were taken over by Norton Cricket Club Trust FC who were formed in 1969, playing on the Trust's own sports complex in Station Road. They took the nickname of the old Stockton club, the Ancients, and when elected to the Northern League became known as Norton and Stockton Ancients FC.

Another club by the name of Stockton FC were formed in 1980 when an old outfit, Stockton Cricket Club FC changed their name. They played two years in the Wearside League at the Grangefield Community Centre before moving to a council-owned ground at Tilery Rec. 1983 saw the then successful club buy the former sports ground of the Head Wrightson engineering company on the south bank of the Tees. It had facilities for football, cricket, bowls and tennis and boasted a pavilion and social club.

The football club spent a small fortune on terraces, floodlighting, dressing rooms and the social club as they converted the cricket ground to a football stadium. More covered areas were planned and a 3,000 crowd saw a pre-season friendly with Middlesbrough in 1986, but with a cocktail of apathy and vandalism the ground has quickly gone to seed to such an extent that in 1995 there were doubts about the very future of the club within the Northern League.

the old committee left, the Northern League suspended the club following a lack of correspondence, although planning permission went through for building work on the ground soon after.

HAZEL GROVE
Cockfield FC

Although the Durham fells village of Cockfield play in nothing grander than the Auckland and District League and the ground is little more than a barriered-off pitch with a decidedly dodgy-looking pavilion for changing rooms, Hazel Grove is one of the more romantic grounds in the country.

Much has been written about Cockfield in the last few years as strangers have discovered the ground after reading of the club's astonishing achievements in the 1920's and early 30's. The village team came to prominence when elected to the Northern League in 1921 and the following year saw a new pavilion opened at the ground as they progressed through to the semi-final of the Amateur Cup. Five years later they went one better, winning the final at Middlesbrough.

A stand was erected behind the near goal and they continued until the war when they disbanded. Hazel Grove has continued to be used, with a smaller version of the pavilion in place and a jerry-built canopy to cover a handful. A group of floodlight pylons have

Cockfield is undoubtedly one of the most atmospheric little grounds anywhere.

lain in the grass for some years, as if waiting for the club's third visit to the Northern League but the neat and tidy post and rails around the pitch set off the ground perfectly. Cockfield have dominated the local league and claimed many scalps in the County Cup over the last few years and this totally atmospheric little ground could yet be the scene of Northern League football in the future.

WELFARE GROUND
Evenwood FC

Evenwood played on a site known as the Gala Field from their formation in 1890 until 1924 when, following the establishment of the Miners' Welfare Commission, the club moved to the newly-established Randolph Colliery Miners Welfare Ground. By then Evenwood Colliery had closed, but Randolph continued until the early sixties when the trusteeship of the ground, which had been leased by the Welfare from Strathmore Estates, was taken over by the Parish Council and leased jointly to the football and cricket clubs.

The original two-sided dressing room complex was destroyed by fire many years ago, but was replaced by the present structure, which caters for both games. The basic 200-capacity covered stand is perched rather awkwardly in the corner nearest the cricket pitch, and the whole ground is enclosed by concrete fencing which is useful protection at this wind-swept location deep amongst the former coal-fields of Durham.

MILLFIELD
Crook Town FC

Empty, the atmospheric Millfield ground is one of the most poignant places on the non-League scene, purely because of its relatively recent history. Although enjoying a mini renaissance the ground and the club are long past the halcyon days of the 50s and 60s when success in the Amateur Cup,

A packed stand at Evenwood for an Easter fixture.

Northern League and Durham Challenge Cup attracted gates which would please many a League club today.

The capacity was set until recently at 9,000, currently reduced to 3,000, which gives an indication as to its size even now, although it is doubtful whether potentially large crowds would be allowed to congregate on its impressive terracing due to present safety regulations.

The football club were formed in 1889 and played initially at the Peases West Welfare Ground at Bankfoot on the outskirts of Crook. In 1898 they acquired a new ground on the site of an old mill which served the Iron Foundry, hence the name. The houses and bungalows on the east side of the ground are known as Foundry Fields. The £625 purchase was completed in November 1898 and five local men were appointed trustees. A new grandstand was built to hold 300 people and two cottages were also acquired for dressing and committee rooms. Over the next few years the tipping of ash created the massive banks which were grassed over and survive today on the east side, behind the north goal and above

the stand on the west side. A 500 plus capacity seated grandstand costing £1,300 was built in 1925 by local contractor T. Walton and Son, replacing the original structure. It was opened by the Hon. Joseph Pease on Saturday October 17th 1925, Town defeating Bishop Auckland 3-1 on the day. Dressing rooms and a committee area were incorporated under the stand which still survives.

In the mid-thirties the ground was sold to the Council when the club got into difficulties after playing semi-professionally in the North-Eastern League, and during the war and up until 1949 they were known as Crook Colliery Welfare FC. However, good times were ahead and they found £3,000 in 1951 to level, drain and re-turf the pitch which was re-opened before a 6,000 crowd against Sunderland. The record crowd ever to see a game at Millfield came later that season when 17,500 packed in to see the Amateur Cup quarter-final against Walton & Hersham on Christmas Eve 1952. It is said that many more got in as the gates were broken down, swelling the attendance to 20,000. The population of the town at the time was 12,000!

Attendances never dropped below 4,000 for a dozen years or more with 9,818 against Derby County in 1955 and 8,309 in 1959 against York City. The grassy banking behind the south goal and around the west side was terraced during 1960-61 and the area of terrace next to the grandstand was covered giving the ground the shape it retains today.

Floodlights, upgraded in 1993, came in 1968 some three or four years after the halcyon days. They were switched on by Manchester City, the reigning champions, on December 16th.

Having been deemed unsafe in the late eighties the 70 year old grandstand spent a number of years covered with ugly scaffolding, but happily, with the brickwork replaced by aluminium sheeting and the wooden steps concreted, she was re-opened during the 1994-95 season. The club hope to terrace the sides of the ground still covered by grass banking in the near future.

Crook Town FC.

The football follower will not see a game any nearer the moon than at Tow Law, and will never be more grateful for a covered stand!

IRONWORKS GROUND
Tow Law Town FC

A visit to the Ironworks ground, high up in the Durham coal fields is an unforgettable experience. The football follower will not see a game any nearer the moon than at Tow Law, and will never be more grateful for a covered stand. It has been home to the club for over 100 years, having previously been laid out by striking miners in 1892 on Coal Board land. Around thirty years later, during another strike it was re-built with banking and dressing rooms, again with help from the miners.

The banked nature of the railway side of the ground has always enabled the club to house big gates, none more so than when 5,500 saw the Lawyers hammer Mansfield Town in an FA Cup tie in 1967.

The Ironworks has changed in appearance if not shape since then, with the wooden grandstand replaced around 1970, while the terracing was completed and changing rooms re-built on the same site. Soon after, the long-awaited and much-needed low cover was erected at the bottom end of the ground, which encloses it but doesn't make it any less breezy!

The site was purchased from the Coal Board in 1966, with the pocket of land just behind the banked terrace bought from British Rail when the railway line, which ran alongside it, was closed. Those standing at the rear of the terrace are actually standing on an old line, as the boundary was moved back to increase the standing room. Floodlights were late arriving, erected in 1992 as the club continued to defy the elements and produce a ground they can be proud of.

HALL LANE
Willington AFC

When Willington memorably triumphed over Bishop Auckland in the Amateur Cup final at Wembley in 1950, some 88,000 people saw the match. Soon after the Wembley visit they transformed the ground which had been home since 1911, with a low-roofed solid stand emblazoned with the club name across the fascia. New dressing rooms were built in 1971, a couple of years after the clubhouse was opened, and in 1973 the first set of floodlights were used. These were improved when the Vane Tempest Colliery donated a set on its closure in 1992.

Hall Lane presently hosts but a handful of spectators each game, but three years after the Wembley win, 10,000 saw a Second Round tie with Bromley in 1953, which remains the record gate at what is now a sleepy Second Division club.

BREWERY FIELD
Spennymoor United FC

Sport was being played at the Brewery Field long before the amalgamation of Spennymoor Town and Weardale Ironopolis spawned the United club in 1904. The ground was formerly used by Tudhoe Rugby Club, until their demise at the precise time the newly-formed football club planned to take the lease on a field and erect a large grandstand.

The Brewery Field already had a wooden pen, a form of open stand, and this remained in use until it was demolished in 1930, to make way for a new and much larger grand-

Willington AFC.

Spennymoor supporters mourn the loss of the Cow Shed during the 1986-87 season.

stand purchased for £300 from Catterick Racecourse. This splendid brick-based jet-black structure stood virtually unchanged in appearance for over 50 years until it was condemned and sadly demolished following the Bradford fire disaster. Opening the stand, on September 1st 1932, Councillor Harry Askew, President of the club, said: "it is one of the proudest moments of my life so far as my football career is concerned". In the summer of 1948, the Supporters' Club erected a massive covered stand, reaching all down the side of the ground opposite the grandstand and providing cover for over 2,000 spectators. This huge building, fondly known as the 'Shed', stood as the focal point of the ground until the 1986-87 season, when it was demolished to make way for the club's 300-seater stand, opened in 1990 and costing £255,000.

During the fifties and sixties, the ground was gradually improved with the introduction of terracing, and it was in 1957 that the record attendance to date was posted, when 7,202 packed into the Brewery Field for the Durham Challenge Cup match against Bishop Auckland. Throughout the seventies the ground was at its peak, and it took the Bradford fire disaster, and successive promotions on the pitch to change the face of the Brewery Field for ever. Happily for the club, they were in a position to complete the required work to be able to take their rightful place. Following the grandstand, a further £50,000 was spent on erecting a full width corrugated covered end, with three steps of terracing, which can hold 1,750 people, and there are plans to construct a further grandstand opposite the existing one, on the site of the late-lamented Catterick Stand, which has been left as flat standing since 1986.

Many long-serving club men mourn the passing of the two old stands, and indeed the reaction to the Bradford fire has accounted for many more around the country, some it has to be said entirely unnecessarily. Spennymoor United are however fortunate to have in their place, the beginnings of a ground which has had some thought put into it, rather than being hastily slung together. The Brewery Field is in a somewhat cramped setting, surrounded by housing, and has little or no parking, which may cause a problem or

two if the club progress, but it is once again a comfortable spot to watch football, and although the memories of the Shed and the Catterick Stand will fade, there are always photos as a permanent reminder of the good old days.

DEAN STREET
Shildon FC

Shildon Football Club enjoyed its heyday just prior to the Second World War when the Northern League title was won five times in seven years. The same can possibly be said of Dean Street, although it is by no means unpleasant today. It started life in the late 1800's as the South Durham Athletic Ground, and was surrounded by steep grass banks, the remnants of which are still in evidence today. Such was the size of the place that a schoolboy match in the twenties is reputed to have attracted a crowd of 13,000, whilst the Durham Senior Cup match against Ferryhill around the same time, brought in 11,000.

The huge pagoda-style grandstand was built during these heady times in 1923 along with the much-used turnstiles. The grandstand is still in excellent shape over seventy years later, having had modernised changing rooms built inside it along with a social club. Floodlights came to Dean Street in 1987 when Manchester United visited. Today the capacity is set at 4,000 for a ground that once

held over three times that amount without the need for segregation or safety licences. It is unlikely ever to be tested, but a full Dean Street ground must be an impressive sight.

DARLINGTON ROAD GROUND
Ferryhill Athletic FC

For a club that have suffered traumatic times in recent years, Ferryhill have managed to maintain their home ground, and even improve it. Surprisingly for a ground which dates from around the 1920's, it is not, and never has been a Welfare Ground, although ironically it has suffered more than most from mining subsidence.

The antiquated stand is still hanging on, though in truth four fifths of it have been replaced over the years, and its corrugated tin overhang no longer bears the club name. The clubhouse in the corner of the ground was built in the late sixties, and the more modern dressing room complex went up ten years ago. The car-park in front of the ground has been improved in recent times, and there is now a fence enclosing the ground from it. The imposing brick wall which runs alongside the main road is still in fine fettle, and gives a good clue as to the age of the ground. Sadly, Ferryhill announced they had sold the old ground in 1995 and moved in with Brandon United, whilst their ground-sharers from last year, Hartlepool Town have moved

The vast pagoda shaped stand at Shildon.

Ferryhill's old ground was sold for development during 1995.

in with Stockton.

High above the ground, on a plateau, is the former Welfare Ground of the Dean and Chapter Colliery which closed in 1966. This barriered-off pitch is now administered by the council, and used by junior clubs.

KINGSWAY
Bishop Auckland FC

Kingsway has been home to the town's cricket club since the middle of the last century, and even if Bishops move off for pastures new as it appears they might, cricket will continue. Kingsway will be left to brood, but will possibly be used for junior football by youngsters who cannot imagine that 17,000 people gathered there for an FA Cup tie with Coventry City in 1952.

Despite the unabated success the club enjoyed throughout its amateur career with finals at Wembley and Northern League and FA Cup success, very little has been documented about the goings on at the club and the chronology of the changes at Kingsway is difficult to compile.

What is known is that an earlier version

of the club, based around the Church Institute, split to form Auckland Town and from that time in 1887, Bishops as they were later known, played at Kingsway.

The Kingsway end in its original form stretched further back but was truncated by a road-widening scheme in 1964 which had already put paid to plans to cover the end four years previously. The grandstand is believed to date from just after the Great War and almost certainly replaced a smaller, less elaborate version. Its mass of railings and stairways give the impression of an old race-course stand, and the two winged extensions, known as Harold's Lugs after the man whose company built them, were added in 1955. They increased the capacity by a further 168 seats.

The terracing either side of the stand and behind the Kingsway goal was in place soon after the war, if not before, for the crowds were regularly into five figures and finances became available for ground improvements. The fifties saw a small covered stand near where the clubhouse, board room and refreshment bar were, but all went up in flames in December 1961. The buildings were

not replaced for a full five years. In 1953 the club obtained some temporary stands which were erected on the cricket pitch side and were in use for several years until lent to West Auckland in 1960 for their Amateur Cup-tie with Hendon. They were subsequently sold to Redcar Council.

The modern Kingsway is little changed with only a new press box and some cosmetic surgery to the grandstand within the last few years. The days of the 15,000 crowds and Wembley appearances are long gone, but unlike so many other large grounds which were once full but are now semi-redundant, Kingsway still retains its charm and is one of the very best of the now maligned three-sided grounds.

DARLINGTON ROAD
West Auckland Town FC

West Auckland have always lived in the shadow of their illustrious neighbours, but have arguably the more impressive name on their honours board in the Thomas Lipton Trophy, known as the first World Cup. Tragically, after being on display in the local working men's club since 1909, it was stolen a couple of years ago and has never been recovered.

Wests emulated their rivals in 1961 by reaching the Amateur Cup final, and although losing to Walthamstow Avenue, they used part of the financial windfall to build the brick-fronted stand and changing rooms soon after.

Darlington Road is far more typical of what a Northern League ground is today when compared with Kingsway, but is none the worse for that.

Photos in this section by: Trevor Beaumont, Andy Dakin, Gavin Ellis-Neville, Dave West and James Wright.

The home of one of the most famous non-League clubs of all, Bishop Auckland.

Durham North and Wearside

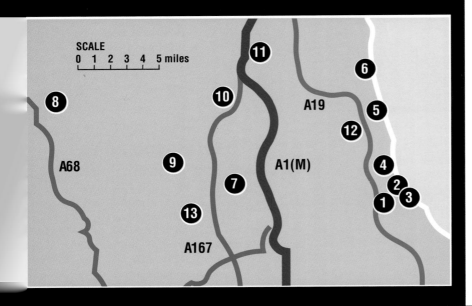

Of the major non-League grounds in this area, only Peterlee, Durham and Consett are unconnected with the pits. Welfare grounds dominate the football scene as they do further south and the majority host Northern League football. Although enthusiasm waned in the sixties and lack of interest in the part time game in the north-east has led to double figure crowds, the Northern League still somehow has a magic all of its own.

DURHAM and NORTHUMBERLAND WELFARE GROUNDS

The boom time for Miners Welfare schemes came after the Great War when miners paid a donation from their weekly wage to fund a function hall or Welfare Institute for the social activities which grew up around the whole culture and life of the pit. With larger pits naturally having bigger communities, more advanced Welfares, which incorporated Welfare or Recreation Grounds sprang up. These varied in size from a small area with a bowls green and a children's play area, through to massive grounds laid out

1	Shotton Comrades FC
2	Peterlee Newtown FC
3	Horden CW FC
4	Easington CW FC
5	Seaham Red Star FC
6	Ryhope CW FC
7	Durham City FC
8	Consett FC
9	Langley Park FC
10	Chester-le-Street FC
11	Washington FC
12	Murton FC
13	Brandon United FC

Welfare grounds at Shotton (above) and Horden, complete with newly refurbished stand (right).

close to the pit with tennis courts, bowls greens, cricket and football pitches, a bandstand and even, in cases such as that at Horden, a swimming pool.

As pits were exhausted and subsequently closed, the Welfare Schemes were wound up, the Institutes no longer financially supported and surplus to demands. In many cases, the property was transferred to the local Council for them to maintain and use as an amenity for the people of the area, while the grounds, complete with their pavilions, reverted to Recreation Grounds, although naturally were still referred to as Welfares by the local inhabitants.

In the case of less-developed football pitches within the Welfares, these were often simply rented out to whoever could pay until, in many instances, the land was bought and subsequently developed when the original amenities became derelict or unwanted.

The opposite scenario saw grounds such as those at Easington, Horden, Seaham, Langley Park, Bedlington and Murton, which thrived due to successful football teams and were eventually developed into Northern League grounds, attracting crowds of many thousands during the boom times after the Second War. Of the many hundreds of pits and Welfares which were scattered all over the North-East until the collapse of the industry, there are only a dozen active schemes still in existence today, although a considerable number of sports grounds are still in use, most in a more abbreviated form than when first opened.

SHOTTON RECREATION
Shotton Comrades FC

The current Shotton team has been around for only 22 years, having left the Peterlee Sunday League in 1976 and switched to Saturdays. They were preceded many years ago by Shotton Colliery who used the Welfare Ground which, since being transferred to the local authorities, has been known as the Recreation Ground.

It was originally laid out in the twenties in the style of so many others of the time, with tennis courts and a bandstand. The football pitch was eventually banked around part of the playing area with an old pavilion sited just to the left of the current dug-outs. Players would change below the old cricket pavilion and walk through to the pitch. The modern ground has been enclosed by replacing the bank with a red brick wall and a stand which can cover 400. A new Swiss-chalet style pavilion and changing rooms are situated behind one goal which has a training area made from the redundant tennis courts alongside.

WELFARE PARK
Horden Colliery Welfare FC

The community which relied so heavily on its collieries around Horden was devastated when Horden pit closed in February 1986. The massive Welfare Grounds had served the people since they were first laid out in the early 1900's with an enclosed football field, rugby pitch, cricket field, band stand, bowling greens, tennis courts and even a swimming pool, all lovingly kept within a park which was surrounded by miners' terraced housing.

The football ground began to develop very early and pre-war maps show a grandstand of some sort roughly where today's version. Indeed, the recently re-vamped and re-roofed stand may well be an original, with its archaic changing rooms below. Banking formed with railway sleepers was laid down and eventually concreted as the club were extremely successful in their Wearside League days in both League and Cup. The ground held around 8,000 for an FA Cup tie in 1937, and in the fifties and sixties the Welfare was a focal point as many cups and trophies came their way. By 1975 the stand was beginning to show signs of wear and tear, and just prior to going into the Northern League it was re-roofed at a cost of £1,500.

By 1981 the huge boundary wall which encircled half the football ground and the terracing itself had seen better days, and when the club drew Blackpool FC at home in the First Round of the FA Cup in 1981 they were refused permission to stage the game on the basis the terracing was unsafe. To their credit it was eventually upgraded at a cost of £4,000 with the walls partly re-built also. Fifteen years later the stand was again in desperate need of repair but the club had reached rock bottom. Hard work has since resurrected them, and although the terraces have not been over-used both Horden and the Welfare Ground are in there fighting.

EDEN LANE
Peterlee Newtown FC

The club have played on the Eden Lane Playing Fields since they were formed, with the approval and backing of the Town Council, in 1976. At the time the ground was home to Peterlee Cricket Club, and had two parallel football pitches during the winter.

However, they soon moved out, and the football club played in the Northern Alliance before enclosing the main pitch. This relegated the second pitch to outside, and they joined the Northern League in 1982. Much graft occurred, with the addition of the perimeter wall and fence, rebuilding of the dressing rooms, a new seated stand, canteen, floodlights and clubhouse. Success on the pitch mirrored the changes, with the club reaching the 4th Qualifying Round of the FA Cup, before losing a replay to Whitby Town in front of 1,500 in 1984. The record crowd was shattered five years later when a Northern League select team played a benefit game following the Hillsborough disaster.

The club continued to expand in the summer of 1995 when a new stand went up across what was the old cricket square.

WELFARE PARK
Easington Colliery FC

Easington has had a football team on and off since 1913 when the Welfare Grounds were first laid out. The first version of the club played until 1937, when they folded for two years, re-starting shortly before the war. They disbanded again in 1964, only for

a new side to spring up in 1973, join the Wearside League and then amalgamate with Easington Rangers in 1980.

Throughout this time home has been the Welfare Ground, a fifteen acre site originally housing two football pitches and a cricket pitch, bowling greens and tennis courts, all served by four pavilions, and built on the site of allotments near to an old quarry.

The football part of the ground was never fully developed although soon after the Second World War, the banking along one side topped by a small stand was terraced with railway sleepers and was sufficient to hold 4,500 for an FA Cup-tie with Tranmere Rovers in 1955. The pitch barrier was replaced in 1965 and outer fencing around the whole ground in 1971. The modern Welfare club eventually constructed its social club and followed with a covered stand and floodlights in 1987, finishing terracing one side soon after. In 1977, following the folding of the Welfare scheme, the grounds were handed over to the council for their administration.

SEAHAM TOWN PARK
Seaham Red Star FC

Seaham Red Star have only been in existence since 1973, when they were formed as a Sunday morning side. After a couple of seasons playing on the Deneside Rec. they switched to Saturdays and joined the Houghton and District League and then the Northern Alliance playing at the Vane Tempest Welfare Ground.

In 1978, they moved onto the semi-derelict Seaham Welfare Ground, a once

Seaham Red Star FC.

BELLE VUE PARK
Consett FC

Belle Vue ground was born in 1950 following the loss of the club's traditional home, called Vicarage Field, above the Consett Iron Company. Such was its close proximity to the works that the noise generated often drowned out the referee's whistle! There was an old Army hut which served as changing rooms and a small much sought-after shelter. In the immediate post-war boom Consett's Iron Works blossomed and they soon announced an extension which erased 50 years of history and reduced Consett FC to playing on a Welfare Ground at Eden Colliery while the new ground was prepared.

impressive place which had fallen foul of both the elements and vandals. It had been the home of Seaham Colliery Welfare and Seaham United, both part of the North-East scene until folding. On moving to the ground the club, as part of the deal, were saddled with the name 'Seaham Colliery Welfare Red Star' which they kept until the ground was transferred to the council, who renamed it Seaham Town Park enabling the club to revert to its original name.

The Welfare was first bought and laid out for cricket in 1925, with additional ground comprising 1.36 acres incorporating a football pitch in 1930. Pavilions were built for football, cricket and tennis and the ground barriered-off. Many years of turmoil saw the Welfare fall into disrepair and when Red Star moved in they were confronted with broken fences, a leaking pavilion and long unkempt grass. The small areas of terracing were crumbling and much work lay ahead. However in 1982 a new changing room complex was built in an updated pavilion to add to the floodlights which were erected following the club's success in winning the Phillips Floodlighting Tournament at Birmingham in 1979. More major changes occurred in 1983 when the club entered the Northern League, with continued smartening of the ground, along with a new £18,000 stand in 1984.

The club's impressive clubhouse, situated lower down towards the town was opened in the early nineties but destroyed by a devastating fire in 1994. It has since been replaced on the same site.

RYHOPE CW and CA

Ryhope presently boasts two grounds, that of the Colliery Welfare which was built in the 1890's, and Meadow Park, home of Ryhope CA.

The Welfare Ground is now used by the latest version of the club, Sunderland Vaux Ryhope CW who, in their various guises, have played there ever since their foundation as Ryhope Villa in 1898. The ground record crowd is believed to be 2,000 for the FA Cup First Round match with Workington in 1967.

Ryhoe Community Association FC were formed as a youth club in 1961, playing friendlies on a field behind the local Co-op until becoming senior and moving to the Welfare Ground. From 1978 the club played four seasons on a roped-off pitch at the local comprehensive school until work had been completed on Meadow Park, which had been transformed from derelict land at a cost of some £30,000 with changing rooms, club house and floodlights. The ground was opened with a friendly against Newcastle United on August 16th 1982 and attracted a crowd of 1,018 that has not yet been beaten. The following year the 200-seater grandstand was built as the club began their career in the Northern League.

Belle Vue was constructed almost entirely with voluntary labour after the Urban Council had given the go-ahead, and banks were created around the ground using cinder from mine workings. Stands were built of concrete, brick and timber either side of the ground and a crowd of some 7,000 witnessed the opening game against Sunderland Reserves in August 1950.

Today Belle Vue is still a proud ground, although suffering like most through lack of ambition but sadly no lack of vandalism. It has gained an eight pylon set of floodlights and a new concrete wall surrounding the pitch, but has lost part of the covered enclosure opposite the stand which is now much reduced in length. Its shape and age are both reminiscent of the ground at Billingham Synthonia which also posted its highest-ever attendance at its opening game.

Aerial view of Consett in the 70s.

The opening of Belle Vue Park in 1950.

MOOR PARK
Chester-le-Street Town FC

Town are a club formed as recently as 1972, when they were named Garden Farm, after the nearby hotel. They played at Ravensworth Welfare, a ground opened in 1925 and known locally as Team Colliery. Since its transfer in 1984 it has been home to junior sides such as Hughwood FC, Thomas Wilson WMC and Portobello.

In 1926 the club moved to the enclosed Welfare ground at Sacriston where they became Chester-le-Street Town and joined the Wearside League. But Sacriston was in the final year of its lease and in 1980 Town moved to the long-abandoned Chester Moor Colliery Welfare Ground just outside the town where they began the awesome task of transforming it into a ground worthy of senior football.

Chester Moor was a small Welfare which had fallen into disrepair along with the social building whilst protracted attempts were made to sell it by CISWO. A widening of the road outside in 1967 meant the removal of a large number of houses in the area and inaccessibility due to fast-moving traffic had rendered the ground virtually useless for some ten years. It was never more than a barriered-off field with primitive changing rooms since it was first laid out in the 1920's and had become neglected, but was given a new lease of life by the club. Since then the newly named Moor Park has seen floodlights, a 200-seater stand, covered accommodation and terracing with updated dressing rooms and a new fence enclosure. The impressive changes were tested when an estimated 3,000 people saw a match between Newcastle United and Sunderland to raise funds for the Bradford Fire Appeal in 1985.

WELFARE GROUND, LOW MOOR ROAD
Langley Park FC

Langley Park has been either been a hotbed of football, or a footballing graveyard, whichever way you look at it, since the original team was formed 100 years ago. Since then there have been around ten different versions of the same side, with two separate Welfare Grounds, one in Bridge Street and one in Low Moor Road.

The first Welfare Ground was developed on land close to the old Witton Gilbert railway station on the Lanchester Valley branch line around 1923, and contained a football pitch and pavilion, with cricket and bowls. The second came in 1953 at Low Moor Road, which is home today. The main bulk of the changes to the ground came on entry to the Northern League, when the new Langley Park, coming out of Sunday football, built cover for 500 to add to the small stand on the

ground. The lack of floodlights appears to have been the next handicap, for the club were forced off the ground for one year, as the facilities were deemed inadequate, but the newly-named Langley Park S & S Utd are back home, although anxious about the future.

The past has seen Langley Park, Langley Park Welfare, Langley Park Villa and Langley Park Rovers all play at the two grounds, plus Hotspur and a new Colliery Welfare who changed their name several times to United, Villa and back to Colliery Welfare in the fifties! The first ground was taken over by Esk Parish Council in 1969, and although still in existence, was barely usable as a pitch with its wrecked pavilion.

ALBANY PARK
Washington FC

Washington FC came into being from the miners of the 'F' pit in 1947, who called themselves Washington Colliery Mechanics and played on the Welfare Ground before moving to Usworth Welfare, whose own team had used the ground until folding shortly before. This ground had a pavilion with bowls and tennis and was in existence from 1925, until Washington Development Corporation bought it to put a road through the middle of the pitch leaving the rest of the facilities intact.

Moving to the Glebe Miners Welfare, which had a cricket and football pitch they set about transforming the place, and soon sectioned off the football area and built a small stand on the half way line. Pitch barriers were installed and an impressive clubhouse with dressing rooms was built. It all went horribly wrong when arsonists destroyed their headquarters some five years ago which led the club into a legal nightmare, eventually resolved, but the equally impressive replacement is now up and running, as are the new floodlights which were obtained from Monkwearmouth Colliery in 1995.

Langley Park FC.

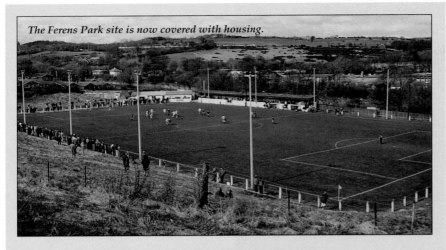

The Ferens Park site is now covered with housing.

BELMONT GROUND and FERENS PARK
Durham City FC

Durham City won the Northern League title for the first-ever time in 1994, ironically playing their last game at the delightful Ferens Park ground in the process. Situated at the Sands, an area of the city close to the River Wear, and not a million miles from two of their previous grounds, Ferens Park was opened in 1950 and named after the late Alderman H.C. Ferens who was President of the club and a generous benefactor when purchasing the land.

It was a delightful setting, now sadly the domain of new housing, and to the casual eye a crowd of 7,000 assembling to watch an FA Cup tie with Tranmere Rovers would seem unlikely. But Ferens Park was big enough and accessible enough for that to happen, and with its steep sloping grass banks able to be utilised long before strict crowd control came in, the horseshoe-shaped ground was a pleasure to behold.

In the 44 years of its existence, it did not change significantly, the clubhouse, dressing rooms, and covered enclosure all being tucked into the corner nearest the city. Terracing stretched around the ground at one end and along one side, while the stand itself, solid brick and iron struts, was topped off by netting, and flanked by old floodlighting poles. Housing and office space had begun to encroach on Ferens Park for some time, but when the end came, it was still very sad that this splendid, if unspectacular, ground was to be lost.

In earlier times Durham played on three previous grounds, the first being in the club's inaugural season at Garden House Park (roughly where the County Hall now stands) and immediately after at Kepier Heughs, a large field near Kepier Farm close to the site of Ferens Park, where they were to remain for four seasons. The original club's final move was to Holiday Park, a stadium alongside the River at Framwellgate Waterside, which was next to the large gasometer. This ground was to stage League Football as well as greyhound racing, and City played here for just fifteen seasons before disbanding shortly before the war. It wasn't until 1950 that football returned to Durham, and 45 years later, it has gone again although this time to Belmont, on a former Civil Service ground close to the A1. The new home is being built to Northern Premier League specifications, which however cosmetically presented, will have to go a long way to match the charm of Ferens Park.

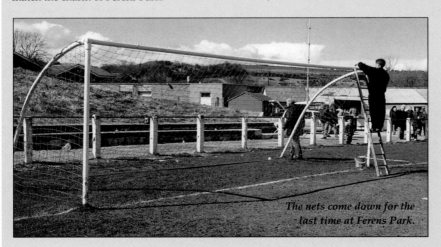

The nets come down for the last time at Ferens Park.

MURTON PARK
Murton FC

Murton boasted one of the biggest and most impressive Welfare Grounds when it was opened in the early twenties. Some twenty acres housed a cricket field, football pitches, a bowling green, tennis courts, a putting green and a playground. There were three separate pavilions and the football pitch was graced by a seated stand. The entire place was tended by a groundsman whose house was also the on site.

From the start, the football pitch was surrounded by a wooden standing rail with the grandstand based on one which stood on a sports field at New Tredegar, in South Wales. Part of the area covered by the football pitch was laid out on an old tip, and this caused some problems in the early days before it settled down. The players changed in the Welfare itself until 1932 when the stand was dragged overnight, using a series of pulleys and chains, some eighty yards to its current position, and dressing rooms and washing facilities were put in place. Much later, as areas of the old grounds became redundant, they were sold off in 1961 for re-building of the local school, and when the pit closed along with the Welfare scheme in 1976, the grounds were transferred over to the council. To the credit of many, Murton Park is still in good condition, although the old stand was partly demolished as it had become unsafe, and was replaced by one opposite. A new concrete post and galvanised rail was put in place in 1970, and some £3,000 was spent on improving the seating arrangements in 1982. Murton FC dropped the Colliery Welfare from their name before joining the Northern League in 1988. The original club played on a ground called Fatten Pasture until moving to the Welfare in 1928.

WELFARE GROUND
Brandon United FC

Brandon United are a relatively new club playing on a fairly established site. Along with many other clubs in Durham and the north-east, theirs is a former Welfare ground, having been taken over by the council following the closure of the Brandon 'C' pit in the sixties.

Brandon were a Sunday side until 1977 when, having won the FA Sunday Cup, they turned to Saturday football. Constant promotion meant the basic old ground had to be upgraded and floodlights were installed with a loan in 1978. In subsequent years, referee's rooms, a new drainage system, and a grandstand were all added, with Sunderland providing the opposition for the opening of the latter on August 15th 1985.

Photos in this section by: Richard Brock,
Gavin Ellis-Neville and Dave West.

Cumbria

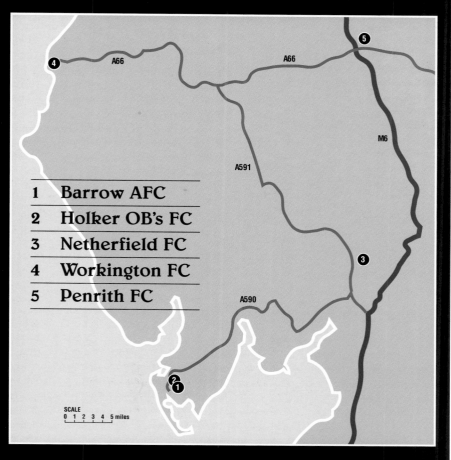

1 **Barrow AFC**
2 **Holker OB's FC**
3 **Netherfield FC**
4 **Workington FC**
5 **Penrith FC**

SCALE
0 1 2 3 4 5 miles

CUMBRIA has only five major non-League clubs, two of which lost their positions in the Football League in the seventies. Penrith played their football in the north-east for many years before switching to the pyramid in 1982. Both Barrow and Workington have struggled since being voted out of the League, and both have ground problems, with areas of Holker Street and Borough Park being out of bounds for a period.

A number of smaller clubs in the area, Cleator Moor Celtic, Windscale and Carlisle City elected to play across in the north-east based Northern Alliance and Wearside Leagues, although the Cleator Moor announced they would play in local Cumbria football during 1995.

HOLKER STREET
Barrow-in-Furness FC

The home of Barrow Football Club since September 1909, Holker Street has seen many changes of shape, as well as good times and bad. The club spent 51 turbulent years in the Football League, before an unexpected demotion saw them return to non-League football. Happily, they have managed to maintain their status in the upper reaches of the pyramid, despite having yo-yo'd between the Conference and the Northern Premier League, and still have aspirations towards returning to League football.

The very early days of Barrow Football Club, from their formation in 1901, were spent on a field called the Strawberry Ground at the edge of town. Players changed in the nearby Strawberry Hotel, and walked to the pitch. At the time, there was another ground within a larger complex called Cavendish Park. This had stands and cover on two sides and had been home to a previous club in the town which folded earlier. This ground was much coveted, but the local athletic and rugby clubs blocked any chance of it being rented, and so Barrow stayed at the Strawberry for three years, until asked to chose a new venue by their landlords, the Railway Company. Somewhat foolhardily, they picked the ground at Ainslie Street. The pitch was worked on and a hut erected for

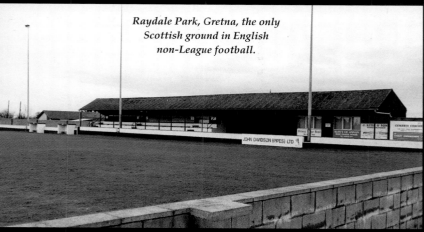

Raydale Park, Gretna, the only Scottish ground in English non-League football.

The old stand at Barrow FC, now demolished.

changing, but the venue was not popular and inside a year the club had moved on to Roose. Little Park had a far superior pitch but access was difficult. The ground was again somewhat basic, with dressing rooms and little else. Eventually, in 1909, a site was found in Holker Street, formerly the home of Hindpool Athletic. The ground was sub-let from the Steelworks Band, who in turn leased it from the owners, the Furness Railway Company.

Many hours of hard graft went into preparing the pitch for play, as the site had once been a rubbish tip and discarded items regularly surfaced. The club's artifacts from the Little Park ground were transported over, and crude earth embankments were shaped around the playing area. The first structure of any note was the seated stand, completed in 1912 and later extended at either end, giving a capacity of 1,500. Between then, and the club's elevation to the Football League after winning the Lancashire Combination, Holker Street was transformed. Opposite the stand was built an area of cover, and the banking was partly terraced all round. The cover was soon on the move however, for Barrow re-sited it at what was called the Gasworks End, and built a larger enclosure, capable of housing 4,000 spectators. Dressing rooms were improved and turnstiles put in place and by the time League football came to Holker Street, the ground could hold 20,000.

The decade up to the Second World War was one of comparative struggle. The geographical position of the town plus the depression meant hard times, and it wasn't until the forties that further work was carried out, the terracing being upgraded at a cost of £3,500. A new enclosure was erected on the Holker Street side, and the old one opposite replaced. At this time in the ground's history, it could boast cover on all four sides.

In 1954, the capacity was tested for the first time when 16,874 saw Barrow draw 2-2 with Swansea Town in the FA Cup Third Round, to date the record attendance for any match at Holker Street. Five years later though it was nearly broken with the visit of Wolverhampton Wanderers in the same round. In 1963 Arsenal replaced their flood-lighting system at Highbury, and sold the old one to Barrow, but it was several years before the debt was paid off.

Despite relegation, Barrow went ahead with their £40,000 Bluebirds Club which is situated behind what is now the Ray Wilkie Stand, and two years later in 1972, made a momentous decision which was to change the shape of Holker Street permanently. Speedway was introduced to the area, and to accommodate this sport, the steelworks end was demolished and the pitch moved westwards to create room for the track. Unfortunately it had the immediate effect of making the ground lop-sided. It was a failure, and for five years the steelworks end remained undeveloped with a disused cinder

THORNCLIFF ROAD
Holker OB's FC

The club was created by the former pupils of Holker Street school and played for many years on a Corporation pitch in Thorncliff Road. In the late 60's an area of pasture land was turned into a new pitch and a small club room was built, later extended in 1981.

There was a temporary stand which sufficed until, having progressed through the Furness League to the West Lancs, the club entered the North-West Counties League. To be eligible, a 220-seater stand, floodlights and turnstiles were all installed and the ground was completely enclosed. A further cover down one side enhances a functional ground which will always be in the shadow of its neighbours at Holker Street.

track between the crowd and the pitch. However in 1979, with the advent of the Alliance Premier League, the pitch was returned to its former position, and a Leisure Centre, complete with squash court, bars and dressing rooms built on the site of the old terracing.

In 1990, the old covered enclosure on the south side was replaced by a seated stand, since re-named the Ray Wilkie Stand in memory of the much-missed former manager of the club. Sadly, at the start of the 1994-95 season, the old wooden stand which had been partly condemned for so long finally gave up the ghost and was demolished. Plans to replace it are in hand when finances permit.

Holker Street comes in the same category as the Buck's Head at Telford, and lower down the scale York Road, Maidenhead, in that parts of the ground are pleasing to the eye and traditional, and even comfortable, whereas areas of it, in this case the unattrac-

tive Leisure Centre complex, ruin the effect. The loss of the main stand, and the resulting naked gap cannot be helped, but the ground viewed as a whole at present is merely a pale shadow of its former self.

SOUTHEND ROAD
Penrith FC

There has been football played on the site since the late 1880's when the area was known as Kilgour's Field, and was also used for agricultural shows, gala days and marching bands. Penrith FC were formed on 27th September 1894 and played at the Field, previously occupied by Carleton Rovers.

Crowds in general were small and facilities lacking, until hurdling was placed around the pitch to give spectators a dry vantage point out of the wet grass. A public footpath which ran across the pitch did not help either as many exercised their right to walk it, thus gaining free entry. A large wooden stand was erected during the early part of the century, and this lasted well into the fifties until it was demolished and eventually replaced with a shelter. There were no changing facilities at the ground until 1947 when officials set about building a club-house, changing rooms and an office - all needed to gain entry to the Northern League. These were heady times for the club, as a new Supporters' Club had been formed and their fund raising exploits had provided a shelter as a replacement for the old dilapidated grandstand plus terracing at the Dog Beck end of the ground.

In 1959 the Council decided, as part of a £12,000 scheme to improve sporting facilities in the area, to enclose the Southend Road ground. Work was finished on the project within a year and the club soon built a grandstand on the opposite side to the original and on the site of the Supporters' Club shelter. A form of lighting was provided as a training aid removing the need for the club to use lighting from the nearby lorry park. These were in place until October 1975 when

Southend Road, Penrith, in the 1950s before it was enclosed.

Three views of Netherfield FC. Here: A super late 1950s shot... supporters standing in orderly rows and policemen watching the match. Below: The same game, looking across to the Clubhouse end and (bottom) a similar view today... little has changed, including the trees.

a campaign to 'sponsor a light' was so successful the club purchased the old security lights from the Black and Decker factory in Spennymoor and erected them in time for a celebration match with Carlisle United. Since that time Southend Road has been regularly brought into line with league regulations, with the lighting improved in 1989 and more recently hard standing added all around the pitch. Penrith's home is a rarity in that it is a town centre ground that has both survived and is looking good. It must be hoped it stays that way.

PARKSIDE
Netherfield FC

Netherfield Football Club came into being in 1919 when the workers from the Somerville Brothers shoe factory got a side together. The company formed a Sports Association into which they and each member of the workforce paid 1d each per week and from these funds the ground first took shape.

They collected £3 10s. from the workers, bought a set of goalposts from Kendal Amateurs FC and began playing on a field in Parkside Road owned by a Mr. Jackson but home to ducks and hens which had to be removed before each game. The players changed in the dinner house at the factory, where they had baths and all modern conveniences, for many years.

The swampy area was originally a refuse tip and both football pitch and adjacent cricket ground suffered until extensive work was carried out to alleviate the problem.

Towards the end of the twenties the company built the dressing rooms which still exist and are in use on the left of the ground. Soon after was added the curious sloping-sided black timber stand, capable of seating around 200, which was extended around 1955.

As funds continued to roll in additional scratching sheds were erected on either side of the ground stretching up from the club end goal-line, and happily these too are alive and well. After the Second World War the club entered the Lancs. Combination and sought to improve Parkside further by laying down extensive terracing which increased the capacity to around 5,000. The area in front of the clubhouse and around the left hand side of the ground benefited from the work which was fully tested when Netherfield reached the First Round of the FA Cup six times in the ten post-war seasons culminating in a record crowd of 5,184 when Grimsby Town visited in November 1955. In the run-up to the match the club built a large covered structure over the terracing to the left of the ground out of old scaffold poles and corrugated sheets and this existed until severely damaged in a storm five years ago. It is since been re-built and is more or less the same as before.

The introduction of floodlighting in 1965 meant Netherfield took their place as founder members of the Northern Premier League in 1968 and with Parkside still owned by the firm (long since known as K Shoes) the club were able to meet the relevant ground requirements, and apart from a brief spell after relegation have been in the league ever since. Today Parkside is everything that nostalgia-lovers look for in a non-League ground, with all the original artifacts still in place and no garish fences or intrusive railing to spoil the place. Only the 1956 vintage 'Park' clubhouse perched on the bank overlooking the ground is the slightest bit clumsy, its austere front clashing with the rest of the ground which, on a good day can look as if it is trapped in a time warp.

Photos in this section by: Mal Keenan, Peter Savage, Colin Stevens, Alan Watson, Phil Yelland and from 'A History of Penrith Football Club'.

BOROUGH PARK
Workington FC

The old offices at Borough Park.

Information on football in Workington in the very early days is sporadic. There is evidence of a new club being formed under association rules in the Westfield area of town in October 1884, and this may well have been the beginning of Workington FC.

The club folded in 1911 and during their absence three other clubs played in the town, Central, United and Athletic, the latter two playing at Ashfield and Lonsdale Park. The club was re-formed following a meeting in January 1921 and trials matches were held at Lonsdale Park, where they had played previously, after moving there in 1909. The ground is still in use today as a greyhound stadium and Workington utilised it in 1986-87 by staging five Northern Premier League matches after Borough Park's main stand was deemed unsafe.

In 1937 the club moved with the help of the council to a brand new ground adjacent to Lonsdale Park - called Borough Park in recognition of the council's contribution. The move had resulted following a row with the owners of the site regarding a bill presented for some damage done to a shelter. The first few matches of the season were played at the Ellis Sports Ground, now home of Workington RUFC, as the new ground was not quite ready. Much work had gone on to construct ash banking all around the playing area and to construct a marvellous new brick and wood main stand with glass sides for protection against the cold and wet. To finance the building, debenture bonds to the extent of £2,000 were issued, United Steel Company and a local brewery buying the majority. The first competitive match was a reserve fixture on September 25th 1937 against Cleator Moor Celtic. Either side of the war extensive work was done on terracing the ground and erecting the covered accommodation which stretches around Borough Park, one end being very similar to that which once covered part of Haig Avenue. The club's entry into the Football League on June 2nd 1951 heralded a completely new era for them and the ground. The 1,000-seat main stand catered for press and directors as well as officials and training staff. Underneath were (and still are) offices, dressing rooms and other ancillary rooms with the entire building centrally-heated. The capacity at the time was around 20,000, and when the popular side shelter was erected in 1956 another 4,000 were able to escape the Cumberland weather. Two railway dining cars, frequently featured by the press and media as being `quaint', were purchased and used firstly for refreshment and latterly as a club shop. Already capable of hosting matches in front of crowds of 17 or 18,000 Borough Park soon became one of the best-appointed grounds in the north-west and when Manchester United were drawn to travel to Workington in the 3rd Round of the FA Cup in 1958, the ground record attendance of 21,000 was set. It is not surprising that the next four highest attendances at the ground are all against local rivals Carlisle United.

Just two months earlier the first floodlighting system costing £12,000 was switched on, the initial game curiously being a friendly with Hamilton Academicals on 20th November 1957.

The covered terrace at Workington is still in good shape.

A new ground and a handsome stand

Top: *The opening of Borough Park in 1937.* Below: *The same view 56 years later.*

Newcastle and the North

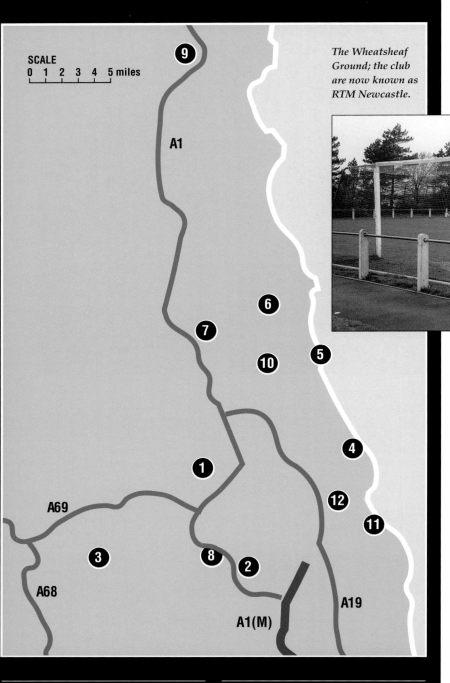

SCALE
0 1 2 3 4 5 miles

A1

A69

A68

A1(M)

A19

The Wheatsheaf Ground; the club are now known as RTM Newcastle.

1	RTM Newcastle FC	7	Morpeth FC
2	Gateshead FC	8	Dunston Feds FC
3	Prudhoe Town FC	9	Alnwick Town FC
4	Whitley Bay FC	10	Bedlington Terriers FC
5	Blyth Spartans FC	11	South Shields FC
6	Ashington FC	12	North Shields FC

NEWCASTLE itself does not have a rich pedigree in non-League circles, although Gateshead, South and North Shields, Whitley Bay and Blyth are close by and have supported clubs with varying degrees of success.

Possibly the most tragic story is the demise of the marvellously atmospheric Appleby Park which was home to the NCEL winners in 1992, before almost overnight being sold for development with the club folding soon after. Blyth Spartans are without doubt the best known of the clubs in this area, after their FA Cup exploits and Northern League championships.

WHEATSHEAF GROUND
RTM Newcastle FC

A sponsorship deal two years ago saw the famous cup-fighting name of Blue Star disappear from the scene. They reached Wembley in the FA Vase Final of 1978 and the semi-final of 1982 simply as Blue Star before adding the city name in 1986.

The Wheatsheaf Ground is situated behind the pub of the same name and was originally set out much further away from the club and dressing rooms, a fact borne out by the skeleton of an old stand which is tucked away near the railway line. The low cantilever seated stand stretches along one side with a post and rail around the pitch, and the dressing rooms and clubhouse, at the entrance behind the pub end goal, are heavily fortified.

APPLEBY PARK
North Shields FC

Appleby Park, tragically, is now no more, its wooden terracing, cavernous enclosures and large imposing main stand swept away following a season of unremitting success that appears to have been to the ultimate detriment of the club.

Tucked away in the main street with a large entrance proudly displaying the club name, the ground once saw a crowd of nearly 13,000 as early as 1936, for a derby match with South Shields. Although little chronological information is available about the

Main stand at Whitley Bay.

ground, it is known that North Shields Athletic played there after a change of name to Preston Colliery. A limited company was formed as North Shields FC in the 20's and it may be assumed that the ground was shaped around that time as the club played in the North Eastern League.

At its peak, Appleby Park could hold 15,000, and even at the end had a capacity for nearly 10,000, over 2,000 of whom could be under cover.

A new North Shields FC was formed in 1992 and for a while played at Appleby Park until forced to move to the less glamorous Percy Main FC. The club now play on the Swallow Sports Ground near the Rising Sun in Wallsend.

HILLHEADS PARK
Whitley Bay FC

Hillheads Park has been so completely altered in its fifty-odd year history that nothing of the original ground remains.

The club first played at the turn of the century as Monkseaton, on a pitch in the Uplands area. The move to Hillheads did not occur until just before the war, and shortly after the facilities began to improve. Timber huts were erected to act as dressing and committee rooms, and two small stands were built on either side of the ground. In 1950, the club became known as Whitley Bay Athletic, and around the same time, the perimeter fence, also timber, was improved.

It wasn't until 1963 that Hillheads began to take on its present shape. The old timber dressing rooms were demolished, and new ones built. The main stand on the ice-rink side of the ground was taken down, and with the help of a generous donation from the FA, plus voluntary labour supplied by players and supporters, the existing stand was constructed.

Even with the help of all and sundry, at one point the project looked doomed for, whilst digging the foundations, bones were discovered on the site, and a pathologist called in to investigate. Fortunately, they

were all revealed as animal, and a horses' mass grave had been unearthed. Current visitors to the ground can rest assured that the grave was fully cleared before the stand was completed!

In 1966, the Seahorse Social Club was erected at a cost of £4,000 on the site of the old dressing rooms, and two years later floodlights were added, first used for a game against Newcastle United. The timber perimeter fence had for some time been eroded by the effects of sea air, and gradually it was replaced by a wall of concrete panelling. The stand on the Creamery side was equally affected, and in 1971 was demolished for safety reasons. The area is now open standing. Ten years later the Seahorse Club was extended by the addition of a lounge, and three years after that two floodlit five-a-side courts were built, and dressing rooms erected behind the main stand. In 1988 a board room and office were built behind the Seahorse Club.

Back in 1965, the club staged an FA Amateur Cup-tie against Hendon when 7,300 turned up. In 1989, Preston were the visitors in the Second Round of the FA Cup

and to accommodate the 4,500 crowd, concrete terracing was laid around the ground, and two new entrances were also added at the Hillheads Road end.

Despite the desperate problems that have faced the club in recent years, the ground is still in good shape.

CROFT PARK
Blyth Spartans FC

Blyth Spartans took over, from Bishop Auckland and Crook Town, the mantle of the North-East's foremost team of the seventies, with runs in Amateur Cup, Trophy, and FA Cup as well as many successful seasons in the Northern League. Despite success, survival has at times been a struggle, reflected in little change to a ground which until recently was in a poor state of repair, the old West Stand being semi-derelict for a time.

Happily, it seems to have caught its second wind and is now good enough for the Northern Premier League, no mean feat.

The club were formed in September 1899 and first played on a field near Percy's Gardens before transferring to a ground called the Spion Kop at Bates Pit for five years until 1906. They then moved to a pitch which stood opposite today's Croft Park (now covered by housing), until another exodus a year later saw Spartans at Thoroton Cottage ground for two years. Finally, in 1909 they decamped to the newly-built Croft Park, named after landlords Thoroton Croft Trustees. The ground was officially opened in September 1909 by Mrs Clark of Bellester Castle before a friendly match with Newcastle United. Spartans actually bought Croft Park for £3,100 in 1921 but were forced to sell it to the council for £4,150 in 1944 to pay off extensive debts.

Blyth's main wooden stand which was as old as the ground was gutted by vandals in 1971, and the council replaced it in 1972 with

Croft Park, Blyth.

SOUTH SHIELDS and GATESHEAD FOOTBALL CLUBS

The history of football in the Newcastle area, Gateshead and South Shields in particular, is so complex it would be foolhardy to attempt to unravel its complexities in such a short space.

The more immediate history of The Mariners from South Shields FC dates from 1974, when the club were re-formed, having been removed lock, stock and barrel from their vast home at Simonside Hall by unwanted factions to the Athletics Stadium where they became Gateshead. The re-hashed club began playing at Jack Clarke Park, ironically a council ground adjacent to a housing estate built on the site of the club's old Horsley Hill ground which staged Football League matches in between the wars. Simonside Hall was a splendid home built in the grounds of an 18th century country mansion of the same name, and existed from 1949 to 1974. The mansion itself became the club headquarters and was separated from the pitch by a wooded area. In its prime, the ground boasted two stands on either side, one of which was extended in later years when floodlighting was introduced. Such was the vastness of the ground that the attendance record stood at 18,500 who crammed in to see the FA Cup tie with York City in 1957. The site of the ground is now covered by a council housing development.

Gateshead played at Jack Clarke Park until 1992 when the club's excellent development at Filtrona Park was opened. A works sports ground was purchased by club chairman John Rundle, and the site soon boasted an enviably fine clubhouse which now has a small area of cover in front of it, with an unusual floodlighting system in that two of its pylons are on a grass verge outside the ground. Another pitch runs behind the far goal and the whole ground exudes an aura of success.

Possibly the ultimate irony for Filtrona Park, is its position at the end of a road which looks directly onto the site of Simonside Hall.

The Gateshead club which played in the Football League until 1960 began life as South Shields Adelaide and played at Horsley Hill when the former occupants, the Rugby League club, folded. The ground eventually developed enough to hold a record crowd of 21,000 for a League game with Luton and remained home until 1930 when the club moved to a new ground close to Redheugh Bridge in Gateshead, 10 miles away. Horsley Hill became a greyhound track and was demolished for housing in the mid-60s.

Redheugh Park was also used for greyhounds although its clumsy paraphernalia made the ground unpopular. It was built close to industry in the Teams area and changed little in its lifetime, since being fashioned from a clay pit. It opened in August 1930 and the club changed their name to Gateshead, and ground improvements were made at Redheugh before a greyhound track was laid in 1935. Two years later, an unbeaten record crowd of over 20,000 saw a match with Lincoln City. In 1953 the first set of floodlights was gained but this did not greatly inspire the club and by 1960, on what by then was an ageing ground, they were surprisingly voted out of the League.

Gateshead continued at Redheugh in non-League football until the club finally folded in 1972. Redheugh had become derelict and weed-strewn and was eventually demolished in the seventies. Until very recently the site was an open space which had been partly filled with rubble and in due course it was turned into a play area. During the mid sixties the death knell for Redheugh had sounded when the Municipal Stadium, later to become the International Stadium, was started, but from the ashes came Gateshead Town playing at the new stadium. By then South Shields had become Gateshead United, but they folded in 1977 to be re-formed as Gateshead FC., the club which today plays at the 11,000 capacity International Stadium. That figure has been reached many times for athletics meetings but the record football crowd so far stands at 5,000 for a testimonial match with Newcastle United.

Gateshead's Redheugh Park, long demolished.

a cantilevered 350-seater brick-built structure at a cost of £15,000. The 1920's-built West Stand opposite can protect 1,500 people and has been re-furbished three times in its lifetime.

Spartans' first-ever floodlights were erected in October 1966 at a cost of £1,200 and Sunderland opened them with a friendly. The second set arrived in October 1980 with further expenditure of £20,000. As the club embarked on their heyday the first clubhouse, recently refurbished, was opened in 1973 at the Kingsway end. The following year some 8,500 crammed in to see Bobby Charlton's Preston North End visit in the FA Cup, only 1,500 short of the all-time record gate which saw an FA Cup tie with Hartlepool United in December 1956. Despite the introduction of concrete terracing added around the ground in 1978, those gates will sadly never be repeated as the limit is now officially 6,000 and even that is unlikely in the modern safety first climate.

PORTLAND PARK
Ashington FC

One of the happier occurrences of recent times has been the rescue and partial resuscitation of Portland Park, the former Football League home of Ashington which has stood in its various forms since 1909.

It had become a pitiful place. A relatively new grandstand was surrounded by barbed wire, the huge covered enclosure roofless, and a general air of decay permeated, alienating many prospective spectators. Portland Park today is changed in outlook. Tidy, without being antiseptic, yet retaining the feel of a very old and historic ground about it.

The greyhound racing paraphernalia is still in situ, but the banked nature of the ground compensates in many ways. Two of the original entrances are still in place, and the enclosure which once ran the length of the ground opposite the stand is now reduced to a third of its size.

The 24-year-old main stand, the third to cover that particular spot, is in use again, albeit partially, the majority of the seats having been taken out of commission following the Popplewell Report.

Ashington first played at Portland Park in 1909, having been at the Recreation Ground in North Ashington from 1883 until 1908, before moving to Station Road (now covered by gardens next to the town library) for a year. The club rented a field further along Station Road which was sub-let via the Duke of Portland and within three years they had provided a grandstand, naming the ground Portland Park. Only twelve years later, Ashington were in the Football League, having terraced the ground on three sides and provided a thousand seats in the improved stand, along with a tea bar and press room. There were three entrances, one of which still exists at the YMCA end, and the steeply-banked surroundings had crash barriers installed, before an FA Cup game with Aston Villa in 1924.

With the advent of greyhound racing after the Second World War, Portland Park changed dramatically. Part of the terracing was removed and the pitch pushed northwards to create the track in a similar way to that at Barrow and Winsford United. The original grandstand was replaced on the same site, covered terracing either side stretching virtually the length of the pitch. Opposite, an equally long covered terrace was built with a committee room and tea bar to the north of it, just by the YMCA entrance. The second grandstand lasted until 1971 when it was destroyed in a massive fire being replaced by a slightly more modest structure. The covered terrace opposite was solid until 1990 when it was found to contain asbestos, and the roof was removed. It has since been partially re-roofed and is the main feature of the ground's nostalgic air. Portland Park has been home to stock car racing and speedway as well as the dogs, which accounts for the banked track, and although the electrical equipment and the Nissen hut which housed the kennels all endure, they don't detract from the ground's appeal.

Portland Park is akin to an ageing blonde movie star - past its sell-by date, a bit tarted up, but well worth a re-visit given half a chance!

The truncated covered terrace at Ashington in 1995 and (below) how it looked, packed to the rafters in 1950.

This rather austere structure at Ashington was built on the site of two previous stands, the first of which can be seen in the 1921 picture below.

KIMBERLEY PARK
Prudhoe Town FC

Formed as Ovington in 1959 by a group of young men from the area, the club began playing on a farmer's field behind Ovington Social Club, before moving to Mickley Welfare Ground in 1968. The club headquarters also transferred, and were then based at the West Wylam Inn at Prudhoe.

After only one season they moved again, this time to Eastwood Park, where the name Prudhoe East End came into being. In 1986 the former rubbish tip at West Wylam was reclaimed and levelled - the combined efforts of Kimberley Clark Ltd, the council and several other local firms who ensured a pitch was laid, a car park provided and a club house erected.

Further improvements were made when the club entered the Northern Alliance, winning promotion in 1984, and changed its name in 1993 to Prudhoe Town. Kimberley Park now has all its facilities down one side, with a curiously-angled seated stand set right back, well away from the action. The playing area is surrounded by a grass bank topped by a ricketty fence, the whole overlooking the former pit area.

FEDERATION PARK
Dunston Federation Breweries FC

Dunston are only 20 years old, but have come a long way, especially after tying up with the brewery, which has afforded the impetus to create an excellent ground and social club in a very short time. For the first ten years the club played on council-owned pitches at Dunston Park, until leasing a piece of fallow land, creating dressing rooms and fencing off the pitch to Northern League standards.

The grandstand, named after local boy Paul Gascoigne, was built in 1990 with the cover opposite erected four years later. The Feds aimed higher during the summer of 1995, adding 150 seats to bring the ground ever nearer Northern Premier League standards. The crowd capacity stands at 2,000, and has already been pushed when well over 1,500 saw the Shipowners Cup-Final in 1988.

DOCTOR PIT WELFARE GROUND
Bedlington Terriers FC

The history of football in Bedlington is so entangled it would need a book in its own right to do it justice. The life of the Doctor Pit Welfare Ground is slightly less complex although it has seen many variations on the same footballing theme since it was originally laid out in 1925.

The five acre plot contained a football pitch, two tennis courts, a bowls green and a playground, with a pavilion for a multitude of uses. The football pitch was precisely that until 1938 when it was re-laid and extended and an ash track and barrier fence was installed around some of it.

Part of the grounds were sold off to the Electricity Board in 1962 but the football continued with the pavilion extended and used as a bar in the mid-sixties. Following the closure of the pit the entire grounds were transferred to Bedlingtonshire UDC in 1975 under the Open Spaces Act and have been locally-run ever since.

The modern version of the Welfare sees the changing rooms and clubhouse next to the entrance with a small 50-seater stand on one side and a group of newer covered areas opposite. The record crowd at the ground is believed to be the 1,013 which saw the Northern League game against local rivals Blyth Spartans in 1986. Over the years a number of Bedlington sides have used the Doctor Pit ground, most of them being more or less the same club. Bedlington Mechanics, Colliery Welfare, Bedlington Colliery, Bedlington United and Bedlington Town are all shown as playing there, as well as the current club who at one stage used the Welfare Ground at West Sleekburn, which was itself home to a senior team which competed in the FA Cup in the early fifties.

ST JAMES PARK
Alnwick Town FC

The origins of football in this Northern outpost are shrouded in mystery, but certainly organised football had begun in the town by 1880. Football has always been based around the area which now houses the three main sporting clubs in the town, with early matches taking place on the cricket field and the midden field, which were either side of the present site.

CRAIK PARK and STOREY PARK
Morpeth Town FC

Situated west of Ashington in Northumberland, Morpeth has seen football since 1880 when Morpeth Harriers were the most prominent team in the area, playing on a field to the north of Dogger Bank. Ten years later, two teams merged to form a new Harriers and in 1909 the club, now Morpeth Town with headquarters at the Phoenix Hotel, were playing on what is the present cricket field.

Between the wars the club played at Stobhill and Grange House Field, moving to a pitch on Lamb's Field in the mid thirties. Storey Park became home in 1954 where they stayed until 1993 when a new ground complete with 100-seater main stand and changing rooms together with a running track and floodlights was opened and named Craik Park in honour of the two members of that family who served the club for over 50 years.

Decreed by its benefactor, Septimus Storey, that football must always be played there, Storey Park was given to the area in 1925. Although home for 40 years it could never be developed to a high standard and when the last match was played on May 1st 1994 the new ground, with facilities good enough for the Northern League, was already in place at Morpeth Common.

St James Park was created around 1900, when a lease was acquired from the Duke of Northumberland and Alnwick United Juniors used the field. After the first war, a longer lease was obtained, and although matches had been held on the Wagonway Field, St James Park has been home to the various Alnwick sides ever since. The first structure, a dressing room building, stood in the corner removed when the roundabout was built. It was followed by the post and rail around 1950. The fearsomely sloping pitch was levelled at the same time, and shortly after the grandstand and dressing room building was built, in a somewhat different form to that which exists today. It had three standing areas, with a brick wall along the front, changing rooms in the rear, and a second storey meeting room. The rescued timber from the old building was used in construction of the new. Much later, the wall was removed, and the middle section extended out to form a small clubhouse, with dugouts filling up most of the remaining space.

Floodlights were installed in 1987 as the club progressed in the Northern League, and a small delicate-looking stand was erected opposite to cater for League ground rulings.

Photos in this section by: Andy Dakin, Gavin Ellis-Neville, Ray C Maule and Dave West.

The original drawing of the stand at Alnwick in 1952. Although altered, the structure is easily recognisable.

Welsh clubs in England

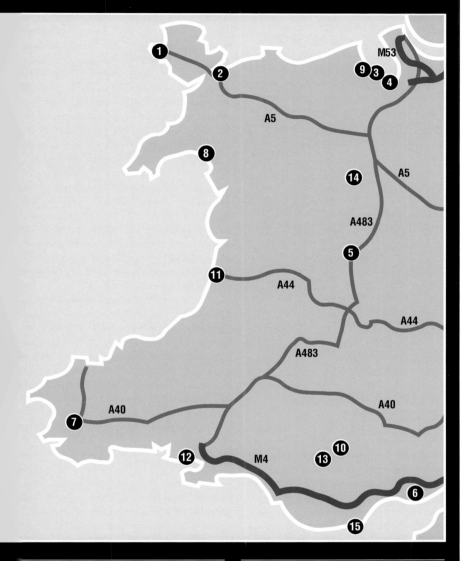

1	Holyhead Town FC	11	Aberystwyth Town FC
2	Bangor City FC	12	Llanelli FC
3	Flint Town FC	13	Ton Pentre FC
4	Connah's Quay Nomads FC	14	Llansantffraid FC
		15	Barry Town FC
5	Newtown FC		
6	Newport AFC		
7	Haverfordwest FC		
8	Porthmadoc FC		
9	Holywell Town FC		
10	Treharris Athletic FC		

IT is the intention to dedicate a sister book to exploring the histories of Welsh football grounds and therefore this final chapter sets out to look at just a few of the grounds which have seen action, in particular those which saw football in English Leagues and Cups.

There are of course many clubs which, for various reasons including the FA Cup, played in England, many of whom now play in minor leagues far away from the squabbling which has gone on since the advent of the new League of Wales virtually ended cross-border sport. Blaenau Ffestiniog, Bethesda, Rhosllaneruchgog, Treodrhiw, Abergavenny Thursdays, Ton Pentre, Bridgend Town, Monmouth and Chepstow are just a few to have had differing fortunes since they last competed in England.

Other than the three League sides, Bangor City are top dog, having won the League of Wales in May 1995 to qualify for Europe once again.

With the League of Wales officially accepted as a National League it is a matter for conjecture whether any of their member clubs should be in this book at all, dependant upon the reader's perception of non-League.

FARRAR ROAD
Bangor City FC

Farrar Road, existing in one form or another since 1920, is arguably the biggest non-League ground in Wales having a current capacity of some 10,000. The club previously played at a well-appointed ground with a wooden stand and changing rooms at Maes y Dref for many years. This ground was in the lower High Street, but was undersized and caused many problems in Cup competitions.

During the Great War it was requisitioned for allotments and never played on again. Builders took over Maes y Dref in 1925 and the site is now covered by housing.

The club, then called Bangor Athletic, moved in with the cricket club, who had been at Farrar Road since 1878, but there were problems over the ground-share and eventually the cricket club moved on to a new site in 1928. The original circular shape of the ground soon disappeared when the first grandstand was bought from Caernarvon Town in 1935 for £80 and erected along the touch-line parallel with the High Street. Only half of the wooden, yellow and blue painted stand with its garish bench seats still survives, as part was lost in 1957 when fire swept through it. Re-built a year later, it now holds the board room and changing rooms, along with the administration areas.

The other three sides are of concrete terracing, upgraded from rough banking in the sixties, and re-laid before the visit of Atletico Madrid in 1985. The covered terrace opposite the main stand put up in the early sixties, stretched almost the length of the ground

FOOTBALL IN HOLYHEAD

When the new synthetic pitch and stadium were opened in October 1988 after substantial grants from the Football Trust and the Welsh Office had helped raise the necessary £600,000, Holyhead Town were hoping to utilise it to move forward in the Welsh pyramid.

The ground with its 500-seater grandstand, floodlighting and modern changing rooms was ideal, but the installation of the synthetic pitch meant once promotion to the Welsh Alliance was achieved they would have to move off the main pitch and on to the adjacent one, similarly railed-off but with no cover. As a result the new stadium is used by the Ynys Mon School of Excellence for Anglesey youngsters. It was named The Oval which continues a tradition begun when Holyhead Swifts played on a field very close to the present one in Cyttir Road. From the club's halcyon 1920's days, home was a remarkable site, surrounded by industry and called Cae Mwd, (Mud Park). Situated in Turkey Shore Road it was owned by British Rail who eventually built their freight terminal over it in 1970. It had covered banking on two sides, extensive grass terraces around the remainder and was capable of hosting matches watched by many thousands.

Cae Mwd, former home of Holyhead Town, now under a railway terminal.

until two large sections were damaged and eventually removed in 1982. In 1968 the council-owned ground was floodlit for the first time and around the same time the clubhouse was built on waste ground to the left of the main stand. Sadly, this is no longer licensed and is now a creche.

Towered over and hemmed in by Victorian tenements, terraced housing and a church, Farrar Road stadium is reached through a series of narrow alleys none of which announce the presence of the club. All this adds to its historic feel and it seems much older than the 60 years since it became a football ground. It is somewhat similar in shape and feel to Stonebridge Road, Gravesend but the homeliness is dramatically disfigured by arguably the most hideous security fence seen anywhere in British football. This fine ground has been ruined since an 8ft steel cage was placed around it ten years ago for the European Cup-Winners' Cup game against Atletico Madrid, and the council owners in their wisdom have shown little inclination to have it removed. On no part of the ground is it possible to view play without peering through the execrable structure which has also ruined any possible photography, and it is to be fervently hoped that someone has the sense to eliminate it, regardless of expense.

HOLYWELL ROAD and CAE Y CASTELL
Flint Town United FC

With no little sadness the author witnessed the last match ever played on this ground which had given such sterling service since 1924.

Having been used for farming until 1921, the land was bought by the textile firm Courtaulds, who immediately leased it to the council, who in turn used the field as a recreation ground, not converting it to a football pitch until 1924. Several years later the pitch was moved across to allow an extension to one of the mills which overlooked the ground. Eventually, Courtaulds gave it to the council, who leased it to Flint Town United until the last match in November 1993.

As is the case with many grounds whose existence is, at best uncertain, the Holywell Road ground was looking a touch shop-soiled on its demise. The splendid main entrance with the club name picked out above the turnstiles was redundant, and access was gained via the gateway in the opposite corner, where the tin fence seemed to be grimly hanging on. The black and white main stand however retained its dignity to the end, and like some fading actress whose best years are behind her, managed to exude an elegance that only lovers of this most basic of architecture can appreciate.

Happily, the club have moved to a new base - which has all possible requirements for the national League of Wales - in the shadow of Flint Castle, close to the Dee Estuary and the railway. The ground is completely walled off with a stand situated above the dressing-rooms straddling the half-way line. Opposite is a small covered area primarily constructed as the television camera gantry

Cae Y Castell is purpose-built and adequate for the needs of modern football, and the club can be proud of it, but history and tradition take many years to develop and unfortunately can be wiped out in a matter of minutes as the Town ground sadly proved. But local councils and supermarket chains gather speed together and once into their stride nothing will stop them, least of all 70 years of history.

HALFWAY GROUND
Connahs Quay Nomads FC

Football has been played behind the Halfway House pub for well over 80 years, but it was not until 1946 when Connahs Quay Juniors were formed that the ground developed an identity.

The post-war club owes its existence to

The old stand at Connah's Quay.

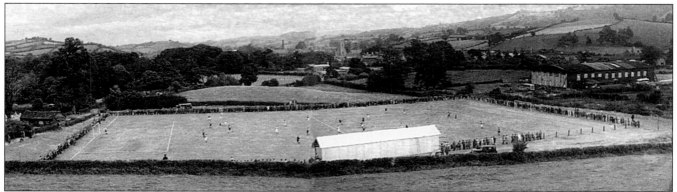

The first ever match at Latham Park in Newtown, a Central Wales League game with Aberystwyth in 1951.

the former Welsh international Tommy Jones, who formed a committee in an effort to resurrect football in the town. Many of the original committee were businessmen, and the inaugural meeting was held in a Scout hut in Chapel Street. Permission to play at the Halfway was granted by the owners Northgate Brewery, and an extended period of success came their way.

A change of name to Nomads came during the 1952-53 season, when they entered the Welsh League (North) Division One.

To comply with league rules, changing rooms were built on the half-way line to the right of the ground. Some years later the concrete walkway was added and a hedgerow removed when housing developments began on the other side.

More recently seating has been installed in the stand and dressing room complex, and membership of the new League of Wales, plus a long lease on the ground from Greenalls, has introduced good times to Halfway House.

LATHAM PARK
Newtown FC

Newtown Football Club are one of the oldest in Wales, having been founded in 1875. Their Latham Park headquarters however, is of 1951 vintage, although it has the pleasant, comfortable feel of a much older ground. The decision to purchase was made in the late 1940's whilst the club were playing at Plantation Lane, a ground just a stone's throw away from Latham Park.

In the early days, a number of grounds were used, all with varying degrees of comfort; Cunnings, Twenty-four Acres, and the Racecourse Recreation ground preceded Plantation Lane, now variously a supermarket, a bowls club with car-park, and an open recreation area .

The first match played was against Aberystwyth, a 4-0 Central Wales League victory in front of 1,211 spectators. The seated stand, still in situ, was provided from the start, and the covered area of terrace opposite dates from 1955. A large grassed bank with concrete standing areas stretches around the corner to the left of the main stand, and on

the other side of it, the canteen and clubhouse are situated. In 1989, a fire destroyed the original clubhouse, a devastating blow to the club who had taken the bold step of entering the Northern Premier League, but a splendid all-round effort by various individuals saw its re-opening just six months later. Floodlighting first came to Latham Park in 1979, when Wrexham provided the opposition, and since then they have upgraded to allow UEFA Internationals to be staged there.

SOMERTON PARK and NEWPORT STADIUM
Newport AFC

The trials and tribulations of Newport County and Newport AFC during the last ten years are well documented elsewhere and it would take a whole book to do them justice. The sad outcome is that Somerton Park is no more and after several years of nomadic existence, the Exiles have still to settle their differences with the FAW, and are playing at Newport Stadium due to a temporary injunction having been granted against them.

Somerton Park was home to Newport County from 1912 until their sad demise during the 1988-89 season when a series of failed

promises and escalating debts hastened closure after loss of their coveted Football League position the season before. The ground was possibly unique in that its bleakness and lack of comfort held an attraction which makes its passing all the more sad. As Simon Inglis observed in his *Football Grounds of England and Wales*, "Once spotted there can be no mistake about whose ground it is; Somerton Park is a splash of amber and black on the landscape".

The ground had a chequered history, being bought and sold several times before eventually finding itself in the hands of the local council in the early seventies. A previous owner, a greyhound racing company had brought the sport to Somerton in 1932, which necessitated wholesale changes at the ground which until then had but one small stand and some cover on the Cromwell Road End. The main stand was built and banking created, and the pitch was moved to allow for the track. The original stand was converted into a race viewing area and all these changes were utilised to the full in 1937 when the record attendance of over 24,000 was posted against Cardiff City.

Due to Saturday afternoon dog racing during the war, County played at the ground of Lovell's Athletic and later at Rodney

The remnants of Newport County's Somerton Park ground in 1995.

Newport Stadium, current home of Newport AFC.

Parade when the Civil Defence took over the ground. Dog racing finally vacated Somerton Park in 1963, moving to the rugby stadium and the company sold the ground to the council who leased it to a speedway franchise. The late seventies saw a minor resurgence in fortune, as the club qualified for Europe by winning the Welsh Cup, and Somerton Park was heaving again for a spell. Sadly the bubble burst and when they lost League status, the club and ground seemed doomed. The loss of County was soon followed by the birth of Newport AFC, created by club men and supporters with the aim of returning to Somerton Park and ultimately the Football League. Whilst the ground was locked and going to seed, and all the club fittings sold, the new club were playing at the London Road home of Moreton Town FC and later at Meadow Park, Gloucester City due to continued political problems with the FAW. The second season saw the return to Somerton after a mammoth operation had rejuvenated the ground and some 2,500 turned up to watch a friendly against Moreton in August 1990. Tragically, the club were again forced off the ground which had finally reached the end of the road after some 80 years, and during the summer of 1993 its innards were bulldozed, leaving just the perimeter walls and turnstiles intact. The remains of the speedway track could still be clearly seen, and the terraced shallow banking was just discernible at the end.

Newport Stadium was completed around the same time and has been home to Welsh League club Albion Rovers since. Newport began playing there also in August 1994, posting a crowd of 2,475 for their second return to Wales against Redditch United.

The stadium was patently not built with football in mind, although it is accessible and comfortable in the stand. The seating area slopes right down to ground level with the administration and dressing rooms and various function areas all behind it rather than underneath, thus leaving no room for any paddock accommodation. Spectators who wish to stand therefore do so to the sides of the stand on ground level or across the other side on a shallow uncovered terrace. The running track and various field apparatus have prevented the curved ends - 60 yards from the action - from being developed. Future plans indicate that a similar stand may be built opposite the current one which would incorporate a clubhouse and should put a completely different complexion on the ground.

Y TRAETH
Porthmadoc FC

Y Traeth (Welsh for beach) has seen football since the 1870's, when it shared the area with cricket. Facilities were originally basic, dressing rooms and the small main stand not being provided until after the war. At one point there was shedding behind the far goal but that was lost to the elements many years ago.

Since 1992 and the inception of the League of Wales, changes have been made to Y Traeth that have transformed it into a comfortable venue. A new stand was built in 1993 behind the town goal, and the perimeter fence infilled. The ground now has three stands, two with seats and one for standing, plus a floodlighting system. The innovations

BRIDGE MEADOW
Haverfordwest County FC

It has become an all too regular occurrence since research began for this book to have to report the loss of yet another delightful ground to the bulldozer and its employer, the superstore. Haverfordwest County's delightful Bridge Meadow ground stood on the junction of the by-pass and Cardigan Road, and even withstood a forced move of 20 yards or so when the by-pass ran too close to the pitch. But the superstore proved irresistible and a new purpose-built ground should soon be ready just 300 yards from Bridge Meadow.

The original ground was built in 1936 and its ramshackle changing rooms survived until the enforced re-alignment of the pitch in 1987, when a new changing room was built to replace the one now under Leo's Supermarket. The long 1000-seater stand was extended as part of the deal, and a car-park created on the area of pitch no longer required.

Overlooked by the castle the area though open is attractive with the river, prone to flooding and the cause of much grief over the years, meandering close by. It is to be hoped that the new ground can in some way emulate the old one although, if recent 'purpose-built' grounds are anything to go by, the odds are not encouraging.

were all fully tested at the end of the second season in the new league, when Y Traeth staged a local derby against Bangor City which decided the Championship in front of 3,000 people.

Once visited, the facts and figures surrounding the ground pale into insignificance. The sheer breathtaking magnificence of Snowdonia watches over Y Traeth from a distance, while on a good day the effortless flight of buzzards and Red Kites top off the scene. Just behind the ground, running alongside it during the relevant months, is the preserved Welsh Highland Railway which steams sedately by, with the Ffestiniog railway a few hundred yards away. With the possible exception of Locomotive Llanberis F.C., whose ground lies at the side of Llyn Padarn at the foot of Mount Snowdon, Y Traeth is the most beautifully-situated football ground in the whole of England and Wales.

ATHLETIC GROUNDS
Treharris Athletic FC

The former pit village of Treharris stands some 11 miles up the Taff-Ely valley from Cardiff and a mile from its neighbouring village of Trelewis. Both villages currently have football clubs in the lower reaches of the Welsh League with Trelewis playing on the most spartan of Welfare grounds, with a post and rail barrier and breeze-block dugouts some distance from the changing rooms.

A certain sparseness is not uncommon amongst valley clubs, possibly because the relatively thinly-populated areas have no need of huge stands and floodlights and with Welsh League requirements being player-based rather than spectator-oriented, the grounds of the slightly less ambitious clubs have changed little. This though, cannot be said of Treharris Athletic's hillside home.

Originally known as the Old Orchard, it stands wedged in on what appears to be a plateau hewn from two steep-sided residential streets, a high mesh fence fighting a losing battle in its attempts to apprehend wayward clearances. The steep walled area immediately outside the ground is in fact the skeletal remains of the Commercial Inn which was the club headquarters until demolished in 1972. The brewery connection goes back further as it was they who originated the ground in 1889. Now council-owned, it is leased to the club who have played there for well over 100 years.

Until recently, an 8ft breeze block wall topped with netting bounded the undeveloped side, but was removed for safety purposes and to fully appreciate this remarkable little ground, it should be viewed from that area. The stand, with its pristine roof, has been renovated many times and has several red-painted iron struts supporting the roof which are in fact old tram rails gifted by the

HALKYN ROAD
Holywell Town FC

The most pleasing aspect of Holywell Town's Halkyn Road ground is the feeling one gets that the stand's structure could quite easily survive another thirty-odd years, despite having been built back in 1958. Simply constructed and covered with corrugated iron, it has freshly-painted struts along the front and a brick-built wall at the back, with a neat and tidy green and white fascia and the club name ornately picked out in white.

When the ground was first laid out at the end of the Second World War, the club was re-formed by returning servicemen, who played on a sloping surface similar to Yeovil's. A barrier around the pitch and a wooden changing room sufficed until the present stand was built.

A further 30 years passed before more alterations were made, when the middle section of the stand wall was removed and the changing room extension built into the gap. Since then bench seats have been added, and a new entrance built. Sadly, the original turnstiles have been consigned to the undergrowth, after giving sterling service. Despite research, it is not known from which club they were originally purchased, and it seems that little mystery may remain unsolved.

Possibly the most ambitious project to date occurred at the turn of the 90's when the playing surface was levelled, chiefly by removing material from the car-park area and building up the pitch as at Bristol Manor Farm. Although still sloping, it is less prominent.

From the open side the ground and, with a little imagination, Halkyn Road is, with its pleasant backdrop of wooded hills and lush valley, reminiscent of Matlock's Causeway. It remains to be seen whether this splendid council-owned ground will survive, for sadly it joins a seldom dormant list of sporting arenas whose acres are constantly coveted by supermarket chains. The thought of this modest but comfortable little ground, which saw the Welsh Alliance League and Alves Cup Winners crowned over the years, going the way of Flint Town United's home and becoming a car-park is one that must sadden the heart of every lover of footballing nostalgia.

Deep Navigation Pit which ceased production a few years ago. Along the front of the stand are a row of wrought iron fencing sections rescued from a villager's garden, painted white and welded on to the stand to form a safety barrier.

To the left of the stand is, with the possible exception of the tiny old stand that once stood at Wrexham, the most remarkable structure on any football ground. Several concrete pillars, now hastily filled in with breeze-blocks, hold up the changing rooms and kitchen which are housed in a concrete shed, with a railing fronting a small walkway protected by a roof which also came from the pit. Some ten feet below and jutting out in front is another verandah which is uncovered but acts as a shelter for the dug-outs beneath. The whole thing houses a tractor for good measure.

The pitch, sadly, is so narrow that the club can never again play in Welsh Cup football, but on the up side, League of Wales football is also impossible and therefore the Athletic Ground should remain untouched.

PARK AVENUE
Aberystwyth Town FC

The present Aber club was formed in 1884, playing the majority of their matches at the Vicarage Field until their tenancy was withdrawn in 1907. A lease was successfully sought through the council, in conjunction

with the cricket, tennis and cycling clubs, to play at Smithfield, a ground which had its first recorded match back in 1881, when Aber Mechanics beat Ardwyn in the semi-final of the Cardigan Cup.

The ground was originally laid out on the site of an old iron foundry which was dismantled for that purpose, but it suffered badly from poor drainage, which meant many matches were transferred to The Vicarage or Barracks Fields.

The college quit the ground after a rent increase, and the local paper noted "as this is the only field where a gate could be taken, it had been for twenty years a gold mine to the college who had sub-let to other clubs. A capital field when dry, but useless when wet and in need of draining." Soon a seating enclosure was made ready, a cinder track laid, and much work accomplished to drain off water. During the Great War, junior football was played at the ground, which in the main was used for drilling, and in 1919 a decision was made which shaped its future. For two years the club closed whilst the whole ground was raised by some four feet. All efforts to keep the River Rheidol at bay had failed, and drastic measures were taken. Debris from the town's infirmary and sewerage works was dumped at Smithfield, along with enormous amounts of refuse from the council, and many tons of sand from Aberdyfi. In all over 100,000 tons of earth and rubble was used for the project. The entrance to the ground was altered and improved, ticket booths erected, the ground fenced off and a stand put up to give a "new and commodious ground" as the *Cambrian Times* reported. All this effort was not without problems as the pitch was found to be too short, and because of this Welsh Cup matches were not on the agenda until 1923, by which time further terracing had appeared at Smithfield. The stand cost over £1,000 and is a testimony to the workmanship of the time remaining intact to this day.

In October 1934 the ground was renamed Park Avenue, as the old Smithfield Road was now known, and this name change heralded a quiet spell up to the Second World War when the Army again took over, erecting two storage sheds either side of the stand. After the war the committee set about paying off the massive debt incurred by the purchase of the stand, and within six weeks had achieved their aim through a well-organised appeal. A new covered enclosure at the Crosville End, two canteens and more terracing were quickly added, with the playing area again being enlarged and levelled.

By 1950 the facilities were impressive and the Welsh Amateur Cup Final was staged there, more than 4,500 people spectating as Caerau beat Llay 3-2. Little changed in the next decade or so, although extra bathing facilities were added under the stand. As the lease would expire in 1968, the club were unable to erect a perimeter fence around the ground, and as a result it remained a common play area and not ideal.

Three factors came together in 1969. A Ground Improvements Committee was formed under the chairmanship of Derrick Dawson, the club drew Cardiff City in the Fifth Round of the Welsh Cup, which attracted 4,000 paying spectators and a thirty year lease was awarded. Improvements were made steadily with a clubhouse, extended three years later, opened in 1973. A further three years on saw floodlights go up at Park Avenue, and a floodlit training area built. With another stand projected soon alongside the new dressing rooms the famous old ground has never looked better.

JENNER PARK
Barry Town FC

Jenner Park has seen more than its fair share of ups and downs with Barry Town suffering long periods without success and then ultimately being forced to leave the town and the ground after the League of Wales saga. It appears to be behind them now as the council-owned Jenner Park has been re-built with a fine 800-seater stand and new running track, the capacity presently being a more than adequate 3,000.

The early Barry clubs had a number of temporary homes, Barry and Cadoxton District AFC playing at the Witchill Athletic Grounds, sharing with rugby, dog-racing, pigeon-shooting, athletics and horse racing. Barry Town were formed in 1893 and played at Castle Farm Fields for one year until disbanding, but District played on, moving to Tynewydd Fields.

In 1897 Barry Unionist Club raised funds for the football club to buy the Unionist Ground near the docks which had pay booths and a press box. District became Barry Unionist Athletic AFC, but the ground was short-lived as they were unable to afford the upkeep and it was sold off, the club moving to Jubilee Fields. Later, as Barry District, they played at the Butrills, an open area still being used for football a hundred years later.

In November 1912 a meeting was called to discuss the possibility of building a new stadium with Barry joining the Southern League. An area of land was leased and named Jenner Park after the family which owned it, and money raised for nets and goalposts by the newly formed Supporters' Club. Local brewers financed the building of two wooden stands as well as changing rooms at the northern end of the ground. The area was banked with one side being terraced ten years later.

Little changed at Jenner Park until after the war when fresh enthusiasm saw plans emerge for a new grandstand, and for many years after, other than the installation of crude floodlights, the place was to remain unaltered. It had a low post and rail around the greyhound track which surrounded the pitch with a large covered bank on one side and seating opposite. The initial enthusiasm waned and Jenner Park began to deteriorate, but a proposition to run stock car racing as a money-making venture was mercifully scrapped as it would undoubtedly have seen the end of the stadium as a football ground. A tidy up would periodically take place but the football and athletics clubs were refused permission to improve the facilities by the council, including floodlights, and when Southern League regulations tightened, Barry reluctantly pulled out and returned to Welsh football.

In 1985 the council had a change of heart and authorised wholesale rebuilding of what was by then a dilapidated ground. A synthetic running track, floodlighting and a new grandstand were all installed during the next couple of years and Barry duly returned to the Southern League in 1989. It was to be a brief sojourn for the ongoing saga of the exiled clubs continued. After being forced to play at Worcester City under the name of Barry FC, fielding another team in the Barry and District League at Jenner Park, the club returned home to Welsh League and eventually League of Wales football - a period which saw them win the Welsh Cup at the National Stadium to qualify for European football.

Right: **Jenner Park before alterations.**

STEBONHEATH PARK
Llanelli FC

Llanelli FC have played on Stebonheath Park since it was converted from an allotment between Stebonheath School and the workhouse in September 1922. Much work was done including the re-erecting of the old grandstand from Llanelli's previous home in Halfway Park. Its official opening was celebrated against Tottenham Hotspur on October 1st when 18,000 are believed to have been present.

The club went under three years later, the ground being used for recreational purposes by the employees of a local store, until Rugby League arrived. The club were re-instated and took over the fixtures of the disbanded Aberdare FC, but in 1930 fire destroyed the grandstand putting them back to square one. In February 1932 a new 1,280-seater stand was opened by the Mayor for the visit of Cardiff City in the Welsh Cup, and soon after a covered 3,000-capacity stand was built over the banking at the Evans Terrace end. Such was the steepness of the banking around the ground, that an estimated 30,000 saw a

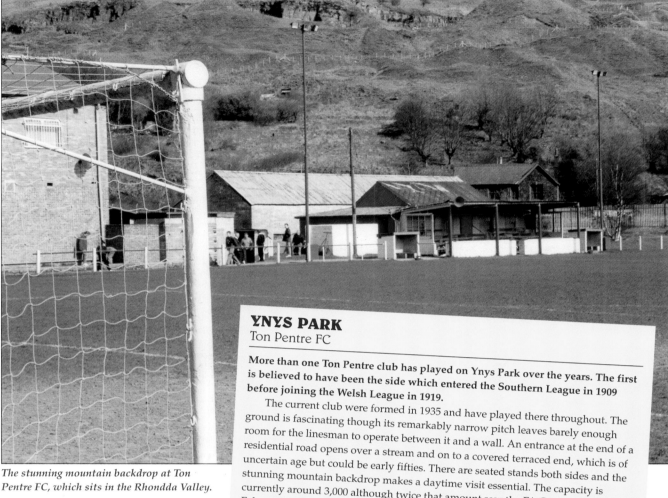

YNYS PARK
Ton Pentre FC

More than one Ton Pentre club has played on Ynys Park over the years. The first is believed to have been the side which entered the Southern League in 1909 before joining the Welsh League in 1919.

The current club were formed in 1935 and have played there throughout. The ground is fascinating though its remarkably narrow pitch leaves barely enough room for the linesman to operate between it and a wall. An entrance at the end of a residential road opens over a stream and on to a covered terraced end, which is of uncertain age but could be early fifties. There are seated stands both sides and the stunning mountain backdrop makes a daytime visit essential. The capacity is currently around 3,000 although twice that amount saw the FA Cup match with Falmouth Town in 1969 and this remains the record attendance.

The stunning mountain backdrop at Ton Pentre FC, which sits in the Rhondda Valley.

Rugby League international against France in 1935. It was used throughout the war, and in 1950 again held a huge crowd when 18,000 saw an FA Cup replay with Bristol Rovers. Ownership passed eventually to the Council, and following the Chester Report, the old ground was extensively altered with a new 700-seater grandstand built and the Evans Terrace removed in 1981. More recently terracing, running the length of the ground opposite the stand, has been laid with floodlighting and an all-weather pitch as Stebonheath Park hosts League of Wales football.

RECREATION GROUND
Llansantffraid FC

The rise of Llansantffraid FC from the obscurity of the Montgomery Amateur League through to the League of Wales has been mirrored by the changes at the modest but comfortable Recreation Ground. Situated a dozen miles south-west of Oswestry in the village of Llansantffraid-ym-Mechain (The Church of St. Brides by the River), the club have only played at the Rec since 1981, when they moved up from their Waen Field home which had been base since the start in 1959.

Waen Field has no facilities and the players changed in the old Village Hall, before the new one was built next to the Rec. Waen Field is still used by the club's third team. Much effort was needed to transform the bowl-shaped field into a relatively flat surface - the slope can be seen by the steepness of the bank on the stand side of the ground. Most of the structural work was started in 1989, when a small stand was erected on the half-way line and a perimeter fence went up. The clubhouse soon followed, having previously seen service as two portable classrooms in a school at Meole Brace in Shrewsbury. The club's acceptance into the League of Wales saw floodlighting erected in 1993 and a new fence and car-park a year later. The original stand was extended on both ends and now has a small standing area at the back of it which to date is the only cover at the ground. Llansantffraid is possibly the smallest village to support a national league side anywhere in the British Isles and the ground, although relatively undeveloped, still retains a village atmosphere on match days.

Photos in this section by: Gareth Davies, Paul Dennis, Ian Morsman and James Wright.

Subscribers

1 KERRY MILLER, East Lyng, Somerset
2 Mrs LYNN MILLER
3 Miss KATE MILLER
4 Mr & Mrs R. MILLER
5 JAMES WRIGHT, Non-League Newsdesk
6 GREG TESSER, Non-League Monthly
7 DEAN WALTON, W.B.A.
8 GAVIN ELLIS-NEVILLE
9 PAUL DENNIS
10 DAVE WEST
11 TREVOR HARTLEY
12 CHRIS BAKER
13 ALLAN BOLTON, Colne, Lancs
14 ANDREW CHITTY
15 GORDON ANDERSON, Tiverton Town FC
16 MIKE AMOS, Northern Ventures, Northern Gains
17 BILL BERRY, Non-League Traveller
18 TOM HARRIS, Taunton Town FC
19 MICHAEL LENIHAN
20 JOHN A. HARRIS, Southgate, London
21 GEOFF ALLMAN, Essington, Wolverhampton
22 DAVID KEATS, Thornton Heath, Surrey
23 DAVID DOWNS, Tilehurst, Reading
24 ALAN DAVIES, Worcester
25 J. RINGROSE, Romford, Essex
26 DAVID LONG, West Knighton, Leicester
27 MARTIN SIMONS, Bekkevoort, Belgium
28 ARTHUR SHAW, Amesbury, Salisbury, Wilts
29 D. BOWLCOTT, Leicester
30 ÖRJAN HANSSON, Helsingborg, Sweden
31 ADAM GREENWAY, Desford, Leics
32 T.J. GRANT, Saffron Walden, Essex
33 WILLIAM A. HARVEY, Nuneaton, Warwicks
34 LEONARD B. CROSS, Leicester
35 GRAEME MALCOLM NORRIS, Rothwell, Northants
36 PETER JACKSON, Church Gresley, Derbyshire
37 JOHN JACKSON, Church Gresley, Derbyshire
38 RICHARD WELLS, Surbiton, Surrey
39 KEN PRIOR, Bitterne, Southampton
40 KEN SHAW, Sunderland, Tyne & Wear
41 DEREK SALE, Hemel Hempstead, Herts
42 MICHAEL PENSON, Northolt, Middlesex
43 JONATHAN HALL, Henleaze, Bristol
44 I. SHARMAN, Burbage, Leics
45 DAVID JOHN HENRY LENTON, Blaby, Leics
46 ALAN W. MEEK, Thorpe St. Andrew, Norfolk
47 PHILIP C. LAWRANCE, Padworth, Berkshire
48 PETER FORD, Allesley Park, Coventry
49 J.D. MARSH, Oxenholme, Kendal, Cumbria
50 CHRIS WIGGINTON, London SW1
51 ALAN MASON, Leicester
52 M.W. FOREMAN, Lowestoft, Suffolk
53 LIONEL FOGERTY, Barford St. Martin, Wiltshire
54 ROBERT RUSSELL, Greenford, Middlesex
55 STEVE DURHAM, Whitehaven, Cumbria
56 BARRY LENTON, Crosby, Liverpool
57 M.G. ROBINS, Bournemouth, Dorset
58 A.F. PEARSON Jnr, Stapenhill, Burton on Trent
59 B.A. FULTON, Barkingside, Ilford, Essex
60 P.E. NUNLEY, Rushden, Northamptonshire
61 ROB BRADING, Horsham, Sussex
62 MARK PUMPHREY, Bournville, Birmingham
63 R.J. FISHER, Great Barr, Birmingham
64 RICHARD J. COOK, Cosby, Leicester
65 ADRIAN MANN, Wallington, Surrey
66 M.J. WILLIAMS, Connah's Quay, Deeside
67 ROBERT LILLIMAN, London SW18
68 RAY MURPHY, Bournemouth, Dorset
69 R.V. CALMELS, Gamlingay, Bedfordshire
70 DEREK MEAD, Guildford, Surrey
71 D.J. COOKE, Churchill North, Redditch
72 RAYMOND FLOOD, London W6
73 GEOFF COMBES, Romford, Essex
74 LES RANCE, HAMPTON F.C.
75 ARTHUR EVANS, Quainton, Aylesbury

76 GARRY CLARKE, Great Sankey, Warrington
77 ANDREW PAUL ROBINSON, Ilkeston, Derbys.
78 ROBERT GILLIGAN, Acton, London
79 JAMES RICHARDSON, Tunbridge Wells
80 D. AYLING, Carshalton, Surrey
81 STEVE MOORE, Blaenplwyf, Aberystwyth
82 ROLAND REEVE, Rainham, Kent
83 DONALD SEABY, Ferndown, Dorset
84 IAN HOWARD, Sittingbourne, Kent
85 PAUL JOHN REX ROTH, Garlinge, Margate
86 NIGEL GIBB, Yarm, Cleveland
87 TERENCE TURNER, Palfrey, Walsall
88 STEVE WHILEY, Stirchley, Birmingham
89 PHILIP C. RICE, York
90 F.J. TAYLOR, Osterley, Middlesex
91 PETER MILES, Westcliff on Sea, Essex
92 STEPHEN WOOD, Eastbourne, E. Sussex
93 J.F. BURRELL, Bristol
94 D. NORTH, Tilehurst, Reading
95 DAVID ROBERTSON, Morecambe, Lancs
96 GRAHAM MITCHELL, Fetcham, Surrey
97 ANDREW ROBERT PHILLIPS, South Witham, Lincs
98 TONY SMITH, Gatley, Cheshire
99 PHILIP SMY, St Peters, Worcester
100 C. ASHLEY, Murdishaw, Runcorn
101 P.W. BROWN, Cheam, Surrey
102 STEVE REANEY, Cricklewood, London
103 JEREMY BIGGS, Leicester
104 BRIAN P. HARDY, Alvaston, Derby
105 MARTYN T. DAVIS, Sheldon, Birmingham
106 ROB DAVIDSON, Bushey, Herts
107 COLIN DEAN, Goring-by-Sea, W. Sussex
108 MARK DAWSON, Crewe, Cheshire
109 TIM TRICKER, Great Bentley, Essex
110 JOHN ALLEN, Lower Bentley, Bromsgrove
111 FREDERICK & MOIRA FURNESS, North Shields
112 MARK TYLER, Rayleigh, Essex
113 DAVID O'CONNOR, Hough Green, Widnes
114 ALLAN MONUMENT, Tan-y-Bryn, Bangor
115 TERRY SPRACKLEN (DORCHESTER TOWN F.C.)
116 STANLEY WILTON, Smalley, Derby
117 BARRIE P.S. ROSS, Baldock, Herts
118 BARRY WORSLEY, Bodicote, Banbury, Oxon
119 GERRY McGILL, Bishopstoke, Eastleigh, Hants
120 ANDREW M. SNEDDON, Lytham St. Annes, Lancs
121 Dr. P.G. LONGHURST, Buckingham
122 T.D. KAY, Luton, Bedfordshire
123 L.I. SCOTT, Morpeth, Northumberland
124 J.K. ANDERSON, Clevedon, Avon
125 S.J. LEVERMORE, Bishops Cleeve, Glos
126 M.J. CRIPPS, Burgess Hill, West Sussex
127 BOB CAIN, Kidbrooke, London
128 COLIN I. SINDEN, Wrestlingworth, Beds
129 CHRIS OAKLEY, London NW3
130 GEORGE McKINSTRY, Southbourne, Bournemouth
131 WAYNE DICKSON, Alton, Hampshire
132 ALAN B. THOMPSON, Whittle-le-Woods, Chorley
133 G.G. PAINE, Chapelfields, Coventry
134 SIMON INGLIS, London NW6
135 DONALD LANCASTER, Pittsburgh, P.A., USA
136 TONY ANDERSON, Nuneaton, Warwicks
137 R.M. IRVING, Hinckley, Leics
138 A.W. HILLBURN, Selsdon, South Croydon
139 A.J. EARL, March, Cambridgeshire
140 K. PINK, Salisbury, Wiltshire
141 PHIL PASSINGHAM, Market Harborough, Leics
142 MARTIN BARTLEY, Ickenham, Middlesex
143 NEIL S. HARTLEY, Manchester
144 JOHN MILLS, Burrington, Umberleigh, Devon
145 JEREMY TAYLOR, Matlock, Derbyshire
146 ALAN MEADOWS, Hadley, Telford, Shropshire
147 MICHAEL MALES, Carpenders Park, Watford
148 MATTHEW EYRE, Cosham, Portsmouth
149 JONATHAN STRANGE, Wembley, Middlesex
150 MARK CAIN, Singapore

151 IAN HARRADEN, Stoneleigh, Epsom, Surrey
152 MICHAEL DODD, Berrylands, Surbiton, Surrey
153 CHRIS FOOTE WOOD, Bishop Auckland
154 RODNEY WALKER, Staveley, Chesterfield
155 DAVID GARNER, Bedford
156 DAVID A. HOWGATE, Southport, Lancashire
157 JACK BONE, Whitton, Middlesex
158 DAVID DICKENS, Braunton, Devon
159 MARTIN OSMAN, Swindon, Wiltshire
160 DEREK ELSTON, Northampton
161 J. GIBBONS, Kempston, Bedford
162 M.R. BLAKEMAN, Codsall, Wolverhampton
163 DEREK PEDDER, North Chingford, London
164 PHILIP DONALDSON, Bexhill-on-Sea, E. Sussex
165 J.R. SOPP, Reading, Berkshire
166 DENNY FULLBROOK, Reading, Berkshire
167 MICHAEL TUBB, Woodley, Reading
168 DON RAINGER, Pendleton, Salford
169 PETER J. STANLEY, Sutton Coldfield
170 MICHAEL W. STANLEY
171 STEPHEN DAGLISH, Burnham, Bucks
172 DAVID LESCOTT, Orton Malbourne, Peterboro'
173 IAN FARRELL, Hove, East Sussex
174 BERNIE KINGMAN, Addiscombe, Croydon
175 B. PEARSON, Skegness, Lincs
176 BRIAN R. PHILLIPS, Liverpool
177 TONY CUNNINGHAM, Greenmount, nr Bury, Lancs
178 ANDREW D. PICKLES, Odsal, Bradford
179 DANIEL MARTIN, Sandbach, Cheshire
180 MARTIN ALSOP, Warren Lodge, Newmarket
181 ˙J. NUNN, East Molesey, Surrey
182 BARRIE DALBY, Thrybergh, Rotherham
183 DAVID HARRISON, Bushey, Herts
184 JOHN BOWER, Lillington, Leamington Spa
185 Mrs A. MORRIS, Ingleby Barwick, Stockton-on-Tees
186 MARTIN WILLIAMS, Thorneywood, Nottingham
187 ROGER HUDSON, Thames Ditton, Surrey
188 DAVID W. MARSH, Tyldesley, Manchester
189 CHRISTOPHER ASHBRIDGE, North Finchley, London
190 ROGER ELDERFIELD, Didcot, Oxon
191 NICK HADKISS, Hoddesdon, Herts
192 DAVID HOLMES, Enfield, Middlesex
193 DAVID WINDROSS, Barlby, Selby, N. Yorks
194 A. ATKINSON, Muswell Hill, London
195 S.J. McCARTHY, London NW1
196 PETER COGLE, Aberdeen
197 D.A. REED, North Cray, Sidcup, Kent
198 GEOFF AUSTIN, Kingston upon Thames
199 ULRICH MATHEJA, Nürnberg, Germany
200 IRVIN MORGAN, Muswell Hill, London
201 C. TIMBRELL, Whiteway, Dursley, Glos
202 GORDON FOWKES, Herne Hill, London
203 SYDNEY H. LEE, Leicester
203 GERALD JOHN HUTCHINSON, Leicester
205 LESLIE HOWELLS, Gwernesney, Usk, Gwent
206 PETER NEALE, Chesterfield, Derbyshire
207 STEWART DAVIDSON, Paisley, Scotland
208 IAN RUDKINS, Billericay, Essex
209 RICHARD S. WELLS, Stratton St Margaret, Witls
210 JANE ALISON OLIVER, Hawkslade, Aylesbury
211 PETER TINDALL, Congleton, Cheshire
212 DAVID EMERY (Assoc. Ed), Daily Express Sport
213 N.R. TAYLOR, Bearsted, Maidstone
214 J.R. ORTON, Barwell, Leics
215 RAY STANTON, Hayes, Middlesex
216 STUART SHEPHERD, Walthamstow, London
217 PETER F. JONES, Upminster, Essex
218 T.D. COLCOMB, Calne, Wiltshire
219 W.D. PHILLIPS, Frogmore, Devon
220 GORDON R. WHITTINGTON, Bedford
221 NIGEL DUDLEY, Witham, Essex
222 THE FOOTBALL TRUST, London NW1
223 NEIL SCOTT, Worksop, Notts
224 RICHARD LAMBERT, Wallington, Surrey
225 KEITH EVEMY, Sanderstead, South Croydon
226 KAREN TOLLADY, Northolt, Middlesex
227 GEOFF SEERS, Northolt, Middlesex
228 STEVE SHIRLEY, Enfield, Middlesex
229 J.T. THORNE, Swindon, Wiltshire
230 IAN J. PICKLES, Knaresborough, N. Yorks
231 C. SUMNER, Kelsall, Tarporley, Cheshire

232 J.W. ONLEY, Chatham, Kent
233 G. TAYLOR, North Cheam, Surrey
234 CROCKENHILL F.C., Swanley, Kent
235 K. PARTLETON, Burton, Christchurch, Dorset
236 BOGNOR REGIS TOWN FOOTBALL CLUB
237 NEIL HARVEY, Impington, Cambridge
238 PETER WOOD, North Hollywood, California
239 GEOFFREY WRIGHT, Ware, Herts
240 S.J. HESTER, Kempston, Beds
241 BRIAN TABNER, Forton, Preston, Lancs
242 T.A. MORRIS, Hendon, London
243 PETER ABBOTT, Springfield, Chelmsford
244 RICHARD LANE, Newark, Notts
245 T.J. GREGORY, Southampton
246 KEN ALLEN, St. Albans, Herts
247 MICHAEL EDROFF, Petts Wood, Kent
248 KEN KENEALY, New Eltham, London
249 S.J. CHAPMAN, Hayes, Middlesex
250 ROBERT NORTH, Langford Village, Oxon
251 KEVIN BARTHROP, Lower Kingswood, Surrey
252 PETER LUSH, London E14
253 N.R. ROBINSON, Peckham, London
254 RICHARD DAWSON, Knebworth, Herts
255 PHILIP HEADY, Billericay, Essex
256 ANTHONY DAVID WARNE, Keighley, W. Yorks
257 VINCENT TAYLOR, Laindon, Basildon
258 ANDREW FLEMING, Wallington, Surrey
259 GRAHAM SMITH, Stanmore, Middlesex
260 BODO SOHMEN, Wesel, Germany
261 STEVE JARVIS, Ravenshead, Notts
262 DAVE GREEEN, Hatfield, Herts
263 ALAN STEWART, Crook, Co. Durham
264 MIKE SPOONER, Stone Cross, Pevensey, E. Sussex
265 RICHARD BUCKINGHAM-SMITH, Eastleigh, Hants
266 ROGER LEWIS, Chippenham Town F.C., Wiltshire
267 PAUL DAVIS, Nailsea, Bristol
268 P.A. GRAHAM, Bury St. Edmunds, Suffolk
269 MARK SOUTHGATE, Thames Hamlet, Grays, Essex
270 C.J. WISHART, Dunfermline, Fife
271 M. GREAVES, Lewisham, London
272 M. PRIDDIS, Allington, Maidstone, Kent
273 S. PRIDDIS, Allington, Maidstone, Kent
274 PAUL HAWKINS, New Southgate, London
275 IAN RUNHAM, Newton, West Kirby, Wirral
276 GARY A. PARLE, Lincoln
277 P.E. HIGH, St Leonards-on-Sea, E. Sussex
278 N.E. CORNWELL, Northampton
279 JOHN STANT, Haddenham, Aylesbury
280 IAN STEWART, Sheffield
281 JOHN A. HIGGINS, Handsworth Wood, Birmingham
282 DAVID A. GOWER, Bushey, Herts
283 JAMES BURROUGH, Bristol
284 KEITH COBURN, Cambridge
285 M.R. PAVEY, Pound Hill, Crawley, W. Sussex
286 ROGER HULBERT, Anlaby, Hull
287 ROGER FRANCIS WHEELER, Leicester
288 S.J. MAILES, South Ockendon, Essex
289 MARK JAMES, Bricket Wood, Herts
290 STEPHEN CARR, Wood Green, Wednesbury
291 CHRISTOPHER MAY, Whitchurch, Bristol
292 NEIL MORRIS, East Croydon, Surrey
293 SOHAM TOWN RANGERS F.C., Ely, Cambs
294 S.T. KING, Chessington, Surrey
295 STEVE CLARK, Chipstead, Surrey
296 RICHARD TANSER, Welford, Northampton
297 S. BLAIN, N.W.C.F.L., Bury, Lancs
298 F. CLAYTON, N.W.C.F.L., Accrington, Lancs
299 DARWEN A.F.C., The Anchor, Darwen
300 A.S. FENNA, Mossley A.F.C., Manchester
301 J.A. FRADLEY, Flixton A.F.C., Manchester
302 A.S. MOFFAT, N.W.C.F.L., Hyde, Cheshire
303 S. STRICKLAND, Burscough A.F.C., Ormskirk, Lancs
304 R.C. BROCKETT, Baildon, Shipley, Yorks
305 ALAN SMITH, Slough, Berkshire
306 PETER WALLIS, Burgess Hill, W.Sussex
307 MARK DADGE, Cheltenham, Glos
308 G. FIRTH, Harlow, Essex
309 DAVID STEVENTON, Darlaston, W. Midlands
310 JOHN JARVIS, Kingswood, Bristol
311 NIGEL HOLLAND, Linslade, Beds
312 NIGEL HANKS, Wombwell, Barnsley

313 TONY MARTIN, Bramhall, Stockport
314 KEITH J. SMITH, Canterbury City F.C., Kent
315 GARETH A. EVANS, Disley, Cheshire
316 DAVID MOON, Little Snoring, Norfolk
317 DAVID BISSET, Preston, Nr Cirencester, Glos
318 PAUL BROOKS, Eastleigh, Hampshire
319 A. DUNMORE, Purley, Surrey
320 CRAIG SAUL, Barton Seagrave, Northants
321 DAVE JODRELL, Crewe, Cheshire
322 RIVA BLACK, Edgware, Middlesex
323 GARETH M. DAVIES, Holyhead, Gwynedd
324 ANDREW MATTHEWS, Worksop, Notts
325 DAVE MASTERS, Solihull, W. Midlands
326 P. MALCOLM, Harpenden, Herts
327 S. HARDY, East Hagbourne, Oxon
328 PAUL WOOD, Enfield, Middlesex
329 PAUL DAVIDSON, Canvey Island, Essex
330 KEVIN O'CONNOR, London N1
331 DOUGLAS J. PEARL, Haverhill, Suffolk
332 BRIAN COOK, Lichfield, Staffs
333 NIGEL FOSTER, Moulsford, Wallingford, Oxon
334 MALCOLM HIGGINS, Hedge End, Southampton
335 STEVE THORNE, Croydon, Surrey
336 NIGEL BISHOP, Doune, Perthshire
337 MICHAEL NELSON, Sheffield
338 A.J. LAYCOCK, Broadfield, Crawley, W. Sussex
339 CRAIG MATTHEWS, Frimley, Surrey
340 ANDY KIMBER, Yateley, Hampshire
341 C. PEEL, Kings Norton, Birmingham
342 N.I.A. LEUTY, Hitchin, Herts
343 D.R. ALLAN, Stourbridge, W. Midlands
344 R.A.C. WOODHEAD, Chesterfield, Derbys
345 TERJE OVREBO, Forde, Norway
346 STEPHEN COULSON, Sawbridgeworth, Herts
347 KEVIN HEALY, Northwich, Cheshire
348 GORDON FRISBY - Merry Xmas 1995
349 ALEC GRAHAM, Stony Stratford, Bucks
350 LEIGH COLTON EXTENCE, Shaldon, Devon
351 DERRICK BATES, Stamford, Lincs
352 A.J. COLE, Durleigh, Somerset
353 G.A. SHOWELL, Welwyn Garden City
354 ANDY DAKIN, Northwich
355 GRAHAM COOKSON, Northwich

356 DAVE CALDWELL, Northwich
357 PETE WILSON, Manchester
358 WILLIAM HUGHES, Weaverham, Cheshire
359 HARRY MERRY, Birkenhead
360 JIM SANDERSON, Romiley, Cheshire
361 IAN KELLY, Maghull, Merseyside
362 NOEL TRUSSLER, Manchester
363 ALAN TOMLINSON, Northwich
364 MICHAEL OLIVER, Hillingdon, Middlesex
365 BRIAN JONES, Copmanthorpe, York
366 STEPHEN FARMERY, Stubbington, Fareham, Hants
367 Miss L M McCARTHY, London W6
368 JOHN BRYAN, Matlock, Derbyshire
369 ROBERT SMITH, New Malden, Surrey
370 KARL SENIOR, Cashes Green, Stroud, Glos
371 TERRY HOPKINS, Cheshunt, Herts
372 TERRY SURRIDGE, Poynton, Cheshire
373 S. PENNY, Watlington, Norfolk
374 R.P.E. WALL, Kesgrave, Suffolk
375 NEIL FOWLER, Cardiff
376 CLIVE ADAMS, St Albans, Herts
377 ROGER TWIDDY, Stamford, Lincs
378 DAVID SALISBURY, Stamford, Lincs
379 M.J. WALKER, Darlington, Co. Durham
380 KEVIN ZUPP, Lutterworth, Leics
381 LES TURLAND, Hounslow, Middlesex
382 D.C. FREER, Saxilby, Lincoln
383 C.J. FREER, Lincoln
384 STEPHEN RUFF, Hare Street, Herts
385 PAUL CLAYDON, Ashingdon, Rochford, Essex
386 RONALD BAGSHAW, Collyhurst, Manchester
387 LES GREEN, Tettenhall Wood, Wolverhampton
388 R.T. SAUNDERS, Hednesford, Staffs
389 TREVOR STEVENS, Redditch, Worcs
390 HORNCHURCH F.C., Upminster, Essex
391 D.C. BARNES, Immingham, South Humberside
392 ADRIAN FRANCE, Bardsley, Oldham, Lancs
393 WILLIAM P. EVANS, Barlborough, Chesterfield
394 HAN VAN EYDEN, Almere, Netherlands
395 BOBBY BASKCOMB, Worth Matravers, Dorset
396 DAVID GASK, Rothley, Leicester
397 GERALD TOON, Thurnby, Leicester
398 JULIAN BASKCOMB, Leicester

With Grateful Thanks To...

David Osborne, Halstead Town; Derrick Kinsey, Gresley Rovers; Paul Burdell, Marlow; Andy Wells, Wantage Town; John Hutter, Chichester City; Mark Smith, Maidenhead United; Jon Weaver, Braintree Town; Mike Wenham, Shoreham; Mike Casey, Treharris; Doug Hand, Clevedon Town; Graham Showell, Hertford Town; Norman Harrison, Northfield Town; Keith Brookman, Bath City; John Ansell, Wokingham Town; Peter Clynes, Moor Green; Joe Mason, Blakenall; Paul Bates, Margate & Ramsgate; Tony Jones, Rushden & Diamonds; Ron Rendall, Radstock Town; Dave Watts, Stourport Swifts; Dave Ward, Swaffham Town; John Lee, Desborough Town; David Tavener, St. Albans City; Harold Whiddon, Finchley; Rod Grubb, Nuneaton Borough & Bedworth; Andy Pace, Nuneaton Borough; Richard Markiewicz, Wembley; Terry Horgan, Barking; Terry Lynes, Lowestoft Town; Roger Leeks, Sudbury Town; Jeff Frank, North Ferriby; Eric Oliver, Leek Town; Paul Carr, Bootle; Graham Etchell, Hendon; Brian Seddon, Atherton LR; E.P. Elmer, Woking; Ian Garland, Welsh Football Historian; Gordon Nicholson, Evenwood Town; Sam Balston, D&C Police; Tony Booth, Harrow Borough; Raymond C. Maule, Eccleshill United; Lionel Ball, Gravesend & Northfleet; Paul Harrison, Gravesend & Northfleet; Andy Dakin, Northwich Victoria; Barry Denyer, Horsham YMCA; John Dunn, Rossendale United; Stan Strickland, Burscough; Ian Bagshaw, Chorley; Paul Vanes, Paget Rangers & Sutton Coldfield Town; Bernard Bagnall, Telford United; David Shelton, Chasetown; Clive Williams, Cheadle Town; Mick Alexander, Norwich United; M. Davis, Wisbech Town; Steve Jupp, Frome Town; David Johnson, Leatherhead; Che Kerin, Nantwich Town; Carl Allen, Harwich & Parkstone; Bill Kings, Bromsgrove Rovers; John Wybrew, Newmarket Town; Steve Moore, Aberystwyth; Mick Marriott, Cogenoe; Jerry Dowlen, Cray Wanderers; David Foulkes, Whitley Bay; John Gillingham, Stowmarket Town; Mike Pavosovic, Hyde United; Tony Milton, Minehead; Colin Sinden, Hoddesdon; Peter Lynn, Waterlooville; Roy Sisley, Tooting & Mitcham; Hugh Clark, Stourbridge; Paul Hughes, Beaconsfield; Mel Hopkins, Kettering Town; Ken Monk, Deal Town; Andrew Pearson, Consett; Steve Addison, Kings Lynn; Gareth Davies, Holyhead Town; Ray Esdale, Haverhill Rovers; Steve Eeles, Eynesbury Rovers & St. Neots; Chris Bedford, Stafford Rangers; Gordon Holland, Hallam; Colin Wilson, Clitheroe; Alan Farmer, Enfield; Bill Holian, Morpeth Town; Mick Jones, Raunds Town; Barry Lenton, Marine; Chris Taley, Alfreton Town; Fred Earnicker, Bognor Regis; Robbie Drummie, Windsor & Eton; Mal Keenan, Chalfont St. Peters; David Elliott, Canterbury City; Joe Townsend, Weymouth; Doug Smith, Herne Bay; Kevin Strangeway, Garforth Town; Peter High, Stamco; Neil Harvey, Cambridge City; Rob Britton, Cambridge City; T. Oliver, Matlock Town; Arthur Evans, Various; Andrew Chitty, Various; Neville Wigglesworth, Ossett Albion; Robert Brassett, Potters Bar; Derik Brookes, Eastleigh; Roy Dalby, Harrogate Town; Harold Stew, Dunstable; Stan Watson, Blyth Spartans; John Self, Bromley; Martin Giles, Hythe United; Eric Winser, Banstead Athletic; Derek Inskip, Potton United; Gareth Stephens, Bishops Stortford; Alan Stewart, Crook Town; Rob Kujawa, Gloucester City; John Haines, Thatcham Town; Colin Barrett, Harlow Town; Andrew Luscombe, Various; R.W. Reeves, Brockenhurst; Mike Floate, Various; Julian Pugh, Worcester City; Joe Reed, East Cowes Victoria; Peter Savage, Netherfield; Peter Bough, Ashfield United; Glyn Davies, Shifnal Town; K. Hunter, Maine Road; Mike Spooner, Langney Sports; The Rev. Wallace Boulton, Bexley United; Alan Timpson, Cheshunt; Bernard Thompson, Whitstable Town; John Bailey, Henley Town; Cyril Skinner, Bridlington Town.